COLLECTED ESSAYS IN LAW

# Family Values and Family Justice

# Collected Essays in Law Series
*General Editor: Tom D. Campbell*

Objectivity in Ethics and Law

*Michael Moore*

ISBN: 978 0 7546 2329 8

Crime, Compliance and Control

*Doreen McBarnet*

ISBN: 978 0 7546 2349 6

Democracy Through Law

*Johan Steyn*

ISBN: 978 0 7546 2404 2

Legal Reasoning, Legal Theory and Rights

*Martin P. Golding*

ISBN: 978 0 7546 2669 5

Meaning, Mind and Law

*Dennis Patterson*

ISBN: 978 0 7546 2749 4

Law as Resistance:
Modernism, Imperialism, Legalism

*Peter Fitzpatrick*

ISBN: 978 0 7546 2685 5

Beyond Law in Context:
Developing a Sociological Understanding of Law

*David Nelken*

978-0-7546-2802-6

Islam and Human Rights

*Abdullahi An-Na'im, edited by Mashood A. Baderin*

978-0-7546-2823-1

Michael Freeman F.B.A.

# Family Values and Family Justice

ASHGATE

Published by
Ashgate Publishing Limited
Wey Court East
Union Road
Farnham
Surrey GU9 7PT
England

Ashgate Publishing Company
Suite 420
101 Cherry Street
Burlington, VT 05401-4405
USA

Ashgate website: www.ashgate.com

**British Library Cataloguing in Publication Data**
Freeman, Michael D.A.
    Family values and family justice. – (Collected essays in
    law)
    1. Domestic relations. 2. Children's rights.
    I. Title II. Series
    346'.015-dc22

**Library of Congress Control Number:** 2009938294

ISBN: 978 0 7546 2663 3

**Mixed Sources**
Product group from well-managed
forests and other controlled sources
www.fsc.org  Cert no. SGS-COC-2482
© 1996 Forest Stewardship Council
FSC

Printed and bound in Great Britain by
TJ International Ltd, Padstow, Cornwall

# Contents

# Acknowledgements

The chapters in this volume are taken from the sources listed below, for which the author and publishers wish to thank the original publishers or other copyright holders for permission to use materials as follows:

**Chapter 1:** Family Values and Family Justice, *Current Legal Problems*, **50**, (1997), pp. 315–59. Copyright © 1997 Oxford University Press.

**Chapter 2:** Disputing Children, *Cross Currents*, S. Katz, J. Eekelaar and M. MacLean (eds), Oxford University Press (2000), pp. 441–70. Copyright © 2000 Sanford Katz, John Eekelaar and Mavis Maclean.

**Chapter 3:** The Best Interests of The Child? Is *The Best Interests of The Child* in the Best Interests of Children? *International Journal of Law, Policy and the Family*, **11**, (1997), pp. 366–88. Copyright © 1997 Oxford University Press.

**Chapter 4:** What's Right with Rights for Children, *International Journal of Law in Context,* **2**, (2006), pp. 89–98.Cambridge University Press.

**Chapter 5:** The End of The Century of The Child? *Current Legal Problems*, **53**, (2000), pp. 505–58. Copyright © 2000 Oxford University Press.

**Chapter 6:** Children Are Unbeatable, *Children and Society*, **13**, (1999), pp. 130–41. Copyright © 1999 John Wiley & Sons.

**Chapter 7:** Saviour Siblings, *First Do No Harm*, Sheila A.M. McLean (ed.), Ashgate (2006), pp. 389–406. Copyright © 2006 Sheila A.M. McLean.

**Chapter 8:** Why It Remains Important to Take Children's Rights Seriously, *International Journal of Children's Rights*, **15**, (2007), pp. 5–23. Copyright © 2007 Koninklijke Brill NV, Leiden.

**Chapter 9:** Legal Ideologies, Patriarchal Precedents and Domestic Violence, *State, Law and Family: Critical Perspectives*, Michael D.A. Freeman (ed.), Tavistock Publications (1984), pp. 51–78. Copyright © 1984 Michael D.A. Freeman.

**Chapter 10:** The Right to Responsible Parents, *Responsibility, Law and the Family*, Jo Bridgeman, Heather Keating and Craig Lind (eds), Ashgate (2008), pp. 21–39. Copyright © 2008 Jo Bridgeman, Heather Keating and Craig Lind.

**Chapter 11:** Does Surrogacy Have a Future After Brazier? *Medical Law Review*, 7, (1999), pp. 1–20. Copyright © 1999 Oxford University Press.

**Chapter 12:** Not Such A Queer Idea: Is There A Case for Same Sex Marriage? *Journal of Applied Philosophy*, **16**, (1999), pp. 1–17. Copyright © 1999 Society for Applied Philosophy.

**Chapter 13:** Questioning The Delegalization Movement in Family Law: Do We Really Want A Family Court? *The Resolution of Family Conflict*, John Eekelaar and Sanford Katz (eds), Butterworths: Toronto (1984), pp. 7–25. Copyright © 1984 Butterworth & Co. (Canada) Ltd.

**Chapter 14:** Is The Jewish *Get* Any Business of The State? *Law And Religion*, Richard O'Dair and Andrew Lewis (eds), Oxford University Press (2001), 365–83. Copyright © 2001 Oxford University Press

**Chapter 15:** Towards A Critical Theory of Family Law, *Current Legal Problems*, **38**, (1985), pp. 153–85.

# Series Editor's Preface

Collected Essays in Law makes available some of the most important work of scholars who have made a major contribution to the study of law. Each volume brings together a selection of writings by a leading authority on a particular subject. The series gives authors an opportunity to present and comment on what they regard as their most important work in a specific area. Within their chosen subject area, the collections aim to give a comprehensive coverage of the authors' research. Care is taken to include essays and articles which are less readily accessible and to give the reader a picture of the development of the authors' work and an indication of research in progress.

**Michael Freeman**

# Introduction

The essays contained in this volume span a quarter of a century, and range from discussions about patriarchy and mediation, to same-sex marriages and saviour siblings. There is much about children's rights and about parental responsibility. If there is an underlying theme it is about the limits of the state so far as the family – that most intimate of relationships – is concerned.

The volume derives its title from an essay contributed to a collection on law and public opinion at the end of the twentieth century.[1] Twelve years on the moral panic is still there, if its ground has shifted. There is still concern about youth crime and misbehaviour (and we now have anti-social behaviour orders[2]), about child support and errant fathers (and the sanctions have been substantially increased[3]), about child abuse (the image of Baby Peter glares at us unforgivingly[4]). The family rights of the gay have been increased: they can now adopt[5] and enter into civil partnerships.[6] We no longer talk of pretended family relationships[7], and we have eased access to fertility treatment for single and lesbian women by removing the requirement that clinics should consider the child's need for a father.[8] But many of these changes were contested.[9] But the trend is towards inclusivity, unimaginable a generation ago, and barely on

---

1  See M. Freeman, *Law and Opinion at the End of The Twentieth Century*, Oxford, Oxford University Press, 1997.

2  But little changes: *see* D. Hayes, 'The Same Old Story', *Community Care*, 11 September 2008, 18–19.

3  I discuss these in *Understanding Family Law*, London, Sweet and Maxwell, 2007, ch.12.

4  See the Laming report, discussed in J. Carvel, ' "Cinderella Service" will be shaken up, minister pledges', *The Guardian*, 13 March 2009, 6–7.

5  Adoption and Children Act 2002 s.144(4), as amended by the Civil Partnership Act 2004 s.79.

6  Civil Partnership Act 2004.

7  The Local Government Act 1988 s.28 was repealed by the Local Government Act 2003, Sch. 8(1), para 1.

8  This direction in Human Fertilisation and Embryology Act 1990 s. 13(5) was replaced by one emphasising the need for 'supportive parenting' in the Human Fertilisation and Embryology Act 2008 s.14(2).

9  See N. Watt, 'MPs Vote for Hybrid Embryos after Brown makes plea to permit "Moral Endeavour"', *The Guardian*, 20 May 2008, 4; J. Randerson *et al*, 'Ethical Concerns in Embryos Bill Divide MPs', *The Guardian*, 12 May 2008, 4.

the horizon even in 1996. The change reflects a new human rights agenda.[10] There have been changes since 'Family Values and Family Justice' was written: the divorce reform was never implemented[11], and a restructuring of the divorce process is now relegated to a distant back seat. The Gender Recognition Act 2004 now allows post-operative trans-gender persons to marry in their new identity, and the gay may regularise their relationships in civil partnerships. The debate about gay marriage continues but it is less prominent in the UK than in California, for example.[12] We are beginning to think 'beyond conjugality', 'outside the marital and conjugal box'.[13] The Law Commission of Canada has gone further, asking whether the distinction between conjugal and non-conjugal relationships is consistent with the value of equality. Autonomy, it argues, will be furthered if 'the state's stance is one of neutrality regarding the individual's choices whether to enter into personal relationships'.[14] The unlikeliest of test cases was fought in 2008 by two elderly unmarried sisters.[15] They had lived together all their lives in a property built on land inherited from their parents. They were concerned that the surviving sister would be forced to sell the property to pay inheritance tax. This, they maintained, was discriminatory, since spouses and civil partners were exempt from this tax. Their claim was rejected by the European Court of Human Rights which held the relationship between siblings was 'qualitatively' different from that between married couples and homosexual civil partners. The court said in marriage and civil partnership there was a public undertaking. This, of course, could easily be introduced. But is the case not rather about the absence of a sexual relationship? The Misses Burdens are the unlikeliest of revolutionaries but they may well be harbingers of reform. But how soon?

The next chapters (2–8) centre on issues relating to children. The Children Act 1989 still governs disputes over children. Concerns that the paramountcy principle would not survive the Human Rights Act 1998 have proved alarmist. This was already apparent in 1982 in *Hendricks* v *The Netherlands*[16], and

---

10 The Human Rights Act 1998 incorporated the European Convention on Human Rights into UK law. On an increasing backlash against it (or rather the Court) see 'Courting Disaster', *The Guardian*, 11 April 2009, 36.

11 On calls to re-activate the divorce law reform debate *see* G. Morris, 'Times They Are A-Changing'. (2009) 159 *New Law Journal* 494–95.

12 Where the legalisation of gay marriages was overturned by popular vote in November 2008.

13 *Beyond Conjugality: Recognizing and Supporting Close Adult Relationships*, 2002.

14 *See* B. Cossman, 'Beyond Marriage' in (ed.) M.L. Shanley, Just Marriage, New York, Oxford University Press, 2004, 97.

15 *Burden* v. *United Kingdom* [2008] 2 FLR 787.

16  (1982) 5 E.H.H.R.223.

was affirmed in *Payne* v *Payne* in 2001 by Thorpe L.J. who noted that 'the acknowledgment of child welfare as paramount must be common to most if not all judicial systems within the Council of Europe'.[17] Subsequently (in 2004), Munby J. described the welfare principle as 'a core principle' of human rights law.[18] In 'Disputing Children' I observed that some of the most hotly contested disputes about children concerned contact arrangements. If anything this problem has got worse. The relationship between domestic violence and contact has come into stronger focus, the Court of Appeal, wrongly I believe, being reluctant to impose a presumption against contact where there has been domestic violence.[19] There has also been more attention paid to the recalcitrant mother, with new initiatives to tackle the problem in the Children and Adoption Act 2006. Parents (it will usually be mothers) can now be made to do up to 200 hours of unpaid work for breach of a contact order.[20] Another change in the law since 'Disputing Children' was written has seen the status of the unmarried father increase. He now acquires parental responsibility if he is registered as the child's father on the birth certificate.[21] There is even now talk of his being given automatic parental responsibility.

When one reads a leading Kantian philosopher writing about a child's main remedy is to 'grow up',[22] and another finding it strange to think of children as having rights,[23] it is perhaps not surprising that influential monographs like those by Goldstein, Freud and Solnit and by Martin Guggenheim can propagate anti-children's rights sentiments. And, as I write, there is an Equality Bill before the UK Parliament which targets just about every discrimination imaginable but strategically omits that against children.[24] Chapters 3 and 4 of this book

---

17 [2001] 1 FLR 1052,1065.

18 In *CF* v. *Secretary for the Home Department* [2004] 2 FLR 556.

19 *Re L, Re V, Re M, Re H* [2001] Fam 260. New Zealand has a presumption against unsupervised contact in cases of violence: see A. Perry, 'Safety First? Contact and Family Violence In New Zealand' (2006) 18 *Child and Family Law Quarterly* 1.

20 Schedule A 1, para. 4 of Children Act 1989, added by Schedule 1 of the Children and Adoption Act 2006. For further commentary see M. Freeman, *Understanding Family Law*, London, Sweet and Maxwell, 2007, 238–40.

21 Children Act 1989 s. 4(1)(a) and (1A), as amended by the Adoption and Children Act 2002.

22 *See* O. O'Neill, 'Children's Rights and Children's Lives' (1998) 98 *Ethics* 445–63.

23 *See* H. Brighouse, 'What Rights (If Any) Do Children Have?' in (eds) D. Archard and C. Macleod, *The Moral and Political Status of Children*, Oxford, Oxford University Press, 2002, 31–52, 37.

24 The Equality Bill 2009. See the discussion in C. Davies, 'Discrimination "a daily fact of life for children"', *The Observer*, 29 March 2009, 14.

respond first to Goldstein, Freud and Solnit[25] and then to Guggenheim.[26] Both
books emanate from the US, which together with Somalia (which doesn't
have a government) has not ratified the UN Convention in the Rights of the
Child. Neither book really addresses the Convention[27], though Guggenheim is
sceptical that ratification by the USA would make any difference. The main
right Goldstein *et al* would give children is the right to autonomous parents.[28]
Guggenheim concludes 'children have the right to be raised by parents who
are minimally fit and who are likely to make significant mistakes in judgment
in childrearing.'[29] I thought there was a typo here, but have been assured that
there is not. What kind of a life does this offer children?

Chapter 5 was written as a response to Ellen Key's *The Century of the
Child*, first published exactly 100 years earlier.[30] It is an audit and a critical
assessment, and its themes still resonate. Child poverty is still endemic[31], such
that *Save The Children* is now targeting child malnutrition in the UK.[32] We've
had a commitment (by Tony Blair) to end child poverty by 2020: this now
looks unattainable, and did even before recession hit us. We are no nearer
conquering child abuse now than we were in 2000. The House of Lords has
in *Re B*[33] upheld its earlier ruling *in Re H*[34], which I criticised in 'The Century
of The Child'.[35] We've had at least two well-publicised scandals since 2000:
the Victoria Climbié case[36] and that of 'Baby Peter'.[37] Both led to inquiries by

---

25 In particular to their *The Best Interests of the Child*, New York, Free Press, 1996.

26 *What's Wrong with Children's Rights*, Cambridge, Mass, Harvard University Press,
2005. Note the title is a statement, hence the omission of a question mark!

27 Guggenheim, when he does so, gets it wrong!

28 *Op cit*, note 25, 90. *See also* 140 (to be represented by parents) and 148 (to parents
who care).

29 *Op cit*, note 27, 43.

30 In Swedish: it was first published in English in 1909.

31 The Government has failed in its goal to reduce it by 50 per cent by 2009. And *see*
L. Elliott, 'Up. Up. Up. Child Poverty, Pensioner Poverty, Inequality', *The Guardian* 11
June 2008, 1–2.

32 *The Guardian*, 2 April 2009.

33 [2008] 2 F L R 141.

34 [1996] A C 563.

35 It also ruled that *Re M and R* [1996] 2 F L R 195 was correctly decided.

36 *See* Lord Laming, *The Victoria Climbié Inquiry* Cm.5730, London, The Stationery
Office, 2003.

37 Who was failed by social workers, the police, doctors (see *The Times*, 28 November
2008, 21), and the legal system. We have been 'assured' it will not happen again! (see
P. Curtis, 'Balls "was irresponsible" to promise Baby Peter case will not happen again',
*The Guardian*, 12 December 2009, 7).

Lord Laming.[38] The latter report significantly quoted the UN Convention on the Rights of the Child, but it was Article 6 (on survival and development) which was seen as significant (as it is). Article 19 is equally pertinent (on abuse), and it got no mention at all. It is rather a pity that the relationship between child abuse and child chastisement is still so little addressed.[39] But, more generally, there is a failure to recognise the link between protecting children and protecting their rights.

Chapter 6 follows on from this. It focuses on the issue of corporal punishment of children by parents. There are now 27 countries which have made it unlawful for parents to hit children.[40] These include one English-speaking country, New Zealand, where there is already a move to reverse the legislation.[41] England now has a 'compromise' position, which essentially permits parents to assault their children so long as actual bodily harm (in lay language, a mark) does not result.[42] This followed a deeply embarrassing so called 'consultation' exercise in which the Swedish model (a total ban) was ruled out, and respondents were asked questions about permissible implements, parts of the body and so on.[43] The 2004 compromise satisfies no one. Those who call for an outright ban continue to do so. Those who see the legislation as unnecessary meddling with parents' rights to rear children as they see fit are critical of, what they see as, bungling interference. The police are unhappy too, so are social workers who cannot offer parents an unequivocal message. Parents cannot know in advance what the limits of what they can do are. But the Government resists change, even going to the extent of prolonging debate on other issues so that a vote on hitting children is not taken.[44]

The chapter on 'saviour siblings' was written contemporaneously with the *Hashmi* case.[45] The use of pre-implantation genetic diagnosis (PGD) and tissue typing (HLA) to create a child to save the life of an existing child gets less controversial, now what is involved is better understood. Nevertheless,

---

38 Lord Laming, *The Protection of Children in England: A Progress Report*, March 2009. For reaction see *Professional Social Work*, April 2009, 5.

39 'Can We Conquer Child Abuse If We Don't Outlaw Physical Chastisement of Children?', paper at ISPCAN Conference, Hong Kong, September 2008 (to be published).

40 *Global Initiative To End All Corporal Punishment of Children* updates data regularly. Croatia and Costa Rica are the latest examples.

41 Which was passed in 2007.

42 *See* Children Act 2004 s.58.

43 *Protecting Children, Supporting Parents: A Consultation Document on the Physical Punishment of Children*, 2000.

44 During a debate on the Children and Young Persons Bill in October 2008.

45 *R (on the Application of Quintavalle) (on behalf of the Prolife Alliance)* v. *Secretary of State for Health* [2003] 2 A C 687.

it fuelled controversy during the passage of the 2008 Human Fertilisation and Embryology Bill. But the end result is that legislation now permits these techniques to be used.[46] The concern about where it will end (designer babies and the like)[47] remains, if now somewhat muted. The question I raise at the end of 'Saviour Siblings' – whether there is a parental obligation to have a saviour sibling – ties in with the debates in chapter 10 of this book on responsible parenting. The new legislation does not, of course, create such an obligation.

The next chapter returns to the theme of children's rights. My writings on this subject go back to 1980[48] and can be traced through two books, *The Rights and Wrongs of Children* (1983)[49] and *The Moral Status of Children* (1997).[50] Essays on 'taking children's rights seriously' have evolved through three versions.[51] The version here is the most recent, though an essay entitled 'The Human Rights of Children' is due to appear in 2010.[52] As we saw earlier, there are those who deny children have human rights at all (even if they admit they may have certain legal rights). Others are prepared to concede that children have welfare rights though not agency rights.[53] I have always argued that children have both welfare rights (to protection and to the provision of certain basic goods, like healthcare and education), and agency rights (participation, freedom of speech, association etc.), even if on occasion it may be necessary to curtail certain freedoms to protect future autonomy.[54] Drawing the line is not easy: when, for example, should a competent child be denied the right to refuse

---

46 Human Fertilisation and Embryology Act 2008 Sch. 2, para. 3.

47 On which see, *inter alia*, R.M. Green, *Babies by Design – The Ethics of Genetic Choice*, New Haven, Yale University Press, 2007, and C. Gavaghan, *Defending The Genetic Supermarket: Law and Ethics of Selecting The Next Generation*, Abingdon, Routledge Cavendish, 2007.

48 'The Rights of Children in the International Year of The Child' (1980) 33 *Current Legal Problems* 1–31 (the text of a lecture to mark the IYC in 1979).

49 London, Frances Pinter, 1983.

50 The Hague, Martinus Nijhoff, 1997.

51 'Taking Children's Rights Seriously' (1987) *Children and Society* 299–319. 'Taking Children's Rights More Seriously' (1992) *International Journal of Law and the Family* 52–71 and the essay which appears in this volume as chapter 8.

52 In (2010) *Current Legal Problems*. It is the text of a lecture given first at the Hebrew University of Jerusalem in June 2009 and then at UCL in October 2009.

53 For example, James Griffin: *see now* his *On Human Rights*, Oxford, Oxford University Press, 2008, 83–95.

54 So argued in note 49, above, ch.2, where I defend, what I call, 'liberal paternalism'.

medical treatment?[55] I have addressed this elsewhere in an essay not included in this volume.[56]

Chapter 9 is about the private and the public,[57] about patriarchy and about why the law had then (in 1984), and also now, failed to conquer domestic violence. Family law, like law generally, has often been seen apart from the values it embodies and helps to structure and restructure. Many of the examples cited in the paper are now relegated to history. The marital rape immunity, for example, was put to rest in 1991.[58] But much remains, and the thesis in this chapter that the law is unlikely to solve the problem of domestic violence[59] so long as it remains part of the problem is, it is submitted, still convincing.

It raises also the propriety and effectiveness of state intervention into the family; as does the next essay. One cannot raise the right to have responsible parents without discussing whether parenthood should be licensed. It looks like a dystopian spectre but, of course, it exists in the context of adoption and fertility treatment[60], and we accept there are circumstances in which a baby has to be removed from parents at birth. We have given too little thought to what parental responsibility means. It is clear that the meaning is shifting: where once it was about authority, now it is about accountability. But the implications of this shift in emphasis have not been thought through. Accountability to whom? Is it to the state or to children? And if the latter, how is it to be enforced, and by whom?

We have never quite made our minds up about surrogacy, the subject of Chapter 11. It started with a moral panic in 1985 with Kim Cotton,[61] a Finchley housewife being prepared to hand over a child she had carried to a 'foreign' commissioning couple for 'money'. The Warnock report had

---

55 *See Re R (A Minor) (Medical Treatment)* [1992] Fam 11; *Re W (Medical Treatment)* [1993] Fam 64. *See further*, M. Freeman, 'Rethinking Gillick' (2005) 13 *International Journal of Children's Rights* 201–17.

56 'Removing Rights From Adolescents' in (eds.) Y. Ronen and C.W. Greenbaum, *The Case for the Child: Towards A New Agenda*, Antwerp, Intersentia, 2008, 309–25.

57 I do not here raise this in relation to children, but see T. Cockburn, 'Partners in Power: A Radically Pluralistic Form of Participative Democracy for Children and Young People' (2007) 21 *Children and Society* 446–57. *See also* J. Ribbens McCarthy and R. Edwards, 'The Individual in the Public and Private: the Significance of Mothers and Children' in (ed.) A. Carling, *Analysing Families*, London, Routledge, 2002, 199–217.

58 R v. R (*A Husband*) [1992] 1 A C 599.

59 See M. Freeman, 'Violence Against Women: Does The Legal System Provide Solutions or Itself Constitute The Problem?' (1980) 7 *British Journal of Law and Society* 215–41.

60 In both of which there is vetting.

61 *See Re C (A Minor) (Wardship: Surrogacy)* [1985] F L R 846.

already condemned surrogacy – in fact surrogacy for convenience – as 'totally ethically unacceptable'.[62] Legislation followed swiftly, targeted at the commercialisation of surrogacy, but it did so obliquely by criminalising not the surrogate or the commissioning parents, but professionals (lawyers and doctors) as well as newspapers and newsagents involved in negotiating arrangements or publicising surrogacy services.[63] Chapter 11 is my response to the Brazier report[64] which thought the best way of getting at surrogacy was to outlaw payments to surrogates. The Brazier report has not been implemented. It is unlikely that it will be. Surrogacy remains an unenforceable contract,[65] but legislation provides for a swift method of transferring parenthood to the commissioning parents.[66] 'Family values' dictated that this provision (the parental order) was only available to married couples[67] but 2008 legislation has extended this to those in civil partnership and to those in an 'enduring family relationship' (that is to gay couples who regularise their relationship and to those in stable cohabiting relationships).[68]

Chapter 12 puts the case for gay marriages. The debate has moved on in the last 10 years.[69] Three European countries (Belgium[70], The Netherlands[71] and Spain[72]) now permit same-sex couples to enter into a valid marriage. They are allowed also in Massachusetts[73] and in Canada[74], and were for a short time in California.[75] But, more significantly, the case against the legal concept of marriage grows. The writings of Fineman feature prominently.[76]

---

62 *Report of the Committee of Inquiry into Human Fertilisation and Embryology.* Cmnd. 9314, 1984, para. 8. 17.

63 Surrogacy Arrangements Act 1985, amended by the Human Fertilisation and Embryology Act 2008, s.59.

64 M. Brazier, A. Campbell and S. Golombok, *Surrogacy Review for Health Minister of the Current Arrangements for Payment and Regulation,* 1998, Cm. 4068.

65 The 1990 Act inserted a new s.IA into the 1985 Act.

66 Section 30 of the 1990 Act was inserted late in the passage of the Bill, as a simpler alternative to adoption.

67 Human Fertilisation and Embryology Act 1990 s.30.

68 Human Fertilisation and Embryology Act 2008 s.54(2).

69 *See* K. Norrie (2008) 4 *International Journal of Law in Context* 411–17.

70 In 2002.

71 In 2001.

72 In 2005.

73 *See Goodridge* v. *Department of Health* 798 N.E. 2d 941 (2003).

74 Civil Marriages Act 2005.

75 It was voted down in November 2008, raising uncertainties about the marriages of those entered into during the period when such marriages were permitted.

76 *The Neutered Mother, The Sexual Family and Other Twentieth Century Tragedies,* New York, Routledge, 1995.

She envisages the interactions of 'sexual affiliates' being governed by the same rules as regulate other interactions in society: contract, tort, property, criminal law. Instead of marriage, she sees 'a new family core connection – that of caretaker-dependent'.[77] And Mary Lyndon Shanley believes we should move to a 'legal regime of universal civil unions for heterosexual and homosexual couples alike'. Unlike Fineman, who wants to shift the emphasis to the mother-child relationship, Shanley still attaches it to adult relationships. Indeed, she accepts that 'publicly recognizing ongoing relationships assigns them a symbolic value distinct from that of individualised contracts, which recognize the separateness of the contracting agents and the quid pro quo nature of their agreement'.[78] And why, of course, should there be only one form of marriage? The gay themselves do not necessarily want marriage, which many of them see as an institution fit only for the 'straight'. But others do, condemning the institution of civil partnership, introduced in the UK in 2004, as a second-class institution, a form of apartheid.[79]

In the early 1980s, when Chapter 13 was written, there was serious discussion about establishing a Family Court in England, though the Finer Report had already been relegated to a back-burner.[80] At the time Chapter 13 was written – for a conference at Harvard – there was a Consultation Paper out for discussion, and there was another one in 1986.[81] There was then a hiatus before the Department of Constitutional Affairs published a further consultation paper, and then a response to the consultation, in 2005.[82] A family court is now envisaged as a long-term objective, and specialist domestic violence courts have already been established. There remains agreement that we need a court more responsive to the needs of families.[83] Discourses about the form of law, a main theme in the Harvard paper, are not now usually encountered in debates about the family court. Talk of the 'triumph of the therapeutic' seem almost perverse today given the failure to implement the divorce reforms of 1996. And who today brings Max Weber into debates about family dispute resolution?[84]

---

77 *The Autonomy Myth*, New York, New Press, 2004, 123.

78 'Afterword' to (ed.) M.L. Shanley, *Just Marriage*, New York, Oxford University Press, 2004, 112, 113.

79 *See* e.g. P. Tatchell, 'Civil Partnerships are Divorced from Reality', *The Guardian*, 19 December 2005.

80 *Report of the Committee on One Parent Families*, London, HMSO, 1974.

81 *See* [1986] 16 *Family Law* 247.

82 Respectively, *A Single Civil Court?*, and *Focusing Judicial Resources Appropriately*.

83 And *see Lomas* v. *Parle* [2004] 1 WLR 1642, 1652.

84 As I do in Chapter 13.

Chapter 14 on one level is of interest only to specialists on the problem of *agunot* (literally chained women). These are Jewish women denied a *get* (a bill of divorcement) by their husbands who, though they may well be civilly divorced, remain unable to remarry according to Jewish law. The problem remains, with Jewish halakhic authorities unable (or unwilling) to find a solution within Jewish law. And so Jews have turned to the states in which they live to find secular solutions. And legal systems have duly obliged. There is no evidence that much use is made of the English remedy (in the Divorces [Religious Marriages] Act 2002), by which the English court may order that a decree of divorce is not to be made absolute until there is a declaration by both parties that they have taken such steps as are required to dissolve the marriage 'in accordance with the usages of the Jews'. But this is not the point: it lets the rabbinical authorities off the hook; it releases them, so they think, from any obligation to find a solution within Jewish law. On another level the *get* problem raises the relationship of church (in this case a minority church) and state. Is religion any business of the state? This would take me far beyond the remit of this essay or this collection, but it raises sensitive issues like why we should have an established church. And this would take us also into big questions of human rights. Whether the *get* is compatible with human rights legislation is dubious. I have little doubt that the 2002 Act is incompatible.

The final chapter in this book began life as an 'Inaugural' lecture, delivered at University College London in 1985. It communicated a vision of family law, which I called 'critical family law'. Others since have been critical of critical family law[85], but I maintain the questions posed about the private and the public, about whether family law had the 'functions' usually attributed to it, in particular whether its protective function could be taken as unproblematic, remain important issues.

---

85 Notably John Eekelaar in 'What is "Critical" Family Law? (1989) 105 *Law Quarterly Review* 244.

# [1]
# Family Values and Family Justice

## Introduction: 'Family Law' in 1900

Family law has come a long way in the twentieth century. When the
century opened there was divorce for adultery only—aggravated
adultery where wives were the petitioners.[1] A wife who committed
adultery forfeited her right to maintenance and to property, even
property she had brought into the marriage. Domestic violence had
been discovered[2] and largely forgotten: it was assumed the
separation order invented in 1878 had solved the problem.[3] A
recent reform was the introduction of separation of property in
1882,[4] fought for by middle-class women[5] and of no relevance to
most. Married women still lacked full contractual capacity, a

---

[1] Matrimonial Causes Act 1857. This Act changed process and procedure: it did
not change the substantive law of divorce. And see Colin S. Gibson, *Dissolving
Wedlock* (London, 1994), chap. 4.

[2] See A. James Hammerton, *Cruelty and Companionship: Conflict In Nineteenth
Century Married Life* (London, 1992); Carol Bauer and Lawrence Ritt, ' "A
Husband is a beating Animal": Frances Power Cobbe Confronts the Wife-abuse
Problem in Victorian England' and 'Wife-abuse, Late-Victorian English Feminists,
and the Legacy of Frances Power Cobbe' (1983) 6 *Int. J. Women's Studies* 99, 195
(on Frances Power Cobbe and her legacy). On the US see Reva B. Siegel, ' "The Rule
of Love": Wife beating as Prerogative and Privacy' (1996) 105 *Yale LJ* 2117, and
Linda Gordon, *Heroes of Their Own Lives: The Politics and History of Family
Violence* (New York, 1988).

[3] Matrimonial Causes Act 1878 (the 'future safety' of the wife had to be 'in
peril'): this proviso was removed in 1895 by the Summary Jurisdiction (Married
Women) Act 1895.

[4] Married Women's Property Act 1882, on which see Lee Holcombe, *Wives and
Property: Reform of the Married Women's Property Law In Nineteenth-Century
England* (Toronto, 1983).

[5] See Dorothy M. Stetson, *A Women's Issue: The Politics of Family Law Reform
in England* (Westport, Conn., 1982).

316

disability that was to survive for more than a third of this century.[6] Not surprisingly the ability of a married woman to pledge her husband's credit for necessary goods and services assumed an importance that seems barely credible today.[7]

The law of marriage was firmly in place: reforms in 1753[8] and 1836[9] had opened the institution to public scrutiny and provided for a centralized system of state regulation.[10] Lord Penzance's definition[11] of 'Christian' marriage as a 'voluntary union for life of one man and one woman to the exclusion of all others' was unchallenged and, it seemed, unassailable. Polygamous marriage was not only denied matrimonial remedies and relief but was judged not to be marriage at all.[12] Of transsexualism[13] we knew nothing: the gay[14] were more likely to find their way into Reading gaol than its register office.[15] Quasi-marital relationships were denied legal status: a case[16] in the early years of this century stigmatized the contract involved as akin to one for prostitution.

Beyond the law of wardship[17]—and this then existed more to

---

[6] It was removed by the Law Reform (Married Women and Tortfeasors) Act 1935, s. 1.

[7] Though the common law presumption has not been formally abolished. The agency of necessity has: see Matrimonial Proceedings and Property Act 1970, s. 40.

[8] Marriage Act 1753 (Lord Hardwicke's Act). Elite public opinion began to favour reform in the 1730s, but Bill after Bill failed: opposition was greatest in the House of Commons.

[9] Marriage Act 1836. The Births and Deaths Registration Act was passed the same year. See further Diana Leonard, 'The Regulation of Marriage: Repressive Benevolence' in G. Littlejohn *et al.*, *Power and the State* (London, 1978). See also the thesis of Jacques Donzelot, *The Policing of Families* (New York, 1979).

[10] For the situation before see Lawrence Stone, *Uncertain Unions: Marriage in England 1660–1753* (Oxford, 1992).

[11] *Hyde* v. *Hyde and Woodmansee* (1866) LR 1 P & D 130. But John Cairncross notes that many prominent thinkers including Milton and perhaps Newton thought polygamy consistent with Christianity: *After Polygamy Was Made A Sin* (London, 1974).

[12] *Re Bethell* (1888) 38 Ch.D 220.

[13] *Corbett* v. *Corbett (orse Ashley)* [1971] P 83 was English law's first confrontation with the phenomenon.

[14] But for evidence of same-sex unions in pre-modern Europe see John Boswell, *The Marriage of Likeness* (New York, 1994).

[15] On the Oscar Wilde trial see Richard Ellmann, *Oscar Wilde* (London, 1987), chap. XVII.

[16] *Upfill* v. *Wright* [1911] 1 KB 506.

[17] On which see John Seymour, 'Parens Patriae and Wardship Powers: Their Nature and Origins' (1994) 14 *OJLS* 159.

protect property than the welfare of children[18]—there was little child law. The child's welfare only became a relevant consideration in custody disputes in 1886: it was not until 1925 that the child's welfare became the 'first and paramount consideration', and this only because of feminist pressure for mothers to have equality with fathers.[19] There was a rudimentary law of child protection in existence[20]—it had taken three generations since a similar law to protect domestic animals[21]—but no understanding of child abuse.[22] As for sexual abuse, incest was not even a crime[23]—for this we had to wait until 1908.[24] There was no law of adoption,[25] no child welfare system,[26] no legitimation by subsequent marriage.[27] The law placed full responsibility on the mother rather than the father for bringing about the undesirable situation of illegitimacy. Laws relating to illegitimacy were emblematic of the negative and

[18] Despite comments such as Lord Cottenham's in *Re Spence* (1847) 2 Ph. 247, 251, and Kay LJ's in *R v. Gyngall* [1893] 2 QB 232, 248. And see N. V. Lowe and R. A. H. White, *Wards of Court* (2nd edn.) (London, 1986), 4, and the Latey Report on the *Age of Majority* (Cmnd. 3342) (London, 1967), para. 193.

[19] See respectively Guardianship of Infants Act 1886 and Guardianship of Infants Act 1925.

[20] The Prevention of Cruelty to Children Act 1889. See for the origins of this C. K. Behlmer, *Child Abuse And Moral Reform in England 1870–1908* (Stanford, Cal., 1982). But Linda Pollock in *Forgotten Children: Parent–Child Relations from 1500 to 1900* (Cambridge, 1983) shows there was public concern about cruelty to children well before the 1889 Act (385 cases in *The Times* between 1785 and 1860 and only 7% resulted in acquittals).

[21] This had been passed in 1823. The sponsor of the 1889 Bill was 'anxious' that children should be given 'almost the same protection' (HC Debs., vol. 337, col. 229).

[22] For this we had to wait until the 1960s: see M. D. A. Freeman, *Violence In The Home* (Farnborough, 1979), chap. 2.

[23] It had been an ecclesiastical offence (except between 1650 and 1660) though ecclesiastical authority was in decline long before 1908 (and see Lord Penzance's remarks in *Phillimore v. Machon* (1876) 1 PD 481).

[24] Punishment of Incest Act 1908. On the origins of the 1908 Act see V. Bailey and S. Blackburn, 'The Punishment of Incest Act 1908: A Study in Law Creation' (1979) *Crim. LR* 708. Prosecutions for incest in church courts seem to have been rare in early modern England. See Martin Ingram, *Church Courts, Sex and Marriage in England 1570–1640* (Cambridge, 1987), 245–9.

[25] For this we had to wait until 1926: see Adoption of Children Act 1926.

[26] This developed after the Second World War: important triggering events were a scandal (the O'Neill death), a famous letter to *The Times* (by Lady Allen of Hartwood on 5 July 1944), and the Curtis Report (*Care of Children*, Cmd. 6922, London, 1946). See further Jean Packman, *The Child's Generation* (Oxford and London, 1975).

[27] Introduced by the Legitimacy Act 1926. It had been rejected by the Barons at the Council of Merton in 1236.

318

punitive approach to family regulation. The law showed no compassion towards the child, who could not even inherit from a mother who died intestate until 1926.[28]

## Family Law: An Academic Discipline

As the century opened there was no academic discipline of family law. For this we had to wait until after the Second World War. The London School of Economics was the first institution to teach family law—the law of domestic relations as they called it. The initiative came from the distinguished comparativist, Otto Kahn-Freund, whose tradition was very different from that just described.[29] UCL did not teach family law until the 1950s: it too called it 'the law of domestic relations'.[30] The subject lacked an academic text until 1957.[31]

## Family Law: A Discrete Entity

As an academic discipline, family law developed much as other law subjects. The early textbooks, particularly *Bromley*, were firmly rooted within a positivistic and legalistic framework. Family 'law' was a discrete entity, not part of a social continuum.[32] Viewing the discipline in this way had a number of consequences.

The law was seen apart from the values it embodied and helped to structure and restructure—and it is by no means a one-way process. Thus, to take an example, the relationship between law and patriarchy,[33] so essential to an understanding of family law, was not understood. Consider the resurrection of the 'one-third rule' in *Wachtel* v. *Wachtel*:[34] Lord Denning MR justified this on

[28] The ecclesiastical courts, however, gave a right of support: see R. H. Helmholz, 'Support Orders, Church Courts and the Rule of Filius Nullius' (1977) 63 *Virginia LRev.* 431.

[29] In a public lecture, he recalled the scepticism with which the innovation was greeted, particularly amongst practitioners for whom divorce was synonymous with family law.

[30] And see Roscoe Pound, *Jurisprudence* (St. Paul, Minn., 1959), vol. III, 68.

[31] When P. M. Bromley's *Family Law* (London, 1957) was published. The main practitioner text (first published in 1910) was called simply *Divorce* until its 16th edn. in 1991.

[32] And see Judith Shklar, *Legalism* (Cambridge, Mass., 1964).

[33] On this see Michael D. A. Freeman, 'Legal Ideologies, Patriarchal Precedents, and Domestic Violence' in Michael D. A. Freeman (ed.), *State, Law and Family: Critical Perspectives* (London, 1984), 51.          [34] [1973] Fam. 72.

the ground that on divorce the ex-husband would have greater expenditure than his former wife. He would 'have to go out to work all day and must get some woman to look after the house', whereas the ex-wife 'will not . . . have so much expense . . . she will do most of the housework herself'.[35] Compare his reasoning in *Button* v. *Button*[36] with that in *Cooke* v. *Head*.[37] Ignore the values involved and the cases may readily be distinguished. Ms Cooke was what we would now call a cohabitant. But look at the values. In *Button* the argument was that 'a wife does not get a share in the house simply because she cleans the walls or works in the garden or helps her husband with the painting and decorating'.[38] In *Cooke* v. *Head*, by contrast, where the female cohabitant did 'quite an unusual amount of work for a woman',[39] using a sledgehammer to demolish old buildings, working a cement mixer, and doing other 'male' activities (in effect demonstrating she was a crafts*man*), her work was richly rewarded. The message is clear: what women normally do, or are expected to do, has no economic value, but 'real' work must be compensated.

### Family Law's Image of the Family

A second consequence of the way family law as a discipline developed was that what emerged as family law, in the eyes of most family lawyers, academics, and practitioners, was a narrow and distorted image both of the subject of the discipline (the family) and of the processes which regulate the family.

First, let me explain this in relation to 'the family'. Family law is about husbands and wives (or those who live in relationships 'like' husbands and wives) and the children they produce. Of course, in part this is true, but I would suggest only in part. Why is it that we take it for granted that the family revolves around a sexual tie? Why is the 'sexual family' invested by our culture and society with exclusive legitimacy? Why is it, and here I quote Martha Fineman,[40]

---

[35] *Ibid.* 94.
[36] [1968] 1 All ER 1064.
[37] [1972] 2 All ER 38.
[38] N. 36 above, 1067.
[39] N. 37 above, 40.
[40] *The Neutered Mother, The Sexual Family and Other Twentieth Century Tragedies* (New York, 1995). Though I agree with this analysis, I do not accept Fineman's maternalist vision of the way in which the family should be conceived and structured. There is an excellent review article by M. M. Slaughter (1995) 95 *Columbia LR* 2156.

320

the 'foundational institution'? The sexual tie may not be a marital bond, it may even exist between members of the same sex, but it remains at the core of our understanding of intimacy and family connection.

In these terms single mothers are deviant: we never talk of married mothers because mothers are assumed to be married or in equivalent relationships.

We define children, even today, in terms of the relationship between their parents. Although the terms 'legitimate' and 'illegitimate' no longer exist in English law[41] and the legislation eschews terms like 'marital' and 'non-marital' (contrary to Law Commission advice[42] which favoured such epithets), the relationship between the child and his/her father still depends on the father's relationship with the mother.[43]

Step-children are only children of the family when 'treated'[44] as such by both their parent and the person to whom their parent is now married, and anything less than marriage will not do. This, it may be thought, is odd: are the 'couple' and their children not a family?

Relationships between parents and adult children, even adult dependent children, for example the many 'twenty somethings' who, in the absence of employment or marriage, have returned home fit ill within conventional concepts of the family. This is well illustrated by the discomfort the law feels when confronted by a family provision application by an adult child. Take the case of *Re Jennings (Deceased)*.[45] Jennings separated from his wife in 1945 and died in 1990. After the separation the only thing he did for his son, who was less than two at the time, was to send him ten shillings in a birthday card on his second birthday. The son from

---

[41] Family Law Reform Act 1987, s. 1.
[42] See Law Commission, *Illegitimacy* (Law Com. No. 118) (London, 1982), para. 4.
[43] Unmarried fathers do not automatically have parental responsibility: see Children Act 1989, s. 2(2)(b). They can acquire it (see s. 4), but very few do (see I. Butler *et al.*, 'The Children Act 1989 and the Unmarried Father' (1993) 5 *JCL* 157).
[44] See Matrimonial Causes Act 1973, s. 52(1). A child born to the wife after a marriage has been dissolved is not a child of the family: *Fisher* v. *Fisher* [1989] 1 FLR 423. There are similar, but not identical, provisions in the Inheritance (Provision for Family and Dependants) Act 1975 and the Marriage (Prohibited Degrees of Relationship) Act 1986 (and see the facts of *Smith* v. *Clerical Medical and General Life Assurance Society* [1993] 1 FLR 47).
[45] [1994] 1 FLR 536.

modest beginnings had done quite well. Now 50, he was comfortably off. Nevertheless, he wanted to claim financial provision from his father's estate. Did Jennings have 'any obligations and responsibilities'[46] towards his son? Wall J thought he did: the phrase was 'not limited to obligations existing solely at the date of death, but is wide enough to include obligations and responsibilities arising in infancy which were not discharged'.[47] The Court of Appeal did not agree: the reference in the Act to obligations and responsibilities which the deceased 'had' could not mean 'had at any time in the past'. Nourse LJ reasoned, '[a]n Act intended to facilitate the making of reasonable financial provision cannot have been intended to revive defunct obligations and responsibilities as a basis for making it',[48] and in answer to an alternative submission that a failure to meet legal obligations imposed a continuing moral obligation, the judge said the 'only factor on which the [son] can rely is the relationship between the deceased and himself as father and son, and this was not the intention of Parliament'.[49] Henry LJ, supporting this conclusion, said that 'it is not the purpose of the 1975 Act to punish or redress past bad or unfeeling parental behaviour when that behaviour does not still impinge on the applicant's present financial situation'.[50] The issue is rendered more complex because, despite twentieth-century reforms,[51] English law, unlike its civilian counterparts, still recognizes freedom of testation, and family provision is but an exception grafted on to this. Nevertheless a conclusion such as that reached in Re Jennings (Deceased) sits uncomfortably with the emphasis we would now wish to place on parental responsibility.

## Family Law and Social Control

If the image of the family was narrow, so too was our understanding of the state's involvement with it. As with other areas of law we saw

[46] See Inheritance (Provision for Family and Dependants) Act 1975, s. 3(1)(d). An excellent discussion is Kate Green, 'The Englishwoman's Castle—Inheritance and Private Property Today' (1988) 51 MLR 187.
[47] N. 45 above, 542.     [48] Ibid. 543.     [49] Idem.
[50] Ibid. 548. And see S. M. Cretney, 'Reforms of Intestacy: The Best We Can Do?' (1995) 111 LQR 77, 96–7.
[51] Beginning in 1938 with the Inheritance (Family Provision) Act. This Act was the initiative of Eleanor Rathbone. Lord Astor had six times failed to get his bill passed. And see Re Coventry (Deceased) [1980] Ch. 461, 474.

322

the law's involvement—thus also the state's—only at the point of breakdown.[52] It is true that the law refrains from intervention in ongoing relationships, though this can be over-emphasized.[53] This relative abstinence is said to reflect the values we place on autonomy, integrity, and privacy.[54] But, in seeing the law as occupying a central hegemonic position, we overlook the ways in which the family is controlled other than by legal rules and principles. Order is not just constructed by law.

We have begun to notice this now with the transfer of child maintenance to a regulatory body (The Child Support Agency)[55] and with the shift in the Family Law Act of 1996 away from law and lawyers and the new emphasis on process and on alternative methods of family dispute resolution, in particular mediation. But, if we had not totally immersed ourselves in the law reports, we would have seen the subtle and less than subtle ways in which family interactions were socially controlled. The boundaries between what is intimate and what is public have become blurred.[56] Marriage has become 'medicalized',[57] subjected to expert knowledge, guidance, and intervention. This has grown out of the interventionist strategies which developed in the nineteenth century to modernize the 'backward' parts of society, the lower social orders.

There are two discourses on marriage. One emphasizes social control, the other autonomy. The social control discourse is dominated by a view of marriage as an institution involving constraints, clear and prescribed social roles, and penalties for those who break the conventions and norms governing marital relations. The autonomy discourse emphasizes choice and depicts

---

[52] See Otto Kahn-Freund, Editorial Introduction to John Eekelaar, *Family Security and Family Breakdown* (Harmondsworth, 1971), 7.

[53] e.g. see John Eekelaar, *Family Security and Family Breakdown* (Harmondsworth, 1971), 76 (see also his *Family Law and Social Policy* (London, 1978) ). But see M. D. A. Freeman, 'Towards A Critical Theory of Family Law' (1985) 35 *CLP* 153.

[54] But see Carole Pateman, *The Disorder of Women* (Cambridge, 1989), chap. 6 on the public/private dichotomy and Freeman, n. 53, 166.

[55] See Child Support Act 1991 and Mavis Maclean, 'Child Support In The U.K.: Making The Move From Courts To Agency' (1994) 31 *Houston LR* 515.

[56] See Richard Sennett, *The Fall of Public Man* (Cambridge, 1974).

[57] See David Morgan, *The Family, Politics and Social Theory* (London, 1985). See also Christopher Lasch, *Haven In A Heartless World* (New York, 1977), referring to the 'new religion of health'.

Family Values and Family Justice 323

the social actor as a rational person empowered to shape family life in accordance with his or her life projects. These discourses express 'ideal-types'; they are ends of a continuum, and marriage and those who work with marriage—institutions ranging from the courts to mediators and counsellors—operate in the space between these polar positions.

If we narrow our focus, as the discipline of family law has tended to do, to family legislation and to what the courts are doing, it is easy to conclude that the autonomy discourse is in the ascendancy. The removal of the matrimonial offence,[58] a relaxed attitude to whom one may marry[59] and now where,[60] greater tolerance of polygamy,[61] even now of polygamous ceremonies by those domiciled in this country,[62] more recognition of quasi-marital relationships,[63] can be seen as freedom-enhancing, humanistic measures giving people greater space to do their own thing. But, even looking just at legal developments, the picture is blurred. Freedom extends only so far: we cannot change our sex[64] (the law is firmly rooted in biological determinism); we cannot marry persons of the same sex as ourselves:[65] countries which allow registered partnerships

[58] By the Family Law Act 1996. See, generally, Ingleby, 'Matrimonial Breakdown and the Legal Process: The Limitations of No-Fault Divorce' (1989) 11 *Law and Policy* 1. On the US see Herbert Jacob, *Silent Revolution* (Chicago, Ill., 1988).

[59] See Marriage (Prohibited Degrees of Relationship) Act 1986. Australia has gone further, removing all restrictions based on affinity (see H. A. Finlay, 'Farewell To Affinity and the Calculus of Kinship' (1976) 5 *Univ. of Tas. LR* 16).

[60] Marriage Act 1994 (civil marriage may take place in 'approved premises' such as stately homes and hotels but not 'behind the bushes', *per* Gyles Brandreth MP, HC Debs., vol. 250, col. 1330).

[61] Matrimonial relief has been available since 1972 (see now Matrimonial Causes Act 1973, s. 47). On succession are *Chaudhry* v. *Chaudhry* [1976] Fam. 148.

[62] See Private International Law (Miscellaneous Provisions) Act 1995, ss. 5 and 6.

[63] See generally Michael D. A. Freeman and Christina M. Lyon, *Cohabitation Without Marriage* (Aldershot, 1983). The Scottish Law Commission has recommended that a former cohabitant should be able to apply to a court within a year of the end of cohabitation for financial provision (*Report on Family Law*, Scot. Law Com. No. 135 (1992)). There are precedents in New South Wales (De Facto Relationship Act 1984, s. 27) and Ontario (Family Law Act 1986, s. 26).

[64] A person's sex is fixed at birth: *Corbett* v. *Corbett* (*orse Ashley*) [1971] P 83. The accepted view is that *Corbett* still represents English law (see *R.* v. *Tan* [1981] QB 1053; *Rees* v. *United Kingdom* [1987] 2 FLR 111).

[65] See Matrimonial Causes Act 1973, s. 11(c): parties must be respectively male and female. In the US see the Defense of Marriage Act, Pub. L. No. 104–199, § 3(a), 110 Stat. 2419 (1996).

324

usually draw the line at same-sex marriages,[66] and a legitimate interpretation of the growth of cohabitation law would see it not so much as an enhancement of autonomy to shape relationships as the thrusting, Malvolio-like, of marriage on those who would wish to escape from it.[67]

If we broaden our focus, we witness not so much a withdrawal of social control but what Stanley Cohen has called its 'dispersal'.[68] An effect of the 'triumph of the therapeutic' has been to 'increase rather than decrease the *amount* of intervention . . . and, probably, to increase rather than decrease the total *number* who get into the system in the first place'.[69] Cohen was writing of the criminal justice system, but the parallels with family regulation are too close to ignore. A generation ago we were flushed with enthusiasm for a Family Court,[70] described as a ' "caring court" with social and welfare services integrated within it as part of a total team operation'.[71] At least then these services were projected as part of a court. Now it is accepted that the focus—and with it the values— should be a clinic.[72] We are told that mediation will not be compulsory, though in practice it will become so, particularly for those who will also require state-subsidized legal services, in effect

[66] See Danish Registered Partnership Act, No. 372 (1989), Norwegian Act on Registered Partnerships for Homosexual Couples, No. 40 (1993), Swedish Law Regarding Registered Partnerships (1994). See also the Hawaii case of *Baehr* v. *Lewin*, 852 P 2d 44, *clarified* 852 P 2d 74 (1993). See also William Eskridge, *The Case for Same-Sex Marriage* (New York, 1996) and David J. Chambers, 'What If?' (1996) 95 *Michigan LRev.* 447).
[67] See Freeman and Lyon, n. 63 above, 183 (see also Freeman and Lyon (1980) 130 *NLJ* 228). A formidable defence of this is Ruth Deech, 'The Case Against Legal Recognition of Cohabitation' in J. Eekelaar and S. Katz (eds.), *Marriage and Cohabitation in Contemporary Societies* (Toronto, 1980), 300.
[68] 'The Punitive City: Notes on The Dispersal of Social Control' (1979) 3 *Contemporary Crises* 339.
[69] *Ibid.* 347. See also S. Cohen, 'Prisons and The Future of Control Systems' in M. Fitzgerald *et al.* (eds.), *Welfare In Action* (London, 1977), 217.
[70] I questioned this in 'Questioning the Delegalization Movement in Family Law: Do We Really Want A Family Court?' in J. M. Eekelaar and S. N. Katz (eds.), *The Resolution of Family Conflict* (Toronto, 1984), 7.
[71] *Per* A. H. Manchester, 'Reform and The Family Court' (1975) 125 *NLJ* 984. The model then was the Finer report, *One-Parent Families*, Cmnd. 5629 (London, 1974), part IV, ss. 13 and 14. It is now accepted that the jurisdictional reforms of the Children Act 1989 are as much as we are likely to get.
[72] And see John Eekelaar, 'Family Justice: Ideal on Illusion?' (1995) 48 *CLP* 190, 193.

## Family Values and Family Justice                325

the poor (and particularly women) whose personal lives have long been more intensively policed than the rest of the population.

### Family Law's Neglect of Family Issues

A third consequence of the way family law developed has been its continuing neglect of areas of life and social regulation, without an understanding of which it is not really possible to grasp what are generally agreed to be its central features. This is less so now of housing law or homelessness legislation or social security law than it was, but it remains the case with what is euphemistically called 'community care'.[73] Perhaps because family law has revolved around a sexual tie, it has been easy to overlook the elderly. In an ageing world, should not family law embrace family relationships with, and responsibilities towards, the elderly?[74] When, for example, will elder abuse (once distastefully called 'granny-bashing') be taken seriously?[75] When will family law acknowledge that this social problem comes within its horizons? The legislation is ahead of the textbook writers on this: elderly relatives come within a category of 'associated persons' and thus may use the domestic violence remedies in the new Family Law Act 1996[76] and, presumably, others may invoke remedies on their behalf.[77] The plight of elderly victims barely featured in the Law Commission Report from which this legislation derives, or in debates, discussions, or commentaries on the new legislation (including mine).[78] But that should not really surprise us: we have not as yet grappled with the problem.

Of greater significance is family law's neglect of community care.

---

[73] See National Health Service and Community Care Act 1990. Richard Titmuss referred to its 'comforting appellation' in *Commitment To Welfare* (London, 1968), 104.

[74] See John Eekelaar and David Pearl, *An Aging World-Dilemmas and Challenges for Law and Social Policy* (Oxford, 1989).

[75] See P. Decalmer and F. Glendenning, *The Mistreatment of Elderly People* (2nd edn.) (London, 1997), and B. Penhale, 'The Abuse of Elderly People: Considerations For Practice' (1993) 23 *British Journal of Social Work* 95, where similarities and differences with child abuse are discussed. On the gendered nature of elder abuse see Simon Biggs, 'A Family Concern' (1996) 47 *Critical Social Policy* 63.

[76] See s. 63(3)(c) and (d).                   [77] Family Law Act 1996, s. 60.

[78] It is mentioned in the Law Commission report. See *Domestic Violence and The Occupation of The Family Home* (London, 1992), para. 3.8.

326

Community care could not be more inappropriately labelled. It is care by the family, which means disproportionately care by women.[79] It raises important questions which family law has barely begun to address. If the state is imposing responsibility for caring for the elderly on to daughters and daughters-in-law, is it also giving them any status? It has taken us long enough to move from parental rights to parental responsibility.[80] Ought we to consider the rights and responsibilities involved in this caring relationship? It is perhaps a relationship best understood by reference to, or at least by analogy with, the trust relationship. This may fit better here than it does with the parent–child relationship, which some have wished to characterize in terms of a trust model.[81] The implications of extending a woman's homecaring role, particularly if she has to give up work (again), similarly needs exposing. In terms of property interests and financial provision, should any significance be attached to whose parent (his or hers) she is looking after? (It is to be assumed that it is a contribution towards the welfare of the family,[82] but this is to give 'family' a broader meaning than it usually has). More broadly, the issue of community care raises all sorts of issues about state regulation and social control, as social workers become increasingly involved with 'normal' as opposed to deviant families, traditionally their clientèle. Could they yet become embroiled in the lives of 'normal' families outside this context? Is the final triumph of a therapeutic state in sight?

[79] See J. Finch and D. Groves, 'Community Care and the Family: A Case For Equal Opportunities?' (1980) 9 *Journal of Social Policy* 487; C. Ungerson, *Policy is Personal: Sex, Gender and Informal Care* (London, 1987); J. Lewis and B. Meredith, *Daughters Who Care* (London, 1988).

[80] Parental responsibility was only encoded into English law in 1989 with the Children Act 1989, ss. 2 and 3. It did, of course, take much longer to recognize the authority of the mother: this was encoded in the Guardianship Act 1973, after attempts to achieve this in 1925 failed (on this see S. M. Cretney, 'What Will The Women Want Next?' (1996) 112 *LQR* 110, and J. Brophy, 'Parental Rights and Children's Welfare' (1982) 10 *Int. J of Soc. L* 149).

[81] See C. Beck *et al.*, 'The Rights of Children: A Trust Model' (1978) 46 *Fordham L Rev.* 669 and the criticisms of Chris Barton and Gillian Douglas, *Law and Parenthood* (London, 1995), 22–8. See also John Eekelaar, 'Are Parents Morally Obliged To Care For Their Children?' (1991) 11 *OJLS* 51.

[82] Matrimonial Causes Act 1973, s. 25(2)(f). And see Julia Twigg, 'Carers, Families, Relatives: Socio-Legal Conceptions of Care-giving Relationships' (1994) *JSWFL* 279.

## Family Values and Family Justice 327

### Family Law and Opinion

In Dicey's view law was based on opinion.[83] In *Law and Public Opinion in England during the Nineteenth Century* he quotes David Hume to the effect that 'the governors have nothing to support them but opinion' of the governed.[84] He also believed, somewhat paradoxically, that legislation could 'foster or create law-making opinion'.[85] He saw the law then both as secondary, taking its moral legitimacy from society, and as a primary force with potential for social engineering. Later writers[86] have shown that law is better able to effect social change in so-called 'instrumental', or morally neutral, areas of life than with so-called 'expressive' activities, of which family living is the quintessential example. Dicey recognized this: 'changes in the law which affect family life always offend the natural conservatism of ordinary citizens'.[87] But he also recognized—and was right to do so—the complex inter-relationship of law and opinion in the process of family law reform.

He uses two examples, the divorce reform of 1857[88] and the married women's property legislation of 1870–93.[89] Of the first divorce legislation he says, 'on the face of it [it] did no more than increase the facilities for obtaining divorce'. However:

in reality [it] gave national sanction to the contractual view of marriage, and propagated the belief that the marriage contract, like every other agreement, ought to be capable of dissolution when it fails to attain its end. This Act and the feelings it fostered are closely related to the Married Women's Property Acts 1870–1893.

Nor, Dicey adds:

can any one doubt that these enactments have in their turn given strength to the belief that women ought, in the eye of the law, to stand substantially

---

[83] *Law and Public Opinion in England During The Nineteenth Century* (2nd edn.) (London, 1914, originally published in 1905), 1.
[84] *Ibid.* 2 (see also 14). [85] *Ibid.* 41.
[86] e.g. Y. Dror, 'Law and Social Change' (1959) 33 *Tulane LR* 787; G. J. Massell, 'Law as An Instrument of Revolutionary Change In a Traditional Milieu' (1968) 2 *Law and Society Review* 179. [87] N. 83 above, 385.
[88] Matrimonial Causes Act 1857.
[89] One of the earliest statements of the need for reform is Eliza Lynn's essay 'One Of Our Legal Fictions', 9 *Household Words* 260 (Apr. 1854). In 1854 also Barbara Leigh Smith published 'A Brief Summary of The Law Concerning Women' (London, 1854).

328

on an equality with men, and have encouraged legislation tending to produce such equality. In this matter laws have deeply affected not only the legislative but also the social opinion of the country as to the position of women.[90]

And he concludes, 'law and opinion are here so intermixed that it is difficult to say whether opinion has done most to produce legislation or laws to create a state of legislative opinion'.[91] It is striking that Dicey should have seen the 1857 reform as a 'triumph of individual liberalism'[92] for it was legislation which upheld the interests of the community and of Christian morality. It was, further, censorious and discriminatory. It is, we would think, to the reform of 1969[93] that we should look to find the beginnings of a divorce law which embodies individualistic rather than collectivist ideology. And the dichotomy ill-suits the latest divorce legislation[94] which straddles the two.

Of married women's property legislation Dicey writes at length. Consistent with his thesis that law-forming opinion emerges from the ideas of great thinkers,[95] he attaches considerable importance to John Stuart Mill whose 'authority among the educated youth of England was greater than may appear credible to the present generation'.[96] Dicey is amazed at the speed with which married women's property rights developed in English law. His explanation was that rather than try to work any 'sudden revolution' in the law, Parliament had been content to engage in 'judicial legislation', that is, 'the reproduction in statutory shape of rules originally established by the courts'.[97] Although 'the simpler mode of proceeding was to enact ... that a married woman should, as regards her property

[90] N. 83 above, 43–4.　　　　[91] *Ibid.* 44.
[92] *Ibid.* 347. But in the 'Introduction To The Second Edition' Dicey uses divorce reform as an example of the contrast between the 'individualistic, or democratic, and the socialistic view of life' (see lxxix). In Dicey's terms Lord Mackay would be 'socialistic'!
[93] The Divorce Reform Act 1969 (if only in the provision allowing divorce on the fact of five years' separation: s.2(i)(e) ).
[94] The Family Law Act 1996. The new law is individualistic in that ultimately s/he who wants a divorce will almost invariably get one irrespective of the wishes of the other: the hurdles erected in the way of this goal, together with much of the language of the law, particularly that embodied in its principles, suggest valorization of the community over the individual.
[95] N. 83 above, 21–6.
[96] *Ibid.* 386 (see also 22, where Mill's *On Liberty* is quoted to the effect that 'wise' 'noble' things come from 'individuals').　　[97] *Ibid.* 362.

Family Values and Family Justice                    329

and rights or liabilities connected with property, stand on the same
footing as an unmarried woman',[98] Parliament instead made the
property of a married woman 'her "separate property" in the
technical sense which that term had acquired in the Courts of
Equity'.[99] At long last the procedures that were 'framed for the
daughters of the rich, have been extended to the daughters of the
poor'.[100] This analysis is interesting but, like many accounts by
lawyers, when they venture into the field of the sociology of law
creation, far from accurate. It is an explanation of legal development
but it is separated off from the political context and hence its
political meaning. What is missing is an understanding of the
existence of an alternative vision of what the law governing married
women's property should be. And this was found in the feminists
who campaigned for the original legislation in 1868: Lydia Becker,
Ursula and Jacob Bright, Elizabeth Wolstenholme Elmy (all of
whom were ignored by Dicey[101]), and John Stuart Mill.[102] The
principle of the original bill was that with respect to her property a
married woman should be able to act as a feme sole. The feminist
reformers sought legal equality between husband and wife: they got
an extension to all women of the protection and special status that
the few wives with 'separate property' had long enjoyed.

These examples draw attention not only to the complexity of the
inter-relationship between law and opinion, and do so from a
historical distance, but they also raise many questions about law
creation: about how a seemingly objective condition becomes a
social problem when it was not one previously,[103] about moral
entrepreneurship[104] and definition, about the impact of different
interest groups and different ideologies,[105] about the relationship
of courts and legislatures.

[98] Ibid. 387.              [99] Ibid. 387–8.              [100] Ibid. 395.
[101] But see Mary Lyndon Shanley, Feminism, Marriage and the Law In Victorian
England (Princeton, NJ, 1989). On these feminist thinkers see Barbara Caine,
Victorian Feminists (New York, 1992).
[102] Dicey lauds Mill, attributing the earliest married women's property legislation
in 1870 to his 'influence' (n. 83 above, 386). Dicey underestimates the importance of
the 1870 Act: he overlooks the fact that for the bulk of women 'earnings' were more
significant than 'property'.
[103] See Willard Waller, 'Social Problems and the Mores' (1936) 1 American
Sociological Review 922.
[104] On which see Howard S. Becker, Outsiders (New York, 1963), 147.
[105] See William J. Chambliss and Marjorie S. Katz, Making Law (Bloomington
Ind., 1993).

330

As a generalization it would be true to say that in the area of family regulation it is social forces which have shaped and altered law, rather than the reverse. But this does not tell us much. Certainly, this was the case with the first adoption legislation in 1926, with attempts at informal adoptions long antedating long-delayed legislation.[106] But this is less so in other areas concerned with the status of children, in particular in relation to children born outside marriage where even a proposal to allow for legitimation by subsequent marriage met resistance as late as 1920.[107] The growth of a law of cohabitation since the 1970s is clearly a response to the upsurge in alternative living arrangements and the perceived need to do justice between such partners:[108] the contrast between what the Court of Appeal was saying in 1959[109] and in the cluster of cases in the early 1970s beginning with *Cooke* v. *Head* could not be stronger. But the treatment of cohabitation as if it were marriage is not applied consistently through National Insurance, the tax system, or the maintenance regime.[110]

The courts are even prepared to accept that words can change their meaning in accordance with common and accepted parlance. Thus, in 1975 the Court of Appeal had no difficulty in construing 'member' of the tenant's family to include a woman who had lived with the deceased tenant for twenty-one years, though Parliament in passing the original legislation would not have had such a person within its contemplation.[111] What society understood as 'family', not what the legislature meant by 'family' more than fifty years earlier, was the determining consideration.[112] When, in the late 1940s, the House of Lords decided that a marriage could be consummated despite the use of a condom, and despite the Book of

---

[106] Though the acceptance by the state of adoption is both co-optation and regulation.

[107] The first Bill sponsored by the National Council for the Unmarried Mother And Her Child (founded in 1918) was introduced by Neville Chamberlain in 1920 and would have allowed for legitimation, as well as increasing the maximum affiliation payment and providing officers to collect such payments (see Jenny Teichman, *Illegitimacy* (Oxford, 1982), 162–4).

[108] It is largely judge-made law. See further Freeman and Lyon, n. 63 above.

[109] In *Diwell* v. *Farnes* [1959] 2 All ER 379.

[110] Or in family law generally: see e.g. *Burns* v. *Burns* [1984] Ch. 317.

[111] See *Dyson Holidays* v. *Fox* [1976] QB 503.

[112] Increase of Rent and Mortgage Interest (Restrictions) Act 1920, s. 12(1)(g).

## Family Values and Family Justice                    331

Common Prayer's admonition about marriage being about procreation of children, it did much the same thing, putting a concept
into the context of common practice.[113] The courts in both these
cases were, it may be thought, right. But was the Court of Appeal
also right to conclude that a woman who lived in council
accommodation with another woman, a secured tenant, and who
shared a 'committed, monogamous, homosexual relationship' with
her was not a 'member of the tenant's family'?[114] Their decision
accorded with common usage (and prejudice): was this an occasion
on which the courts should have taken a lead? Is it within the
judicial province even to contemplate doing so?[115]

To attribute a change and development in family law to social
forces does not advance our understanding by much and is, above
all, simplistic. There can be few areas of life upon which there is less
consensus. As a result family law reform is commonly controversial
and contested. The major divorce reforms this century (in 1923,
1937, 1969, and 1996) have all encountered opposition. The
reforms of 1937—though not the three-year bar on divorce—had
been recommended by a Royal Commission as long ago as 1912.[116]
At least the reforms of 1969 and 1996 were immune from
organized clerical opposition (indeed, the Church acted as a
catalyst for reform in 1969).[117] The passage of the latest Act was so
stormy that a government eager not to lose its 'pro-family' divorce
measure was forced into concessions on a variety of matters
including pension-splitting.[118]

---

[113] In *Baxter* v. *Baxter* [1948] AC 274.

[114] See *Harrogate BC* v. *Simpson* [1986] 2 FLR 91.

[115] The House of Lords in *R* v. *R* [1992] 1 AC 599 thought it could remove the
very long-standing marital rape immunity, and rejected what had existed for more
than 300 years because of social change ('marriage is in modern times . . . a
partnership of equals').

[116] Royal Commission On Divorce and Matrimonial Causes (Cd. 6478) (the
Gorell report) (London, 1912).

[117] See Archbishop of Canterbury Group, *Putting Asunder: A Divorce Law For
Contemporary Society* (London, 1966): this was a major source of the Divorce
Reform Act 1969. Contemporaneously, the Archbishop of Canterbury told the
House of Lords that the matrimonial offence existed for historical reasons and not
'for any reasons of Divine necessity' (HL Debs., vol. 278, col. 271).

[118] On pension splitting see s. 16, the result of a government defeat in the House
of Lords (see HL Debs., vol. 569, cols. 1610–35). In the House of Commons it was
made 'crystal clear' that the Family Law Bill would not pass without this provision
being added.

332

Change in law is a complex subject. Changes can be subtle and not so subtle. These can be changes in function without change in form with tenacity of conceptual thinking cloaking the uses to which those concepts are put.[119] Major changes can result from seemingly minor alterations in process: the introduction of the 'special procedure' in 1973 may have had greater impact on the reform of divorce than the Divorce Reform Act in 1969, but it was not even debated in Parliament and attracted little interest and less controversy.[120] The growth of legal aid and its subsequent near-withdrawal may have had greater effects on divorce than any alterations in grounds or judicial interpretations.[121]

It is common to talk about law and social change in terms of lag. Dicey was one of the first to attempt to explain why the law was often in arrears of social change, and critics are apt to seize upon the perceived gap between law and society and attribute this to the law's 'natural' conservatism. The American sociologist Ogburn built a theory around 'lag', what he called 'cultural lag'.[122] He tried to show how legal culture could hang over after material conditions had changed: one example he gave was the doctrine of common employment and industrial world in which it developed.[123] But resistance to change can only be characterized as 'lag' where there is one 'true' definition of a problem and one, and only one, 'true' solution.[124] The legal process is part of the total culture and in the normal case can only, and will, respond to demands levelled at it.

There are areas concerned with family regulation where it is difficult to believe that there is more than one 'true' solution. The 1923 divorce reform, giving wives the same rights as husbands, is such an example—at least from our perspective, though it was not so perceived then.[125] The removal of a wife's domicile of

[119] See Karl Renner, *The Institutions of Private Law and Their Social Functions* (London, 1949).
[120] See P. T. O'Neill, 'Divorce: A Judicial or An Administrative Process?' (1974) 4 *Family Law* 71.
[121] See C. Gibson, 'The Effect of Legal Aid on Divorce In England and Wales' (1971) 1 *Family Law* 90, 122.
[122] See W. G. Ogburn, *Social Change With Respect To Culture and Original Nature* (New York, 1950). [123] *Ibid.* 236.
[124] Lawrence Friedman and Jack Ladinsky, 'Social Change and The Law of Industrial Accidents' (1967) 67 *Columbia LR* 50.
[125] It was the fourth attempt at reform since the ending of the War. It gained support from the fact that married women had recently been granted the vote: see Lawrence Stone, *Road To Divorce: England 1530–1987* (Oxford, 1990), 394–6.

## Family Values and Family Justice                333

dependency[126] (Lord Denning called it the 'last barbarous relic of a wife' servitude'[127]) is another. The final extirpation, by judicial[128] and legislative reform,[129] of the marital rape immunity is perhaps a third example, but then we are reminded that the Criminal Law Revision Committee, as recently as 1984, recommended by a majority to retain the immunity in all cases except where the parties were living apart.[130]

These cases—and of course there are others—are the exception. Today, as before, across a range of family issues there is little or no consensus. The new divorce law remains controversial (should the period for reflection and consideration be longer where there are children of the family under sixteen?[131] Should there be no circumstances in which the basic waiting period can be reduced?[132] Why a waiting period at all when reflection and consideration have already taken place? Why, some will still say, is adultery not a ground for divorce?). Financial provision remains controversial (for example, many would think its assessment ought to take greater account of matrimonial misconduct.)[133] The rights of first and reconstituted families remains contentious: the controversies ignited by the Child Support Act in 1991 have not died away despite reforms.[134] The attitude the law should adopt towards those who live together outside marriage continues to excite passions, as witnessed by the angry, at times irrational, response to the domestic

---

[126] By the Domicile and Matrimonial Proceedings Act 1973.

[127] In *Gray* v. *Formosa* [1963] P 259, 267.

[128] See n. 115. This withstood challenge in the European Court of Human Rights: see *CR* v. *United Kingdom* [1996] 1 FLR 434.

[129] In the Criminal Justice and Public Order Act 1994, s. 142.

[130] *Sexual Offences* (Cmnd. 9213) (London, 1984).

[131] The Law Commission rejected the idea that the period should be longer if there were children (see *The Ground for Divorce*, Law Com. No. 192, para. 28). Cf. s. 7(11), (13), but note s. 7(12)(b).

[132] It cannot be reduced in any circumstances: the government adamantly resisted amendments to allow for abridgement (see HL Debs., vol. 568, col. 961; vol. 570, col. 18).

[133] This may be taken into account if in the opinion of the court it would be 'inequitable to disregard it' (Matrimonial Causes Act 1973, s. 25(2)(g), as amended by the Family Law Act 1996, Sched. 8, para. 8(3)(b) ). It is now emphasized that conduct may be taken into account whatever its nature, though in most cases where it has been taken into account it has been extreme (e.g. *Evans* v. *Evans* [1989] 1 FLR 351; *H* v. *H* [1994] 2 FLR 801; *A* v. *A* [1995] 1 FLR 345: cf. *F* v. *F* [1996] 1 FLR 863).

[134] See M. Horton, 'Improving Child Support—A Missed Opportunity' (1995) 7 *CFLQ* 26.

334

violence bill in 1995,[135] and the eccentric provision in the Family
Law Act 1996 stating as a normative proposition the 'fact' that
couples who live together outside marriage have not shown the
'commitment' that is involved in marriage.[136]

On child law issues, similarly, the consensus, where it exists, is
thin. There is agreement that child abuse is a 'bad thing', but not
upon what constitutes child abuse.[137] There is a 'spectrum of
abuse' and an 'index of harm'; that much is acknowledged.[138] But
there is a belief among some, not only the leading thinkers
Goldstein, Freud and Solnit, that sexual abuse and psychological
and emotional abuse are too vague and value-laden to warrant state
intrusion.[139] There is even less consensus on corporal chastisement
by parents, though a number of countries have followed Sweden's
lead and outlawed the practice.[140] It might have been thought that
legislation to ban corporal punishment in state schools[141] would
have had the effect of fostering or creating law-making opinion as
regards the hitting of children by parents, but it has not done so. On
adoption too there are big differences, so much so that the then
government abandoned its plans to implement adoption reform in
the 1996–7 session fearing it would provoke dissent on race and
sexual orientation issues.[142] The issue of 'open' adoption also
divides, including in constituencies within the child welfare
movement.[143]

[135] See Teresa Gorman, 'No Backbenchers in the Bedroom', *Independent*, 7 Nov.
1995.                                    [136] See Family Law Act 1996, s. 41(2).
[137] *Working Together* (London, 1991) lists four categories for the register and for
statistical purposes (neglect, physical injury, sexual abuse—which was not recognized
officially in 1980—and emotional abuse). Domestic violence is not included (on
which see Audrey Mullender and Rebecca Morley, *Children Living With Domestic
Violence* (London, 1994) ).
[138] *Per* Ward LJ in *Re B* [1990] 2 FLR 317.
[139] See Joseph Goldstein, Albert J. Solnit, Sonja Goldstein and Anna Freud, *The
Best Interests of the Child* (New York, 1996), 112, 122. See the critique by Michael
Freeman, 'The Best Interests of the Child?' (1997) 11 *Int. J. of Law, Policy and the
Family* 360.
[140] Sweden was the first country to do so (in 1979): others to follow are Finland
(1983), Norway (1987), Austria (1989), and Cyprus (1994).
[141] Education (No. 2) Act 1986, largely a response to *Campbell and Cosans* v.
*United Kingdom* (1982) 4 EHRR 293.
[142] See *Adoption—A Service for Children* (London, 1996), containing a
consultative Adoption Bill.
[143] See Murray Ryburn, *Open Adoption: Research, Theory and Practice*
(Aldershot, 1994). Secrecy has a relatively short history (it dates from 1949 in
England).

## Family Values and Family Justice                335

The development of family law does reflect the felt necessities of powerful interest groups, both their ability to construct law to further their meanings and interests and their ability to keep alternative agendas out.[144] Laws are arenas for the contestation of meaning. Those with the power to impose their meanings, and block out alternative visions/revisions, can present these meanings as more than consensual, as natural. There is no better example than the notorious section of the Local Government Act 1988 (section 28) which defined lesbian and gay relationships as 'pretended families'.[145] Such imagery is calculated to defuse conflict: who can believe in 'pretended' as opposed (presumably) to real families? Just as, in relation to the recent campaign, it would be difficult to find good reasons to object to 'family values' if one had no knowledge of the meanings packed into this symbol of political legitimation.[146]

The pivot for change may seem to be outside this structure of power. Often the *fons et origo* has been scandal, the Dennis O'Neill case leading to the Children Act in 1948,[147] the death of Maria Colwell being instrumental in helping to forge the Children Act of 1975,[148] the sex abuse explosion in Cleveland in 1987 becoming an effective source of the Children Act in 1989;[149] the birth of 'Baby Cotton' (as a result of supposedly the first commercial surrogate pregnancy) providing the spark for the Surrogacy Arrangements Act of 1985.[150] Sometimes there has been moral panic over real folk devils; at other times over fictive ones (for example, the large

[144] See Alison Diduck, 'The Unmodified Family: The Child Support Act and the Construction of Legal Subjects' (1995) 22 *Journal of Law and Society* 527.

[145] See Jeffrey Weeks, 'Pretended Family Relationships' in David Clark (ed.), *Marriage, Domestic Life and Social Change* (London, 1991), chap. 9.

[146] See as examples and for contrast David Willetts, *The Family* (London, n.d.); Patricia Hewitt and Penelope Leach, *Social Justice, Children and Families* (London, 1993). See also Kate Marshall, *Moral Panics and Victorian Values* (London, 1986).

[147] See the Monckton report (Cmd. 6636, London, 1945). Interesting insights may be found in Nigel Middleton, *When Family Failed* (London, 1970).

[148] On which see Nigel Parton, *The Politics of Child Abuse* (Basingstoke, 1985), chap. 4. For the growth of understanding in the US see Barbara J. Nelson, *Making An Issue of Child Abuse* (Chicago, Ill., 1984) and Lela B. Costin, Howard J. Karger and David Stoesz, *The Politics of Child Abuse in America* (New York, 1996).

[149] On which see M. D. A. Freeman, 'Cleveland, Butler-Sloss and Beyond' (1989) 42 *CLP* 85.

[150] On which see M. D. A. Freeman, After Warnock—Whither The Law' (1986) 39 *CLP* 33.

336

number of unmarried women queuing up for *in vitro* fertilization
that led to the passing of section 13(5) of the Human Fertilisation
and Embryology Act in 1990 which requires that a woman shall
not be provided with treatment services unless account has been
taken of the welfare of any child who may be born as a result of the
treatment (including the need of that child for a father) ).[151]

Sometimes, as Dicey wrote, change can be attributed to the
thinking of 'some one man of originality or genius'[152] (he had in
mind Adam Smith or Jeremy Bentham). In family law it is difficult
to construct such a pantheon; John Stuart Mill and Harriet Taylor
perhaps;[153] the women's suffrage movement;[154] the modern
feminist movement;[155] Goldstein, Freud and Solnit.[156] All these
persons (and movements) have influenced the development of
family law, but often their ideas have been redefined to fit goals or
programmes or have been used piecemeal (thus Goldstein, Freud
and Solnit's 'psychological parent' found its way into the Children
Act 1975 when permanency planning was on the agenda,[157]
together with a 'child's sense of time',[158] though this was not
understood by the legislature,[159] and the 'least detrimental alternative'[160] is encoded into the 1989 legislation, where there is less of an
emphasis on psychological parenthood).[161]

---

[151] See Gillian Douglas, 'Assisted Reproduction and the Welfare of the Child'
(1993) 46 *CLP* 53.

[152] N. 83 above, 22.

[153] See Barbara Caine, 'John Stuart Mill and the English Women's Movement'
[1978] *Historical Studies* 52.

[154] See Sandra Holton, *Feminism and Democracy: Women's Suffrage and
Reform Politics in Britain 1900–1918* (Cambridge, 1986); Jill Liddington and Jill
Norris, *One Hand Tied Behind Us: The Rise of the Women's Suffrage Movement*
(London, 1978).

[155] A good discussion is Dale Spender, *Women of Ideas And What Men Have
Done To Them from Aphra Behn to Adrienne Rich* (London, 1983).

[156] See n. 139 above, and see on their influence Peggy C. Davis, ' "There Is a
Book Out . . .": An Analysis of Judicial Absorption of Legislative Facts' (1987) 100
*Harvard LR* 1539.

[157] On which see June Thoburn, Anne Murdoch, and Alison O'Brien, *Permanence
in Child Care* (Oxford, 1986).

[158] See n. 139 above, 41–5.

[159] See the time limit provisions of the Children Act 1975 (ss. 29, 56, 57) which
take no account of the age of the child. The Children Act 1989 is more conscious of
this: see s. 1(2) and the time-tabling provisions in ss. 11 and 32.

[160] See n. 139 above, 50–61.

[161] See Children Act 1989 s. 1(5).

Family Values and Family Justice                    337

## The Family Today

To understand current debates about the family, the 'back to basics' campaign, the emphasis on family values, the concern with responsible reproduction and parenthood, the panic about divorce as well as about cohabitation and illegitimacy, some facts have to be established.

When this century opened there were 600 divorce petitions in its first year. The century has witnessed 'the emancipation of divorce'. As Gibson says:

> Marriages in Victorian times were regulated by a morally and socially divisive system which sanctioned separation but harshly restricted divorce. Only a combination of statistical ignorance, historical incomprehension and legal disregard could set the 600 petitions of 1900 against some 189,000 petitions in 1992 as evidence of earlier family permanency.[162]

Until the First World War divorce was largely confined to the middle and upper classes: changes in aid given to poor petitioners in 1914, together with the effects of the war, produced an increase in the divorce rate after 1918.[163] Even so, the rate was under one per 1,000 of the married population until the Second World War. It was 5.9 in 1971. It is now 13.1 (a decline from a peak of 13.7 in 1992). Such a rate, if it continues at the 1987 divorce level and pattern, suggests that about 37 per cent of newly formed marriages will ultimately end in divorce.[164] Almost three million children under 16 experienced parental divorce in the twenty years between 1971 and 1990.[165] It is probable that if trends continue, one in four children will have first-hand knowledge of parental divorce before

---

[162] 'Contemporary Divorce and Changing Family Patterns' in Michael Freeman (ed.), *Divorce: Where Next?* (Aldershot, 1996), 9. A good example of moral regulation is the warning in *Fisher* v. *Fisher* (1861) 2 Sw. & Tr. 410 that a petitioning wife would receive no more maintenance that was necessary for her support, and that it should be assessed on a more moderate basis than for alimony in cases of judicial separation.

[163] See Jane Lewis, *Women In England 1870–1950* (Hemel Hempstead, 1984). In France in 1891, where the assistance to the poor to undertake litigation was more generous, there were 13 times more divorce petitions per 1,000 marriages than in England.

[164] See J. Haskey, 'Current Prospects for the Proportion of Marriages Ending In Divorce' (1989) 55 *Population Trends* 34.

[165] See Gibson, n. 162 above, 15.

338

they reach the school-leaving age.[166] Fewer divorcing couples have dependent children than was the case in 1970 (57 per cent in 1992, compared to 62 per cent in 1970); even so the annual number of dependent children involved in divorce has more than doubled to some 168,000 in 1992 as a consequence of the increase in the number of divorces.[167]

Only Denmark of Western European countries has a higher divorce rate than England.[168] However, the rate of increase in divorce numbers between 1970 and 1989 is more than twice as high as Denmark (1.7 as opposed to 0.8[169]), suggesting that it is likely that we will soon overtake Denmark and become Western Europe's divorce capital. The median duration of marriage at divorce is about 9½ years.[170] But, if the trend is observed, this time span is deceptively high. Kiernan and Wicks noted in 1990 that 10 per cent of couples who married in 1951 had divorced by their twenty-fifth wedding anniversary; for those marrying in 1961 10 per cent had divorced by their twelfth wedding anniversary, whilst amongst those marrying in 1971 and 1981 the analogous durations of marriage were 6 and 4.5 years.[171]

The number of persons marrying is also in decline, though England still has the second highest marriage rate (6.8 per 1,000 per year of the eligible population) of countries in Western Europe.[172] The peak year for marriage was 1971. The median age for marriage then was 24.6 for men and 22.6 for women, two years

---

[166] See A. Cherlin, *Marriage, Divorce, Remarriage* (Cambridge, Mass., 1992), 26. W. J. Goode, *World Changes In Divorce Patterns* (New Haven, Conn., 1993) believes it may be twice this proportion.

[167] N. 162 above, Table 2.2.

[168] Central Statistical Office, *Social Trends* (London, 1993). Incidence is higher in the US (see J. Goldthorpe, *Family Life In Western Societies* (Cambridge, 1987) ). It was 21 per 1,000 in 1991. On Canada and Australia see Lorraine Fox Harding, *Family, State and Social Policy* (Basingstoke, 1996), 58.

[169] N. 162 above, Table 2.6.

[170] This is based on the length of time a marriage has existed as a legal entity. The evidence is that about a third of divorcing couples separate within five years of marrying. See Office of Population, Censuses and Surveys, *Marriage and Divorce* (London, 1992). See also B. Thornes and J. Collard, *Who Divorces?* (London, 1979) and Gibson, n. 1 above, 143–5.

[171] *Family Change and Future Policy* (London, 1990), 13.

[172] It is higher only in Portugal. In 1994 there was more than one divorce for every two marriages (158,200 divorces and 291,100 marriages): see *Population Trends* No. 85 (London, 1996).

Family Values and Family Justice                    339

less than it had been in 1951.[173] The sex ratio was more even (in the first half of this century and in the last century women outnumbered men). There was increasing economic prosperity and close to full (male) employment. Couples were thus enabled to marry and begin families earlier with the resources to do so and a reasonable prospect of a secure economic future.

Since 1971 the median age for marriage has risen: by 1991 it was well over 26 for men and well over 24 for women.[174] The fall in first marriage rates after 1970 was largely due to people under 25: the marriage rate declined steeply for men and even more dramatically for women. Teenage marriage rates also fell.[175] The trend has changed the prediction of those ever marrying/never marrying. According to the Family Policy Studies Centre, 'if present marriage rates continue, then the expected proportions of men and women married by age 50 would be around 77% for men and 78% for women, compared with 93% of women and 96% of men in 1971'.[176] The percentage of those marrying in church has also declined.[177] The increase in civil marriage is connected with the rise in the number of second and subsequent marriages,[178] and the general secularization of society. But it also masks a change in the understanding and meaning of marriage: there has been an ideological shift in which marriage is seen more as a terminable contract rather than a life-long and religiously sanctioned commitment. Marriage has become what Giddens refers to as a 'pure relationship', that is 'a social relation which is internally reverential, that is, depends fudamentally on satisfactions or rewards generic to

[173] See B. J. Elliot, 'Demographic Trends In Domestic Life 1945–1987' in D. Clark (ed.), *Marriage, Domestic Life and Social Change* (London, 1991).

[174] Office for Population, Censuses and Surveys, *Marriage and Divorce Statistics*, Series FM No. 19 (London, 1991).

[175] N. 173 above, 88 (in 1970 one in 10 teenage women and one in 40 teenage men were married: in 1987 it was one in 40 women, and one in 200 men).

[176] Fact Sheet: The Family Today; One Parent Families No. 3 (London, 1991), 1. But *Social Trends* No. 27 (London, 1997) projects that by 2020 the population of those over 16 who are married will fall to 49%.

[177] 51% of marriages were in register offices and 32% in Anglican churches in 1993 (see *Population Trends*, No. 80 (London, 1995). The proportion of civil marriages is likely to increase with the Marriage Act 1994.

[178] More than one-third of marriages are remarriages for one or both spouses. In the perspective of history this is not surprising, though in the 18th century, when the proportion was similar, most first marriages had ended on death (see L. Stone, *The Family, Sex and Marriage in England 1500–1800* (Harmondsworth, 1977).

340

that relation itself'.[179] It has freed itself from the traditional
influences which used to shape it, such as tradition, religious
dogma, and kin bargaining. The companionate, rather than the
institutional, marriage is part of this quest for self-identity and self-
fulfilment.[180] Other unions, gay ones for example, are part of this
same quest, as is divorce, with the opportunity this presents to
discover diverse family forms.

Companionate marriage, both as ideal and ideology, may have
contributed to divorce, raising expectations, increasing anger and
frustration, fuelling a cause of disappointment. Changes in attitudes
towards marriage (and divorce) have had their effect also on
counsellors, therapists, and others concerned with marriage guidance, so that there has been a shift from adopting a social control
stance, where the emphasis was on marriage-saving, to one of social
support, where the stress is on individual problem-solving.[181] And,
where once marriage guidance took a distinctly moral Christian
viewpoint, it is now less judgmental and more appreciative of the
needs of those who seek its help.[182] Sometimes, in reading the
debates on the Family Law Act 1996 one had to wonder whether
our legislators were aware of this shift in role: certainly, they often
acted as if the clock could be turned back. The 'right' sees divorce
as a societal rather than an individual problem, as a problem of
social order and welfare expenditure. There are those on the 'right'
who are prepared to argue that the welfare benefits system should
be used to coerce people into remaining married, even into getting
married in the first place.[183]

It also deplores the rise in the number of people living together
outside marriage. Cohabitation is common today as, of course, it
was in the past when the line between marriage and cohabitation

[179] *Modernity and Self-Identity* (Cambridge, 1991), 244. See also Janet Finch and
David Morgan, 'Marriage in the 1980s: A New Sense of Realism?' in n. 173, 55.

[180] See Janet Finch and Penny Summerfield, 'Social Reconstruction and the
Emergence of the Companionate Marriage, 1945–1959' in n. 173, 7. See also M.
Young and P. Wilmott, *The Symmetrical Family* (London, 1973).

[181] See Jane Lewis, David Clark, and David Morgan, *Whom God Hath Joined
Together: The Work of Marriage Guidance* (London, 1992).

[182] The writings of Herbert Gray and Dr E. F. Griffith, discussed by Jane Lewis in
n. 181, chap. 2 capture the flavour of early marriage guidance, including its
association with the eugenics movement.

[183] eg. Patricia Morgan, *Farewell To The Family: Public Policy and Family
Breakdown in Britain and the USA* (London, 1995).

## Family Values and Family Justice 341

was not clear.[184] We tend to think of marriage and cohabitation as discrete entities: our ancestors saw them, perhaps more accurately, as part of a social continuum. Cohabitation was not common in the 'permissive' 1960s. Only 2 per cent of women marrying before the age of 30 (both bride and groom being single) in the period 1965–9 had lived with their husbands before marriage. For those marrying in the period 1985–9 the proportion had risen to almost half (47 per cent).[185] Fewer than one in ten of those under 40 regard living together outside marriage as morally wrong.[186] Over a half of all men (55 per cent) and women (58 per cent) aged 25–29 report having lived in a extra-marital relationship.[187] It is estimated that in 1992 there were 1.3 million cohabiting couples.[188]

Cohabitation is no more stable than marriage, and is probably less so. Cohabitations tend to be short-lived, after which they either break up or are transformed into marriages. There is a finding[189] that divorce is more probable if the couple cohabits first: married couples who had cohabited were about 60 per cent more likely to have divorced or separated within fifteen years than those who had not cohabited. Whether such people by cohabiting indicated a weaker commitment to marriage or whether it is that cohabitation is practised more by less conventional people who are also for that reason more willing to divorce is not known. Nor, I suspect, would the disparity look as great if the years spent cohabiting were included in the calculation of the length of the marriage.

People are having children also outside both marriage and cohabitation. Although the law does not distinguish births within a

[184] See Phillipe Ariès, 'Marriage' (1980) 2 *London Review of Books* No. 20, 8. See also Freeman and Lyon, n. 63, chap. 1.

[185] Office of Population, Censuses and Surveys, *General Household Survey* 22 (London, 1993), 230. By 1993 it had leapt to 70% (*Population Trends* No. 80, London, 1995).

[186] Central Statistical Office, *Social Trends* (London, 1995), 75. The Protestant Reformation Society found in 1996 that 70% of members of the Church of England and 56% of active members did not believe it was 'sinful' for a man and a woman to live together without being married. Amongst those aged 25–35 the proportion disapproving was 12%. See *Independent*, 28 Aug. 1996.

[187] See British Household Panel Survey, *Changing Households: The British Household Panel Survey 1990–1992* (Colchester, 1994), 75, 78.

[188] *Social Trends*, No. 27 (London, 1997).

[189] See John Haskey, 'Premarital Cohabitation and the Probability of Subsequent Divorce: Analyses using New Data from the General Household Survey' (1992) 68 *Population Trends* 10.

342

stable cohabitation from those to single and unpartnered women, there are big differences. The global statistic that a third of births in this country are outside marriage[190] cloaks the distinction between children born to parents who are living together and those born to mothers without male partners. In 1990 75 per cent of out-of-wedlock births were jointly registered, and three quarters of these joint registrations were by couples at the same address.[191] Well over half of such births are thus likely to be cohabiting couples. About 4 per cent of all dependent children are reared in non-marital, cohabiting relationships.[192]

There has been a decrease in the proportion of households filling the 'traditional' family structure of a couple with dependent children: the proportion of families meeting this was 31 per cent of households in 1979 but only 25 per cent in 1991.[193] The proportion of families headed by a lone parent increased from 8 per cent in 1971, when there was sufficient concern to establish a Royal Commission under Sir Morris Finer,[194] to 21 per cent in 1992.[195] The United Kingdom has one of the highest rates of lone parenthood in Europe. A figure of 1.5 million lone parent families has been estimated for the year 2005: that could be close to a 300 per cent increase in a generation.[196] The number has gone up through divorce, but equally because of the number who do not marry. In 1989 one third of all lone parent families were headed by a never-married mother (there was 360,000 never-married mothers out of 1.2 million single-parent families in 1989, and they are

[190] The percentage is now 34%: (1996) 85 *Population Trends*. The sharpest increase occurred in the early to mid-1980s: see J. Cooper, 'Births Outside Marriage: Recent Trends and Associated Demographic and Social Changes' (1991) 63 *Population Trends* 8.
[191] See John Haskey, 'Estimated Numbers and Demographic Characterisations of One-Parent Families in Great Britain' (1991) 65 *Population Trends* 35.
[192] See John Haskey and Katherine Kiernan, 'Cohabitation In Great Britain—Characteristics and Estimated Numbers of Cohabiting Partners' (1989) 58 *Population Trends* 23.
[193] Office of Population, Censuses and Surveys, *General Household Survey* (London, 1991).
[194] *Report of Committee on One-Parent Families*, Cmnd. 5629 (London, 1974).
[195] Office of Populations, Censuses and Surveys, *General Household Survey* (London, 1994). 2.3 million children are growing up in lone-parent families.
[196] Family Policy Studies Centre, n. 176 above. It was 570,000 in 1971: see n. 194 above.

Family Values and Family Justice                343

growing at a rate of about 17 per cent a year).[197] Concern,
particularly on the 'right' has been voiced about this new
'underclass'.[198] The family behaviour of the poor and of marginal
members of society has caused alarm throughout history.[199] In the
1980s and 1990s there has been particular moral panic about this
'fatherless' underclass. In the United States, though less so in
Britain, this is tangled with issues of race.[200]

## Family Values

In Britain the underclass 'debate' is associated with a series of
polemical publications of the Institute of Economic Affairs.[201] A
principal concern is welfare dependency. This is said to undermine
the family. As Segalman and Marsland explain:

the family is the crucial—indeed indispensable—mechanism in producing
autonomous, self-reliant personalities, capable of resisting the blandishments
of welfare dependency. It is . . . only in the context of loving support and
rational discipline which the family offers . . . that children can be reliably
socialised . . . anything at all which weakens the fabric of families
inevitably generates and escalates welfare dependency. . . . Social policies
which . . . weaken the legitimate authority of parents in the socialisation of
their children are likely to create environments in which only exceptional
children are capable of growing up into genuinely mature and autonomous
adults.[202]

I have quoted this at length both because it is so representative of
'underclass' literature and because it has so many questionable
assumptions. I will look at just one: the underlying assumption that
the two-parent model of the family is essential for the normal
development of children. Without a father present, the children will

---

[197] See L. Burghes, One-Parent Families: Policy Options for the 1990s (York,
1993).
[198] See Charles Murray, The Making of The British Underclass (London, 1990);
Norman Dennis and G. Erdos, Families Without Fathers (London, 1992).
[199] For insights see Gareth Stedman Jones, Outcast London (Oxford, 1971).
[200] As in Charles Murray and Richard Herrnstein, The Bell Curve (New York,
1994). For a critique see R. Jacoby and N. Glaubermann (eds.), The Bell Curve
Debate (New York, 1995).
[201] e.g. n. 198 above and J. Davies, B. Berger, and A. Carlson, The Family: Is It
Just Another Lifestyle Choice? (London, 1993).
[202] Cradle To The Grave: Comparative Perspectives On The State of Welfare
(London, 1989), 121.

344

be improperly socialized. Implicit in this is the view that the mother's values and expectations will vary by type of family. But the only researchers to test this hypothesis, Acock and Demo,[203] did not so find. They found that parenting values held by mothers do not vary by family type. All family types had mothers who stressed the importance of following 'culturally valued guidelines for behavior'.[204] There was no statistically significant difference across family types for parental difficulties with children. Though 'first married'[205] mothers were twice as likely to be involved in school activities as continuously single mothers, there was little difference in maternal interaction across family types for pre-school children, or in mothers' involvement in the leisure activities of their school-age children. Single parenthood was found to be less stressful than pre-divorce parenthood. Divorced women living as single parents reported an improvement both in their parental status and in their functioning. The 'right' seems to assume that families without fathers account for a range of social problems, notably teenage sexual activity, drug use, and delinquency.[206] Acock and Demo show evidence of technically present but 'functionally absent fathers',[207] suggesting it is not in one type of family only that fathers are absent as active participants.

Acock and Demo found few statistically significant differences across family types on measures of the socio-emotional adjustment and well-being of children. When samples were controlled for social background, there were no significant differences across family types in academic performance. They conclude:

teachers, politicians and popular commentators are simply wrong if they assume that single mothers do not value their children's education, do not have high educational expectations for their children, or do not impose family rules. What is needed to support these families is not rhetoric but changes in social policy and the provision of social programs and special services to meet their needs.[208]

---

[203] *Family Diversity And Well-Being* (Thousand Oaks, Cal., 1994).
[204] *Ibid.* 219.
[205] Where both mother and father were in their first marriage and they had one or more biological children under 19 living at home (see *ibid.* 51).
[206] e.g. Gertrude Himmelfarb, *The Demoralization of Society: From Victorian Virtues To Modern Values* (London, 1995). See the critique of Linda C. McClain, ' "Irresponsible" Reproduction' (1996) 47 *Hastings LJ* 339.
[207] N. 203 above, 217.                   [208] N. 203 above, 231.

Family Values and Family Justice 345

What they get is rhetoric. In 1993 it was 'back to basics'.[209] The world was captured by the Bulger case, the trial of two 11-year-olds for the abduction and savage murder of a toddler.[210] The case was thought to illustrate graphically the supposed malaise in family life—neither Thompson nor Venables came from a traditional or functioning family. The case equally illustrated the absence of civic responsibility[211] as forty plus adults watched a distressed toddler dragged to his death, and none intervened. Would this have happened had James Bulger been a dog?

The 'back to basics' campaign lasted barely a year. It tripped on innumerable banana skins, as successive prominent government ministers were found not to know that the seventh commandment was central to the traditional values that they themselves were preaching. Its final demise, like his, came in February 1994 when a Tory MP was found hanging with an orange in his mouth and clad only in stockings and suspenders. The campaign itself was soon resurrected, this time using the catch phrase of 'family values'.[212] It is difficult to spell these out exactly. It is a moral campaign and it is pro-family. It is against welfare dependency.[213] It evokes an image of a past society characterized by stable monogamous marriage. It is a snapshot perhaps of the 1950s before liberalism, permissiveness, and feminism challenged and problematized conventional behaviour. It is a campaign directed particularly against men who fail to fulfil their parental obligations. In this respect it is more than a moral campaign: the Child Support Act can be understood as a dual discourse, in part injecting moral virtue but equally concerned with

---

[209] See M. D. A. Freeman, 'Back To Basics' (1995) 33 *University of Louisville Journal of Family Law* 329.

[210] See M. D. A. Freeman, 'The James Bulger Tragedy: Childish Innocence and the Construction of Guilt' in Anne McGillivray (ed.), *Governing Childhood* (Aldershot, 1997), 115. See also Blake Morrison, *As If* (London, 1997).

[211] On which see Suzanna Sherry, 'Responsible Republicanism: Educating for Citizenship' (1995) 62 *Univ. of Chicago LR* 131.

[212] A slogan rather than a concept. This is noted also by Steven H. Hobbs, 'In Search of Family Value: Constructing A Framework For Jurisprudential Discourse' (1992) 75 *Marquette LR* 529. He offers clues to an explanation of the concept.

[213] But see Nancy Fraser, *Unruly Practices: Power, Discourse and Gender in Contemporary Social Theory* (Cambridge, 1989): women dependent on state welfare as 'the negatives of possessive individuals' (152). Wider implications are traced in Jan E. Dizard and Howard Gadlin, *The Minimal Family* (Amherst, Mass., 1990).

346

saving public money.[214] It cannot be said to have succeeded in
either its symbolic or instrumental goals. It subjected a vast
population to a social security formula, many for the first time. It
scrutinized their behaviour and their finances, not surprisingly
provoked a backlash,[215] and led to some reforms.[216] It remains,
until the Family Law Act 1996 is implemented, the most concrete
example of family values in action. But its attempt to impose moral
and financial order seems likely to fail.

But it is not just a campaign against errant fathers. It is directed
against much in recent change: divorce 'the great destroyer'[217]
(there are too many and they can be gained too easily[218]), freer
sexual morality (cohabitation should be discouraged, abortion
restricted[219]), single parenthood (irresponsible reproduction is
particularly censored[220]). They want to restore traditional gender
roles, so that women should not be in paid employment but in the
home and available to care for children (as well as to undertake

[214] It was based on a White Paper called *Children Come First* (London, 1990),
Cm 1263, soon dubbed 'Taxpayers Come First' by John Eekelaar, *Independent*, 2
Nov. 1990.
[215] Though much of the criticism was misconceived or distorted the scheme came
close to provoking opposition on 'poll-tax' scale. A particular legal problem—the
conflict between the clean break principle and a continuing obligation to support
children—was seen in *Crozier* v. *Crozier* [1994] 1 FLR 126.
[216] See Child Support (Miscellaneous Amendments and Transitional Provisions)
Regulations 1994 (SI 1994 No. 227); Child Support and Income Support
(Amendment) Regulations 1995 (SI 1995 No. 1945); Child Support Act 1995 (and
see Michael Freeman, 'Family Justice and Family Values In 1995' in Andrew
Bainhaim (ed.), *The International Survey of Family Law* (The Hague, 1997), 142–6.
[217] *Per* Patricia Morgan, 'Conflict and Divorce: Like A Horse and Carriage?' in
Robert Whelan (ed.), *Just A Piece of Paper? Divorce Reform and the Undermining
of Marriage* (London, 1995), 31.
[218] Divorce reform was heralded by the Lord Chancellor before the Law
Commission report was published in 1990. In a speech to the Family Conciliation
Council (see *The Times*, 18 Oct. 1990) he called for a brake on 'easy' divorce. He
talked of the need to strengthen marriage and make the divorce process more
rigorous.
[219] Attacks on abortion are not necessarily motivated by pro-life considerations.
They may equally be targeted at what are considered to be the dangers of giving
women, reproductive freedom. See (in the US context) Walter Dellinger and Gene B.
Sterling, 'Abortion and the Supreme Court: The Retreat from *Roe* v. *Wade*' (1989)
138 *Univ. of Pennsylvania LRev.* 83.
[220] A critical assessment is Nancy Dowd, 'Stigmatizing Single Parents' (1995) 18
*Harvard Women's LJ* 19. We should not ignore, she argues, 'implicit stories of race
and gender that reek of oppression' (45). See also Martha L. A. Fineman, 'Masking
Dependency: The Political Role of Family Rhetoric' (1995) 81 *Virginia LRev.* 2181.

'community care'). The family values movement is also associated with an anti-gay backlash and a moral panic about AIDS.[221]

In the name of family values the Family Homes and Domestic Violence Bill was killed off in the autumn of 1995.[222] The Bill, based on a Law Commission report,[223] was proceeding smoothly and uncontroversially under the 'Jellicoe' procedure when it encountered the opposition of the *Daily Mail*, in particular its columnist William Oddie. He was able to whip up a frenzy of opposition among a cabal of back-bench Conservative MPs. His initial blast, 'How MPs Fail To Spot This Blow To Marriage',[224] was followed by an attack on the Law Commission, 'Legal Commissars Subverting Family Values'.[225] Much of their fury was misplaced or very late: some of what they attacked has been law since 1976.[226] A novel provision[227] to which they took exception would have extended to cohabiting couples the summary procedure in section 17 of the Married Women's Property Act 1882, and presumably also by implication its case law.[228] Not only would this have given them a quicker, more informal remedy. It would also have been cheaper for them and for the state. How insisting that such property disputes be determined by High Court judges upholds family values is beyond my comprehension. Anyone reading a case like *H* v. *M*[229] would soon realize that the determination of such disputes cries out for a simpler process. Though most of the lost Bill was retrieved in the Family Law Act 1996, the Government was unwilling to court further disaster by attempting this reform again.

[221] In relation to gay parenting see Helen Reece, 'The Paramountcy Principle: Consensus or Construct?' (1996) 49 *CLP* 267. An interesting case study is Phyllis Burke, *Family Values* (New York, 1993).
[222] See Clare Dyer, 'Homes and Guardians', *Guardian*, 31 Oct. 1995.
[223] See n. 78 above.
[224] 23 Oct. 1995.
[225] 1 Nov. 1995. For rational responses see leading articles in the *Guardian*, 28 Oct. and 3 Nov. 1995: see also Paul Vallely, 'How The Right Wing Went For Lord Mackay', *Independent*, 2 Nov. 1995 and Helen Wilkinson, 'Fundamentally Wrong on Families', *Independent*, 3 Nov. 1995.
[226] See Domestic Violence and Matrimonial Proceedings Act 1976, s. 1(2).
[227] See Family Homes and Domestic Violence Bill 1995, cl. 26 (in the Bill as amended on Report).
[228] Notably *Pettitt* v. *Pettitt* [1970] AC 777.
[229] [1992] 1 FLR 229. See, in support, Waite J's remarks at 242.

348

## Family Justice

The 'right' (or much of it) is also opposed to modern trends in divorce law. It would not see a link between a moral campaign on family values and the family justice embodied in the latest divorce reform (the Family Law Act 1996). The personal opinions of the Lord Chancellor, so clearly articulated in an unprecedented credo placed in the foreword in *Looking To The Future*,[230] are only partly reflected in the practical blueprint of the legislation. But he does not subscribe, nor does the Act give effect, to the view of marriage and divorce such as is found in 'family values' documents.

For them the new Act is the final nail in the coffin of marriage. It turns marriage into a 'provisional agreement, terminable at whim'.[231] It 'abolishes marriage'.[232] The end of fault, so one of them argues:[233]

will virtually kill marriage off as a concept with any legal meaning. Fault describes what happens when someone is held responsible for their bad behaviour. Abolishing fault abolishes the concept of personal responsibility. It effectively declares that the breakdown of the marriage is no-one's responsibility. Marital breakdown becomes instead something that just happens to unfortunate individuals, like meningitis or an earthquake.

She further argues that:

civil marriage does not set out the obligations of one spouse to another. They are inferred instead from the legal remedies in divorce. Duties such as staying together, being faithful to each other or treating each other reasonably exist only by virtue of the fault that accrues to desertion, adultery or unreasonable behaviour. Remove these defaults, and marriage becomes a vapid concept.[234]

This is a shallow, simplistic, and pathological view of law. Of course the law appears more visible when it is broken, just as the laws of grammar do. But sanctions do not create obligations: sanctions exist to support obligations.[235] Without sanctions (divorce

---

[230] *Looking To The Future: Mediation and the Ground For Divorce* (London, 1995), Cm 2799.

[231] Norman Barry, 'Justice and Liberty In Marriage and Divorce', n. 217 above, 39.

[232] *Per* Melanie Phillips, 'Death Blow To Marriage', n. 217 above, 13.

[233] *Ibid.* 14.                                                              [234] *Idem.*

[235] See H. L. A. Hart, *The Concept of Law* (Oxford, 1961), 193.

Family Values and Family Justice                       349

for adultery, for example) the obligation (in this instance marital fidelity) may be weakened (that is an empirical question, thus far untested[236]), or redefined (adultery, these critics seem to forget, is currently defined very narrowly[237]). The truth is we do not know. However, it seems unlikely that spouses currently desist from fornicating outside their marriage because of the sanction attached to adultery.[238]

Despite what these right-wing critics and moralists think, the new divorce law does embody a vision of the family which is consistent with some of the ideals with which we associate family values. It is a divorce Act which is pro-marriage; it encourages counselling, mediation, reconciliation, the promotion of good continuing relationships. The Act begins by setting out general principles, the first one of which is that 'the institution of marriage is to be supported'. Section 1 also emphasizes marriage saving and the promotion of good continuing relationships between the parties and any children affected. It should be noted that the reference is to the 'institution' of marriage, not the marriage which is the subject of the proceedings. Marriage is an ideological enclosure, the prescribed relationship against which all else is measured, and in comparison to which all else is found wanting.[239] That cohabitation is different from marriage is stressed in section 41(2): when dealing with the relationship of cohabitants (before making an occuptaion order) the court is directed to have regard to the 'fact' (it is so stated) that the couple 'have not given each other the commitment involved in marriage'. The courts may find it as difficult to unravel this as they have previously found the concept of living together 'as husband and wife'.[240]

---

[236] There is, however, some evidence of an increase in spousal abuse in American states which have removed fault from their divorce laws.

[237] There must be vaginal penetration: see *Dennis* v. *Dennis and Spillett* [1955] P 153. So (in Scotland) A I D was held not to amount to adultery (*Maclennan* v. *Maclennan*, 1958 SLT 12).

[238] We cannot assume that the literature in commercial law recounting the necessity for preserving incentives for good faith behaviour in long-term commercial relationships has any force in the domestic context: see, e.g., Scott, 'Conflict and Co-operation In Long-Term Contracts' (1987) 75 *California L Rev.* 2005. But note Milton C. Regan, *Family Law And The Pursuit of Intimacy* (New York, 1993), 139.

[239] See Carol Smart, *The Ties That Bind* (London, 1984), 141–6.

[240] *McLean* v. *Nugent* (1980) 1 FLR 26; *Tuck* v. *Nicholls* [1989] 1 FLR 283; *Adeoso* v. *Adeoso* [1981] 1 All ER 107; and in, the context of marriage, *Fuller* v.

350

The new Act emphasizes marriage in other ways too. It slows up
the process of divorce. 'Quickie' divorces, available when the
adultery or behaviour facts are used, as they have been in 75 per
cent of divorces, become a thing of the past.[241] It will now take a
minimum of eighty weeks to end a marriage where there are
children of the family under 16.[242] The Act is full of waiting
periods: the one-year absolute bar on divorce is retained[243] (though
the justifications posited for this are weak[244]); at least three months
must elapse between attending an information meeting and making
a statement of marital breakdown which commences the divorce
process; a period of nine months and fourteen days (fifteen months
and fourteen days where there is a child of the family under 16) is
set aside for reflection on whether the marriage can be saved and to
give space to effect a reconciliation, and for consideration of future
arrangements.[245] The standard period for reflection and consideration can be extended:[246] it can never be reduced, not even in cases
of extreme violence or moral turpitude, not even where the delay
will detrimentally affect the health or welfare of children, not even
when the applicant is terminally ill and will not survive long enough
to get a divorce order, perhaps to remarry and legitimate
children.[247] What does this moral absolutism imply? It can only be
an attempt to convey that marriage is not to be relinquished lightly.
So couples who have done their reflecting and considering and
couples incapable of reflecting and considering on anything for
fifteen minutes will still have to wait for fifteen months (if they have
school-age children). Many, of course, will already be in other

*Fuller* [1973] 1 WLR 730 and *Santos* v. *Santos* [1972] Fam. 247. See also Mary
Hayes, ' "Cohabitation Clauses" In Financial Provision and Property Adjustment
Orders—Law, Policy and Justice' (1994) 110 *LQR* 124.

[241] See Gwynn Davis and Mervyn Murch, *Grounds For Divorce* (Oxford, 1988):
see chap. 5 on the choice of 'fact'.

[242] See Family Law Act 1996, s. 7(11), (13).

[243] See Family Law Act 1996, s. 7(6).

[244] The Law Commission dodged the issue (see *The Ground For Divorce*
(London, 1992), Law Com. No. 192, para. 5.82): *Looking To The Future*, n. 230
above, though it would help 'to protect couples rushing into re-marriage too soon
without having had time to think why their previous marriage was so short-lived'
(para. 4.42).

[245] See Family Law Act 1996, s. 8(2), 7(3), (11), (13).

[246] See Family Law Act 1996, s. 7(13) (for circumstances where it cannot be
extended are s. 7(12)).

[247] Because, allegedly, to do so would be to re-introduce considerations of fault.

Family Values and Family Justice                      351

relationships, and many of these will have broken up before the marriage is ended. Oddly, the Act encourages extra-marital cohabitation (also perhaps abandonment and bigamy) by extending the uncoupling process.

Central to this new system of family justice is mediation.[248] The Law Commission recommended it, though it conceded that there were dangers in relying 'too heavily upon . . . mediation instead of more traditional methods of negotiation and adjudication'. It listed these as

exploitation of the weaker by the stronger . . . considerable potential for delay, which is damaging both to the children and often to the interests of one of the adults involved . . . and the temptation for the court to postpone deciding some very difficult and painful cases which ought to be decided quickly.[249]

The government's view, nevertheless, was that a 'greater use of mediation . . . will help achieve the objectives of a good divorce system'.[250] There were fears that mediation would be compulsory. It is not to be, though there is a clear 'encouragement'[251] to use family mediation.

Concern has been expressed about the move to mediation.[252] It constitutes a shift in the paradigm of dispute resolution away from law and lawyers.[253] Mediation is couched in the language of responsibilities—it is said to enable spouses to take responsibility for the breakdown of their marriage and to encourage them to look to their future responsibilities[254]—and there is no denying that these are important. But so are rights,[255] and law and lawyers, whatever the faults of the institution and its practitioners, have a reasonable record in protecting these. It is perfectly consistent with the move away from moral judgment (at least that found in the

---

[248] See Simon Roberts, 'Mediation In Family Law Disputes' (1983) 46 *MLR* 537. On the need for lawyers and mediators to offer a complementary service see Janet Walker, 'Is There A Future For Lawyers In Divorce?' (1996) 10 *Int. J of Law, Policy and the Family* 52.                              [249] N. 244 above, para. 5.34.
[250] N. 230 above, para. 5.21.              [251] N. 230 above, para. 5.21.
[252] See John Eekelaar, n. 72 above; S. Cretney, 'Divorce Reform in England: Humbug and Hypocrisy or a Smooth Transition?' in Freeman (ed.), n. 152 above, 39. See also C. Piper in Freeman (ed.), n. 162 above, 63.
[253] See M. Freeman, n. 70 above.              [254] See n. 230, above, para. 5.21.
[255] Particularly to the weak: see Kimberlé Crenshaw, 'Race, Reform and Retrenchment: Transformation and Legitimation In Anti-Discrimination Law' (1988) 100 *Harvard L Rev.* 1331.

352

evaluation of conduct that the fault fact represented) that a process which looks to the future rather than judging the past should become dominant. But if rights are not publicized—and many mediators will not fully understand legal implications—and not protected, who will lose out? The fear is that most victims will be women. You cannot negotiate decisions and renegotiate relationships without access to full and competent information. Without it important legal rights may be unknowingly relinquished, entire issues may be overlooked, and time and money may be wasted mediating an agreement which subsequently has to be rewritten when legal advice is obtained. We do not know what attitude the courts will take to agreements negotiated during a mediation, particularly where there is a gross imbalance in bargaining power.[256]

There is concern also in the context of domestic violence[257]— perhaps the grossest example of where unequal power distorts bargaining relationships. It may be that cases of domestic violence will be exempted from mediation. But why just cases of violence? What of other forms of abuse? What of cases where there has been, and is likely therefore still to be, economic exploitation? Concern has been expressed also about the impact of mediation on children. As Martin Richards has noted, 'mediation is an adult business and, although adults may be bargaining in the shadow of their children's needs as they perceive them, children cannot be party to it.'[258] The government's response was that 'mediation services are very conscious of children's needs'.[259] It thought that soon mediators will be specifically trained to deal appropriately with the interests of children, even to receive guidance on when it is appropriate to involve children in mediation.[260] It is ironic that when the

---

[256] For evidence of pressures to agree to settlements see Gwynn Davis *et al.*, *Simple Quarrels* (Oxford, 1994). And see *Edgar* v. *Edgar* [1980] 3 All ER 887.

[257] See Trina Grillo, 'The Mediation Alternative: Process Dangers for Women' (1991) 100 *Yale LJ* 1545; Penelope Bryan, 'Killing Us Softly: Divorce Mediation and the Politics of Power' (1992) 40 *Buffalo L Rev.* 441; Felicity Kaganas and Christine Piper, 'Domestic Violence and Divorce Mediation' (1994) *JSWFL* 265.

[258] 'But What About The Children? Some Reflections On The Divorce White Paper', (1995) 7 *CFLQ* 223, 225.

[259] N. 230 above, para. 5.32. See also Adrian L. James, 'Social Work in Divorce: Welfare, Mediation and Justice' (1995) 9 *Int. J of Law and the Family* 256, arguing that mediation is becoming synonymous with child welfare.

[260] N. 230 above, para. 5.33.

Family Values and Family Justice                353

competence of children to participate is more and more being recognized,[261] when they are granted more and more rights to independent representation in legal proceedings, that a shift away from law and lawyers should see this snatched away from them, particularly in an Act which strengthens their status.[262]

What the effects of the new Act will be on divorce remains contentious. It will lengthen the process of divorce. There will be some reconciliations. We may never learn how many, any more than we know why at present there are many more divorce petitions that decrees nisi, and why there is a significant shortfall between the number of decrees nisi and absolute.[263] Perhaps more cases will fall by the wayside than now. If so there will be a growing number of persons living in a status of limbo. Whether the number of divorces will go up depends on a number of matters. It is commonly said that with each divorce reform, divorce increases.[264] But this is not strictly so. To take only the most obvious example, it would seem that the number of divorce petitions rose substantially with the implementation of the Divorce Reform Act in 1971. But the 1960s saw an annual rise of 9.5 per cent to a peak of 70,575 petitions in 1970. If this yearly increase had continued there would have been over 200,000 petitions by 1990, when there were in fact 189,000.[265] Both Schoen and Baj[266] and Haskey[267] have followed birth cohorts, and each found that successive generations register a higher rate of divorce. The structure and processes of divorce law

---

[261] See Elizabeth S. Scott, 'Judgment and Reasoning In Adolescent Decisionmaking' (1992) 37 *Villanova L Rev.* 1607; Priscilla Alderson, *Children's Consent To Surgery* (Buckingham, 1993); *Gillick* v. *West Norfolk and Wisbech AHA* [1986] AC 112; and the Children Act 1989.

[262] See Family Law Act 1996, s. 11 (and see also s. 64). The significance of s. 11 can, however, be over-emphasized, as the Lord Chancellor did (see HL, Debs., vol. 567, col. 703) when he stressed that 'all arrangements will have to be decided before divorce', which is in this context is not true.

[263] Davis and Murch, n. 241 above, 53, point to a 'fall-off' rate of about 2% between nisi and absolute: the 'fall-off' from petition to decree nisi is even more pronounced (perhaps as high as 15%).

[264] Notably by Ruth Deech, 'Divorce Law and Empirical Studies' (1990) 106 LQR 229, 242.

[265] As observed by C. Gibson, n. 162 above, 32.

[266] 'Twentieth Century Cohort Marriage and Divorce in England and Wales', *Population Studies* 38, 439 (1984).

[267] 'First Marriage, Divorce and Remarriage: Birth Cohort Analyses', *Population Trends* 72, 24 (1993).

354

have little impact on the incidence of divorce or marital breakdown. What then does?

We live in a privatized world: Mrs Thatcher's notorious remark about there being no such thing as society, only individuals, was ideological, not sociological. But the society she helped to forge, one built on egoism and selfishness, was one in which divorce could be expected to flourish. We also live increasingly in a secularized world, less constrained by religious and traditional codes of morality. There is a backlash against this, and some attempt is being made to reinject a sense of community. It is in part upon the success of this that we wait to see whether the number of those getting divorced will increase or not.

It is short-sighted to think that our answers lie in systems of family justice. It is not to marital law that we should look to create better or happier families. It can play a role, but it is subsidiary to a basket of other policies. In the coda to this article I address a few of these.

### Justice For The Family

Anyone who studies the family in Britain today cannot fail to be struck by the absence of a family policy, particularly when we examine the ways that our neighbours treat the family.[268]

The family values rhetoric, with its emphasis on moral malaise, on family disintegration, on the growth of an underclass, leads to policies placing greater emphasis on family obligations and responsibilities, to punitive welfare policies and to other forms of social control. There is a weak commitment in Britain towards creating the infrastructure on which an explicit and coherent family policy can be built. We lack strong institutional support for mothers' labour market chances. We are laggard in our provision of socialized child care facilities. Our provision of cash benefits subsidizing the costs of children is poor. We have long panicked

---

[268] In particular France: see Linda Hantrais, 'Comparing Family Policy in Britain, France and Germany' (1994) 23 *Journal of Social Policy* 135 and Jane Lewis, 'Gender and the Development of Welfare Regimes' (1992) 2 *Journal of European Social Policy* 159. Though dated, Sheila Kamerman and Alfred Kahn's *Family Policy: Government and Families in Fourteen Countries* (New York, 1978) is still an invaluable source. S. Zimmerman, *Family Policies and Family Well-Being* (Newbury Park, Cal., 1992) is also useful in relation to the US.

Family Values and Family Justice 355

over lone mothers. It was their heavy dependence on the social security system that motivated the establishment of the Child Support Agency. Of course men should meet their obligation to children they have fathered. But more could be done to enable these women to work. Currently, they have a very low employment rate: compare Sweden where 87 per cent of lone mothers are in the labour force and, when not working full-time, hold jobs which provide the legal entitlement to work three quarters of the normal day, with all the occupational benefits accruing to full-time employees, while their children are small.[269] In France (as well as Belgium), 95 per cent of 3 to 5-year-olds have places in publicly funded childcare facilities: ten times as many French women work through their child bearing years as those in Britain.[270] We are the only country in Europe where lone mothers have a lower full-time employment rate than mothers in two-parent families.[271] The nursery voucher scheme showed the Conservative government may have begun to understand the problem, though it did not find the solution. And low pay remains a consistent feature of women's work. Britain is 'one of three countries in the EC which have the highest proportion of female low paid'.[272]

We need to find ways of assisting entry to the labour market for lone parents. Instead we have concentrated on ways of finding savings in the social security budget. So the Child Support Act of 1991 was introduced to substitute private transfers for public ones, not to augment family income for poor lone-parent families.

On maternity leave we now compare favourably. But until October 1994 we were the only country in the EC which insisted on a 'length of service' condition to maternity leave. We have not

[269] See A. Leira, 'The Woman Friendly Welfare State? The Case of Norway and Sweden' in Jane Lewis (ed.), *Women and Social Policies in Europe* (Aldershot, 1993).
[270] See A. Phillips and P. Moss, *Who Cares for Europe's Children? The Short Report of the European Childcare Network* (Brussels, 1988).
[271] See S. Dex and P. Walters, 'Women's Occupational Status in Britain, France and the USA: Explaining The Difference' (1989) 20 *Industrial Relations Journal* 203.
[272] S. Dex, S. Lissenburgh and M. Taylor, *Women and Low Pay: Identifying The Issues* (Manchester, 1994), p. vii. In 1995 women manual workers' hourly pay was 72% of men's (with non-manual workers it was 68%). Since women work a shorter week, their gross weekly earnings were lower (67%; and 65% respectively: see Central Statistical Office, *New Earnings Survey* (London, 1995), Table 20.1.

356

hitherto given entitlement to parental leave. The Conservative Government refused to comply with the EC Directive on this,[273] consistent with its decision (now likely to be revoked by the new Labour Government) to opt out of the Social Chapter of the Maastricht Treaty.[274] In France by comparison, parental levae from work can be taken by either men or women until a child is 3 and extend up to a period of three years. In Denmark parental leave is a statutory right (ten weeks at 90 per cent of earnings). Germany allows eighteen months' leave, but pays a low flat-rate payment for only six months. Italy pays 30 per cent of earnings for six months.

These examples could be multiplied. What they show is what family values could look like. We can deplore and despise the right's stand on 'family values' and still support family values. We need a policy which values the family, which upholds the integrity of all of its members, which enhances the opportunities of its members to fulfil their life chances, which offers support rather than discipline. If family law is to play a part in this reconstruction it will have to break beyond the conventional boundaries to examine social policies as they affect family members. It will also have to look beyond the boundaries of this country to Maastricht and beyond.

## The Future

I doubt whether the future—certainly the short-term future—will see the development of any such family policy, though the new Labour Government is committed to adopting the Social Chapter of the Maastricht Treaty.[275] What it will see is both resistance to change and pressure for change. The new divorce law will be seen as meddlesome and onerous. The mediation system will not be able to cope and there will be demand for the new processes to be relaxed. In time the period for reflection and consideration will be reduced, probably to six months. Nor will the differential for those

---

[273] (1996) 96/34/EC: OJL 145, 4.
[274] See Peter Lange, 'Maastricht and the Social Procotol: Why Did They Do It?' (1993) 21 *Politics and Society* 5. But see Brian Burkitt and Mark Baimbridge, 'The Maastricht Treaty's Impact on the Welfare State' (1995) 42 *Critical Social Policy* 100.
[275] Bribes (tax allowances) to keep women (probably only married women) at home is a distinct possibility, but hardly a welcome one.

with children be sustained. The information meeting will disappear, to be replaced by a booklet or, as likely, the internet. By the time of the next divorce law, in 2020 or thereabouts, divorce is likely to be an administrative procedure, nothing more.

Cohabitation will become more and more like marriage, or marriage more and more like cohabitation. The pressure may be for the latter, but so long as the family is seen as an instrument of state policy, assimilation is likely to be in the direction of marriage. Same-sex marriages, though barely on the agenda in this country,[276] will be allowed. So, of course, will the marriage of transsexuals. These concessions to pluralism will liberalize, but will also colonize—the state gaining control of a wider range of relationships. Divorce law, in as much as such 'law' exists, will extend to these newly-recognized marriages and, by analogy, to cohabitation as well. We will continue to struggle to define cohabitation, but those relationships embraced by whatever definition is adopted will find a marriage-like regime imposed on them. This could lead to courts acquiring a discretion over money and property issues[277] when cohabitation is brought to an end. But the discretion the courts have now with marriage is likely to come under increasing scrutiny[278] and if fixed rules emerge, as I think they are likely to do, they will apply to cohabitation also.[279] This would be a case of marriage adopting the current legal practices of cohabitation, though, of course, the rules originate in marriage.[280] Though some will continue to call for the end of maintenance, it is more likely

[276] In contrast to Scandinavia, the Netherlands, and the United States. On the US see Mark Strasser, *Legally Wed: Same-Sex Marriages and the Constitution* (Ithaca, NY, 1997) and contrast Lynn Wardle, 'A Critical Analysis of Constitutional Claims for Same-Sex Marriage' (1996) *Brigham Young L Rev.* 1.

[277] Including pension issues: see *The Treatment of Pension Rights On Divorce* (London, 1996), Cm 3345. A comparative prospective (and warning) is David L. Baumer and J. C. Poindexter, 'Women and Divorce: The Perils of Pension Division' (1996) 57 *Ohio State LJ* 203.

[278] As in the United States: see Jane C. Murphy, 'Eroding The Myth of Discretionary Justice in Family Law: The Child Support Experiment' (1991) 70 *NCLRev.* 209 and Carl E. Schneider, 'Discretion, Rules and Law: Child Custody and the UMDA'S Best-Interest Standard' (1991) 89 *Mich. L Rev.* 2215; 'The Tension Between Rules and Discretion in Family Law' (1993) 27 *Family LQ* 229.

[279] But see Grace Blumberg, 'Cohabitation Without Marriage: A Different Perspective' (1981) 28 *UCLA L Rev.* 1125.

[280] And see S. M. Cretney and J. M. Masson, *Principles of Family Law* (6th edn.) (London, 1991), 231–4.

358

that the concept will extend to cohabitation: English law may yet come to know of 'palimony'.[281]

The driving force is likely to be the concept of responsibility. Now well entrenched in child law and child support law, it will make inroads into the law governing adult domestic relationships.[282] This will include relationships with the elderly. Family law will as assuredly embrace 'community care' as it now does children.

Students of the family values debates of the 1990s and the ensuing 1996 Act cannot fail to have been struck by the contrasting ideology and images of the family in the Children Act 1989.[283] They should therefore not be surprised that by 1996 the Children Act was coming under attack:[284] extravagant claims were made that its ideology, supposedly associated with increasing children's rights, was undermining the stability of the family. Attention was drawn to the spectre of children divorcing their parents[285] and taking parents to courts—and European ones to boot—for smacking them.[286] Concern about juvenile crime—the Bulger case[287] was a catalyst—was further fuelled by these tensions. The Children Act adopted parental responsibility[288] (as it did the concept of partnership[289]) as a central concept, refusing to withdraw it from those who acted irresponsibly or abusively.[290] Whether a future Children Act will be as committed to upholding responsibility as a normative goal where factually it is absent may be doubted. The pendulum may swing from partnership with parents to greater protection of children, with parental responsibility being upheld as an ideal but being scrutinized more intensively and removed more

[281] *Cf. Windeler* v. *Whitehall* [1990] 2 FLR 505, *per* Millet J.

[282] See Christine Piper, *The Reasonable Parent* (Hemel Hempstead, 1993).

[283] See Lorraine Fox Harding, 'The Children Act 1989 In Context: Four Perspectives In Child Care Law and Policy' [1991] *Journal of Social Welfare and Family Law* 179 and 285.

[284] See, e.g., the leading article in the *Daily Telegraph*, 13 Feb. 1997.

[285] See Michael Freeman, 'Can Children Divorce Their Parents?' in Michael Freeman (ed.), n. 162 above, 159.

[286] See the *Independent*, 9 Sept. 1996. See also the case in *The Times*, 4 Sept. 1996.

[287] See n. 210 above.

[288] Children Act 1989, ss. 2 and 3.

[289] Not in the Act but see Department of Health, *Principles and Practice In Regulations and Guidance* (London, 1990), 8.

[290] See John Eekelaar, 'Parental Responsibility: State of Nature or Nature of The State?' [1991] *Journal of Social Welfare and Family Law* 37.

readily. Adoption is likely to become more 'open'[291] but a concomitant of this may be a greater reliance upon it.

When the state of family law comes to be reviewed a generation from now the audit will look very different—so, it may be predicted, will the concerns and the agenda.

[291] See n. 143 above.

# [2]
# Disputing Children

Fifty years ago there were disputes over children—many fewer than there are now because there were many fewer divorces and we were a less rights-conscious society—but their character was very different from those of today. Society in 1950 was more stable and less questioning. A consensus had been forged, initially perhaps by the deprivations of war and subsequently by a reforming Labour Government. Marriage was the bedrock of the family. People knew their place and did what they were told. Feminism had not (re)emerged and, though the world had focused on children in the aftermath of World War I,[1] there was no talk of children's rights.[2] There were few reported cases relating to children and these often related to issue of legitimacy.[3] Cases did not need to go to court: the divorcing couple bargained in the shadow of legal and psychological truths—by the 1950s the former undoubtedly a reflection of the latter—and this was encapsulated in the writings of John Bowlby.[4]

In 1945 the leading case on children was *Re Thain*.[5] This had decided in 1926 that the parental right of an unimpeachable parent should take priority over considerations of a child's welfare. A father, unable to cope after the death of the mother, had handed his eight-month-old daughter to his brother-in-law and wife and had sought six years later her return. Eve J, ordering the delivery up of the child, remarked:

It is said that the little girl will be greatly distressed and upset at parting from Mr and Mrs J. I can quite understand it may be so, but, at her tender age, one knows from experience how mercifully transient are the effects of partings and other sorrows, and how soon the novelty of fresh surroundings and new associations effaces the recollection of former days and kind friends, and I cannot attach weight to this aspect of the case.

Whether *Re Thain* would have been decided the same way if a mother had handed her child to relatives in similar circumstances may be doubted: she would have been expected to put caring for her child before her career. But mothers who surrendered children for adoption and then changed their minds were held to be acting unreasonably only where they

---

[1] Reflected in the Declaration of Geneva of 1924.
[2] Writers like Kate Douglas Wiggin, Janusz Korzcak, and Ellen Key had no impact on policy makers.    [3] And, in effect, to questions of property transmission.
[4] Originally a WHO publication in 1951, it was popularized as J. Bowlby, *Child Care and the Growth of Love*. Harmondsworth: Penguin Press (1953).    [5] [1926] Ch 676.

442

could be said to be callous or culpable in some way.[6] The law prioritized parental rights over children's interests and welfare. As late as 1966 the ideology of *Re Thain* was being upheld.[7] It was the end of that decade before welfare was held to prevail over the right of an unimpeachable parent. The child's welfare is 'the first consideration because it is of first importance and paramount because it determines the course to be followed', proclaimed Lord MacDermott.[8] And this interpretation was held to apply to disputes between parents and non-parents as well as to those between parents themselves. Stephen Cretney has convincingly shown that the House of Lords misinterpreted the legislation,[9] but it was undoubtedly a construction consonant with an emergent image of children.

In 1945 disputes about children were about rights. It was the mid-1970s before the right of the so-called 'unimpeachable' parent was finally scotched There were several cases[10] of which the most important were *Re K*[11] and *S(BD) v S(DJ)*.[12] Only fifteen years before, in *Re L*,[13] the Court of Appeal had denied a mother who had left her husband for another man, care and control of the daughters. As Lord Denning MR reasoned, in an outburst of moral fundamentalism:

> It would be an exceedingly bad example if it were thought that a mother could go off with another man and then claim as of right to say: 'Oh well, they are my two little girls and I am entitled to take them with me. I can not only leave my home and break it up and leave their father, but I can take the children with me and the law will not say me nay'. It seems to me that a mother must realise that if she leaves and breaks up her home in this way she cannot as of right demand to take the children from the father.

It may well be that the father had been wronged, but, it will be observed, there is no reference in Lord Denning's peroration to the children's best interests. It is significant that twice in his judgment he used the expression 'as of right', and he went on to refer to the case as 'a matter of simple justice' between mother and father. 'The claims of justice', he insisted, 'cannot be overlooked.' But, with the legislation interpreted so that 'first and paramount'[14] meant 'only', the effect of *J v C*,[15] there could be no space for 'justice', and in *S(BD) v S(DJ)* Ormrod LJ retorted that the question was not what the 'essential justice of the case' requires but 'what the best interests of the children' demand.[16] In 1977, the date of this judgment, 'best interests' was essen-

---

[6] This remained the law until *Re W* [1971] 2 All ER 49 (an earlier attempt was Lord Denning MR's judgment in *Re L* (1962) 106 Sol Jo 611).
  [7] *Re C (MA)* [1966] 1 All ER 838.      [8] In *J v C* [1970] AC 668, 710.
  [9] Stephen Cretney, *Law, Law Reform and The Family*. Oxford: Clarendon Press (1998), ch 7.
  [10] See also cases reported as news items in *The Times*, 11 Nov 1975 and 18 Nov 1975.
  [11] [1977] 1 All ER 647.      [12] [1977] 1 All ER 656.      [13] [1962] 1 WLR 886.
  [14] Guardianship of Minors Act 1971 s 1.      [15] n 8 above.      [16] n 12 above.

tially a brocard with little normative content, but its emphasis was significant in providing a focus: it was the child's interests which counted, and no one else's.

## THE EMERGENCE OF CHILDREN'S RIGHTS

The *Gillick* decision did not emerge out of thin air[17] and, as Eekelaar showed shortly after the House of Lords' decision,[18] it was consistent with principle. But it shocked and it also offended.[19] Popular opinion supported parental rights, and *Gillick* undercut them. The issue in *Gillick* concerned the lawfulness of a notice issued by the Department of Health and Social Security which enabled a doctor to give contraceptive counselling and treatment to children under 16 without consulting a parent. At first instance, Woolf J held the notice to be lawful. The Court of Appeal reversed, unanimously, though the three judges concerned used different arguments (none of which, it may be said, was convincing).[20] The House of Lords, by 3–2, upheld the lawfulness of the notice.[21]

The decision accepted that growing up is a process. As Lord Scarman put it:

The law relating to parent and child is concerned with the problems of growth and maturity of the human personality. If the law should impose upon the process of 'growing up' fixed limits where nature only knows a continuous process, the price would be artificiality and a lack of realism in an area where the law must be sensitive to human development and social change.

The majority of the Lords thus rejected a status test in favour of one which looks to capacity. For them Gillick competence, as it has come to be called, hinged on understanding and intelligence. Thus, for Lord Scarman, 'parental right yields to the child's right to make his own decisions when he reaches a sufficient understanding and intelligence to be capable of making up his own mind on the matter requiring decision'. Elsewhere in his judgment he referred to a competent child as one who 'achieves a

---

[17] Earlier indications are *Hewer v Bryant* [1970] 1 QB 357, and *R v D* [1984] AC 778.
[18] J. Eekelaar, 'The Emergence of Children's Rights', (1986) 6 *Oxford Journal of Legal Studies* 161.
[19] A national campaign 'to protect the family from interference from officialdom' was established. See *The Times*, 28 May 1985. The concerns (pre-Gillick) were voiced by the 'right' in such texts as F. Mount, *The Subversive Family*. London: Jonathan Cape (1982).
[20] [1985] 2 WLR 413. For Eveleigh LJ the notice contravened a parental right which pertained to the upbringing of a child. For Parker LJ a child's consent was a nullity so that presumably an intelligent 15-year-old could not have a sore throat examined without a parent's consent.              [21] [1986] AC 112.

444

sufficient understanding and intelligence to enable him or her to understand fully what is proposed', and also (and this is often overlooked by
commentators on the case) has 'sufficient discretion to enable him or her
to make a wise choice in his or her own interests'.[22] In these terms, competence combines understanding and knowledge with wisdom and experience. There are dangers in conflating knowledge and wisdom, but this
is commonly done. Few adults are Gillick competent if competence is to
hinge upon abilities fully to understand what is involved in a decision.
But many children, far below the age with which Gillick competence is
conventionally associated, are competent within the test articulated by
Lord Scarman if 'wise choice' is genuinely situated within the child's
personal, experiential knowledge of his or her own interests. Alderson
and Goodwin have noted that we tend to value highly 'professional,
textbook knowledge',[23] whilst discounting the importance of personal
experiential knowledge. And, once such 'wisdom' is devalued, the child
can be assumed to be ignorant, except in so far as he or she can recount
medical or other professional information.

That *Gillick* is a watershed decision cannot be denied, but from the
perspective of 2000 it begins to look like a false dawn. Writing shortly
after the decision, Eekelaar predicted that its effect was to overturn
parental authority once an adolescent had acquired competence;[24] and
not just parental authority but logically also that of a wardship court,
the jurisdiction of which was based both in history and on principle in
its acting as *parens patriae*. Children now had, Eekelaar claimed, 'that
most dangerous but most precious of rights: the right to make their
own mistakes'. Yet, when the opportunity presented itself for the
courts to test the implications of this they flinched. In *Re R*[25] and *Re W*[26]
(and subsequently in other cases,[27] most recently the heart transplant
case of *Re M*[28]), they held that, although a Gillick competent child
could consent to medical treatment on her own behalf, she could not
refuse to consent to treatment. As a result, as Brazier and Bridge
observe, 'the right to be wrong applies only where minors say yes to
treatment'.[29]

But, both here and elsewhere,[30] the courts have raised the level of
Gillick competence beyond that which is required to consent to treat-

---

[22] At 188.
[23] P. Alderson and M. Goodwin, 'Contradictions within Concepts of Children's Competence', (1993) 1 *International Journal of Children's Rights* 303, 305.        [24] n 18 above, at 181.
[25] [1992] Fam 11.        [26] [1993] Fam 64.
[27] *Re E* [1993] 1 FLR 386; *Re S* [1994] 2 FLR 1065.        [28] [1999] 2 FLR 1097.
[29] M. Brazier and C. Bridge, 'Coercion or Caring: Analysing Adolescent Autonomy',
(1996) 16 *Legal Studies* 84, 88 ; see also C. Smith, 'Children's Rights: Judicial Ambivalence
and Social Resistance', (1997) 11 *International Journal of Law, Policy and the Family* 103.
[30] eg *Re E*, n 27 above; *Re K, W and H* [1993] 1 FLR 854.

ment. Indeed, the more far-reaching the effects of refusal, the higher the level of competence is raised. In *Re R*,[31] where the evidence was that without treatment the girl would lapse into a dangerously psychotic state, Lord Donaldson MR said that what was required was not merely an ability to understand the nature of the proposed treatment, but a full understanding and appreciation of the consequences both of the treatment in terms of intended and possible side effects and, equally important, the anticipated consequences of a failure to treat. This goes way beyond what was envisaged in *Gillick* and is also more stringent than the test laid down for mentally disordered adults.[32] That test (first formulated in *Re C* by Thorpe J)[33] has been used by courts to test the competence of 16–18-year-olds,[34] but not to supplant that articulated in *Re R* for children under 16. Lord Donaldson MR's test in *Re R* demands more of children than is required of adults in another respect too. Lord Donaldson himself accepts that an adult's capacity to decide about treatment has to be assessed at the time the decision is made.[35] But in *Re R* he required a permanent state of competence: where this fluctuates, as it did in *Re R*, the adolescent cannot be judged by her capacity on her 'good days'.[36]

Despite *Gillick* and in the face of legislation (both the Family Law Reform Act 1969 and the Children Act 1989),[37] the courts evince reluctance to give rein to a child's autonomy. Where the child is under 16 they do this by concluding that the child is not Gillick competent. This is well illustrated by two Jehovah's Witnesses' 'blood transfusion' cases. In *Re E*[38] a boy of 15¾, though of sufficient intelligence to be able to take decisions about his own well-being, was not, it was held, Gillick competent because there was a range of decisions confronting him which lay outside his full comprehension. Said Ward J: 'He may have some concept of the fact that he will die, but as to the manner of his death and the extent of his and his family's suffering I find he has not the ability to turn his mind to it nor the will to do so[39].' In *Re S*,[40] a girl of 15½ who had suffered from thalassaemia virtually since birth became a Jehovah's Witness and decided to cease having blood transfusions. Forcing them on her was, as she described it, 'like rape'.[41] To Johnson J: 'There are those who are children

[31] n 25 above.   [32] In *Re C* [1994] 1 FLR 31.
[33] In *Re C*, n 32 above: applied in *Re JT* [1998] 1 FLR 48 to a 25-year-old learning-disabled adult held competent to refuse life-saving renal dialysis.
[34] *A Metropolitan Borough Council v DB* [1997] 1 FLR 767, 773 *per* Cazalet J and *Re C* [1997] 2 FLR 180, 195 *per* Wall J.   [35] *Re T* [1992] 2 FLR 458, 470.
[36] n 25 above at 26. And see J. Montgomery, 'Parents and Children in Dispute: Who Has the Final Word?' (1992) 4 *Journal of Child Law* 85.
[37] See sections 38(6), 43(8), 44(7). However, note the courts' interpretation in *South Glamorgan County Council v W and B* [1993] 1 FLR 574.   [38] n 27 above.
[39] *Re E* at 391.   [40] n 27 above.   [41] *Re S* at 1072.

446

and there are those who are adults and those who are in-between'.[42] He did not see S as in-between. She was 'a child' with the 'integrity and commitment of a child and not of somebody who was competent to make the decision that she tells me she has made. She hopes still for a miracle. My conclusion is, therefore, that she is not "*Gillick*-competent"'. Her capacity, he concluded, was not 'commensurate with the gravity of the decision which she has made'. She needed greater understanding of the manner of the death, the pain, and the distress. In *Re E* the boy died shortly after his eighteenth birthday—when treatment could no longer be imposed upon him.[43] It is possible that the same fate befell the girl in *Re S*. Both cases were decided upon what courts deemed to be in the child's best interests, but whether either of the children involved would have seen it that way or, had they lived, would have come to see it in that way, may be doubted.

When the child is over 16 Gillick competence is not the issue. It was thought that legislation[44] had made the law clear: at 16 a child could take his or her own decisions in relation to medical care.[45] But in *Re W*[46] the Court of Appeal decided we laboured under a misapprehension, and, even though the girl was 16, the local authority was granted leave to make an application for the exercise by the court of the inherent jurisdiction of the High Court. An anorexic, with sufficient understanding to make an informed choice, could be force-fed.[47]

## THE CHILDREN ACT 1989

Of children's legislation passed since the end of World War II,[48] only the 1989 Act addresses the status of children. The Act has a number of sources, of which *Gillick* is one and Cleveland[49] another, and is the product of a number of value positions. For Fox Harding[50] dominant are paternalism and defence of the birth family: in my view the non-interventionist strand in the Act is overarching.[51] To Cleveland's assertion

[42] *Re S* at 1076.      [43] This fact was revealed in *Re S*, n 27 above, 1075.
[44] Family Law Reform Act 1969 s 8(1).
[45] But s 8(3) was ambiguous, thus leaving open the possibility that someone else could consent on behalf of a child of 16 or 17.                          [46] n 26 above.
[47] See also *A Metropolitan Borough Council v DB*, n 34 above; *Re C*, n 34 above.
[48] Other Acts of importance are/were Children Act 1948, Children and Young Persons Act 1963, Children and Young Persons Act 1969, and Children Act 1975.
[49] *Report of Inquiry into Child Abuse in Cleveland*. London: HMSO Cm 62 (1988); below p 584.
[50] L. Fox Harding, 'The Children Act 1989 in Context: Four Perspectives in Child Care Law and Policy', (1991) *Journal of Social Welfare and Family Law* 179 and 285.
[51] M. Freeman, 'In the Child's Best Interests: Reading the Children Act Critically', (1992) 45 *Current Legal Problems—Annual Review* 173.

that 'the child is a person and not an object of concern', the Act responds with a package of children's rights measures, but it does so within a framework which emphasizes family autonomy[52] and within a network of practices which prioritizes family support over child protection.[53] Perhaps, therefore, it is not surprising that there should have been the retreat from *Gillick* just described, or that those provisions in the Act which emphasize the participatory powers of children should have been interpreted so restrictively.[54]

It would be wrong to conclude that the Act empowered children, as some commentators believed.[55] But it certainly gives children a number of powers which they lacked previously. For example, the power to initiate court actions. Thus, a child may challenge an emergency protection order,[56] seek contact when in care,[57] ask for a care order to be discharged[58] and, most importantly in the context of this chapter, seek the court's leave to obtain a s 8 order making decisions where s/he is to live or with whom have contact, or deciding a specific issue relating to his or her upbringing or prohibiting a parent from exercising parental responsibility in a particular way.[59]

The ability to seek leave to apply for a residence order led to suggestions (and criticisms) that this offered a facility for children to divorce their parents.[60] The image arrived neatly packaged from the United States[61] and what threatened for a short time to be a moral panic erupted. Gym-slipped folk-devils—that as many of them were boys as girls was conveniently ignored—were destroying the family. The reality is that there were very few cases and the courts kept a tight rein (indeed, an over-tight) on them. To apply for a residence order, the child, and no age is specified, requires leave to make the application, and the court must be satisfied that s/he has 'sufficient understanding'.[62] This in itself may be difficult enough to establish, but in *Re SC*[63] Booth J ruled that a court has discretion whether to grant leave even if it has been established that the child has sufficient understanding to make the application. The likely success of the substantive application is also to be considered. It has also been suggested (by Johnson J in *Re C*[64]) that the welfare principle

[52] See in particular s 1(5).
[53] M. Freeman, 'The End of the Century of the Child?' (2000) 53 *Current Legal Problems* (forthcoming). [54] See below pp 449–52.
[55] D. Hodgson, 'Power to the Child', *Social Work Today* 12 July (1990) 16.
[56] Children Act 1989, s 45(8). [57] *ibid* s 34(2). [58] *ibid* s 39(1). [59] *ibid* s 10(8).
[60] And see M. Freeman, 'Can Children Divorce Their Parents?' in M. Freeman (ed), *Divorce: Where Next?* Aldershot: Dartmouth (1996) 159.
[61] After publicity surrounding the Gregory Kingsley case: *Kingsley v Kingsley* 623 So 2d 780 (1993). [62] Children Act 1989 s 10(8).
[63] [1994] 1 FLR 96, 98.
[64] [1994] 1 FLR 26, 28. Neither Booth J in *Re SC*, n 63 above, nor Stuart Smith J in *Re C* [1995] 1 FLR 927 agree.

448

should operate at the stage of the leave process. But this cannot be right, for at the filter stage it must be the child's wishes that are in issue.[65] Best interests would then come into play at the trial of the substantive issue.

The Act also emphasizes the importance of a child's wishes and feelings.[66] But a concern remains that children are not able to put their views to a court as readily as should be the case. Their views will often reach the court only through the filter of a welfare officer's report and may not, as a result, coincide with the child's views, particularly where these are not consistent with what the welfare officer believes to be in the child's best interests.[67] The case of *Re M*[68] graphically illustrates these difficulties. M was 12½ and deemed by the court to be able, intelligent, articulate, and having an attractive personality. She wanted to live with her father who had been denied a residence order. But she was not allowed to swear an affidavit supporting her father's appeal. On one level this is understandable: the welfare officer's report had already conveyed to the court what M's views were. But, since the welfare recommendation went against these views, it undermined the participatory rights of the person most affected by the decision. Butler-Sloss LJ was clearly concerned to prevent children becoming entangled in their parents' litigation, and alarmed that a child might be manipulated by a parent. But the end result—the silencing of an intelligent adolescent— sends out the wrong messages about the status of children.

On several occasions since the Children Act judges have positively discouraged children from participating in proceedings which related directly to them. In *Re C*,[69] where the views of a 13-year-old girl were discounted (she was, it was said, 'too young to carry the burden of decisions about her own future, and too young to have to bear the weight of responsibility for a parent who lacks authority and plays on her feelings of protectiveness'), the judge commented that 'to sit for hours, or it may even be days, listening to lawyers debating one's future is not an experience that should in normal circumstances be wished upon any child as young as this'. In *Re W*,[70] the liberty of a boy of 10 was at stake. The local authority was applying for a secure accommodation order. For the child it was contended that this was the equivalent of a custodial order in a criminal court, and that natural justice dictates that he should be allowed

[65] I expressed the opposite view in Freeman, n 60 above, at 169, but now concede that I was wrong to do so. See further M. Hayes and C. Williams, *Family Law: Principles, Policy and Practice*. London: Butterworths (1999) 101–4.

[66] Children Act 1989 s 1(3)(a). These must be considered in the light of the child's age and understanding.

[67] See, further, M. Freeman, 'The Next Children's Act?' (1998) 28 *Family Law* 341 and A. L. James and A. James, 'Pump up the Volume: Listening to Children in Separation and Divorce', (1999) 6 *Childhood* 189.                        [68] [1995] 2 FLR 100.

[69] [1993] 1 FLR 832.        [70] [1994] 2 FLR 1092.

to be in court before an order is made which will have that effect. But the judge could not see 'any analogy between orders made in [the Family] Division and orders made by the criminal court'. And he added, in what may be thought a give-away line, 'the purpose of the criminal court is to deal with criminal offences committed *by people or children*' (my emphasis). By contrast, this jurisdiction is 'a benign jurisdiction'. That is how lawyers see it, but it is doubtful whether most adults, let alone most children, would so perceive it.

The judiciary has been hardly more receptive to allowing children to communicate their views in private. Back in 1981, Ormrod LJ said that whether a judge should see a child in private was a personal matter for himself to determine.[71] Earlier still, in 1974, Megaw LJ commented that it was 'of course most desirable . . . that the judge hearing the case should see the children and should see the children otherwise than in open court'.[72] But, despite the Children Act and the United Nations Convention (in particular Article 12), there is now an ambivalence, with a greater willingness to see children in public law proceedings than in private law cases. Thus, in *Re M*,[73] Wall J suggested that an 'intelligent and articulate 12 year old who had an excellent grasp of the issues and who had discussed the matter fully was entitled to see the judge who was to decide his future'. But the same judge, in *B v B*,[74] detected an inherent contradiction in seeing children to ascertain their wishes whilst being obliged to report to their parents anything material they said. The ambivalence also appears when the judiciary allow themselves the jurisdiction to see children in private but deny this to magistrates, who hear the bulk of the cases. Booth J thus thought it was only in 'rare and exceptional cases'[75] that magistrates were entitled to see children privately.

A striking difference between contemporary child litigation and that even a generation ago is the understanding of the importance of the child being independently represented. But how much autonomy should the child be given? In *Re S*[76] the then Master of the Rolls, Sir Thomas Bingham, addressed two considerations:

First . . . the principle that children are human beings in their own right with individual minds and wills, views and emotions, which should command serious attention. A child's wishes are not to be discounted or dismissed simply because he is a child. He should be free to express them and decision-makers should listen. Second is the fact that a child is, after all, a child. The reason why the law is particularly solicitous in protecting the interests of children is that they are liable to be vulnerable and impressionable, lacking the

---

[71] *D v D* [1981] 2 FLR 74.     [72] *H v H* [1974] 1 All ER 1145, 1147.
[73] [1994] 1 FLR 749, 755.     [74] [1994] 2 FLR 489.     [75] *Re M* [1993] 2 FLR 706, 709.
[76] [1993] 2 FLR 437.

450

maturity to weigh the longer term against the shorter, lacking the insight to
know how they will react and the imagination to know how others will react
in certain situations, lacking the experience to match the probable against the
possible.

The case concerned a boy of 11. An application had been made by his
father for residence and contact orders. He was made a party to the
proceedings, and the Official Solicitor was appointed to act as his
guardian ad litem.[77] The Official Solicitor recommended that V should
continue to live with his mother (he had done so since he was 5), and
should see his father less frequently. It was the father's contention, which
S supported, that S should live with him in the United States. S contended
from the outset of the proceedings that the Official Solicitor would not
represent him, and that he should be able to act independently through a
solicitor. The Court Rules allow this but they stipulate that the child must
have 'understanding'. In line with the reasoning in *Gillick*, Sir Thomas
Bingham MR emphasized understanding rather than age, and he
accepted that this increased with the passage of time. He noted that
'different children have differing levels of understanding at the same age.
And understanding is not an absolute. It has to be assessed relatively to
the issues in the proceedings.'[78] But he concluded that 'where any sound
judgment on these issues call for insight and imagination which only
maturity and experience can bring both the court and the solicitor will be
slow to conclude that the child's understanding is sufficient'. The boy's
application was rejected. He may have been influenced, even over-
influenced, by his father, and he may have been impressionable. But the
Rules provide for children to be able to make such decisions and these
decisions do not belong to the category of decisions where a mistake
might harm them severely or irreparably.

A similar conclusion could have been reached in *Re H*,[79] but it was not.
A 15-year-old boy was warded by his parents after the man with whom
he was living was charged with sexual offences against another boy. He
had been left in England when his parents moved to France. He now
wished to stay in England, and ran away each time he was taken to
France. It was his view that the Official Solicitor was not representing his
views. He wished him to be removed and to be able to continue to defend
the proceedings without the Official Solicitor acting as his guardian ad
litem. There was a difference of psychiatric opinion. The psychiatrist
instructed by the Official Solicitor considered that H lacked sufficient
understanding to participate in the proceedings because he did not
appreciate the dangers posed by a suspected sex offender. The psychia-

[77] On the role of which see D. Venables, 'The Official Solicitor', (1990) 20 *Family Law* 53.
[78] n 76 above, 444.        [79] [1993] 2 FLR 552.

trist treating H considered that the views expressed were those of H, and that having his own representative would assist him to feel that justice was being done, and so would ease his acceptance and compliance with the provisions made for him and reduce the risk of rash and unwise decisions. It was the latter opinion which Booth J preferred. She held that H had the understanding necessary to instruct his own legal advisor without the services of the Official Solicitor. This is a liberal conclusion, the more so since, if anything, one might have supposed that H was in greater need of protection than S. She also adopted a broader approach to competence than Sir Thomas Bingham MR did in *Re S*. She noted:

The court must be satisfied that H . . . has sufficient understanding to participate as a party . . . without a guardian ad litem. [This] . . . means much more than instructing a solicitor as to his own views. The child enters the arena among other adult parties. He may give evidence and he may be cross-examined. He will hear other parties, including in this case his parents, give evidence and be cross-examined. He must be able to give instructions on many different matters as the case goes through its stages and to make decisions as need arises. Thus a child is exposed and not protected in these procedures.

Of course, many adults do not have these abilities.

### FROM RIGHTS TO RESPONSIBILITY

The second half of the twentieth century also saw a shift in the way parent–child relations were characterized, though the change can be exaggerated. The language and the symbolism altered, but there was not all that much substance to the change. The most significant change was effected by the Children Act 1989, some fifteen years after it was first recommended in a *Justice* report.[80] Parent–child relations were now to be characterized in terms of parental responsibility rather than parental rights. The 1980s, the dismal years of Thatcher, were a period in which we were supposed to believe that there was no such thing as society, only individuals. This is not an environment in which an emphasis on responsibility could be expected to emerge. That it did may say something for the relative autonomy of the law-making process. It may also explain why the change was more apparent than real. The new 'politics of the common good',[81] with responsibility as one of its key features, does not seem to have been a major influence.

---

[80] *Parental Rights and Duties and Custody Suits*. London: Stevens (1975).
[81] M. Sandel, 'Morality and the Liberal Ideal', *New Republic* (7 May 1984) 15.

452

The shift from parental rights to parental responsibilities was generally welcomed. It also led to a questioning of where rights, and to a lesser extent, responsibilities came from. That the debate emerged at all may partly be explained by the reproduction revolution.[82] The fact that the 'private'[83] (and hence the family) was being opened up to theoretical analysis was equally, if not more, significant.[84] Rights are redolent of property, whereas responsibility conjures up an image of trusteeship.[85] By emphasizing parental responsibility rather than rights, the 1989 Act conveyed three messages. First, that responsibility is more important than rights. Even where parents have rights they may have responsibilities not to exercise them.[86] The courts have long stressed the importance of parental responsibilities: parental rights being justified because they enabled a parent to perform duties towards the child.[87] Second, that it is parents, and not therefore children, who are the decision-makers. This and the *Gillick* decision send out conflicting messages. Interestingly, the Lord Chancellor responsible for the Children Act 1989 gave assurances that the new emphasis on parental responsibility did not overturn the *Gillick* principle.[88] The retreat from *Gillick*, discussed above, suggests the courts may think otherwise. Third, the emphasis on parental responsibility conveys the all-important message that it is parents, and not the state, who have responsibility for children. The consequences of this are that parents have responsibility in a normative sense even when they act with complete disregard for that responsibility.[89] Thus, English law now only allows a parent to be divested of parental responsibility when the child is transplanted into another family by adoption.[90] The grossly abusive parent retains parental responsibility even where the child is subject to a care order and is removed from parents.[91]

Who has parental responsibility? Mothers always do, but as far as fathers are concerned, English law has moved little in the last fifty years. Indeed, with births outside marriage now more than a third of all births

[82] J. L. Hill,'What Does it Mean to be a "Parent"? The Claims of Biology as the Basis for Parental Rights', (1991) 66 *New York University Law Review* 353.

[83] N. Rose, 'Beyond the Public/Private Divide: Law, Power and the Family', (1987) 14 *Journal of Law and Society* 61.

[84] K. Bartlett, 'Re-expressing Parenthood', (1988) 98 *Yale Law Journal* 293.

[85] And see C. Beck, G. Glavis, M. Barnes Jenkins, and R. Nardi, 'The Rights of Children: A Trust Model', (1978) 46 *Fordham Law Review* 669. Also see C. Barton and G. Douglas, *Law and Parenthood*. London: Butterworths (1995) 22–8.

[86] M. Brazier, 'Liberty, Responsibility, Maternity', (1999) 52 *Current Legal Problems* 359.

[87] eg Lord Scarman in *Gillick*, n 21 above.

[88] *House of Lords Debates (Hansard)*, vol 502, col 1351.

[89] J. Eekelaar, 'Parental Responsibility: State of Nature or Nature of the State?', (1991) *Journal of Social Welfare and Family Law* 37.

[90] Or after surrogacy (see Human Fertilisation and Embryology Act 1990 s 30).

[91] Children Act 1989 s 33(3)(b), (4).

Disputing Children 453

(though most of these take place in stable cohabitations),[92] a higher percentage of men today do not require parental responsibility than had parental rights vested in them in 1945. In the period in between, illegitimacy ceased to have the legal significance or social stigma that it once had. Legislation in 1987[93] has meant that the fact of marriage between parents is irrelevant unless statute expressly provides to the contrary. An example is the British Nationality Act 1981 under which a person born in the United Kingdom shall be a British citizen if at the time of his birth, his father or mother is a British citizen or is settled in the United Kingdom.[94] But 'the relationship of father and child shall be taken to exist only between a man and any legitimate child born to him'.[95] Gay men cannot inter-marry and thus can never pass on citizenship to any child. This problem arose in acute form at the beginning of 2000, when a child was born by a surrogacy arrangement in California and was denied entry to the United Kingdom even though the homosexual couple involved were both British citizens.[96] But, short of amending legislation, it is likely to happen again and again.

Fathers are only ascribed parental responsibility when at the date of the child's birth they are married to the mothers.[97] Whether married or not, they come within the definition of 'parent' in the Children Act. This means that they are in the same position as all other parents for the purposes of succession.[98] An unmarried father without parental responsibility has an obligation to maintain.[99] There is a presumption of reasonable contact in his favour.[100] He has the right to be consulted by a local authority about decisions taken in relation to his child where the local authority is providing accommodation for the child.[101] He can apply without leave for a s 8 order.[102] On the other hand, his agreement is not required for adoption.[103]

Thus, English law emphasizes the importance of parental responsibility but withholds it from more than one-third of fathers. And it may be supposed that most of these men live in stable cohabitations and remain blissfully unaware that they are denied responsibility.[104] Only where there is a dispute (about education or medical treatment, for example) or when the relationship breaks down is the significance of their defective status likely to bite. The justifications offered for discriminating against unmarried

[92] Three-quarters of births to unmarried women are jointly registered and three-quarters of these registrations are by couples at the same address.
[93] Family Law Reform Act 1987 s 1(1).    [94] s 1(1).    [95] s 50(a)(b).
[96] See *The Independent*, 12 Jan 2000.    [97] Children Act 1989 s 2(2)(b).
[98] Famly Law Reform Act 1987 s 1(1).    [99] Under the Child Support Act 1991.
[100] Children Act 1989 s 34(1)(a).    [101] *ibid* s 22(4).    [102] *ibid* s 10(4)(a).
[103] See *Re C* [1993] 2 FLR 260.
[104] As also the mothers: see S. McRae, *Cohabiting Mothers: Changing Marriage Parenthood*. London: Policy Studies Institute (1993).

454

fathers in this way are weak,[105] were countered by the Scottish Law
Commission in 1992,[106] and are no longer seriously advanced.[107] Most
hyped was the thin end of the wedge argument that to confer rights on
all fathers would amount to a 'rapists' charter'. But, as Barton and Douglas conclude, the rapist is a 'phantom figure'.[108] English law is likely to
change early in the millennium, very possibly to ascribe parental responsibility to all fathers whose names appear on the register of births.[109]
Until it does, the law offers fathers a number of ways of acquiring
parental responsibility. This (since the Children Act 1989) can be done
by private agreement[110] (although there are formalities, these are of an
administrative rather than judicial nature and so scrutinize neither
whether the man is indeed the father nor whether the sharing of parental
responsibility will be in the child's best interests). If the mother is unwilling to share responsibility voluntarily, the father may apply to the court
for a parental responsibility order[111] (or, if he wishes to take over the
physical care of the child, for a residence order[112]). There are few reported
cases where parental responsibility orders have been refused.[113] The
overriding consideration is the child's welfare: so, for example, acrimony between the parents is not, it has been held, a good reason to
refuse an order.[114] And an order can be made where a contact order is
refused.[115] The courts are clear what the father needs to satisfy to be
granted an order (commitment, attachment, and good reasons for applying[116]) but are not so clear as to what orders are for. They will eventually
disappear with emerging reforms, leaving us with greater scope for
parental disputes to be decided by specific issue and prohibited steps
orders.

English law is also rather poor at defining parental responsibility. It
does not even lay down the standards of care which children can expect

[105] A. Bainham, 'When is a Parent not a Parent? Reflections on the Unmarried Father and
His Child in English Law', (1989) 3 *International Journal of Law and the Family* 208. But for a
contrary view see R. Deech, 'The Unmarried Father and Human Rights', (1992) 4 *Journal of
Child Law* 3.
[106] Scottish Law Commission, *Report on Family Law*. Edinburgh: HMSO (1992) paras
2.36–2.51.
[107] The views of Ruth Deech, n 105 above, are isolated and dated.          [108] n 85 above, 93.
[109] Lord Chancellor's Department, *The Law on Parental Responsibility for Unmarried Fathers*.
London: HMSO (1998).
[110] Children Act 1989 s 4(1)(b). In 1996 there were 3,590 agreements registered, a ludicrously low figure, suggesting that the facility is not known about.
[111] Children Act 1989 s 4(1)(a).        [112] *ibid* s 12(1).
[113] Examples of refusals are *Re P* [1997] 2 FLR 722 (where the father had a long term of
imprisonment); *Re H* [1998] 1 FLR 855 (where he had injured the child in a sadistic manner);
and *Re P* [1998] 2 FLR 96 (father's motivation inappropriate). Contrast *Re S* [1995] 2 FLR 648
(order despite possession of obscene literature and failure to pay child maintenance).
[114] *Re P* [1994] 1 FLR 578.        [115] *Re H* [1993] 1 FLR 484.        [116] *Re H* [1991] 1 FLR 214.

Disputing Children 455

from parents,[117] which puts it in breach of the United Nations Convention which requires States Parties to 'render appropriate assistance to parents and legal guardians in the performance of their child-rearing responsibilities'.[118] The Children Act simply defines parental responsibility as 'the rights, duties, powers, responsibilities and authority which by law a parent has in relation to the child and his property'.[119] This, of course, begs the question and leaves the courts to provide content in the context of disputes. Perhaps no other solution was practicable. Certainly a comprehensive list would be difficult.[120] But there remains the feeling that English law has sacrificed principle to pragmatism. Scottish law, by contrast, at least attempts to formulate some parental responsibilities.[121] This incoherence is well illustrated also by the vast amount of recent litigation testing the rights of mothers to change children's surnames. The Children Act 1989, short of a residence order, would seem to have enabled one parent to change the child's surname without the other's consent.[122] But that surely cannot have been intended and so Holman J held in *Re PC*,[123] where any suggestion that a parent with parental responsibility could unilaterally change his or her child's surname was criticized as 'little short of bizarre'.[124] This would put the unmarried mother into a stronger position than her married counterpart. Only she can register the child's surname[125] and she can change it by deed poll without the father's consent (only the consent of those with parental responsibility is required). Or so we thought.[126] But the House of Lords recently held that the Court of Appeal was right to conclude that:

the registration or change of a child's surname is a profound and not a merely formal issue, whatever the age of the child. Any dispute on such an issue must be referred to the court for determination whether or not there is a residence order in force and whoever has or has not parental responsibility. No disputed registration or change should be made unilaterally.[127]

There is, accordingly, 'a heavy responsibility on those who seek to effect the change, first, as a matter of prudence if not of direct law to take the issue of dispute for the resolution of the judge and to appreciate that

---

[117] C. Lyon, 'The Definition of, and Legal and Management Responses to, Child Abuse in England and Wales', in M. Freeman (ed), *Overcoming Child Abuse: A Window on a World Problem*. Aldershot: Ashgate (2000) 95.          [118] Article 18(2).

[119] Children Act 1989 s 3(1) and see N. Lowe, 'The Meaning and Allocation of Parental Responsibility—A Common Lawyer's Perspective', (1997) 11 *International Journal of Law, Policy and the Family* 192.

[120] In the past attempts were made to define parental rights: the best was J. Eekelaar, 'What are Parental Rights?' (1973) 89 *Law Quarterly Review* 210.

[121] Children (Scotland) Act 1995 s 1(1). Parental rights are defined in s 2(1).

[122] By s 2(7).          [123] [1997] 2 FLR 730.          [124] At 736.

[125] Births and Deaths Registration Act 1953 s 10(1).

[126] This was the view of the textbook writers; indeed, it passed barely noticed and certainly as uncontentious.          [127] *Dawson v Wearmouth* [1999] 2 All ER 353 at 358.

456

good reasons have to be shown before the judge will allow such a change'. On one level this is understandable, for what it does is to circumscribe the exercise of parental responsibility to the promotion of a child's welfare. But on another level all that it achieves is to prevent the mother from changing the child's surname where the father contests the change. It may seem odd to ordinary people that someone with parental responsibility cannot do what someone without it can seek to stop. The cases confirm how unclear the concepts are and, most importantly, the way children's welfare has continued to eclipse parental responsibility.

### DISPUTES ABOUT CHILDREN

In the period under consideration there have been enormous changes in the ways adults have disputed about children The language has changed. No longer are children regarded as packages or pieces of property to be moved about.[128] The concepts have changed.[129] In 1945 one sought the custody of a child (this has a broader and narrower meaning, though this was rarely recognized[130]). There must have been disputes over access (as it was then called[131]) but there is no evidence in the law reports that this was a live issue. Wardship had only just emerged as an institution to protect a child's welfare,[132] rather than family property, but for a quarter of a century thereafter was used primarily to target elopement.[133] The law operated with presumptions: young children should be placed in the custody of their mothers;[134] older children, especially boys, should be brought up by their fathers.[135] Whether the law favoured mothers, as is often claimed, or whether decisions to give custody to the mother reflected an understandable desire to protect the residential status quo— it being commonly the case that it is fathers who leave when a marriage breaks down—it was (and still is) mothers who usually got/continued to care for children after divorce.[136] This was what nature had 'ordained', as Stamp LJ put it in 1978. And he added: 'however good a man may be, he cannot perform the functions which a mother performs by nature in relation to her own little girl.'[137]

---

[128] *Re B* [1992] 2 FLR 1, 5 *per* Butler-Sloss LJ.
[129] Since the Children Act 1989 concepts like 'custody' and 'access' have been replaced by 'residence' and 'contact'.          [130] It was in *Dipper v Dipper* [1980] 2 All ER 722.
[131] Since the Children Act the word 'contact' has been used.
[132] See N. V. Lowe and R. A. H. White, *Wards of Court*. London: Barry Rose (1986) ch 1.
[133] See G. Cross, 'Wards of Court', (1967) 83 *Law Quarterly Review* 200.
[134] *Re B* [1962] 1 All ER 872; *Re S* [1958] 1 All ER 783; *Re O* [1971] ch 748 (the more so when she did not work: see at 752).          [135] *Re C (A)* [1970] 1 All ER 309.
[136] J. A. Priest and J. C. Whybrow, *Custody Law in Practice in the Divorce and Domestic Courts*. London: HMSO (1986).          [137] *M v M* [1978] 1 FLR 77.

The presumptions have gone, replaced by 'considerations'. Thus, Butler-Sloss LJ in *Re S* could still talk, in 1991, of its being 'natural' for young children to be with their mothers, but, she added, 'where it is in dispute, it is a consideration . . . not a presumption'.[138] She explained this further in *Re A*.[139]

> In cases where the child has remained throughout with the mother and is young, particularly when a baby or a toddler, the unbroken relationship of the mother and child is one which it would be very difficult to displace, unless the mother was unsuitable to care for the child. But where the mother and child have been separated, and the mother seeks the return of the child, other considerations apply, and there is no starting-point that the mother should be preferred to the father . . .

And she stressed again that there is no presumption which requires the mother, 'as mother', to be considered as the primary caretaker in preference to the father. Even so, it is rare for the father to be preferred to the mother where the child is young. When this happened in 1998 in *Re K*[140] the case attracted considerable media attention.[141] The child had been with his mother for 'a good deal of his life, but not the whole of it, and had never been in the exclusive care of his father'. In the United States the tender years presumption may have been displaced because of feminist demands that men and women be treated equally.[142] There is no evidence that the attenuation of the doctrine in England—for that is what the replacement of presumptions by considerations amounts to—can be similarly explained.

Throughout the period under consideration the courts have purported to decide disputes about children guided by their best interests. The governing legislation in 1945 was the Guardianship of Infants Act 1925. This was passed to inject some equality into the rights of parents.[143] It certainly was not passed to make the child's best interests the only consideration, nor was it intended to apply to disputes between parents and third parties (foster parents, relatives). But the House of Lords in *J v C* in 1969 put both these constructions on the legislation.[144] Legislation in 1969[145] did not change the test and the child's welfare remained 'first and paramount' until the Children Act 1989 replaced this by 'paramount',

---

[138] [1991] 2 FLR 388, 390.    [139] [1991] 2 FLR 394.    [140] [1999] 1 FLR 583.
[141] Thus 'Mother's Day Has Gone, says Custody Judge' said *The Times*, 27 Nov 1998. It noted that twice as many men were looking after their children compared with 1993.
[142] M. A. Mason, *The Custody Wars*. New York: Basic Books (1999) ch 1.
[143] J. Brophy, 'Parental Rights and Children's Welfare: Some Problems of Feminists' Strategy in the 1920s', (1982) 10 *International Journal of the Sociology of Law* 149; I. Théry, '"The Interest of the Child" and the Regulation of the Post-Divorce Family' in C. Smart and S. Sevenhuijsen (eds), *Child Custody and the Politics of Gender* (1989) 78–99; See also S. Cretney, n 9 above.                                        [144] [1970] AC 668.
[145] Guardianship of Minors Act 1969.

458

thus endorsing the Lords' construction of twenty years earlier.[146] Section 1 of the 1989 provides that:

When a court determines any question with respect to
(a)  the upbringing of a child; or
(b)  the administration of the child's property or the application of any income arising from it,
the child's welfare shall be the court's paramount consideration.

The courts have construed 'upbringing' narrowly. For example, where what is in issue is the child's paternity, this only indirectly concerns a child's upbringing and so falls outside the paramountcy test.[147] So, it has been held, do applications to restrict the publication of a book that might be harmful to a child:[148] the courts apparently still think that free speech is more important than the protection of a child's interests. Although the paramountcy principle has come under attack in recent years, in particular for allowing other policies and principles to 'smuggle themselves' into children's cases,[149] it has been extended in the latest divorce legislation to guide courts into refusing to make a divorce order.[150] The paramountcy principle is, of course, an indeterminate notion. Without the injection of normative content it is exposed to the criticism that decisions will be atomistic, or worse, idiosyncratic.[151] English law accordingly made a major advance in 1989 (a practice followed in the 1996 Act too[152]) when it structured the discretion of the courts by laying down a checklist of factors to be considered before making a decision about a child.[153] This checklist requires a court to have regard in particular to such matters as a child's wishes and feelings; needs; the likely effect of any change of circumstances; age, sex, and background; any harm suffered or risk of harm; the capability of his parents (and any other relevant person) of meeting his needs; and the range of powers open to the court. The list can be said

[146] It is generally acknowledged that the removal of the words 'first and', leaving the child's welfare as the 'paramount consideration' merely confirmed the *J v C* interpretation of the previous language.   [147] *S v Mc (formerly S)* [1972] AC 24.
[148] *Re Z* [1997] Fam 1. See generally J. Moriarty, 'Children, Privacy and the Press', (1997) 9 *Child and Family Law Quarterly* 217.
[149] H. Reece, 'The Paramountcy Principle: Consensus or Construct?' (1996) 49 *Current Legal Problems* 267, 268.   [150] Family Law Act 1996 s 11(3).
[151] On indeterminacy see R. Mnookin, 'Child Custody Adjudication: Judicial Functions in the Face of Indeterminacy', (1975) 29 *Law and Contemporary Problems* 226; S. Parker, 'The Best Interests of the Child—Principles and Problems' in P. Alston (ed), *The Best Interests of the Child*. Oxford: Clarendon Press (1994).   [152] Family Law Act 1996 s 11(4).
[153] Children Act 1989 s 1(3). 'Best interests' is applied in areas of medical law as well (eg to decisions about sterilization of the learning disabled: *Re B* [1988] AC 199; *Re F* [1990] 2 AC 1) but without a structuring or an injection of normative content, each case is decided on its merits as individual judges see it. This is criticized by I. Kennedy, *Treat Me Right: Essays in Medical Law and Ethics*. Oxford: Oxford University Press (1992).

to reflect a broad-based consensus of both professional and popular opinion. It is child-centred: there is thus no reference to parental conduct, sexual orientation, or new relationships. In many cases those factors which
are relevant may all point in the same direction. But obviously there are
cases where different items in the guidelines will suggest different conclusions. The legislation does not prioritize any factor, though many will
take comfort from its placing of the ascertainable wishes and feelings of
the child as first in the list.

Inevitably, areas of controversy still exist, and however constrained the
discretion there will remain an irreducible element of value judgment. A
good example is the case where the judge made a residence order in
favour of the father because he disapproved of the attitude of the mother
and her new partner to nudity and communal bathing. The Court of
Appeal, not surprisingly, allowed the mother's appeal.[154] A high profile
area of controversy in recent years—and one where values necessarily
intrude—concerns a parent's sexual orientation.[155] In one case[156] Balcombe
LJ advised that it was necessary to apply the moral standards of the
community. He continued:

> It is still the norm that children are brought up in a home with a father, mother
> and siblings (if any) and, other things being equal, such an upbringing is most
> likely to be conducive to their welfare. If, because the parents are divorced, such
> an upbringing is no longer possible, then a very material factor in considering
> where the child's welfare lies is which of the competing parents can offer the
> nearest approach to the norm.

It was, he said 'clearly the father' since the mother was living in a lesbian
relationship. The father would offer 'a normal home by the standards of
our society'. The court was concerned with both the stigma a child would
suffer if brought up in a lesbian relationship and the effect this would
have on the child's own sexuality.[157]

It has come to be accepted that an important consideration in a dispute
over where the child shall live is which of the parents will be best able to
encourage a continuing relationship between the child and the absent
parent and the wider family.[158] But shared parenting lacks the profile that
it has in the United States. There is no evidence that the early Wallerstein
and Kelly research *Surviving the Break-up* had any impact in Britain.[159] In

---

[154] *Re W* [1999] FLR 869.
[155] And see K. Standley, 'Children and Lesbian Mothers', (1992) 4 *Journal of Child Law* 134;
H. Reece, n 149 above.                    [156] *C v C* [1991] 1 FLR 223.
[157] Cf *B v B* [1991] 1 FLR 402. Curiously, the courts take a much more liberal attitude to
homosexuality in the context of adoption: *Re W* [1997] 2 FLR 406.
[158] See J. Pryor and F. Seymour, 'Making Decisions about Children after Parental Separation', (1996) 8 *Child and Family Law Quarterly* 229.
[159] But see M. Freeman, 'How Children Cope With Divorce—New Evidence on an Old
Problem', (1981) 11 *Family Law* 105.

460

1945, and for most of the period under consideration, shared parenting
was not even discussed in Britain. In 1986 the Court of Appeal decided
that it was not open to a court to make what was then called a joint care
and control order.[160] The 1989 Act, however, does allow for such orders to
be made.[161] Few are. Initially, the view taken was that such orders were to
be made only in 'exceptional circumstances'.[162] The Court of Appeal later
ruled that they may be made in 'unusual' circumstances'.[163] It is a way of
conferring parental responsibility on a step-parent and this, it has been
held,[164] is an example of such an unusual circumstance (though the reality
is that such reconstituted families are very common). The Court of
Appeal has given guidance on when a shared residence order is not
appropriate: this would be when there are concrete issues still to be
resolved, such as the type and amount of contact and education
questions.[165] The probability is that shared parenting works best where
the parties do not need to go to court for any order.[166]

It is recognized now—it certainly wasn't in 1945—that parents, with
or without help,[167] can make post-separation child arrangements themselves. This has led to what is perhaps the greatest change in the English
approach to disputes about children. Before the Children Act 1989 court
orders were sought and made in almost all divorce cases involving children.[168] But, following the view of the Government that 'families should
generally be left to sort out matters for themselves unless it is shown
that without an order the child's welfare will suffer',[169] section 1(5) of the
Children Act provides: 'Where a court is considering whether or not to
make one or more orders under this Act with respect to a child, it shall
not make the order or any of the orders unless it considers that doing so
would be better for the child than making no order at all.' Orders are
accordingly only to be made where they resolve disputes or in some
other way benefit a child, for example to facilitate the grant of public
housing and thus ensure the child is properly housed. Also, if the child
is to be looked after by someone who would not otherwise have
parental responsibility (a grandparent, for example), then making an
order (a residence order in favour of the grandparent which would
confer parental responsibility on her) may well benefit the child, since

---

[160] *Riley v Riley* [1986] 2 FLR 429.
[161] s 11(4).        [162] *Re H* [1994] 1 FLR 717.        [163] *A v A* [1994] 1 FLR 669.
[164] *Re H* [1995] 2 FLR 883.        [165] n 163 above, at 677.
[166] So that where they seek an order, it probably should not be made (it will not be better
for the child than making no order).
[167] Counselling, conciliation, and mediation. See *Practice Direction: Conciliation—Children*
[1992] 1 FLR 228. See also G. Davis, *Partisans and Mediators: The Resolution of Divorce Disputes.*
Oxford: Clarendon Press (1988).
[168] See J. A. Priest and J. C. Whybrow, n 136 above, 222.
[169] Lord Mackay, 'The Joseph Jackson Memorial Lecture', (1989) 139 *New Law Journal* 505.

Disputing Children 461

the person with whom he is now living will be able to take decisions about his upbringing.[170]

Some of the most hotly contested disputes about children concern contact. Disputes arise about frequency and about venue[171] and also over the quality of the contact (for example, whether staying contact is to be allowed). Until the Children Act came into operation the normal practice was to order reasonable access (as it was then called) and leave it to the parties to agree on what was reasonable. With the adoption of the minimal intervention principle in s 1(5), the reasonable contact order has fallen into desuetude. In 1962 the Court of Appeal was clear that access was a non-custodial parent's right.[172] By 1973 it was being viewed as the right of the child, so that no court was to deprive a child of access to a parent unless wholly satisfied that it was in the child's interest that there should be none.[173] This was the earliest judicial pronouncement on children's rights, and it has been repeated many times.[174] The importance of contact is reflected in the development of contact centres, and in the encouragement of indirect contact (letters, presents, telephone calls) where direct contact is impracticable or undesirable.[175] Also, courts have imposed obligations on the residential parent to send photographs, school reports, and the like, and to read the non-residential parent's letters to the child.[176] The courts have also increasingly recognized the importance to a child of retaining or regaining contact with persons other than parents. In one recent case,[177] the court ordered contact to resume between a man (a father figure) and his former stepson, whilst at the same time denying him contact to his own son.

There is a perception that disputes over contact (and probably over residence as well) have intensified in the 1990s.[178] This may be explained in a number of ways. First, with almost no divorces being defended and with the growth of mediation, divorce has become much more a private affair, less visible and less controlled.[179] Second, whether or not men are taking on more child care responsibilities, many now think differently about their role as fathers and their relationship with their children, which, not surprisingly, they wish to survive their

[170] *B v B* [1992] 2 FLR 327.
[171] Hence the development of contact centres, on which see E. Halliday, 'The Role and Function of Child Contact Centres', (1997) 19 *Journal of Social Welfare and Family Law* 53.
[172] *S v S and P* [1962] 2 All ER 1, 3 *per* Willmer J.
[173] *M v M* [1973] 2 All ER 81, 85 *per* Wrangham J.    [174] eg in *Re R* [1993] 2 FLR 762.
[175] As in *Re M* [1994] 1 FLR 272. See also *Re P* [1999] 2 FLR 893.
[176] *Re O* [1995] 2 FLR 124.    [177] *Re C and V* [1998] 1 FLR 392.
[178] R. Bailey-Harris, G. Davis, G. J. Barron, and J. Pearce, *Monitoring Private Law Applications under the Children Act 1989.* Bristol: University of Bristol (1998).
[179] See J. Roche, 'Children and Divorce: A Private Affair?' in S. D. Sclater and C. Piper (eds), *Undercurrents of Divorce.* Aldershot: Ashgate (1999) 55–75.

462

divorce.[180] Third, we have become much more aware of domestic violence:[181] this only re-emerged as a social problem in the 1970s and may now feature in a quarter of the marriages which end in divorce.[182] Domestic violence has also come to be accepted as a form of child abuse.[183] Fourth (and ironically) as mediation and counselling grow to take the heat out of divorce, they may also fuel or rekindle anger as couples relive the past even as they disentangle themselves.[184] Whatever the explanation, we have seen the emergence of the 'implacably hostile' parent (invariably the mother), of a growth of allegations of sexual abuse,[185] and of domestic violence being raised in the context of contact.

The courts do not react favourably to implacable hostility. Thus, in *Re O*,[186] Sir Thomas Bingham MR said: 'Neither parent should be encouraged or permitted to think that the more intransigent, the more unreasonable, the more obdurate and the more unco-operative they are, the more likely they are to get their own way.' In *Re P*[187] this reluctance to allow implacable hostility to prevail led the Court of Appeal to order supervised contact to a father with a history of psychiatric illness, alcohol and drug abuse and who had Nazi sympathies,[188] despite the fact that contact was thought likely to cause the mother stress and anxiety which would communicate itself to the children whose welfare would as a result suffer detriment. But, in another case where a court welfare officer concluded that it would not be in a 10-year-old boy's best interests to be forced into a situation which for him was 'fraught with anxiety and insecurity',[189] the judge allowed the mother's implacable hostility to prevail. Balcombe LJ acknowledged that the father might feel he is suffering injustice. He was,

---

[180] See B. Lupton and L. Barclay, *Constructing Fatherhood Discourses and Experiences.* London: Sage (1997).

[181] See M. Kaye, 'Domestic Violence, Residence and Contact', (1996) 8 *Child and Family Law Quarterly* 285.

[182] The Law Commission in 1998 said 22% (*Facing The Future*, Law Com. No. 170, Appendix C), L. Anderson, 'Contact between Children and Violent Fathers—In Whose Best Interests?' *Rights of Women Bulletin* (Summer Issue, 1997) reports nearly one-third of cases involve violence *after* proceedings commenced. See also R. Ingleby, *Solicitors and Divorce.* Oxford: Clarendon Press (1992).

[183] A. Mullender and R. Morley (eds), *Children Living with Domestic Violence: Putting Men's Abuse of Women on the Child Care Agenda.* London: Whiting and Birch (1994).

[184] See C. Piper, *The Responsible Parent.* Hemel Hempstead: Harvester Wheatsheaf (1993).

[185] On which see N. Thoennes and P. G. Tjaden, 'The Extent, Nature and Validity of Sexual Abuse Allegations in Custody/Visitation Disputes', (1990) 14 *Child Abuse and Neglect* 151. C-A. Hooper, *Mothers Surviving Child Sexual Abuse,* London: Routledge (1992) refers to the suggestion that allegations are false as a 'new myth' (at 18).          [186] [1995] 2 FLR 124.

[187] [1996] 2 FLR 314.

[188] Rather disappointingly the judge held that a father who is a racist cannot be denied contact to his children on that ground alone (see at 320). Given that he dressed his sons (aged 5 and 8) in Nazi regalia this is a quite unacceptable conclusion.

[189] See *Re J* [1994] 1 FLR 729, 732.

but 'this is yet another example where the welfare of the child requires the court to inflict injustice upon a parent with whom the child is not resident'.[190]

Because there are so many allegations of implacable hostility there is a danger that opposition to contact by a mother will attract this label even where she has genuine and rationally held fears for her child or herself. The two situations must be distinguished.[191] In *Re D*, where there had been domestic violence, the Court of Appeal agreed with the judge that the mother's fears of the father were genuine and that contact should not be restored in the immediate future.[192] The child was of mixed parentage (Ghanaian father, Canadian mother): unfortunately, the court addressed only the negative features of this (since the child thought his father 'nasty', he might accept racial stereotyping), and not the positive (denying the child contact would deprive him of cultural heritage and identity). The courts have been reluctant to refuse contact because of domestic violence. In an early case[193] in which it was refused, the mother had left the father before the child was born (because of his violence) and the father had not seen the child since his birth. In *Re A*[194] there were assaults on a child of 3 (for which there had been police cautions) and domestic violence. In *Re K*[195] there had not only been violence but a particularly brutal kidnap of the child before his second birthday. Indirect contact only was allowed. It may be that the court paid insufficient attention to the fact that the child (now nearly 6) actually enjoyed contact.[196] Most recently has come the firmest denunciation of domestic violence in a contact case. In *Re M*[197] Wall J said:

Often in these cases where domestic violence has been found, too little weight . . . is given to the need for the father to change. It is often said that, notwithstanding the violence, the mother must nonetheless bring up the children with full knowledge and a positive image of their natural father and arrange for the children to be available for contact. Too often . . . the courts neglect the other side of the equation, which is that a father . . . must demonstrate that he is a fit person to exercise contact; that he is not going to destabilise the family, that he is not going to upset the children and harm them emotionally.

[190] At 736. Balcombe LJ may have been over-sympathetic to a man who had used violence against his son and who was a pimp.
[191] See to this effect Hale J in *Re D* [1997] 2 FLR 48, 53.
[192] It was envisaged that the father might reapply for contact in three to four years, when it might succeed since he was becoming 'gentle, considerate and caring'.
[193] *Re D* [1993] 2 FLR 1. For cases involving domestic violence and contact, 1993 must be regarded as 'early'.                                        [194] [1998] 2 FLR 171.
[195] [1999] 2 FLR 703.
[196] The child's confusions were expressed in guilt feelings: it was clear to him that contact distressed the mother.                                        [197] [1999] 2 FLR 321.

464

## RELIGION AND RACE

Neither religion nor race is specifically referred to in the welfare checklist
to which reference has already been made, but both are clearly embraced
by 'background'.[198] In the past, religion has assumed what to us today is
a disproportionate and disruptive influence on decisions about a child's
upbringing.[199] Until recently, questions of race (and concomitantly of
culture and colour) were not issues. But one of the main differences
between the England of 1945 and today is that it is now a multicultural
society with nearly 6 per cent of the population belonging to non-white
ethnic minorities. There is also considerable religious diversity. One
result is that both religion and race issues have thrown up some of the
most difficult, and certainly some of the most controversial, questions in
relation to children.

The courts have consistently declined to discriminate between one
faith and another.[200] Nor have they throughout the period under consideration been prepared to favour a religion over none at all.[201] They
have occasionally taken the view that a particular form of religious
upbringing is intrinsically harmful to the child, because it isolates him
socially and educationally.[202] Even stronger opposition was taken in one
case[203] to the cult of scientology, and it was held that its harmful effects
necessitated transferring the care of the children from the father to the
mother (a scientology court having given the father custody), even
though they had lived with him for five-and-a-half years in a stable relationship.[204] But in general the view prevailing is that it is not for the
court to pass any judgment on the beliefs of a parent where they are
socially acceptable and consistent with a decent and respectable life.[205]
Where the residential parent has a religious practice which could potentially harm a child (for example, a Jehovah's Witness who will not countenance blood transfusions), courts have imposed undertakings. Courts
have sometimes required persons looking after a child to bring him up
in his religion even where it is not theirs. This happened in the leading

---

[198] Children Act 1989 s 1(3)(d). In *Re P* [1999] 2 FLR 573, Ward LJ said that 'Religious
beliefs must not be devalued' (at 596). Religion also comes within 'educational needs', see
s 1(3)(b) and *Re J* [1999] 2 FLR 678, 685 *per* Wall J.

[199] See eg *Hawksworth v Hawksworth* (1871) 6 Ch App 539, where reference was made to the
need to have 'sacred regard to the religion of the father'.      [200] *Re Carroll* [1931] 1 KB 317.

[201] They once showed antipathy to atheism: *Shelley v Westbrooke* (1817) Jac 66n; *Re Besant*
(1879) 11 Ch D 508.

[202] This view was taken of the Exclusive Brethren in *Hewitson v Hewitson* (1977) 7 *Fam
Law* 207.

[203] *Re B and G* [1985] FLR 134 (Latey J). He was affirmed by the Court of Appeal: see [1985]
FLR 493.

[204] Latey J described scientology as immoral, socially obnoxious, corrupt, sinister, and
dangerous.      [205] *Re T* [1981] 2 FLR 239; *Re R* [1993] 2 FLR 163.

case of *J v C*:[206] English foster parents who were Anglicans were ordered to continue to bring up the son of Roman Catholic Spanish parents as a Roman Catholic and were not allowed to send him to an Anglican choir school.[207] But now it has been said that only in unusual circumstances would a court require that a child be brought up in a religion which was not that of the parent with whom the child was residing.[208]

Such circumstances occurred in the most graphic recent example of religious conflict about a child's upbringing to challenge an English court. In *Re J*,[209] a Turkish Muslim father sought specific issue orders from the court in relation to his 5-year-old son, one requiring the nominally Christian mother to raise the child as a Muslim, and another requiring her to have the boy circumcised. The mother and the guardian ad litem opposed both applications. The father was not a devout Muslim. The court refused to make either order. As far as upbringing was concerned it was 'not practical to make an order that a child whose home is with a mother who is a non-practising Christian should be brought up as a Muslim'. The judge saw this as an application of the minimal intervention principle.[210] He held that male[211] circumcision was lawful—the first authority to this effect in England—but that to circumcise a son was not a decision that a parent could take alone, despite legislation[212] which provides that each person with parental responsibility 'may act alone and without the other (or others) in meeting that responsibility'. This judicial inroad on a clear legislative provision was justified by the judge because circumcision is 'an irrevocable step'.[213] The only other issue relating to parental responsibility which divided the parents concerned the eating of pork, a matter, thought the judge, for compromise and agreement. But, whatever, it was not 'in J's welfare interests . . . to make a specific order in relation to it':[214] that is, presumably, it was not better for J that an order be made. If the circumstances had been such that an order was appropriate, the court would have had to decide whether the eating of pork was in this child's best interests. The boundaries of justiciability are fast being approached!

The imperatives of religion were tested also recently in the heart-rending case of *Re P*.[215] The case has echoes of *Re Thain*, with the added complications of a handicapped (Down's Syndrome) child and religion—

---

[206] [1970] AC 668.
[207] See also *Re E* [1963] 3 All ER 874 (Jewish couple required to bring up ward as Roman Catholic). [208] *Re J* [1999] 2 FLR 678.
[209] n 208 above. [210] In s 1(5) of the Children Act 1989, discussed above.
[211] Female circumcision is prohibited by the Prohibition of Female Circumcision Act 1985. Unlike in France, there have not been any prosecutions for breaking this law.
[212] Children Act 1989 s 2(7). [213] n 208 above at 702.
[214] n 208 above, at 687; upheld by the Court of Appeal: [2000] 1 FLR 571.
[215] [1999] 2 FLR 573.

466

and it has a different conclusion. The case records the end of a battle by orthodox Jewish parents to recover their 8-year-old from Roman Catholic foster parents with whom the child had lived for seven years and with whom she had clearly bonded, though contact had not been lost with her family of origin. The child had been placed with the particular foster parents when the biological parents could not cope and attempts to find a suitable Jewish family had failed. The court accepted that the final loss of their daughter was tragic, but the conclusion was inevitable. There couldn't be a clearer case of foster parents having become psychological parents. The evidence was plain that a move back now would bewilder and distress the child who might see it as 'punishment'. What a contrast with the reasoning of Eve J in *Re Thain*! Butler-Sloss LJ thought the residential *status quo* argument was 'sometimes over-emphasised' but had no doubt that it had 'real validity in this case'. Religion was a 'relevant' consideration: here it was an 'important factor' since 'no one would wish to deprive a Jewish child of her right to her Jewish heritage'.[216] But— and here there was a nod in the direction of European jurisprudence,[217] 'in the jurisprudence of human rights, the right to practise one's religion is subservient to the need in a democratic society to put welfare first'.[218]

At the end of a century which has seen religion decline—at least the religion which purports to be *the* religion in Britain—it continues to exercise the court's careful judgment. Only in the final decades of the century did issues of race assume the same (or greater) importance. The Children Act 1989 is the first children's legislation to be alert to the issue.[219] Two years before, the courts were saying—rather as they have now done with religion—that they would not prioritize it over other aspects of a child's welfare.[220] The child, a Nigerian girl of 9 who had been with white foster parents for five-and-a-half years was 'adamant' that she wished to remain with her foster parents. But this was not what tilted the balance: 'one must, of course, approach the statements of young children with a degree of caution' said Swinton Thomas J.[221] The decision that the child should remain with her foster parents was dictated by paramountcy considerations. And significantly it was in striking contrast to the somewhat over-ideologized expert evidence to the effect that 'any child of West African background, regardless of the length of time that a child has been in an alternative family, must be placed back with a West

---

[216] n 215 above at 585.     [217] *Hoffmann v Austria* [1994] 17 EHRR 293.
[218] n 215 above at 598 *per* Ward LJ.
[219] See in particular s 22(5)( c) and Sch 2, para 11 (discussion of which falls outside the remit of this chapter).                              [220] *Re A* [1987] 2 FLR 429.
[221] n 220 above, at 436. Children cannot dictate decisions relating to their welfare, he added.

African family'. This expert had 'not met or spoken' with either the foster parents or the child.[222]

Another illustration of the conflict is *Re N*,[223] a case which contains a trenchant condemnation of the domination of social services departments by political correctness. The case related to a Nigerian child of 4½ ('a person in her own right and not just an appendage of her parents') who had lived with white foster parents since she was three weeks old. They wished to adopt: the father (by birth Nigerian but now a naturalized American living in the USA) wanted care and control (the child had been warded). Bush J, after commenting that he had been 'bombarded by a host of theories and opinions by experts who derive their being (*sic*) from the political approach to race relations in America in the 1960s and 1970s', concluded that to separate the child from her foster parents would cause serious psychological damage both at present and in the future. The compromise—which seems to have given greater weight to the father's interests than the child's—was to reject adoption. This is not an institution known in Nigerian culture and to the father it was redolent of 'slavery'. The foster parents were given care and control (which left the court, in whom were vested major decisions, and the mother, who played no part in the child's life, as the only persons with parental rights).[224]

These two cases are evidence of a judicial commitment to welfare over colour. And there are other instances.[225] But there are also cases which have gone the opposite way. One,[226] which was particularly controversial, had the Court of Appeal refusing to interfere[227] with a trial judge's decision to remove a child of mixed race aged sixteen months from a white foster mother with whom he had been since he was five days old. The Court of Appeal held the judge had been entitled to conclude that the advantages of bringing up a child of mixed race in a black family—one of Jamaican origin had been found—outweighed the importance of maintaining the *status quo* for the child who was thriving in a stable home. The most recent case suggests that this emphasis on colour or culture—the two are not clearly distinguished and Bush J in *Re N* ridiculed this—has assumed new importance since the Children Act 1989. In *Re M*,[228] a Zulu boy of 10 was being brought up by an Afrikaans foster mother in London (he had been in London for four years). She wished to adopt or at least keep him in England by obtaining a residence

---

[222] It remains an article of faith (or political correctness) that transracial placements are intrinsically bad for children. A good critique is P. Hayes, 'The Ideological Attack on Transracial Adoption in the USA and Britain', (1995) 9 *International Journal of Law and the Family* 1.      [223] [1990] 1 FLR 58.

[224] Today, a residence order in favour of the foster parents would be made.

[225] For example, *Re JK* [1991] 2 FLR 340.      [226] *Re P* [1990] 1 FLR 96.

[227] See *G v G* [1985] 2 All ER 225.      [228] [1996] 2 FLR 441.

468

order. She was undoubtedly his psychological parent (or at least one of them, for his mother could also be so characterized[229]). The Court of Appeal was impressed by the trial judge's view that the boy's development 'must be, in the last resort and profoundly, Zulu development and not Afrikaans or English development'. There was expert evidence to the effect that a swift return to South Africa would cause him severe trauma. Astonishingly, the views of the boy were not sought. The court, following a passage in Waite LJ's judgment in *Re K*,[230] saw the immediate return of the child as one of his rights as part of his welfare: 'to have the ties of nature maintained wherever possible with the parents who gave [him] life'. The boy certainly did not see it this way. He had to be removed forcibly, and subsequently returned to England. It is an interesting reflection on our times that where once the courts would have justified their decision in terms of the sacred rights of parents a generation ago in terms of the pseudo-scientific 'blood tie', now they invoke the rights of the child.

WHERE NEXT?

Disputes about children have been, and will continue to be, controversial. They will also continue to be bitter. The tensions that currently exist, for example between determinate rules and individualized decision-making, each having its advantages and drawbacks, will persist. Domestic violence will not disappear and in more and more cases it will be an issue. So will sexual abuse. Conflict over contact could get more intense: there is no sign that the implacably hostile mother will go away or that courts will find better ways of dealing with her congruent with promoting the child's best interests.[231] The courts will be forced into paying more attention to the wishes and feelings of (at least) the maturer child. The backlash against *Gillick* is temporary.

The checklist (in section 1(3) has been invaluable, but disputes still arise as to the weight to be attached to different factors, to the balancing exercise, and to evaluation. Does the future lie in trying to find a better way of determining what is best for, what one writer called, these 'children of Armageddon'?[232] If, as I suspect, children will emerge best where arrangements for their caretaking can be reinforced rather than

---

[229] *Per* Thorpe J, quoted at 452.      [230] [1990] 2 FLR 64, 70.

[231] See Julie Wallbank,'Castigating Mothers: The Judicial Response To "Wilful" Women in Disputes over Paternal Contact in English Law', (1998) 20 *Journal of Social Welfare and Family Law* 357.

[232] A. Watson, 'The Children of Armageddon: Problems of Custody Following Divorce', (1980) 21 *Syracuse Law Review* 55.

disrupted, then the need to identify paramountcy with caretaking (rather than residential) *status quo* becomes critical. Nor should it be difficult to form an opinion as to who the caregiver is. It will not necessarily be a parent, but it usually will be—and this will usually mean the mother. This is not a retreat to the maternal presumption. Nor will it work to the detriment of fathers (it is possible that more men will be awarded their children under such a standard). And there will need to be important exceptions to cater for domestic violence and sexual abuse, to take account of the views and preferences of maturer children, to tackle the obstructive or obdurate parent who wishes (without justification) to cut the other parent out of the child's life. It may be objected that this is to look to the past, but on such matters as parenting competence, emotional ties, and commitment to the child's welfare, the past is as good guide as any to what will happen in the future. There is a model for the standard suggested here: the state of Washington's Parenting Act gives first priority to 'the strength, nature, and stability of the child's relationship with each parent (including which parent has taken more responsibility for daily care)'.[233]

Washington and Montana in addition require a parenting plan.[234] There has been as yet no call for this to be introduced in England. This is a surprising omission given the presumption against an order unless it can be shown that the requested order is better for the child than not making an order,[235] and given the development of the care plan where a local authority is seeking a care order. It may be predicted that the parenting plan will be mandated in England—and sooner rather than later. The value of the plan is that it makes parents focus on their plans for their children for the future. As such it is consonant with the new divorce model—the implementation of which has been postponed—which requires divorcing couples to look to the future.[236] It may be assumed that the ideal plan will be jointly submitted. Where this is impossible and separate proposed plans are designed, it will give the court more information upon which to base its decision than is often the case now. Plans will, of course, need to be both flexible and dynamic, to cope with change both foreseen and unpredicted. The relationship of plans to counselling and to mediation, for there will be an inevitable link, will need to be worked out. It may be predicted also that the parenting order, introduced in England in 1998 in a different context[237]—as a way of assisting parents

---

[233] See J. Ellis,'The Washington State Parenting Act in the Courts: Reconciling Discretion and Justice in Reconciling Parenting Plan Disputes', (1994) 69 *Washington Law Review* 679.

[234] A number of other states in the US require such plans as a condition of a joint custody order.                                          [235] Children Act 1989 s 1(5).

[236] The Family Law Act 1996. This will not come into force until after the next General Election (if at all).                        [237] Crime and Disorder Act 1998 s 8(1)(a).

470

to prevent their children offending—will find its way into the legal
structure for the post-divorce family. Parenting classes loom on the near
horizon. At a certain point there will be resistance. The refusal by the
Labour Government even to contemplate making corporal punishment
by parents unlawful is in part a recognition that even the 'nanny state'
has some limits.[238] But we have long accepted that its tentacles can
intrude further into the deviant and the dysfunctional, and governments
may push on despite resistance.

[238] Department of Health, *Protecting Children, Supporting Parents. A Consultation Document
on the Physical Punishment of Children* (2000).

# [3]
# The Best Interests of the Child?
# Is *The Best Interests of the*
# *Child* in the Best Interests of
# Children?

ABSTRACT

The writings of Goldstein, Freud and Solnit, particularly some of the concepts they developed, have exercised a profound influence on our thinking about children. A new, revamped, final, authoritative edition presents the opportunity for critical re-assessment. The author finds a partial analytical framework, a dated image of children, a narrow concept of children's rights, triggers for intervention which leave children dangerously exposed and, above all, a sense that events have moved on leaving the most influential text of this generation firmly rooted in the ideas, problems and concepts of the last.

The publication in one revised volume of the landmark trilogy of *Beyond*, *Before* and *In*[1] provides an excuse, if one were needed, to assess the impact and re-evaluate the arguments contained within the three monographs and now compressed and updated. Whether or not one agrees with all, or even any, of the ideas contained within *Best Interests* (as I shall now call the collection), and I shall criticize both applications and implications, the concepts have impressed themselves, perhaps indelibly, on our thinking about children. Like it or not, anyone thinking about child law or policy, the relation between parents and children, the state and family, has to grapple with concepts like 'least detrimental alternative', the 'psychological parent', a child's sense of time and others of the rich ideas which permeate *Best Interests*.[2]

## 1.  SOME INITIAL THOUGHTS

*Best Interests* is an essay which links psychoanalytic theory to public, in particular social, policy. Therefore, before examining the impact of the books on public policy, a few comments will be offered on the relevance of psychoanalytic theory, in particular on the psychoanalytic theory embedded within *Best Interests*, to the public policy issues. This may be

THE BEST INTERESTS OF THE CHILD                361

interpreted as an act of folly on any part, even *chutzpah* given the audience,[3] but I am convinced that decision-makers have not confronted the
limitations of psychoanalytic theory, indeed may have embraced one
interpretation as if it embodied incontestable scientific truth and was
therefore beyond any challenge.

*Best Interests* states at its outset (5) that it uses psychoanalytic theory
to develop 'generally applicable guidelines to child placement'. This
theory is, its authors say, 'reinforced by common sense' (87). Adopting
a particular version of psychoanalytic theory (they quote Freud and
Bentham, curiously attributing to the latter an observation of his
allegedly made eight years after he died) (89), they point to the infant's
long period of physical dependence and they state that this physical tie
is turned into a mutual psychological attachment. They continue:

What begins as the experience of physical contentment . . . develops into a
primary attachment to the persons who provide it. This again changes into the
wish for a parent's constant presence irrespective of physical wants. Help-
lessness requires total care and over time is transformed into the need or wish
for approval and love . . . It provides a developmental base upon which the
child's responsiveness to educational efforts rests. Love for the parents leads to
identification with them, without which impulse control and socialization could
be deficient. Finally, . . . comes the . . . adolescent struggle to attain a separate
identity with physical, emotional, and moral self-reliance.

These complex and vital developments thrive in the protective enclave of
family life under guardianship by parents who are autonomous . . . When
family integrity is broken or weakened by state intrusion, her needs are
thwarted, and her belief that her parents are omniscient and all-powerful is
shaken prematurely. The effect on the child's developmental progress is likely
to be detrimental. The child's need for security within the confines of the family
must be met by law through its recognition of family privacy as the barrier to
state intervention upon parental autonomy. (90)

These 'needs', now called 'rights' – three are listed, namely, parental
autonomy, a child's entitlement to autonomous parents, and privacy –
are 'essential ingredients of family integrity' (90). They continue:

Two purposes underlie the parents' right to be free of state intrusion. The first
is to provide parents with an uninterrupted *opportunity* to meet the developing
physical and emotional needs of their child in establishing the familial bonds
critical to every child's healthy growth and development. The second purpose
. . . is to safeguard the continuing *maintenance* of these family ties – of psychological parent-child relationships. (90)

Footnotes, which I necessarily omit, point to the support of a number
of psychoanalytic writers – interestingly all sources cited ante-date 1973
when *Beyond* was first published – and acknowledge that a number of
'behavioural' psychologists including Rutter, Kagan, Tizard and the
Clarkes emphasize the resilience of cognitive functions. But to the

authors of *Best Interests*, to rely on the resilience of cognitive function as evidence of the child's well-being is 'simplistic' (20). This is to ignore that this research points also to social resilience.

*Best Interests* rests on a particular version of psychoanalytic theory. It is therefore important to see this in its context and to understand its implications (and its limitations as an instrument for social policy). Psychoanalytic theory is derived from the clinical practice of psychoanalysis of adults and children. In analysis the patient is removed from the context of everyday life. He talks and the analyst interprets. Unconscious processes are brought to consciousness and can be reconnected to the original experience and situations that produced them. They cease as a result to act as unconscious determinants of behaviour.

The basis of psychoanalysis is thus clinical, but *Best Interests*, and it is not alone in this, purports to transcend the practice from which it emerges and draw out therefrom universal or scientific conclusions. The patients, the source material for the theory, are not, and they have never been, a representative sample of the population. Although I do not base this on empirical evidence – I am not even aware whether there is any— intuition tells me that most patients are middle-class, wealthy and come from stereotypical family units. Its application must therefore be limited: in particular, in the context of *Best Interests* its relevance to the complex, often reconstituted, families to whom the new guidelines and framework are directed is questionable.

The authors of *Best Interests* place great emphasis on the child's need for the continuous presence of an autonomous and omniscient parent: the non-custodial parent cannot, so they believe, be an effective 'psychological parent' because the relationship between such a parent and a child is intermittent. The model adopted here is highly idealized and distantly removed from the realities of everyday parent-child interactions. It looks more like the relationship between analyst and patient in the consulting room than between parent and child outside it (and see Chodorow, 1978). It is, of course, true that some continuity and quality of care is essential for the adequate development of the child, but quite what requires empirical psychological investigation rather than inference drawn from psychoanalytic practice (and see Rutter, 1972). Surprisingly, *Best Interests* makes no reference to the childrearing practices of the *kibbutz*.[4]

A further important claim in much psychoanalytic thought is that a child enters into a relationship with a father only when he has perceived that the father is emotionally important to the mother. It is the close attachment of mother and father that gives the father a key role in the child's emotional development. Although the authors of *Best Interests* do not specially articulate this, it is this understanding which must, at least in part, explain why they state that children have difficulties in relating to parents who do not have a close emotional involvement with each other. There are two problems with this: first it idealizes intact families –

the sharing of a domestic household is no guarantee of inter-parental emotional contact. Secondly, it may well be that the child acquires a special relationship with the father because of his position as the social father, and not because of the father's relationship with the mother. Indeed, a child's relationship with his father may be better when the parents have split up: a husband-wife relationship may obstruct or frustrate the husband/father's relationship with his child.

One final initial thought concerns the glaring omission from *Best Interests* of any discussion of gender. There is nothing on the effects of the gender of a parent, nor is gender within the dynamics of the relationships between parents or parents and children commented upon. 'Gender issues' appears twice in the index but the 'issues' are not explored in the text. Both references are to reported cases (*Ross* v *Hoffman*[5] and *Derby* v *Derby*[6]: in the former there is reference to 'mothering' as a *'function'* rather than identifying a person; in the latter an understanding that the primary care-giving parent may be identified regardless of gender). These are important recognitions and important decisions. But their incorporation into *Best Interests* does not disguise – if anything it draws attention to – the fact that gender is glossed over. True, even though they adopt very traditional views of the family throughout, they are agnostic about which of the two parents is best suited to head a single parent household. Are we to assume that on gender the authors of *Best Interests* reject Freud? Freud of course emphasized the importance of the father playing a dominant role within the home. Others stress the role of the primary relationship with the mother in determining psychological outcomes. There is empirical evidence against the Freudian position: children growing up in a home without the presence of a father do not appear to suffer in the way the theory might anticipate. But other questions remain. Evidence suggests that the gender of a single parent may be of significance for some aspects of a child's development: for example, among children living in single-parent households, boys may develop better self esteem when living with fathers and girls with mothers (Santrock and Warshak, 1979); children from single-parent households may have difficulties in heterosexual relationships at adolescence (Hetherington, 1979) (it may even be one of the reasons why divorce rates are higher for children whose own parents divorced (Wadsworth, 1986)). There does not appear to be room for empirical evidence in *Best Interests*, particularly where it would seem to deflect from the guiding light of psychoanalytic inference. This point could be generalized, but the issue of gender reveals its realities and complexities. If, as seems likely, on this the authors of *Best Interests* reject Freud and do so because the Freudian position is incompatible with empirical evidence, then why do they shy clear of examining empirical findings elsewhere?

## 2. SOME REFLECTIONS ON RIGHTS

The authors of *Best Interests* come from two traditions: Freudianism and liberalism. On the question of rights it is clear that their liberalism takes

364

a back seat. *Best Interests* must be the only book on the best interests of children published in the 1990s which totally – one almost might say disdainfully – ignores the United Nations Convention on the Rights of the Child of 1989. No international document in world history has attracted more interest (virtually the whole world,[7] except the United States has ratified it) but it ignites no passion for the authors of *Best Interests*. If they think it is a deeply flawed instrument of policy let them say so. What, for example, do they think of Article 12?[8] Their own code (the Child Placement Code), an appendix to *Before*[9] but omitted from *Best Interests* formulates one child right (to autonomous parents) and the right of a child to be represented by parents is in the text of *Before* (114). Children's rights is also indexed in *Before*, and *Re Gault*,[10] the landmark US Supreme Court decision, is discussed, though to see it as reaffirming 'the right of a child to have his own parents make decisions about what he needs' (129) is about as perverse an interpretation of a case as it would be possible to imagine.

In *Best Interests* the following children's rights are identified:
— to autonomous parents (90)
— to be represented by parents (140)
— to parents who care (148) (see also 228)

Somewhat more equivocally, children are given the right to independent representation but only between an adjudication and final disposition, save in cases of emergency when such an appointment may be made at the stage of invocation (140). Counsel so appointed are to 'represent a child's legal needs by safeguarding her rights . . .' (140). Of course, this question begs: what rights does she have?

In the 'Reflections' at the end of *Best Interests* the concern is expressed, curiously for the first time, that 'the law's commitment to respect parental rights does not mean that children are to be regarded as property'. In the very next sentence we are told that 'sometimes they are treated as such' (227). Unfortunately, as I will show when I analyse the grounds for intervention, the authors of *Best Interests* are themselves, unwittingly perhaps, guilty of just this.

Another reference in the text to children's rights is the castigation of the development in a number of legal systems (Freeman, 1997) that visitation or contact is the right of a child, not of the parents. This, they say, is 'misleading' in that it shifts the power to deprive the child of that 'right' from the custodial to the non-custodial parent (26) (I retain the terms 'custodial' and 'non-custodial', though English law rejects them, as it should, since they are redolent of a property relationship).[11] Courts, they say, are 'powerless . . . to order non-custodial parents to visit their "waiting" children' (27). This ignores the moral force of law. It also refuses to confront the fact that if contact is a child's right then children will take the initiative to re-establish relationships. If contact is to be a gift in the hands of the 'custodial' parent, the child becomes a commodity, the very thing that in their 'Reflections' the authors are concerned to avoid.

*Best Interests'* position on parental rights is equivocal. The essential thesis of the book is that children's best interests are served when parents' rights to be free of state intrusion are optimally upheld. 'Two purposes' are said to underlie this right. They have been quoted earlier is this paper. In the 'Reflections' the authors candidly admit that they 'respect the parental rights that are based on the fact of reproduction' (225). They should, and we all do. We also know that far too often parents misuse the rights vested in them by biology and abuse children – *Best Interests* is part of the debate on where the rule of biology ends. In the 'Reflections' there seems to be greater acknowledgement than anywhere in the text (though see 10–11) that, to quote it, 'parental authority is frequently abusive, harmful, and detrimental to the child' (225): the example is given of families 'torn internally by parental violence or indifference' (225).

It is perhaps for this reason that in the 'Reflections' there is an emphasis for the first time on parental responsibility. The 'misperception' that children are to be regarded as property is attributed, 'reinforced', the authors say, 'by language that emphasizes the rights rather duties of adults' (227). Their illustrations are instructive:

The filing of a birth certificate is thought of as an assignment of a child to adults rather than the other way round. Likewise, divorce decrees award custody of the child to one of the competing adults rather than awarding a custodial parent to the child. (227–8)

But it is not just 'language' which creates these images: they are structured and restructured by institutional practices to which the authors of *Best Interests* have given influential support. If they now wish to resile from this position, so much the better. But the 'Reflections' and the text do not send out consistent messages. If 'custody' is to be seen as in the quotation from the 'Reflections', then why is visitation to remain a parent's right rather than a child's? By the end of the book (literally its last page), the authors are talking of parental 'responsibility.'

The vocabulary of placement ought to be reconceptualized to force focus where it belongs – on parental responsibility to satisfy a child's fundamental right to caring parents. (228)

Why this afterthought? It would be uncharitable to suggest that the authors were merely climbing a trendy bandwagon, climbing into bed (if I may change the metaphor) with Mary Ann Glendon ('rights talk' has 'impoverished' political discourse) (Glendon, 1991; Sunstein, 1995; Wardle, 1996). Parental responsibility, on which English and Scottish law now focuses (see Children Act 1989, Children (Scotland) Act 1995),[12] is more important than parental rights, though it too emits

366

conflicting messages (Freeman, 1992). The authors of *Best Interests* need to address the implications of their new understanding of the importance of parental responsibility. It is more, I assume, than a conversion on the road to Jerusalem.

## 3. IMAGES OF THE CHILD

*Best Interests* employs a particular, and I will argue, narrow and static image of the child. Although children of different ages are distinguished both when the effect of discontinuity is in issue (19–20) and for the purpose of understanding a child's sense of time (41 *et seq*), in general children are not distinguished by age, nor, until the very end of the book in the 'Reflections' and in a Transcript from an A B C programme,[13] are cultural differences (226) or 'different backgrounds' (227) recognized.

The child is seen by the authors of *Best Interests* as incompetent. As already indicated, a very incompetent Bentham and Sigmund Freud are cited in support of this image. Children, they say, 'are presumed in law to be incomplete beings during the whole period of their development' (8). Children – presumably all children – are 'not adults in miniature. They differ from their elders in their mental nature, their functioning, their understanding of events, and their reactions to them' (9). Although 'the enormous variations in the quality and degree of such differences' (9) are acknowledged, essentially children are lumped together.

Not surprisingly, *Best Interests* is critical of emancipation statutes. Whilst conceding one could be drafted (California's is reproduced at 281–2), the authors do not 'recommend' one, because they 'do not believe that there are or can be circumstances which justify emancipating children to meet their own legal care needs in the child placement process' (147).

A view of the child's mind and body as temporary, and relatively worthless, pervades the history of childhood. (Hendrick, 1990). Reformers, I noted in 1983, have usually treated children as 'things, as problems, but rarely as human beings with personality and integrity' (Freeman, 1983). Thus, one of the authors of *Best Interests* could write of children as if they were not fully human, seeing them as 'unrestrained, greedy and cruel little savages,' and not yet 'civilized beings', (Freud, 1958).

A distinction between adults and very young dependent children is obviously needed. Yet distinctions which are too rigid and sweeping, which attribute all wisdom, knowledge and prudence to adults, and all folly, ignorance and self-destructiveness to children, do not fit true reality. And history (Ariès, 1962; Cunningham, 1991), sociology (James and Prout, 1990; Qvortrup *et al*, 1994; Brannen and O'Brien, 1996; Jenks, 1996), psychology (Melton, 1987; Stainton Rogers, 1992); educa-

THE BEST INTERESTS OF THE CHILD                367

tion (Alderson, 1993), as well as developments within the law (see, in particular, the *Gillick* decision, discussed below) pose a challenge to the concept of childhood, which *Best Interests* does not take up.

Insights from the history and sociology of childhood show how childhood is socially constructed. An emergent sociology of childhood has revealed how it is the most intensively governed sector of personal relations (Rose, 1989) and yet how the study of children has been submerged in the study of families; usage of the term 'families', as in family autonomy, has too often come to be identified with 'parents'. And so children have been objects of social concern and intervention, rather than persons in their own right.

There has been important work on children's competence. Weithorn and Campbell compared the responses of nine, fourteen, eighteen and twenty-one-year-old participants to hypothetical decision-making problems concerning medical and psychological treatment. The fourteen-year-olds did not differ from the adult groups on any of the major standards of competency to consent: evidence of a choice; understanding of the facts; reasonable decision-making processes; reasonable outcome of choice. Even the nine-year-olds were as competent as the average adult, according to the standards of evidence of a choice and reasonableness of choice. (Weithorn and Campbell, 1982). This is consistent with Lewis's finding that, when elementary schoolchildren were given essentially unlimited access to the school nurse for routine medical care, their health-care behaviour was very similar to adults with similar demographic characteristics (Lewis, 1983). These findings, Gary Melton observes, present 'a conservative estimate of children's capacities' (Melton, 1984). The reason for this is that where children have experiences with, and overt permission for, participation in decision-making, their competence in reasoning increases: the more autonomy children are given, the better they are able to exercise it (see also, Belter and Grisso, 1984; Tapp and Melton, 1983). Anne Solberg's research with Norwegian twelve-year-olds shows how the ones whose parents expect them to take on adult responsibilities can do so, but the ones who are treated as immature and irresponsible tend to remain so (Solberg, 1990 and 1994).

Priscilla Alderson's research on consent to surgery by children is also extremely important (Alderson, 1993). She interviewed 120 children between the ages of eight and fifteen. At the beginning of the study she quotes ten-year-old Amy who informed her that she was 'only a metre high' and had decided to have her legs lengthened. 'When asked, "So you are having the tops of your legs made larger?", she replied, "I suffer from achondroplasia and I am having my femurs lengthened".' As Alderson comments, 'she raised the conversation to a level suited to her intelligence and dignity'. She also notes that children 'clearly did

368

not realize how incompetent they were supposed to be, because they insisted that research interviews should not be conducted during soap opera viewing times'. She explains:

Almost everyone was enthralled by *Neighbours* and *Eastenders*. Each series shows a large cast connected by confusing inter-marriage and inter-generational networks, and long-standing friendships and feuds, grappling with a constant onslaught of ethical dilemmas. One example is a black headmistress deciding whether to agree to an abortion after her foetus has been diagnosed as having sickle cell disease. Her husband, a church elder, threatens to leave her because he cannot accept abortion. Her children anxiously wait her decision. A further complication is that each scenario lasts only a few seconds. A police raid fades into a scene of a teacher reprimanding pupils, followed by an argument about rain forests, then back to the police. Each series demands acute observation, rapid interpretation of numerous understated details, sophisticated knowledge of wide-ranging social issues, and formidable powers of concentration, association and memory. Otherwise, each episode is a bewildering, boring kaleidoscope. Yet children can discuss the characters' biography and motives.

Alderson admits that researching with children had changed her views. She began with the idea that competence to consent to surgery might 'evolve at around 10–12 years'. She did not expect to find the range of experience, ability, or of the desire to make, or share in making, or to delegate decisions in school-age children. Her study suggests that 'competence develops, or at least is demonstrated, in response to experience and reasonably high expectations, rather than gradually over time or through ages or stages'.

Research on the criminal justice process also throws light on the competence of children. Research by Peterson-Badali and Abramovitch found that a 'majority of even the youngest subjects [those between nine and eleven] demonstrated an adequate understanding of the concept of defence counsel as an advocate in the criminal process'. By contrast, even much older children, those of fourteen and fifteen, showed substantial ignorance of the principle of lawyer-client confidentiality when pushed regarding the lawyer's ability to reveal information to specific parties, but then so did young adults (Peterson-Badali and Abramovitch, 1992). In a second study (Peterson-Badali and Abramovitch, 1993) the same researchers found that 'a majority of even the ten-year-old subjects used legal rather than moral criteria in making their plea decisions'. The authors commented: 'The actions of these children clearly indicate their ability to distinguish a legal domain, with its own set of rules and principles, from the domain of morality'.

Ellen Greenberg Garrison's research into children's competence to participate in divorce custody decision-making also offers valuable insights into children's abilities. She found that fourteen-year-olds performed as well as eighteen-year-olds in stating a custodial preference: hardly a startling conclusion. More interestingly, she found that nine

THE BEST INTERESTS OF THE CHILD 369

and ten-year-olds were as competent as the fourteen and eighteen-year-olds according to the reasonableness of preference or the rationality of reasons standard, a conclusion consistent with the Weithorn and Campbell work referred to previously. (Garrison, 1991).

And we could increase children's competence. It is increasingly obvious that, when sufficient understanding is tested, the way questions are asked will have an impact on the answers. For an adult, poorly worded questions may simply be a nuisance: for a child, they may be a potentially serious source of miscommunication. An important recent study identifies three sources of communicative mischief: (i) age-inappropriate vocabulary; (ii) complex syntax; and (iii) general ambiguity (Walker, 1993). Anne Griffam Walker is surely right to observe that:

the real question of children's linguistic competence in evidentiary settings belongs not the children, but to the adults. It is our adult legal system that the children are caught up in, it is our adult language in which proceedings are conducted, it is our adult assumptions about both law and language upon which communication in the courts is based.

She concludes 'we are not doing as well as we might in integrating children linguistically into a system not built for them'. But, if the argument of *Best Interests* prevail, why should we?

Competence (or capacity) as a basis for rights is a hostage to fortune and I would not advocate it. It allows critics such as the authors of *Best Interests* (see also, Goldstein, 1977) to argue that childhood is a time of dependency and incompetency and champion extensive parental authority (Federle, 1993 and 1994). Competence can also be looked at in a number of different ways: at its highest level few are competent (Beauchamp and Childress, 1994). Certainly many adults lack competence and many children are more competent than many adults.

Despite this we cannot ignore – it is rather a pity that *Best Interests* does – developments in English (and now Scottish)[14] law which tie children's decision-making abilities to their competence. The *Gillick* case[15] is important not because it gave adolescent girls the right to seek contraceptive advice and treatment without their parents' permission, but because it accepted that a competent child was one who 'achieves a sufficient understanding and intelligence to enable him or her to understand fully what is proposed' and also has 'sufficient discretion to enable him or her to make a wise choice in his or her own interests' (*Gillick* v *West Norfolk and Wisbech Area Health Authority*, 1986; see also Eekelaar, 1986; Bainham, 1986). What Lord Scarman said in *Gillick* is important, not only because it enables us to distinguish babies and fifteen-year-olds (this point is easy to grasp but, it seems, less easy to accept), but because so much previous discussion has emphasized professional, textbook knowledge and devalued personal, experiential 'wisdom' (see, for example, Faden and Beauchamp, 1986 and compare Alderson and

370

Goodwin, 1993). And many children, as Alderson's important study on children undergoing surgery shows (Alderson, 1993) are 'Gillick-competent' in this sense at very early ages.

The authors of *Best Interests* are wrong to dichotomize children and adults in the way they do, and wrong to lump all children together. Children are often like adults and adults like children in their rationality, maturity and interdependence.

## 4. PARENTAL AUTONOMY AND STATE INTERVENTION

Parental autonomy is important. Parents do generally act in their children's best interests. Two parents together are the ideal setting for a child and the State is a second best alternative, no real substitute for flesh and blood parents. *Best Interests* is thus right to state:

the law does not have the capacity to supervise the fragile, complex interpersonal bonds between child and parent. As *parens patriae* the state is too crude an instrument to become an adequate substitute for flesh-and-blood parents. The legal system has neither the resources nor the sensitivity to respond to a growing child's ever-changing needs and demands. It does not have the capacity to deal on an individual basis with the consequences of its decisions, or to act with the speed that is required by the child's sense of time. (91)

On this much we can agree. On where the barriers to state intervention into child-rearing should be erected we differ markedly.

*Best Interests* gives four reasons for adopting a non-interventionist approach. It emphasizes biology, psychology, the law's limited capacities (as just cited) and the authors' liberalism. As regards the last of these strands, the authors of *Best Interests* state: 'A policy of minimum intervention by the state . . . accords . . . with our firm belief as citizens in individual freedom and human dignity' (91). This political credo may be attractive to some, but in a world of basic structural inequalities individual freedom can be so exercised as to undermine not only the liberty of others but also their human dignity. The parent-child relationship is not an equal one. Bill Jordan put the point well when he wrote that 'the case against intervention in family life often rests on the freedom of more powerful members (usually husbands in relation to wives and parents in relation to children) to exercise their power without restriction'. (Jordan, 1976). Failure to intervene can, therefore, ensure the prevailing of a parent's will over a child's legitimate interests and, though some of these interests may seem relatively trivial, others may be fundamental (abortion, sterilization, life-saving surgery).

*Best Interests* takes a simplistic view of autonomy. It is something that is 'there'; it is discrete, taken for granted and unproblematic. What is ignored are the ways in which autonomy is constructed and regulated by legal processes. The law is the cultural and institutional underpinning of autonomy. It gives and its takes away. Families – that is of course parents, though the two concepts are not always distinguished – have as much autonomy as the law allows them. Long ago it imposed restrictions on parental views regarding child-rearing. It is for this reason that we have today compulsory restrictions on child labour, that we insist on children attending school and upon certain vaccinations. In their day each of these policies was resisted, and each is by no means uncontroversial to-day. Why do the authors of *Best Interests* not question such state intrusions? Is it because the status quo, particularly when well-entrenched, is beyond recall?

*Best Interests*, nevertheless, accepts that the family 'enclave' (in *Before* the word 'privacy' was used) may become a 'cover' for exploiting the 'inherent inequality' between adult and child. It may 'prevent detection of parental abuse or neglect' (in *Before* of 'unconscious or conscious hatred') (92). A balance has to be struck. All legal systems have to strike one: the current English compromise in the Children Act 1989 reflects the position adopted in *Best Interests*. The trigger for state intervention is significant harm (see s 31 (2)) and a court cannot make an order unless to do so would be better for the child than leaving 'well alone' (s 1 (5)). It is, of course, right that state officials must not impose their 'personal' views upon unwilling parents (92), though *Best Interests* now accepts they can impose their 'professional' views. *Best Interests* also reveals greater concern about discrimination against non-traditional families, including gay unions, than the authors demonstrated in previous manifestations of their thesis. It is not clear what Freud (Sigmund or Anna) would have thought about this. Nor am I clear whether it can be squared with the psychoanalytic framework which encases the principles for non-intervention. But I am sure it would be welcomed.

Before examining some of *Best Interests*' grounds for intervention, a few further observations may be made. First, *Best Interests* does not address the standard of proof to be satisfied before a ground can be established,[16] nor does it consider the problems of establishing the truth or how these may be overcome. Secondly, it is not clear whether a child can be protected against future harm. It is true that 'ground 5' includes a threat to inflict serious bodily injury and the repeated failure of parents to protect a child from exposure to such injury. But it is doubtful whether this would allow state intervention to protect an as yet uninjured child where parents had already seriously injured another of their children. English law permits intervention where a child is 'likely' to suffer significant harm.[17] *Best Interests*, unwisely I think, does not go this far. Of course, there are standard of proof problems, graphically illustrated in the recent case of *Re H and R* (1996).[18] The existence of these should not deflect us from wishing to protect by prevention. Thirdly, *Best Interests* neglects to confront the question of liability of the state when it fails to intervene. This is a problem of major concern in

372

both the United States (see *De Shaney* v *Winnebago County Department of Social Services*[19] 1989) and England (see *X* v *Bedfordshire County Council*,[20] 1995). The conclusion reached by the courts in both countries is disappointing. If, however, we are to shift our horizons to emphasize responsibility, a view with which the authors of *Best Interests* clearly now sympathize (see the discussion of their 'Reflections' above), the responsibilities of state institutions needs to be re-assessed. It has even been suggested that there should be a new principle of tort law, a duty to care for others in distress (see Gabel *et al*, 1996).

5. THE GROUNDS FOR INTERVENTION

A sustained examination of all the grounds for intervention set out in *Best Interests* is not possible given time and space constraints. I will accordingly concentrate most of my affection on two of the grounds: that concerned with serious bodily injury (or abuse) and that which relates to medical decision-making.

*Best Interests* sets out (as Ground 5) the following:

Serious Bodily Injury Inflicted by Parents Upon Their Child, an Attempt or a Threat to Inflict Such Injury, or the Repeated Failure of Parents to Protect the Child from Exposure to Such Injury. (111)

We are told that this ground is designed to establish 'a minimum standard of care below which no parents may go . . . It is meant to give the State the authority to identify and to provide protection to children who are kicked, beaten, raped, or otherwise brutally attacked by their parents' (111). It is also designed to safeguard children from attempts to injure them: the examples given are of starvation, poisoning and strangling, though it has to be said that the distinction between injuring and attempting to injure in these three examples may be more apparent than real.

It is what is excluded from this standard of intervention that causes concern. First, *Best Interests* refuses to accept that corporal punishment by parents (the authors acknowledge that school beatings come into a different category) can be targeted by the State. The authors accept it is 'harmful, humiliating and disadvantageous to the child's development' (112), but they look to 'gradual enlightenment and humanizing of public attitudes', not legislation, to remove the practice from our homes. They are aware of Swedish legislation, passed as long ago as 1979, and they could also cite similar legislation in Norway, Finland, Austria and Cyprus.[21] I have no doubt that *Best Interests* is wrong on this. Wrong to look to enlightenment (can the enlightened not take the lead?). Wrong to fail to see that the line between physical abuse and corporal chastizement is wafer-thin? (Since it is very difficult, if not impossible, to tell parents in advance on which side of the line their action will come, the

refusal to include corporal punishment is almost certainly an infringement of their 'fair warning' injunction (93–4)). Wrong to refuse to
acknowledge that acts of corporal punishment often lead to serious
abuse (much abuse is corporal punishment which has gone awfully
wrong). It is noteworthy that with female genital mutilation *Best Interests*
is more equivocal whether the practice should be outlawed or left to
'enlightenment' that comes with being part of American society (270–
1). I leave others to judge whether the USA is an enlightened society.
Whether Congresswoman Patricia Schroeder thinks so or not I do not
know but she introduced a Female Genital Mutilation Bill in 1993.[22]
The United Kingdom, Switzerland and Sweden have already banned
the practice (James, 1994).

The refusal to address corporal punishment (and the equivocation on
female genital mutilation) may be considered marginal – though they
say much about the status of children – in comparison with other parental failures with which *Best Interests* fails to grapple.

The most significant of these is child sexual abuse. There is an important shift in opinion between *Before* and *Best Interests*. In *Before* (see 62–
72) conviction (or acquittal by reason of insanity) of a sexual offence
against one's child was a ground for intervention. This was criticized
by me (Freeman, 1983) and others (Appleton, 1980; Katz, 1981) as a
ham-fisted response to sexual abuse. By insisting that protective intervention could follow only after a criminal conviction, the ground was
over restrictive. It was difficult to see how authors concerned with family
integrity and protection of the family from invasion of its privacy could
possibly want to encourage the use of the criminal law to tackle sexual
offences against children within the family. And, given the delays in the
criminal process, it was difficult to see how the ground would tackle the
traumatization of a child over whom the matter would hang perhaps
for a couple of years. *Before* at least addresses sexual abuse: *Best Interests*
dismisses it in a few words. It is 'too vague' (112) and there is 'neither
professional nor societal consensus' (113) about it.

Of course, the definition of sexual abuse in practice is complex. There
are few clear-cut medical signs of such abuse (the controversies over
Cleveland demonstrated this all too clearly) (and see Freeman, 1989).
By its nature it is secretive (Fürniss, 1991). As a result the child's
account of events becomes crucial. Children do not usually fabricate
stories of sexual abuse, but there are cases and situations where children
can and do make false allegations (Mantell, 1988). The Cleveland report
(1988) considered that social workers and clinical psychologists were
too uncritical in their adherence to belief in the child, and saw this
as contributing to their generally overzealous approach in 'disclosure
interviews'. Despite these problems sexual abuse can be defined and
recognized and acted upon, and children can be protected from one of
the gravest infringements of their personality and integrity. The abuser

374

'pre-empts the rights and individuality of the victim' (Hartman and Burgess, 1989). A commonly-cited, and authoritative, definition deems:

Any child below the age of consent . . . to have been sexually abused when a sexually mature person has, by design or neglect of their usual societal or specific responsibilities in relation to the child, engaged or permitted the engagement of that child in any activity of a sexual nature which is intended to lead to the sexual gratification of the sexually mature person. This definition pertains whether or not it involves genital contact or physical contact, and whether or not there is discernible harmful outcome in the short-term (Glaser and Frosh, 1988).

I think this definition is comprehensive and helpful. The only uncertainty in it relates to what is meant by a 'sexually mature person'. There is increasing evidence of abuse by older siblings and doubt as to whether they should be categorized as victims or abusers. But whichever, even in this difficult case, is there not justification for state intervention?

Not only is sexual abuse excluded from *Best Interests'* grounds of legitimate intervention, but so too, and for the same reason, are 'unwarranted intrusions authorized by neglect statutes that use such undefined terms as "denial of proper care", "psychological abuse" or "serious emotional damage"' (112). These concepts are, *Best Interests* claims, 'too vague'. I agree that emotional abuse is difficult to define and it is vague. But it can be defined. The Department of Health in England offers: 'actual or likely severe adverse effect on the emotional and behavioural development of a child caused by persistent or severe emotional illtreatment or rejection' (Department of Health, 1991). It should have identifiable serious consequences linked to parenting behaviour before it can be responded to by state action (and see Montgomery, 1988). But there are clear examples of emotional abuse. A commonly-used example is the refusal to recognize a child's gender, making him/her dress and adopt the role of the other sex. It has been suggested by a leading child psychiatrist that three things should be looked for (Wolkind, 1988): parental behaviour that is deviant; a form of child behaviour that is persistently and severely impairing the child's full attainment of mental health; appropriate treatment offered and rejected by the parents. The focus on the child's abnormal behaviour distinguishes emotional abuse from other forms of abuse, but I do not see this as any reason why intervention should not take place in the appropriate case.

If the problem is with vagueness and the value-laden nature of emotional abuse, then similar concerns could be voiced at the criterion of serious bodily injury. What is a 'serious' injury? The answer to this surely depends on values upon which no consensus can be guaranteed. What is a 'brutal' attack? Is the parent's motive relevant? Suppose this is to punish. Can cultural background be considered relevant? There is

THE BEST INTERESTS OF THE CHILD                    375

newly-discovered sensitivity to cultural issues in the coda to *Best Interests*. This is a problem with which English law has had to grapple: thus, in one case the practices of a mother who was by origin Vietnamese was judged against 'reasonable objective standards of the culture in which the children have hitherto been brought up', though the judge was careful to add, 'so long as these do not conflict with our minimal acceptable standards of child care in England' (*Re H*,[23] 1987; Neate, 1991). How would the authors of *Best Interests* deal with such a case? How would they deal with cases of serious injury which result from accidents which occur in the course of punishing a child? The emphasis on 'serious' bodily injury may also mean that danger signs may not be spotted: minor injuries often forewarn of more dangerous traumas (Bourne and Newberger, 1977).

Apart from the 'abuse' which *Best Interests* excludes from its grounds for intervention, there is a range of parental behaviour which can be seen, and is classified by some, as abuse. The list is endless: it includes locking a child in a cupboard or chaining him to a bed (Mary Ellen I believe was so found)[24] which are presumably not grounds for intervention because they do not (usually) cause serious bodily injury. But it also ranges over such activities as indulging in domestic violence (Mullender and Morley, 1994) smoking in the child's presence (Ezra, 1993), the repeated hospitalization of a child by a parent suffering from Munchausen's syndrome by proxy (Meadow, 1982; Bools, Neate and Meadow, 1994), as well as the controversial (though why?) use of drugs whilst pregnant (see the English case of *D* v *Berkshire County Council*,[25] 1987). None of these problems is discussed in *Best Interests*, though they are important test cases for its standard of intrusion. If any or all of these activities would not trigger intervention, is it because they are not abusive to children, or because something is wrong with the guideline?

The second of the grounds upon which I concentrate is refusal by parents to authorize lifesaving medical care. Ground 6 is set out thus:

A Parent's Refusal to Authorize Medical Care When (1) Medical Experts Agree That Treatment is Non-experimental and Appropriate for the Child, and (2) Denial of That Treatment Would Result in Death, and (3) the Anticipated Result of Treatment Is What Society Would Want for Every Child – a Chance for Normal, Healthy Growth or a Life Worth Living (128).

This is controversial. Adequate medical care is defined in as narrow a way as possible: the child must be faced with death and not, for example, the prospect of blindness or lameness; there must be medical consensus on the type of intervention and on the fact that it is therapeutic; and, dealing specifically but not exclusively with 'defective neonates', the child must have a chance to live 'a normal life' or a life worth living (again a consensual standard is assumed).

The ground raises profound ethical, legal, social and medical issues. The reasons for limiting intervention are similar to those addressed

376

elsewhere in *Best Interests*. The authors do not want the views of professionals, be they doctors, social workers or judges substituted for parents. They are not convinced that outside professionals are any more capable of taking decisions than parents. Indeed, they believe that decisions other than life or death are only reflections of a 'preference for one style of life over another' (129). Further, they argue that 'the law cannot find in medicine (or, for that matter, in any science) the ethical, political, or social values for evaluating health care choices' (129). 'A prime function of law', they say, 'is to prevent one person's truth . . . from becoming another person's tyranny' (129).

It is noteworthy, indeed, ironic, that, as I wrote this paper, Britain was rocked by a case (*Re T*,[26] 1996) in which the Court of Appeal allowed ordinary, decent devoted parents, themselves coincidentally health care workers, to refuse to consent to a liver transplant for their baby of eighteen months, despite medical evidence being clear that the operation was in the child's best interests. Without the transplant the child would die within a year. This decision is wrong on *Best Interests'* Ground 6 and I am sure that its authors would have overruled the parents (strictly speaking, the mother because the parents were not married and, in English law, the father has no parental rights). But – and here is the irony – the case oozes with the ideological sentiments we associate with *Best Interests*. Thus Butler-Sloss LJ said:

This mother and this child are one for the purpose of this unusual case and the decision of the court to consent to the operation jointly affects the mother and son . . . The welfare of this child depends upon his mother. The practical considerations of her ability to cope with supporting the child in the face of her belief that this course is not right for him, the requirement to return probably for a long period to this country, either to leave the father behind and lose his support or to require him to give up his present job were not put by the [first instance] judge into the balance when he made his decision [to authorize the operation].

She concluded that the 'best interests of this child require that his future treatment should be left in the hands of his devoted parents'. Waite LJ thought it was not an occasion 'even in an age preoccupied with "rights" to talk of the rights of a child . . .' He thought that 'in the last analysis the best interests of every child include an expectation that difficult decisions affecting the length and quality of life will be taken for it [in parenthesis I note "it", itself significant] by the parent to whom its care has been entrusted by nature'.

It is possible, though I think unlikely, that these judges have read the trilogy authored by the Goldsteins, Anna Freud and Al Solnit, but whether they have or not, their views are close to the sentiments of *Best Interests*. Natural conservatism (dressed up as common sense) and pseudo-science (the blood tie now masquerading as the rights of devoted parents), rather than one model of psychoanalytic theory, lead the judges to adopt this ideology. But the route, though relevant, is not as important as the destination.

It is interesting that the first group to praise this decision are the Jehovah's Witnesses who assume, almost certainly wrongly, that their decisions to deny blood transfusions to their children will not be gainsaid by courts. Again, of course, *Best Interests* would have no problem: on Ground 6 it would be easy to counter the objections of Jehovah's Witnesses objecting to blood transfusions, at least – and this is where I would part company with *Best Interests* – where these are necessary to save a child's life (there are situations short of the life-threatening where I would overrule them).

However, once outside this relatively non-controversial area, cases arise which expose the limits of Ground 6. For example, what is 'non-experimental' treatment? Is a procedure experimental because it is not orthodox? Are we not to allow an adolescent to take the risk of being cured by treatment which is still at the experimental stage? What is a 'life worth living'? How long does such a life last? In *Re T* the prognosis was fifteen years of normal, healthy development. Who should take the decision as to which lives are worth living? There is surely a distinction, which *Best Interests* does not acknowledge, between giving parents some autonomy, and allowing someone else to review the decisions they take. They are thus critical of the decision in the Connecticut case of *Hart* v *Brown* (1972) (see 137–9).[27] The case arose out of a decision by parents to save an eight-year-old daughter's life by a kidney transplant from her healthy twin-sister. Acting on medical advice, the parents consented to surgery, but the hospital would not operate without a court review. The court upheld the parents' decision, though not their 'autonomy to decide'. *Best Interests* is critical: neither doctors nor judges are trained or in any other way qualified to impose their values about what is right for children or families in such situations.

The standard in *Best Interests* is more suspect where failure to treat leads to irreparable harm, but not death. The Pennsylvania Supreme Court decision of *Re Green*[28] is a case in point. The child was sixteen and suffered from a curvature of the spine as a result of polio. A spinal fusion was required to straighten his spine and prevent his becoming totally bedridden. The mother, a Jehovah's Witness, refused her consent to blood transfusions essential to the operation. The court considered the boy's wishes (though a dissenting judge thought that a crippled child 'under the direct control and guidance of his parents' could not make an independent judgment) and, after finding that he didn't want the operation, honoured his wishes. The majority opinion is close in sentiment to that in *Best Interests* (though its authors would not have consulted the child). Thus, Chief Justice Jones states: 'We are of the opinion that as between a parent and the state, the state does not have

378

an interest of sufficient magnitude outweighing a parent's religious beliefs when a child's life is *not immediately imperilled* by his physical condition'. If spinal surgery could be ordered, what, he asked, about a hernia or gall bladder operation or a hysterectomy? The implication – that these are decisions to be left to parents – is surely not acceptable. The dissent in *Re Green* is far more persuasive: Justice Eagen wrote that 'by the decision of this Court today, this boy may never enjoy any semblance of a normal life which the vast majority of our society has come to enjoy and cherish'.

The sterilization of children with learning disabilities poses yet a further problem. Ground 6 is based on parental failure to meet particular standards. But parents who wish to have their daughters sterilized do not see themselves as neglectful or abusive: they believe they are protecting them from dangers they think lack the capacity to tackle. Bernard Dickens (1981) expresses this particularly well:

> The tests in [*Best Interests*] seem to lack the fine tuning required to deal with the situation presented by *Re D*[29] [in the first English litigation on the subject in 1976], since they are directed primarily at decisions to remove children entirely from parental custody and control. Further, they are concerned with parents whose treatment of their children falls short of legislated or judicially set minimum standards of care. They seem not to address parents whose well-meaning and conscientious initiatives are misguided or insensitive in ways denying children future rights. The tests set by [Best Interests] are illustrated by failure to come up to the standards and do not consider deviation from norms of child-rearing, by, for instance, over-protectiveness. They do not deal with causing harm to children by violating or pre-empting their human rights, such as their rights of reproduction.

*Best Interests* refers to sterilization only twice, and then only in the endnotes (278, 284). The second reference is to the Carrie Buck case (*Buck v Bell*,[30] 1927) and the dangers of 'scientific' consensus. All sorts of lessons can be learnt from a quite disgraceful judgment – and the case has implications for psychoanalytic theory where 'scientific' consensus has also had ill effects – but I do not think we can draw useful conclusions from the case about state interference with parenting. The other reference is to two cases in the 1970s. The only opinion ventured is that it 'may be that parental consent to surgery for the irreversible sterilization of a child ought not to be sufficient to authorize the operation without court review' (278, n 21).

It is a pity that *Best Interests* does not develop this question further. It is controversial: legal opinion is divided (cf *Re B*,[31] 1987, with *Re Eve*,[32] 1986). And it is a critical test case for the theory and practice of *Best Interests*. If it 'may' be that parental consent is insufficient—and why sit on the fence—whose consent is required? Doctors, courts? And what criteria should they apply? Of what importance are parental concerns and wishes, or convenience? Would the authors distinguish thera-

peutic and non-therapeutic sterilizations? Is the age of the child important? Would they apply the same considerations to mentally handicapped
adult children in the care of their parents? (see further Freeman, 1988).

## 6.   SOME THOUGHTS ABOUT CONTINUITY

The importance of continuity and its implications for placement
decisions is stressed in *Best Interests* (19–27). I am sure 'Continuity of
Relationships' is essential for a child's healthy development' (19). Many
of the supposed implications of this are less convincing. A close examination of the reasoning reveals a rigidity of thinking, even at times (though
this is denied) some inconsistency.

Thus the treatment of adoption looks at this as a one-dimensional
institution. There is no discussion of the implications of the guidelines
for children of different ages (where does the child's sense of time come
in?). All references are to 'children' and it seems not to matter whether
the child is six weeks or six-years-old. Does history play no part in the
understanding of continuity? Are decisions about older children not
more difficult and therefore delays before adoptions are finalized more
readily justifiable? *Best Interests* is trapped in a time warp when adoption
was a service for the infertile. The views expressed on adoption fit ill
with the contemporary institution which sees adoption as a child care
service. Post-adoption contact makes little (I refrain from saying 'no')
sense when the adoptee is a baby, but there is every reason, not least
continuity, for believing it has an important function where the child
concerned has a sense of his/her being, his/her relationships and his/
her status. *Best Interests* does not discuss 'open' adoption at all; clearly
its authors are opposed at least to court-imposed open adoptions, but
in effect many, perhaps most, adoptions today are open. Children know
about their biological families; is it really consistent with the continuity
principle to cut a child off perhaps from siblings, or any evidence that
open adoption harms children? Recent work in England (Ryburn, 1996)
suggest families engineer open adoption even where courts and adoption
agencies refuse to countenance it.

The authors of *Best Interests* acknowledge that their stand on post-
divorce visitation has been the most controversial (they add 'most misunderstood' and 'most resisted') aspect of their prescriptions. They say
it has been 'misread to mean that we oppose the continuation of contact
between a child and her non-custodial parent' (24). I have not so misread it, but I have always thought it wrong to transfer the decision as
to whether the absent parent should retain a relationship with a child
away from courts to residential parents. I think *Beyond* underestimated
the moral force of the law. A law which adopts the position that residential parents are the arbiters stamps with legitimacy post-divorce
decision-making which removes the absent parent from the child's life.

380

The law is an important symbol of what is right and wrong: its educative force should not be underestimated. A clear reading of *Beyond* would not have led anyone to conclude that its authors were opposed to the continuation of contact between a child and his (now her) non-custodial parent. But in the bitterness and turmoil of post-divorce situations people do not read clearly and readers drew conclusions they wanted to find.

Even so, two of the challenges *Best Interests* identifies in my opinion remain as potent criticisms; namely, first that the position adopted in *Best Interests* conflicts with the continuity guidelines; and secondly it deprives a child of his/her basic right to maintain ties with a non-custodial present. In most cases – I accept far from all because it is all too common that one parent will have drifted away or even blatantly abandoned his family – both parents are the child's psychological parents. Divorce terminates marriage: not parenthood or psychological parenthood. The children who come out of divorce least damaged are the ones able to maintain a continuing relationship with both parents (Wallerstein and Kelly, 1980). The English Family Law Act of 1996 recognizes this.[33] *Best Interests* accepts this but draws the line at compelling the custodial/residential parent to allow the child contact with the other parent. I deliberately put it this way round, and not as Maccoby and Mnookin (1992) do. It is the child's contact with the absent parent that anyone concerned with the best interests of the child must see as primary, not any parental right to see his child. I do, however, agree with Maccoby and Mnookin that 'because most divorced fathers have established a substantial relationship with their children before the breakup . . . the father should ordinarily have the legal right to maintain some sort of ongoing relationship with the children . . ., even though he was not the primary parent and no longer gets along with the mother . . .' – though, as I have indicated, I would not so conceptualize it. *Best Interests* is unduly dismissive of the empirical findings in *Dividing The Child* (Maccoby and Mnookin, 1992) and seemingly more so of those in *Surviving the Breakup* (Wallerstein and Kelly, 1980). *Best Interests* is also wrong to equate court-ordered visitation and joint parenting orders. The latter, however desirable (and cf Wallerstein and Kelly, 1980 with Wallerstein and Blakeslee, 1989) are difficult to operationalize and will not work in default of amicable cooperation between parents.

*Best Interests* also rejects the argument for court-ordered visitation that it is a recognition of the fact that contact with an absent parent is a child's right. To the authors of *Best Interests* this is a 'misleading assertion' (26). The reason is that conceptualizing contact as a child's right (which English law does: see Children Act 1989 s 8) 'merely shifts the power to deprive the child of that 'right' *from* the custodial parent to the non-custodial parent. Visitation orders make the non-custodial parent – rather than the parent who is responsible for the child's day-to-day care – the final authority for deciding whether to visit' (26). But in arguing in this way it is *Best Interests* that misleads. It is wrong to reject the moral argument for a concept by pointing to difficulties in operationalizing it. We do not reject orders ousting a violent or sexually abusive father because he may come back – with the mother's connivance or authority – despite such an order being made. To say, as *Best Interests* does, that the 'non-custodial parent remains, free not to visit' (26) puts a construction on freedom which few lawyers or philosophers would accept. Of course, a non-custodial parent who refuses to have contact with his child is in contempt. Why is his situation any different from that of the custodial parent who defies a court order to grant her child contact with his or her father? I think part of *Best Interests*' problems is to see this issue through the prism of divorce. For *Best Interests* it is the paradigm case. But I ask: are we to leave decisions about whether a child in care sees parents entirely in the hands of the authority in whom care of the child is vested? Or are we to do, as English law has done since the Children Act 1989 (see s 34), presume contact to be in a child's best interests and deny the authority (save for emergency situations and then only for a very short period of time) the right to deny the child contact? If there is a difference between the two cases, we are owed an explanation. Part of the reason that we do not get one is that throughout *Best Interests* concentrates on one sort of family (married or formerly married flesh and blood parents in the literal sense) and overlooks a variety of other family-type situations.

Were they to focus more prominently on other situations, further questions about psychological parenthood would also be raised. *Best Intentions* hints at a difficulty by bringing up the 'Holocaust' cases (82) – a number arose in the Netherlands when deported Jews returned from concentration camps to reclaim children and Dutch courts, wisely the authors of *Best Interests* and I agree, returned them to biological parents.[34] The 'special case' nature of the Holocaust should not, however, deflect us from considering the not inconsiderable number of cases at least as complex as the Holocaust examples where there is a conflict between two psychological parents.

A graphic illustration is the so-called 'Zulu' case which was decided by the English Court of Appeal in 1996 (*Re M*,[35] 1996). The case concerned Sifiso, a boy of ten, whose parents were Zulus from the Leboa area of Transvaal in South Africa. The mother was initially employed by an Afrikaner woman in South Africa as nanny cook/housekeeper for her daughters. The Afrikaner woman (who had British nationality by virtue of having married an Englishman, now dead) returned to England in 1992. The mother, and it seems the father, agreed to Sifiso going with her. The Afrikaner woman had become strongly attached to him (there is an inference that the boy was similarly attached but this is not brought out as clearly in the law report). How long the arrangement

382

was supposed to last, and what were its terms, subsequently became matters of disagreement.

In 1992 Sifiso's psychological parent was his mother, though there was clearly a close relationship with the Afrikaner woman. By 1996 the Afrikaner woman had become Sifiso's psychological parent, but had his mother ceased to be his psychological mother? *Best Interests* would argue that a child can only have one psychological parent, unless two are living together and together rearing the child. But is not a case, as one of the judges himself, ironically, of South African origin, characterized it where there was a claim between two psychological mothers? Will it do to classify it as a dispute between the claims of a biological mother and a psychological one? Does 'continuity' not recognize the ties of culture, of heritage, of language (Sifiso was forgetting his 'mother' language), of race? If the Afrikaner woman were allowed to adopt (even to acquire a residence order, her second preference), what were the chances of an identity crisis during adolescence?

The court decided that other things being equal (whatever that means) it was in the best interests of the child that he should be brought up by his biological parents. On this basis and on the basis also that Sifiso's development should be Zulu development, not Afrikaans or English development, and also having regard to the fact that the parents and the Afrikaner woman could not co-operate, the court ordered Sifiso's return to South Africa. There is no suggestion that the child's wishes and feelings were taken into account. His views were clear: he refused to board the plane (he was forcibly returned to South Africa the following day). I have no doubt that Sifiso's views were important but *Best Interests* would deny their relevance. The follow-up to the case suggests Sifiso has not settled and six months on he has returned to England, it seems with his parents' blessing.

This is a difficult case and like all different cases has no easy solution. I do not know what conclusion I would have come to. I know I would not have allowed the Afrikaner woman to adopt – the via media of a residence order being more appropriate. I certainly would have listened to the child. The authors of *Best Interests* would have taken neither of these courses. I would also have imposed conditions on the Afrikaner woman, requiring her, for example, to obtain Zulu lessons for Sifiso to promote continuity with his heritage (in English law conditions can be attached to a residence order). I would have made a contact order (presumably the authors of *Best Interests* would not – they do not discuss imposed visitation outside of the context of divorce). All this assumes I would have decided that staying in England with the Afrikaner woman was best for Sifiso. And, on balance, I think it is. I think in coming to this conclusion I come to the same conclusion as Goldstein, Freud and Solnit would. It may be that I come to the same conclusion as Solomon.[36] But I would employ neither the reasoning of Goldstein, Freud and Solnit nor Solomon.

Sifiso's case is a graphic illustration of the complexity of disputes about children. There are no simple cases and reductionist one-dimensional rules and principles may obstruct more than they assist.

### 7. CONCLUSION

Like *Best Interests* I will end with a 'Reflection'. Reading *Best Interests* in 1996 has been a stimulating experience, but it leaves me with a sense of *déja vu*. Its authors will think this right. I think an opportunity to reassess the principles in the light of social changes in the last twenty-five years has been missed. I do not wish to repeat what I have written in this paper. Let me therefore draw attention to some of these changes and the issues they raise.

In the last decades we have to recognize that children are persons and have rights (Farson, 1975; Holt, 1974; Freeman, 1983; Franklin, 1986; Veerman, 1990; Van Bueren, 1995). We have come to recognize that childhood is a social construction (was there a sociology of childhood when *Beyond* and *Before* were written?) (James and Prout, 1990; Mayall, 1994; Jenks, 1996; Brannen and O'Brien, 1996). We have even come to ask questions about how children make sense of family and kinship (O'Brien, Alldred and Jones, 1996). There has been a 'reproduction revolution' (Singer and Wells, 1984). It is disappointing that *Best Interests* totally ignores surrogacy (how would its authors have decided 'Baby M'?[37]) How much importance do believers in freedom and dignity attach to the surrogacy contract? (Wertheimer, 1996). There is a brief reference to artificial insemination (a 1977 case) (252) but none to in vitro fertilization or any of the child-centred problems this has produced. How would *Best Interests* decide custody disputes over frozen embryos?

References to culture in the reflections at the end of *Best Interests* makes me yearn to hear how its authors would tackle inter-racial adoption. What is their view on Bartholet's work? (Bartholet, 1993, 1996). Do they have a view on inter-country adoption? This transplant of children lacked prominence in the days of *Beyond*, but today is of major significance (Jaffe, 1995). *Best Interests* also ignores international child abduction, which constitutes a graphic test-case for its theories. Would its authors adopt The Hague Convention solution or allow the courts of the country to which the child is taken to investigate the best interests of the child?[38] Can abduction cases be decided on continuity and psychological parent principles? And suppose the allegation is that the parent from whom the child has been abducted has 'sexually abused' the child or perpetrated some other 'vague' act on her?[39]

384

*Best Interests* steers clear of abortion (*Roe* v *Wade*,[40] was decided the same year as *Beyond* was published), thus avoiding such questions as to whether the decision to produce children with genetic faults should be left to parents (Shepherd, 1995) of the problems of AIDS and HIV (which emerged in the 1980s), of drug addiction, of domestic violence. It pays almost no attention to the growth of one-parent families. The world has changed, or at least our understanding of it has. And the changes pose new challenges. Too often reading *Best Interests* I have been left with a feeling of being trapped in a time warp. Not least I sense that *Best Interests* has an almost cereal package image of the family. It is not just that those on whom the authors initially focused, in the main two-parent (divorcing) parents, were two-parent families, whereas so many of today's 'problem families' are one-parent families, but also that the families of the days of *Beyond* in the main shared the authors' values. Today there are fewer shared values, more problems, and fewer resources made available to tackle those problems.

Not only have families moved on, and governments back, but methods of resolving family dispute have too. I looked in vain to see where ADR, in particular family mediation, would fit into *Best Interests*' structure. I wondered also what were their views of family group conferences, a system pioneered in New Zealand, where the family plays a part in decision-making (Hudson *et al*, 1996). These are institutions and practices which advocates of family autonomy and privacy must grapple with: unfortunately they do not do so.

*Best Interests* concludes with Gilmore's Biblical or Marxian observation that 'in Heaven there will be no law and the lion will lie down with the lamb', whereas 'in Hell there will be nothing but law and due process will be meticulously observed' (Gilmore, 1975). We do not live in Heaven and many of our children live in Hell. I venture to suggest that the implementation of a children's rights agenda will bring out children closer to Heaven than the putting into practice of the principles of Best Interests is likely to do.

NOTES

[1] Joseph Goldstein, Albert J. Solnit, Sonja Goldstein and the late Anna Freud, *The Best Interests of the Child: The Least Detrimental Alternative*, New York: Free Press, 1996.
[2] On early reactions to their theses see Strauss and Strauss (1974), Freeman (1983(a)) and Davis (1987). An early examination of the arguments is Richards (1986).
[3] This article was delivered as a paper at a conference to commemorate twenty-five years since the publication of *Beyond the Best Interests of the Child*, in Jerusalem, Israel, in November 1996 (albeit two years early!) The audience was predominantly 'psy' professionals.
[4] On which see Spiro (1958) who notes that, although parents do not play an outstanding role in their children's socialization or in providing for their physical needs, they are of crucial importance in the psychological development of the child. He thought attachment to parents greater in such a society that in the United States.
[5] 364 A 2d 596 (Md 1976).
[6] 571 P 2d 562 (Or App 1977).

THE BEST INTERESTS OF THE CHILD 385

[7] Only Somalia (which lacks a government) joins in American obstinacy.

[8] This states in its first paragraph: 'States parties shall assure to the child who is capable of forming his or her own views the right to express those views freely in all matters affecting the child, the views of the child being given due weight in accordance with the age and maturity of the child.'

[9] Appendix II (see *Before*, 187–96).

[10] 387 US 1 (1967).

[11] These were rejected in the Children Act 1989, residence orders (see s 8) replacing custody orders.

[12] See Children Act 1989 s 2 and s 3 and Children (Scotland) Act 1995 s 1. Scottish legislation sets out parental responsibilities (it also sets out parental rights in s 2).

[13] 'We Want Our Children Back', transmitted by ABC News 20/20 on 18 August 1995.

[14] Children (Scotland) Act 1995 s 6: this relates to 'any major decision'.

[15] [1986] AC 112.

[16] In English law the standard of proof is the ordinary civil standard of balance of probability. See *H* v *H*, *K* v *K* [1990] Fam 86 at 94 and 100, approved by the House of Lords in *Re H and R* [1996] 1 FLR 80, 97.

[17] See Children Act 1989 s 31 (2).

[18] [1996] 1 FLR 80.

[19] 109 S Ct 998 (1989).

[20] [1995] 2 FLR 276.

[21] Denmark has not passed such legislation, though it is common to assume it has (see Nielsen and Frost, 1996).

[22] The Bill is discussed by Mary Ann James (1994).

[23] [1987] 2 FLR 12.

[24] The *Mary Ellen* is commonly thought of as the *fons et origo* of the discovery of child abuse in the United States, though many myths surround the case.

[25] [1987] AC 317.

[26] [1997] 1 FLR 502.

[27] 289 A 2d 386 (1972).

[28] 292 A 2d 387 (1972).

[29] [1976] Fam 185.

[30] 274 US 200 (1927).

[31] [1987] 2 All ER 206.

[32] (1986) 31 DLR. (4th edn) 1.

[33] See s 1 (c)(ii).

[34] This is not a subject which has been investigated or written about. Even Dwork (1991), who is cited by the authors of *Best Interests*, ignores the problems.

[35] [1996] 2 FLR 441.

[36] See 1 Kings 3, 16–28: a brilliant critical insight is Ashe (1991).

[37] In *Re Baby M* 525 A 2d 1128 (NJ Super 1987), affirmed in part, reversed in part, *Matter of Baby M* 537 A 2d 1227 (NJ 1988).

[38] See Hague Convention on the Civil Aspect of International Child Abduction 1980. Also Article 35 of the United Nations Convention on the Rights of the Child.

[39] Despite Article 13.

[40] 410 US 113 (1973).

REFERENCES

Alderson, Priscilla (1993) *Children's Consent to Surgery*, Buckingham: Open University Press.
Alderson, Priscilla and Goodwin, Mary (1993) 'Contradictions within Concepts of Children's Competence', 1 *International Journal of Children's Rights* 303.
Appleton, Susan F. (1980) 'Growing Up with Goldstein, Freud and Solnit', 58 *Texas Law Review* 1443.
Ariès, Phillippe (1962) *Centuries of Child*, London: Cape.
Ashe, Marie (1991) 'Abortion of Narrative: A Reading of the Judgment of Solomon', 4 *Yale Journal of Law and Feminism* 81.
Bainham, Andrew (1986) 'The Balance of Power in Family Decisions', *Cambridge Law Journal* 262.

386

Bartholet, Elizabeth (1993) *Family Bonds: Adoption and the Politics of Parenting*, Boston: Houghton Mifflin.
Bartholet, Elizabeth (1996) 'What's Wrong with Adoption Law?', 4 *International Journal of Children's Rights* 263.
Beauchamp, Tom L. and Childress, James F. (1994) *Principles of Biomedical Ethics* (4th edn), New York: Oxford University Press.
Belter, R.W. and Grisso, Thomas (1984) 'Children's Recognition of Rights Violations in Counselling', 15 *Professional Psychology: Research and Practice* 899.
Bools, Christopher, Neale, Brenda, and Meadow, Roy (1984) 'Munchausen Syndrome by Proxy: A Study of Psychopathology', 18 *Child Abuse and Neglect* 73.
Bourne, Richard and Newberger, Eli. H. (1977) ' "Family Autonomy" or "Coercive Intervention" ' 57 *Boston University Law Review* 663.
Brannen, Julia and O'Brien, Margaret (1996) *Children in Families*, London: Falmer Press.
Chodorow, Nancy (1978) *The Reproduction of Mothering: Psychoanalysis and the Sociology of Gender*, Berkeley, University of California Press.
Cleveland Report (1988) *Report Of The Inquiry into Child Abuse In Cleveland*, London: HMSO (Cm 412).
Cunningham, Hugh (1991) *The Children of the Poor: Representation of Childhood Since the Seventeenth Century*, Oxford: Basil Blackwell.
Davis, Peggy C. (1987) ' "There is a Book Out . . .": An Analysis of the Judicial Absorption of Legislative Facts', 100 *Harvard Law Review* 1539.
Department of Health (1991) *Working Together*, London: HMSO.
Dickens, Bernard (1981) 'The Modern Function and Limits of Parental Rights', 97 *Law Quarterly Review* 462.
Dwork, Deborah (1991) *Children with a Star*, New Haven: Yale University Press.
Eekelaar, John (1986) 'The Emergence of Children's Rights', 6 *OJLS* 161.
Ezra, David B. (1 993) 'Sticks and Stones can Break My Bones, but Tobacco Smoke can Kill Me: Can We Protect Children from Parents that Smoke?' 13 *Saint Louis University Public Law Review* 547.
Faden, Ruth R. and Beauchamp, Tom L. (1986) *A History and Theory of Informed Consent*, New York: Oxford University Press.
Farson, Richard (1978) *Birthrights*, Harmondsworth: Penguin.
Federle, Katherine Hunt (1993) 'On the Road to Reconceiving Rights for Children: A Postfeminist Analysis of the Capacity Principle', 43 *DePaul Law Review* 983.
Federle, Katherine Hunt (1994) 'Rights Flow Downhill', 2 *International Journal of Children's Rights* 343.
Franklin, Bob (1986) *The Rights of Children*, Oxford: Blackwell.
Freeman, Michael (1983(a)) 'Freedom and the Welfare State: Child-Rearing, Parental Autonomy and State Intervention', *Journal of Social Welfare Law* 70.
Freeman, Michael (1983(b)) *The Rights and Wrongs of Children*, London: Frances Pinter.
Freeman, Michael (1988) 'Sterilising the Mentally Handicapped' in Michael Freeman (ed) *Medicine, Ethics and The Law*, London: Stevens.
Freeman, Michael (1989) 'Cleveland, Butler-Sloss and Beyond', 42 *Current Legal Problems* 85.
Freeman, Michael (1992) *Children, Their Families and the Law*, Basingstoke: Macmillan.
Freeman, Michael (1997) *The Moral Status of Children*, The Hague: Kluwer.
Freud, Anna (1958) 'Child Observation and Prediction of Development: Memorial Lecture in Honour of Ernst Kris', 13 *The Psychoanalytic Study of the Child* 97.
Fürniss, Tilman (1991) *The Multi-Professional Handbook of Child Sexual Abuse: Integrated Management, Therapy and Legal Intervention*, London: Routledge.
Gabel, Peter (1996) 'Plank on Law', 11(5) *Tikkun* 31.
Garrison, Elizabeth Greenberg (1991) 'Children's Competence To Participate In Divorce Custody Decisionmaking', 20 *Journal of Clinical Child Psychology* 78.
Gilmore, Grant (1995) 'The Storrs Lectures: The Age of Anxiety', 84 *Yale Law Journal* 1022.
Glaser, Danya and Frosh, Stephen (1988) *Child Sexual Abuse*, Basingstoke: Macmillan.
Glendon, Mary Ann (1991) *Rights Talk*, New York: Free Press.
Goldstein, Joseph (1977) 'Medical Care for the Child at Risk: On State Supervision of Parental Autonomy', 86 *Yale Law Journal* 645.
Hartman, Carol R. and Burgess, Ann W. (1 989) 'Sexual Abuse of Children: Causes and Consequence' in Dante Cicchetti and Vicki Carlson (eds) *Child Maltreatment*, Cambridge, Mass, Cambridge University Press.

THE BEST INTERESTS OF THE CHILD                387

Hendrick, Harry (1994) *Child Welfare: England 1872–1989*, London: Routledge.
Hetherington, E. Mavis (1979) 'The Development of Children in Mother-Headed Families' in D.
   Reiss and H. Hoffman (eds) *The American Family: Dying or Developing*, New York: Plenum Press.
Holt, John (1975) *Escape from Childhood*, Harmondsworth: Penguin.
Hudson, Joe; Morris, Allison; Maxwell, Gabrielle and Galway, Burt (1996) *Family Group Conferences*,
   Annadale, NSW: Federation Press.
Jaffe, Eliezer D. (1995) *Intercountry Adoptions*, Dordrecht: Martinus Nijhoff.
James, Mary Ann (1994) 'Federal Prohibition of Female Genital Mutilation', 9 *Berkeley Women's
   Law Journal* 206.
James, Stephen (1994) 'Reconciling International Human Rights and Cultural Relativism: The
   Case of Female Circumcision', 8 *Bioethics* 1.
James, Allison and Prout, Alan (1990) *Constructing and Reconstructing Childhood*, Basingstoke: Falmer
   Press.
Jenks, Chris (1996) *Childhood*, London: Routledge.
Jordan, Bill (1976) *Freedom and the Welfare State*, London: Routledge.
Katz, K.D. (1981) 'When in Doubt, the Parents Win Out', 45 *Albany Law Review* 525.
Lewis, C.E. (1983) 'Decision Making Related to Health: When Could/Should Children Behave
   Responsibly?' in Gary L. Melton, Gerald P. Koocher and Michael J. Saks, *Children's Competence
   to Consent*, New York: Plenum Press.
Maccoby, Eleanor E. and Mnookin, Robert H. (1992) *Dividing the Child: Social and Legal Dilemmas
   of Custody*, Cambridge, Mass: Harvard University Press.
Mantell, D. (1988) 'Clarifying Erroneous Child Sexual Abuse Allegations', 58 *American Journal of
   Orthopsychiatry* 618.
Mayall, Berry (ed) (1994) *Children's Childhoods: Observed and Experience*, London: Falmer Press.
Meadow, Roy (1982) 'Munchausen Syndrome by Proxy', 57 *Archives of Disease in Childhood* 92.
Melton, Gary (1984) 'Developmental Psychology and the Law: The State of the Art', 22 *Journal of
   Family Law* 445.
Melton, Gary (1987) *Reforming the Law*, New York: Plenum Press.
Montgomery, Jonathan (1988) 'Children as Property', 51 *Modern Law Review* 323.
Mullender, Audrey and Morley, Rebecca (1994) *Children Living with Domestic Violence*, London:
   Whiting and Birch.
Neate, Polly (1991) 'Bridging the Cultural Divide', 890 *Community Care*, 12.
Nielsen, Linda and Frost, Lis (1996) 'Children and the Convention: the Danish Debate' in Michael
   Freeman (ed) *Children's Rights: A Comparative Perspective*, Aldershot: Dartmouth.
O'Brien, Margaret, Allred, Pam and Jones, Deborah (1996) 'Children's Constructions of Family
   Kinship' in Brannen and O'Brien, above.
Peterson-Badali, Michelle and Abramovitch, Rona (1992) 'Children's Knowledge of the Legal
   System: Are they Competent to Instruct Legal Counsel?' 34 *Canadian Journal of Criminology* 139.
Qvortrup, Jens; Bardy, Margatta; Sgritta, Giovanni and Wintersberger, Helmut (1994) *Childhood
   Matters: Social Theory, Practice and Policy*, Aldershot: Avebury.
Richards, Martin P.M. (1986) 'Behind the Best Interests of the Child: An Examination of the
   Arguments of Goldstein, Freud and Solnit Concerning Custody and Access at Divorce', *Journal
   of Social Welfare Law* 77.
Rose, Nikolas (1989) *Governing the Soul: The Shaping of the Private Self*, London: Routledge.
Rutter, Michael (1972) *Maternal Deprivation Reassessed*, Harmondsworth: Penguin.
Ryburn, Murray (1996) 'A Study of Post-Adoption Contact in Compulsory Adoptions', 26 *British
   Journal of Social Work* 627.
Santrock, J.W. and Warshak, R.A., (1979) 'Father Custody and Social Development in Boys and
   Girls', 35 *Journal of Social Issues* 112.
Shepherd, Lois (1995) 'Protecting Parents' Freedom to have Children with Genetic Differences',
   *University of Illinois Law Review* 761.
Singer, Peter and Wells, Deanne (1984) *The Reproduction Revolution*, Oxford: Oxford University
   Press.
Solberg, Anne (1990) 'Negotiating Childhood: Changing Constructions of Age for Norwegian
   Children' in James and Prout, above.
Solberg, Anne (1996) 'The Challenge in Child Research: From "Being" to "Doing" ' in Brannen
   and O'Brien, above.
Spiro, M.E. (1958) *Children of the Kibbutz*, Cambridge, Mass: Harvard University Press.
Stainton Rogers, Rex and Stainton Rogers, Wendy (1992) *Stories of Childhood*, Hemel Hempstead:
   Harvester Wheatsheaf.

388

Strauss, Peter L. and Strauss, Joanna B. (1974) 'Review of Beyond the Best Interests of the Child', 74 *Columbia Law Review* 281.

Sunstein, Cass R. (1995) 'Rights and their Critics', 70 *Notre Dame Law Review* 727.

Tapp, June and Melton, Gary (1983) 'Preparing Children for Decision Making: Implications of Legal Socialization Research' in Melton, Koocher and Saks, above.

Van Bueren, Geraldine (1995) *The International Law on the Rights of the Child*, Dordrecht: Martinus Nijhoff.

Veerman, Philip E. (1992) *The Rights of the Child and the Changing Image of Childhood*, Dordrecht: Martinus Nijhoff.

Wadsworth, M. (1986) 'Evidence from Three Birth Cohort Studies for Long-Term and Cross-Generational Effects on the Development of Children' in Martin P.M. Richards and P. Light (eds) *Children of Social Worlds*, Cambridge: Polity Press.

Walker, Ann Griffam (1993) 'Questioning Young Children in Court', 17 *Law And Human Behaviour* 59.

Wallerstein, Judith S. and Kelly, Joan Berlin (1980) *Surviving the Breakup*, New York: Basic Books.

Wallerstein, Judith S. and Blakeslee, Sandra (1989) *Second Chances: Men, Women and Children a Decade after Divorce*, New York: Ticknor and Fields.

Wardle, Lynn D. (1995) 'The Use and Abuse of Rights Rhetoric: The Constitutional Rights of Children', 27 *Loyola University Chicago Law Journal* 321.

Weithorn, Lois A. and Campbell, S. (1982) 'The Competency of Children and Adolescents to make Informed Treatment Decisions', 53 *Child Development* 1589.

Wertheimer, Alan (1996) *Exploitation*, Princeton, New Jersey: Princeton University Press.

Wolkind, Stephen (1988) 'Emotional Signs', *Journal of Social Welfare Law* 82.

# [4]
# What's Right with Rights for Children

I will start this review with a lengthy statement, setting out what I believe is the importance of a rights agenda. The language of rights can make visible what has too long been suppressed. It can lead to new stories being heard in public. As Carrie Menkel-Meadow (1987, p. 52) has put it: 'Each time we let in a new excluded group, each time we listen to a new way of knowing, we learn more about the limits of our current way of seeing.'

One cannot underestimate the centrality of rights. Rights are important because they are inclusive. They are universal, available to all members of the human family. In the past, they have depended on gender and on race. Women were non-persons, black people were kept in subservience by policies which justified 'separate but equal' practices (and worse, of course, by slavery). But just as concepts of gender inequality have been key to understanding womanhood and women's social status, so 'the concept of generation is key to understanding childhood' (Mayall, 2002, p. 120: see also Alanen, 2001). It has always been to the advantage of the powerful to keep others out. It is not, therefore, surprising that adults should want to do this to children; that they should wish to keep them in an often imposed and prolonged dependence which history and culture show to be neither inevitable nor essential. Think of the other side of inclusion, of exclusion and what this generates both on the part of the excluders and their victims, the socially excluded. Note the way the powerful regulate space (social, political, geographical[1]), define participation, marginalise significance, and hamper development.

Rights are indivisible and interdependent. Human rights – for that is what children's rights are – include the whole range of civil, political, social, economic and cultural rights. Denying certain rights undermines other rights. So, for example, if we do not put in place structures to tackle domestic violence, we will not protect children from child abuse. And *mutatis mutandis*. We are highly unlike to further children's rights if we deny the population as a whole its political freedom.

Rights are important because they recognise the respect the bearers are owed. To accord rights is to respect dignity: to deny rights is to cast doubt on humanity and on integrity. Rights affirm the Kantian principle that we are ends in ourselves and not means to others' ends (Kant, 1997).

It is, therefore, important that, as Ronald Dworkin so eloquently reminded us, we see rights as 'trumps'. They cannot be knocked off their pedestal because it would be better for others, or even society as a whole, were these rights not to exist. Of course, for the powerful – and for children adults are always powerful – rights are an inconvenience. The powerful would find it easier if those below

---

1   See further, Gill Valentine (2004).

them lacked rights. It would be easier to rule, decision-making would be swifter, cheaper, more efficient, more certain. It is hardly surprising that we have had to fight for the rights we have.

Rights are important because those who have them can exercise agency. Agents are decision-makers. They are people who negotiate with others, who alter relationships or decisions, who can shift social assumptions and constraints. And there is now clear evidence that even the youngest can do this (Alderson, 2002; Alderson, Hawthorne and Killen, 2005). We won't believe this because we don't wish to do so. As agents, rights-bearers can participate. They can make their own lives, rather than having their lives made for them. And participation is a fundamental human right. It enables us to demand rights. We are better able to do so where there is freedom of speech and orthodoxies can be challenged,[2] freedom of association and our understandings can be nourished, and freedom of information.

Rights are an important advocacy tool, a weapon to use in the battle to secure recognition. Giving people rights without access to those who can present those rights, without the right of representation, is thus of little value. But this is to acknowledge that we must get beyond rhetoric. Rights without remedies are of symbolic importance, no more. And remedies themselves require the injection of resources, a commitment on behalf of all of us that we view rights with respect, that we want them to have an input on the lives of all people, and not just the lives of the powerful and the privileged.

Rights offer legitimacy to campaigns, to pressure groups, to lobbies, to direct and indirect action, in particular to those who are disadvantaged or excluded. They offer a way in, they open doors.

Rights are also a resource: they offer a reasoned argument. They can put a moral case. Too often those who oppose rights can offer little in response. I am reminded of Devlin's invocation of 'widespread intolerable indignation, and disgust' (Devlin, 1965, p. 17) – as if this were a rational basis for policy-makers. And of some of the simply ludicrous ripostes to those who would allow gay marriage from distinguished thinkers like John Finnis (1994). Or, closer to the subject of the book review, of those whose only response to the demand that violence should not be used against children in the name of punishment is the incantation 'it never did me any harm' (to which it is difficult to avoid adding *sed quaere!*) (cf. Newell, 1989).

Rights offer fora for action. Without rights the excluded can request, they can beg, rely on *noblesse oblige*, on others being nice or generous or co-operative, or even foresighted. But they cannot demand (see Feinberg, 1966, p. 9).

What the excluded lack most is a right one rarely finds articulated. This is the right to possess rights. Hannah Arendt has postulated this better than anyone. She observed, à propos the Holocaust, that 'a condition of complete rightlessness was created before the right to live was challenged' (Arendt, 1986, p. 296). Before the Nazis robbed the Jews of their lives, they robbed them of their humanity, just as generations had done with slaves. To quote Arendt again: 'Slavery's fundamental offense against human rights was not that it took liberty away … but that it excluded a certain category of people even from the possibility of fighting for freedom – a fight possible under tyranny, and even under the desperate conditions of modern terror (but not under any condition of concentration-camp life)' (Arendt, 1986, p. 297).

In relation to children, Guggenheim would accept none of this. This is not because he is anti-rights, for the book oozes with passionate defences of the rights of the parents. He goes so far as to call parental rights 'sacred' (p. 71) And, where he attacks rights, nowhere does he do so with the sophistication of, for example, Mark Tushnet (1984, 1992) or Mary Ann Glendon (1991). His arguments have affinities with the writings of Lynn Wardle, who thought children's rights advocates were overvaluing the capacity of children's rights 'to make things right' (Wardle, 1996, p. 326).

---

2    As John Stuart Mill argued (1989, Ch. 2).

And, although he is critical of their influential emphasis on the 'psychological parent' (see p. 100) there are similarities also with Goldstein, Freud and Solnit's writings (1996, pp. 111–13). Goldstein, Freud and Solnit identify three children's rights: to autonomous parents; to be represented by parents; and to parents who care (1996, pp. 90, 140, 148, and see Freeman, 1997). The only right Guggenheim seems prepared to concede to children is 'to be raised by parents who are minimally fit and who are likely [*sic*] to make significant [*sic*] mistakes in judgment in childrearing' (see p. 43). It is most unfortunate that a typo (or typos) as major as this should occur in such a pivotal sentence. All sorts of conclusions could be drawn. And, despite the fact that there are other careless slips in the book – so little attention does he pay to proponents of children's rights that he can't be bothered to check the name of Katherine Hunt Federle and so parochial is he that he does not know that the Universal Declaration of Human Rights is so called[3] – one must be charitable and assume he is endorsing the first of the rights articulated by Goldstein and his colleagues.

Of course, autonomous parents are important. The United Nations Convention on the Rights of the Child recognises this. States Parties are to 'respect the responsibilities, rights, and duties of parents' (Article 5) and to 'ensure that a child shall not be separated from his or her parents against their will, except where competent authorities . . . determine . . . that such separation is necessary for the best interests of the child' (Article 9(1)). But there is so much more to children's rights. Can one really write a book entitled *What's Wrong With Children's Rights* – and note the absence of a question mark, for this book is a statement – and not at least investigate the U.N. Convention? Guggenheim has purported to do just this. We all, of course, know that Somalia, because it does not have a government, and the U.S.A, presumably because it does,[4] have not ratified the Convention (I say 'we all', but Guggenheim, who does not know the difference between signing and ratifying treaties, states, at one point, that the U.S.A. has not 'signed' the Convention, when in fact it has). Guggenheim makes only cursory reference to the Convention. He purports to quote Article 3(2) but succeeds only in paraphrasing Article 12(1) and (2), which he joins together (see p. 160). And he argues, but at no length, that the U.S.A.'s refusal to ratify the U.N. Convention 'has very little to do with children's rights, and certainly is no proof of their repudiation' (see p. 15). The reasons why the U.S.A. has not ratified the Convention have been explored by others (Levesque, 2002); its ambivalence to international treaties has been brilliantly exposed by Philippe Sands (2005).

Many think it would make no difference, even that U.S. law already upholds Convention obligations. That this is patently untrue can be seen by contrasting *Parham v. J.R.*[5] with Article 12, or *Hazlewood School District v. Kuhlmeier*[6] with Article 13, or *DeShaney v. Winnebago County Department of Social Service*[7] with Article 19, or *Ingraham v. Wright*[8] with Article 28(2), or *San Antonio Independent School District v. Rodriguez*[9] with Article 29, or *Prince v. Massachussets*[10] with Article 30, or *Stanford v. Kentucky*[11] with Article 37(a), or *Flores v. Reno*[12] with Article 37(b) – and this is just a selection of the

3    See appears as Kathleen (p. 8, 270 and the Index) and as Katherine, correctly, on p. 159. It is cited as the United Nations Declaration of Human Rights (p. 14).

4    Though the First Lady for eight years of the period under consideration, Hillary Rodham, was an early advocate of children's rights. Her advocacy of children's rights (1973) has been very influential.

5    442 U.S. 584 (1979).

6    484 U.S. 260 (1988).

7    489 U.S. 189 (1989).

8    430 U.S. 651 (1977).

9    411 U.S. 1 (1973).

10   321 U.S. 158 (1944).

11   492 U.S. 361 (1989).

12   113 S. Ct 1439 (1993).

most egregious examples of American decisions falling short of Convention norms. Of these
decisions, Guggenheim discusses only *Parham v. J.R.* He does not defend the Supreme Court's
decision but he explains it (away) as making clear the 'result-oriented base of children's rights' (see
p. 241). He alleges that 'the Court could comfortably rely on physicians to review parental choice
because the Court understood that physicians would tend to err on the side of admitting children
into mental hospitals' (p. 241). Guggenheim can seek succour in the reasoning of the Court of Appeal
(in England) in *Re W*: a 16-year-old could not refuse treatment (and therefore a pregnancy termination) if it was in her best interests, but 'medical ethics' would come to her rescue, and doctors would
not force her to have an abortion.[13]

Back in 1983, I described *Parham* as 'a low watermark for children's rights' (Freeman, 1983, p. 267),
and I would not resile from that position now. The court favoured the 'traditional presumption that
the parents act in the best interests of the child' (p. 604) – exactly Guggenheim's view. It ignored the
moral status of the children involved. Re-reading *Parham* now, I am struck that its opening questions
should have concerned the protection of parental decision-making rather than children's liberty
interests. And that the court could draw analogies with tonsillectomies, appendectomies and other
similar medical procedures. That these are not apposite was pointed out by Andrew Watson: a child's
medical symptoms of mental illness may stem from parental problems, and 'the child may serve as
the scapegoat and a symbolic focus for intrafamily conflicts. This sort of admission differs from
hospitalisation for other medical purposes because it presents the question under what circumstances the state should intervene into family psychological or social difficulties that hinder the
development of the child' (Watson, 1980, p. 676). Thomas Szasz (1977), writing before *Parham*, raised
similar concerns.

One of the best test cases for children's rights is in the area of health care. It is thus not surprising
that the leading English case on children's rights should have arisen in this area.[14] Guggenheim does
not discuss *Gillick*, although he does refer briefly to legislation in four U.S. states which enunciate a
similar principle, and to *Carey v. Population Services International*, which centred on the same issue as
*Gillick* – adolescent access to contraceptives.[15] There is also a substantial study of adolescents' rights
to abortion. Characteristically, Guggenheim sees the 'net result of the Supreme Court's pronouncements in the abortion cases concerning minors [as] a denial of constitutional rights to parents, not a
granting of rights to children' (p. 233). The cases, he says, are a 'public health challenge ... not an
issue about the rights of children' (p. 237). Would he see the denial of powers to husbands to prevent
their wives having abortions as an infringement of husbands' rights rather than being about the
rights of women? And if not, why not? AIDS (Bayer, 1989), SARS (Fidler, 2004) and Bio-Terrorism
(Moreno, 2003) are public health issues: is adolescent pregnancy to be so categorised?

It is a pity that concentration on the abortion issue – an American obsession – deflects attention
away from other health care conflicts. Goldstein, Freud and Solnit stumbled on this (1996, p. 128).
One looks in vain to see how Guggenheim would resolve the dilemma. Put starkly, can one leave
decisions about very sick children to their parents? (see Freeman, 2000). English jurisprudence has
had to come to grips with this very regularly in the immediate past: the severely disabled newborn
child;[16] the baby requiring an intestinal blockage to be removed;[17] the small child in need of a liver

---

13  [1993] Fam 64.

14  *Gillick v. West Norfolk and Wisbech A.H.A.* [1986] AC 112.

15  431 US 678 (1977).

16  *Re C* [1990] Fam 26; *Re J* [1990] 3 All ER 930. This is more complicated where there are conjoined twins: *Re A*
    [2001] 1 FLR 1.

17  *Re B* [1981] 1 WLR 1421.

transplant;[18] the adolescent anorexic who does not want treatment;[19] controversies about the sterilisation of learning disabled adolescents (and young adults).[20] Guggenheim discusses only American case law, so that in effect his book is largely about the uses and iniquities of recourse to children's rights in American litigation, but even so there is no discussion of key cases where parental decisions have trampled on children's rights. Cases like the Pennsylvania Supreme Court decision in *Re Green.*[21]

This case is a striking test of children's rights because what the 16-year-old and his mother wanted was, most of us would think, not in his best interests. Ricky suffers from a curvature of the spine as a result of polio. A spinal fusion was required to straighten this and prevent his becoming totally bedridden. The mother, a Jehovah's Witness, refused her consent to the blood transfusion essential to his operation. The court considered the boy's wishes (though a dissenting judge thought that a crippled child 'under the direct control and guidance of his parents' could not make an independent judgment), and, after finding that he didn't want the operation, honoured his wishes. The majority opinion is close in sentiment to that found in Goldstein, Freud and Solnit, though they would not have consulted the child. It must be assumed that Guggenheim would have come to the same conclusion also. He surely would endorse what Chief Justice Jones wrote (at 391): 'we are of the opinion that as between a parent and the state, the state does not have an interest of sufficient magnitude outweighing a parent's religious beliefs when the child's life is *not immediately imperiled* by his physical condition.' If spinal surgery can be ordered, what, he asked, about a hernia or gall bladder operation or a hysterectomy? What, indeed? Surely these are not decisions which can be left to parents. This was recognised by a dissenting judge who noted (at 392) that: 'By the decision of this Court today, this boy may never enjoy any semblance of a normal life which the vast majority of our society has come to enjoy and cherish.'

Of course, the most difficult feature of the case revolves around the importance to be attached to the child's views. In what circumstances, if any, is it justifiable to protect a child against the exercise of autonomy? And how are the child's views to be presented? On the second question Guggenheim is clear: he is unhappy about the separate representation of children. This does not, he believes, add the child's 'voice' but rather the lawyer's. 'Amazingly enough', he comments, 'courts sometimes believe the position really is the child's, when it is nothing more than the lawyer's' (see p. 95). That this can happen also when the client is an adult is blithely overlooked. In both cases it may be the result of bad lawyering.

Of course, it is true that law schools do not 'adequately prepare' law students to handle cases involving children (Kell, 1998, p. 690). But rather than concluding from this that attention should focus on training better child lawyers, and identifying their role, Guggenheim opposes lawyers for children. In earlier writing (1996) he appeared to favour a lawyer arguing a child's case where, as with abortion, she possessed a 'substantial constitutional right' – a clear right under the United Nations Convention narrowly being insufficient – but even this concession is absent now. But children need representation. First, because the judge cannot adequately protect children's interests, s/he is not in a position to appreciate the child's perspective. Nor are parents adequate representatives of a child's interests: there will often be a conflict of interests (Walter, 1999). And social welfare bodies cannot perform the job: they are overwhelmed, under-funded and highly bureaucratic, and their interests may not necessarily coincide with those of the child. Their ideological frameworks also may conflict with what is best for this child.

---

18   *Re T* [1997] 1 FLR 502.

19   *Re W* [1993] Fam 64; *Re C* [1997] 2 FLR 180.

20   *Re D* [1976] Fam 185; *Re B* [1988] AC 199; *Re F* [1990] 2 AC 1.

21   292 A. 2d 387 (1972).

The emphasis should be on better practice. Too rarely do lawyers understand their clients' lives. A test like 'best interests' will be opened up, its subjectivity reduced, if this understanding were broadened. There is a need, for example, for cross-cultural training (Duquette and Ramsey, 1987): social and family therapy both recognise this, but law is only now coming to do so (Mandelbaum, 2000).

Children need to be represented for many reasons. Representation redresses the 'imbalance of power', and addresses the need to minimise the risk of harm to the child that 'flows from contact with the legal system' (Fordham Conference, 1986, p. 1327). An equitable result is best achieved through 'zealous and effective representation of all sides of the issue' (Wilker, 1983, p. 354).

The question remains as to how best representation is to be achieved so as to maximise child participation. I have argued previously for the invocation of substituted judgment. It is child-focused, but it does not give much guidance as to how to determine the child's perspective and, as a result, can end up invoking a type of reasonable child test. The uniqueness of this child thus gets glossed over. Although, there is not the space to develop it here, Jean Koh Peters' 'child-in-context' approach is appealing. The concept of the child-in-context understands the child 'on her own terms in ways she would be able to understand and endorse' (1997, pp. 53–54). Peters is for maximising a child's participation. Even a newborn child, she believes, can contribute some amount to her lawyer's representation (see also Alderson et al., 2005), and 'the lawyer must strive to incorporate every percentage of the client's contribution into the representation' (1997, p. 54). In order to represent children well and enhance their participation in proceedings, lawyers must open themselves up, listen, question when they do not understand, and recognise difference. They must understand their child clients' lives and the communities within which they live. Child representation can be achieved: Guggenheim's concerns can be overcome.

Reconciling welfare and autonomy is more difficult. It is a problem that Guggenheim alludes to but does not grapple with. There is a brief reference to one of my own arguments (see pp. 93, 277 n. 36) – and I should be flattered because in this Americo-centric book I am one of only two contemporary non-American writers acknowledged – but this is not to my defence of liberal paternalism.[22] John Eekelaar's situating of children's rights within dynamic self-determinism, an approach designed 'to bring a child to the threshold of adulthood with the maximum opportunities to form and pursue life-goals which reflect as closely as possible an autonomous choice' (1994, p. 53) is ignored. So is Jane Fortin's argument. She recently wrote that 'the claim that a rights-based approach must necessarily be devoid of any element of any paternalism or "welfare" misconstrues the concept of rights' (2004, p. 259). Guggenheim may not be convinced by the arguments of any of the three of us: I suspect he is not. But he must counter them, not ignore them. And the debate is, I would reiterate, an important one. There is much which hinges on whether one adopts a rights-based or welfare-based approach, not least who one regards as the primary decision-maker.

One of Guggenheim's principal concerns is that an emphasis on children's rights relegates the interests of others. He is not the first to complain about the way emphasis on the paramountcy principle, for example, has discriminated against particular groups: Stephen Toope (1991) has written about its effect on minority cultures and Helen Reece (1996) has criticised the way it is used against lesbians. Guggenheim prays in aid the well-known case of *Painter v. Bannister*.[23] This is a case in which the values of a conservative judiciary prevailed but the same conclusion would have been reached applying any rule[24] other than one which prioritised the right of a biological parent. Is

---

22   Inter alia, in M. D. A. Freeman (1983, Ch. 2).

23   140 N. W. 2d 152 (Iowa 1966).

24   Guggenheim considers the alternatives.

this a call for a return to an unimpeachable parent presumption[25] or the pseudo-science of the blood-tie?[26]

There are good reasons why the interests of the child should rule. And this is so even if this will lead to an order which will only marginally improve the child's welfare at the expense of parents (or a parent), other family members or, indeed, the wider community. These have been rehearsed often. Briefly, children are especially vulnerable: they have fewer resources – material, psychological, relational – to rely on in adversity; they are usually blameless, and certainly did not ask to come into the world; for too long children have been treated as objects of concern (or worse, objects) rather than as persons, and even today they remain voiceless, even invisible, when disputes are fought over them.

It is important to realise that emphasising children does not necessarily mean that the interests of adults will be neglected. As Barbara Bennett Woodhouse eloquently reminds us (1993, p. 1825): 'A truly child-centred perspective would . . . expose the fallacy that children can thrive while their care-givers struggle, or that the care-givers' needs can be severed from the child's, which can lead to the attitude that violence, hostility, and neglect toward the care giver are somehow irrelevant in the best interests calculus.'[27] Herring (1999a; see also 1999b) can find no difficulty in interpreting the welfare principle so as to take account of the rights or interests of others. He describes this interpretation as relationship-based welfare. It may not be in the child's interests to be raised in a relationship in which a parent's rights were being wrongly ignored. As Kavanagh (2004; see also Czapanskij, 1999) pointed out recently, there is necessary reciprocity so that support for a child necessarily involves supporting that child's care-giver and vice versa. It is easier to express a formula than apply it in practice. I do not pretend the answers are simple, and there are dangers, as I would see them, of losing sight of children's interests if an emphasis on relationship places too much emphasis on adults. This concern has been forcefully expressed by John Eekelaar (2002, 2004). If there is to be a balancing exercise, how is this to be carried out, by whom, and how much weight is to be given to children's interests? Try applying relationship-based welfare to the 'Baby Jessica' case,[28] the subject of Guggenheim's third chapter, or to the so-called 'Zulu boy' saga in England in the mid 1990s[29]. But Guggenheim does none of this and, nor, within his terms, does he need to do so, because it is parental rights which concern him.

Although he is at pains to deny that Jessica (a 3-year-old removed from the only parents she knew to be raised by her biological father and his partner) was treated as a piece of property – and even property wrongfully detained is sometimes more difficult to get restored to rightful owners, as witness cases involving art looted by the Nazis (Petropoulos, 2000) – from the child's perspective that is exactly what she was. Guggenheim analyses the case in a scrupulously careful lawyer-like way. And he conducts a semi-Socratic dialogue with us. Suppose Jessica has been snatched from her hospital crib and only found after three years: surely there would have been no objection by 'the children's rights lobby' to her being returned to her biological parents? And he invokes the example of Jewish children hidden by righteous gentiles during the Second World War – there were notable examples in the Netherlands.[30] But there are good reasons to take account of the interests of adults in both these cases: in both, in the second case egregiously so, there was a gross violation of the human rights of the parents and the children.

---

25   A good illustration of which is *Re Thain* [1926] Ch 676.

26   As in *Re C (MA)* [1966] 1 All ER 838.

27   Since Woodhouse is one of the few advocates for children's rights with whom Guggenheim admits to having familiarity, it is a pity that this article is not discussed by him.

28   See *Clausen v. Schmidt* 502 N. W. 2d 649 (Mich, 1993): *Dauber v. Dauber and Schmidt* 509 U. S. 1301 (1996).

29   [1996] 2 FLR 441.

30   He alludes to this at p. 204, but does not discuss the cases.

Guggenheim's thesis is clear. By means of a number of case studies of American, largely private law, litigation he is able to argue that children's rights supply 'a convenient argument for adults who seek an advantage in court' (p. 132). They have 'elasticity', and so 'can be invoked by almost anyone' (p. 130). He builds on his own experience as a practitioner when he thought he was the 'true children's rights advocate' (p. 180): the book is his defence of a position that he feels should have prevailed but has not always done so. Although he is a defender of parental rights, there is a fuzzy utilitarianism to be found running through his book. Thus, the doctrine of parental rights is said to 'further vital interests of American society' (p. 47). And he holds up *West Virginia Board of Education v. Barnette*[31] and *Brown v. Board of Education*[32] as examples of the ways in which children's rights can be furthered without articulating them as such. The emphasis in *Barnette* was 'on the cost to society as a whole', and in *Brown* the Supreme Court 'emphasized education's significance to *society as a whole*' (p. 257). The trouble with this argument is that, for example, the execution of juvenile murderers,[33] the detention of juveniles in Guantánamo Bay, or corporal punishment in schools could all be justified in crude utilitarian terms, and doubtless have been.

There is no doubt that Guggenheim has a genuine concern for children. He is distressed that so many poor children die when with a better health care system they would not. He is troubled by the number of gun facilities. Of course, arms-bearing is a right in the United States: health care (like education) is not. He is concerned about poverty, the cause so often of children going into substitute care. But, because he is so unprepared to think in terms of children's rights, there is no attempt to articulate a right to an adequate standard of living (Sandbaek, 2005; Evans, 2004) or even one to nutrition (see Article 27 of the UN Convention and Jonssen, 1997). Is it a defence of Guggenheim that this is not an American way of thinking? Surely not. This book is not entitled *What's Wrong with Children's Rights in the United States*, though I suspect it should be.

There is very little attempt to look beyond the United States, to examine other policies, other institutions. Thus, the first chapter is a history, albeit rather selective, of children's rights 'in the United States'. There is thus no necessity to consider Ellen Key (1909) or Janusz Korzcak (see Lipton, 1988). There is not a single reference to the *International Journal of Children's Rights*, the leading journal in the field, or to *Childhood*, the main organ of childhood studies. There is no discussion of the ombudsman concept (Flekkøy, 1991) or of anti-spanking laws (Taylor, 2005).[34] Instead, we are offered some rather bland and not particularly original analysis of some leading U.S. decisions. Thus, not only is the view narrow, but it is a distorted one. On the larger plain of children's lives, is grandparent visitation of such major concern? Or whether unwed fathers have rights? (Note Guggenheim always talks of these people's rights, never of their responsibilities.)

And his thesis is thin: a children's rights agenda is a recipe for state intrusion. Children don't need rights within the family: children's rights – it is not clear which – are served best 'by restricting the conditions under which their lives are subject to review by state officials' (p. 248). That he wants fairness and justice comes out on the very last page of the book (see p. 266). But he fails to realise that it is through taking children's rights seriously that this is most likely to be achieved.

---

31    319 U.S. 624 (1943).

32    347 U.S. 483 (1954).

33    As Guggenheim predicts, the Supreme Court has in 2005 ruled against this (see *Roper v. Simmons*).

34    16 countries now ban the hitting of children by their parents: see Nicola Taylor (2005). A radical critique is Phillips and Alderson (2003).

# References

ALANEN, Leona (2001) 'Explorations in Generational Analysis' in L. Alanen and B. Mayall (eds.) *Conceptualizing Child-Adult Relations.* London: Routledge, Falmer.

ALDERSON, Priscilla (2000) *Young Children's Rights.* London: Jessica Kingsley.

ALDERSON, Priscilla, HAWTHORNE, Joanna and KILLEN, Margaret (2005) 'The Participation Rights of Premature Babies', *International Journal of Children's Rights* 13: 31–50.

ARENDT, Hannah (1986) *The Origins of Totalitarianism.* London: Andre Deutsch.

BAYER, Ronald (1989) *Private Acts, Social Consequences.* New York: Free Press.

CZAPANSKIY, Karen (1999) 'Interdependencies, Families and Children', *Santa Clara Law Review* 39: 957–1034.

DEVLIN, Patrick (1965) *The Enforcement of Morals.* Oxford: Clarendon Press.

DUQUETTE, Donald and RAMSEY, Sarah (1987) 'Representation of Children in Child Abuse and Neglect Cases: An Empirical View at what Constitutes an Effective Representation', *University of Michigan Journal of Law Reform* 20: 341.

DWORKIN, Ronald (1977) *Taking Rights Seriously.* London: Duckworth.

EEKELAAR, John (1994) 'The Interests of the Child and the Child's Wishes: The Role of Dynamic Self-Determinism', *International Journal of Law and The Family* 8: 42–63.

EEKELAAR, John (2002) 'Beyond the Welfare Principle', *Child and Family Law Quarterly* 14: 237–50.

EEKELAAR, John (2004) 'Children Between Cultures', *International Journal of Law, Policy and the Family* 16: 178–94.

EVANS, G. W. (2004) 'The Environment of Childhood Poverty', *American Psychologist* 39(2): 77–92.

FEINBERG, Joel (1966) 'Duties, Rights and Claims', *American Philosophical Quarterly* 3: 137–44.

FIDLER, David (2004) *SARS, Governance and the Globalisation of Disease.* London: Palgrave Macmillan.

FINNIS, John (1994) 'Law, Morality and "Sexual Orientation"', *Notre Dame Law Review* 69: 1049–76.

FLEKKØY, Malfrid Grude (1991) *A Voice for Children: Speaking Out As Their Ombudsman.* London: Jessica Kingsley.

Fordham Conference (1996) 'Proceedings of the Conference on Ethical Issues on the Representation of Children, Recommendations of the Conference', *Fordham Law Review* 64: 1301–23.

FORTIN, Jane (2004) 'Children's Rights: Are the Courts Taking Them More Seriously?', *King' College Law Journal* 15: 253–72.

FREEMAN, Michael (1983) *The Rights and Wrongs of Children.* London: Frances Pinter.

FREEMAN, Michael (1997) 'The Best Interests of the Child? Is *The Best Interests of the Child* in the Best Interests of the Children?', *International Journal of Law, Policy and the Family* 11: 360–88.

FREEMAN, Michael (2000) 'Can We Leave the Best Interests of Very Sick Children to their Parents?' in Michael Freeman and Andrew Lewis (eds.) *Law and Medicine.* Oxford: Oxford University Press, 257–68.

GLENDON, Mary Ann (1991) *Rights Talk.* New York: Free Press.

GOLDSTEIN, Joseph, FREUD Anna, GOLDSTEIN, Sonja and SOLNIT, Albert (1996) *The Best Interests of the Child.* New York, Free Press.

GUGGENHEIM, Martin (1996) 'A Paradigm of Determining the Role of Counsel for Children', *Fordham Law Review* 64: 1399–433.

HERRING, Jonathan (1999a) 'The Human Rights Act and the Welfare Principle in Family Law – Conflicting or Complementary?', *Child and Family Law Quarterly* 11: 223.

HERRING, Jonathan (1999b) 'The Welfare Principle and the Rights of Parents' in A. Bainham, S. Day Sclater and M. Richards (eds.) *What Is A Parent?* Oxford: Hart Publishing, 89–106.

JONSSON, Urban (1997) 'An Approach to Assess and Analyse the Health and Nutrition Situation of Children in the Perspective of the Convention on the Rights of the Child', *International Journal of Children's Rights* 5: 367–81.

98

KANT, Immanuel (1997) *Groundwork of the Metaphysics of Morals.* Cambridge: Cambridge University Press, (originally published in 1783).

KAVANAGH, Matthew M. (2004) 'Re-Writing The Legal Family: Beyond Exclusivity to a Care-Based Standard', *Yale Journal of Law and Feminism* 16: 83–143.

KELL, William A. (1998) 'Voices Lost and Found: Training Ethical Lawyers for Children', *Indiana Law Journal* 73: 635–58.

KEY, Ellen (1909) *The Century of the Child.* New York: Putnam's (originally published in Swedish in 1900).

LEVESQUE, Roger (2002) 'Child Advocacy in the United States and the Power of International Human Rights Law' in K. Alaimo and B. Klug (eds.) *Children As Equals.* Lanham, Maryland: University Press of America.

LIFTON, Betty Jean (1988) *The King of Children.* London: Chatto and Windus.

MANDELBAUM, Randi (2000) 'Revisiting the Question of Whether Young Children in Child Protection Proceedings Should be Represented by Lawyers', *Loyola University Chicago Law Journal* 32: 1–90.

MAYALL, Berry (2002) *Towards a Sociology of Childhood.* London: Routledge, Falmer.

MENKEL-MEADOW, Carrie (1987) 'Excluded Voices: New Voices in the Legal Profession Making New Voices in the Law', *University of Miami Law Review* 42: 29–53.

MILL, John Stuart (1989) *On Liberty.* Cambridge: Cambridge University Press (originally published 1859).

MORENO, Jonathan (2003) *In The Wake of the Terror.* Cambridge, Mass: MIT Press.

NEWELL, Peter (1989) *Children Are People Too.* London: Bedford Square Press.

PETERS, Jean Koh (1997) *Representing Children in Child Protection Proceedings: Ethical and Practical Dimensions.* Charlottesville, VA: LEXIS Law Publishing.

PETROPOULOS, Jonathan (2001) *The Faustian Bargain.* New York: Oxford University Press.

PHILLIPS, Ben and ALDERSON, Priscilla (2003) 'Beyond "Anti-Smacking": Challenging Violence and Coercion in Parent-Child Relations', *International Journal of Children's Rights* 11: 175–97.

REECE, Helen (1996) 'The Paramountcy Principle: Consensus or Construct?', *Current Legal Problems* 49: 267–89.

RODHAM, Hillary (1973) 'Children Under the Law', *Harvard Educational Review* 43: 487–514.

SANDBAEK, Monica (2005) 'Children's Right To A Decent Standard of Living' (Oslo, unpublished paper).

SANDS, Philippe (2005) *Lawless World.* Harmondsworth: Penguin.

SZASZ, Thomas (1977) 'The Child as Involuntary Mental Patient: The Threat of Child Therapy to the Child's Dignity, Privacy and Self Esteem', *San Diego Law Review* 14: 1005.

TAYLOR, Nicola (2005) 'Physical Punishment of Children', *New Zealand Family Law Journal* 5: 14–22.

TOOPE, Stephen (1991) 'Riding The Fences: Courts, Charter Rights and Family Law', *Canadian Journal of Family Law* 9: 55–78.

TUSHNET, Mark (1984) 'An Essay On Rights', *Texas Law Review* 62: 1363–1403.

TUSHNET, Mark (1992) 'The Critique of Rights', *Southern Methodist University Law Review* 47: 23–34.

VALENTINE, Gill (2004) *Public Space and the Culture of Childhood.* Aldershot: Ashgate.

WALTER, Jennifer (1999) 'Averting Re-victimisation of Children', *Journal of the Center for Children and the Courts* 1: 45.

WARDLE, Lynn (1986) 'The Use and Abuse of Rights Rhetoric: The Constitutional Rights of Children', *Loyola University Chicago Law Journal* 27: 321–48.

WATSON, Andrew (1980) 'Children, Families and Courts: Before the Best Interests of the Child and *Parham* v. *J.R.*', *Virginia Law Review* 66: 653–79.

WILBER, Shannan L. (1993) 'Independent Counsel for Children', *Family Law Quarterly* 27: 349–64.

WOODHOUSE, Barbara Bennett (1993) 'Hatching The Egg: A Child-Centered Perspective on Parents' Rights', *Cardozo Law Review* 14: 1747–864.

# [5]
# The End of The Century
# of The Child?

The twentieth century was to have been the century of the child: Ellen Key, the author of the book with this title, so assured us in her book, which was published in Sweden in 1900.[1] It was to be the century of the child, just as the nineteenth century had been the century of the woman. She actually says as much.[2] I suppose we should have been warned.

Now, as the century closes, and as we celebrate the tenth anniversary of the United Nations Convention on the Rights of the Child and, in England and Wales, the tenth anniversary also of our most child-centred legislation, the Children Act 1989, it is appropriate to take an audit, to examine the century's achievements and its failings, and to ask whether it has lived up to its billing.

Has the twentieth century been the century of the child?

## This Century

This was the century of the Holocaust with its systematic extermination of one and a half million children.[3] It was the century of the

---

[1] Ellen Key, *The Century of the Child* (New York, 1909), a translation of the original edition published in Sweden as *Barnets Århundrate* in 1900. On Key see Louise Hamilton-Nyström, *Ellen Key: Her Life and Work* (New York, 1913). See also Philip Veerman, *The Rights of The Child and The Changing Image of Childhood* (Dordrecht, 1992), ch. V.

[2] Note 1 above, 45, quoting 'a much discussed drama called *The Lion's Whelp*'.

[3] See Deborah Dwork, *Children With a Star* (New Haven, 1991) and also Raul Hilberg, *Perpetrators Victims Bystanders* (New York, 1992). On the grotesque 'twin' experiments of Dr Mengele see Lucette Matalon Lagnado and Sheila Cohn Dekel, *Children of the Flames: Dr Josef and the Untold Story of the Twins of Auschwitz* (London, 1991).

506

Communist experiment[4] of totalitarian social systems which destroyed the lives of children in the Soviet Union, China and elsewhere, and of the grisly aftermath of abandonment and neglect that we associate with institutions for children in Romania, Bulgaria, and Albania. It was the century of Hiroshima and Chernobyl. The century ends with children being sold into slavery in Africa and dying in Iraq because the West prevents medicines getting to them.[5] It was the century of racism,[6] in particular of apartheid which humiliated, divided, and deprived the majority of the population of South Africa of its basic liberties, including its children of their education. It was the century of two world wars and of many uncivil conflicts. These still continue, and children continue to be victimized by them, in particular in parts of Africa, where wars are waged by children and children are hacked to death often by other children, or have limbs amputated or worse, as in Sierra Leone.[7] And this has been the century of the displaced person, of the refugee,[8] of children 'exported' to the 'colonies',[9] of children who 'disappear'. It has been the century too of the phenomenon of 'street children'[10] and, if it is the concept rather than the phenomenon which is new, what is novel is the use of extermination squads—these have operated in Brazil and Guatemala and doubtless elsewhere—to sanitize the shanties.[11]

---

[4] On which see Orlando Figes, *A People's Tragedy* (London, 1996). For its effect on children see Judith Harwin, *Children of the Russian State* (Aldershot, 1996). On children as informers in Stalin's Soviet Union see Mikhail Heller, *Cogs in the Soviet Wheel: The Formation of Soviet Man* (London, 1988). On Russia's unwanted children see Clementine Creuziger, 'Russia's Unwanted Children' (1997) 4 *Childhood* 343.

[5] On Iraq, see John Pilger, 'Squeezed To Death', *The Guardian* (Weekend), 4 March 2000, 26.

[6] Interestingly not predicted by nineteenth-century prophets such as Karl Marx.

[7] Philip Veerman, 'The Children's Rights Crisis in Sierra Leone' (1999) *International Children's Rights Monitor* (Summer Issue) 10. See also Jørgen Pauli Jensen, 'War-Affected Societies and War Affected Children' (1996) 3 *Childhood* 415, and *The Independent*, 9 May 2000 (20 million children left orphaned, abused and brutalized by war).

[8] Dallas Stevens, 'Refugee Law and The Rights of the Child', in (eds.) Nigel Lowe and Gillian Douglas, *Families Across Frontiers* (The Hague, 1996), 449.

[9] John Eekelaar, ' "The Chief Glory": The Export of Children from the United Kingdom' in n. 8, above, 539.

[10] See *Childhood*, vol. 3(2) (1996) 'Children Out of Place' (special issue on street children).

[11] Martha K. Huggins and Myriam Mesquita P. de Castro, 'Exclusion, Civic Invisibility and Impunity as Explanations for Youth Murders in Brazil' (1996) 3 *Childhood* 77.

*The End of the Century of the Child?*      507

Children with learning disabilities have been sterilized in the United States, in Britain, in France, in the Nordic countries and, of course, in Nazi Germany.[12] Ellen Key would not have supported the brutality, but with the ideology she was at one.[13] Throughout the century there has been widespread discrimination against, and abuse of, children with handicaps, even to the extent of punishing blind children by putting them with deaf children.[14] We cannot know whether there has been more or less abuse of children in the twentieth century than previously, but we do know it has been practised in this century on a scale that few imagined was possible. And children with disabilities have been far more vulnerable to both physical and sexual abuse than are other children.[15] The scale of institutional abuse, of which we have become aware only in the last decade of this century, makes uncomfortable reading, particularly as we come to realize that it is a lot nearer home than Romanian orphanages.[16] We have also sensitized in the last third of this century to a range of discriminatory practices against the girl child: rape, forced prostitution and coerced marriages, trafficking, genital mutilation, perpetrated in vast swathes of Africa, Asia, and in the Islamic world,[17] and son preference leading to gendericide in India,[18] for example, and in China, where the 'one child per family' policy has led commonly to the killing of new-born daughters with the connivance of state authorities.[19] And, if the twentieth century has generally been good for childhood illnesses (when the century

---

[12] On Sweden, see Torbjörn Tännsjö, 'Compulsory Sterilization In Sweden' (1998) 12 *Bioethics* 236. It continues in China: see Linda Johnson, 'Expanding Eugenics or Improving Health Care In China' (1997) 24 *Journal of Law and Society* 199.             [13] Note 1 above, 24.

[14] This example is drawn from Michael Rosen, *The Penguin Book of Childhood* (Harmondsworth, 1995), 127, citing a school in Stoke in *c*.1916.

[15] See Helen Westcott and Merry Cross, *This Far and No Further: Towards Ending The Abuse of Disabled Children* (Birmingham, 1996). See also Mark Priestley, 'Childhood Disability and Disabled Childhoods' (1998) 5 *Childhood* 207.

[16] The Waterhouse report (February 2000) will become the *locus classicus* on this. See *The Times*, 16 February 2000.

[17] Human Rights Watch Women's Rights Project, *The Human Rights Watch Global Report on Women's Human Rights* (New York, 1995).

[18] C. Sleightholme and I. Sinha, *Guilty Without Trial* (Calcutta, 1996); P. Jeffrey and A. Basu, *Appropriating Gender* (New York, 1998).

[19] Discussed by Betsy Hartmann, *Reproductive Rights and Wrongs* (Boston, 1995), ch. 9. See also J. Mirsky, 'The Infanticide Tragedy in China', *The Nation*, 2 July 1993 and John Aird, *Slaughter of the Innocents: Coercive Birth Control in China* (Washington, D.C., 1990).

508

opened two-thirds of children did not survive adolescence), it has
also witnessed the birth (or discovery) in its last twenty years of the
plague of HIV infection and of AIDS. In 1998 2.5 million people
died from AIDS; over half a million of these were children. In
Zimbabwe it has been estimated that in 2005 there will be 900,000
'AIDS orphans'.[20] Many of these will become street children and
will turn to prostitution, only to perpetuate the cycle. A litany
which began with the Holocaust may appropriately end with
AIDS, which will soon kill as many children in a year as Hitler's
policies did throughout their duration.

### Children's Rights As An Achievement

This is a gloomy picture. But many of the aspects of children's
lives to which I have drawn attention are not features of the past
but continuing problems. Whatever the century's achievements
these cannot be ignored. Nor should we pass over them because
often they affect children outside our immediate horizons more
than those with whom we come into contact.

### INTERNATIONAL CHILDREN'S RIGHTS

When the history of the child in the twentieth century comes to be
written, the Convention adopted by the United Nations in 1989
may well be seen as its greatest achievement.[21] And yet a decade
on it begins to look as if it may also be seen as a false dawn. The
Convention has been ratified by all but two states (Somalia and
the United States). It had sixty-one signatories on its first day and
was in force in under a year. Never before had the world community embraced a convention with such enthusiasm or alacrity. The
International Covenant on Civil and Political Rights, by contrast,
took ten years to come into force. And the Convention has set a
standard for others to follow: we now have in force a Charter on
the Rights and Welfare of The African Child,[22] and a European

[20] Information compiled from *AIDS Information Newsletters*. For another
example (Brazil) see Miguel B. Fontes, Janette Hillis, and Glenn K. Wasek, 'Children Affected by AIDS in Brazil' (1998) 5 *Childhood* 345.
[21] On the Convention see Geraldine van Bueren, *The International Law on the
Rights of the Child* (Dordrecht, 1995).
[22] It is reproduced in Veerman, n. 1 above, 579. It dates from 1990 and came
into force on the tenth anniversary of the UN Convention, 20 November 1999.

*The End of the Century of the Child?*          509

Convention on the Exercise of Children's Rights.[23] And it contains important innovations. The Convention has influenced the jurisprudence of both international courts (for example, the European Court of Human Rights)[24] and national courts (for example the High Court in Australia). Children's rights have been recognized too in national constitutions, particularly in societies such as South Africa when they are involved in reconstruction.[25] But the plight of children world-wide does not seem to have got any better. If anything it is worse now than in 1989. That there is heightened concern for this condition—and given the world's response to the United Nations Convention it could hardly be otherwise—may constitute the light at the end of the tunnel. But, as yet, this remains a glimmer.

We could have anticipated some of this. The Convention underwent a long drafting process—it was ten years in gestation— and there were drafting difficulties as well as real areas of controversy.[26] The Convention permits the making of reservations, provided these are compatible with the aims and purposes of the Convention.[27] However, there are far too many reservations, particularly where States Parties invoke either religious or national laws as reasons for not considering themselves bound by provisions of the Convention.[28] The Convention also has a weak enforcement mechanism, the linchpin of which is a reporting system which operates within a framework of constructive dialogue. But there is no scope for national or individual petition. Nor does the International Court of Justice have jurisdiction over the interpretation and application of the Convention. The Committee on the Rights of the Child is grossly under-resourced, severely overwhelmed by the volume of work with which it is

[23] See Margaret Killerby, 'The Draft European Convention on the Exercise of Children's Rights' (1995) 3 *International Journal of Children's Rights* 127.
[24] See Ursula Kilkelly, *The Child and the European Convention on Human Rights* (Aldershot, 1999).
[25] Julia Sloth-Nielsen, 'The Contribution of Children's Rights To The Reconstruction of Society' (1996) 4 *International Journal of Children's Rights* 323.
[26] On which see David Johnson, 'Cultural and Regional Pluralism in the Drafting of the UN Convention on the Rights of the Child', in (eds.) Michael Freeman and Philip Veerman, *The Ideologies of Children's Rights* (Dordrecht, 1992), 95.                                           [27] Article 51(2).
[28] Lawrence J. LeBlanc, 'Reservations to the Convention on the Rights of the Child: A Macroscopic View of State Practice' (1996) 4 *International Journal of Children's Rights* 357.

510

expected to cope, and, not surprisingly, is years behind. Perhaps taking a cue from this, many States Parties are overdue with their initial reports (these are due two years after ratification) and many more are overdue in submitting their periodic reports. In short, the system is breaking down.

What conclusion should be drawn from this? That rights are a smokescreen, with the language of rights undermining efforts to accomplish genuine social change by diverting attention from the real abuses, the imbalance of power, economic disparities, social oppression?[29] In these terms the Convention would be nothing more than an exercise in symbolic politics and we would not be entitled to take seriously the commitment to children's rights in the Convention. Certainly, States Parties spoke as if committed to the Convention's provisions. Of course, it may be responded that no state could possibly be seen not to believe in children's welfare. But the UN Convention goes beyond rudimentary welfare protection, to protect children's autonomy and participation rights. Governments would have lost no face with their electorates in not endorsing this tranch of rights. But if this is not the explanation, what is? Two other explanations have been posited. Their ideological sources (conservatism and autopoiesis) are very different, but their argument is not far apart.

Lynn Wardle believes that children's rights advocates are overvaluing the capacity of children's rights 'to make things right'.[30] They are said to 'manifest the lingering hubris of the belief in the infinite and invincible capacity of the law to do good. They see law as a secular Messiah, a care-all for every social ill, a big yellow social bulldozer that can shove away the old problems and build new temples of goodness.'[31] We are, in other words, expecting too much of law. It is an old argument, going back to Savigny and W. G. Sumner. 'Stateways cannot make folkways,' wrote Sumner.[32] International conventions cannot alter the bedrock of public opinion, Wardle would retort. There are limits to effective international legal action, as there are to effective legal action within municipal legal systems. But

---

[29] As argued, though not in relation to children's rights specifically, by Mark Tushnet, 'An Essay on Rights (1984) 62 *Texas Law Review* 1363.

[30] 'The Use and Abuse of Rights Rhetoric: The Constitutional Rights of Children' (1996) 27 *Loyola University Chicago Law Journal* 321, 326.

[31] Ibid., 332.                    [32] W. G. Sumner, *Folkways* (Boston, 1906).

*The End of the Century of the Child?*          511

the social engineering potential of international legislation should not be discounted. Law, whatever its source, is an important symbol of what is right and wrong.

This is recognized, albeit obliquely, by Michael King, another critic of children's rights to attempt an explanation of why the Convention is not working. He argues that 'the reason for this faith in the power of law may stem more from a disillusionment and a lack of faith in other systems, such as politics, economics, science and religion, to protect children and their future well-being than from any widespread popularity of law or lawyers'.[33] It is likely that we invest in internationalism and constitutionalism because this is 'all that is now available to modern society for the task of creating such moral communities'.[34] Law, King argues, is able to operate 'only upon the second order, legal reconstructions of harms to children and not upon the harms themselves'.[35] Of course that is true, but it is also platitudinous. All law acts in this way but it is neither a good reason for not investing in law nor anything more than the mildest warning that we should not expect change to result from law alone. Other systems have failed children and continue to do so. Politics and economics clearly so: children lack political clout; they are a minority interest group which has never been well represented and they have often been invisible in policy-making, even in the evidence (for example the statistics) used as a basis for this. Religion too has failed children: its most famous pronouncement requires them to honour parents in return for which they are promised long life but not, for example, a protected environment.[36] And religion is clearly a cultural root of corporal punishment and hence of childhood abuse.[37] Science too has let children down. Many examples could be given: the development of the IQ test and the '11-Plus' examination, eugenics, Freud's theories being used to retard our understanding of child sexual abuse.[38] Law does have the

---

[33] *A Better World for Children?* (London, 1997), 171.          [34] Ibid., 172.
[35] Ibid., 183.
[36] Exodus 20:12; Deuteronomy 5:16 (the *quid pro quo* is only offered in the latter).          [37] Philip Greven, *Spare The Child* (New York, 1992).
[38] *The Complete Introductory Lectures on Psychoanalysis* (New York, 1965) (ed. and trans. J. Strachey) (originally published 1933). See also A. M. Arkin, 'A Hypothesis Concerning The Incest Taboo' (1984) 71 *Psychoanalytic Review* 375.

512

capacity to effect change, even change in the way other disciplines think. And it can be both a positive and a negative force.
It must send out consistent messages. It must work in conjunc-
tion with other strategies and policies. We must invest in it,
both ideologically and with resources. We must be committed
to enforcement.

That the Convention has not been the success that we might
have hoped is not due to any inherent failing in the rights strategy.
We should no more reject it than we do race relations laws or
equal pay legislation, neither of which have had the anticipated
impact. Rights, as Alan Hunt importantly noted, have the 'capacity to be elements of emancipation, but they are neither a perfect
nor exclusive vehicle'.[39] They can only assist to engineer a social
transformation as they become 'part of an emergent "common
sense" and are articulated with social practices'.[40] A régime of
rights is one of the weak's greatest resources.[41] As Federle pithily
puts it, 'rights flow downhill'.[42]

We can debate over which rights it is best to have, or how best
to actualize them, but not, I think, over whether rights are 'perni-
cious'[43] merely by virtue of being rights.

The Convention is far from being a perfect instrument, and
there are many ways it can be improved by revision, reform and
innovation. It does insufficient to advance the status of a number
of marginalized groups, disabled children,[44] gay children,[45] street

[39] 'Rights and Social Movements: Counter-Hegemonic Strategies' (1990) 17
*Journal of Law and Society* 309, 325.                                    [40] Ibid.
[41] See, for example, Kimberlé Crenshaw, 'Race, Reform and Retrenchment:
Transformation and Legislation In Anti-Discrimination Law' (1988) 101 *Harvard
Law Review* 1331.
[42] Katherine Hunt Federle, 'Rights Flow Downhill' (1994) 2 *International Journal of Children's Rights* 343.
[43] Cf. Cass R. Sunstein, 'Rights and Their Critics' (1995) 70 *Notre Dame Law
Review* 727, 729.
[44] M. Jones and L. A. B. Marks, 'The Dynamic Developmental Model of Emerging Rights In Children' (1994) 2 *International Journal of Children's Rights* 265;
ead., 'Beyond The Convention on the Rights of the Child: the Rights of Children
With Disabilities in International Law' (1997) 5 *International Journal of Children's Rights* 177; J. Morris, *Still Missing? Disabled Children and the Children Act*
(London, 1998).
[45] D. Monk, 'Sex Education and HIV/AIDS: Political Conflict and Legal
Resolution' 12 *Children and Society* 295; C. Lind and C. Butler, 'The Legal
Abuse of Homosexual Children' (1996) 7 *Journal of Child and Family Law*
3.

## The End of the Century of the Child? 513

children,[46] girls,[47] refugees,[48] indigenous children,[49] children in trouble with the law.[50] Many of the rights it endorses could be articulated better, flushed out more fully or thought through again. And there are gaps which need to be plugged.[51] The Convention remains an achievement. That supplementary Protocols are being considered, that one has now been drafted raising the minimum age for child soldiers,[52] is a recognition that it is but a beginning. But if the Convention is truly to succeed we must commit ourselves and our resources to it in ways not hitherto attempted.

The Convention has a built-in implementation mechanism.[53] This centres on a Committee on the Rights of the Child and a system of periodic reporting (reports themselves are often inadequate: this is especially so in relation to social and economic issues). The context is one of critique and dialogue, but there are no real teeth in the enforcement provisions. If international children's rights are to have a real future, the Convention must be more intensively policed. If the fulcrum of enforcement is to be the Committee, it must have more powers. Thus, it ought to be a Permanent Bureau. It ought to be pro-active, with the ability to

[46] Note 10 above.
[47] Alice Armstrong et al., 'Towards A Cultural Understanding of the Interplay Between Children's Rights and Woman's Rights: An Eastern and Southern Africa Perspective' (1995) 3 International Journal of Children's Rights 333; Savitri Gooneskere, Women's Rights and Children's Rights: The United Nations Conventions as Compatible and Complimentary International Treaties (Florence, 1992).
[48] G. S. Goodwin-Gill, 'Unaccompanied Refugee Minors: The Role and Place of International Law in the Pursuit of Durable Solutions' (1995) 3 International Journal of Children's Rights 405.
[49] R. B. Douglas and E. Te K. Douglas, 'The Rights of the Indigenous Child: Reconciling the UN Convention on the Rights of the Child and the (Draft) Declaration on the Rights of Indigenous People with Early Education Policies for Indigenous People' (1995) 3 International Journal of Children's Rights 197.
[50] For example, it does not prescribe a minimum age of criminal responsibility. England pitches this ludicrously low (at 10); Scotland even lower (8), but it subjects children to a children's hearing. In most European countries, the age is considerably higher.
[51] See Michael Freeman, 'The Future of Children's Rights' (2000) 14 Children and Society 277.
[52] Rädda Barnen, Children of War, No. 4/99, December 1999. This raises the age of non-recruitment and non-deployment to 18: the UK (and Bosnia-Hercegovina) are the only European countries in favour of volunteers at 16. See also Security Council Resolution 1261 (document S/1999/911), 25 August 1999.
[53] Articles 42 and 45.

514

conduct strategic investigations and garner evidence. It ought to
have access to children and young people. They should have the
opportunity to present evidence. This would amount to a realization of the principle of Article 12 of the Convention and would
present States Parties with a real challenge. But I would go further
than this and allow for inter-state complaints, and for complaints
by individuals who consider themselves aggrieved by shortcomings
in the laws and practices of their own countries. The model of
individual petition in the European Convention on Human Rights
is instructive. The image of children hauling their own states in
front of an international court would serve to impress upon the
world the importance of the rights and lives of children. It may be
that international petition will come—there is talk of a Protocol to
this effect—but it remains on the horizon, and there is no sense
that there is progress towards actualization of any such system.

## NATIONAL CHILDREN'S RIGHTS

Although there was some discussion of children's rights in the nineteenth century, the emphasis was on child-saving, on protecting
children rather than their autonomy, on nurturance rather than
self-determination.[54] This saw the growth of the orphanage, the
development of compulsory schooling and the construction of
separate institutions like the reformatory and the juvenile court.
The latter part of the century also passed the first child protection
legislation, in England this was in 1889.[55] This is the time also of
the earliest child-centred thinking, of Kate Douglas Wiggin[56] in the
United States, Janusz Korczak[57] in Poland and Ellen Key[58] in
Sweden. Wiggin wrote of the 'divine right to be gloriously dirty' (in
effect promoting the child's right to be curious and explore).[59] She
also looked forward to the 'rod of reason' replacing the 'rod of
birch'.[60] Korczak's *How To Love a Child*[61] took as one of its main

[54] C. M. Rogers and L. S. Wrightman, 'Attitudes Toward Children's Rights:
Nurturance or Self Determination?' (1978) 34 *Journal of Social Issues* 59.
[55] On which see George K. Behlmer, *Child Abuse and Moral Reform In England*
(Stanford, California, 1982).                    [56] *Children's Rights* (Boston, 1892).
[57] On Korczak see B. J. Lifton: *The King of Children* (London, 1988). See also
Philip E. Veerman 'Janusz Korczak and the Rights of the Child' (1987) *Concern*
(Spring Issue), 7.                                            [58] Note 1 above.
[59] Note 56 above, 11.                                        [60] Ibid., 19.
[61] In *Selected Works of Janusz Korczak* (ed. M Wolins) (Warsaw, 1920).

## The End of the Century of the Child?   515

theses the idea that you cannot possibly love a child—your own or another's—until you see him as a separate being with the inalienable right to grow into the person he was meant to be. It was more than half a century before others were to recognize the importance of a child's autonomy[62]—and this was thirty years after Korczak, in this 'century of the child', had led the children of the Warsaw ghetto on their fateful journey to Treblinka.[63] Ellen Key looked for 'increasing limitations of the right of parents over children',[64] to the end of corporal punishment (she described this 'as humiliating for him who gives it as for him who receives it')[65] and to treating a child as 'really one's equal, that is . . . show[ing] him the same consideration, the same kind confidence one shows to an adult'.[66]

But it was not to these thinkers that legislators looked. The child-saving movement had an impact—and may have ensured that the century was more aptly characterized as the century of the children's expert—but there is little or no sign that either legislature or judiciary anywhere was impressed by thinking that children were persons. Not surprisingly, children do not feature in the constitutions which follow any of the great modern revolutions, the American, the French, and the Russian. It is the 1960s before we get the earliest judicial pronouncements on children's rights.

It was because it was becoming 'painfully obvious'[67] that the dream behind the juvenile court was falling short of realization because of 'inadequate resources, imprecise legal standards, poorly trained personnel, and unchecked discretion'[68] that one of two solutions pressed itself: either the court was abolished and there would be a return to a single system of criminal justice or there would need to be an extension to children of those rights that safeguarded an individual's position in an adult court. The United States Supreme Court in *Re Gault*[69] decided that the latter (or we subsequently

---

[62] P. Adams, Children's Rights, *Toward the Liberation of the Child* (New York, 1971); J Holt, *Escape from Childhood* (Harmondsworth, 1975); R Farson, *Birthrights* (Harmondsworth, 1978).
[63] Note 57, above, ch. 37 and Epilogue.   [64] Note 1 above, 317.
[65] Ibid., 327.   [66] Ibid., 109.
[67] *Per* Hillary Rodham, 'Children's Rights: A Legal Perspective', in (eds.) Patricia A. Vardin and Ilene N. Brody, *Children's Rights: Contemporary Perspectives* (New York, 1978) 21, 28.   [68] Ibid.
[69] 387 U S 1 (1967), And see Barry C. Feld, 'Criminalizing the Juvenile Court: A Research Agenda For the 1990s', in (ed.) Ira M. Schwartz, *Juvenile Justice and Public Policy* (New York, 1992), 59.

516

discovered parts of the latter) was the better solution. It ordered that juveniles threatened with deprivation of liberty were entitled under the due process clause to notice, the right to counsel, the privilege against self-incrimination, and the right to confront these accusers and to cross-examine witnesses. The Court subsequently decided that children were not entitled to jury trial.[70] And, within a space of three years, that a child could not be expelled or suspended from school without being given an adequate chance to respond to the charges against him,[71] but could be paddled, absent excessive physical harm, because corporal punishment was permissible under the Eighth Amendment of the Constitution.[72] As Hillary Rodham wrote (in 1979): 'These decisions represent the confusion and conflicting goals besetting the Court as it tries to strike a balance between a child's alleged rights and the administrative needs of institutions against whom those rights would be exercised.'[73]

*Gault, Tinker,* and *Goss v Lopez* had no impact on thinking about children in this country. Our education law was at the time highly rudimentary: it emphasized parents' duties and was only later to stress their rights,[74] but even now the rights of consumers of education are virtually ignored.[75] As for the rights of children who do wrong,[76] this was barely addressed. The absence of a written constitution may in part explain the failure to engage with children's rights in education matters. Its failure in the juvenile justice context is more complex. In the United Kingdom at the time of *Gault* decriminalization was the goal:[77] this was effected in Scotland with the children's hearing system[78] and bungled in England and Wales with the partial implementation of the Children and Young Persons Act 1969.[79] In England and Wales the

---

[70] *McKeiver v Pennsylvania* 403 U S 528 (1971).

[71] *Tinker v Des Moines School District* 393 U S 503 (1969); *Goss v Lopez* 419 U S 565 (1975).                 [72] *Ingraham v Wright* 430 U S 651 (1977).

[73] Note 67 above, 29.         [74] Education Act 1980 s. 6 began this process.

[75] An account is Jane Fortin, *Children's Rights and the Developing Law* (London, 1998), ch. 6

[76] Cf. M. D. A. Freeman, 'The Rights of Children Who Do Wrong' (1981) 21 *British Journal of Criminology* 210

[77] *The Child, The Family and the Young Offender,* Cmnd. 2742 (London, 1965).

[78] But see A. Morris and M. McIsaac, *Juvenile Justice?* (London, 1978).

[79] See A. E. Bottoms and S. Stevenson, 'What Went Wrong? Criminal Justice Policy In England and Wales 1945–1970; in (ed.) D. Downes, *Unravelling Criminal Justice* (Basingstoke, 1992).

The End of the Century of the Child?          517

*Bulger* case may yet prove the watershed with the European Court of Human Rights holding that the 11-year-olds convicted of the toddler's murder did not receive a fair trial.[80] As yet the Scottish hearings system has escaped outright attack in the European Court, but whether it can withstand challenge in the future is dubious.[81] The impact of the Human Rights Act 1998 on children's rights in education and within the juvenile justice systems (in the latter in the light particularly of increased authoritarianism)[82] must be awaited. It could be at least as great as that effected by the classic 1960s and 1970s US decisions.

In England the earliest judicial assertion of a child's right was in 1973 in the case of *M* v *M*.[83] Speaking of access Wrangham J said he would prefer to call it 'a basic right in the child rather than a basic right in the parent'.[84] But he explained that this only meant that 'no court should deprive a child of access to either parent unless it is wholly satisfied that it is in the interests of the child that access should cease'.[85] This has been reiterated many times. Sir Stephen Brown P described it as 'a fundamental right of a child',[86] and Butler-Sloss LJ found legitimacy for the right in the United Nations Convention and in the Children Act 1989.[87] Although Wrangham J expressed the right subject to a best interests qualification (as indeed does the UN Convention),[88] it nevertheless affirmed contact as child-centred. By contrast, the same year Goldstein, Freud, and Solnit in their highly influential *Beyond The Best Interests of the Child* gave the decision to the custodial parent. Somewhat surprisingly, they too identified contact as a child's right but, since 'the custodial parent should have the right to decide whether it is desirable for the child to have such rights',[89] it is not a right of much substance. There were

---

[80] Application 24274/94 (1999) and Application 24888/94 (1999). The response is the Practice Direction (Crown Court: Trial of Children and Young Persons) *The Times*, 17 February 2000.

[81] Though, interestingly, this is not a problem anticipated by K. Norrie, *Children's Hearings in Scotland* (Edinburgh, 1997).

[82] The context is depicted by Tim Newburn, 'Youth, Crime and Justice' in (eds.) M. Maguire, R. Morgan, and R. Reiner, *The Oxford Handbook of Criminology* (Oxford, 1997), 613.          [83] [1973] 2 All ER 81

[84] Ibid., 85.                                                                      [85] Ibid.

[86] *Re H* [1992] 1 FLR 148; see also *Re H* [1998] 2 FLR 42.

[87] *Re R* [1993] 2 FLR 762.                                      [88] Article 9(3).

[89] J. Goldstein, A Freud, and A. Solnit, *Beyond The Best Interests of the Child* (New York, 1973), 38.

518

other examples too in the 1970s of the English judiciary proclaim-
ing the paramountcy of children's interests (for example, in the
determination of custody disputes,[90] disputes over the matrimonial home[91] and in relation to education)[92] but never was the
interest categorized as a right and none of the cases used the
rhetorical flourish of the American cases of this era.

It was the mid-1980s before the highest court in the United
Kingdom addressed the legal personality of children. The *Gillick*
case is the watershed but it was anticipated in *R v D*[93] when Lord
Brandon argued that a child with 'sufficient understanding and
intelligence' could so consent to being taken away by a stranger as
to provide a defence to a charge of kidnapping. The *Gillick* case
builds upon this reasoning.[94] Lord Scarman's judgment is so
forward-looking that he himself is unable to grasp how much
progress it makes. He denies that English law has ever treated the
child as 'other than a person with capacities and rights recognised
by law'.[95] In theory this might be true: in practice the law fell very
short of this, and sometimes still does.

The *Gillick* decision accepts that growing up is a process. As
Lord Scarman puts it:

The law relating to parent and child is concerned with the problems of
growth and maturity of the human personality. If the law should impose
upon the process of 'growing up' fixed limits where nature only knows a
continuous process, the price would be artificiality and a lack of realism
in an area where the law must be sensitive to human development and
social change.[96]

The majority of the Lords thus rejects a status test in favour of
one which looks to capacity (or competence). Some, Fortin for
example, are critical of this. She argues that 'the inherent weak-
ness of the concept of Gillick competence is its uncertainty'.[97] On
the contrary, the reasoning process is insightful. The importance
of *Gillick* lies in its rejection of rigid categories, of dichotomies,
and in its recognition of adolescence. Adolescents are not all the
same and rigid dividing-lines can only be arbitrary.

---

[90] *J v C* [1970] AC 668, *S(BD) v S(DJ)* [1977] Fam 109.
[91] A trend reversed by House of Lords in *Richards v Richards* [1984] AC 174.
But see Family Law Act 1996 s. 33(7), 35(8), 36(8).
[92] *Re S* [1978] QB 120.                                    [93] [1984] AC 778.
[94] *Gillick v West Norfolk and Wisbech AHA* [1986] AC 112.
[95] Ibid., 184.              [96] Ibid., 186.              [97] Note 75 above, 73.

*The End of the Century of the Child?*          519

For the majority in *Gillick* competence hinges on understanding and intelligence. Thus, for Lord Scarman 'parental right yields to the child's right to make his own decisions when he reaches a sufficient understanding and intelligence to be capable of making up his own mind on the matter requiring decision'.[98] Elsewhere he refers to a competent child as one who 'achieves a sufficient understanding and intelligence to enable him or her to understand fully what is proposed',[99] and also, and this is often overlooked, has 'sufficient discretion to enable him or her to make a wise choice in his or her own interests'.[100] In these terms, competence welds together understanding and knowledge with wisdom and experience. There are dangers in conflating knowledge and wisdom, but this is commonly done. Few adults are Gillick competent if competence is to hinge upon abilities to understand fully what is involved in a decision. But many children, well below the age with which we tend to associate Gillick competence, are competent within the test articulated by Lord Scarman if 'wise choice' is genuinely situated within the child's personal, experiential knowledge of his or her 'own interests'. Alderson and Goodwin noted that we tend to value highly 'professional, textbook knowledge',[101] whilst discounting personal experiential knowledge. Once such 'wisdom' is ignored, the child is assumed to be ignorant, except insofar as he or she can recount medical or other professional information.

The *Gillick* decision sent out a strong message to parents—who only four years later were to be told that they had parental responsibility[102]—and to the judiciary and the legislature. The former retreated.[103] The latter grappled with some of the implications of *Gillick* in formulating the most child-centred legislation of the century, the Children Act of 1989. Some wanted to read *Gillick* narrowly, as being about medical treatment or even only contraception. But John Eekelaar predicted that its effect was to overturn all parental rights once an adolescent had acquired

---

[98] Note 94 above, 186.        [99] Ibid., 189.        [100] Ibid., 188.
[101] P. Alderson and M. Goodwin, 'Contradictions Within Concepts of Children's Competence' (1993) 1 *International Journal of Children's Rights* 303.
[102] Children Act 1989 s. 2.
[103] See *Re R* [1992] Fam 11; *Re W* [1993] Fam 64; *Re E* [1993] 1 FLR 386; *Re S* [1994] 2 FLR 1065; *Re M* [1999] 2 FLR 1097. And see Carole Smith, 'Children's Rights: Judicial Ambivalence and Social Resistance' (1997) 11 *International Journal of Law, Policy and the Family* 103.

520

*Gillick* competence. Even the right to decide where the child should live. In his view, children now had 'that most dangerous but most precious of rights: the right to make their own mistakes'.[104] And the right to do what others think is wrong, Ronald Dworkin has famously reminded us, is at the root of 'taking rights seriously'.[105]

The Children Act 1989 was not the first English legislation to be child-centred, or the first to be described as a children's charter. In their own ways Acts of 1908, 1933, 1948, 1969, and 1975 were all significant.[106] And there were important Acts too on adoption (in 1926 and 1958),[107] on legitimacy (in 1926, 1959, and 1987)[108] and, after the 1989 Act, on child support (in 1991 and 1995).[109] Only the 1989 Act can be read as a statement of children's rights. There is a greater recognition of the child as a participant in the decision-making process affecting him or her. The Act gave children a number of new rights. Some commentators saw it as empowering children.[110] Some empowerment is there, though this is not the dominant ideology of the Act.[111] Children were given the power to initiate court actions, for example to challenge an emergency protection order, to seek a contact order when in care, to ask for a care order to be discharged, to seek the court's leave to obtain a section 8 order making directions about where he or she is to live or with whom to have contact.[112] It is usually a pre-condition that the child is Gillick competent, but not always. There is also greater recognition of a child's wishes and feelings.[113] A child of sufficient understanding to make an informed decision has the right to refuse to submit to a medical or psychiatric examination or other assessment in the context of a child assessment order, emergency protec-

---

[104] 'The Emergence of Children's Rights' (1986) 6 *Oxford Journal of Legal Studies* 161, 182.      [105] *Taking Rights Seriously* (London, 1977).
[106] Children Act 1908; Children and Young Persons Act 1933; Children Act 1948; Children and Young Persons Act 1969; Children Act 1975.
[107] Adoption of Children Act 1926; Adoption Act 1958.
[108] Legitimacy Act 1926; Legitimacy Act 1959, Family Law Reform Act 1987.
[109] Child Support Act 1991; Child Support Act 1995.
[110] For example, D. Hodgson, 'Power to the Child' (1990) *Social Work Today* 16 (12 July).
[111] Lorraine Fox Harding sees this as paternalism and the defence of birth parents' rights. See 'The Children Act 1989 in Context: Four Perspectives In Child Care Law and Policy' (1991) *Journal of Social Welfare and Family Law* 179 and 285, at 299.      [112] See ss. 45(8), 34(2), 39(1) 10(2), (8).
[113] See s. 1(3)(a).

*The End of the Century of the Child?* 521

tion order or other similar protective measure.[114] The courts, however, have severely undercut this right.[115] And there is more extensive use of separate representation of children by guardians *ad litem*.[116] The concept of the guardian *ad litem* is without question one of the most significant developments in child law in this century, though its failure to penetrate the private law arena remains a cause for concern.[117]

Legislation elsewhere goes further. An example is Finland where the Child Custody and Right of Access Act of 1983 states that before a parent who has custody

makes a decision on a matter relating to the person of the child, he or she shall, where possible, discuss the matter with the child taking into account the child's age and maturity and the nature of the matter. In making the decision the custodian shall give due consideration to the child's feelings, opinions and wishes.[118]

Both Sweden and Scotland have followed this precedent.[119] The Scottish Law Commission found it attractive because it saw value in the provision 'even if it was vague and unenforceable'.[120] It thought it would have an 'influence on behaviour'. And not, I would maintain, only the behaviour of parents, but also that of public authorities, where paternalism would dilute as the need for dialogue developed.

Other legal changes outside the United Kingdom which have furthered children's rights have been the development of anti-corporal punishment laws, starting in Sweden in 1979,[121] and the growth of the institution of the children's ombudsman which Norway pioneered in 1981.[122] It is likely that both Scotland and

[114] See ss. 38(6), 43(8) and 44(7).
[115] *South Glamorgan C.C. v W and B* [1993] 1 FLR 574.
[116] See s. 41. See also Judith E. Timms, *Children's Representation* (London 1995).
[117] N. W. Wyld, 'Children's Participation—Myth or Reality?' (1991) 3 *Journal of Child Law* 83.
[118] This is discussed by Matti Savolainen, 'Finland: More Rights for Children', (1986) 25 *Journal of Family Law* 113.
[119] Scotland in the Children (Scotland) Act 1995 s. 6.
[120] Scottish Law Commission Discussion Paper, *Parental Responsibilities and Rights* (Edinburgh, 1990) para 2.1 *et seq*; 2.60 *et seq*.
[121] These are discussed by Michael Freeman, 'Children Are Unbeatable' (1999) 13 *Children and Society* 130.
[122] On which see Malfrid Flekkøy, *A Voice for Children: Speaking Out As Their Ombudsman* (London, 1991).

522

Wales will have children's commissioners quite soon—an early positive outcome of devolution—and that England will follow in time. But hitherto there has been resistance, as there has to a parallel innovation, the child impact statement.[123] And, in the land of *le vice anglais*, the *Volksgeist* would resist—or at least so we are told—an anti-spanking law. But the end of corporal punishment in schools was effected within a generation[124] and there is no reason to suppose that a law to ban physical chastisement by parents will take longer.

## But The Welfare State Fails Children

The welfare state is, of course, one of the century's greatest achievements—in those countries able and willing to resource one. It should have meant the end to child poverty. Poverty is at the root of so much else—disease, homelessness, crime, bad education, abuse—that the century of the child should have seen its eradication. Of course, it hasn't. In what follows I discuss only Britain.

We are an unequal country, not a poor one. Child poverty in the UK has increased more nearly fourfold in the last twenty years. The proportion of children living in households with an equivalent income of less than 50 per cent of the average increased from 9 per cent in 1979 to 35 per cent in 1996/7.[125] A total of 2.7 million children were dependent on income support in 1998 (less than one million depended on supplementary benefit in 1979). A recent UNICEF analysis of twenty-five countries shows that in 1995 the UK had the third highest child poverty rate, after Russia and the United States.[126] Only Italy of the EU countries surveyed ran us close (its percentage point per annum increase is greater

[123] M. D. A. Freeman, 'Taking Children's Rights Seriously' (1987–8) 1 *Children and Society* 299; see also Peter Newell and Martin Rosenbaum, *Taking Children Seriously* (London, 1991), rev. Peter Newell (London, 2000).

[124] Moves began in the early 1970s (see, for example, Peter Newell, *A Last Resort?* (Harmondsworth, 1972)) and led to abolition in state schools, independent schools receiving public funding and for pupils with assisted places in 1986 (Education (No.2) Act 1986, ss. 47 and 48). It was removed from other schools by the Schools Standards and Framework Act 1998 s. 131.

[125] Department of Social Security, *Households Below Average Income: A Statistical Analysis 1979–1995/96* (London, 1998).

[126] B. Bradbury and M. Jantti, 'Child Poverty Across Industrialised Countries', *Innocenti Occasional Papers, Economic and Social Policy Series*, No. 71 (Florence, 1999).

*The End of the Century of the Child?* 523

than the UK's). In France, the child poverty rate is less than half that in the UK; in the Netherlands it is one-third; in Belgium one-quarter; and in Sweden about one-eighth.

Why is Britain's child poverty so much worse than that of almost all other comparable countries?[127] The answer does not lie in economic restructuring, globalization, or family demography. The percentage of children in households without a full-time paid worker is higher than the overall unemployment rate. It has been diverging from the unemployment rate since the late 1980s.[128] The OECD has shown that non-employment in Britain (that is households without a worker) is very high for lone parents (61 per cent) and for couples with children it is as high as 11 per cent.[129] One hypothesis is thus that the level of unemployment compensation may be to blame for the high child poverty rate. Bradshaw quotes research which shows that in 1992 the short-term insurance-based compensation package for a couple with two children in the UK was the lowest among the 'twelve' in the EU before and after housing costs. And similar conclusions have been reached comparing social assistance, and comparing provision for lone parents.[130]

Britain's poverty record is equally bad where parents (and lone parents) work. Twenty per cent remain in poverty and, significantly, the poverty rate barely falls after the impact of taxes and benefits is accounted for (it is then 18 per cent).[131] Both pre-transfers and post-transfers Britain's poverty rate is higher than all its European partners. And the reduction in poverty as a result of transfers is 12 per cent compared with, for example, 77 per cent in Finland and 72 per cent in Sweden.[132] Britain's tax/benefit package

---

[127] The latest OECD evidence suggests UK poverty rates and long-term experience of poverty may outstrip even the United States (*The Guardian*, 12 January 2000).
[128] A. B. Atkinson, 'Macroeconomics and Children', *Innocenti Occasional Papers*, No. 68 (Florence, 1998).
[129] OECD, 'Recent Labour Market Developments and Prospects', *Employment Outlook*, June 1998.
[130] J. Bradshaw, 'Comparing Child Poverty' (1999) 104 *Poverty* 15, 17–18.
[131] T. Eardley, J. Bradshaw, J. Ditch, I. Gough, and P. Whiteford, *Social Assistance in OECD Countries: Synthesis Report* (DSS Research Report 46) (London, 1996); J. Bradshaw, S. Kennedy, M. Kilkey, S. Hutton, A. Corden, T. Eardley, H. Holmes, and J. Neale, *Policy and the Employment of Lone Parents in 20 Countries* (York, 1996).
[132] J. Bradshaw and J-R Chen, 'Poverty in the U.K.: A Comparison With 19 Other Countries' (1997) *Benefits* 18, 13.

524

in respect of children is below average among EU countries, and is considerably less generous than Belgium, France, and Finland.

In March 1999 Blair announced that child poverty would end in twenty years.[133] In attempting to do so Britain is starting from a very disadvantaged base. Some of the statistics quoted are necessarily out of date and do not take account of the measures introduced by the Labour government since 1997. The 'New Deals', the minimum wage, the working families tax credit, increases in child benefit, a new improved child support system[134] will have done (or will do) a little to mitigate the hardships. But there will still always be families with children who cannot get employment or prefer to commit themselves to bringing up their children. Income support will have to rise. So will child benefit. The 1p cut in income tax which took effect in 2000 would fund a 40 per cent increase in benefit for all children, or alternatively would enable benefit levels to be substantially increased.[135] Poverty can be defined out of existence but it cannot be eradicated without redistributive policies. Hitherto, this government has been reluctant to pursue such policies. Children have a right to an adequate standard of living. Four million plus children in Britain today are denied this. As a result, they are marginalized, socially excluded, and unable to participate in basic social goods.

### Health Questions—How Much Better Off Are Children?

In some ways the twentieth century has been a good one for children's health. Many childhood killers of the past have been controlled, though some are re-emerging, and AIDS is having a devastating effect on children, particularly in Sub-Saharan Africa. Inequalities in health remain, even within the population of a developed country such as Britain, where a national health service created universal access to health care over fifty years ago. The Black Report documented inequalities in health in 1980.[136] The

---

[133] *The Times*, 20 March 1999. It increased by 100,000 in his first three years as Prime Minister.

[134] The Child Support, Pensions and Social Security Act 2000 (likely to be implemented in late 2001).

[135] Martin Barnes, 'Comment' (1999) 103 *Poverty* 1.

[136] Peter Townsend and Nick Davidson, *Inequalities In Health* (Harmondsworth, 1982) (the Secretary of State refused to endorse it: see p. 39).

*The End of the Century of the Child?*          525

Acheson Report in 1998 returned to the same theme.[137] Very little had been done in the interim to redress health inequalities.

There is a 'continuum of disadvantage from pre-conception through pregnancy, birth, childhood to adult life'.[138] The health and welfare of children is inextricably linked to the health of their family, particularly that of their mother. As a result 'inequalities in the health of teenage girls and young women will be reflected in the survival and morbidity of their offspring'.[139] So, as Woodroffe, Glickman, Barker, and Power demonstrated, still-births, low birth weight, infant death, congenital anomalies, chronic childhood illness, respiratory infections, accidents, and behavioural problems all continue to show steep socio-economic gradients.[140]

The key to unlock the solution lies only partially in improving health services. It requires also a network of policies to reduce poverty, improve access to education and to improve housing and social services. And children's needs and rights to good health need to be taken seriously. School health services, which are breaking down, need to be strengthened.[141]

Campaigns to alert and to change behaviour have a differential impact. Thus, smoking remains more common in the lower socio-economic classes. The campaign to reduce 'Sudden Infant Death' has had less effect on the socially disadvantaged.[142] In 1996 the highest rate of SIDSs was for babies born to mothers under 20 and for those born outside marriage.[143] On breast feeding too there are socio-economic inequalities. Ninety-one per cent of social class I mothers initiate breast feeding: only 40 per cent in social class V do. By six months, 48 per cent of mothers in social class I are still breast feeding but only 22 per cent of those in social class V are.[144] Lynch has pointed to the ways local initiatives can raise breast feeding rates in disadvantaged communities: in 1991 only 53 per cent of mothers left one inner London hospital (King's

---

[137] D. Acheson, *Independent Inquiry into Inequalities in Health* (London, 1998).
[138] Margaret Lynch, 'Making Health Equality A Reality' (1998) 101 *Poverty* 8, 9.                                                                    [139] Ibid.
[140] C. Woodroffe, M. Glickman, M. Barker, and C. Power, *Children, Teenagers and Health: The Key Data* (Bury St Edmunds, 1993).
[141] See Berry Mayall and Pamela Storey, 'A School Health Service for Children?' (1998) 12 *Children and Society* 86.
[142] Office for National Statistics (London, 1996).          [143] 1.5 per thousand.
[144] Note 138 above, 9.

526

College) breast feeding. By 1996, as a result of a strategy which included the appointment of a breast feeding advisor, 86 per cent of mothers were breast feeding at 10 days.[145] Breast feeding exerts a strong influence on the health of babies (and mothers): even in the United Kingdom it significantly reduces the risk of the baby contracting gastro-enteritis and being admitted to hospital.[146]

A number of diseases have been shown to correlate with social disadvantage. Cardiovascular disease in adults is related to birth weight and to health in early childhood.[147] Iron deficiency anaemia—which may have consequences for cognitive development which are not fully reversible—is found in as many as one in three children from poor social backgrounds.[148] This is the result of poor diets. Education can tackle this only in part. Nutritional foods may be unaffordable or inaccessible, or the money which might go to purchase these may be diverted to adults' recreational needs. The problem can be addressed by iron supplementation—iron-supplemented milk and cereals can reduce the risk of anaemia—but under current free welfare milk provision only cow's milk is available.[149]

Respiratory diseases too are found unequally spread. They are more common where there is poor housing. Bronchitis, pneumonia, and chronic coughs all show a strong socio-economic gradient, with increasing evidence that poor housing, especially with damp and moulds, has an effect on respiratory symptoms in children. Two 1997 studies showed asthma and respiratory symptoms to be associated with living in damp houses.[150]

Fewer children are dying from injury and poisoning. But accidental injury is nevertheless the leading cause of death in children over one and of hospital admissions in children over 5. The social

[145] Idem.
[146] P. W. Howie, J. S. Forsyth, S. A. Ogston, A. Clark, and C. du V. Florey, 'Protective Effect of Breast Feeding Against Infection' (1990) 300 *British Medical Journal* 11.
[147] D Barker (ed.), *Fetal and Infant Origin of Adult Disease* (London, 1993).
[148] B. Lozoff, E. J. Jimenez, and A. W. Wolf, 'Long Term Developmental Outcome of Infants with Iron Deficiency' (1991) 325 *New England Journal of Medicine* 687. [149] See Lynch, n. 138 above, 10.
[150] I. J. Williamson, C. J. Martin, G. McGill, R. D. H. Monie, and A. G. Fennarty, 'Damp Housing and Asthma: A Case Control Study' (1997) 52 *Thorax* 229; C. Yang, J. Chui, H. Chui, and W. Kao, 'Damp Housing Conditions and Respiratory Symptoms In Primary School Children' (1997) 24 *Pediatric Pulmonology* 73.

*The End of the Century of the Child?*          527

class gradient for injury is steeper than for any other cause of child death. Nine times as many children in Social Class V die from fire and fumes than in Social Class I.[151] The chance of so dying is closely related to the type of housing, and those in temporary accommodation, particularly in bed and breakfast hostels, or in poor local authority accommodation are most at risk. In 1996 there were over 120,000 households which were homeless: the Housing Act 1996 has increased the number of children in temporary accommodation.[152] Homelessness has profound health implications for children.[153] For example, immunization rates of such children are lower.[154] Since most will be registered, if at all, with their original doctor, accessing health services is more difficult and is unlikely to be attempted. Nevertheless, people in poor housing use the NHS fifty times more than the average member of the population. This is a clear reflection of their higher health needs.[155]

Other children in special needs are those of travelling families[156] and refugee children.[157] Health services for refugee families must be made readily accessible as well as culturally sensitive, and must be disentangled from immigration processes. There are Key Recommendations on Refugee Children by the European Council on Refugees and Exiles. These must be implemented to ease some of the disadvantages which these children suffer.

It is also important that we do not overlook the health care needs of the 50,000 'children of the state'.[158] Two-thirds of these children are in foster care: the rest in residential homes. Their health care needs can easily be overlooked. Many of these, for

---

[151] S. Jarvis and E. Towner, 'Accidents' in (ed). B. Botting, *The Health of Our Children: A Review of the Mid-1990s* (London, 1995).

[152] M. Benzeval, K. Judge, and M. Whitehead, *Tackling Inequalities In Health: An Agenda For Action* (London, 1994).

[153] Gillian Burton, Mitch Blair, and Nicola Crown, 'A New Look at the Health and Homeless Experience of a Cohort of Five Year Olds' (1998) 12 *Children and Society* 349.

[154] Burton *et al.*, n. 153 above, found 77 per cent of homeless children had been immunized (see 356). This is higher than in other studies but well below the childhood average of 95 per cent.

[155] Standing Conference on Public Health Working Group Report, *Housing, Homelessness and Health* (London, 1994).

[156] A neglected group. See Cathy Liddle, *Traveller Children* (London, 1999).

[157] G. Karmi, 'Refugee Health' (1992) 305 *British Medical Journal* 205.

[158] The term is Mick Stein's.

528

reasons already given, will come into care with severe health deficits. There are dangers that these will be overlooked, insufficiently attended to or aggravated. These children will have had discontinuities in health care and gaps in treatment, the result of parental neglect, mobility, and other factors connected with deprivation and inequality. With divisions of responsibility in care, often with multiple placements, healthcare problems can easily slip through the net. Health education is also imperative since we know that alcohol and drug abuse, including glue-sniffing, and unsafe sex, including the selling of sexual services, are prevalent amongst this population.[159]

At the end of the century of the child, fifty years after the introduction of the National Health Service, this audit on the health of our children should set alarm bells ringing. To the commitment to end poverty by 2019 should be added one to eliminate health inequalities.

### Child Abuse Better Understood—But Still With Us

When Lloyd de Mause wrote in 1964 of childhood as 'a nightmare from which we have only recently begun to awake',[160] it was to child abuse that his remarks were most appropriately directed. Child abuse has always been with us. We gained some understanding of the physical abuse of children in the latter third of the nineteenth century. England outlawed cruelty to domestic animals two-thirds of a century before it passed its first child cruelty legislation (in 1889). The sponsor of the 1889 Act was 'anxious that we should give children almost the same protection that we give . . . domestic animals'.[161] The Bill encountered resistance, since it was thought to undermine the sacred rights of fathers.[162] Violence against children is firmly rooted in our history and culture.

The 1889 Act—followed by further Acts in 1894, 1904, and 1908, which consolidated and extended it[163]—seemed to have had

---

[159] See further A Dennehy et al., *Not To Be Ignored: Young People, Poverty and Health* (London, 1997).

[160] *The History of Childhood* (London, 1976), 1.

[161] Philip Mundella M.P., Hansard HC vol. 337, col. 229.

[162] On which see *Re Agar—Ellis* (1883) 24 Ch. D 317.

[163] 'There have been virtually no fundamental changes in the categories of children covered by interventionist legislation since 1984', maintain R. Dingwell et al., 'Childhood As A Social Problem' (1984) 11 JLS 202, 220.

*The End of the Century of the Child?*          529

an effect. By 1913–14, although the NSPCC was seeing more cases, the percentage of prosecutions was in decline. The Home Office was in no doubt as to the reason: children of the poorer classes were being better cared for.[164]

There are other explanations: a decline in the birth rate; the First World War and the depression may have diverted attention from the issue; complacency, attributable to misplaced confidence that the NSPCC had dealt with the problem. But most convincing is the analysis of Dingwall *et al.* that child protection, save in the last decade of the nineteenth century, had never been a major concern of the state. Its real worry was the threat provided by inadequate moral socialization of children to the social order.[165] Their view is that the state recoiled from the (supposed) attack on the family (and particularly on patriarchal authority), and redirected its efforts towards effecting change—particularly preventing neglect which it saw as leading to delinquency—by means of support services which it focused on mothers. Whatever the reason, as Linda Gordon, puts it, 'violence was de-emphasized' and child neglect 'conceived primarily in terms of economic neglect, such as malnutrition or inadequate medical care' became the focus.[166]

On sexual abuse, a discreet veil was drawn.[167] Its existence was acknowledged but it was not brought to public attention in the way physical abuse and neglect were. A report of the London SPCC in 1884 referred to twelve cases which concerned 'an evil which is altogether too unmentionable'.[168] The public was, however, sensitized to the problem of child prostitution by William Stead in 1885, and the age of lawful consent to sexual intercourse for girls was increased from 13 to 16.[169] Child sexual abuse within the family was not discussed publicly. It was thought to be exclusively a vice of the poor, linked to low intelligence and a product of overcrowded sleeping conditions. Incest did not become a crime until 1908.[170] There were few prosecutions:

---

[164] *Report of the Work of the Children's Branch* (London, 1923), 69–70.

[165] R. Dingwall, J. Eekelaar and T. Murray, *The Protection of Children: State Intervention and Family Life* (Oxford, 1983).

[166] *Heroes Of Their Own Lives: the Politics and History of Family Violence* (London, 1989), 22–3.

[167] This veil became all the thicker as Freud's explanations/rationalizations took root.             [168] London SPCC, *First Annual Report* (London, 1884) 5–6.

[169] Criminal Law (Amendment) Act 1885.

[170] Punishment of Incest Act 1908.

530

twenty-four in the first year, rising to 101 in 1939 and 516 in 1987, the year of Cleveland.[171] A Royal Commission on Venereal Diseases in 1916 took childhood infections for granted.[172] When gonorrhoea was noticed to be prevalent amongst girls in institutions, an editorial in *The Lancet* offered a simplistic explanation and simple advice. 'No towels, baths, or bedroom chambers should ever be shared by girl children in institutions.'[173] There was not even the hint of a suspicion that these girls might have been sexually abused. But, as Carol Smart has demonstrated, though the orthodoxy may have been innocent transmission, 'there were counter-discourses available from within the medical profession itself', mainly from prominent women doctors. She draws attention too to the belief, 'reported as "fact"' in the Report of the Royal Commission, that sex with a virgin would cure a man of venereal disease. And so it was, neither abuse nor rape, but 'misdirected medical effort'.[174]

There were calls for legal reforms in the 1920s and the 1930s. It was in fact the 1990s before these reforms were implemented.[175] The legal response at the time, and for decades after, was to blame the victim. A report in 1925 recommended radical reforms but these met legal resistance.[176] It was a remarkable document. It would have put this country in the forefront of the fight against sexual abuse, but it outraged the legal establishment. The stance of this was said by Smart to rest 'upon a specific understanding of childhood as a phase of both resilience and insignificance. Children did not matter in this scheme of things, at least the working class girls they were likely to see did not matter. On the other hand men ... did matter; they were recognized as legal subjects'.[177] When, more than sixty years later, the Butler-Sloss report looked forward to a time when

[171] See Brian Corby, *Child Abuse: Towards A Knowledge Base* (Buckingham, 1993), 162 (drawing on Home Office Criminal Statistics).
[172] *Final Report* Cd. 8189 (London, 1916).
[173] *The Lancet*, 11 July 1925, 101–2.
[174] 'A History of Ambivalence and Conflict in the Discursive Construction of the "Child Victim" of Sexual Abuse', (1999) 8 *Social and Legal Studies* 391, 397–8.
[175] After the Pigot Report on Video Evidence (London, 1989), some of the recommendations of which were implemented in the Criminal Justice Act 1991. See also J. Morgan and L. Zedner, *Child Victims: Crime, Impact and Criminal Justice* (Oxford, 1992).
[176] *Departmental Committee on Sexual Offences Against Young Persons*, Cmd. 2561 (London, 1925).          [177] Note 174 above, 403.

The End of the Century of the Child?          531

children would be persons in their own right, not merely objects of concern,[178] what may have been overlooked was that in relation to sexual abuse they had hardly become even objects of concern.

For something to be recognized as a social problem a whistle has to be blown—it also has to be heard. It was the 1960s before we rediscovered the phenomenon of the physical abuse of children—originally explained as 'battered baby syndrome'[179]—and it was the mid-1980s before we began to take child sexual abuse seriously.[180] There have been over seventy enquiries into cases of child abuse since the Maria Colwell case took us by storm in 1973–4.[181] Social work practices have been criticized, and there have been reforms, both legislative (Acts of 1975 and 1989) and in terms of practice (working in partnership was an unknown concept a generation ago).[182] Prevention may have been best practice as long ago as the 1950s[183] but it took on a new emphasis after the rediscovery of abuse and particularly after the 1989 Act encoded the concept of 'children in need'.[184] A network of practices has developed to tackle the problem: the child protection conference,[185] the register,[186] but, unlike a number of countries,

[178] Report of the Inquiry Into Child Abuse in Cleveland 1987, Cm. 412 (London, 1988), 245.

[179] On the discovery (or rediscovery—see Behlmer, n. 55 above) see S. Pfohl, 'The Discovery of Child Abuse' (1977) 24 Social Problems 310.

[180] In the 1970s, far from its being discussed, almost the only reference I can find is to an unpublished paper by M van Stolk (2nd World Congress of International Society of Family Law, 1977) which suggested that the circumcision of male babies was sexual abuse. Early articles are M. D. A. Freeman, 'Sexual Abuse of Children' (1978) 8 Family Law 221, and the first report of BASPCAN, Child Sexual Abuse (Rochdale, 1981). Cleveland was, of course, the catalyst (and see n. 178 above).

[181] See P. Reder, S. Duncan, and M. Grey, Beyond Blame: Child Abuse Tragedies Revisited (London, 1993).

[182] Department of Health, Principles and Practice In Regulations and Guidance (London, 1990). A thoughtful comment is Martin C. Calder, 'Child Protection: Balancing Paternalism and Partnership' (1995) 25 British Journal of Social Work 749.         [183] Jean Packman, The Child's Generation (Oxford, 1981), ch. 4.

[184] In s. 17: see Michael D. A. Freeman, Children, Their Families and the Law (Basingstoke, 1992), ch. 4; P. Hardiker, K. Exton and M. Barker, 'The Social Policy Contexts of Prevention in Child Care' (1991) 21 British Journal of Social Work 341.

[185] See Department of Health, Working Together (London, 1999) (there were earlier editions in 1988 and 1991).

[186] On selection processes operating here, which serve to screen out many cases, see J. Gibbons, S. Conroy, and C. Bell, Operation of Child Protection Registers (Norwich, 1993).

532

not mandatory reporting.[187] Nor have we followed the Dutch example and channelled cases through the medical profession:[188] even though for long our dominant model of child abuse was a medical one (the so-called psycho-pathological model), social services have remained at the forefront of the battle.[189]

Like the categories of negligence, the categories of child abuse never close. There is greater cognizance today of emotional abuse than hitherto, though its incidence is still underestimated.[190] And new examples constantly emerge. An example is Munchausen's disease by proxy.[191] Behaviour, not previously so considered, attracts the label of 'child abuse': domestic violence,[192] parental smoking,[193] the consumption of drugs whilst pregnant,[194] the use of children in prostitution,[195] and pornography.[196] We have rid ourselves of one form of institutional abuse—corporal punishment in schools—only finally last year.[197] But over the last ten years we have become aware of institutional abuse on a wide scale: for too long we refused to believe or did not listen. Or we covered up. The cancer went deep: the fraud and deceit even deeper.[198]

[187] See Susan Maidment, 'Some Legal Problems Arising Out of the Reporting of Child Abuse' (1978) 31 *Current Legal Problems* 149. It has been discussed: see DHSS, *Review of Child Care Law* (London, 1985) para. 12.3–12.4.
[188] This model has been followed in Belgium: see C. Marneffe, E. Boemans, and A. Lampoo, in M. Davies and A. Sale (eds.), *Child Protection Policies and Practice in Europe* (London, 1990).
[189] This is reflected in the Children Act 1989 s. 47.
[190] Celia Doyle's research (an unpublished University of Leicester Ph.D., 1996) found it the most prevalent form of abuse. See C. Doyle, 'Current Issues In Child Protection' (1996) 26 *British Journal of Social Work* 565.
[191] See J. A. Libow, 'Munchausen By Proxy Victims In Childhood' (1995) 19 *Child Abuse and Neglect* 1131. It can be seen as a form of emotional abuse.
[192] See A. Mullender and R. Morley, *Children Living with Domestic Violence* (London, 1994), and H. Cleaver, I. Unell, and J. Aldgate, *Children's Needs—Parenting Capacity: The Impact of Parental Mental Illness, Problem Alcohol and Drug Use, and Domestic Violence On Children's Development* (London, 1999).
[193] See D. Ezra, 'Sticks and Stones Can Break My Bones, But Tobacco Smoke Can Kill Me' (1993) 13 *St Louis University Public Law Review* 347.
[194] See D. Johnsen, 'The Creation of Fetal Rights: Conflicts with Women's Constitutional Rights to Liberty, Privacy and Equal Protection' (1986) 95 *Yale Law Journal* 599.
[195] See R. Edgington in (ed.) D. Barrett, *Child Prostitution in Britain—Dilemmas and Practical Responses* (London, 1997).
[196] The growth of the internet has aggravated this problem.
[197] School Standards and Framework Act 1998 s. 131.
[198] See the Utting Enquiry, *People Like Us* (London, 1997) and now the Waterhouse report, n. 16 above.

*The End of the Century of the Child?* 533

In this century of the child, it is estimated that in England perhaps 20 per cent of girls are sexually abused (there are suggestions that it may be as many as one in three). Though fewer boys are abused in this way, it is by no means uncommon. A third of sexually abused children are the victims of other children or adolescents.[199] Perhaps 120 children a year die at the hands of parents (or step-parents).[200] About one child in 300 is placed on a child protection register.[201] This is about 20 per cent of those referred to social services and other child protection agencies.[202] Suspicion of physical injury accounts for 40 per cent of children on registers.[203] Of course, whether a child will be registered depends on a number of variables, including local practice and resources. The registration of a child is a reflection of a number of process decisions. Many children on registers have not been abused but are deemed to be 'at risk'. Many children not on registers are victims of abuse: some are not registered because they have not come to attention.

Of course, the question of 'how many' depends upon how abuse is defined. The National Commission of Inquiry into the Prevention of Child Abuse and Neglect returned to David Gil's definition of 1970: 'anything which individuals, institutions or processes do or fail to do which directly or indirectly harms children or damages their prospects of safe and healthy development into adulthood'.[204] No legal system does, or should, define child abuse in this way, but it identifies a broader range of potentially harmful actions than most legal systems regard as child abuse. It may also fit victims' experiences of abuse better than those laws which are based on professional perceptions. And it would

[199] See L. Horne, D. Glasgow, A. Cox, and R. Callum, 'Sexual Abuse of Children by Children' (1990) 3 *Journal of Child Law* 147.
[200] See A. Falkov, *Study of Working Together Part 8 Reports: Fatal Child Abuse and Parental Psychiatric Disorder* (London, 1996). Babies and toddlers are more at risk of homicide than any other age group, and this has been the case for (at least) the last 20 years: see S. J. Creighton, 'Fatal Child Abuse: How Preventable Is It?' (1995) 4 *Child Abuse Review* 318.
[201] See Department of Health, *Children and Young People on Child Protection Registers* (London, 1996).
[202] See Department of Health, *Messages from Research* (London, 1995).
[203] And see *Childhood Matters—Report of the National Commission of Inquiry Into the Prevention of Child Abuse* (London, 1996).
[204] See ibid. (1997), following D. Gil, *Violence Against Children* (Cambridge, Mass., 1970).

534

certainly encourage those legal systems, like the English, which do not regard corporal chastisement as abuse to think about it differently. Even acts which do not result in significant harm (the legal threshold for abuse in England)[205] may damage developmental prospects.

*Working Together*—the official practitioners' guide to social work with children at risk—categorizes child abuse (there are now four categories and 'grave concern' has been removed), but it does not define.[206] Legislation—the Children Act of 1989—gives social services and the NSPCC the power to intervene in families and seek a care order where it can be shown that 'the child is suffering or is likely to suffer significant harm' and that this is 'attributable' to a lack of reasonable parental care.[207] But the Act does not lay down the standards of care which children can expect from their parents. This leaves English law, as Lyon points out,[208] in breach of the United Nations Convention which requires States Parties to 'render appropriate assistance to parents and legal guardians in the performance of their child-rearing responsibilities'.[209]

There is concern that English law and social work practice— and they are inextricably linked—are doing too little to protect children from abuse. The strategy of tackling abuse has changed recently in line with a shift in ideology from child protection to family support. The dominant approach until the mid-1990s, which emphasized child protection, was thought to focus attention on securing the safety of a small number of children at risk of 'serious' abuse, whilst at the same time drawing into the bureaucratic net many more cases for which it was not appropriate. In 1995, the Department of Health, after noting this, commented:

Protection issues are best viewed in the context of children's wider needs. It is important to ensure that inappropriate cases do not get caught up in the child protection process, for this could have several undesirable

---

[205] See Children Act 1989 s. 31(2).

[206] Note 185 above, 14–15. The Scottish equivalent (Scottish Office, *Child Protection In Scotland: Management Information* (Edinburgh, 1992)) is broader (it includes non-organic failure to thrive).

[207] And see M. Adcock and R. White (eds.), *Significant Harm: Its Management and Outcome* (Croydon, 1998).

[208] Christina M. Lyon, 'The Definition of, and Legal and Management Responses to, the Problem of Child Abuse in England and Wales', in (ed.) Michael Freeman, *Overcoming Child Abuse: A Window on a World Problem* (Aldershot, 2000), 95.

[209] Article 18(2).

*The End of the Century of the Child?* 535

consequences. Of particular concern is the unnecessary distress caused to family members who may then be unwilling to co-operate with subsequent plans. Professionals ... may have to rebuild a sense of trust with family members to enable them to participate. Ultimately, it will be necessary to decide when and how to permit a case to leave the child protection arena'.[210]

The premise is that serious abuse is rare, that rehabilitation is a challenge that more often than not can be successfully embraced, and that permanent placement outside the family is necessarily a bad thing.

By adopting the family support model, the English approach to child abuse has moved closer to the dominant strategy found in other parts of Europe.[211] The Dutch may have been the first to see intervention in terms of support as well as protection. Their confidential doctor (or medical referee) system developed in the early 1970s,[212] and has since spread to Belgium. Hetherington *et al.*, describing the Belgian system, say that confidential doctor centres 'accept and follow up referrals from other agencies and from individuals, while preserving their anonymity, but will only intervene with the agreement of the parents and children. It is not impossible for referral to be made to the legal system but it is very unusual'.[213] Germany too follows this model. Its child protection centres exist to help the affected family and work with it to solve its problems. The family is free to decide whether it accepts offers of assistance.[214] Like the Dutch system, there is strict confidentiality: 'the intervention of a third party only takes place with the agreement of the family and as a rule with the family itself present'.[215] Austria too has come under this influence: child protection centres are said to operate 'without the threat of punishment'.[216] The family support model is found also in the

---

[210] Department of Health, *Child Protection: Messages From Research* (London, 1995), 32.
[211] Though there is no hint in *Messages From Research* that this assimilation is deliberate.
[212] An early English account is M. D. A. Freeman, 'The Dutch Confidential Doctor System' (1977) 7 *Family Law* 53.
[213] R. Hetherington *et al.*, *Protecting Children: Messages from Europe* (Lyme Regis, 1997), 59.  [214] See P. Hutz in n. 188, above.
[215] See W. Wustendorfer, 'Violence Against Children in Germany', in C. Birks (ed.), *Child Abuse in Europe* vol. 1 (Nuremberg, 1995).
[216] H. Planicka, 'Child Abuse In Austria' in n. 215 above, 68.

536

Nordic world.[217] The structure in France is different but the philosophy is very similar.[218] And New Zealand's family group conference,[219] increasingly influential in other countries including England, espouses a similar family-oriented model, making the family pivotal to decision-making.

The child protection model may be thought to reify child abuse and to separate it from issues of child care generally. But it is possible to promote positive child care, for example to discourage corporal punishment, whilst acknowledging that child abuse is a thing apart and has to be tackled separately. The new orthodoxy, however, sees the switch from child protection to family support as right. But does not an emphasis on family support conflate the interests of parents (and they may not be identical) with that of the child (whose interests may well conflict with those of her parents or, at least, one of them)? There is a danger that a system of family support can serve to reaffirm and perpetrate power differentials within the family, those of age and, in the context of sexual abuse especially, of gender. There is a danger also that the child's voice will be suppressed. Article 12 of the UN Convention emphasizes the importance of the child's participation in the decision-making process, a value re-emphasized in the European Convention on the Exercise of Children's Rights. But what space does the family support system afford the child victim? Not surprisingly, the system is being questioned within those countries in which it is firmly entrenched. There is concern in France that the child's perspective is often unheard by the *juge des enfants*.[220] Of the Netherlands Van Montfoort has commented that the welfare approach risks 'overlooking power relationships within the family'.[221]

---

[217] See, for example, in relation to Finland, R. Tuomisto, and E. Vuori-Karvia, 'Child Protection in Finland' in M. Harder and K. Pringle (eds.), *Protecting Children In Europe: Towards a New Millennium* (Aalborg, 1997).

[218] See Michael King and Judith Trowell, *Children's Welfare and the Law: The Limits of Legal Intervention* (London, 1992).

[219] A valuable study of which is M. Gilling, L. Patterson, and B. Walker, *Family Members' Experiences of the Care and Protection Family Group Conference* (Wellington, 1995).

[220] See H. Armstrong and A. Hollows, 'Responses to Child Abuse in the EC', in M. Hill (ed.), *Social Work and the European Community* (London, 1991).

[221] A. Van Montfoort, 'The Protection of Children in the Netherlands: Between Justice and Welfare', in (eds.) H. Ferguson, R. Gilligan, and R. Torode, *Surviving Childhood Adversity* (Dublin, 1993), 62.

*The End of the Century of the Child?*        537

Strategies and solutions pre-suppose an understanding of a problem. The earliest interpretation of child abuse—the psychopathological model—endows the medical profession with the answer. Even if its exponents were right and abusers were sick, we were not attracted by the solutions or their implications. The socio-environmental stress model requires us to find ways of reducing the stress which follows, *inter alia*, from poverty. The removal of poverty and its correlates (broadly social exclusion) may well have an effect on child abuse, but it will not eliminate it. The cultural model looks forward, in effect, to a cultural revolution. The different approaches adopted in different countries at different times reflect different interpretations of abuse, its aetiology and its implications. If abuse is interpreted as a system of family dysfunction, then solutions will be looked to which work to rehabilitate the family as a functioning unit. Thus, Cooper *et al.*, writing of child protection work in France, can describe it as 'first and foremost a family affair'. They add: 'It is not the individual child who is the primary focus of concern and intervention but the child-as-part-of-the-family, and the whole thrust of the French system is towards maintaining children as part of their families of origin.'[222] Of Finland, Tuomisto and Vuori-Karvia write: 'Traditional, individual-oriented forms of care have been criticised for being expert-dominated, time-consuming and apparently ineffective. These traditional forms of care have been widely replaced by approaches based on systems theory.'[223]

But does a family systems explanation satisfactorily account for child abuse? Whilst conceding that there is no one explanation and that the causes of child abuse are multi-layered, the family systems model woefully underplays the agency and responsibility of the abuser, disempowers the non-abusing parent and, in the case of sexual abuse, glosses over the power issues related to masculinity which are now generally agreed to be central to our understanding of this.

Since sexual abuse dominates thinking about abuse today, I will examine the recent shift in English thinking and the policies this engenders in the context of sexual abuse.

[222] D. Cooper, R. Hetherington, K. Bristow, J. Pitts, and A. Spriggs, *Positive Child Protection: A View from Abroad* (Lyme Regis, 1995), 6.
[223] Note 217 above, 89.

538

As with other abuse, the tendency has been to locate the causes within individuals (and now dysfunctioning families) or within socio-environmental factors (it was once thought that incest behaviour was inversely related to socioeconomic status). One factor in child sexual abuse does, however, stand out and separate such abuse from other forms. Most perpetrators are men, and most victims are female.[224] Abuse, Campbell reminded us at the time of Cleveland, is 'an expression of a patriarchal sexual culture'.[225] Its source is in masculine sexuality. Until recently, discussion of sexual abuse rarely made the gender of the perpetrator explicit. The Cleveland affair was invariably about 'parents'.[226] It is still common to find mother blaming in the orthodox literature on child sexual abuse. Nelson notes that 'professionals cling to the collusion wife theory like drowning men grasping at flotsam'. 'Could it be', she asks, 'because it is such a powerful defence against admitting the male abuse of power?[227] Of course, without this assumption of the role of the wife/mother, the family therapist begins to look like the emperor without clothes.

Feminism offers greater insight into child sexual abuse because it makes us ask questions about culture and power (which are equally relevant to an understanding of other forms of abuse). Feminism not only offers a different interpretation of child sexual abuse, but also challenges the responses of orthodoxy, which new English 'official' thinking and practices now encode. Family systems theory asks what is wrong with the functioning of the family, and how its fragmented pieces can be successfully reconstructed. But it refuses to indict, to blame: instead, it prefers to share responsibility. But, as one feminist critic puts it: 'The father rapes, abuses, brutalises and assaults the children and the mother, but somehow it is the mother's or child's fault.'[228] An understanding of abuse requires an understanding of power. Sex, dominance, and abuse do not have to be linked: there is no biological

---

[224] Boys are more commonly victims of physical abuse, neglect and emotional abuse than girls. Sexual abuse by women is thought to be on the increase: see R. Krug, 'Adult Male Report of Childhood Sexual Abuse by Mothers' (1989) 13 *Child Abuse and Neglect* 111.       [225] *Unofficial Secrets* (London, 1988), 62.
[226] Typified by the Butler–Sloss report itself (n. 178 above).
[227] *Incest: Fact and Myth* (Edinburgh, 1987), 108.
[228] E. Wattenberg, 'In a Different Light: A Feminist Perspective on the Role of Mothers In Father-Daughter Incest' (1985) 64 *Child Welfare* 203, 206.

The End of the Century of the Child?          539

inevitability. But in our culture they are, and they produce the conditions in which the sexual abuse of children is perpetrated, and in which excuses are offered. The relationship needs to be deconstructed. The family support model is not calculated to do this.

It presupposes a family systems theory, leading to the legitimate concern that its endorsement will lead more to the protection of adults than to the securing of the safety or the promotion of the welfare of children. One of the ironies of the British move towards the tackling of the problem in the way adopted in so many continental countries is that understanding of the causes of abuse seems more advanced in the English-speaking world. Certainly, also, we were aware of the problem and of its prevalence before our continental counterparts. This is in part why the Dutroux case in Belgium, the Roum affair in Denmark, the scandals in Ireland, all recent, provoked such concern and media attention in these countries. Pringle and Harder have, rightly I believe, pointed to the 'real tragedy of the situation in England and Wales' that 'the enormity of the problem has been more realised there than elsewhere in Western Europe but the system designed to deal with it is wholly inadequate'.[229] That abuse, particularly sexual abuse but also sexual violence against women generally, is better known about in Britain is in large part because the problem has been politicized by feminists and others who have challenged the very cosy arrangements which (unintentionally) family systems theorists and practitioners endorse.

The attempt to embrace a more continental approach may be wrong for another reason too. It presupposes that solutions can be isolated from ideologies and from structures. But we have a different context, a different view of society and the individual (perhaps more individualistic), a different vision of the role of the state and of community. This point is addressed well by Hetherington et al.: 'When services for children are enshrined by the principles of social solidarity, subsidiarity and citizenship, one consequence is that the institutions which organise, deliver, and shape local responses to child protection are structured into, and derive their authority from a total conception of society.'[230] These principles, they argue, are absent from a Britain which has not (yet) recovered from eighteen

[229] Note 217 above, 168.          [230] Note 213 above, 34.

540

years of Conservatism, 'a period which witnessed a consolidation of ideologies of individual rights . . . and a general decline in ideas of collective responsibility'.[231] In fact, the roots of this go even deeper, grounded as they are in a set of assumptions about the relationship of the individual to society and to government.

The child protection model did not work, but that is only part of the reason why we recently rejected it. The family systems model does not work either. There is evidence of that from countries where, given their assumptions about society, it was more likely to work. Given the enormity of the problem it cannot be expected to work in Britain any more than elsewhere. And it is not just a question of resources.

Both models over-rely on professionals to solve the problem. This is not to downplay the pivotal role of professional expertise: the emergence of the family group conference alarms me because it vests the family, and potentially the abuser, with too much decision-making power. We must find a role for the family, but it must be a role in prevention, not one assigned to decision-making. We must find ways of empowering non-abusing family members. There are ways the law can assist this process: for example, making residence orders in favour of relatives, rather than care orders. But where the opportunity arose for the House of Lords to take the lead and endorse such a practice, it inexplicably and inexcusably failed so to do.[232]

A role in prevention must also be found for non-family members. There are many lessons to be learnt from the James Bulger case but one that can all too easily be overlooked is that he would not have died had one of the thirty-eight (or more) adults who witnessed his fateful walk intervened.[233] What Gerrilyn Smith has called 'a protected environment'[234] needs investigation. She argues that 'Our prevention programmes should be aimed first at the adults who surround children in their day-to-day lives: parents, extended family members, childminders, nursery workers,

[231] Note 213 above, 85.
[232] *Re M* [1994] 2 AC 424; and see Judith Masson, 'Social Engineering In the House of Lords' (1994) 6 *Journal of Child Law* 170.
[233] See M. Freeman, *The Moral Status of Children* (The Hague, 1997), ch. 12. Blake Morrison's description in *As If* (London, 1997), ch. 4 repays attention.
[234] 'Reassessing Protectiveness', in D. Batty and D. Cullen (eds.), *Child Protection: The Therapeutic Option* (London, 1996), 77.

The End of the Century of the Child?            541

and teachers among others.'[235] The Bulger case, she observes, shows that 'we, as a community of adults, are reluctant to take responsibility for protecting other people's children. Hence protectiveness has become increasingly professionalised and more removed from the natural networks that surround children where it would be most effective.'[236] Whether such networks are effective depends on a number of variables. It depends on children 'telling'—but it is more likely that they will tell persons known to them than statutory agencies—and it depends on how such persons perceive abuse—they are more likely to respond to sexual abuse, which generally appals, than to physical abuse, which is commonly interpreted as punishment and therefore acceptable. And it depends also on education: of adults, and also of children.

More than twenty years ago Kempe and Kempe wrote that 'before [child abuse] could be acknowledged as a social ill, changes had to occur in the sensibilities and outlook of our [in their case American] culture'.[237] If child abuse is to wither away, many changes in sensibilities and outlook are needed. We must ask why children's bodies are still exploited, sexually molested and subjected to physical and psychological violence. The answer is complex, but can be partly explained in the way childhood has been constructed. If we are to eradicate the abuse of children we must learn to take children's rights seriously, we must acknowledge their entitlement to 'equal concern and respect',[238] we must accept that children are not property or pretty play things or (literally) whipping boys, but individuals whose physical, sexual, and psychological integrity is as important, if not more important, than that of the adult population.

We must also inject more content into the 'protected environment' than Gerrilyn Smith envisages. We must learn to take abuse more seriously. Far too many children are left in, or indeed put into, abusive environments. The abuse legislation needs to be interpreted purposefully and expansively to protect children's integrity rather than parents' privacy.[239] The Human Rights Act 1998 will not stand in our way of doing this if our courts, like the

---

[235] Ibid.                                            [236] Ibid., 85.
[237] R. Kempe and C. H. Kempe, *Child Abuse* (London, 1978), 17.
[238] Note 105 above, 272–8.
[239] But there is a danger that, with the implementation of the Human Rights Act 1998, privacy (see Article 8) will be prioritized.

542

European Court of Human Rights, come to realize the importance
of using principles derived from the United Nations Convention in
its interpretation.[240] And the European Commission has now
ruled that children were subjected to 'torture or inhuman or
degrading treatment' when a social services department failed for
more than four years to remove them from 'horrific' neglect.[241]
The House of Lords had ruled that it would be contrary to public
policy to allow the children to sue the local authority.[242] A
common law duty of care would 'cut across the whole statutory
scheme set up for the protection of children at risk'.[243] The task of
social services in dealing with children at risk was 'extraordinarily
delicate. Legislation requires the local authority to have regard not
only to the physical well-being of the child but also to the advantages of not disrupting the child's family environment' (and here
the Cleveland report is quoted in support). . . . If liability in
damages were allowed, local authorities might adopt a 'more
cautious and defensive approach to their duties.'[244] Then there
was the 'spectre of vexatious and costly litigation'[245] as well as the
existence of other remedies (though these have not proved efficacious) and precedents against in supposedly analogous cases
regarding the police.[246] The European Commission has now said
this stance breaches Article 6 of the European Convention: the
right to a fair hearing. The significance of the Commission ruling
cannot be underestimated. The European Court of Human Rights
can be expected to affirm it. The floodgates will not open: social
work practices have improved since the late 1980s and early
1990s and this case will have a further positive impact.

So will the *Barrett* decision.[247] The House of Lords refused to
strike out a claimant's action for negligence against a local authority
which, it was alleged, having secured a care order did not make
satisfactory arrangements thereafter, causing him to experience
alcohol problems, a tendency to self-harm, behavioural problems
and a failed marriage. The Lords held that it was not necessarily
unjust or unreasonable to impose a duty of care on a local authority

[240] In particular Article 12.
[241] *Z v United Kingdom* [2000] 2 FCR 245.
[242] *X v Bedfordshire C.C.* [1995] 2 FLR 276.          [243] Ibid., 301.
[244] Ibid.                                              [245] Ibid., 302.
[246] *Hill v Chief Constable of West Yorkshire* [1989] AC 53.
[247] *Barrett v Enfield L.B.C.* [1999] 2 FLR 426.

## The End of the Century of the Child?                543

in relation to children in its care. The court appreciated there were difficulties. As Lord Slynn put it:

Both in deciding whether particular issues are justiciable and whether if a duty of care is owed, it has been broken, the court must have regard to the statutory context and to the nature of the tasks involved. The mere fact that something has gone wrong or that a mistake has been made, or that someone has been inefficient does not mean that there was a duty to be careful or that such a duty has been broken. Much of what has to be done in this area involves the balancing of delicate and difficult factors and courts should not be too ready to find in these situations that there has been negligence by staff who largely are skilled and dedicated.[248]

The Lords accepted that, unless the courts exercised their jurisdiction to consider these questions, the interests of the child would not be sufficiently protected. But will they be protected if the courts once more invoke the heresy, now firmly quashed in medical cases,[249] that there is a distinction between errors and negligence? Both Lord Slynn and Lord Hutton make this distinction. Of equal concern is Lord Slynn's assertion that social workers are entitled to rely on the *Bolam* principle[250] (in *X v Bedfordshire CC* Lord Browne-Wilkinson had taken it for granted that educational psychologists were also to be so judged).[251] In *Barrett* the headnote writer in the *Family Law Reports* refuses to believe this. It concludes: 'Requiring that the conduct of the local authority be measured against the standards of the reasonable man, was in the public interest, not opposed to it.'[252] And so it should be. Further, the Lords take it for granted that a child is not able to sue her parents for negligence in relation to care-giving decisions (as opposed quite obviously to injuries which are the result of a parent's negligent driving). Lord Slynn grounds the distinction in the fact, as he sees it, that local authorities have 'to take decisions which parents never or rarely have to take (for example, as to adoption or as to an appropriate foster-parent or institution)'.[253] But some parents do have to take these or similar decisions: whether to give up a child for adoption, whether to

---

[248] Ibid., 445.
[249] Lord Denning invented it (see *Roe v Minister of Health* [1954] 2 QB 66). It was finally buried in the House of Lords in *Whitehouse v Jordan* [1981] 1 All ER 267).
[250] *Bolam v Friern Barnet Management Committee* [1957] 1 WLR 582.
[251] Note 242 above, 314.                                    [252] Note 247 above, 427.
[253] Ibid., 446.

544

have a child accommodated or seek the return of a child so placed, whether to place a child with foster parents or with a relative. And parents have other decisions to take as well. Why should there not be an actionable duty of care against a mother who decides to live with a known sex abuser or against parents who smoke in the presence of an asthmatic child[254] or against a mother with HIV who insists on breast feeding her baby?[255]

*X v United Kingdom* and *Barrett v London Borough of Enfield* are landmark decisions. So was *A v United Kingdom* in 1998.[256] The European Court of Human Rights unanimously held that the law in the United Kingdom, which allows parents to inflict reasonable corporal chastisement, breaches Article 3 of the European Convention. The Court found that the law in the United Kingdom did not provide 'adequate protection' to children. The court proclaimed:

> Children and other vulnerable individuals, in particular, are entitled to State protection, in the form of effective deterrence, against serious breaches of personal integrity.[257]

The case in question related to a boy repeatedly beaten by his stepfather with a garden cane. The stepfather had been acquitted on the ground that his assaults amounted to reasonable chastisement. It is difficult to state what constitutes moderate and reasonable corporal punishment. The test is open-textured and vague, deliberately so. Thus, the law says nothing about the part of the body on which the chastisement may be inflicted, whether an implement may be used, whether age is relevant or the child's gender material. It is surprising that, with corporal punishment so institutionalized (it has only been finally extirpated from the school setting in 1999), it was so little regulated.

If we are to create a protected environment, we must respond positively to the European Court's ruling. The Government's initial response was not promising. They distinguished the 'safe smack' from corporal punishment and pledged that the former would remain a parental privilege.[258] The promised Consultation Paper

---

[254] The Congenital Disabilities (Civil Liability) Act 1976 rules out actions against a mother whose alcohol or drug abuse harms an unborn child. But this exception may need to be reconsidered.                    [255] *Re C* [1999] 2 FLR 1004.
[256] [1998] 2 FLR 959.                                            [257] Ibid., 964.
[258] *The Times*, 8 November 1997 (reacting to the Commission ruling).

The End of the Century of the Child?          545

took sixteen months to materialize. Putting a 'spin' on a 'safe smack' was not easy! The task of definition is elusive. As for moral justification, try justifying the safe smacking of wives (or servants).

Informed opinion could write a Consultation Paper in an afternoon. But just imagine the knots being tied by the draftsman who has to define a 'loving' or a 'safe' smack! Is it lawful to smack babies? Or disabled children? Are you to be allowed to hit a child's head, or face, or 'box' his ears? And what of his bottom, given the sexual connotations? Is there to be a maximum age? Can you strike a Gillick competent child? Will it be permissible to remove a child's clothes? Will there be any circumstances in which an implement will be allowed? And who is to be allowed to hit children? Only parents? Or all those with parental responsibility? What of the unmarried father? What of grandparents? Will stepparents be able to smack children? What of 'live-in' boyfriends? Nannies? Au pairs? Baby-sitters?

The Consultation Paper[259] would have been a profound disappointment if anything better had been anticipated. It is couched entirely in terms of parents' rights and responsibilities: never once does it allude to children as persons or as rights-bearers,[260] and once again they are objects of social intervention, social problems. Today's children may 'shape tomorrow's future society'[261] but they must be disciplined to do so. The 'Swedish model' is explicitly ruled out: it is 'quite unacceptable'.[262] But there must, the Government accepts, be reform, though only, it seems, because the European Court has forced the issue. It therefore sets out the 'minimum steps needed to clarify the law in the light of the European Court's ruling'.[263] It does this by offering a checklist which will assist no one,[264] and may not even satisfy the European jurisprudence. For example, it would not necessarily rule out the use of a cane. But because public opinion,[265] not it seems the

---

[259] Department of Health, *Protecting Children, Supporting Parents* (London, 2000).
[260] The only right it gives children is to be protected from harm, as it sees it.
[261] Note 259 above, 1, 8.                                    [262] Ibid., 1.5, 2.14.
[263] Ibid., 5.5.
[264] It is vague and open-ended. It certainly does not provide a 'doctrine of fair opportunity': see H. L. A. Hart, *Punishment and Responsibility* (Oxford, 1968).
[265] This was elicited by a survey conducted by the Office for National Statistics. See n. 259, above, Annex A. It should be added that the responses—often to loaded questions—are out of line with other survey responses.

546

Government, would want children to have greater protection, a number of other options are set out. First, the ruling out of physical punishment which causes, or is likely to cause, injury to the head (including injuries to the brain, eyes, and ears)[266] and/or the use of implements. Secondly, the restriction of the reasonable chastisement defence to cases of common assault only, in effect making it an offence to cause a child actual bodily harm.[267] And thirdly, limiting those able to claim the defence of reasonable chastisement, possibly to those with parental responsibility (which would rule out about a third of fathers[268] and nearly all stepparents, grandparents, and relatives) or conceivably to those who act on behalf of parents where express permission has been given physically to punish the child.[269] We will make it unlawful to hit children: this lacklustre Consultation Paper merely postpones the inevitable.

Sweden made it unlawful to hit children twenty years ago. Their Children and Parents Code, as amended in 1983, provides

Children are entitled to care, security and a good upbringing. They shall be treated with respect for their person and their distinctive character and may not be subject to corporal punishment or any other injurious or humiliating treatment.[270]

The anti-spanking law is only part of a strategy to create a new culture of childhood, one in which children are identified as persons and rights-holders, but it is an important part.[271]

The law was passed as social engineering, rather than as a measure to intrude upon family privacy or haul parents before courts. Prosecutions are very rare. Finland followed the Swedish

[266] Note it does not rule out all striking of the head or face and perhaps not even boxing of the ears (this only rarely causes injury and would not therefore satisfy the House of Lords' test in *Re H* [1996] AC 563).

[267] But on the Offences Against the Person Charging Standard, see n. 259 above, 3.5.

[268] Those not married to the mother, without a parental responsibility agreement or order. Reform is anticipated but cannot be expected in the immediate future.

[269] The Government seems to overlook s. 1(7) of the Children and Young Persons Act 1933 (which it quotes at para. 3.14). This gives anyone having lawful control or charge of a child or young person an independent right to administer punishment.                                   [270] Ch. 6 s. 1.

[271] See J. E. Durrant and G. M. Olsen, 'Parenting and Public Policy: Contextualizing The Swedish Corporal Punishment Ban' (1997) 19 *Journal of Social Welfare and Family Law* 443. Ulrich Beck sees in Sweden a different attitude towards children: 'Democratization of the Family' (1997) 4 *Childhood* 151, 161.

The End of the Century of the Child?          547

example in 1983,[272] Norway in 1987.[273] Austria was the first non-Nordic country to outlaw corporal punishment, doing so in 1989 and by unanimous vote.[274] As in Sweden, the legislation is targeted at education of parents rather than the use of criminal penalties. There is no evidence of any increase in prosecutions, but clear evidence that community sentiment has shifted in line with the legislation. Cyprus outlawed the corporal punishment of children in 1993.[275] The Cypriot law is particularly interesting for two reasons. First, penal sanctions attach, and are increased because the violence is used against a member of the family. Secondly, because not only is force against children prohibited, but so is violence in the presence of children, an acknowledgement unique in legislation that domestic violence is a form of child abuse. In 1997 Denmark joined the other Nordic countries in prohibiting all corporal punishment of children.[276] There has been legislation also in Latvia in 1998, Croatia in 1999, and Germany in 2000, and it is imminent in Belgium. Belgium is responding to the child sex murders scandal with, *inter alia*, legislation guaranteeing children the right to 'respect for [their] person . . . and individuality', and stressing that 'they shall not be subjected to degrading treatment, nor to any other form of physical or psychological violence'.[277]

In Italy there has not been legislation, but, in 1996, the Corte dei Cassazzione ruled that the use of violence by parents for educational purposes was no longer lawful.[278] The judges were influenced by the Italian Constitution of 1948 and laws built upon it, and by international law, particularly the UN Convention on the Rights of the Child. The Court's opinion found support in a number of articles of the Convention, in particular the non-discrimination principle in Article 2, the emphasis on a child's best

---

[272] See P. Newell, *Children Are People Too* (London, 1989), 87.
[273] Parent and Child Act Art 30 s. 3.
[274] E. Bernat, 'Austria: the Final Stages of Three Decades of Family Law Reform' (1990-1) 29 *Journal of Family Law* 285.
[275] Act of 17 June 1994, Law 147(1).
[276] Parental Custody Amendment Act ns. 416 s. 1. Denmark bowed to the inevitable: its earlier legislation (in 1985) allowed light corporal punishment.
[277] Belgian Senate 1997–8 Session: Proposal For a Law Inserting an Article 371 bis into the *Code Civil*.
[278] Foro It II 1996, 407 (the case of Natalino Cambria). The Israeli Supreme Court in early 2000 has followed the Italian example.

548

interests in Articles 3 and 18, and Article 19's prohibition on the use of violence against children. The Convention does not proscribe corporal punishment but Article 19 clearly indicts it. The Committee on the Rights of the Child is unequivocal on the practice:

> the Committee has paid particular attention to the child's right to physical integrity . . . It has stressed that corporal punishment of children is incompatible with the Convention and has often proposed the revision of existing legislation, as well as the development of awareness and education campaigns, to prevent child abuse and the physical punishment of children.[279]

It has criticized many countries, the laws of which allow the corporal punishment of children, including the United Kingdom.[280]

If we are to create a protected environment we must make it unlawful to hit children. There is a concern that this would lead to greater intervention into the family, more prosecutions of parents, more care proceedings. But this is not the experience of countries which have passed such legislation. Nor is it the reason why those who favour legislation want it. Legislation is needed to change attitudes, and you do not change attitudes by half-measures, or by sending out incoherent or inconsistent messages. Arguably you do not even make 'law'.[281] Legislation can mould moral behaviour, even in expressive areas of life like parent-child relations. The Swedish experience is testimony to this. Of course, legislation by itself is not enough and must be accompanied by an education programme, as in Sweden. It is important too that children are reared in an environment free of violence. Outlawing corporal punishment will more likely lead to fewer prosecutions—because there will be less abuse—to fewer care proceedings, and also to less delinquency and violent crime, and thus a reduction in the prison population, because corporal punishment teaches violence and the victims of today become tomorrow's violent criminals.

---

[279] UN Committee on the Rights of the Child, *Report of Seventh Session* UN Doc CRC/C/34 (Geneva, 1994), Annex iv, 63.

[280] The UK in 1995 (UN Committee on the Rights of the Child, Concluding Observations of the Committee on the Rights of the Child: United Kingdom of Great Britain and Northern Ireland, 8th Session. UN Doc CRC/C/15 Add. 34) (Geneva, 1995), paras. 16 and 31.

[281] Cf. Lon L. Fuller, *The Morality of Law* (New Haven, Conn., 1964), 33.

The End of the Century of the Child?        549

Banning corporal punishment could thus be justified on utilitarian grounds. But, even were it to work, even if it could be shown that it acted as a deterrent to bad behaviour, naughtiness or whatever, it could not be justified on moral grounds.

We must rid ourselves of our habit of hitting children because it is wrong. It is wrong to hit children as it is wrong to hit adults. That is why we abolished it as a judicial punishment, in prisons, in the armed services, and why it is no longer lawful to hit wives (or servants). Much abuse is corporal chastisement which has gone awfully wrong. The early reformers, Wiggin, Key, and Korczak, were right to condemn it. That nine countries have now outlawed it is one of the century's achievements as far as children are concerned. The twenty-first century must consign it to history.

A protected environment requires other measures too. Policies to target domestic violence,[282] child pornography,[283] child prostitution,[284] sex tourism.[285] We have awoken to each of these evils, but we are far from eradicating any of them. And abuse itself must be taken more seriously. Legislation should spell out parental responsibilities:[286] there should be greater guidance on good parenting practices. We should be less chary of intervening. Too many children are left in abusive homes. Care orders should be easier to obtain. They have become more difficult since the House of Lords' ruling in Re H.[287] Although all their Lordships agreed that the ordinary civil standard of proof applied to proof of the threshold test, that is that the child is suffering or is likely to suffer significant harm, the majority refused to accept a simple balance

[282] Where contact is a problem: see H. Saunders, 'Child Contact and Domestic Violence' (1999) 156 Childright 19.

[283] The Criminal Justice Act 1991 has had a minimal impact on the possession and distribution of child pornography. Gaps in the law remain (one is the use of encryption to hide computer pornography).

[284] See D. Barrett, Child Prostitution in Britain: Dilemmas and Practical Responses (London, 1997); Patrick Ayre and David Barrett, 'Young People and Prostitution: an End to the Beginning?' (2000) 14 Children and Society 48. Guidelines in December 1998 recommend that children under 18 be treated as victims rather than offenders. As a result the number of convictions are likely to fall but the case for decriminalization remains.

[285] Some progress has been made: see Sexual Offences (Conspiracy and Incitement Act) 1996 and Sexual Offences Act 1997. The 'sex offender' order introduced by the Crime and Disorder Act 1998 may also assist the management of these perverts.

[286] It already does in Scotland: Children (Scotland) Act 1995 s. 1.

[287] [1996] AC 563.

550

of probabilities test. Lord Nicholls reasoned that a court, when assessing probabilities, should have in mind that 'the more serious the allegation the less likely it is that the event occurred and, hence, the stronger should be the evidence before the court concludes that the allegation is established on the balance of probability'.[288] John Spencer's comment on an earlier case was:

> The consequence of finding that the parents nearly killed their child when they did not will be that the child will be removed from them. The consequence of finding that they did not do it when they did is likely to be the refusal to make a care order, and the child being returned to the people who nearly killed her ... [This theory] about the standard of proof is worse than just not sensible: it is actually perverse. In practice it means that the worse the danger the child is in, the less likely the courts are to remove her from it.[289]

Lord Lloyd, who dissented, pointed to an obvious implication. It was, he thought, 'a strong argument in favour of making the threshold test lower rather than higher'.[290] He thought it 'bizarre' that the more serious the anticipated injury, the more difficult it became for the local authority to satisfy the initial burden of proof, and thereby secure protection for the child. The majority may have believed that the sexual abuse of step-daughters was a rare event—in which case they are wrong. But the question at issue was not the probability of any step-daughter being abused, but the ones in this case. A better comparator population than step-daughters as a whole would be step-daughters in cases where other girls within the family have complained.[291]

The problem is further illustrated by the Court of Appeal decision in *Re M and R*.[292] Although, to quote Connell J at first instance, there was 'a real possibility that [sexual] abuse' had happened, he held, following *Re H* that 'such a possibility cannot justify a conclusion that the threshold criteria are satisfied'.[293] It was argued on appeal that the judge, having found that there was

---

[288] [1996] AC 586.
[289] 'Evidence In Child Abuse Cases—Too High a Price for Too High a Standard' (1994) 6 *Journal of Child Law* 160, commenting on *Re M* [1994] 1 FLR 59. See alse Mary Hayes, 'Reconciling Protection for Children With Justice for Parents' (1997) 17 *Legal Studies* 1. [290] Note 287 above, 577.
[291] See to like effect Mary Hayes and Catherine Williams, *Family Law: Principles, Policy and Practice* (London, 1999), 208.
[292] [1996] 2 FLR 195. [293] Ibid., 199.

*The End of the Century of the Child?*          551

a real possibility of sexual abuse, had erred in not taking into account the allegations of sexual abuse in his assessment of the children's welfare at the discretionary stage. This was despite the balance of psychiatric evidence being unanimously to the effect that sexual abuse had probably occurred. Counsel for the local authority, with the support of the guardian *ad litem*'s counsel, urged that section 1 could be approached differently from section 31 because under section 1 the welfare of the child was the paramount consideration, and this 'justified and indeed required the court to act on possibilities rather than proof on the preponderance of probability'.[294] Butler-Sloss LJ rejected these arguments: 'They amount to the assertion that under s. 1 the welfare of the child dictates the court should act on suspicion or doubts, rather than facts. To our minds the welfare of the child dictates the exact opposite.'[295] *Re H* was followed. 'If . . . the court concludes that the evidence is insufficient to prove sexual abuse in the past, and if the fact of sexual abuse in the past is the only basis for asserting a risk of sexual abuse in the future, then it follows that there is nothing (except suspicion or mere doubts) to show a risk of future sexual abuse.'[296]

Whether these decisions are right or not—and I believe they are wrong—they are obstructing efforts to protect children or delaying the inevitable. It may well be that they are consonant with the dominant ideology of the Children Act. Local authorities are under a duty to provide services for children who would otherwise be at risk of sustaining impaired health or development, and such services must be directed to preventing the need to take care proceedings. The aspiration is liberal, even noble—children should be brought up by their own parents—the reality is that many of these children continue to be abused or neglected (or both) by parents who lack and will never develop acceptable parenting skills. Children are allowed to drift—not in care as was the case pre-Children Act 1975—but in their home environment. 'Children who wait' has taken on a new meaning.[297] We are failing these children. And we do less about children who are victims than children who victimize others. This has always been so, but is strikingly illustrated now by the invention of the parenting order in the

---

[294] Ibid., 202.          [295] Ibid., 203.                    [296] Ibid.
[297] Cf. Jane Rowe and Lydia Lambert, *Children Who Wait* (London, 1973).

552

Crime and Disorder Act 1998.[298] This may be made in a number
of circumstances, including where a child safety order has been
made. The purpose of the order is to require parents to attend
courses which will assist them to prevent their children offending.
The child safety order is a flawed concept and it will not work,[299]
but where one is made a parenting order may also be made. A
parent can be required to attend counselling or guidance sessions
where *inter alia* his child has acted in a manner that caused or was
likely to cause harassment, alarm or distress to someone outside
his household, but not where that parent is rearing his child in a
dysfunctional environment. And this is despite evidence that such
children are more likely to commit the delinquent acts targeted by
the child safety order. Parenting orders—we might have called
them 'parental responsibility orders' were this not already bespo-
ken—should be seen as a weapon in the war against abuse and
neglect. Let us not forget the normative in responsibility.

We might also take up Lord Lloyd's suggestion, whether it was
rhetorical or not, that the threshold test may have to be lowered.
The DHSS *Review of Child Care Law*, the immediate source of
the concept of 'significant harm', argued

Having set an acceptable standard of upbringing for the child, it should
be necessary to show some substantial deficit in that standard. Minor
shortcomings in the health and care provided or minor defects in physical,
psychological or social development should not give rise to any compulsory intervention unless they are having or likely to have, serious and lasting effects upon the child.[300]

Of course, our legislation does not set an acceptable standard of
upbringing. The focus on 'significant' harm can hardly be said to
provide any real guidance to parents. The Act—unlike the Scottish
equivalent[301]—does not even identify what responsibilities a
parent has. Nor has this been addressed in later legislation where
the 'parenting order' has been invented.

That these are difficult questions does not relieve us of responsibility for trying to grapple with them. There are clearly very

[298] In ss. 8–10.
[299] The purpose is to facilitate a balance between protecting the child and the
community. The new order seems to lean further in the direction of the latter than
other contemporary legislation (though see Children Act 1989 s. 25, particularly as
interpreted in *Re M* [1995] 1 FLR 418).
[300] Note 187 above, para. 15.15.   [301] Children (Scotland) Act 1995 s. 1.

## The End of the Century of the Child?    553

many children in our society who suffer from a 'substantial deficit' in their parents' child-rearing skills. However, finding an alternative to 'significant harm' is not easy. Its replacement by a welfare test simpliciter is obviously unacceptable.[302] 'Significant' is a lesser standard than 'serious'; certainly, a lesser standard than 'severe'. To substitute 'considerable' or 'noteworthy' would not assist over much. To replace 'significant' with 'unacceptable' or 'unreasonable' would beg questions. I like Ward LJ's reference to a 'spectrum of abuse' and an 'index of harm'.[303] It occurred in a judgment of sensitivity and it contained real insight into what is meant by 'significant harm'. But it is not language which could find its way into legislation. There is merit in a rethink even if one reaches no decisive conclusion. If there is to be a change, if we are to reconsider our concept of abuse, we must look at these negative features of child rearing within the framework of what we can expect of parents and we must make it clear what responsibilities parents have and what are and what are not acceptable or appropriate child-rearing practices. A more valuable exercise, I think, than trying to define a 'safe smack'!

### Conclusion—The Next Century as the Century of the Child

Ellen Key had a vision that the twentieth century would be the 'century of the child'. No one today would want to adopt this as a blueprint: her views on eugenics and on women, particularly on women and work, betray the era in which she wrote. Many of her proposals have been accepted: the end of illegitimacy (surely we could remove its final vestiges?), the development of anti-corporal punishment laws (which we will inevitably adopt sooner rather than later in the twenty-first century), more child-centred education (but when will we give children, as opposed to their parents, rights in the education system?).

The century has not been the century of the child. We are clearly more child-conscious now than in previous centuries. Our children normally live, and we have created all sorts of structures for them, institutions and expert practices. We have created a

[302] This was rejected by the Review of Child Care Law, n. 187 above, para. 15.10.          [303] *Re B* [1990] 2 FLR 317.

554

childhood which is essentially a protectionist experience.[304]
Perhaps the century has been the century of correct childhood,
with ideas of childhood frequently used as control mechanisms.[305]
And it has been a century in which the child expert has flourished.
There have been enormous achievements too. An understanding
that children have rights, both to protection and welfare and to
autonomy and participation, that children's best interests trump
other considerations, are important achievements. The UN
Convention on the Rights of the Child, which would have been
beyond Ellen Key's wildest dreams, is a pinnacle in twentieth-
century history. In this country the *Gillick* decision, the latest
Children Act—its Scottish counterpart is better—the end of corporal punishment in schools are significant landmarks. And, elsewhere, the development of the children's ombudsman concept and
the passing of anti-spanking laws will be remembered as major
achievements for children in the twentieth century.

But neither we in this country nor the world as a whole can rest
on our laurels. The UN Convention is but a beginning. It focuses
on a number of marginalized groups insufficiently, many of the
rights it endorses could be better formulated, and there remain
gaps to fill. There are far too many reservations. Too many countries, including the United Kingdom, are in breach of too many of
the articles. The implementation mechanisms are far too weak.

In the United Kingdom we have achieved much. But child
poverty remains—indeed, it has got worse. And, so long as it is
with us, so will its correlates. Its impact on health has been
discussed. Child abuse, not addressed by Ellen Key outside the
context of punishment, remains a major problem. Its extirpation
requires the development of a new culture of childhood, one from
which violence, in the presence of and not just against children,
has been removed and one in which children are no longer seen as
sexual objects. Part of this agenda requires us to take children and
their rights more seriously. The *Gillick* decision, and the Children
Act 1989, could have been the beginnings of this with implications
for all areas of children's lives. But the retreat from this ideology

---

[304] See Berry Mayall, *Children's Childhoods Observed and Experienced*
(London, 1994).
[305] See, further, Judith Ennew, *The Sexual Exploitation of Children* (Cambridge,
1986), 21.

*The End of the Century of the Child?*          555

in medical law,[306] in the Education Acts,[307] in measures to target children's deviancy has turned the clock back.[308] It is more likely that we will remember the image of *Bulger* than the argument of *Gillick*.

A new 'Century of The Child' needs to be written. We can learn both from Ellen Key and from this century's experiences. It would address some of the same issues (education, labour, punishment), but many others which have emerged. Poverty, health, and abuse, those issues which I have identified in this paper, are central concerns. The participation of children in war will remain a scarring image of the 1990s. Thirty-five per cent of recruits to the British army even today are under 18 (two of our very few fatalities in the Gulf War were aged 17).[309] The new Protocol to the UN Convention may have some impact but not it seems here.[310] The phenomenon of street children, their existence and their exploitation, is another issue of great concern. In Britain there are relatively few and new legislation[311] imposing strengthened after-care services on local authorities, if interpreted sensitively, may reduce their number. But others may also be refugee children and they constitute yet another of the uncomfortable images of a century of war and dislocation. Half the world's refugees are children, and the concept of 'refugee' employed by the Convention is outdated.[312] Another marginalized group are indigenous children. The Convention innovatively protects them but does so only negatively: they are not to be denied the right to enjoy their own language and culture,[313] but there are no positive obligations to facilitate the practice of these individual and

---

[306] See n. 103, above.

[307] Where children's and parents' interests are conflated. This problem is aggravated where the child is learning disabled and is therefore more reliant on parental decision-making (and see Fortin, n. 75 above, ch. 13).

[308] See Home Office, No More Excuses—A New Approach to Tackling Youth Crime in England and Wales Cm. 3809 (London, 1997); the Crime and Disorder Act 1998; C. Piper, 'The Crime and Disorder Act 1998: Child and Community "Safety"' (1999) 62 *Modern Law Review* 397.

[309] *The Independent*, 22 October 1999.

[310] We will continue to allow 16-year-olds to volunteer. Many, of course, will be care-leavers.                              [311] Children (Leaving Care) Act 2000.

[312] For example, there is no legal definition of an unaccompanied minor. See, further, E. Diane Pask, 'Unaccompanied Refugee and Displaced Children: Jurisdiction, Decision-Making and Representation' (1989) 1 *International Journal of Refugee Law* 2.                              [313] Article 30.

556

community rights. Another category of children, insufficiently addressed in legislation and in the Convention, are disabled children. The model of disability employed tends to emphasize non-discrimination rather than inclusion, and thus to legitimate segregation.[314] Gay children too are marginalized. The non-discrimination provision in the Convention does not extend to sexual orientation.[315] English education law blatantly fails to address the special needs of gay pupils.[316] Half or more of the world's children are girls and too many, even in Britain, are genitally mutilated, forced into marriage or prostitution or sexually abused or exploited or their health needs inappropriately tackled[317] (it is not insignificant that the leading cases establishing that refusal to consent to medical treatment can be overridden both concern female adolescents).[318] If the twenty-first century is to be the century of the child, all these questions, issues and groups will need to be addressed and many changes effected both within and outside this country.

There are other more immediate steps that can and should also be taken. A number of countries have now followed the Norwegian precedent and established a children's ombudsman. I first recommended that we should create one in this country in 1987.[319] It was part of an agenda, which included also the introduction of a 'child impact statement', designed to enable us, in language reminiscent of Dworkin, to take children's rights seriously. The idea was taken up by Newell and Rosenbaum[320] and it is now a central demand of a coalition of children's groups.[321] Whether England adopts the institution or not—and I prefer children's ombudsman to children's commissioner, though nothing of substance hangs on the title—Wales and Scotland will. It is time for us to take the institution seriously. It would give children a higher profile and more political clout. It would offer a channel

---

[314] Articles 2, 23. Even the opposition to sterilization is oblique (see Articles 37 (a), 16, 23(1)).

[315] This is not specified in Article 2, and is not included within 'status'.

[316] See Education Act 1996 s. 403(1) and the Local Government Act 1988 s. 28 (the Government has promised to repeal this but is finding it difficult to do so).

[317] The UN Convention prescribes no minimum age for marriage.

[318] *Re R* [1992] Fam 11; *Re W* [1993] Fam 64.      [319] Note 123 above.

[320] Note 123 above.

[321] The Government resists this. A Private Member's Bill failed to make progress in March 2000.

## *The End of the Century of the Child?* 557

through which representations, complaints, and perceived injustices could be directed. The ombudsman's investigative powers would undoubtedly expose bad practices that might otherwise remain invisible. Would we, to take an obvious example, have had to wait this long and would so many children have had to have suffered so much abuse in institutions, had a children's ombudsman been in office? I would see the institution also vetting legislation, in effect encouraging the development of child impact statements. Too rarely do our legislators consider the implications of laws that they are making for the largest disenfranchised section of the population. As a minority group, children have less purchase on our legislature's considerations than aliens: discrimination on grounds of nationality is at least unlawful. I would see the ombudsman concerned also with law reform. This in relation to children is all too often disjointed and incoherent. Children need 'joined up government' too.

The child impact statement is also worth serious consideration. We are compelled every five years to audit the state of children in this country and, unlike some countries, we take this duty seriously. The audit is our Report to the UN Committee on the Rights of the Child. Am I alone in finding this glossy but insubstantial, combative but eschewing genuine dialogue? It is important that all policies, not just those which obviously affect children, should be subjected to analysis to see what effect that will have on children's lives. I use the word 'policy' rather than 'law' deliberately. It is wider and embraces a congeries of activities which affect our lives, intentionally or unintentionally or indirectly. All too rarely is consideration given to what policies formulated at the level of government, bureaucracy or local state level do to children. Even in children's legislation the unintended or indirect effects of changes are not given the critical attention they demand. But where the policy is not 'headlined' children, immigration policy or housing policy for example, the impact on the lives of children is all too readily glossed over.

Finally, if we are truly to create a century of the child, we should consider passing legislation which might bring the realization of such a goal closer. A Children's Act[322]—rather than a Children Act (the case for this has been put elsewhere). More

---

[322] Michael Freeman, 'The Next Children's Act?' (1998) 28 *Family Law* 341.

558

child-centred policies in areas where children's interests are marginalized, in education law and in the law governing children's deviancy. An anti-spanking law, certainly. But we need something more. I would like to see us enter the new Millennium with a Bill of Rights for Children. We have now 'brought home' the European Convention on Human Rights, but this is largely for adults.[323] We could, of course, follow this up by bringing home the UN Convention on the Rights of the Child. But we could also do better than and give our children a package of rights which goes beyond the Convention, which fully takes account of the interests of marginalized groups and which rethinks rights that have been imperfectly formulated and fills in gaps created by inadvertence or compromise.

   Children do not do well among us. But they are our nation's future. There are few better ways of judging a society than seeing how it treats its weakest and most disadvantaged members. We can do better for our children than we have done, much better, and we can leave a legacy of which we can be proud.

[323] But see Jane Fortin, 'Rights Brought Home for Children' (1999) 62 *Modern Law Review* 350.

# [6]
# Children Are Unbeatable

*The European Court on Human Rights has recently held that the law in the United Kingdom, which allows reasonable corporal punishment to be administered by parents, gives insufficient protection to children. Is the answer to distinguish between inhuman or degrading punishment (for example, with an implement) and ordinary safe smacks or is it to outlaw corporal chastisement by parents altogether? The author argues for the latter which he shows is in line with developments in European jurisprudence. It is also argued that the United Kingdom law is in breach of a number of international law norms, including the United Nations Convention on the Rights of the Child. And, far from this proposal leading to greater intervention into the family, it is argued that the removal of the parental right to smack will lead to less abuse and therefore less interference with parental autonomy.*

I n September 1998 the European Court of Human Rights in *A v. United Kingdom* ([1998] 2 FLR 959) unanimously held that the law in the United Kingdom, which allows parents to inflict reasonable physical chastisement, breaches Article 3 of the European Convention on Human Rights (in effect, when this becomes law, the Human Rights Act 1998). Article 3 states that 'No one shall be subjected to torture or to inhuman or degrading treatment or punishment'. The Court found that the law in the United Kingdom did not provide 'adequate protection' to children.

> Children and other vulnerable individuals, in particular, are entitled to State protection, in the form of effective deterrence, against serious breaches of personal integrity.

proclaimed the Court. The case in question related to a boy repeatedly beaten, between the ages of five and eight, by his step-father with a garden cane. The step-father had been acquitted on the ground that his assaults amounted to reasonable chastisement. Parents and others are regularly so acquitted.

## English law

English law is found in the Children and Young Persons Act 1933 (its roots are of course much deeper: on religious roots see

Greven, 1991). The corporal punishment provision itself can be traced back to the Prevention of Cruelty to Children Act 1889. Section 1 of the 1933 Act makes it a criminal offence, inter alia, wilfully to assault a child. Liability is limited by sub-section 7 which states:

> nothing in this section shall be construed as affecting the right of any parent, teacher or other person having the lawful charge of a child or young person to administer punishment to him.

Legislation goes no further: it is the common law which stipulates that the punishment must be 'moderate and reasonable' (in recent discussion the epithet 'moderate' seems to have got lost). In the leading case of *R. v. Hopley*, Lord Chief Justice Cockburn emphasised that

> by the law a parent ... may, for the purpose of correcting what is evil in the child, inflict moderate and reasonable corporal punishment—always, however with this condition: that it is moderate and reasonable (see (1860) 2 F and F 202).

It is difficult to state definitively what constitutes moderate and reasonable corporal punishment (Freeman, 1988; McGillivray, 1997). The test is open-textured and vague, deliberately so (Katz, 1998). Thus, the law says nothing about the part of the body on which the chastisement may be inflicted, whether an implement may be used, whether age is relevant or the child's gender material. It is surprising that, with corporal punishment so institutionalised (it will only disappear from the school setting completely with the coming into effect of the School Standards and Framework Act 1998, S. 131) that, outside the former approved school context, it was so little regulated.

## Earlier responses

The Government's view is clear: it does not believe that the right way forward is to ban all physical punishment (Department of Health, 1998, para 5.10). It will therefore respond to the European Court's decision by outlawing inhuman or degrading punishment by parents. There is a clear precedent in the response to the *Costello-Roberts* decision ([1994] E.H.R.R. 112): in that case the European Court found there was no breach of Article 3 when a seven-year old at a 'prep' school was slippered (the minimum level of severity had not been reached), but the case was 'at or near the borderline'. The result was the inclusion within the Education Act 1993 (see now Education Act 1996, S. 548(2)) of the Convention concept and independent schools were warned that they could not lawfully administer 'inhuman or degrading' corporal punishment. And they were advised that, when determining whether punishment is inhuman or degrading

> ... regard shall be had to all the circumstances of the case, including the reason for giving it, how soon after the event it is given, its nature, the manner and circumstances in which it is given, the persons involved and its mental and physical effects. (S. 549(2)).

The response to *Costello-Roberts* decision can have satisfied few. It certainly did not satisfy the United Nations Committee on the Rights of the Child (1995a), and it is doubtful whether independent schools can have found it helpful. Given its formal, institutionalised setting, it is questionable whether any corporal punishment in a school would have conformed with the legislation (for agreement, see Fortin, 1998).

The last Government had two further opportunities to tackle physical chastisement. The Scottish Law Commission had distinguished 'an ordinary smack by loving parents' (1992,

132

para 2.89) from punishment with an implement. It accordingly recommended that the law should remove the defence of reasonable chastisement in the exercise of parental rights, if the conduct complained of involved hitting the child with an implement, or in a way that actually injured the child or involved a risk of injury, or caused, or risked causing, pain or discomfort lasting more than a very short time (1992, para 2.105). Faced with such casuistry, hardly surprisingly the Government simply omitted any reference to corporal punishment or to this proposed reform in the Children (Scotland) Act 1995. And the Education Act 1997, which addressed the issue of school discipline and gave teachers the ability to use 'such force as is reasonable in the circumstances' (for example to break up fights or exclude pupils from the classroom) simply did not pronounce on the issue of corporal punishment, although arguably the provision quoted legitimates it (see S. 4, inserting S. 550A into Education Act 1996 and Hamilton, 1997).

## The smack of statism?

The recent European Court decision thus offers a golden opportunity to end the 'century of the child' (Key, 1909) by striking a blow for children. Can we really begin a new era of human rights if we deny children such a fundamental one? The time has come to acknowledge that half-measures will not do. Conceptual distinctions (between ordinary safe smacks and inhuman or degrading punishment) do not work, and are morally bankrupt (imagine legislation which allowed husbands to smack their wives but withheld from them the power to use an implement!). We must follow the examples of other countries and make it unlawful to assault children. This is one 'smack of statism' (Amiel, 1988, criticising the author of this article) which we should be eager to embrace.

## The experiences of other countries

We should be encouraged, and not deterred, by the experiences of other countries. In eight the corporal chastisement of children by parents is outlawed by legislation. In a ninth, Italy, the Supreme Court ruled in 1996 (Foro It. II 1996, 407) that the use of violence by parents for educational purposes was no longer lawful. A tenth, Belgium, is about to respond to the child sex murders scandal, inter alia, with legislation guaranteeing children the right to 'respect for [their] person ... and individuality' and stressing that 'they shall not be subjected to degrading treatment, nor to any other form of physical or psychological violence' (Belgian Senate, 1997–8 Session: Proposal for a Law Inserting an Article 371 bis into the Code Civil).

Sweden was the first country to ban all corporal punishment of children (Newell, 1989; Olson, 1984; Durrant and Olsen, 1997). It did so nearly 20 years ago in 1979 (*Children and Parents Code*, ch. 6, §1(2)). Their statute, as amended in 1983, provides

> Children are entitled to care, security and a good upbringing. They shall be treated with respect for their person and their distinctive character and may not be subject to corporal punishment or any other injurious or humiliating treatment. (*Children and Parents Code*, ch. 6, §1.)

The 1979 law was passed by a vote of 259 to six. It is clear that, although there was opposition to the law (Ziegert, 1983), by 1981 three quarters of the population supported it. It will have been observed that the Swedish punishment law does not provide for legal sanctions in case of violation. The law was passed as social engineering (Pound, 1954;

Cotterrell, 1992; Agell, 1998) rather than as a measure to intrude upon family privacy or haul parents before courts (compare Goldstein and others, 1996). But parents can be prosecuted under the penal code (and the child could seek damages if injured). Prosecutions are very rare. But children can be taken into care and parents can lose custody in divorce disputes. The Swedish law has worked and it continues to be supported (in 1995 78 per cent of Swedish adults thought corporal punishment of children unaccept-able) (Statistics Sweden, 1996) and this despite the move away from permissiveness in child-rearing, with which we associate Sweden (Haeuser, 1992; Pringle, 1998). The Swedish law is only part of a strategy to create a new culture of childhood, one in which children are identified as persons and rights-holders, but it is an important part (Ziegert, 1987).

Finland followed the Swedish example in 1983 (its legislature passing the ban unanimously) (Child Custody and Right of Access Act). Savolainen, who drafted the legislation, explained it thus:

> ... the Act attempts to establish certain "positive" guidelines for the upbringing of the child. [It] makes it absolutely clear that all violations against the child's integrity (whether "physical" or "spiritual") which would constitute a criminal offence if committed by a third person ... are equally punishable ... when committed by a parent with the intent to discipline the child ... The Act explicitly forbids also any degrading treatment ... (quoted in Newell, 1989, p. 87).

Corporal punishment is also a breach of Finland's penal code (ch. 21(5)). In 1993 Finland's Supreme Court found a guardian guilty of petty assault because he pulled his child's hair and slapped his fingers (1993: 151, Helsinki 1994, 685). The Court held that the penal code was to be applied 'when parents or guardians employ physical violence on their child, even if they consider it a means of upbringing'. As in Sweden, children may seek damages and, as in Sweden, courts may be influenced by parents' use of physical discipline in deciding on custody cases.

In 1987 Norway too outlawed the corporal punishment of children (Parent and Child Act, Art. 30 §3). The model employed is the Swedish one: so no sanctions are attached to the law, the principal objective of which is to effect social change. Prosecutions can take place under Norway's Criminal Act (for which there must be bodily injury) (Criminal Act, Art. 228 §1). There is also a statutory prohibition against neglect or maltreatment of children. Again, a tort action can be brought (Tort Act 1969, nr. 26, Arts 3–5), and a parent's use of corporal punishment may affect the outcome of a custody dispute.

Austria became the first non-Nordic country to outlaw corporal punishment, doing so in 1989 and by a unanimous vote (Bernat, 1990–1). The law provides that the child must obey the instructions of his parents. However, in their orders parents must consider the age, development and personality of the child; the use of force and the infliction of physical and psychological harm are not permitted (ABGB, Section 146(a)). The Act provides no legal remedies for the corporally punished child, but parents may be prosecuted under provisions of the penal code. Again, the legislation is targeted at education of parents rather than the use of criminal penalties. There is no evidence of any increase in prosecutions but there is clear evidence that community sentiment has shifted in line with the legislation. A study commissioned by the Ministry of the Environment, Youth and the Family found (in the early 1990s) that 67.5 per cent of mothers and 68.8 per cent of fathers categorically rejected serious corporal punishment as a means of education (Division for Children's Rights, 1996).

134

The most interesting case to emerge from corporal punishment legislation is from Austria, where the Supreme Court in 1993 had to interpret the ban in the context of a custody dispute. The parents had agreed that the father should have custody of the two sons. He was a strict disciplinarian and used quite severe corporal punishment. The court found no bodily injury had occurred to either boy. The mother challenged the custody arrangement on the basis that the child-rearing methods used by the father were not in the best interests of the children. Most interestingly, the argument was raised that the boys themselves were not offended by their father's method of raising them. Nevertheless, the Court took the view that the 1989 law not only proscribes bodily injury and physical torture but any other form of ill-treatment which fails to respect human dignity, even though the child affected does not consider it to be 'harm'. It accordingly concluded that the boys' best interests were in jeopardy and granted the mother's application for a transfer of custody (Bernat, 1993–4; Freeman, 1993).

Cyprus outlawed the corporal punishment of children in 1993 (Act of June 17, 1994, Law 147(1)). The Cypriot law is interesting for two reasons: first, penal sanctions attach, indeed are increased because the violence is used against a member of the family (S. 4(1)); and, secondly, because not only is force against children prohibited, but so is violence in the presence of children (S. 3(3)), an acknowledgement unique in legislation that domestic violence is a form of child abuse (Mullender and Morley, 1994).

It is commonly thought that Denmark outlawed corporal chastisement in its Minors' Act 1985 (compare Nielsen and Frost, 1996). The Act provided that 'Parental custody implies the obligation to protect the child against physical and psychological violence and against other harmful treatment'. But this did not abolish parents' rights to inflict corporal punishment: what was known as legally inflicted punishment ('loving revselse') remained (indeed, an explanatory memorandum accompanying the 1985 law indicated that light corporal punishment was allowed) (Graversen, 1986–7). But in 1997 Denmark joined the other Nordic countries in prohibiting totally all corporal punishment of children. The child is to be 'treated with respect for its personality and may not be subjected to corporal punishment or any other offensive treatment' (Parental Custody Amendment Act, ns. 416 §1). As with the other Nordic models, prosecutions may take place under the Criminal Code for assault and battery and other related crimes, but the goal of the legislation is to educate rather than to subject parents to penal sanctions.

There has been legislation also in Latvia (this came into force on 8 July 1998) and Croatia (operative at the beginning of 1999) and it is imminent in Belgium and Germany (where the Minister for Families in the new Government is committed to prohibiting all corporal punishment). It is also promised elsewhere. More dramatic is the Italian Supreme Court's intervention. In the absence of a strict system of precedent it cannot be stated with certainty how its ruling will be regarded, though it must be assumed to be of high authority and concomitantly influential. The Court upheld the conviction of Natalino Cambria for maltreating his ten-year old daughter (he subjected her to beatings, he said to correct her behaviour). Although there was serious violence in *Cambria's* case, the Court did not limit itself to ruling upon the facts of the case (unlike the European Court in *A. v. United Kingdom*). Rather, it attempted to establish the legal principle that the use of violence against children even for educational purposes is never permissible. The judges who decided *Cambria* were influenced by the Italian Constitution of 1948 and laws built upon this and by international law, particularly the UN Convention of the Rights of the Child. The Court's opinion relies on a number of articles of the Convention, notably the non-discrimination principle in Article 2, the emphasis on a child's best interests in Articles 3 and 18, and Article 19's prohibition on the use of violence against children. If our legislature does not take the initiative, an English court so minded, particularly with the Human Rights Act such an influential backdrop, could construe our common law similarly (and see Lord Scarman's judgment in *Gillick v. West Norfolk and Wisbech AHA* [1986] AC 112). In Italy the uprooting of corporal punishment is seen as part of the move away from authoritarianism: our experiences of this may not be as profound (we didn't experience Fascism) but they remain pervasive (particularly in the family context). And it may be, accordingly, to the courts that we need to look.

## International law and corporal punishment

The arguments can be found in the experiences of other countries. They can also be found in international law. I reject the public/private distinction in interpreting international human rights instruments (Clapham, 1993, pp. 91–4; and for a feminist critique, Romany, 1993). If these apply to schools, then they apply equally to parents. The UN Convention on the Rights of the Child acknowledges this. Throughout it is clear that its articles apply to states parties and private actors. And this applies elsewhere as well.

The UN Convention on the Rights of the Child has been ratified by every state except Somalia and the United States. The Convention established the Committee on the Rights of the Child to monitor compliance with the Convention. This Committee is unequivocal on corporal punishment

> ... the Committee has paid particular attention to the child's right to physical integrity ... It has stressed that corporal punishment of children is incompatible with the Convention and has often proposed the revision of existing legislation, as well as the development of awareness and education campaigns, to prevent child abuse and the physical punishment of children. (UN Committee on the Rights of the Child, 1994, Annex IV, 63.)

It has criticised many countries, the laws of which allow corporal punishment of children. The United Kingdom was so censured in 1995 (UN Committee on the Rights of the Child, 1995a, paras 16 and 31).

Of the provisions in the Convention, it is Article 19 which offers the clearest indictment of corporal punishment.

> States Parties shall take all appropriate legislative, administrative, social and educational measures to protect the child from all forms of physical or mental violence, injury or abuse, neglect or negligent treatment, maltreatment or exploitation, including sexual abuse, while in the care of parents, legal guardians or any other person who has the care of the child.

It must be clear that this article proscribes corporal punishment, though it does not refer to it as such (and see Newell, 1995). If the article targets only beating, as some would claim, then why does it refer separately to 'all forms of physical ... violence' as well as to 'injury or abuse'? The Committee's Guidelines on the Form and Content of Periodic Reports requires reports to indicate 'whether legislation (criminal and/or family law) includes a prohibition on all forms of physical and mental violence, including corporal punishment' (UN Committee on the Rights of the Child, 1996). And the Committee's criticisms of states parties on corporal punishment including the report on the United Kingdom (UN Committee on the Rights of the Child, 1995a, para 31) have referred to Article 19

136

specifically. It was the United Kingdom, perhaps predictably, which argued that there was a justification for reasonable corporal punishment within the Convention (in Article 5). This provides that states parties are to respect the rights of parents to direct and guide the child.

But the response could not have been clearer.

> It must be borne in mind, however, that article 19 of the Convention required all appropriate measures, including legislative measures, to be taken to protect the child against, inter alia, physical violence. A way should thus be found of striking the balance between the responsibilities of the parents and the rights and evolving capacities of the child that was implied in article 5 of the Convention. There was no place for corporal punishment within the margin of discretion accorded in article 5 to parents in the exercise of their responsibilities (UN Committee on the Rights of the Child, 1995a).

Support for the view that corporal punishment infringes the human rights of children can be found in other articles of the Convention as well.

Thus, Article 37, proscribing 'torture or other cruel, inhuman or degrading treatment or punishment' (the language of the European Convention's Article 3) clearly embraces disciplinary measures which fall within the category of 'inhuman' or 'degrading' punishment. And, in the light of a construction which applies such provisions to the so-called 'private' sphere, there is no reason why the prohibition should not apply to family life, as well as, for example, to the school system. Article 28, paragraph 2, which applies to school discipline is also relevant: it stresses the child's human dignity, a value which is found throughout the Convention. Article 39 is also relevant. This directs that states parties shall take all appropriate measures to promote the physical and psychological recovery of children who have been victims of cruel or degrading treatment such that 'recovery ... shall take place in an environment which fosters the ... dignity of the child'. What 'dignity' can a child have if he is not guaranteed bodily integrity (see Cohen, 1984)? As we saw, the Italian Supreme Court certainly understands this. Article 24, paragraph 3, which requires states parties to take 'all effective and appropriate measures with a view to abolishing traditional practices prejudicial to the health of children', though not specifically targeted at corporal punishment, can also be read in support of the end of this practice. Its target is, of course, female genital mutilation (Detrick, 1992), but the language used in the article can be interpreted more broadly.

A child's right to be free from corporal punishment can also be read from other principles within the Convention. The non-discrimination principle in Article 2 should be read not just to exclude discrimination between children (for example on grounds of race or gender) but also against children. In the United Kingdom, as in most of the civilised world, only children can be lawfully subjected to corporal punishment. The principle in Article 3 that 'in all actions concerning children ... the best interests of the child shall be a primary consideration', though not specifically directed to parents, must constrain the autonomy allowed parents by the state. It offers a framework for parent-child relations that excludes the corporal punishment of children. And, the provision in Article 12 that the child should be allowed to participate in all matters affecting his or her life cannot be consistently upheld in the context of a practice which turns the child into an object rather than a social actor. Participation implies dialogue, negotiation, peaceful resolution of conflict, not the imposition of a 'solution' by force.

Support for the child to be free from corporal punishment can be found also in inter-national instruments which ante-date the UN Convention on the Rights of the Child (Van Bueren, 1998). There can be no doubt that these international instruments protect children's human rights (It is astonishing that the question is even debated (Bennett, 1987; Heintze, 1992)). Thus, Article 7 of the International Covenant on Civil and Political Rights which prohibits torture and cruel, inhuman or degrading treatment or punishment should rule out the corporal punishment of children. This is the view also of the UN Human Rights Committee (1996), which is charged with monitoring compliance with the Covenant, though it stops short of condemning all corporal punishment—in its view it has to be excessive—and it emphasises the protection of children in educational institutions—an unfortunate limitation.

The applicability of the Torture Convention is in more doubt. Orthodox interpretation would limit this to state actors and exclude private perpetrators. Thus interpreted, it would apply to schools but not to parents. But it has been suggested, for example, that it applies to domestic violence against women. Why, it may be argued, should it not apply to states which fail to take steps to avert private violence, whether this be domestic violence, the sexual abuse of children or corporal punishment (Copelon, 1994; Paust, 1992)? The Torture Convention prohibits torture, defined as 'any act by which severe pain or suffering, whether physical or mental' is caused to the victim. English law complies with this prohibition. But it also prohibits cruel, inhuman or degrading treatment or punishment. The Committee Against Torture has stated, as recently as 1997, that corporal punishment is incompatible with the Convention, and has said that it need not be excessive to come within the prohibition (UN Committee on Human Rights, 1997).

Article 3 of the European Convention has already been referred to. Although the European Court did not interpret the ban on inhuman or degrading punishment to rule out all corporal punishment—an omission immediately seized upon by defenders of corporal punishment—it limited its ruling to the facts before it. This is the approach usually adopted, as it would be by an English court, and it would be wrong to read too much into this. It is true that the European Commission in this case stressed that its finding—which the Court upheld—

> does not mean that Article 3 is to be interpreted as imposing an obligation on States to protect, through their criminal law, against any form of physical rebuke, however mild, by a parent of a child.

It is significant that the Court did not repeat this.

The Court in *A. v. United Kingdom* did not find it necessary to consider whether Article 8 of the European Convention had been breached. This Article provides that 'Everyone has the right to respect for his private ... life'. In *Costello-Roberts* the Court observed that the

> possibility that circumstances might exist in which Article 8 could be regarded as affording a protection which went beyond that given by Article 3 was not excluded.

And, in an earlier case, the Commission concluded that a complaint was actionable under Article 8 where children were struck with a leather strap on the hand and the buttocks at school (*App. No. 10592/83 v. United Kingdom* 9 EHHR 278). The Commission in *A v. United Kingdom* agreed with this interpretation but did not consider the applicability of Article 8 on its merits to the facts of the case. By contrast, Swedish parents who took their government to the European Court claiming their privacy rights were infringed by the Swedish ban on corporal punishment failed (*X Y and Z v. Sweden*, 1983 5 EHRR 147). This decision should not be overlooked: it demonstrates that banning corporal punishment does not breach the norms of European jurisprudence.

Challenges to corporal punishment using Article 8 may prove more fruitful. The 'concept of privacy encompasses the concept of bodily integrity' (Van Bueren, 1995, p. 251) and the punishment would not have to be severe to come within Article 8's scope. If corporal punishment breaches Article 8, it must also breach privacy guarantees in other conventions, for example Article 12 of the Universal Declaration and Article 17 of the Covenant on Civil and Political Rights. And, as to the latter, the Human Rights Committee is of the view that the non-discrimination principle in Article 24 applies throughout its articles and thus to Article 17, and in effect this too rules out corporal punishment of children on privacy grounds (UN Human Rights Committee, 1989).

English law is thus out of line with the increasing trend in Europe, is in breach of the UN Convention on the Rights of the Child and is in conflict with a number of other norms of international law. And yet at a time when we are putting on the statute book our most important human rights legislation ever (the Human Rights Act 1998), it appears the government is not prepared to grasp the nettle and pass legislation outlawing corporal punishment by parents. It continues to take refuge in a narrow interpretation of the UN Convention and of European jurisprudence. We can expect legislation modelled on the 1993 Education Act and, no doubt, there will be accompanying guidance.

## Drafting a compromise—the third way?

Who would want to be the civil servant charged with drafting this? What is a 'loving' smack? Or a 'safe' smack? Is it lawful to smack babies? Or disabled children? Are you to be allowed to hit a child's head, or face, or 'box' his ears? And what of his bottom, given the sexual connotations? (A whole industry has grown up on the back of this practice, as a gaze at any telephone booth in Central London tells us, and see Anthony, 1995). Is there to be a maximum age? (Can you strike a Gillick competent child?) (cf. Eekelaar, 1986 and Sedley, 1986). Will it be permissible to remove a child's clothes? Will an implement be totally ruled out? (Odd, isn't it, that some would countenance a punch with a fist or a powerful blow with the hand but rule out a strap on the palm of the hand or the back of a leg?)

And who is to be allowed to hit children? Parents? Those with parental responsibility? Those to whom limited parental responsibility is delegated (a grandparent whilst parents take a weekend break)? Will step-parents to able to smack children? What of 'live-in' boyfriends? Nannies? Au pairs? Baby-sitters? It is not an enviable task.

And it is—everyone must realise this—a short-term measure. Even if a 'loving smack' (a classic oxymoron if ever there was one) is not currently contrary to Article 3 of the European Convention, the development of the European Convention is such that it can only be a matter of years, three perhaps or five, before it is so held. And it may be found to breach Article 8 even sooner. The UN Committee on the Rights of the Child, when it next reports on the United Kingdom in 1999, is bound to condemn our reluctance to free children from corporal chastisement. Our resistance is likely to be as unsuccessful as

Canute's. Would it not be better if our government took the initiative now, rather than being forced to do so in a few years' time? Already, the Health Education Authority, in a pamphlet sent to all pregnant women, advises against smacking, and a leaflet, produced by the NSPCC and sponsored by the Department of Health, emphasises that 'it's never OK to shake or smack a baby'.

There is a concern that making it unlawful to hit children will lead to greater intervention into the family, more prosecutions of parents, more care proceedings (Thompson, 1993). But this is not the experience of countries which have passed such legislation. Nor is it the reason why those who favour legislation want it. Legislation is needed to change attitudes, and you do not change attitudes by half-measures. Because we believe that racism is morally wrong, we have made racial discrimination in most areas of life unlawful; we did not distinguish serious discrimination from more trivial varieties. Legislation can mould moral behaviour, even in expressive areas of life like parent–child relations (Olivecrona, 1939 but compare Dror, 1959). The Swedish experience is testimony to this. Of course, legislation by itself is not enough and must be accompanied by an education programme, as in Sweden (Justice Department, 1979; see also Leach, 1997 and Straus, 1994). It is important too that children are reared in an environment free of violence (Nilsson, 1991). Outlawing corporal punishment will more likely lead to fewer prosecutions—because there will be less abuse—to fewer care proceedings, and also to less delinquency and violent crime and thus a reduction in the prison population, because corporal punishment teaches violence and the victims of today become tomorrow's violent criminals. Banning corporal punishment could thus be justified on utilitarian grounds. But even were it to work, even if it could be shown that it acted as a deterrent, it could not be justified on moral grounds.

We must rid ourselves of our habit of hitting children because it is wrong. It is wrong to hit children as it is wrong to hit adults. That is why we abolished it as a judicial punishment, in prisons, in the armed services, and why it is no longer lawful to hit wives or servants. Governments must lead. They must send out clear messages. The 'loving smack' offers instead contradiction and confusion. There is only one answer to the European Court's decision: it did not go far enough and we will finish its job. There can be no better way of greeting the passage into law of the Human Rights Act 1998 than by affirming we have respect for all persons, their dignity and their bodily integrity, and demonstrating this by making it unlawful to hit children.

# References

Agell, A 'Should and can family law influence social behaviour?', *in* Eekelaar, J and Nhlapo, T *eds* (1998) *The Changing Family.* Oxford: Hart Publishing

Amiel, B (1988) 'The smack of statism', *The Times*

Anthony, E (1995) *Thy Rod and Staff.* London: Little Brown

Bennett, WH (1987) 'A critique of the emerging Convention on the Rights of the Child', *Cornell International Law Journal,* **20**, 1–64

Bernat, E (1990–1) 'Austria: the final stages of three decades of family law reform', *Journal of Family Law,* **29**, 285–295

Bernat, E (1993–4) 'Austria: legislating for assisted reproduction and interpreting the ban on corporal punishment', *University of Louisville Journal of Family Law,* **32**, 247–253

Clapham, A (1993) *Human Rights in the Private Sphere.* Oxford: Clarendon Press

140 ]

Cohen, CP (1984) 'Freedom from corporal punishment: one of the human rights of children', *Human Rights Annual*, **II**, 95–130
Copelon, R (1994) 'Regaining the egregious in the everyday: domestic violence as torture', *Columbia Human Rights Law Review*, **25**, 291–367
Cotterrell, R (1992) *Sociology of Law: An Introduction*. London: Butterworths
Department of Health (1998) *Supporting Families*. HMSO
Detrick, S (1992) *The United Nations Conventions on the Rights of the Child: A Guide to the Travaux Préparatoires*. Dordrecht, Martinus Nijhoff
Division for Children's Rights (1996) *Initial Report of Austria in Accordance with Article 44 of the UN Convention on the Rights of the Child*. Vienna
Dror, Y (1959) 'Law and social change', *Tulane Law Review*, **33**, 787–802
Durrant, JE and Olsen, GM (1997) 'Parenting and public policy: contextualizing the Swedish corporal punishment ban', *Journal of Social Welfare and Family Law*, **19**, 443–461
Eekelaar, J (1986) 'Gillick: further limits on parents' right to punish', *Childright*, **28**, 9–10
Fortin, J (1998) *Children's Rights and the Developing Law*. London: Butterworths
Freeman, M (1988) 'Time to stop hitting our children', *Childright*, **51**, 5–8
Freeman, M (1993) 'Austria interprets its punishment ban', *International Journal of Children's Rights*, **1**, 393–394
Goldstein, J and others (1996) *The Best Interests of The Child*. New York: Free Press
Graversen, J (1986–7) 'Denmark: custody reform', *Journal of Family Law*, **25**, 81–89
Greven, P (1991) *Spare the Child*. New York: Alfred A Knopf
Haeuser, A (1992) 'Swedish parents don't spank', *Mothering*, **63**, 42
Hamilton, C (1997) 'Physical restraint of children: a new sanction for schools', *Childright*, **138**, 14–16
Heintze and H-J 'The UN convention and the network of international human rights protection by the UN', in Freeman, M and Veerman, P eds (1992) *The Ideologies of Children's Rights*. Dordrecht, Martinus Nijhoff
Justice Department, Sweden (1989) *Can You Bring Up Children Successfully Without Smacking and Spanking?* Stockholm: Justice Department
Katz, SN 'Parental rights and social responsibilities in American child protection law', in Eekelaar, J and Nhlapo, T eds (1998) *The Changing Family*. Oxford, Hart Publishing
Key, E (1909) *The Century of the Child*. New York: Putnam (originally published as Barnets Århundrade, Albert Bonniers Förlag, Stockholm, in 1900)
Leach, P (1997) *Why Speak Out Against Smacking?* London, Barnardo's
McGillivray, A (1997) ' "He'll learn it on his body": Disciplining childhood in Canadian law', *International Journal of Children's Rights*, **5**, 193–242
Mullender, A and Morley, R (1994) *Children Living with Domestic Violence*. London: Whiting and Birch
Newell, P (1989) *Children Are People Too*. London, Bedford Square Press
Newell, P 'Respecting children's rights to physical integrity', in Franklin, B ed (1995) *Handbook of Children's Rights*. London, Routledge
Nielsen, L and Frost, L 'Children and the convention: the Danish debate', in Freeman, M ed (1996) *Children's Rights: A Comparative Perspective*. Aldershot, Dartmouth
Nilsson, N (1991) 'Children and the commercial exploitation of violence in Sweden' *Current Sweden 384*. Stockholm, Swedish Institute
Olivecrona, K (1939) *Law As Fact*. Copenhagen: Ejaar Munksgaard
Olson, DA (1984) 'The Swedish Ban of Corporal Punishment', *Brigham Young University Law Review*
Paust, JJ (1992) 'The other side of right: private duties under human rights law', *Harvard Human Rights Journal*, **5**, 51–86
Pound, R (1954) *Philosophy of Law*. New Haven: Yale University Press
Pringle, K (1998) *Children and Social Welfare in Europe*. Open University Press
Romany, C (1993) 'Women as aliens: a feminist critique of the public/private distinction in international human rights law', *Harvard Human Rights Journal*, **6**, 87–124
Scottish Law Commission (1992) *Report on Family Law*. Edinburgh: HMSO
Sedley, S (1986) 'Child welfare limits parents' rights to punish', *Childright*, **26**, 17–19

Statistics Sweden (1996) *Demography, The Family and Children: Spanking and Other Forms of Physical Punishment—A Study of Adults' and Middle School Students' Opinions, Experience and Knowledge.* Stockholm, Statistics Sweden

Straus, M (1994) *Beating The Devil Out of Them.* New York: Lexington

Thompson, RA 'Developmental research and legal policy: toward a two way street', *in* Cicchetti, D and Toth, SL *eds* (1993) *Child Abuse, Child Development and Social Policy.* Norwood, NJ, Ablex

United Nations Committee on the Rights of the Child (1994) *Report of Seventh Session.* UN Doc CRC/C/34. Geneva

United Nations Committee on the Rights of the Child (1995a) *Concluding Observations of the Committee on the Rights of the Child: United Kingdom of Great Britain and Northern Ireland.* 8th Session. UN Doc CRC/C/15 Add 34. Geneva

United Nations Committee on the Rights of the Child (1995b) *Summary Record of the 205th Meeting.* UNGAOR, Committee on the Rights of the Child, 8th Session. UN Doc CRC/C/SR 205

United Nations Committee on the Rights of the Child (1996) *General Guidelines Regarding The Form and Contents of Periodic Reports to be Submitted by States Parties Under Article 44, para 1(b) of the Convention.* UNGAOR, 343rd Meeting. UN Doc CRC/C/58. Geneva

United Nations Human Rights Committee (1989) *General Comments Under 40, Paragraph 4 of the Covenant.* UNGAOR, 35th Session, 891st Meeting, General Comment (35) 3/(Art 24). UN Doc CCPR/C/21/Add 7. Geneva

United Nations Human Rights Committee (1996) *Compilation of General Comments and General Recommendations Adopted by the Human Rights Treaty Bodies.* UNGAOR, Human Rights Committee, General Comment. UN Doc HRI/GEN/1/Rev 2. Geneva

United Nations Human Rights Committee (1997) *Report of The Special Rapporteur.* UN Committee on Human Rights, 53rd Session, Provisional agenda, Item 8(a). UN Doc E/CN 4/1997/7. Geneva

Van Bueren, G (1995) *The International Law on the Rights of The Child.* Dordrecht: Martinus Nijhoff

Van Bueren, G (1998) *Childhood Abused.* Aldershot: Ashgate

Ziegert, KA (1983) 'The Swedish prohibition of corporal punishment: a preliminary report', *Journal of Marriage and the Family*, **45**, 917–926

Ziegert, KA (1987) 'Children's rights and the supportive function of law: the case of Sweden', *Journal of Comparative Family Studies*, **18**, 157–174

## Contributor's details

**Michael Freeman** is Professor of English Law at University College London and editor of the *International Journal of Children's Rights.*

# [7]
# Saviour Siblings

## Introduction

The advent of medically assisted reproduction has had many consequences barely anticipated at the time of the Warnock report[1] and not provided for in the Human Fertilisation and Embryology Act 1990. Cell nucleus replacement is one such example – this is now the subject of legislation[2] – and pre-implantation genetic diagnosis (PGD) and tissue typing (HLA) is another.[3] PGD was first successfully used in 1989 by removing a single cell at the eight-cell stage of embryonic development and testing the sex of the cells, so that a female embryo could be implanted and a sex-linked disorder that occurred only in males avoided.[4] Two years later, the same doctor tested for a genetic mutation that causes cystic fibrosis and enabled a high-risk couple to implant an embryo free of the disease. Today, PGD is used to screen for a handful of genetic diseases, including beta thalassaemia, sickle-cell disease, haemophilia, Tay-Sachs and fragile X syndrome. The procedure is expensive, is not available everywhere, and can be used to target only a small number of conditions.[5] But it is foreseeable that none of these limitations will last long.

How are we to respond to PGD? It has clearly proved controversial in two areas: sex selection,[6] where this is not for therapeutic purposes, and where it is used to

---

1   *Report of the Committee of Inquiry into Human Fertilisation and Embryology*, Cmnd. 9314/1984 (Warnock Report) chapter 12 of which looks at 'Possible Future Developments in Research including "selective breeding"' (para 12.16).

2   Human Reproductive Cloning Act 2001.

3   See Botkin, J.R., 'Ethical Issues and Practical Problems in Preimplantation Genetic Diagnosis', (1998) 26 *Journal of Law, Medicine and Ethics*, 17-28.

4   See HFEA/ACGT Consultation Document, *Pre-Implantation Genetic Diagnosis*, London, 1999, para 10.

5   And see Wells, D. and Sherlock, J.K., 'Strategies for Preimplantation Genetic Diagnosis of Single Gene Disorders by DNA Amplification', (1998) 18 *Prenatal Diagnosis*, 1389-1401. There have been only 500 cases involving PGD since the 1990 Act was passed (see H.C. Science and Technology Committee, *Human Reproductive Technologies and the Law*, 5th Report of Session 2004-05 (March 2005), para.109).

6   The Warnock Report, *supra cit.*, contains an early discussion of this: see paras 9.4-9.12; see also The House of Commons Select Committee, *supra cit.*, at paras 131-142. The

produce a child to save the life of an existing child. The latter is the subject of this chapter. But first a few preliminary points.

As has already been indicated, PGD is not specifically tackled in the 1990 Act. But since it involves the creation and use of embryos, it must be licensed by the Human Fertilisation and Embryology Authority (HFEA) to be lawful.[7] The HFEA has licensed PGD for certain severe or life-threatening disorders at a limited number of clinics.[8] It has also firmly rejected the use of PGD for sex selection for social reasons.[9] Some jurisdictions, for example Victoria, Australia, have specifically banned sex selection, in Victoria's case unless it is necessary for the child to be of a particular sex so as to avoid the risk of transmission of a genetic abnormality or a disease to the child.[10] There is legislation in some US states too, and also (and importantly) in the Indian state of Maharashta.[11] The United Kingdom legislation does not ban sex selection being carried out for social purposes – it was not an issue in 1990. The HFEA does prohibit sperm sorting, although it is difficult to see on what legal basis,[12] and in 2003 it recommended a ban on sex selection.[13] It may be that a new 'reproduction' Act will ban it, although the House of Commons Select Committee can find 'no adequate justification for prohibiting the use of sex selection for family balancing'.[14] Indeed, if and when the European Convention on Human Rights and Biomedicine comes to be ratified, it will have to be outlawed. Article 14 of this states: 'the use of techniques of medically assisted procreation shall not be allowed for the purpose of choosing the future child's sex, except where hereditary sex-related disease is to be avoided'. And this, in my opinion, is right.

The HFEA also allows for PGD is situations where abortion legislation would permit the termination of a pregnancy, that is where there is 'a substantial risk that if the child were born it would suffer from physical and mental abnormalities as

---

Government response is to find no adequate justification for prohibiting the use of sex selection for 'family balancing' Cm 6641/2005, at p. 19.

7   See Human Fertilisation and Embryology Act 1990 s 3(1). The problems the HFEA had with PGD generally were partially attributable to the fact that it 'does not appear on the face of the legislation' per Suzi Leather, Chair of HFEA, quoted in House of Commons Select Committee Report, *supra cit.*, at para 248.

8   This is said to be 'implicit' in the Act.

9   For an example see the Louise and Alan Masterson case, *The Guardian*, 16 October 2000. See also the House of Commons Select Committee report, *supra cit.*, at para 138.

10   Infertility Treatment Act 1995 s 50.

11   Regulation of Pre-Natal Diagnostic Techniques Act 1988.

12   No licensed activity is performed where there is sperm sorting before artificial insemination in a woman receiving treatment together with a man whose sperm underwent this process.

13   See HFEA, *Sex Selection; Options for Regulation*, November 2003.

14   Select Committee Report, *supra cit.*, at para.142.

to be seriously handicapped'.[15] This too must be right[16] and, although he does not discuss PGD, it would have the support of Ronald Dworkin, for whom the wasting of 'natural investment'[17] would be so very much less at pre-implantation stage.

Hesitantly, it has also allowed PGD to be employed to produce a child who would be a good tissue match for a sibling who needed a bone marrow transplant.[18] PGD and HLA had already been used for this purpose in Colorado in the USA in the *Nash* case,[19] and a British couple had taken advantage of the facility there to do the same thing,[20] before HFEA gave the go-ahead to the Hashmis in Leeds in 2001.

In doing so, did HFEA exceed its remit? When PDG was developed it was envisaged that embryos would be selected for their own intrinsic merit and not for their utility to another person. The 1990 Act offers little guidance. A licence can be granted only if the activity is 'necessary or desirable'.[21] This hardly assists since it leaves open the ethical assessment. In addition, there is the welfare provision in s 13(5), which requires account to be 'taken of the welfare of any child who may be born as a result of treatment ... and of any other child who may be affected by the birth'. This is a much-criticised provision,[22] and is unlikely to survive any review[23] of the 1990 Act. But it may be a useful resource in helping the determination of a case like that of the Hashmis. Indeed, it is difficult to think of a better example of where treatment service will impact upon the welfare of an existing child, and do so positively. Ironically, the legislature's concern was that existing children might be harmed by the addition of a new child.[24]

But what of the welfare of the child created to save the life of an existing sibling?

---

15  See Abortion Act 1967 s 1(i)(d).

16  There is a useful discussion of this in Steinbock, B., 'Preimplantation Genetic Diagnosis and Embryo Selection', in Burley, J. and Harris, J. (eds), *A Companion To Genethics*, Oxford, Blackwell, 2002, 175-190, at pp. 175-181.

17  *Life's Dominion*, London, Harper Collins, 1993, at p. 87.

18  Ethics Committee of HFEA, *Ethics Issues in the Location and Selection of Pre-Implantation Embryos to Produce Tissue Donors*, 22 November 2001.

19  See Dobson, R., '"Designer Baby" Cures Sister', (2000) 321 *British Medical Journal*, 1040. Stem cells from Adam Nash's umbilical cord were used to treat his sister Molly, who was suffering from Fanconi Anaemia.

20  See Gottlieb, S., 'US Doctors Say Selection Acceptable for Non-Medical Reasons', (2001) 323 *British Medical Journal*, 828.

21  Schedule 2, para 1(3).

22  For example, Jackson,E.,'Conception and the Irrelevance of the Welfare Principle', (2002) 65 *Modern Law Review*, 176-203. See also her 'Fertility Treatment: Abolish the "Welfare Principle"', *Spiked Online*, 11 June 2003.

23  One is currently (2005) being conducted: see Human Fertilisation and Embryology Authority, *Tomorrow's Children*, London, 2005. See also the criticism by the House of Commons Select Committee, *supra cit.*, at paras 94-107.

24  See s 13(5)'s reference to 'any other child who may be affected by the birth'.

392                                    *First Do No Harm*

**The Hashmi Decisions**

A first instance court in England ruled that HFEA was wrong to allow PGD to be used in the *Hashmi* case to select an embryo, which could be tissue-typed to find the best match for an existing child, Zain Hashmi, who has beta thalassaemia major.[25] Maurice Kay J held that the only embryo testing permitted by the legislation is PGD in so far as that is necessary to ensure that the woman can carry the child successfully to full term; that is, embryonic screening to eliminate those genetic defects which might affect the viability of the foetus, and no other.

The Court of Appeal[26] and the House of Lords,[27] correctly in my opinion, disagreed, and as a result have given the green light to an attempt to save Zain Hashmi's life. The Court of Appeal's decision is the more fully argued and I will look at it first. Significantly, one of the judges, Mance LJ, was influenced by the welfare imperative in s 13(5) of the 1990 Act.[28] This, he said, 'points towards a wider concern for the future child and siblings, which is better served if the legislation is read as permitting (the) screening'[29] envisaged in the *Hashmi* case. He had no doubt that 'the language of [s 13(5)] does not exclude positive effects'.[30] Lord Phillips of Worth Matravers MR was persuaded that if the Act permitted the licensing of embryo research activities for the purpose of 'developing methods for detecting the presence of gene or chromosome abnormalities in embryos before implantation',[31] the clear inference was that Parliament approved of PGD to avoid implantation of embryos carrying genetic defects. 'Parliament chose to permit the licensing of research. It makes little sense for Parliament, at the same time, to prohibit reaping the benefit of that research, even under licence'.[32]

The Court of Appeal also had no doubt that genetic analysis for the purpose of tissue typing was 'necessary or desirable for the purpose of providing treatment services'.[33] Lord Phillips of Worth Matravers conceded that his 'initial reaction'[34] was the same as the first instance judge;[35] that is that the phrase suggests 'treatment designed to assist the physical processes from fertilisation to the birth of a child'.[36]

---

25   *R (on application of Quintavalle) v. Human Fertilisation and Embryology Authority*, [2003] 2 All ER 105.

26   *R (on application of Quintavalle) v. Human Fertilisation and Embryology Authority*, [2003] 3 All ER 257.

27   *R (on application of Quintavalle) v. Human Fertilisation and Embryology Authority*, [2005] 2 All ER 555.

28   He is the only judge in either the House of Lords or Court of Appeal to refer to it.

29   See p. 283.

30   *Ibid.*, at p. 286.

31   See Schedule 3, para 3(2)(e).

32   See p. 269.

33   *Ibid.*, at p. 270.

34   *Id.*

35   *Quintavalle* (2003), *supra cit.*, at p. 111.

36   See p. 270.

But he now saw that 'if the impediment to bearing a child is concern that it may be born with a hereditary defect, treatment which enables women to become pregnant and to bear children in the confidence that they will not be suffering from such defects can properly be described as "for the purpose of assisting women to carry children"'.[37] He concluded that:

> whether the PGD has the purpose of producing a child free from genetic defects, or of producing a child with stem cells matching a sick or dying sibling, the IVF treatment that includes PGD constitutes 'treatment for the purpose of assisting women to bear children'.[38]

Of the three judges in the Court of Appeal, only Mance LJ grasped the nettle of the so-called 'designer baby'.[39] Lord Phillips of Worth Matravers appeared to leave decisions regarding this entirely to the discretion of the HFEA.[40] Mance LJ, on the other hand, saw a clear distinction between 'screening out abnormalities' and 'screening in preferences' (for example, and most immediately,[41] as to sex on social grounds only). 'Preferences', he noted, 'suggests personal indulgence or predilection and the luxury of a real choice', and, of course, the last thing that desperate families like the Hashmis were trying to do was 'indulge themselves'.[42] Mance, LJ, did, however, note that Parliament did not include 'any absolute prohibition in the area of sex selection for "social purposes"'.[43] And he added, the Hashmi request was 'much less obviously problematic'.[44]

The House of Lords agreed.[45] There are only two speeches (Lord Hoffmann and Lord Brown of Eaton-under-Heywood). Lord Brown, rather like Lord Phillips of Worth Matravers in the Court of Appeal, confesses that he was initially attracted by the CORE[46] argument:

> that PGD screening is one thing ... tissue typing a completely different concept and impermissible. It is one thing to enable a woman to conceive and bear a child which will itself be free of genetic abnormality, quite another to bear a child specifically selected for the purpose of treating someone else.[47]

---

37 *Id.*
38 *Ibid.*, at p. 271.
39 On designer babies see Mance LJ who discusses the concept at p. 287.
40 See p. 271.
41 The issue has become more urgent with the publication of the House of Commons Select Committee report, *supra cit.*, which despite identifying the objections (see para 134) thought the 'onus should be on those who oppose sex selection for social reasons using PGD to show harm from its use' (para 142).
42 See p. 287.
43 *Ibid.*, at p. 289.
44 *Id.*
45 See *Quintavalle* (2005), *supra cit.*
46 Comment on Reproductive Ethics.
47 See para 51.

394                                    *First Do No Harm*

But neither he nor Lord Hoffmann did come to this conclusion.

The question, as formulated by Lord Hoffmann, is whether PGD and HLA typing are 'activities which (HFEA) can authorise to be done "in the course" of providing her with IVF treatment'.[48] These activities include 'practices designed to secure that embryos are in a suitable condition to be placed in a woman or to determine whether embryos are suitable for that purpose'.[49] The Act does not say – it could hardly do so since PGD and HLA were unknown when it was passed – that PGD or HLA should constitute treatment services.[50] But they must be activities 'in the course' of such services, that is in the course of providing IVF treatment.

CORE's argument against this interpretation invoked the slippery slope. As summarised by Lord Hoffmann:

> It would enable the authority to authorise a single cell biopsy to test the embryo for whatever characteristics the mother might wish to know: whether the child would be male or female, dark or blonde, perhaps even, in time to come, intelligent or stupid.[51]

In other words, it could lead to 'designer babies'. On CORE's interpretation 'suitable' cannot just mean 'suitable for that particular mother'.[52] For CORE, it was argued that 'suitable' meant 'capable of becoming a healthy child, free of abnormalities'.[53] Thus, it believed – or its counsel so argued – that PGD to establish that an embryo is free from genetic abnormalities is acceptable, but not HLA typing. Of course, what the Hashmis want is not just a healthy child, but one that would meet the needs of Zain.

'Suitable', of course, is context-dependent: 'a suitable hat for Royal Ascot is very different from a suitable hat for the Banbury cattle market'.[54] The Warnock report only addresses the issue of suitability in the context of sex selection, upon which it made no positive recommendation.[55] Importantly, it did not recommend that sex selection on social grounds should be banned, leaving the decision on this to, what became, the HFEA. Lord Hoffmann inferred that:

> the Warnock Committee did not intend that selection of IVF embryos on grounds which went beyond genetic abnormality should be altogether banned.[56]

---

48  Para 10.
49  Human Fertilisation and Embryology Act 1990 Sch. 2, para 1(3)(d).
50  PGD was foreseen, but HLA was not. And see Lord Hoffmann at para 29.
51  Para 13.
52  *Id.*
53  *Id.*
54  Para 14.
55  It 'should be kept under review'. In fact there was no reconsideration until the HFEA report in 2003, *supra cit.*, and the discussion in the House of Commons Select Committee Report, *supra cit.*, in 2005.
56  Para 19.

The White Paper which examined the Warnock report, prior to the 1990 Act, was adamant that designer babies should not be permitted,[57] as it was with cloning, although neither it nor the legislation which followed anticipated the 'Dolly' technique.[58] However, as Lord Hoffmann acknowledges, there was no proposal to ban 'the testing of embryos to enable the mother to choose to carry a child with characteristics of her choice'.[59] This is not entirely true, for it was clear that she could not choose 'designer'-type characteristics. In the arguments before the Lords everything hinged on the choice of what characteristics were permissible, on the drawing of a line between saviour siblings and designer babies (and 'more sinister eugenic practices'[60]).

In Lord Hoffmann's view these ethical distinctions were left to the HFEA. He thought it inconceivable that the 1990 Act:

> said nothing on the subject … because Parliament thought it was clearly prohibited by the use of the word 'suitable' or because it wanted to leave the question over for later primary legislation.[61]

It was thus his view that the only reasonable inference is that Parliament intended to leave the matter for the Authority to decide.[62] It could decide to allow sex selection on social grounds, he thought. And once the concept of suitability could be so interpreted:

> it is impossible to say that selection on the grounds of any other characteristics which the mother might desire was positively excluded from the discretion of the authority, however unlikely it might be that the authority would actually allow selection on that ground.[63]

Lord Hoffmann therefore concluded that both PGD and HLA typing could lawfully be authorised by HFEA as 'activities to determine the suitability of the embryo for implantation within the meaning of paragraph 1(1)(d)'.[64]

It is only at the end of his judgment that Lord Hoffmann addresses what many will consider to be the principal ethical question. A concern of CORE's, as formulated by its counsel, is the way HFEA's policy has changed so as to allow the use of bone marrow rather than umbilical cord blood.[65] It may have had little option since,

---

57 *Human Fertilisation and Embryology: A Framework for Legislation*, Cm.259/1987, para 37.

58 It only considered cell nucleus substitution.

59 Para 22.

60 Para 25. A more positive view is Mehlman, M.J., *Wondergenes*, Bloomington, Indiana, Indiana University Press, 2003.

61 Para 29.

62 *Id.*

63 *Id.*

64 Para 35.

65 The HFEA endorsed with amendment a recommendation of its Ethics and Legal Committee to this effect on 21 July 2004.

once an embryo had been implanted and a child conceived, the case goes outside its remit. Nevertheless, there is a real dilemma posed, because the taking of bone marrow, though relatively straightforward and otherwise uncontentious, is invasive. The HFEA itself, in authorising the extension, noted that the threshold for permitting medical procedures to be performed on a child where they were non-therapeutic was higher, and that courts could overrule parental consent where the procedure was not in the child's best interests.

Lord Hoffmann contended himself with saying, '[t]hese reasons appear to be valid'.[66]

He had no doubt that 'medical practitioners' take very seriously the law:

that any operation upon a child for which there is no clinical reason relating to the child itself must be justified as being for other reasons in the child's best interests.[67]

He added, '[t]he Authority is entitled to assume that a child conceived pursuant to its licence will, after birth, receive the full protection of the law'.[68]

This is a real concern and one insufficiently addressed by the House of Lords. Was the one authority that might conceivably have been relevant (*Re Y*[69]) cited to the Lords? It is not referred to in either of the two judgments. It is, of course, a controversial decision, not least because of the expansive meaning given to a learning disabled adult's best interests, one that would need to be extended further to embrace bone marrow donations by a saviour sibling who clearly would not have the psychological ties which Connell J in *Re Y* found to exist in the unusual family circumstances of that case.[70]

Lord Brown does not address this question, and his judgment broadly mirrors Lord Hoffmann's. But rather than trying to distinguish therapeutic from social embryo selection, he attempts to distinguish the two by jurisdiction. As he puts it, 'whereas ... suitability is for the woman, the limits of permissible embryo selection are for the authority'.[71] He assumes that HFEA would not license selection for purely social reasons. If it did, he envisages Parliament intervening or 'in an extreme case' (he does not specify what would be extreme) the court's supervisory jurisdiction being invoked.[72]

In the Hashmi case the intention was for blood to be taken from the baby's umbilical cord, which is rich in stem cells, and infused into the sick child. Zain

---

66 Para 38.
67 *Id.*
68 *Id.*
69 [1997] Fam. 110.
70 The learning disabled young woman would suffer psychologically if her mother's visits decreased as they were likely to do if her sister did not receive bone marrow from her.
71 Para 62.
72 *Id.* On the legality of PGD elsewhere see Shaun Pattison's very helpful table in *Influencing Traits Before Birth*, Aldershot, Ashgate, 2002, Appendix 2. The Committee believes the regulation of pre-implantation testing is highly satisfactory (see para 244).

Hashmi had a hereditary and fatal blood disorder. Other children involved in other similar cases have suffered from rare blood disorders like 'Diamond Blackfan anaemia' from which Charlie Whitaker suffered.[73] A more emotionally fraught scenario, or ethical dilemma, it would difficult to imagine.

## The Ethical Questions

I turn now to the ethical questions. I start from the premise that in a liberal society autonomy – in this case reproductive autonomy – is important.[74] The principle of autonomy is clearly enunciated in Mill's *On Liberty*: 'Over himself, over his own body and mind, the individual is sovereign'.[75] It is a cornerstone of medical law (and ethics). As Lord Goff noted in *Re F*, 'we have to bear well in mind the libertarian principle of self-determination'.[76] Autonomy is clearly related to dignity,[77] which is an equally important principle to observe.[78] So unless it harms, or misuses or abuses the new child, I start from the position that parents like the Hashmis (or the Whitakers[79] or Fletchers[80]) should be able to exercise their reproductive autonomy.

It should be stressed – for autonomy can all too easily be seen in individualistic terms – that what these desperate parents want is, what has been called, 'relational autonomy';[81] that is to say the exercise of reproductive decision making made with reference to others. It is not that they want their views to prevail, so much as wanting

---

73 See Hall, C., 'Two Cases Have Similarities and Vital Differences', *The Daily Telegraph*, 3 August 2002.

74 And so obviously no prenatal screening should be carried out without consent. On issues relating to this see Andrews, L., 'Prenatal Screening and the Culture of Motherhood', (1996) 47 *Hastings Law Journal*, 967-1006.

75 First published in 1859.

76 [1990] 2 AC 1, 73.

77 On the relationship see Raz, J., *The Authority of Law*, Oxford, Clarendon Press, 1979, at p. 221. 'Respecting human dignity entails treating humans as persons capable of planning and plotting their future. Thus, respecting people's dignity includes respecting their autonomy, their right to control their future'. But see Gill, R. and Stirrat, G. (2005) 31 *Journal of Medical Ethics*, 127-130, who argue that 'conceptions of individual autonomy cannot provide a sufficient and convincing starting point for ethics within medical practice'. But compare Macklin, R., 'Dignity Is a Useless Concept', (2003) 327 *BMJ*, 1419-1420.

78 And see Brennan J in *Secretary, Department of Health v. JWB and SMB*, (1992) 66 ALJR 300, 317: 'each person has a unique dignity which the law respects and which it will protect'.

79 The Whitaker case is discussed by the House of Commons Select Committee report, *supra cit.*, at paras 246-248).

80 The HFEA Licence Committee granted a licence to HRGC to provide HLA tissue typing for the Fletchers on 6 September 2004.

81 See Nedelsky, J., 'Reconceiving Autonomy: Thoughts and Possibilities', (1989) 1 *Yale Journal of Law and Feminism*, 7-36.

to improve the welfare of one of their children and thus the welfare of the whole family.[82]

We must therefore ask whether this is an exercise of autonomy which harms, misuses or abuses the new child. We must not ignore the dignity of the child-to-be. Will his/her interests be compromised in any way to promote those of the existing sick child?

Is it a valid objection that parents are having a child for the wrong reasons? Those who are against bringing a child into the world to save another child believe the 'saviour sibling' will be treated as a commodity rather than as a person; as a means to cure a sick sibling rather than as an end in him/herself. This argument resounds to echoes of Kant's dictum – quoted invariably out of context and often misunderstood – that you should 'never use people as a means but always treat them as an end'.[83]

However, Kant was not against treating people as a means, but rather was opposed to treating them *solely* or *merely* as a means. Few of us get through life without treating others as a means. Should we stop organ transplants or blood transfusions on the grounds that we are treating the donors as a means to our ends? As Hans Ever commented the creation of a child to save another child 'is morally acceptable if the use as a donor is not the only motive for the parents to have a child: i.e. they intend to love and care for this child to the same extent as they love and care for the affected child and if the planned procedure would be acceptable for an existing donor child'.[84]

This commodity argument also fails to identify and explain what is wrong with creating a child as a 'saviour sibling' when creating a child for other instrumental purposes is allowed. We do not normally investigate the reasons why people decide to have children. We do not condemn those who have a baby to provide a companion for an existing child or even those who do so to save a failing marriage. There may be all sorts of less-than-worthy motives for having a child. Of course, we must not ignore the dignity of the child-to-be. But will his/her interests be compromised in any way to promote those of the existing sick child? If the stem cells used are from the umbilical cord blood, there will not even be physical intrusions upon the baby – there is with a bone marrow donation, but these have been relatively uncontroversial for many years.[85] Whether they will remain uncontroversial where the bone marrow is sought from a 'saviour sibling' is less clear.

---

82  See Bennett, B., 'Choosing a Child's Future? Reproductive Decision-Making and Preimplantation Genetic Diagnosis', in Gunning, J. and Szoke, H. (eds), *The Regulation of Assisted Reproductive Technology*, Aldershot, Ashgate, 2003, 167-176.

83  Lord Winston is cited by Lord Brown (at para 43) as believing that it commodifies the child-to-be. He is also quoted in BBC News, 13 December 2001.

84  Quoted in Sheldon, S. and Wilkinson, S., 'Hashmi and Whitaker: An Unjustifiable and Misguided Distinction?', (2004) 12 *Medical Law Review*, 137-163, at pp. 146-147. Professor Hans Ever is Chairman of the European Society of Human Reproduction and Embryology.

85  And see C.H. Baron *et al.*, 'Live Organ and Tissue Transplants from Minor Donors in Massachusetts', (1975) 35 *Boston University Law Review*, 159-193, at p. 159.

Provided, as is very likely to be the case, that the new child is wanted and will be loved and nurtured in his/her own right, it is difficult to see how his/her dignity can be thought to be compromised in any way. If there were no intention to bring the child up, the case would look different, albeit little different from a surrogacy arrangement and, though we deprecate these,[86] we do not ban them.[87] Even so, there would remain the argument that it is better to be an adopted child than a non-existent one. However, I would not defend the parents who had a saviour sibling, solely as such, and intended to reject the child once he/she had served the purpose for which he/she was procreated. What would such a child be told about his/her origins? That he/she was indeed a means to someone else's end.

The commodity objection is posed another way as well. It is sometimes said that the more choice parents have as a result of reproductive techniques, the more likely they are to develop 'consumerist' attitudes towards children, which in turn will affect the relationship between parents and children. This may well lead to a value, even a monetary value, being put on children, as, indeed, I have argued elsewhere:[88] perhaps the main objection to surrogacy arrangements is their potentiality to commodify children.[89] However, whether it also leads to children being maltreated or rejected is dubious to say the least. There is no evidence to show that children born as a result of assisted reproduction are more likely to end up as abused children. Psychological research studies have identified that children born through assisted reproduction technology have just as close a loving relationship with parents and just as full a psychological development as children born in the more conventional way.[90] On the commodity argument the jury is out – and I suspect is likely to be unable to return a verdict for a very long time. But intuition suggests there is no basis to the argument. And, of course, the alternative to being a 'saviour sibling' – or a commodity – is non-existence. Is this preferable?

Another argument adduced by those who oppose 'saviour siblings', as was observed in CORE's arguments in the *Hashmi* case, is that by allowing this to happen we will step on to the slippery slope[91] that will end with designer babies[92] – with parents selecting height or hair or eye colour or intelligence.

---

86 See Surrogacy Arrangements Act 1985, which was hurriedly passed to meet a moral panic.

87 Surrogacy agreements are, however, unenforceable and also contrary to public policy.

88 'Is Surrogacy Exploitative?', in McLean, S.A.M. (ed), *Legal Issues in Human Reproduction*, Aldershot, Dartmouth, 1989, 164-184.

89 On which see Radin, M., 'Market – Inalienability', (1986) 100 *Harvard Law Review*, 1849-1937 and *Contested Commodities*, Cambridge, Mass., Harvard University Press, 1996.

90 An interesting discussion is Schultz, K., 'Assisted Reproduction and Parent-Infant Bonding' in Evans, D. (ed) *Creating the Child*, The Hague, Martinus Nijhoff, 1996, 229-238.

91 The concern, more generally, of Francis Fukuyama, *Our Posthuman Future: Consequences of the Biotechnology Revolution*, New York, Farrar, Strauss and Giroux, 2002.

92 On which see Gosden, R., *Designing Babies*, New York, W.H. Freeman, 1999.

There are, of course, different versions of the slippery slope argument.[93] One approach looks to the horrible mess at the bottom of the slippery slope. As Josephine Quintavalle, the initiator of the *Hashmi* challenge, put it: 'the new technique is a dangerous first step towards allowing parents to use embryo testing to choose other characteristics of the baby, such as eye colour and sex'.[94] The second version of the argument emphasises consistency. It suggests that allowing the creation of 'saviour siblings' is not morally different from allowing people to choose babies with designer attributes such as a particular hair or eye colour. Logic dictates that if we reject one – as of course we should – we should reject the other.

There are different ways of challenging the slippery slope argument. The easiest is to question the supposed evilness of the end product, to say in effect 'so, what is wrong with designer babies?'[95] This would be an interesting argument to run, but it is outside the scope of the chapter, and I will not attempt it here. Or, one could argue that there is no moral equivalence between 'saviour siblings' and 'designer babies', so that it is perfectly possible to legitimise the creation of 'saviour siblings', whilst opposing the creation of 'designer babies'. In comparison to the goal of creating a 'saviour sibling', which is to save life, the reasons for seeking to 'design' a baby pale into insignificance. The 'saviour sibling' may eliminate an abnormal characteristic: the designer baby merely filters out what most would regard as a normal characteristic, albeit one to which those parents object. It may be difficult in the hard case to define a genetic defect but that is not so here.

The third objection to the slippery slope argument is that it is possible to allow the creation of 'saviour siblings' without giving the green light to 'designer babies'.

Why? First, because those who object to saviour siblings have given no evidence as to why allowing 'saviour siblings' will lead to the creation of 'designer babies'. Secondly, it is probably easier to create a 'saviour sibling' than a 'designer baby'. To create a 'designer baby' a large number of embryos would be needed as a pool for the selection process. The probability is thus that it would be expensive (itself an argument against it because it would be limited to the rich and to those in rich countries[96]). And, thirdly, because regulation can ensure that selection is restricted to acceptable goals. The HFEA's remit enables it to regulate and to draw distinctions,

---

93  See Williams, B., 'Which Slopes Are Slippery?', in Lockwood, M., *Moral Dilemmas in Modern Medicine*, Oxford, Oxford University Press, 1987.

94  Quoted in Sheldon, S. and Wilkinson, S., 'Should Selecting Saviour Siblings Be Banned?', (2004) 30 *Journal of Medical Ethics*, 533-537, at p. 534.

95  The natural corollary of today's common emphasis (e.g. Robertson, J., *Children of Choice*, Princeton, N.J. 1994) on reproductive autonomy. But see, further, Stock, G., *Redesigning Humans*, London, Houghton Mifflin, 2002.

96  A point made (in a slightly different context) by Parens, E., 'Justice and the Germline', in Stock, G. and Campbell, J. (eds), *Engineering the Human Germline*, New York, Oxford University Press, 2000, 122-124, at p.123. He points to the 'already obscene gap between those who have and those who don't'. This raises the question of the extent to which these new techniques should become part of social medicine, an issue that NICE had recently to grapple when it recommended IVF on the NHS.

and this role should continue.[97] At present, parents have to apply for a licence from HFEA to go through the procedure of PGD and HLA tissue typing to create a 'saviour sibling', and the procedures are permitted on a case-by-case basis using strict guidelines. The HFEA has ruled that the disease needs to be very serious and life threatening, and in effect that the creation of a 'saviour sibling' must be a last resort: if there is another way of treating the child, this should be used.[98] Also, it did not until recently allow parents who suffer from a genetic disease to create a baby to treat their own disease.[99] I think it was wrong to make this change which is not defensible in the way in which having a child to save a child is. Those who object to the creation of 'saviour siblings' have not demonstrated that this system of regulation is likely to fail, though there may be concerns with the way HFEA exercises its powers. The slippery slope criticism thus lacks any real support, and must be rejected.

The third argument adduced against the creation of 'saviour siblings' focuses on the welfare of the child. Reference has already been made to the way this argument was used constructively by Mance LJ in the Court of Appeal in the *Hashmi* case.[100] For as long as section 13(5) remains part of the law,[101] all treatment services must be guided by a welfare principle. But, of course, this was inserted with one-parent families and lesbian couples in mind,[102] not 'saviour siblings' (or for that matter other new developments like fertility treatment for post-menopausal women[103]). Where 'saviour siblings' are to be created, the treatment proposed involves benefits to another person. Is it for the baby-to-be's welfare to be born to save the life of a person who will become his/her sibling? In so far as life, almost any life, is a good, valuable in itself, it may be said that the issue does not arise. Nevertheless, the HFEA uses the 'welfare' provision in the 1990 Act to make a risk/benefit calculation.[104]

Those who oppose creating a baby to save a child's life point to two possible harms that may be caused to the new baby. These are damage to physical health, and psychological harm.

As far as physical health is concerned, when the baby is born it does not suffer any harm, since the taking of stem cells from the umbilical cord blood is not an

---

97   Though in the wake of the House of Commons Select Committee report, *supra cit.*, it may not do so.

98   See Chair's letter: CH (04) 05 (4 August 2004). The criteria are set out more fully in the House of Commons Report, *supra cit.*, at Table 14 on p. 112.

99   It has recently changed its policy so as to allow this now.

100  See above, xx.

101  As already indicated, it seems likely that it will be repealed in future legislation.

102  When the Human Fertilisation and Embryology Bill was before Parliament an amendment was proposed (and lost by one vote in the House of Lords) which would have limited fertility treatment to married couples.

103  On which see Fisher, F. and Sommerville, A., 'To Everything There is a Season? Are There Medical Grounds for Refusing Fertility Treatment To Older Women?', in Harris, J. and Holm, S., *The Future of Human Reproduction*, Oxford, Clarendon Press, 1998, 203-220.

104  See House of Commons Report, *supra cit.*, para 247.

invasive procedure. Nothing is done to the baby him/herself. If the creation of 'saviour siblings' were not to be allowed, the invasive procedure of taking cells from an existing child's tissue-matched bone marrow would have to be undertaken (a procedure already used, unsuccessfully, in all the much-publicised cases). As Vivienne Nathanson of the British Medical Association said, commenting on the *Whitaker's* case:

> As doctors we believe that where technology exists that could help a dying or seriously ill child without involving major risks to others, then it can only be right that it is used for this purpose.[105]

Of course, PGD will lead to the destruction of some embryos during the selection process. Those who object to this object also to in vitro fertilisation, embryo research, abortion and probably to contraception.[106] Their arguments have been countered elsewhere,[107] and it would be superfluous to this chapter to examine them here. It would be different were there to be any detrimental effects to the embryos used in the reproductive process. The evidence thus far does not point to any short-term detriments. However, the use of PGD to create 'saviour siblings' is new – the technology of PGD itself is relatively so – and more research is needed before we can rule out any long-term effects. An editorial in *The Lancet* has made much of this point: 'whilst embryo biopsy for PGD does not seem to produce adverse physical effects in the short term … it is too early to exclude the possibility of later effects'.[108] We can say with confidence that a child created to save the life of another will suffer no more physical health deficits than any other child born as a result of selection during pre-implantation genetic diagnosis.

Opponents of the creation of a child to save another also point to, what they consider, the psychological harm that may be inflicted on the new baby. There are two arguments.

The first is that if the child finds out that he/she was not wanted for him/herself but rather for the ulterior purpose of assisting a sibling to live, this may cause psychological harm. But it is just as likely that such a child will feel pride and contentment in the knowledge that he/she is responsible for saving the life of a sibling. By contrast, an existing child who finds out that he/she is unable to act as a tissue donor for a sibling is much more likely to be psychologically damaged. It is also argued, equally unconvincingly, that psychological harm may occur because a 'saviour sibling' may experience a less close or loving relationship with their

---

105 Quoted in Bhattacharya, S., 'Banned "Designer Baby" is Born in UK', *New Scientist*, 14 June 2003.

106 It is extraordinary that we even question the loss of embryo in the saviour sibling process when we allow experimentation on embryos for 14 days and, of course, allow for the destruction of surplus embryos, and permit abortion. See further Hursthouse, R., *Beginning Lives*, Oxford, Open University Press, 1987.

107 For example, in Harris, J., *The Value of Life*, London, Routledge, 1985.

108 Editorial: 'Preimplantation Donor Selection', (2001) 358 *Lancet*, 1195.

parents. This is supposedly explained by the 'fact' that parents will value such a child less because he/she was born only to save another child. Presumably, those who believe this will think this even more likely when the 'saviour sibling' has failed to do this. I think these sorts of arguments fail to understand that these are parents who have demonstrated love, care, devotion and who have acted with the highest motives. They are parents for whom the concept of parental responsibility has true meaning.[109] As excellent parents they are as likely to be aware of these concerns as any critic of the procedure and to be on their guard against it happening. They are compassionate, not heartless, and are ill served by this blunt criticism.

Overall, then, if child welfare is the issue, it would make the case for, and not the case against, the practice of creating a child to save the life of an existing child. It is in the interests of a child to be born to save another child of the family. The HFEA accordingly was right to approve the creation of a child to attempt to save Zain Hashmi, and to do so also for Joshua Fletcher. It gave the latter approval in September 2004 even though Joshua Fletcher suffered from a non-genetic disease (Diamond Blackfan anaemia).[110] It had previously refused permission in a similar case (that of Charlie Whitaker) because, since the disease cannot be screened for, the tissue typing would be carried out solely for the benefit of the existing child and not in order to identify whether the embryos carried a genetic disorder.[111] In the *Fletcher* case, the parents have been allowed to go through HLA tissue typing to ensure the embryo will be a tissue match for Joshua, even though there can be no guarantee that the new baby will be free from the disease. This may be more difficult to justify than the *Hashmi* case but I believe it can be justified. The HFEA will continue to vet and act on a case-by-case basis. It has stated also that the disease needs to be serious and life-threatening before it will give a go-ahead, and that if there are other courses of action open to parents these options must first be explored first.[112]

There are thus many objections adduced to the creation of saviour siblings: the commodity argument, that which fears a slippery slope; and that which emphasises welfare and points to the harm it believes the donor child may suffer. As I have shown, none of these is convincing. Are there any other arguments which could be constructed? I discount the concern that some have with innovation. The precautionary principle has value, but scientific advancement can be stifled by over-caution.[113] Nothing ventured, nothing gained can be expected to be the response of the parent with the very sick child. And even if, as I believe has happened in

---

109 That is, they behave with responsibility. See, further, Eekelaar, J., 'State of Nature or Nature of the State?', (1991) *Journal of Social Welfare Law*, 37.

110 See the decision of the HFEA Licence Committee, *supra cit.*

111 That the distinction between the *Hashmi* and *Whitaker* cases is wrong is argued by Sheldon, S. and Wilkinson, S., '*Hashmi* and *Whitaker*: An Unjustifiable and Misguided Distinction?', (2004) 12 *Medical Law Review*, 137-163.

112 See Chair's letter, *supra cit.*

113 A critical discussion of which is Furedi, F., 'The Dangers of Safety', (1996) *Living Marxism*, 16-22. The House of Commons Select Committee, *supra cit.*, discusses it at paras 273-276.

he *Hashmi* case, the existing child has not yet been cured,[114] the experiment will not be totally in vain if the lessons learned assist other children in the future.

Just as weak is the argument that parents are seeking to create children as much for their own benefit or, indeed, primarily for their own benefit and to their detriment of their child, existing or to-be. The cynical response to this is to ask why any parents have children. We do not inquire into their motives. But in the case under examination this seems unlikely. These parents are not acting for their own benefit, as, for example, the deaf parents who deliberately want to create a deaf child are doing[115] – and many,[116] though not myself,[117] support their decision. The plausibility of the argument that parents create saviour siblings for their own benefit would be stronger if parents could not go through the process of PGD and HLA tissue typing in order to treat an illness of their own.[118] Until very recently they were not permitted to do so but, as slippery slope opponents of saviour siblings warned, PGD and HLA would be extended to allow for this. I think the HFEA has now erred in permitting parents to do this, but also think it is wrong to use this to argue against saviour siblings.

Finally, there is the argument, heard so often in other contexts, that the process necessarily involves the destruction of embryos, and thus life. To some this is akin to murder. An examination of this argument will take me into well-trodden terrain, and unnecessarily so.[119] This is a weak argument and it has been knocked down many times. Were it to prevail, there would be no abortion, fertility treatment or embryo research. United Kingdom law allows experiments on embryos (and therefore their destruction) for 14 days,[120] and pregnancy terminations in exceptional cases to term.[121] How then can we object to embryo wastage which is incidental to the creation of a 'saviour sibling'?

---

114  See *The Guardian*, 20 April 2004.

115  There is 'an asymmetry between the limitations on opportunity that deafness brings and the goods of membership in the deaf community' per Buchanan, A., *et al.*, *From Chance to Choice: Genetics and Justice*, Cambridge, Cambridge University Press, 2000, at p. 283.

116  For example, Holm, S., in Harris, J. and Holm, S., *The Future of Human Reproduction*, Oxford, Clarendon Press, 1998, 28-47.

117  The case is arguably comparable to deliberately deafening a hearing baby (which would be seen as child abuse by everyone). But see, Hayry, M., 'There is a Difference Between Selecting a Deaf Embryo and Deafening a Hearing Child', (2004) 30 *Journal of Medical Ethics*, 510-512.

118  This is now permitted.

119  A good discussion is Lee, R. and Morgan, D., *Human Fertilisation and Embryology Regulating the Reproductive Revolution*, London, Blackstone Press, 2001, ch. 3.

120  See Human Fertilisation and Embryology Act 1990 s 3(3)(a), (4).

121  See Abortion Act 1967 s 1(b), (c), (d).

## Is There a Parental Obligation to Have a Saviour Sibling?

There is another question which is less commonly raised.[122] Do parents like the Hashmis or the Fletchers have an *obligation* to have another child in order to save an existing child? The legal answer is clear. It must be their choice. We should not investigate their reasons for not doing so. They cannot be compelled by doctors to do so, or by a court, any more that they can be compelled to donate blood, tissue or organs to save a child of theirs.[123] It is clear that there is no legal obligation. And, although the concept of a legal obligation has been stretched somewhat by cases such as *Re Y*,[124] I doubt whether the common law is capable of accommodating such an obligation. It might lead to specific performance of sexual intercourse!

But do parents with a sick child who might be cured by a saviour sibling have a *moral* obligation to create a new child? Could we see this as an element of parental responsibility?[125] There have been several investigations as to the basis of parental rights;[126] fewer of the reasons for vesting responsibility in parents. Does the chance to save a child trump reproductive autonomy? How far are parents required to go? Would we say that parents like the Hashmis, if they refused to attempt to create a saviour sibling, were being unreasonable? Would we censure them? Has the *Hashmi* case and its successors created a new standard which others can be expected to follow?[127]

And there are other questions too. Suppose an embryo which is to be a 'saviour sibling' is created: can the mother change her mind and refuse to have it implanted? The ultimate decision must belong to the woman,[128] though we might censure her if

---

122 Savulescu, J., 'Procreative Beneficience: Why We Should Select The Best Children', (2001) 15 *Bioethics*, 413-426 does raise it briefly (at p. 415). Robertson, J.A., *et al.*, 'Conception To Obtain Haematopoietic Stem Cells', (2002) 32 (3) *Hastings Center Report*, 34-40 say the question 'can be put swiftly to rest' and provide a negative conclusion (at p. 36).

123 The analogy is the medically-indicated Caesarean section, on which see Rhoden, N.K., 'The Judge in the Delivery Room: The Emergence of Court-ordered Caesareans', (1986) 74 *California Law Review*, 1951-2030. See also *McFall v. Shimp*, (1978) 10 Pa D & C 90 (CE Comm PS, Pa).

124 [1997] Fam 110. See also *Curran v. Bosze*, (1990) 566 NE 2d 1319 (Illinois Supreme Court).

125 See Children Act 1989 s 3.

126 For example, Hill, J., 'What Does It Mean To Be A "Parent"? The Claims of Biology As The Basis For Parental Rights', (1991) 66 *New York University Law Review*, 353. See also Barton, C. and Douglas, G., *Law and Parenthood*, London, Butterworths, 1995, ch. 2.

127 In Hart's sense (see Hart, H.L.A., *The Concept of Law*, Oxford, 1961).

128 This is also the view of John Harris (see Harris, J. and Holm, S. *The Future of Human Reproduction*, Oxford, Clarendon Press, 1998, 5-37, at p. 33). Of course it is not as simple as this. Why shouldn't the male partner have rights at least at the pre-implantation stage? Suppose he wants PGD and she doesn't. And what of the gamete donor who says you can have my gametes but I object to pre-implantation testing (or I suppose to abortion)? There are many questions which have not been considered, but which would require investigation further in another paper.

she refused. The 'father' presumably would have no rights.[129] Nor can it be argued that doctors have a legal duty to implant the embryo.[130]

And what of the converse case – doctors do not wish to implant the embryo but the woman wants to take the chance? Can she insist? Draper and Chadwick have argued that once women have parted with their gametes and the resulting embryos have been tested, 'it is possible for them to lose control over what happens next', and 'she cannot compel him to implant embryos against his wishes'.[131] But though this may not impugn her bodily integrity, it certainly undermines her reproductive autonomy, and arguably also her dignity. But one would not expect any court to compel a doctor to implant an embryo against his clinical judgment, nor, I suggest, would it have the authority to do so. As ever with medico-ethical questions the questions are endless – and the answers often elusive!

129  The abortion analogy may not always work, but I think it must hold here. In relation to abortion see *Paton v. Trustees of British Pregnancy Advisory Service*, [1998] 2 All ER 987.

130  But see the arguments of King, D., 'Preimplantation Genetic Diagnosis and the "New" Genetics', (1999) 25 *Journal of Medical Ethics*, 176-182, at p. 180.

131  'Beware! Preimplantation Genetic Diagnosis May Solve Some Old Problems But It Also Raises New Ones', (1999) 25 *Journal of Medical Ethics*, 114-120, at p. 119.

# [8]
# Why It Remains Important To Take Children's Rights Seriously

It was Ronald Dworkin who, nearly 30 years ago, urged us to 'take rights seriously' (1977). It is a pity that his argument did not specifically extend to children. Indeed, that in a little noticed passage a decade later he stumbled on the dilemma of what 'Hercules' (the ideal superhuman judge) should do when he thought 'the best interpretation of the equal protection clause outlaws distinctions between the rights of adults and those of children that have never been questioned in the community, and yet he . . . thinks that it would be politically unfair. . . . for the law to impose that view on a community where family and social practices accept such distinctions as proper and fundamental' (Dworkin, 1986, 402). Nor has he ever returned to this dilemma; a pity because it beautifully encapsulates the problem of what to do when the supposedly 'right answer' is morally the 'wrong answer'.

When *Taking Rights Seriously* was published we were in the heyday of the children's liberation movement. This was the era of Farson (1978) and Holt (1975). Their thesis is ripe for reassessment, but it is clear that at the time its impact was limited. Dworkin was clearly unaware of it, as indeed he was of other children's rights literature of the 1970s and earlier.[1]

My own first foray into writing on children's rights was in 1980, the text of a lecture given to celebrate the International Year of The Child in 1979 (1980). *The Rights and Wrongs of Children* (1983) emerged four years later. Then followed the Brian Jackson Memorial Lecture in Huddersfield in 1987 (1988) which advocated that we take children's rights seriously, and a paper at a workshop on 'children, rights and the law' at the ANU in 1991 which emphasised the need to take children's rights' more seriously' (1992). By then, of course, there was the United Nations Convention on the Rights of the Child, which was swiftly ratified by virtually the whole world[2], and there were developments in legal systems which suggested that children's rights were indeed being taken seriously or at least a lot more seriously than previously.[3]

There has since been a backlash: in part this is because rights themselves have come under attack. But this cannot be the sole reason. Many of today's critics of children's rights are passionate defenders of the rights of others, notably of the rights of parents.[4] An example is the recent–and deeply- flawed–book by the American lawyer, Martin Guggenheim (2005, and see Freeman, 2006).

The language of rights can make visible what has for too long been suppressed. It can lead to different and new stories being heard in public. Carrie Menkel-Meadow explains that 'Each time we let in an excluded group, each time we listen to a new way of knowing, we learn more about the limits of our current way of seeing' (1987, 52). An illustration from a recent English case may assist.

The *Williamson* case[5] revolved about whether parents (as well as teachers) could exercise their right, as they saw it, to continue the practice of corporal punishment in their Christian schools. Legislation had outlawed it,[6] but they claimed this was incompatible with their human rights to freedom of religion and to ensure that education was in conformity with their religious convictions.[7] The case was fought right up to the highest court in the land, the House of Lords. And throughout it was conceived as a dispute between the State–its right to ban corporal punishment from schools–and parents and teachers. Children were the objects of concern, not subjects in their own right. They were not represented: their views were not sought or known. Yes, there is a clear suspicion that they would have agreed with their parents–echoes of the famous U.S. Supreme Court case of *Wisconsin* v. *Yoder*[8]. And this raises a problem, which I discuss later. But that is not the issue. More significant than what these children want is the potential impact of the decision on children as a class. The courts found against the parents and teachers. But suppose they hadn't. Children would once again have been exposed to the rod to uphold the human rights of adults. It is significant that the state did not argue that corporal punishment necessarily involved an infringement of any of the rights of children. The practice is a clear breach of the UN Convention.[9] But Arden L.J. was astute enough to observe that the common law 'effectively treats the child as the property of the parent'[10]–corporal punishment by parents is still permitted in English law–and she adds 'the courts may one day have to consider whether this is the right approach'.[11]

The clearest appreciation of these issues is in Baroness Hale's judgment in the House of Lords. Her judgment begins: 'This is, and always has been, a case about children, their rights and the rights of their parents and teachers. Yet there has been no one here or in the courts below to speak on behalf of the children. The battle has been fought on ground selected by the adults'. What she then has to say is 'for the sake of the children'.[12] From this perspective the case is about 'whether the legislation achieves a fair balance between the rights and freedoms of the parents and teachers and the rights, freedoms and interests, not only of their children, but also of any other children who might be affected by the persistence of corporal punishment in some schools'.[13] However, instead the argument focused on 'whether the beliefs of the parents and teachers qualified for protection'.[14] How could it be otherwise? There was no litigation friend to represent children's rights. Nor any NGO. Had it been possible to argue this case from a children's rights perspective, it would have looked very different, even though, of course, the conclusion would have been the same.[15]

The *Williamson* case draws attention to the importance of children's rights. But I see these as no more or less important than rights generally. It is impossible to underestimate the centrality of rights. Rights are important because they are inclusive: they are universal, available to all members of the human race. In the past, they have depended on gender and on race. Women were non-persons–the US Supreme Court even said this on one notorious occasion.[16] Black people were kept in subservience by policies which justified institutions like slavery and apartheid and other discriminatory policies. And it is surely not insignificant that the word 'boy' was not infrequently applied to black men.

But, just as concepts of gender inequality have been key to understanding womanhood and woman's social status, so the 'concept of generation is key to understanding childhood' (Mayall, 2002, 120). It has always been to the advantage of the powerful to keep others out. It is not, therefore, surprising that adults should want to do this to children, and that they should wish to keep them in an often imposed and prolonged dependence, which history and culture shows to be neither inevitable nor essential. Think of the other side of inclusion–of exclusion, and what this generates both on the part of the excluded and their victims, the socially excluded. And observe how the powerful regulate space–social, political (Archard, 2004), geographical (Valentine, 2004)–define participation, marginalise significance, and frustrate development.

Rights are invisible and inter-dependent. Human rights–for that is what children's rights are–include the whole range of civil, political, social, economic and cultural rights. Denying certain rights undermines other rights. So, for example, if we deny children the right to be free from corporal chastisement, we so undermine their status and integrity that other rights fall as well. And this point applies across classes of potential rights-holders. Thus, if we do not put in place structures to tackle domestic violence, we will not protect children from child abuse. And if we do not eradicate child abuse, we can never hope to conquer domestic violence.

Rights are important because they recognise the respect their bearers are entitled to. To accord rights is to respect dignity: to deny rights is to cast doubt on humanity and on integrity. Rights are an affirmation of the Kantian basic principle that we are ends in ourselves, and not means to the ends of others (Kant, 1997).

What the excluded often most lack is a right one rarely finds articulated. It is Hannah Arendt who has explained this 'right' better than anyone. Her context is very different from ours. Commenting on the Holocaust, she observed that 'a condition of complete rightlessness was created before the right to live was challenged' (1986, 296). Thus, before the Nazis robbed Jews–and gypsies, homosexuals and others–of their lives, they robbed them of their humanity, just as generations had done with slaves. The most fundamental of rights is the right to possess rights. This is a right we deny animals: some are concerned about this. We deny it also to trees, rain forests, mountains: this is less controversial, but they have their supporters too. And we do of course deny it to humans until they are born, which constitutes a major moral dilemma.[17]

For the powerful, and as far as children are concerned adults are always powerful, rights are an inconvenience. The powerful would find it easier if those below them lacked rights. It would be easier to rule, decision-making would be swifter, cheaper, more efficient, more certain. It is hardly surprising that none of the rights we have were freely bestowed: they all had to be fought for. It is, therefore, important that we see rights, as Dworkin so appositely put it, as 'trumps' (1977, ix). This is to emphasise that they cannot be knocked off their pedestal, chipped away at, because it would be better for others (in the case of children, perhaps their parents or teachers) or even for society as a whole were these rights not to exist.

Rights are important because those who have them can exercise agency. Agents are decision-makers. They are people who can negotiate with others, who are capable of altering relationships or decisions, who can shift social assumptions and constraints. And there is now clear evidence that even the youngest can do this (Alderson, Hawthorne and Killen, 2005 and Alderson, Sutcliffe and Curtis, 2006). As agents, rights-bearers can participate. They can make their own lives, rather than having their lives made for them. And participation is a fundamental human right. It enables us to demand rights. We are, of course, better able to do so where there is freedom of speech, so that orthodoxies (for example, about children and their abilities and incapacities) can be challenged; freedom of association, so that understandings can be nourished; and freedom of information. It is common to deny children all three of these freedoms.

Rights are also an important advocacy tool, a weapon which can be employed in the battle to secure recognition. Giving people rights without access to those who can present those rights, and expertly, without the right to representation, is thus of little value. But this is to acknowledge that we must get beyond rhetoric. Rights without remedies are of symbolic importance, no more. And remedies themselves require the injection of resources, a commitment on behalf of all of us that we view rights with respect, that we want them to have an impact on the lives of all people, and not just the lives of the powerful and privileged, who are often the first to exploit rights for their own purposes.

Rights offer legitimacy to pressure groups, lobbies, campaigns, to both direct and indirect action, in particular to those who are disadvantaged or excluded. They offer a way in; they open doors. It is thus hardly surprising that some of the best statements of the case for rights have come from minority scholars like Mari Matsuda (1987) Kimberlé Crenshaw (1988) and Patricia Williams (1997), or from those arguing the case for the excluded like Martha Minow (1990). For Crenshaw, adopting a rights-based discourse is a vehicle in which social movements can enter a debate into the validity of the dominant ideology as part of a counter-hegemonic strategy. And for Alan Hunt (1990): 'rights . . . have the capacity to be elements of emancipation'. He cautions, however, that they are neither 'a perfect nor exclusive vehicle' for such a loosening of bonds. They 'can only be operative as constituents of a strategy for social transformation as they become part of an emergent common sense and are articulated within social practices'. The message is, as Federle so eloquently puts it (1994, 343), 'that rights flow downhill'.

The task of the children's rights advocate is thus manifest, though no one can pretend it is easy. We must show that the case we are making is morally right, so right in fact that people will come to wonder how they can ever have thought–or more likely felt–otherwise. And we can help to negotiate this common sense through our social practices: certainly, the social practices of those who work with children can help to construct a new culture of childhood.

Rights then are also a resource: they offer reasoned argument. They support a strong moral case. Too often those who oppose rights can offer little if anything in response. For example, the opponent of anti-smacking laws who tells us that it never did him any harm (or perhaps none that he recognises!) Or, for that matter the one who, rather like the claimants in the *Williamson* case, reels off epigrams from the Book of Proverbs as if the 'wisdom' of an earlier millennium offered closure to a contemporary debate (and see Greven, 1992).

Rights then offer fora for action. Without rights the excluded can make requests, they can beg or implore, they can be troublesome; they can rely on, what has been called, noblesse oblige, or on others being charitable, generous, kind, co-operative or even intelligently foresighted. But they cannot demand, for there is no entitlement (Bandman, 1973).

Everyone concedes children must have some rights. I have not seen any purported defences of the torture of children. But many, including influential thinkers, either cannot see the point in talking about children's rights or are prepared to identify only the most limited range of rights so far as children are concerned. Thus, Goldstein, Freud and Solnit, for example, identify only three rights which they believe should be available to children: to autonomous parents, to be represented by parents and to parents who care (1996, 90, 140, 148). And Guggenheim, in his recent onslaught on children's rights, seems to offer children only one right. His concern for this right is so attenuated that he states it wrongly– there is a gross typo in this pivotal sentence. But I understand him to be offering children the right 'to be raised by parents who are minimally fit and

10          *Freeman / International Journal of Children's Rights 15 (2007) 5–23*

who are unlikely to make significant mistakes in judgment in childrearing' (2005, 43). Guggenheim, like Goldstein, Freud and Solnit before him, is defending parents' rights, not children's rights, which he is candid enough to admit are an inconvenience which obstruct the greater good.

It is easy to show that this line of thinking is wrong. Indeed, it is only one stage on from conceptualising children as the property of their parents. I have critiqued this elsewhere both generally (1997(a)) and in particular in relation to health care decision-making (2000).

The other argument—that there is no point or value in talking about children's rights—is more substantial and must be addressed. Could it really be that to believe in children's rights, to believe that they can achieve something positive for children, is misguided? Could we improve children's lives—I think we all accept this is a worthwhile goal—in some better way?

One who believes we can is Onora O'Neill (1988). In her view the key lies in obligation. It is her opinion that 'taking rights as fundamental in ethical deliberation about children has neither theoretical nor political advantage' (1988, 25). It is her contention that if we care about children's lives, we should identify what obligations parents, teachers and indeed the wider community have towards children. It is worth examining O'Neill's restatement in the light of a case such as the *Williamson* one, which has already been considered. How would we identify the parental obligation in this case? From the perspective of the child, the parents, Christianity (as interpreted by the parents and these particular schools)? If, as I suspect, it would be the parents' perspective that would count, the obligation would be to raise children in an environment which encouraged physical chastisement. What rights would this give the children? An emphasis on obligations places parents, not children, centre stage.

O'Neill believes that the child's 'main remedy is to grow up' (1988, 39). But this overlooks the impact on adult life that parenting and socialization leave. A child deprived of the sort of rights accorded by the United Nations Convention will grow up very differently from one to whom such rights are granted. And some, because of the way parents conceive their obligation will not grow up at all. I think of cases like that of the 'liver transplant' child[18] or that of the 'Maltese conjoined twins'.[19]

O'Neill's model of childhood is the conventional deficit one. As such, she underestimates the capacities and maturity of many children: for example, their ability to represent themselves and, indeed, other children. There is now evidence that this can promote resilience and positive self-conception (see Grover, 2005). She also ignores the fact that we are prepared to impose responsibility on children, including criminal responsibility, often long before we are disposed to confer rights on them (see, in relation to the U.S., Shook, 2005). The *Bulger* case (Freeman, 1997(b); King, 1995) will remain living testament to this, but its impact may even be exceeded by to-day's ASBOs (Antisocial Behaviour Orders), and these are often imposed on the least competent of children, the learning disabled.

Another critique of the importance of children's rights and of rights-language generally suggests that we should be looking rather to other morally significant values, love, friendship, compassion, altruism (Kleinig, 1982). These, it is said, raise relationships to a higher plain than one based on the observance of duty. There is a strand to this line of thought which associates rights–thinking with maleness and urges us to see, what has been called, an 'ethics of care' (Gilligan, 1982, and see also Arneil, 2002). This argument may be thought particularly apposite to children's rights, particularly in the context of family relationships. And, perhaps, in an ideal moral world this is a tenable position to hold. But we all know that this world is not an ideal one for children. It is rather one in which children suffer in many ways and in which the articulation of rights at the very least establishes targets to alleviate distress. An example is the Protocol to the UN Convention which addresses the use of child soldiers. It is not surprising, that leading minority scholars and some of their most important supporters see the value of rights-discourse.

A further argument–related to the previous one–assumes that adults already relate to children in terms of love, care and altruism, so that the case for children's rights ceases to be important; indeed, becomes otiose. This idealizes adult–child relations: it emphasises that adults (and parents in particular) consider only the best interests of children. There is a tendency for those who believe this to adopt a *laisser-faire* attitude towards the family. This can be seen clearly in the influential writings of Goldstein, Freud and Solnit (1973, 1980, 1996), and in Guggenheim's recent book (2005).

Guggenheim does not contest the value of thinking about rights: he is a passionate defender of parents' rights, even describing them as 'sacred' (2005, 71). And Goldstein, Freud and Solnit advocate a policy of minimum coercive intervention by the state. This accords with their commitment to 'individual freedom and human dignity'. But it hardly needs to be asked *whose* freedom and *what* dignity this is thought to uphold. It is difficult to see how the creation of a private space in this way can be said to protect the humanity of the child. Of course, they impose limits on parents' freedoms, and these shifted as they became conscious of the need to protect children more, but, for reasons I have given elsewhere (1997(a)), these are couched in a dangerously restrictive way.

A further argument equally rests on a myth. It sees childhood as a golden age, as the best years of our life. Childhood is seen as synonymous with innocence. It is the time when, spared the rigours of adult life, we enjoy freedom, adventure, play and joy. And the argument runs: just as we avoid the responsibilities and adversities of adult life in childhood, so there should be no necessity to think in terms of rights, a concept we have to assume is reserved for adults. Whether or not the premise underlying this were correct or not, it would represent an ideal

12                 *Freeman / International Journal of Children's Rights 15 (2007) 5–23*

state of affairs, and one which ill-reflects the lives of many of to-day's children and adolescents. For many children in the world today, this mythic 'walled garden of "Happy, Safe, Protected Innocent Childhood" ' (Holt, 1975) is just plain wrong, with poverty, disease, malnutrition, exploitation and abuse characterising the lives of children across the globe.

Some of those who argue against children's rights make a more fundamental objection. They argue that children are just not qualified to have rights; they lack the capacity to do so. 'Competence' is one of those concepts so easily grasped, or apparently so, that it has tended to be treated as if it were unproblematic. But is not an easy concept, a point that first hit home to me when I was grappling with the problem of learning disability nearly 20 years ago (Freeman, 1988). Intellectual disability is so relative (Wikler, 1979). In reality there are levels of incompetence. Beauchamp and Childress (2001) distinguish seven levels of incompetence (Buchanan and Brock, 1989):

i. The inability to evidence a preference or a choice;
ii. The inability to understand one's situation or relevantly similar situations;
iii. The inability to understand disclosed information;
iv. The inability to give a reason;
v. The inability to give a rational reason;
vi. The inability to give reasons where risk and benefit have been weighed;
vii. The inability to reach a reasonable decision, as judged, for example, by a reasonable person standard.

Even small children can show a preference, and most children can 'understand' a situation. Many can 'understand' disclosed information, and many can give reasons, though we might not be convinced by them. But how many adults get any further? Most of the adult population cannot think rationally or think in such a way as to maximise benefit or minimise loss or reach a reasoned decision. If rights were to hinge on competence at any of the higher levels depicted here, few would have them. But, of course, we do not do this. We may deprive 16-year olds of the vote because of their lack of competence (there may additionally be other reasons), but we give the vote to all (or virtually all) of those of 18 and over irrespective of their competence (at whatever level) or lack thereof.

Competence has become something of a buzz word. This may be attributed in part to the *Gillick* decision (1986). '*Gillick*–competence' has become a measuring– rod, sometimes I think a talisman. To judges and others concerned with what they believe to be its implications–and note the backlash against it in a number of decisions concerned with medical treatment–it has become a concept to narrow or explain away. In the heat generated, it is as well to remember what

*Freeman / International Journal of Children's Rights 15 (2007) 5–23* 13

Lord Scarman actually said. He tied in empowerment to competence. A competent child is one who 'achieves a sufficient understanding and intelligence to enable him or her to understand fully what is proposed' (1986, 188–189). The test does not end here, but a pause is required to take in what has been said. Note the level at which Lord Scarman has pitched understanding and intelligence. If the 'Gillick–competence' test was to be applied to the adult population, what proportion of this would be allowed to make decisions?

But a pause is required for a second reason. Most do not pursue Lord Scarman's reasoning any further. But his judgment continues: and 'has sufficient discretion to enable him or her to make a wise choice in his or her own interest' (1986, 190). In these terms competence incorporates understanding and knowledge with, for want of a better term, 'wisdom'. There are dangers in conflating knowledge and wisdom, but this is commonly done. Many children who are well below the ages with which we tend to associate *Gillick*-competence are competent within Lord Scarman's test if 'wise choice' is genuinely situated within the child's experiential knowledge of his or her 'own interest'. The English courts which, in a series of recent cases, have held that a child's right to consent to medical treatment does not extend to a right to refuse such treatment have failed to appreciate this (see Freeman, 2005).

As Alderson and Goodwin noted, 'professional, textbook knowledge is highly valued, personal experiential knowledge is discounted' (1993, 305). And, once such 'wisdom' is ignored, the child is assumed to be ignorant, except insofar as he or she can recount medical or other professional information, and accordingly incompetent.

It is then an answer to the capacity objection that it underestimates the competences that children, even young children, have. Evidence going back 20 years or more demonstrates that young children can be highly competent, technically, cognitively, socially and morally. I stress 'can' because many are not. But some can be agents. This was shown quite convincingly by Priscilla Alderson in her work on children's consent to surgery (1993). Her recent paper, co-authored with Joanna Hawthorne and Margaret Killen, is equally significant, demonstrating as it does the abilities of even young premature babies to 'participate' in decisions (2005; see also Alderson, Sutcliffe and Curtis, 2006). The article constitutes a real challenge to orthodox opinion, represented by Peter Singer and Helga Kuhse (1985), John Harris (1985) and Michael Tooley (1972), which holds that babies are not even persons, let alone rights-bearers, as Alderson and her colleagues argue.

There is a rather different answer to the capacity objection. It is put most clearly and constructively by Kate Federle (1994). She argues

'Having a right means the power to command respect, to make claims and to have them heard. But if having a right is contingent upon some characteristic, like capacity, then holding the right becomes exclusive and exclusionary: thus, only claims made by a particular group of (competent) beings will be recognized. The confining effects of this kind of rights-talk is apparent when the obverse is considered: claims made by those without the requisite characteristics of a rights holder *need not be recognised*, although specific claims which reinforce existing hierarchies may be acknowledged. There is historicity to the claim that rights for excluded groups evolve from paternalistic notions of the need to protect the weak and ignorant to recognition of capacity and autonomy, for this has been the experience of women and people of colour. Children however, have been unable to redefine themselves as competent beings; thus, powerful elites decide which, if any, of the claims made by children they will recognize' (1994, 344).

Federle concludes that there is a need to reconceptualise the meaning of having and exercising rights. The kind of rights she envisions 'are not premised upon capacity but upon power, or more precisely, powerlessness' (1994, 366). She sees rights more as inhibitions on the ability of those with power. This, she argues, creates 'zones of mutual respect for power that limit the kind of things that we may do to one another' (1994, 366). Her message that 'rights flow downhill' (1994, 365) is one we should take more seriously.

A further argument sometimes adduced against children's rights is that their exercise may not be either in their best interests or in the interests of others. The first of these criticisms pits the two sides of children's rights against each other. How are we to respond when the exercise of autonomy by a child will, in the opinion of adults, harm that child or not be in that child's best interests? Should we protect the child or his or her rights? It is, of course, fundamental to believing in rights that one accepts there is a right to do wrong, to make mistakes, to let others do things which we would not do (Dworkin, 1977, 188–189).

The classic illustration–through he did not come to this conclusion–is in Mill's *On Liberty*: the dilemma of what to do when you see someone crossing an unsafe bridge (1859). Mill was in no doubt: you pulled him back. But suppose the bridge-crosser is intending to commit suicide? Do we have the right to frustrate this exercise of autonomy when the act will mean there is no more autonomy?[20] Imagine our bridge-crosser is instead a 13-year-old Jehovah's Witness who needs a blood transfusion and is refusing it, or a 16-year-old anorexic who is refusing her consent to treatment.[21] Let us assume that both are competent in the *Gillick* sense. I will illustrate the problem by reference to a recent English case.[22] Angela Roddy was nearly 17, and a mother. She wanted to sell her story to a tabloid newspaper. There were injunctions to stop this, to protect her and her family from undue publicity by prohibiting their identification. The judge allowed Angela to proceed. He followed the *Gillick* ruling, and defended the 'right of the child who has sufficient understanding to make an informed decision to make her own choice' (2004, 968). There was a need, he said, to recognise 'Angela's dignity and integrity as a human being' (2004, 968).

She was, of course, almost an adult, but she had had the baby when 13, and in a glare of considerable publicity, though her identity was not revealed, because the Roman Catholic Church had paid for her not to have an abortion. Suppose she had tried to sell her story to the press then. Under pre-Human Rights Act jurisprudence–wardship principles–the court would have applied the best interests test and prevented her from so doing. But to-day any decision would need to be grounded in the European Convention on Human Rights. And she would clearly have rights under this to publish her story. The judge however found she also had rights 'as (her) parents or the court might wish to assert them on her behalf, (a) to keep her private life private and (b) to preserve and protect the family life she enjoys with her parents and other members of her family' (2004, 963). The court, in other words, would not allow her to make a mistake.

This injection of paternalism is explained by John Eekelaar, though not in relation to the *Roddy* case, as the situating of children's rights within dynamic self-determinism. The goal of this is 'to bring a child to the threshold of adult-hood with the maximum opportunities to form and pursue life-goals which reflect as closely as possible an autonomous choice' (1994, 53). It is explained also by Jane Fortin, in a comment on *Roddy* and indeed on this dictum, 'as gen-tle paternalism which bears the hallmarks of commonsense' (2004, 258). There are, she adds, 'respectable jurisprudential arguments for maintaining that a com-mitment to the concept of children's rights does not prevent interventions to stop children making dangerous short-term choices, thereby protecting their poten-tial for long-term autonomy'(2004, 259).

My own view is similar (though closer to Eekelaar than to Fortin). It was explained, 24 years ago, in *The Rights and Wrongs of Children* to be rooted in 'liberal paternalism' (1983, 54–60). I have since been critical of decisions which have removed rights from adolescents when they refuse to consent to medical treatment (1997(c), 2005). But others have argued that where such a dangerous, potentially life-threatening choice is made, 'liberal paternalism' requires adult intervention (Lowe and Juss, 1993). There is not a simple answer to this, or a simple solution. However, there undoubtedly needs to be less emphasis on what these young persons know–less talk in other words of knowledge and under-standing– and more on how the decision they have reached furthers their goals and coheres with their system of values. We need to understand their experiences and their culture. We must engage with them. Merely imposing treatment on them, as had happened all-too-frequently, by itself achieves nothing in the long-term. And we have to look at these decisions not just in terms of what impact they have on the young person in question, but with an understanding of what they say about our concept of childhood.

The promotion of children's rights may undermine the interests of others. This is common criticism: for example, it is at the forefront of Guggenheim's recent critique (2005). There are good reasons why the interests of children should rule. These have been rehearsed often and a brief statement is all that is required here. Children are especially vulnerable. They have fewer resources–material, psychological, relational-upon which to call in situations of adversity. They are usually blameless, and certainly did not ask to come into the world. For too long they have been regarded as objects of concern (sometimes, worse, as objects), rather than as persons, and even to-day they remain voiceless, even invisible, and it matters not that the dispute is about them.

However, it is important to realise that emphasising children does not necessarily mean that the interests of adults must be neglected. As Barbara Bennett Woodhouse eloquently reminds us: 'A truly child-centred perspective would . . . expose the fallacy that children can thrive while their care-givers struggle, or that the care-givers' needs can be severed from the child, which can lead to the attitude that violence, hostility and neglect toward the care-giver are somehow irrelevant in the best interests calculus' (1993, 1825). It is not in a child's interests to be raised in an environment in which a parent's rights are being wrongly ignored. Support for a child necessarily involves supporting that child's care-giver, and vice versa. It is, of course easier to express a formula than apply it in practice. The answers are not simple, and there are dangers of losing sight of children's interests if an emphasis on relationships places too much emphasis on adults. We may end up in a balancing exercise. Then questions arise–which I will not tackle here–as to who is to carry this out and how, and how much weight is to be given to children's interests?

Another criticism of children's rights, though it is not far removed from the one just considered is found in the writings of Laura Purdy (1992, 1994). Her case is postulated as one against children's liberation, but it is more than this. There are, she argues, sufficiently large differences in instrumental reasoning between most children and most adults to justify their being treated differently. An acceptance of the 'liberationist demand' would, she maintains, 'resign' us to a world where 'many people function worse, and take less account of the needs of others' (1994, 236). She sees the roots of children's liberation as lying in 'overly–individualistic theories' (1994, 237). And libertarianism cannot 'make room for the kind of cooperation and sacrifice necessary for a decent world' (1994, 237). Nor can children be provided with the 'intellectual and emotional pre-requisites for that kind of cooperation and sacrifice in the libertarian society' that, she believes, is envisaged by child liberationists. But this is to cast rights 'as the antithesis rather than the essence of relationship and responsibility' (McGillivray, 1994). Purdy conflates children's rights with children's liberation. She sees autonomy 'not in terms of respect and freedom of will and connection

Michael Freeman 213

with the collectivity, but as an impossible licence to do what you want freed of any sort of relational or situational constraint' (McGillivray, 1994). Advocates of children's rights are not arguing for this.

A more articulate critic of children's rights is Michael King (1994). His approach is different. He works within autopoietic theory (with which I confess to having little empathy), so that his most interesting exploration of children's rights is as much an essay in applied autopoietic theory. He has tried to remedy the gap in children's rights literature as he sees it, 'by examining how law becomes important for transforming the concept of rights from dignified statements and "manifesto rights" into rules designed to regulate relationships' between children and adults within social organisations (1994, 385). He asks why it was that those instrumental in producing the UN Convention thought it was important that the document was accepted as 'law'. I think there are answers to this question. Law is an important symbol of legitimacy. It is an accomplished fact, which it is difficult to resist. And it change attitudes as well as behaviour (Freeman, 1974, 68). For King, law is one version of reality, and whether it is experienced as 'real' hinges upon whether it can 'deliver the goods', that is improve the welfare and promote the interests of children. But how are we to get from 'rhetoric' to 'rights'? As King notes, 'the peculiar property of rights invocations in non-legal settings is that they create the expectation of law' (1994, 393).

But if the 'law'–in this instance the UN Convention–disappoints, as, of course, it has, are we to explain this as a result of the fact that 'socially perceived "problems" over children's suffering and defencelessness are so diffuse and their perceived causes so diverse that it is difficult to see how law could possibly reconstruct the issues according to its lawful/unlawful coding'? (King, 1994, 394) Or isn't this to reduce law to a superficial bipolarity? The reasons why the Convention disappoints are many. Its scope is too narrow– King is hardly likely to agree with this. Its enforcement procedures are weak–can this be explained within King's theoretical structure? Many countries have considered rhetoric and symbolism to be sufficient. King's explanation is that 'once political and economic rights have been reconstructed as legal communications, it is possible and indeed appropriate, for governments to respond by further legal communications, declaring that their policies are "lawful" within the terms of the Convention' (1994, 398). This has happened but it does not stop others, children's organisations and other NGOs, from establishing that this is not so, and campaigning for change.

It is striking how little attention has been given by philosophers and political theorists to children. Where are they in Rawls' theory of justice (1971) or in Nozick (1974) or Dworkin (2000) or Walzer (1983)? It is therefore gratifying that a recent collection edited by David Archard and Colin Macleod (2002) takes children as its focus. Again, the concept of children's rights is subject to criticism.

18 *Freeman / International Journal of Children's Rights 15 (2007) 5–23*

Thus, James Griffin argues that human rights are best reserved for 'agents'. Infants are not capable of agency, though children are. He therefore sees children as acquiring rights in stages–'the stages in which they acquire agency' (2002, 28). He lumps infants together with patients in an irreversible coma or with advanced Alzheimer's and with the severely mentally defective, as if these persons didn't have human rights. But of course they do. Consider our reaction to research being conducted on the comatose or the putting of Alzheimer's patients into a circus (would we tolerate the 'elephant man' to-day?) Or that which greeted involuntary sterilisation of the learning disabled when it surfaced to attention 20 years ago[23] (How would we react to-day to a judge like Holmes saying 'three generations of imbeciles are enough'[24]). Griffin is horrified that if we give human rights to infants, the comatose etc, we may have to give them to foetuses. But perhaps the answer to this is that we should: at the least this would have implications for late abortions. Griffin's arguments link too much to capacity/ agency (*cf* Federle, 1994) and, as has been shown, underestimate this anyway (*cf* Alderson, Hawthorne and Killen, 2005).

Agency (or its absence) is central to Harry Brighouse's arguments too. There is, the asserts, 'something very strange about thinking of children as bearers of rights' (2002, 31). 'The further an agent departs from the liberal model of the competent rational person, the less appropriate it seems to be to attribute rights' (Brighouse, 2002, 31). It goes without saying that it was once thought odd to attribute rights to women, who were certainly thought to fall short of the 'liberal model'. Brighouse does not have difficulty with seeing children as bearers of welfare rights but, like Griffin, he has problems with agency rights, at least as far as 'young children' are concerned. Of course it is easier to justify welfare rights and of course there must be some limitations to agency rights, as already indicated, but welfare rights work better in a rights culture where agency–participation, for example–is acknowledged. Protection works best where rights are also protected. The dichotomy, to which Farson (1978, 9) drew attention, between protecting the child and his/her rights, collapses in practice. Take child abuse as an example: the causes of this are undoubtedly many, but one is without question the status which children enjoy.

Brighouse is happier with the interest explanation of the basis of rights. It is certainly, a better explanation of why children have rights than the will or choice theory (MacCormick, 1982). But it does not mean, as is sometimes thought, that children cannot have agency rights. Brighouse believes such rights for children are ill-conceived and cites three such 'purported' rights in particular; to culture (Art. 30 of the Convention), religion (Art. 14) and freedom of expression (Art. 13). But why should children not have these rights? Why would (he uses the example of culture) 'jeopardize the family as an institution' (2002, 29)?

Carol Brennan's approach is more novel. To her the model that makes most sense is 'the gradualist one': children pass through a process in which initially they are 'creatures' whose interests are protected by rights to being persons 'whose rights protect their choices' (2002, 54). She has interesting things to say about the debate between the will and interest theories–which repay examination–concluding that neither of them is correct, but it is her conclusions which I find more dubious. The main reason, as she sees it, for not acknowledging that children have autonomy is that 'often children do not choose well or wisely' (2002, 59). She agrees that adults can also fail to make the right decisions.

Barbara Arneil takes a different approach. She argues that we have put too much faith in the power of rights and rights discourse and that this has bad consequences for children. This is not a novel critique: indeed, it is one to unite the 'New Right', communitarians and feminists, as well as many on the left (Freeman, 1997, 391–395). It is Arneil's view that an ethic of care, emphasizing responsibilities over rights, offers a better way of answering children's needs than relying on rights to achieve this. In Arneil's view 'rights theories do not see children as children' (2002, 93). This is a real criticism and, although I have not previously seen it made so starkly, it is one commonly voiced. In effect it amounts to regarding children's rights as an oxymoron. Arneil's vision, by contrast, views

'... The child's development in holistic terms, going beyond the capacity for rationality. Each child is included, from infancy to adolescence, and the state's role goes beyond both education to social welfare to a fully integrated set of services focused on the child's need for care and the parent's responsibility for care-giving .... The child's growth towards an independent adulthood would be seen as an organic process that unfolds within the context of a multitude of interdependent relationships within both the family and society at large. Such a vision would embrace children as full beings' (2002, 93).

There are a number of responses to this. It describes/prescribes a future so far from present realities that one wonders whether it is attainable. It envisions, as so often, the child as an object of concern rather than a subject or a participant. It over-simplifies the distinction between adults and children, perhaps neglecting even Brennan's 'gradualist' model. It fails to see the importance of rights where relationships, for whatever reason, are poor: how would Arneil deal with the 15-year-old who cannot discuss contraception or an abortion with her parents? It underestimates the part that a rights agenda can play in forging relationships. It overlooks the asymmetry of relationships where rights, and therefore power, is on one side only.

These are just some, and some of the most prominent, arguments of those who reject the case to take children's rights seriously. They have not convinced me and I know I am not going to convince them. It is important that the debate should be kept alive and healthy. The opponents have not yet toppled political initiatives of which the UN Convention is only the best-known example. The case for children's rights will prevail. We have to believe this because out of it will emerge a better world for children and this will redound to the benefit not only of children but of all of us.

## Notes

[1] I discuss some of this further in Freeman, 2001(a), 1402.

[2] Only Somalia and the U.S.A. have not done so.

[3] In England the *Gillick* decision ([1986] AC 112) and Children Act 1989 stand out.

[4] For example, see the work of Goldstein, Freud and Solnit, (1973, 1980, 1996).

[5] *R (Williamson) v. Secretary of State for Education and Employment* [2005] 2 FLR 374.

[6] Education (No.2) Act 1986 s.47; Education Act 1996 s. 548, as amended by School Standards and Framework Act 1998.

[7] Under Article 9 and Article 2 of Protocol of the European Convention on Human Rights.

[8] 406 US 205 (1972).

[9] See Article 19 of the UN Convention on the Rights of The Child. The UN Committee on the Rights of The Child issued a General Comment in June 2006. It states 'giving children equal protection from assault is 'an immediate and unqualified obligation under the Convention'.

[10] *R (Williamson) v. Secretary of State for Education and Employment* [2003] 1 FLR 726, 793.

[11] N.10, above, 793.

[12] N.5, above, 392.

[13] *Ibid*, 393.

[14] *Ibid*.

[15] For a case that would have looked different, see *R (Kehoe) v. Secretary of State for Work and Pensions* [2005] 2 FLR 1249, in particular Baroness Hale's dissent.

[16] *Bradwell v. Illinois* 83 U S (16 Wall.) 130 (1872).

[17] But the morality of abortion goes beyond the remit of this article.

[18] *Re T* [1997] 1 WLR 242.

[19] *Re A* [2001] Fam.147 (And see Freeman, 2001(a)).

[20] Mill discusses this in relation to selling oneself into slavery (see at 79).

[21] As in *Re W* [1993] Fam 64.

[22] *Re Roddy* [2004] 2 FLR 949.

[23] In *Re B* [1988] AC 199 and see Freeman, 1988 (a).

[24] See *Buck v. Bell* 274 US 200 (1927).

## References

Alderson, P. (1993) *Children's Consent To Surgery*, Buckingham: Open University Press.

Alderson, P. and Goodwin, M. (1993) 'Contradictions within Concepts of Children's Competence' *International Journal of Children's Rights*, 1, 303–314.

Alderson, P., Hawthorne, J. and Killen, M. (2005) 'The Participation Rights of Premature Babies' *International Journal of Children's Rights*, 13, 31–50.

Alderson, P., Sutcliffe, K. and Curtis, K. (2006) Children as Partners with Adults in their Medical Care *Archives of Disease in Childhood*, 91, 300–303.

Archard, D. (2004) *Children, Rights and Childhood*, London: Routledge, 2004 (2nd ed).

Arendt, H. (1986) *The Origins of Totalitarianism*, London: André Deutsch.

Arneil, B. (2002) Becoming versus Being: 'A Critical Analysis of the Child in Liberal Theory' in Archard, D. and Macleod, C. (eds), *The Moral and Political Status of Children*, Oxford: Oxford University Press, 70–94.

Bandman, B. (1973) 'Do Children Have Any Natural Rights?' *Proceedings of the 29th Annual Meeting Of Philosophy of Education Society*, 234–246.

Beauchamp, T. and Childress, J. (2001) *Principles of Biomedical Ethics*, Oxford: Oxford University Press.

Brennan, S. (2002) 'Children's Choices or Children's Interests: Which Do Their Rights Protect?' in Archard, D. and Macleod, C. (eds), *The Moral and Political Status of Children*, Oxford Oxford University Press, 53–69.

Brighouse, H. (2002) 'What Rights (If Any) Do Children Have? In Archard, D. and Macleod, C. (eds), *The Moral and Political Status of Children*, Oxford: Oxford University Press, 31–52.

Buchanan, A. and Brock, D. (1989) *Deciding for Others: The Ethics of Surrogate Decision Making*, New York: Cambridge University Press.

Crenshaw, K. (1988) 'Race, Reform and Retrenchment: Transformation and Legitimization in Anti-Discrimination Law', *Harvard Law Review*, 101, 1331.

Dworkin, R. (1977) *Taking Rights Seriously*, London: Duckworth.

Dworkin, R. (1986) *Law's Empire*, London: Fontana.

Dworkin, R. (2000) *Sovereign Virtue*, Cambridge, Mass: Harvard University Press.

Eekelaar, J. (1994) 'The Interests of The Child and the Child's Wishes: The Role of Dynamic Self-Determinism' *International Journal of Law and the Family*, 8, 42–63.

Farson, R. (1978) *Birthrights*, Harmondsworth: Penguin Books.

Federle, K.H. (1994) 'Rights Flow Downhill', *International Journal of Children's Rights*, 2, 343–368.

Fortin, J. (2004) 'Children's Rights: Are The Courts Taking Them More Seriously?' *King's College Law Journal*, 15, 253–273.

Fortin, J. (2006) 'Children's Rights: Substance or Spin?' *Family Law*, 36, 759–763.

Freeman, M. (1974) *The Legal Structure*, Harlow: Longman.

Freeman, M. (1979) *Violence In The Home: a Socio-Legal Study*, Aldershot: Gower.

Freeman, M. (1980) 'The Rights of Children in The International Year of the Child', *Current Legal Problems*, 33, 1–31.

Freeman, M. (1983(a)) *The Rights and Wrongs of Children*, London: Frances Pinter.

Freeman, M. (1988(a)) 'Sterilising The Mentally Handicapped' in Freeman, M. (ed), *Medicine, Ethics and Law*, London: Stevens, 55–84.

Freeman, M. (1988(b)) 'Taking Children's Rights Seriously', *Children and Society*, 1, 299–319.

Freeman, M. (1992) 'Taking Children's Rights More Seriously', *International Journal of Law and the Family*, 6, 52–71.

Freeman, M. (1997(a)) 'Is *The Best Interests of the child* in the Best Interests of Children?' *International Journal of Law, Policy and the Family*, 11, 360–388.

Freeman, M. (1997(b)) 'The James Bulger Tragedy: Childish Innocence and the Construction of Guilt' in Freeman, M., *The Moral Status of Children*, The Hague: Kluwer Law International, 235–253.

Freeman, M. (1997(c)) 'Removing Rights From Adolescents' in Freeman, M., *The Moral Status of Children*, The Hague: Kluwer Law International, 345–356.

Freeman, M. (2000) 'Can We Leave The Best Interests of Very Sick Children To their Parents?' in Freeman, M. and Lewis, A. (eds) *Law and Medicine*, Oxford University Press, 257–268.

Freeman, M. (2001(a)) 'Whose Life Is It Anyway?' *Medical Law Review*, 9, 259–280.
Freeman, M. (2001(b)) *Lloyd's Introduction To Jurisprudence*, London: Sweet and Maxwell (7th edition).
Freeman, M. (2005) 'Rethinking *Gillick*', *International Journal of Children's Rights*, 13, 201–217.
Freeman, M. (2006) 'What's Right with Children's Rights', *International Journal of Law In Context*, 2, 89–98.
*Gillick* v *West Norfolk and Wisbech Area Health Authority* [1986] A.C. 112.
Gilligan, C. (1982) *In Another Voice*, Cambridge, Mass: Harvard University Press.
Goldstein, J., Freud, A. and Solnit, A. (1973) *Beyond The Best Interests of The Child*, New York: Free Press.
Goldstein, J., Freud, A. and Solnit, A. (1980) *Before The Best Interests of The Child*, New York: Free Press.
Goldstein, J., Freud, A. and Solnit, A. (1996) *The Best Interests of The Child*, New York: Free Press.
Greven, P. (1992) *Spare The Child*, New York: Vintage Books.
Griffin, J. (2202) 'Do Children Have Rights' in Archard, D. and Macleod, C. (eds) *The Moral and Political Status of Children*, Oxford: Oxford University Press, 19–30.
Grover, S. (2005) 'Advocacy by Children As A Causal Factor in Promoting Resilience', *Childhood*, 12, 527–538.
Guggenheim, M. (2005) *What's Wrong With Children's Rights*, Cambridge, Mass: Harvard University Press.
Harris, J. (1985) *The Value of Life*, London: Routledge, Kegan Paul.
Holt, J. (1975) *Escape From Childhood*, Harmondsworth: Penguin Books.
Hunt, A. (1990) 'Rights and Social Movements: Counter-Hegemonic Strategies', *Journal of Law and Society*, 17, 309–337.
Kant, I. (1997) *Groundwork of The Metaphysics of Morals*, Cambridge: Cambridge University Press Originally published in 1783.
King, M. (1994) 'Children's Rights as Communication: Reflections on Autopoietic Theory and the United Nations Convention', *Modern Law Review*, 57, 385–401.
King, M. (1995) 'The James Bulger Murder Trials: Moral Dilemmas and Social Solutions' *International Journal of Children's Rights*, 3, 167–187.
Kleinig, J. (1982) *Philosophical Issues In Education*, London: Croom Helm.
Lowe, N. and Juss, S. (1993) 'Medical Treatment–Pragmatism and the Search for Principle' *Modern Law Review*, 56, 865–872.
MacCormick, N. (1982) *Legal Rights and Social Democracy*, Oxford: Clarendon Press, 1982.
McGillivray, A. (1994) 'Why Children Do Have Equal Rights in Reply to Laura Purdy' *International Journal of Children's Rights*, 2, 243–258.
Matsuda, M. (1987) 'Looking To The Bottom: Critical Legal Studies and Reparations', *Harvard Civil Rights–Civil Liberties Law Review*, 22, 338.
Mayall, B. (2002) *Towards A Sociology of Childhood*, London: Routledge, Falmer.
Menkel-Meadow, C. (1987) 'Excluded Voices: New Voices in the Legal Profession Making New Voices In The Law' *University of Miami Law Review*, 42, 29–53.
Mill, J.S. (1989) *On Liberty*, Cambridge: Cambridge University Press (Originally published 1859).
Minow, M. (1990) *Making all The Difference*, Ithaca, N.Y: Cornell University Press.
Nozick, R. (1974) *Anarchy, State and Utopia*, Oxford: Blackwell.
O'Neill, O. (1998) 'Children's Rights and Children Lives', *Ethics*, 98, 445–463.

Purdy, L. (1992) *In Their Best Interest?*, Ithaca, N.Y: Cornell University Press.

Purdy, L. (1994) 'Why Children Shouldn't Have Equal Rights', *International Journal of Children's Rights*, 2, 223–258.

Rawls, J. (1971) *A Theory of Justice*, Cambridge, Mass: Harvard University Press.

Shook, J.J. (2005) 'Contesting Childhood in the US Justice System: The Transfer of Juveniles to Adult Criminal Court'. *Childhood*, 12, 461–478.

Singer, P. and Kuhse, H. (1975) *Should The Baby Live?* Oxford: Oxford University Press.

Tooley, M. (1972) 'Abortion and Infanticide', *Philosophy and Public Affairs*, 2, 37–65.

Valentine, G. (2004) *Public Space and The Culture of Childhood*, Aldershot: Ashgate.

Walzer, M. (1983) *Spheres of Justice*, New York: Basic Books.

Wikler, D. (1979) 'Paternalism and The Mildly Retarded', *Philosophy and Public Affairs*, 8, 377–392.

Williams, P. (1997) *The Alchemy of Race and Rights*, Cambridge, Mass: Harvard University Press.

Woodhouse, B.B. (1993) 'Hatching The Egg: A Child-Centered Perspective on Parents' Rights' *Cardozo Law Review*, 14, 1747–1864.

# [9]
# Legal Ideologies, Patriarchal Precedents, and Domestic Violence

## Introduction

In the last dozen years there has been considerable interest in the problem of violence against women (Binney, Harkell, and Nixon 1981; Borkowski, Murch, and Walker 1983; Bowker 1983; Davidson 1978; Dobash and Dobash 1980; Freeman 1979; Gelles 1974 and 1979; Langley and Levy 1977; Martin 1976; Moore 1979; Pagelow 1981; Pizzey 1979; Pizzey and Shapiro 1982; Schechter 1983; Straus, Gelles, and Steinmetz 1980; Walker 1979; Wilson 1976, 1983). One response to this concern has been the development of various legal remedies designed to provide women with protection and relief. There is, however, no indication that the legal remedies are efficacious or that they are contributing to the conquest of, what all agree is, a severe social problem. Does this reflect on the limits of effective legal action or are we faced with an ambivalent form of social deviance – a form which is not susceptible to eradication through legal means so long as the law reflects an ideology supportive of the behaviour? Can the law provide solutions to the problems of violence against women when it constitutes part of that problem? In many areas, as Klein notes, 'the law *itself* constitutes the harm' (1981:66).

This article investigates this problem using, as a case study, English law and practice, appropriately since the private ills of battered women were recognized as a public problem in England before they were recognized elsewhere (Freeman 1977; May 1978). Furthermore, remedies developed in England to tackle the problem have provided a model for other legal systems. I argue that the legal system is a cultural underpinning of patriarchy. Though mindful of the dangers of developing conspiratorial models (see Coward 1983; Rowbotham

The State, the Law, and the Family

1981), I show in this article how the English legal system is permeated by ideological considerations that express the subordination of women to the patriarchy.

The debate about violence against women needs to be removed from deliberations about strategies for social, including legal, intervention and placed firmly within the arena of sexual politics. Violence by husbands against wives should not be seen as a breakdown in the social order, as orthodox interpretations perceive it, but as an affirmation of a particular sort of social order. Looked at in this way domestic violence is not dysfunctional; quite the reverse, it appears functional. But violence against women must not be viewed as an abstract, unproblematic concept. Nor can it be taken out of its historical context and perceived as some kind of transhistorical activity. It must be considered in a particular cultural context.

### The position of women in England today

In *Capitalism, the Family and Personal Life*, Zaretsky has described how the family and the familial role of women became idealized, the home became a refuge from the demands of capitalist society, 'a separate realm for the economy' (1976: 30; see also Foreman 1977) – a private place to which people, but especially men, could withdraw. In Lasch's graphic phrase, the family became a 'haven in a heartless world' (1977: 6). 'The family', Lasch has written, 'found ideological support and justification in the conception of domestic life as an emotional refuge in a cold and competitive society' (1977:6). But the home became not only a 'walled garden' but also a 'stifling menagerie' (Davidoff, L'Esperance, and Newby 1976: 163). Man became the breadwinner; his wife the dependent home-maker. The ideology encapsulated by this was adopted first by the middle classes and only later by working-class people. That we can speak of 'the family' today as a single entity is in major part the product of the gradual bourgeoisification of the working class who, as Barrett puts it, 'acknowledged the moral legitimacy of the bourgeoisie by adopting its family structure' (1980: 203; see also Flandrin 1979). Poster has described this as 'one of the unwritten aspects of the political success of bourgeois democracy' (1979: 196).

The position of women in British society today is closely related to their role within the family. An understanding of women's oppression accordingly requires a description and analysis of the position of women in today's privatized family. As McIntosh has observed,

Ideologies and domestic violence

'ultimately the very construction of men and women as separate and opposed categories takes place within, and in the terms of, the family' (1979: 154). Women are expected to be dependent on men. Their role is geared to the household. They are responsible for child care, as well as for the care of the aged and handicapped. Their domestic labour is seen as non-productive, not real work. Women, particularly married women, have to be housewives: if they do not carry out the service roles depicted here they are 'bad' housewives, but housewives nevertheless. Furthermore, as Millett notes, 'sex role is sex rank' (1969: 343). As long as woman's place is defined as separate, a 'male-dominated society will define her place as inferior' (Brown *et al.* 1971: 873).

In fact most women are also engaged in remunerative employment. For well over a century, women have constituted about one-third of the formal labour force in Great Britain; 32 per cent of women in paid employment in Britain work part-time (*Social Trends* 1984: 60). Women workers are not dispersed throughout all sectors of the economy, but are heavily concentrated in four occupational groups: clerical workers, service, sports, or recreational workers (mainly cooks, canteen assistants, and office cleaners); professional and technical workers such as teachers and nurses; and shop assistants. It is noticeable that women are over-represented in work which resembles domestic work in the house: ideological divisions within the family are reproduced in the labour market. To Alexander (1976: 59), this represents an extension of the division of labour in the patriarchal family. Nor is this new: Pinchbeck's evidence from the early Victorian period indicates similar work patterns (1977: Appendix) and Clark's *Working Life of Women in the Seventeenth Century* (1919) suggests that even where goods were being produced in the household there was a division of labour along gender lines. The ideology of gender and divisions of work tasks antedate capitalism. Capitalism is nevertheless a watershed, for it divided the work force into wage-earners and those dependent upon the wage of others. In Barrett's words, 'capitalism did not create domestic social relations in which pre-existing divisions were not only reproduced but solidified in the wage-labour system' (1980: 182). Divisions of work tasks along gender lines also exist in so-called 'socialist' countries such as the Sòviet Union, Czechoslovakia (Heitlinger 1979), and China (Croll 1978).

In trying to understand the position that women occupy in the labour market as a secondary labour force (Barron and Norris 1976), it is difficult to avoid the conclusion that family structure and the

The State, the Law, and the Family

ideology of domestic responsibility are significant factors. Barrett puts it this way:

> 'It is clear . . . that women's involvement in the highly exploited areas of part-time work and home-work is the direct consequence of their responsibility for child care. This type of work is not only most convenient for a worker with responsibility for children, it is often (in the absence of nursery or after-school provision) literally the only work available. In addition to this, the categories of work primarily undertaken by women have clearly been constructed along the lines of an ideology of gender which poses servicing and caring work as pre-eminently "feminine". Furthermore, the construction of a family form in which the male head of household is supposedly responsible for the financial support of a dependent wife and children has militated against demands for equal pay and equal "right to work" for women. The "right" of married women to take jobs at the expense of male workers has frequently been explicitly challenged .... Family responsibilities play a direct role in the structure of women's wage labour and in setting limits on women's participation.
>
> (Barrett 1980: 157-58)

But the process is not one way. The weak position of women on the labour market has the effect of reinforcing their subordination in the home. The notion of the 'family wage' has as its concomitant female dependence. A privileged male wage has usually meant an under-privileged female one. Women's wages are generally seen as supplementary to those of husband wage-earners, even by many women themselves.

The family wage notion is usually justified in terms of the sexual division of labour. Thus, it is said to rest on a fair distribution of responsibilities between the sexes, to uphold complementarity of roles. But the sexual division of labour is, as Molyneux notes, 'more than a mere technical division in that it helps to enforce relations of domination and subordination creating structures of privilege and discrimination' (1979: 24). Women are expected to perform household duties even when they are employed on the labour market. Most are poorly paid. These two considerations together act as a deterrent to women seeking remunerative employment and encourage them to seek fulfilment in the home. Female unemployment is also frequently justified by invoking the family wage notion: family income should be provided by its 'head'. An effect of this ideology is that women are not expected to enter the labour market but to become housewives and mothers, or at best part-time workers earning 'pin-money'. Both their formal and informal education tends to be oriented toward these skills and expectations (David 1980). This in turn is reinforced by the sexual division of labour which, as already noted, allocates women in the main to jobs designed to utilize their 'natural', 'feminine' capabilities.

## The law and ideological practice

Where does the legal system fit into this? How do its rules, principles, and administration reflect the practice discussed in the previous section? It is common for lawyers to believe that the law does not play an active role in regulating family relationships. 'The normal behaviour of husband and wife or parents and children towards each other', wrote Kahn-Freund, 'is beyond the law – as long as the family is healthy. The law comes in when things go wrong' (Eekelaar 1971: 7). In the same book Eekelaar wrote of 'English practice', which, he said, 'has been to refrain from formulating general principles as to how families should be managed' (1971: 76). Seven years later, he wrote in *Family Law and Social Policy* of the law's 'minor role in creating conditions which are hoped to be conducive to the successful creation of families' (Eekelaar 1978: xxvii).

This view completely distorts reality. It is clear that not only does the law serve to reproduce social order, but it actually constitutes and defines that order. The legal form is one of the main modalities of social practice through which actual relationships embodying sexual stratification have been expressed. Law defines the character and creates the institutions and social relationships within which the family operates. The legal system is constantly recreating a particular ideological view of relationships between the sexes, best expressed as an ideology of patriarchalism.

That law operates as a form of ideological practice was propagated by Marx and Engels (Cain and Hunt 1979: Chapter 4) and articulated more fully by Gramsci (1971) and Althusser (1971). Such a view has gained currency in the last decade largely through its propagation by social historians. Hay (1975), Thompson (1975), and others, as well as in the writings of critical legal theorists such as Fraser (1978) and Klare (1979). Law plays a primary and significant role in producing social order. The power of law is as a symbol. This power is based on

The State, the Law, and the Family

an ideology of law and an ideology of women supported by law. Relationships between the sexes are expressed 'through the forms of law' (Thompson 1975: 262). One function of ideology is to mystify social reality and to obstruct social change. Law functions, in Gramsci's expression (Boggs 1976: 36-54), as a form of 'ideological hegemony'. For example, it states that women are dependent home-makers and this helps to induce people to consent to this state of affairs, to see it as natural, even just (Peattie and Rein 1983: Chapter 1). Because law has this effect, it acts as a powerful ideological force supportive of social stability. What the law says is so, is 'reality'. The ideology of law is additionally part of its form as a set of principles embodying a notion of rationality. For, as Gouldner has argued, 'freezing ideas and information in words makes it possible to assess more coolly and rigorously the validity of an argument' and this reinforces 'a certain kind of rationality' (1976: 41). The law in relation to women is seen to reflect a rational set of beliefs.

It is important to recognize the power of law as ideology when social engineering efforts to change the status of women are examined. Beliefs in the power of legislation or the results of litigation to effect social reform reflect the pervasive belief in law as a source of social change (see Marris and Rein 1972). But this ignores the ideological power of law to mask social reality and to obstruct real social change. Even the creation of a new corpus of rights for women, as seems to have happened with, for example, equal opportunities or abortion legislation, does not undermine basic sexual hierarchies. The passage of an Act like the Domestic Violence and Matrimonial Proceedings Act of 1976, the victory of Jennifer Davis in a highly publicized case (*Davis* v. *Johnson* 1979), the use of terms like a 'battered mistresses' charter' or 'new rights for women assaulted by their cohabitants', common after a successful piece of litigation, divert potential public consciousness away from the deeper roots of the problem. The power of law is such that by framing the issue in terms of individual rights the real problem is obscured. With domestic violence, as we shall see, the tendency has been to individualize the problem, so that social and psychological analysis has been very much in tune with legal thinking. Both have concentrated on a small sample of known batterers, on 'official deviants' (Box 1981). None of these disciplines has done much to improve the overall position of women.

Ideologies and domestic violence

## Women, law, and ideology

A study of the relationship between the law and the family today gives us insight into the modern forms of patriarchy. The law both serves and legitimizes patriarchal power. Many justifications are posited for treating men and women differently in law (Okin 1979). These may rest on sex differences, but usually gender role differences are called upon to justify differential treatment. But the law itself is a major instrumental force in constructing the gender role differences themselves. 'Legal institutions support the ordering of society on a gender role basis . . . The law defines and reinforces gender roles for individuals which do not necessarily have an inevitable connection with sex differences' (O'Donovan 1979: 135). Very few of the rights and duties of husband and wife are laid down in legislation in England, but there is a consensus among lawyers, judges, and governmental bureaucrats about the legal nature of family relationships. Barker comments that 'the lack of specification reflects the totality of the relationship . . . and that it is a relationship of *personal* dependency' (1978: 242). 'Women cannot at one and the same time be married as we understand marriage, and independent,' Wilson (1977: 153) observes, speaking of the cohabitation rule as a particular instance of this 'general principle'.

Women are supposed to be dependent and to lack power and control over themselves. Their domestic work is seen as non-productive. There are ideals to which 'a good wife' must conform. Her status, her standard of living, her expectations, her life-style, and much of her identity are governed by her husband, even by her cohabitant as the law gradually assimilates the rights and obligations of quasi-marital relationships to those of marriage (Freeman and Lyon 1983). Married women are not autonomous individuals, but are defined in legal institutions in terms of marriage.

There is no better illustration of this relationship, particularly since it demonstrates direct intrusion by the state apparatus, than in fiscal policies (Lister 1980) and social security arrangements (Allatt 1981). These affect the economic dependence of women at every turn. Men and women are not treated equally. Both are stereotyped and discrimination is a necessary concomitant, for women do not fit the female stereotype upon which such laws and other institutional arrangements are predicated. Assumptions about the place of married women derive from economic and demographic concerns of the 1930s (Land 1976), though they are rooted in an ideology that developed

The State, the Law, and the Family

with industrialization in the nineteenth century. The woman's place is in the home, and this 'cult of domesticity' is supported throughout in the tax and social security systems.

The law in Britain relating to national insurance, pensions, supplementary benefit, sickness and unemployment benefit, family income supplement, and income tax are all based on stereotypical sex classifications that impute a dependent role to women. The system assumes that women's earnings are supplementary to the male breadwinner's, and women and children dependent on the man's income. The social security system strengthens the subordinate position of women as domestic workers inside the family and as a secondary labour force outside it. They are, even with recent reforms, largely excluded from independent rights to benefits because they are assumed to be dependent on their husband's income. Women not conforming to the norm of dependence on men are often relegated to a low level of benefits. At the same time, social security policies nurture the position of women as low-paid, casual, or part-time workers, or even home-workers with low pay and insecurity. Parker and Land have commented that 'in reading the social security legislation it would be hard to deduce that the "typical" family consisting of a man in full-time employment, the woman as a full-time housewife, and two dependent children has been at any point a minority of families' (1978: 342). In fact, few families conform to this stereotype.

In reality many women are not dependent on men. Some are wage-earners who do not need men to support them; and many widows, separated and divorced women, and unmarried mothers do not have and may not want men to support them. But, as Ginsburg notes, 'support of these women by the state has been such as to encourage, if possible, the renewal of dependence on men and to discourage the break-up of marriage by rendering single motherhood less eligible and attractive' (1979: 79). Unsupported women (that is, those not barred by the cohabitation rule) tend to fall back on supplementary benefit but supplementary benefit authorities, and before them the poor law, have consistently attempted to shift the burden of support from the state (or parish) to 'liable relatives'. They have attempted to re-establish economic dependence on husbands and fathers. In fact the authorities have had little success. Thus, the cost to the state of providing benefits where there were 'liable relatives' was £486 million in 1978 and only £35½ million of this sum was recovered from 'liable relatives' (Supplementary Benefits Commission 1979: table 12.8). Not surprisingly, many women are not especially co-operative in

Ideologies and domestic violence

helping the authorities to establish paternity or locate a separated husband. The invitation to re-establish dependence is quite properly rejected by many women. This is not entirely true, for when a marriage breaks up there are implicit pressures on a woman to remarry. Having been (if that is the case) a housewife for a number of years, a woman has decreasing value on the labour market. Thus, as Delphy has noted:

> 'from the woman's standpoint, marriage creates the conditions for its own continuation and encourages entry into a second marriage if a particular union comes to an end. . . . For the majority of women the contrast between the standard of living that they enjoy while married and that which they can expect after divorce simply redoubles the pressures in favour of marriage or remarriage depending on the circumstances.'
>
> (Delphy 1976: 81)

The roots of the social security system are embedded in the Beveridge Report published during the Second World War. Women were not treated equally in this report. Man and wife were seen 'as a team' (Beveridge 1942: 45). The married woman was to be treated as a dependent of her husband, and as entitled to economic support by him, both for herself and their children. Thus, it was argued that 'it should be open to any married woman to undertake [paid employment] as an exempt person, paying no contribution of her own and acquiring no claim to benefit in unemployment or sickness' (Beveridge 1942: 50). Those who opted to contribute were to receive benefits at a reduced rate. For Beveridge, 'maternity [was] the principal object of marriage' (1942: 50) and his proposal that maternity benefits should be higher than normal unemployment or disability benefits (as Wilson notes, 'reproduction was . . . tacitly defined as a disability' (1977: 151)) was adopted by the legislature in 1948, though repealed in 1953. Beveridge's conception of the family 'articulated ideas which already commanded a good deal of support' (Harris 1977: 415).

A number of Beveridge's initiatives have succumbed to recent reforms. Women entering employment now have to pay full contributions and can receive full benefits. The new state pension scheme has introduced protected state pension rights for women: years of 'home responsibility' count as contribution years. There are new maternity rights for women though these are mainly conditional on contributions, continuity, and hours of employment – thus excluding the majority of mothers from them. But increasing formal recognition

The State, the Law, and the Family

of equality can obscure discriminatory structures which continue to
exist.

For all the reforms, the social security system still embodies the
concept of women's dependence on men and emphasizes their maternal
and domestic duties. Countless examples remain, two of which will
be examined. The most notorious principle of the social security
system is the cohabitation rule. It has been described by Ginsburg as
'the implicit reinforcement of patriarchy within the social security
system' (1979: 87). The rule – which applies to a wide range of
benefits, though criticism tends to centre on its application to supplementary benefits, where it is policed most stringently – states that
where a husband and wife live together as members of the same
household their requirements and resources shall be aggregated and
treated as the husband's. Only he then may claim the relevant
benefits. Though this is susceptible to criticism, it is the extension of
the rule to men and women who 'live together as a man and wife' that
has provoked most censure (Lister 1970). What is meant by 'cohabitation' is not defined in statute or case law. A number of considerations
are taken into account in determining whether a man and a woman
are living together as man and wife, though more than a lurking
suspicion remains that the primary consideration in the minds of
officials and investigators is a sexual relationship between the couple.
The now defunct Supplementary Benefits Commission itself admitted
that 'in the last resort, it is a matter of personal judgement' (DHSS
1971: para. 15).

The cohabitation rule is symptomatic of the ideology structuring
family relationships, for it assumes that if a man lives with a woman
he supports her. The rule is often justified on the basis that an
unmarried couple should not get more favourable treatment than a
married man and his wife would. This is in many ways a boot strap
argument for it assumes and does not question that marriage should
contain a breadwinner and a dependent. In this sense the removal of
the cohabitation rule would reveal starkly the dependence and inequality inherent in the marriage relationship. This aside, the way the
rule operates, a married woman is treated 'more favourably' than her
cohabiting sister. The rule puts women, who are often in tenuous
personal and economic circumstances, into a position where it is
difficult for them to establish stable and viable relationships with
men. It subjects them to widespread invasions of privacy from those
policing the system. It is thoroughly anomalous. A man has no
obligation to maintain a woman with whom he is living, even if he has

fathered children by her, though he may be compelled to support any such children through affiliation payments. A cohabiting woman has no legal means of compelling support. On the other hand, a married man gets a tax allowance for his wife, irrespective of whether there are dependent children: a man receives no tax allowance for the woman with whom he cohabits. The cohabitation rule succours the institution of marriage (in itself a strange moral argument), but undoubtedly also reinforces the ideology of dependence which so permeates the legal system and its administration.

A second example of arrangements that embody notions of dependence is to be found in several statutory provisions governing tax and social security. As already indicated, a married man gets a tax allowance for his wife. It is assumed that a wife 'or some female person' should care for that man's children and do his housework. An additional personal allowance is paid where wives are incapacitated. But married women with incapacitated husbands are denied this additional allowance. As O'Donovan has noted:

'The allowance reflects the assumption that it is a married woman's unpaid job to care for children and that if she cannot do so, her husband is entitled to financial assistance for someone else to perform the job. In contrast, a woman on her own, even if working, is not considered by the courts as in need of an allowance for a substitute childminder'.

(O'Donovan 1979: 145-46)

Similar examples can be found in other social security provisions. The invalid care allowance is not paid to married women. This can only be because they are expected to do such work without compensation. Where additions for adult dependents are given to those who get the allowance, these are limited to a wife or 'some female person . . . who . . . has care of a child or children of the beneficiary's family' (Social Security Act 1975, s.37 (3)): in other words, a male dependent caring for children is excluded. It is also notable, though perfectly consistent with a system which emphasizes women's domestic duties, that a disabled married woman is not eligible for the non-contributory invalidity pension 'except where she is incapable of performing normal household duties' (Social Security Act 1975, s.37 (2)). This test has been described as an 'unjust and illogical anachronism,' (Glendinning 1980: 13). The assumption behind the 'household duties' test is that a married woman is by definition a 'housewife',

The State, the Law, and the Family

who is dependent on her bread-winner husband for financial support
and whose contribution to the family is the unpaid work she does in
the home. Indeed, the 1974 British Government white paper which
first proposed a non-contributory invalidity pension for married
women says as much (*Social Security Provision for Chronically Sick
and Disabled People* 1974). The retention of the 'normal household
duties' test is virtually impossible to defend but it limps on, as one of
the most stereotypically sexist of social security provisions (Equal
Opportunities Commission 1981).

These examples illustrate the way in which fiscal policies and social
security arrangements impose a particular structural form, patriarchy,
on social relationships between men and women. Sachs discusses the
reasoning used by the judiciary in the nineteenth and early twentieth
centuries to deny women rights to participate in the professions and
in public affairs and demonstrates the use of a strikingly similar
ideology. For sixty years the judiciary strongly denied that women
were 'persons'. Accordingly, they were denied voting rights, rights to
higher education, and other rights. The judges even accepted the
absurd argument that 'women were persons for the purpose of legal
disabilities but non-persons for the purpose of legal rights' (Sachs
1976: 107). A reversal came in 1929 (*Edwards* v. *A.-G. for Canada*
1930). Sachs (1976: 114) suggests that there is no explanation of the
change in terms of judicial reasoning, in 'legal logic'. He and Wilson
argue that 'a study of sexism in the legal systems of Britain and the
United States . . . explodes the notion that legal systems evolve
according to inherent principles of logic and procedure'. They continue:

'the structures of the law were part of the wider social structures
rather than apart from them. The inequality in public life which
the women complained about was as present inside the legal
system as outside of it, while the stake which the male judges had
in maintaining gender exclusiveness was in some ways more direct
than any interest they might have had in maintaining race or class
inequality.'

(Sachs and Wilson 1978: 225)

They show how it was the prevailing concept of 'womanhood' that
determined how the courts would decide the arguments. The judges
put forward a theory of sexual complementarity. Sachs and Wilson
argue that this was 'merely a gracious way of explaining subjection'
(1978: 52). The judges couched their language, their justifying reason-

Ideologies and domestic violence

ing in terms of refinement, decorum, and delicacy. They stressed that women were not being deprived so much as exempted. They claimed to be endorsing women's favoured position as elevated spiritual beings. The exemption was said to be based on respect. The clearest statement of this comes in Willes J.'s judgement in the notorious Manchester voters' case, *Chorlton* v. *Longs* (1869). 'Far from being impartial arbiters,' Pearson and Sachs argue, '... the Judges appear to have been part of the very problem the women and their male supporters were complaining about . . . the judges believed in the principle of gender exclusiveness, and said as much, both on and off the Bench' (1980: 401).

The bias in the 'persons' cases that glares at us today was just as clearly impartial justice to the judges and the majority of society 100 years ago. 'What was self-evident truth to feminists, however, was manifest absurdity to most judges' (Sachs and Wilson 1978: 6). How, then, is this particular change to be explained? Sachs argues that 'what had altered was the ideology of the Judges' (1976: 108). It is not necessary here to examine why this had altered. But what the history of the male monopoly cases puts beyond question is the way that judicial reasoning both reflected dominant male interests (it was, for example, important for middle-class men and their status position to have an unemployed wife) and reinforced patriarchalism.

It is not unusual for judicial modes of reasoning to define issues in terms favourable to dominant groups. There can be few better examples of this than Lord Denning's reasoning in the leading divorce case of *Wachtel* v. *Wachtel* in 1973. Earlier, in a lecture at Liverpool University, he had warned of the dangers of women being given equality. He had pointed to, what he saw as, the Roman example (Denning 1960) (see further Freeman 1984). In *Wachtel* v. *Wachtel*, Lord Denning defended the resuscitation of the 'one-third rule' as a starting point for the reallocation of assets on divorce in this way:

'When a marriage breaks up, there will thenceforward be two households instead of one. The husband will have to go out to work all day and must get some woman to look after the house – either a wife, if he re-marries, or a housekeeper, if he does not. He will also have to provide maintenance for the children. The wife will not usually have so much expense. She may go out to work herself, but she will not usually employ a housekeeper. She will do most of the housework herself, perhaps with some help. In

The State, the Law, and the Family

> any case, when there are two households, the greater expense
> will, in most cases, fall on the husband than the wife.'
>
> > (*Wachtel* v. *Wachtel* 1973: 94)

Of course, this reasoning is totally unrealistic. Most men whose
marriages founder do not employ housekeepers. And, even if this
argument were relevant, it would not explain why wives are not
allowed the value of their housekeeping services. The fact that a wife
will not employ a housekeeper hardly seems a justification for cutting
down on her share. Lord Denning's reasoning makes a number of
assumptions and none of them is right. First, that all women perform
household duties and that no men do housework. Second, that only
fathers maintain their children. Mothers who do not take remunerative
employment, do so in kind rather than in cash. Indeed, they often
forgo paid employment and lose promotion to do so. Third, that
housework is not real work.

Lord Denning is the most influential of contemporary English
judges (see Jowell and McAuslan 1984). He thinks, as do much of the
public, that his decisions are some form of 'wives' charter' (Denning
1980). It is as well to remind ourselves of Thompson's insight that 'the
dominated and oppressed have often perceived their grievances in
legal terms and articulated their needs and interests in terms of rights
thought to be promised or owed by law'. In fact, he adds, rather
wryly, 'some of them had the impertinence, and the imperfect sense
of historical perspective, to expect justice' (1975: 268). Thompson is
making the point, expressed throughout this section, that if law is to
be effective in its function as ideology it must appear to be just.
Indeed, he notes that this cannot be the case where it does not uphold
'its own logic and criteria of equity; indeed, on occasion, by actually
*being* just' (1975: 263).

Lord Denning's reasoning in *Wachtel* v. *Wachtel* was not 'just',
though other parts of his judgement dealing with a woman's contribution to the welfare of the family and his comments on the effect of
adultery on financial provision are instances of actual justice, in
Thompson's terms. Lord Denning's reasoning otherwise is an apt
example of what Barker (1978) has called 'repressive benevolence'.
There have been a number of reforms in the recent past. For
example, the duty to maintain now is mutual. But this, like many
other changes, remains only formal until women are given substantial
equality. Even today, the law refuses to intervene in a married
couple's financial relationship when they are living together. It

Ideologies and domestic violence

supports the notion that the husband sets the standard of living. The wife, in other words, may be a dependent, but the legal system shows marked reluctance to afford her economic protection during marriage. Conditions of domestic production remain outside the purview of the law.

A limited exception is the rule contained in s. 1 of the Married Women's Property Act 1964 that money derived from an allowance given to the wife by the husband or anything bought with that allowance is shared equally by the spouses. The Act only applies if the housekeeping allowance is provided by the husband. Cases have indicated that if the wife gives her money to her husband for use in the home, she is deemed to give it to him as the head of the family, so that the money becomes his (*Edward* v. *Cheyne* 1888; *Re Young* 1913). It is doubtful, to say the least, that the courts would take such a view today though the cases remain interesting for their ideological assumptions. But it is not only the gender assumption of the 1964 Act that invites critical comment. It is also significant that the Act, despite these assumptions, does nothing to compel a husband to make his wife any allowance. It concentrates instead on penalizing a thrifty wife by compelling her to share half of what she saves, or buys with what she saves, with her husband. In past times women managed the domestic economy (Tilly and Scott 1978). The allowance system itself is thus a relatively recent innovation. The 1964 Act now enshrines it.

Many more examples could be given to illustrate the point. More significant is the fact that in England today (and English law is not untypical) there is but one type of marriage. Its nature is not negotiable. Rights and obligations are fixed by operation of the law, not by agreement between the parties. Weitzman (1974: 1170) has, with considerable justification, described the conception of a single structure for all marriages as 'tyrannical'. I view with some alarm the increasing tendency to treat cohabitation as if it were marriage. It seems that many who avoid marriage because of its ideological notions of subordination and dependence find the consequences attaching to marriage thrust on them whether they like it or not. It is almost as if women were being told that they were not allowed to escape by cohabiting. The extension to relationships outside marriage of 'marriage type' law merely reinforces the outmoded views discussed in this section and transfers their application to settings where they are even less appropriate (Freeman and Lyon 1983). However, it is common to find arguments which support such an extension based on the idea that such an assimilation will protect cohabitants, especially

65

The State, the Law, and the Family

female cohabitants. One of the main 'functions' of family law is often said to be its 'protective function' (Eekelaar 1978: 44). The ideological assumptions underlying protection are worth examining.

Stang-Dahl and Snare (1978) regard claims that the law is a protector of women's integrity as a myth. Referring to the state's role, they use the suggestive phrase the 'coercion of privacy' (1978: 8-26). They see the family as a private prison for women. The state, they argue, need not use formal methods of repression and control when women are constrained by a more primary and informal control within the family. The relegation of women to the private sector, documented in Stang-Dahl and Snare's article, is significant also as it becomes an alternative to granting women greater public rights. Sachs, whose exposure of the myth of male protectiveness has been referred to, draws attention to this idea in his discussion of the Married Women's Property Act of 1882. This allowed married women to retain control over their own property. Sachs argues convincingly that:

'the law went some way towards protecting wives from being abused inside the home; it did not create opportunities for them to be useful outside the home. A curb on spending by husbands was not the same as a licence to earn independently by wives. Thus the destiny of woman as wife rather than as independent person was enhanced rather than reduced by the Act.'
(Sachs and Wilson 1978: 137)

The question must be raised as to whether law protects or controls women. The analogy with measures to protect children, for example, the invention of the juvenile court (Platt 1969) or intelligence testing (Mercer 1974: 328-44), looms large far too often. Child-saving has been a cloak to control a 'problem population' (Spitzer 1975: 642). The Victorian conservative judge, Stephen, understood the meaning of protection. In his mind, 'submission and protection' were 'correlative'. 'Withdraw the one,' he argued in *Liberty, Equality, Fraternity*, 'and the other is lost, and force will assert itself a hundred times more harshly through the law of contract then ever it did through the law of status' (Stephen 1873: 289).

Hanmer (1978) has shown how violence or its threat is used to control women both within and outside the home. Women, for example, are taught to avoid certain areas. 'Urban space for women is compartmentalised, to deviate from women's allocated space is to

Ideologies and domestic violence

run the risk of attack by men' (1978: 228). The fear of violence, particularly rape, has the effect of driving women to seek protection from men, of making them dependent. There is a certain irony here for women are supposed to feel safer in the company of husbands and boyfriends though the evidence suggests that they are more likely to be attacked or raped by them than by the dangerous strangers whom they are taught to fear. 'Chivalry', Griffin has noted, 'is an age-old protection racket which depends for its existence on rape' (1971: 28). She equates it with the sort of relationship the Mafia established with small businessmen in the United States earlier in this century.

The problematic nature of protection is forcefully to the fore in legislation regulating employment conditions of women (and children), which is usually called 'protective legislation'. Whom does this legislation protect? It was introduced in the nineteenth-century 'reform era', not in all areas of work but rather, it has been argued (Alexander 1976), in areas where women competed with male workers. Coyle has called protective legislation a 'protection racket'. It did not

'bring women equal pay, it did not bring equality and it has not provided adequate protection at work . . . The very existence of legislation serves as a recognition of . . . inequality . . . The problem with the current legislation is that it does not genuinely 'protect' women but rather operates paternalistically to reinforce women's conditions of inequality'.

(Coyle 1980: 10)

Why was protective legislation passed? Indeed, why was it that when challenged in the USA it was upheld as constitutional when similar restrictions on male labour were held to violate constitutional rights of personal liberty and liberty of contract?

On the face of it limiting the hours of female labour was not in the immediate interests of capital. But it was of concern that if women were worked too hard they would be unable to produce the next generation of workers. No individual firm would benefit from stopping the exploitation of female labour, 'but the state under pressure from the Ten Hours movement, as well as from elements of the bourgeoisie, was able to restrict hours of work, especially for women and children' (McIntosh 1978: 262). The state, in other words, as the 'ideal collectivity of capitals', had to concede limitations on hours of work to ensure the reproduction of labour power.

Another interpretation of the emergence of protective legislation,

The State, the Law, and the Family

sometimes posed as an alternative view and sometimes as a supplementary one, stresses that such legislation was supportive of the
interests of male workers. It suggests that working men were fearful
that women, being cheaper and more pliable, would infiltrate industry,
taking men's jobs and lowering rates of pay for all. Not only would
this be a disaster in terms of men's position within commodity
production but it would also liberate women from dependence on
men and obliterate gender labour divisions in the home. Hartmann
argues that women and children in the labour force 'undermined
authority relations'. She continues:

> 'Not only were women "cheap competition" but working women
> were their very wives, who could not "serve two masters" . . .
> While the problem of cheap competition could have been solved
> by organising the wage-earning women and youths, the problem
> of disrupted family life could not be. Men reserved union protection
> for men and argued for protective labour laws for women and
> children.'                                    (Hartmann 1980: 15-16)

On the other hand, as Humphries (1981) shows in her study of the
1842 Mines Regulation Act, which she agrees may be an atypical
instance, hewers neither individually nor collectively feared competition
from female labour and many had an interest in the retention of
female and child labour underground as it increased their family's
income. Despite this 'male colliers almost universally wanted state
intervention to regulate the labour of women and children, and the
overwhelming majority of hewers believed that women should be
prohibited from working below ground' (1981: 15). She also shows
that the other strand in the Hartmann (Hartmann and Markusen
1980) 'patriarchy first' approach, which emphasizes patriarchal privileges in having wives at home, is inconsistent with the realities of
collier life. 'Existing theorisations', she concludes, 'have proven
inadequate to the understanding of an important historical example.'
Her conclusions are rather negative though she draws attention to the
contradiction between the exploitation of women workers and the sex
role standards prevailing among the bourgeoisie, 'themselves conditions
of existence of the *sexual* oppression of women within that class'
(Humphries 1981: 28). In so far as this might suggest that the
legislation supports the transformation of working-class family structure to something like that found in the bourgeoisie, it reinforces a
view presented earlier in this article.

Ideologies and domestic violence

Protective employment legislation is likely to disappear quite soon. In 1979 the British Equal Opportunities Commission (EOC) submitted a report to the Government proposing the removal of much of it governing the conditions of work for women, though retaining it for young people. It argues:

> 'that the hours of work legislation constitutes a barrier – often an artificial one – to equal pay and job opportunities for women. So long as this legislation remains as it is at present, women as workers will be disadvantaged. Therefore we cannot accept the retention of legislation in its present form, because discrimination will continue to arise out of it.
>
> (Equal Opportunities Commission 1979b: 92)

Unfortunately, a number of matters are not unquestioned by the EOC. For example, their report 'poses the question of shift work as a choice for women to make, rather than recognising the economic circumstances which *force* people into the night shift' (Coyle 1980: 7). There is a strong case for making work conditions equal by extending protective legislation to male workers but that is not a likely reform.

## Domestic Violence

This is the context within which domestic violence must be located. But it has not been understood in this way by the majority of those investigating the problem or those engaged in finding solutions to it. The result has been that 'solutions' remain superficial. Responses hitherto have made few inroads into the problem.

The most common interpretations of domestic violence individualize it (considered in Freeman 1979). They emphasize that men are violent toward the women with whom they live 'because of some internal aberration, abnormality or defective characteristic' (Gelles and Straus 1979: 561). These characteristics are variegated but include inadequate self-control, often linked to problems of alcoholism, psychopathic personality types, and various undifferentiated types of mental illness. The research tends to look for 'inner traits' rather than social or cultural context. A second view of marital violence attributes it to stress, frustration, and blocked goals. It assumes an uneven distribution of the deviance in the social structure, with violence being more common among those in lower socio-economic strata. The precise causal relationship between the stresses caused by economic

The State, the Law, and the Family

conditions and domestic violence is not analysed. The lives of the poor are, of course, more susceptible to public scrutiny and social intervention than those of middle-class people who are better able to preserve their privacy. This theory of wife battering also individualizes the problem. The psycho-pathological model gave us 'sick people'; the environmental stress model posits instead 'a sick society' (McGrath 1979: 17). Both, however, privatize the violent event.

It is of course true that only certain violence is recognized as such. Klein has noted that 'a man's laying hands on a woman can be seen as necessary discipline, proof of manhood, a felony or hideous sin, depending on the relationship (wife, slave, stranger) which itself is socially constructed' (1979: 28). It is a fact of some significance, though one frequently neglected, that some violence against women is regarded as legitimate and not deviant at all. This is the case also with violence against children, for corporal punishment is culturally sanctioned in most societies. Ariès (1962) has shown how, at the time when the conception of childhood evolved, being subject to the infliction of corporal punishment was a badge of inferior status. Dobash and Dobash (1980) have traced the relationship between the growth of the nuclear family and the chastisement of wives. They describe (1980: 56) the period from the sixteenth century until the nineteenth as the 'great age of flogging'. Flogging was used throughout society 'as a means of controlling the powerless: children, women and the lower classes'. Wife beating was acceptable and widespread. At common law a husband was said to have the legal right to beat his wife. The expression 'rule of thumb' is thought to have derived from the belief that he could only use a stick of the thickness of his thumb. Blackstone's rationalization saw a correlativity between the husband having to be answerable for his wife's misbehaviour and his having the power of restraining her by 'domestic chastisement, in the same moderation that a man is allowed to correct his apprentice or children, for whom the master or parent is also liable in some cases to answer' (1765: 444).

Blackstone's formulation was the guide when the first American states formed their wife beating laws in the early nineteenth century. They have since repealed them. In England domestic chastisement is obsolete, though no statute has ever as such repealed the privilege. But throughout the century there are dicta from judges and magistrates affirming its continued existence (Freeman 1979: 178). Most recently, a sheriff in Scotland, having fined a husband for hitting his wife in the face, is reported as having remarked, 'It is a well known fact that you can strike you wife's bottom if you wish, but you must not strike her on the face.' He expressed support for the ancient principle that 'reasonable chastisement should be the duty of every husband when his wife misbehaves' (*Ms*, August 1975: 4).

It is not merely that wives have long been legitimate victims of domestic chastisement. They have been, and remain in England today, liable to forced sexual intercourse by their husbands, which in law is not regarded as rape (Freeman 1981: 8). John Stuart Mill commented on this over 100 years ago that

> 'a female slave has (in Christian countries) an admitted right . . . to refuse to her master the last familiarity. Not so the wife [whose husband] can claim from her and enforce the lowest degradation of a human being, that of being made the instrument of an animal function contrary to her inclination.'
>
> (John Stuart Mill 1869: 32)

So long as marital rape is considered legitimate, it is difficult to see how violence against women in the home can ever be eliminated. There is now a proposal in England to qualify the husband's immunity from prosecution. Marital rape, it is proposed, is to become a crime but only where the spouses are living separately (Criminal Law Revision Committee 1984). The Committee in its working paper of 1980 had suggested that a prosecution should require authorization from the Director of Public Prosecutions but this proposal has been dropped. Marital rape is still to be regarded as different from other rape: as such the proposal may be criticized.

Attitudes described here permeate not just the courts but the helping professions and the police as well. According to Nichols, case-workers often uphold a position that 'supports a belief that the wife encourages, provokes or even enjoys abusive treatment' (1976: 27). As far as the police are concerned, what they tend to call euphemistically 'domestic disturbances' take up considerable time and the 'role of the police is a negative one. We are,' the Association of Chief Police Officers told the House of Commons Select Committee on Violence in Marriage, 'after all dealing with persons bound in marriage, and it is important, for a host of reasons, to maintain the unity of the spouses.' They go on to express their approval of the provision of refuges for battered wives, but add 'every effort should be made to re-unite the family' (House of Commons 1974-75: 366, 369). They and many social workers also seem to take it for granted

The State, the Law, and the Family

that preserving family relationships is a desirable goal. Often it seems that social workers particularly are concerned that a family should be kept together for the sake of the children. Many helping professionals are imbued with a belief that an intact family is preferable to a broken one regardless of the quality of the relationship within it.

## Conclusion

Violence against wives has been described by a leading English judge (Sir George Baker in *Davis* v. *Johnson* 1979: 283) as 'domestic hooliganism'. There is no evidence that it is more prevalent today than in the past. But contemporary society recognizes it as a problem. It looks to the legislature, the courts, the helping professions, and the police to root it out. Some contemporary observers, Pizzey being a prime example, see the remedy as lying with the medical profession and not, for example, in courts of law because, she argues, 'the men act instinctively, not rationally' (House of Commons 1974-75: 2). But given the position of women in society the behaviour of violent husbands is rational, if extreme. It is not necessary for husbands to have formal rights such as to chastise their wives. That they once had this right and exercised it is sufficient. It helped to form and then to reinforce an ideology of subordination and control of women. The ideology remains imbricated in the legal system even if one of its grosser manifestations has virtually disappeared. Wife battering remains one of its legacies and if this too is to go the ideology must be dismantled. The legal system has been committed to a patriarchal ideology. It is this that must be challenged if violence against women is to diminish and ultimately to cease. It is a challenge for which resistance can be expected, for the stakes are high and there are considerable vested interests in the *status quo*. Success is important for through it will come improvement of the position of women in the home, in the economy, and in society in general.

## References

Alexander, S. (1976) Women's Work in Nineteenth Century London: A Study of the Years 1820–50. In J. Mitchell and A. Oakley (eds) *The Rights and Wrongs of Women*. Harmondsworth: Penguin.
Allatt. P. (1981) Stereotyping: Familism in the Law. In B. Fryer *et.al.* (eds) *Law, State and Society*. London: Croom Helm.

Ideologies and domestic violence

Althusser, L. (1971); Ideology and Ideological State Apparatuses. In *Lenin and Philosophy and Other Essays*. London: New Left Books.

Ariès, P. (1962) *Centuries of Childhood* (translated from French). London: Jonathan Cape.

Barker, D.L. (1978) The Regulation of Marriage: Repressive Benevolence. In G. Littlejohn, J. Wakeford, B. Smart, and N. Yuval-Davis (eds) *Power and the State*. London: Croom Helm.

Barrett, M. (1980) *Women's Oppression Today*. London: Verso Books.

Barron, R. and Norris, G. (1976) Sexual Divisions and the Dual Labour Market. In D.L. Barker and S. Allen (eds) *Dependence and Exploitation in Work and Marriage*. Harlow: Longman.

Beveridge, Sir W. (1942) *Social Insurance and Allied Services*. Cmd 6404. London: HMSO.

Binney, V. Harkell, G., and Nixon J. (1981) *Leaving Violent Men*. London: WAF, England.

Blackstone, Sir W. (1765) *Commentaries on the Law of England*. London: Tegg.

Boggs, C. (1976) *Gramsci's Marxism*. London: Pluto Press.

Borkowski, M., Murch, M., and Walker, V. (1983) *Marital Violence*. London: Tavistock.

Bowker, L. (1983) *Beating Wife-Beating*. Lexington: Lexington Books.

Box, S. (1981) *Deviance, Reality and Society*. London: Holt, Rinehart & Winston.

Brown, B., Emerson, T.I., Falk, G., and Freedman, A.E. (1971) The Equal Rights Amendment: A Constitutional Basis for Equal Rights for Women. *Yale Law Journal* 80: 891–985.

Cain, M. and Hunt, A. (1979) *Marx and Engels on Law*. London: Academic Press.

Clark, A. (1919) *Working Life of Women in the Seventeenth Century*. London: G. Routledge.

Coward, R. (1983) *Patriarchal Precedents*. London: Routledge & Kegan Paul.

Coyle, A. (1980) The Protection Racket. *Feminist Review* 4: 1-12.

Criminal Law Revision Committee (1984) *Sexual Offences*, 15th Report, Cmnd 9213. London: HMSO.

Croll, E. (1978) *Feminism and Socialism in China*. London: Routledge & Kegan Paul.

David, M. (1980) *The State, The Family and Education*. London: Routledge & Kegan Paul.

Davidoff, L., L'Esperance, J., and Newby, H. (1976) Landscape with Figures: Home and Community in English Society. In J. Mitchell and

The State, the Law, and the Family

A. Oakley (eds) *The Rights and Wrongs of Women*. Harmondsworth: Penguin.

Davidson, T. (1978) *Conjugal Crime*. New York: Ballantine.

Delphy, C. (1976) Continuities and Discontinuities in Marriage and Divorce In D.L. Barker and S. Allen (eds) *Sexual Divisions and Society*. London: Tavistock.

——(1977) *The Main Enemy* (translated from French). London: Women's Research and Resources Centre.

Denning, Lord (1980) *The Due Process of Law*. London: Butterworths.

——(1960) *The Equality of Women*. Liverpool: Liverpool University Press.

Dobash, R. and Dobash, R. (1980) *Violence Against Wives*. Shepton Mallett: Open Books.

DHSS (1971) *Cohabitation*, Report by the Supplementary Benefits Commission. London: HMSO.

Eekelaar, J. (1971) *Family Security and Family Breakdown*, Harmondsworth: Penguin.

——(1978) *Family Law and Social Policy*. London: Weidenfeld & Nicolson.

Equal Opportunities Commission (1979a) *Third Annual Report*. London: HMSO.

——(1979b) *Report on Health and Safety Legislation: Should We Distinguish Between Men and Women?* London: HMSO.

——(1981) *Behind Closed Doors*. London: HMSO.

Flandrin, J.-L. (1979) *Families in Former Times* (translated from French). London: Cambridge University Press.

Foreman, A. (1977) *Femininity as Alienation*. London: Pluto Press.

Fraser, A. (1978) The Legal Theory We Need Now. *Socialist Review* 40-1:147-88,

Freeman, M.D.A. (1977) Le Vice Anglais? – Wife Battering in English and American Law. *Family Law Quarterly* 11: 199-251.

——(1979) *Violence in the Home – A Socio-Legal Study*. Farnborough: Gower Press.

——(1981) But if You Can't Rape Your Wife, Who[m] Can You Rape? *Family Law Quarterly* 15: 1–29.

——(1984) Family Matters. In J. Jowell and J. McAuslan (eds) *Lord Denning and the Law*. London: Sweet & Maxwell.

Freeman, M.D.A. and Lyon, C.M. (1983) *Cohabitation Without Marriage: An Essay in Law and Social Policy*. Aldershot: Gower Press.

Gelles, R. (1974) *The Violent Home*. Beverly Hills: Sage.

——(1979) *Family Violence*. Beverly Hills: Sage.

Ideologies and domestic violence

Gelles, R. and Straus, M. (1979) Determinants of Violence in the Family: Toward a Theoretical Integration. In W.R. Burr and R. Hill (eds) *Contemporary Theories About the Family – Research-Based Theories*. New York: Free Press.

Ginsburg, N. (1979) *Class, Capital and Social Policy*. London: Macmillan.

Glendinning, C. (1980) *After Working All These Years*. London: The Disability Alliance.

Gouldner, A.W. (1976) *The Dialectic of Ideology and Technology: The Origins, Grammar and Future of Ideology*. London: Macmillan.

Gramsci, A. (1971) *Prison Notebooks* (translated from Italian). London: Lawrence and Wishart.

Griffin, S. (1971) Rape – the All-American Crime. *Ramparts* 10: 26-35.

Hanmer, J. (1978) Violence and the Social Control of Women. In G. Littlejohn, B. Smart, J. Wakeford, and N. Yuval-Davis (eds) *Power and the State*. London: Croom Helm.

Harris, J. (1977) *William Beveridge: A Biography*. Oxford: Oxford University Press.

Hartmann, H. (1976) Capitalism, Patriarchy and Sex Segregation. *Signs* 1: 137-70.

——(1980) The Unhappy Marriage of Marxism and Feminism: Towards a More Progressive Union. *Capital and Class* 7: 1-33.

Hartmann, H. and Markusen, A.R. (1980) Contemporary Marxist Theory and Practice. *Review of Radical and Political Economists*.

Hay, D. (1975) Property, Authority and Criminal Law. In D. Hay, P. Linebaugh, J.G. Rule, E.P. Thompson, and C. Winslow (eds) *Albion's Fatal Tree*. London: Allen Lane.

Heitlinger, A. (1979) *Women and State Socialism: Sex Inequality in the Soviet Union and Czechoslovakia*. London: Macmillan.

Home Office (1980) *Criminal Law Revision Committee Working Paper on Sexual Offences*. London: HMSO.

House of Commons (1974-75) *Select Committee on Violence in Marriage*. HC 553. London: HMSO.

Humphries, J. (1981) Protective Legislation, the Capitalist State and Working Class Men: The Case of the 1842 Mines Regulation Act. *Feminist Review* 7: 1-33.

Hunt, A. (1968) *A Survey of Women's Unemployment*. London: HMSO; Office of Population Censuses and Surveys.

Jowell, J. and McAuslan, J. (eds) (1984) *Lord Denning: The Judge and the Law*. London: Sweet & Maxwell.

Klare, K. (1979) Law-making as Praxis. *Telos* 40: 123-35.

The State, the Law, and the Family

Klein, D. (1979) Can This Marriage Be Saved? Battery and Sheltering. *Crime and Social Justice* 12: 19-33.
——(1981) Violence Against Women: Some Considerations Regarding Its Causes and Elimination. *Crime and Delinquency* 27: 64-80.
Land, H. (1976) Women: Supporters or Supported? In D.L. Barker and S. Allen (eds) *Sexual Divisions and Society*. London: Tavistock.
——(1980) Social Policies and the Family: Their Effect on Women's Paid Employment in Great Britain. In R.S. Ratner (ed.) *Equal Employment Policy for Women*. Philadelphia: Temple University Press.
Langley, R. and Levy, R.C. (1977) *Wife-beating – the Silent Crisis*. New York: Dutton.
Lasch, C. (1977) *Haven in a Heartless World*. New York: Basic Books.
Lister, R. (1970) *As Man and Wife*. London: London Child Poverty Action Group.
——(1980) Taxation, Women and the Family. In C.T. Sandford, C. Pond, and R. Walker (eds) *Taxation and Social Policy*. London: Heinemann.
McGrath, C. (1979) The Crisis of Domestic Order. *Socialist Review* 45: 11-30.
McIntosh, M. (1978) The State and the Oppression of Women. In A. Kuhn and A.-M. Wolpe (eds) *Feminism and Materialism*. London: Routledge & Kegan Paul.
——(1979) The Welfare State and the Needs of the Dependent Family. In S. Burman (ed). *Fit Work for Women*. London: Croom Helm.
Marris, P. and Rein, M. (1972) *Dilemmas of Social Reform*. 2nd edn. Harmondsworth: Penguin.
Martin, D. (1976) *Battered Wives*. San Francisco: Glide Publications.
May, M. (1978) Violence in the Family: An Historical Perspective. In J.P. Martin (ed.) *Violence and the Family*. Chichester: Wiley.
Mercer, J. (1974) A Policy Statement on Assessment Procedures and the Rights of Children. *Harvard Educational Review* (Reprint Series No. 9): 328-44.
Mill, J.S. (1869) *The Subjection of Women*. London: Longmans, Green.
Millett, K. (1969) *Sexual Politics*. London: Hart Davis.
Molyneux, M. (1979) Beyond the Domestic Labour Debate. *New Left Review* 116: 3-27
Moore, D. (1979) *Battered Women*. Beverly Hills: Sage.
Nichols, B. (1976) The Abused Wife Problem. *Social Casework* 57: 27-35
O'Donovan, K. (1979) The Male Appendage – Legal Definitions of

Ideologies and domestic violence

Women. In S. Burman (ed.) *Fit Work for Women*. London: Croom Helm.

Okin, S.M. (1979) *Women in Western Political Thought*. Princeton: Princeton University Press.

Pagelow, M.D. (1981) *Woman-Battering*. Beverly Hills: Sage.

Parker, R. and Land, H. (1978) Family Policy in the United Kingdom. In S.B. Kamerman and A.J. Kahn (eds) *Family Policy*. New York: Columbia University Press.

Peattie, L. and Rein, M. (1983) *Women's Claims – A Study in Political Economy*. London: Oxford University Press.

Pinchbeck, I. (1977) *Women Workers and the Industrial Revolution, 1750–1850*. London: Cass.

Pizzey, E. (1979) *Scream Quietly or the Neighbours Will Hear*. Revised edn. Harmondsworth: Penguin.

Pizzey, E. and Shapiro, J. (1982) *Prone to Violence*. London: Hamlyn.

Platt, A. (1969) *The Child Savers*. Chicago: University of Chicago Press.

Poster, M. (1979) *Critical Theory of the Family*. London: Pluto Press.

Rowbotham, S. (1981) The Trouble with 'Patriarchy'. In R. Samuel (ed.) *People's History and Socialist Theory*. London: Routledge & Kegan Paul.

Sachs, A. (1976) The Myth of Judicial Neutrality: The Male Monopoly Cases. In P. Carlen (ed.) *The Sociology of Law*. Keele: University of Keele.

Sachs, A. and Pearson, R. (1980) Barristers and Gentlemen: A Critical Look at Sexism in the Legal Profession. *Modern Law Review* 43: 400-14.

Sachs, A. and Wilson, J.H. (1978) *Sexism and the Law*. London: Martin Robertson.

Schechter, S. (1983) *Women and Male Violence*. London: Pluto Press.

*Social Trends* (1984) Vol. 14. London: HMSO, Central Statistical Office.

Spitzer, S. (1975) Toward a Marxian Theory of Deviance. *Social Problems* 22: 638-51.

Stang-Dahl, T. and Snare, A. (1978) The Coercion of Privacy: A Feminist Perspective. In C. Smart and B. Smart (eds) *Women, Sexuality and Social Control*. London: Routledge & Kegan Paul.

Stephen, Sir J.F. (1873) *Liberty, Equality, Fraternity*. London: Smith, Elder.

Straus, M., Gelles, R., and Steinmetz, S. (1980) *Behind Closed Doors – Violence in the American Family*. New York: Doubleday.

The State, the Law, and the Family

Supplementary Benefits Commission (1980) *Annual Report 1979.* Cmnd 8033, London: HMSO.

Thompson, E.P. (1975) *Whigs and Hunters.* London: Allen Lane.

Tilly, L.A. and Scott, J.W. (1978) *Women, Work and Family.* New York: Holt, Rinehart & Winston.

Walker, L. (1979) *The Battered Woman.* New York: Harper & Row.

Weitzman, L. (1974) Legal Regulation of Marriage; Tradition and Change. *California Law Review* 62: 1169-288.

Wilson, E. (1976) *The Existing Research Into Battered Women.* London: NWAF.

——(1977) *Women and the Welfare State.* London: Tavistock.

——(1983) *What Is to Be Done About Violence Against Women?* Harmondsworth: Penguin.

Zaretsky, E. (1976) *Capitalism, the Family and Personal Life.* London: Pluto Press.

## Cases

*Chorlton* v. *Lings* (1869) 4 LRCP 398

*Davis* v. *Johnson* [1979] AC 264

*Edward* v. *Cheyne* (No 2) (1888) 13 App Cas 385

*Edwards* v. *Attorney-General for Canada* [1930] AC 124

*Wachtel* v. *Wachtel* [1973] Fam 72

*Re Young* (1913) 29 TLR 319

# [10]
# The Right to Responsible Parents

## Introduction

Sitting on a *Justice* committee more than 30 years ago I urged the members to think about parental responsibilities rather than, as was then the currency, parental rights (*Justice* 1975). There were precedents, in Norway and West Germany.[1] The Committee was persuaded and so recommended. This was not, I hasten to add, why the Children Act in 1989 adopted the language of responsibilities rather than rights.[2] But it is the beginning of my association with the concept of parental responsibility. In 1993 I gave a public lecture at the University of Essex entitled 'Do Children Have the Right Not To Be Born?' (Freeman 1997). This explored the concept of parental responsibility further. This chapter builds on some of the ideas formulated there.

Thinking about responsibility has shifted from the liberal paradigm that was dominant at the time of the *Justice* committee and even at the time of the Essex lecture. Post-liberalism, manifested in communitarianism[3] and the feminist ethics of care,[4] has called for a re-evaluation of what responsibility involves. Tronto argues that the moral question central to an ethic of care is not what we owe others but 'rather – How can we best meet our caring responsibilities?' (Tronto 1993, 137). Reece explains

> Post-liberal responsibility is no longer about discrete decisions; responsible behaviour has become a way of being, a mode of thought; the focus has shifted from the content of the decision to the process of making the decision. (Reece 2003, 232)

What is required, Gillies has argued in a recent paper, is

> ethical self-management within the moral parameters of normative definitions of "successful parenting". Reasonable, rational moral citizens ... seek to do the best for their children. (Gillies 2005, 75)

---

1  On West Germany see Frank 1990.
2  This was the recommendation of the Law Commission, 1988, Law Com. 172.
3  A good discussion of which (in the context of family law) is Eekelaar 2001a. See also Eekelaar 2000 (an article I only discovered after I wrote this chapter but wish I had seen earlier).
4  Which is usually traced to Carol Gilligan (1982), and see Smart and Neale 1999.

At the same time parental responsibility has expanded, and has been redefined. The introduction of the parenting order by the Crime and Disorder Act 1998,[5] and its subsequent extension by the Anti-social Behaviour Act 2003,[6] imposes on parents responsibility for the anti-social behaviour of their children. This can be looked at simplistically as taking the rap. But it is more than this. The 'good' parent is constructed as resourceful and ethically responsible 'able to recognize or learn what is best for their children and tailor their behaviour accordingly' (Gillies 2005, 85). 'Good' parenting, as Reece interprets it is 'an attitude, and an important part of that attitude is being prepared to learn' (Reece 2006, 470). From being about authority – as it certainly became with the passage of the Children Act 1989 (Eekelaar 1991a) – current governmental initiatives identify parental responsibility with accountability.

English law does not define parental responsibility very fully. The formulation in section 3 of the Children Act 1989 is clumsy and inchoate.[7] Of course, a non-definition allows the policy-maker to mould it to meet changing imperatives: no one was thinking of the parenting order in 1989. The Scottish formulation is, by contrast, fuller.[8] Does the absence of a definition make it more difficult for a child to bring a parent to account? It has certainly not prevented the state from so doing. Does it deprive a parent of fair opportunity (see further, Hart 1968) to know what standards are expected of him or her (Lyon 2000)? This is particularly important where there is an allegation of child abuse or neglect.[9] But could it be defined? Of course, some content can clearly be poured into it. However, this does little more than reaffirm jurisprudence which has emerged from isolated pieces of litigation.[10] Acting responsibly is to act ethically. Benhabib puts this well:

> To be a family member, a parent, a spouse or a brother means to know how to reason from the standpoint of the concrete other. One cannot act within these ethical relationships ... without being able to think from the standpoint of our child, our spouse, our sister or brother, mother or father. (Benhabib 1992, 10)

And this requires, as Reece acknowledges, 'far more than the simple assertion of rights and duties in the face of the other's needs' (Reece 2003, 231). It is not enough to 'be' family: it is necessary also to 'do' family. This was recognised by the judiciary when it formulated the test for the granting of a parental responsibility order in 1991.[11]

---

5   See s. 8.

6   See s. 18.

7   This states that parental responsibility comprises 'the rights, duties, powers, responsibilities and authority which by law a parent has in relation to the child and his property'. Lord Meston (Hansard, H.L. vol. 502, col. 1172) described this as a 'non-definition'.

8   It is in the Children (Scotland) Act 1995 s. 1(1) (responsibilities); s. 2(1) (rights).

9   And particularly so in the less-than-obvious case. These include (unfortunately) cases of 'excessive' physical chastisement (*Re R (Care: Rehabilitation in Context of Domestic Violence)* [2007] 1 FLR 1830) and excessive feeding (see *The Guardian*, 13 July 2007).

10  This does not necessarily offer a coherent theory. Whether 'parental responsibility' as such does is debatable. One thoughtful view is John Eekelaar's that it creates a new legal status of 'social parenthood' (2001b).

11  *Re H* [1991] 1 FLR 214. See also *D v Hereford and Worcester CC* [1991] 1 FLR 205.

## Parental Rights

We didn't always think this way. Throughout most of our history children were treated as the property of their fathers (unless illegitimate – such children were the 'children of no one').[12] Parental rights vested in him. In the *Gillick* decision in 1985 the concept of the child as property of the father was deemed 'a historical curiosity'.[13] The Lords acknowledged that parental rights (we were no longer talking of paternal rights) existed but not for the benefit of the parent. Lord Fraser said:

> They exist for the benefit of the child and they are justified only in so far as they enable the parent to perform his duties towards the child, and towards other children in the family. (at 170)

There are similar, if more overtly Dworkinian, sentiments in Lord Scarman's speech.

> The principle of the law ... is that parental rights are derived from parental duty and exist only so long as they are needed for the protection of the person and property of the child. (at 184)

The father's powers – he was the natural guardian of a legitimate child – limped on until this status was finally abolished in 1989.[14] Few will even have noticed this, and its passing was not mourned. Parents still have parental rights, but these are subsumed in parental responsibilities.

## Is there a Right to Have Children?

One right which is still aired is the right to have children. Parenting is an activity which is 'potentially very harmful to children' (LaFollette 1980, 182). We are not allowed to drive a car unless we pass a driving test. We do not license parenthood. Do we depreciate parenting because it is not regarded as having economic value (Westman 1994, 3), or is it because it is largely done by women? A society's children are its future citizens. The public, therefore, has 'a legitimate concern with the selection of child rearers' (Blustein 1982, 119). Should parenting be a privilege? Rather than criticising the welfare norm that governs fertility treatment[15] (Jackson 2002), should we be urging its adoption across the board? Is this to urge a utopian solution or to envisage a ghastly dystopia?[16]

---

12 A good account (in the US context) is found in Mason 1994.

13 *Gillick v West Norfolk and Wisbech A.H.A* [1986] AC 112.

14 Children Act 1989 s. 2(4).

15 Human Fertilisation and Embryology Act 1990 s. 13(5), on which see Jackson 2002. For differing views contrast HC Science and Technology Committee, 2005 (it 'discriminates against the infertile and some sections of society'), and the Joint Committee on the Human Tissue and Embryos (Draft) Bill Report, 2007, 65.

16 See Gray 2007.

There is a school of thought that urges the licensing of parenthood (Covell and Howe 1998; Eisenberg 1994; LaFollette 1980; Mangel 1988; Westman 1994). Is this to think the unthinkable? For Covell and Howe parents must demonstrate that they can be responsible for their own lives 'before being allowed to assume responsibility for a child's life' (1998, 34). The questions are at the very least worth asking. Should there be a minimum age requirement – there is for marriage,[17] for voting, even for purchasing tobacco products. And, if a minimum, why not a maximum age too?[18] Is it responsible to bring children into the world when it is unlikely that you will see them into adulthood? Or when you don't have adequate income to provide for a child's basic necessities? Should those who have abused a child previously be allowed to parent further children? If we could identify potential child abusers in advance should we deny them the freedom to procreate? Predictive screening questionnaires have been developed (see Schneider et al. 1972, discussed in Freeman 1979, 108-111). But it has been shown that false positive errors could potentially be as high as 85 per cent, with the result that many would-be parents would be mistakenly labelled (Light 1973). There would also be false negatives, so that abusers would fall through the net. Together this suggests low practical ability for an unacceptably high social cost (Daniel et al. 1978). But not only do we not know what causes abuse – if the cultural explanation of child abuse is accepted we are all potential child abusers (Gil 1978) – but there is no consensus on what constitutes child abuse. We can list categories, certainly. We can agree on the worst cases. But what of the 'penumbral' case (see further, Hart 1958)? Is 'vulgar but inappropriate horseplay' sexual abuse?[19] Is feeding a child inappropriately so that he becomes obese neglect?[20] Is causing a male child to be circumcised physical abuse (Fox and Thomson 2005)?[21] How relevant is the cultural and religious context? Should those who put serious barriers in the way of the child's capacity for autonomous decision-making (for example, Christian fundamentalists, Hasiddim, racists, etc., etc.) forfeit their freedom to create another generation? And what then about those who would deny their children immunisations (the MMR vaccine, for example[22]), or blood transfusions because

---

17  Marriage Act 1949 s. 2.

18  On fertility treatment for post-menopausal women see Cutas 2007. On 30 December 2006, a 67-year-old Spanish woman gave birth to twins. I believe this is the record, but I do not expect it to stand.

19  See *C v C (Child Abuse: Access)* [1988] 1 FLR 462.

20  See Jenkins, 'Obese girl taken into care because of her weight', *The Times*, July 13 2007 and Templeton, 'Fat boy may be put into care', *Sunday Times*, 25 February 2007.

21  The English courts have said 'no': *Re J (A Minor) (Prohibited Steps Order: Circumcision)* [2000] 1 FLR 571, though in this case they did hold that ritual circumcision of a five-year-old child was not in his best interests. He was being brought up by a nominally Christian mother and had a Muslim father who barely practised his religion. Viens (2004, 246) is surely right to stress the need 'to differentiate between rituals and practices that are in fact grievously harmful and those which relate to the enhancement of a child's religious and cultural identity'.

22  *Re B (A Child) (Immunisation)* [2003] 3 FCR 156.

they are Jehovah's Witnesses,[23] or the celebration of Christmas because they are Plymouth Brethren[24] or, worse, Jews!

Eisenberg calls his proposal 'modest'. He argues

> It is time to say aloud what many people are saying privately: society must be much more proactive in assuring that only people who can properly raise children are allowed to become and remain parents. (Eisenberg 1994, 1416)

Eisenberg's is a detailed blueprint. Earlier proposals by LaFollette (1980) and Mangel (1988) had tried to identify and screen out 'bad parents'. And critics like Frisch (1981), commenting upon LaFollette, had attacked this proposal as being inconsistent with usual licensing requirements, for example to drive a car, which focuses on the knowledge and skills of the applicant, not his or her lack of suitability. Earlier proposals have also been criticised because they rely on the assumption that 'bad parents' can be identified in advance. Adoption panels and clinics offering assisted reproduction services already screen out certain applicants:[25] would-be foster parents, child-minders and teachers are carefully scrutinised before they are permitted to care for (or educate) children.[26] In the United Kingdom some 30 years ago, a parliamentary select committee endorsed screening, though, unsurprisingly, it gave little attention to the concept or its implications (Select Committee 1977). I suspect few remember this.

Eisenberg's model is different. It makes no effort to evaluate subjectively who will be a 'good parent' (1994, 1440). Rather it puts a premium on providing prospective parents with knowledge and skills relevant to parenting. But it is, I think, equally flawed. As he concedes, one of the principal problems is what to do with the children of unlicensed parents. He puts his faith in adoption and in communal institutions (the Israeli Kibbutz model appeals to him), but, even if practical problems could be surmounted, ethical ones would remain. Any proposal that would have a disproportionate impact on those already disadvantaged by low income, poor education, race or disability would be very difficult to defend.

Whether there is 'a right' to have children remains contentious. John Robertson (1983; 1994) is one who argues that we do have such a right. Although he concedes that the desire to reproduce is in part socially constructed, he sees personal identity, meaning and dignity as at the root of the right. But as Purdy (1996, 218) points out, 'is it really such a good idea to conceptualise the relationship between childbearing

---

23 *Wright v Wright* (1981), 2 FLR 276; *Re T (Minors) (Custody: Religious Upbringing)* [1981] 2 FLR 239.

24 *Hewison v Hewison* (1977), 7 Fam Law 207; *Re S (A Minor) (Medical Treatment)* [1993] 1 FLR 377. A striking contrast is the Illinois case of *Re Brown* 689 NE 2d 397 (Ill, 1997) (court refused to order a blood transfusion for a pregnant woman to save the life of her foetus).

25 See Adoption Agency Regulations 2005 on adoption panels and above, n. 14 in relation to fertility clinics (see also *R v Ethical Committee of St Mary's Manchester ex parte Harriott* [1998] 1 FLR 512).

26 See Fostering Services Regulations 2002 and Care Standards Act 2000 s. 79 (and Day Care and Child Minding (National Standards) (England) Regulations 2001, SI 2001/1818).

status and one's core self the way Robertson does?' And she argues that 'it encourages people to care too much about their ability to have children'. If, she adds, 'a person's whole self-concept depends on having them, they are set up for devastating disappointment' (1996, 219). This is especially so for women who 'because of their socialization – as well as continuing sexist and pronatalist pressure – will more likely adopt this understanding of the meaning of life without seriously questioning it' (ibid.). Another to argue the case for a right to have children is Dan Brock (1996). He appeals to self-determination and individual well-being. His argument is couched within the question of access to the new reproductive technologies, but what he says can be generalised. But neither Robertson nor Brock claims that the right to have children is an absolute right. Thus, Robertson requires the capacity to appreciate the meaning of parenthood (which may be absent in people with severe learning disabilities), and the absence of what he calls 'manifest unfitness' (1994, 127). This would certainly be manifested where there was a real risk of harm to the child. The argument against the natural right to have children was put – before either Robertson or Brock presented their case – by Floyd and Pomerantz (1981). They criticise both the self-determination argument (now associated with Brock), and the bodily autonomy argument. They reject the self-determination argument: 'one can have a relational right based on self-determination only if all the parties to the relation consent, and no one consents to be introduced into the world by someone else'. From this it follows that while there might be a right to marry, provided the potential partner consents, there is 'no relational right to be parent'. And they find it even easier to dispose of their bodily autonomy argument. It treats the child as a 'mere appendage', but a child is, of course, a distinct person, a rights-bearing individual. A different argument for the right to have children is the 'desire' argument. There is a thorough examination of this by Ruth Chadwick (1987). She shows that the desire for a child may be one of a number of different desires, or even a combination of them: a desire to rear, a desire to bear, a desire to beget (used more commonly of men than women), a desire to have a child with someone, a desire to be (or appear to be) a 'normal' family, a desire for an heir. There are questions as to whether the desire is socially induced, and is natural or artificial. But do any of these desires generate a right to have a child? Chadwick does not think so. And why should she or we? That something is desired does not turn this into a right in other contexts. Those who desire wealth or an honour (a knighthood, for example) do not thereby acquire a right to it.

These debates in the recent past took place in the context of sterilisation.[27] A book on sterilisation policies was even entitled *The Right to Reproduce* (Trombley 1988). Indeed, my own critique of the notorious case of 'Jeanette' (*Re B*)[28] argues, naively perhaps, for her right to reproduce (Freeman 1988). Most discussion of the 'right to reproduce' today focuses on the infertile and the obligation to provide fertility treatment at state expense. As we have seen, Robertson and Chadwick situate their discussion in this context, and come to different conclusions. That the state assists

---

27 The Brock report of 1934, which now has a discreet veil placed on it, planned the sterilisation of 3.5 million people – in Britain, I hasten to add, not Nazi Germany (Brock 1934).

28 *Re B (A Minor) (Wardship: Sterilisation)* [1988] 1 AC 199.

people to have children in a myriad of other ways does not mean that it ought to assist with IVF treatment (Uniacke 1987). Nor does it mean that the government rejection of the recommendation of NICE that three cycles of IVF should be available on the NHS – it substituted one – was right. There is a difference between arguing for a right to reproduction when the issue is whether this should be taken away from someone on grounds of lesser intelligence or parenting abilities and where what is being argued for is a positive right. The latter falls outside the remit of this chapter: the former firmly within it.

But this is about the right to responsible parents and so we must question whether talking about the right to reproduce is ever an appropriate way of thinking. Should we not reject the rights framework when the issue is about having children, and substitute instead the language of responsibility?[29]

**Procreation as a Responsibility**

To see procreation as a huge responsibility rather than as a right or a privilege is, I believe, relatively uncontentious – and surely less so if we accept the norm of 'ethical self-management' to which reference was made at the beginning of this chapter. We may differ over the implications of this, but not, I suggest, over the characterisation of procreation as a serious responsibility.

This responsibility will increase in the future when it becomes possible to choose the characteristics of our children. We are moving – I use this relatively neutral language, but others might say advancing, which I think begs the question – into a future shaped by assisted reproduction, cloning and other reprogenetic opportunities (Knowles and Kaebnick 2007). Parents will increasingly be accorded the opportunity to select embryos according to their characteristics. It is already possible to screen out genetic disease by using the technique of preimplantation genetic diagnosis (PGD).[30] We have the ability to use this technique (and others) to enable prospective parents to choose the sex of their children. Some fear that this could lead to gendercide, particularly amongst Asian populations.[31] It is also already possible to combine PGD with tissue matching technologies (HLA – human leukocyte antigen) to provide a 'saviour sibling' (Freeman 2006; McLean 2006, Ch. 3) for an existing seriously ill child.[32] PGD is not as yet used commonly: about 100 babies have been born in the UK after the use of PGD and some 1,000 worldwide (Human Genetics Commission 2006, para. 4.1).

It may be that eugenics is 'inescapable' (Kitcher 1996). It is a real concern. One suggestion (by Kitcher) is for what he calls 'utopian eugenics', offering prenatal testing to all, and educating people about the decisions they may take and the implications of those decisions. It should not be forgotten that these private decisions

---

29  In line with the emphasis on responsibility elsewhere (see e.g. Reece 2003 and 2006).

30  The fullest discussion of this is Franklin and Roberts 2006.

31  It is allowed in Israel: see Siegel-Itzkovich 2005.

32  This was challenged by a pro-life pressure group in the 'Hashmi' case. The challenge was unsuccessful, see *R (Quintavalle) v Human Fertilisation and Embryology Authority (Secretary of State for Health Intervening)* [2005] 2 AC 561.

affect the population as a whole. There are also concerns that parents may select embryos for non-medical reasons beyond the sex of the child: intelligence, height, athletic potential, eye colour, perhaps even sexual orientation. And what if – in the future – we could select not just the characteristics of our children but, by altering genetic make-up, also effect a change in the human germ line (Stock and Campbell 2000). The private would become not just public, but also 'future'. Fukuyama (2002) is not alone in being concerned about the possibility of altering 'human nature' (but compare Stock 2002).

But, of course, it has altered already. We have eliminated diseases which in previous generations decimated populations. Life expectancy is now considerably greater than it was only a generation ago. Infertile women can now have children. We can live with someone else's heart, kidney, even face.[33] Kurzweil asks: 'If we regard a human modified with technology as no longer human, where would we draw the defining line? Is a human with a bionic heart still human? How about someone with a neurological implant?' (Kurzweil 2005, 374).

The questions raised – the implications for dignity, for example (and see Bostrom 2005) – go beyond the remit of this chapter. Our concern is with what, if any, are the implications for parental obligation.

Savulescu coined the expression 'procreative beneficence' (Savulescu 2001). Under this principle

> couples or single reproducers should select the child, of the possible children they could have, who is expected to have the best life, or at least as good a life as the others, based on the relevant, reliable information. (Savulescu 2001, 415)

This implies that 'couples should employ genetic tests for non-disease traits in selecting which child to bring into existence and that we should allow selection for non-disease genes in some cases even if this maintains or increases social inequality' (ibid.). There can be little doubt that there will be an increase in social inequality. But it will not necessarily lead to greater discrimination against those with disabilities. Savulescu believes we can distinguish between disability and persons who have disabilities: 'selection reduces the former, but is silent on the value of the latter' (ibid., 423). And there are, he believes, better ways to make statements about the equality of people with disabilities. There will be always be people with disabilities even if procreative beneficence becomes the norm and it is interpreted so that disability is screened 'out' (and not 'in' as some disabled people would apparently prefer). Not all disability has a genetic cause – most does not; accidents will always occur; people will become disabled as a result of, for example, strokes.

Nevertheless, there are question marks over procreative beneficence. Should one be able to select for disability? If you are deaf and belong to the community of the deaf, is there anything wrong in wanting to bring a child into the world who can glory in this deaf culture? Is the fact that you use assisted techniques of reproduction to achieve this – destroying embryos with the capability of hearing in the process – deliberately selecting a deaf embryo – unethical? Many do not think so (for example,

---

33  See Swindell 2007; Hartman, 2005; Freeman and Abou-Daudé 2007.

Holm 1998). They (for example, Häyry 2004) distinguish deliberately selecting a deaf embryo from deafening a hearing child. We all accept that the latter is child abuse. I think we would all accept it would be child abuse if a pregnant woman deliberately ingested a liquid that she knew would have the effect of causing her child to be born without hearing.[34] That the alternative to being selected is not to become a person at all – the standard defence – is not a satisfactory answer to anyone who is concerned with parental responsibility. The intention (in the ingestion example it is recklessness) in all three cases is the same: to produce a deaf child, and this is to act irresponsibly. More difficult is the case of the deaf couple (or couple where one of them is deaf) who know (because of the genetic tests) that if they have a child he/she will be deaf. Should they refrain from reproducing? Use the new reproductive techniques and have a child who is not genetically related to them? Counselling may assist them to come to an informed decision. And it must be their decision, freely reached without coercion or inducement. Too many of those sterilised in the name of eugenics allegedly consented (Kevles 1985; Trombley 1988).

A second problem with 'the perfect baby ideal' (McGee 2000) is what this does to the children. Robertson captures this concern well.

> The very concept of selection of offspring characteristics or "quality control" reveals a major discomfort – the idea that children are objects or products chosen on the basis of their qualities, like products in a shop window, valued not for themselves but for the pleasure or satisfaction they will give parents. (Robertson 1994, 150)

Children are persons, not property; individuals with rights, not commodities (Freeman 2007). A major – I have suggested *the* major – objection to the institution of surrogacy is that it commodifies children (Freeman 1989; Radin 1987). If a child is chosen to be 'intelligent' and turns out to be dull, or is selected to have athletic prowess and is instead slow and clumsy, if in other words parental expectations are thwarted, how will disappointment be expressed. In the worst case scenario the child may be rejected. There is a real danger that children may be damaged as a result.

In the future, as already indicated, it may be possible not merely to choose characteristics but to change them: to manipulate the genetic make-up of the embryo to programme in the desired characteristic. And we may transcend somatic gene therapy to embrace human germ-line therapy, enabling us to enhance the characteristics not just of our children, but of their children and grandchildren. This has caused alarm: George Annas and his colleagues have indicted this as a crime against humanity (Annas, Andrews and Isasi 2002), and such gene therapy has been outlawed in Australia and Canada.[35] The European Convention on Human Rights and Biomedicine also does not permit human germ-line therapy. Article 13 of this states:

---

34 The question has not been considered by any court. The pregnant woman who uses heroin has been considered, in the controversial case of *Re D (A Minor)* [1987] 1 AC 317.

35 See Australian Act 2005, Canadian Act of 2006.

An intervention seeking to modify the human genome may only be undertaken for preventative, diagnostic or therapeutic purposes and only if its aim is not to produce any modification in the genome of any descendants.

UNESCO's Universal Declaration on Bioethics and Human Rights purports to offer a justification for such a ban. In Article 3 it states 'human dignity' is to be 'fully respected'. But it also acknowledges that 'the impact of the life sciences on future generations, including in their genetic constitution, should be given due regard'. There is a concern that we may lose our sense of what is human. But do we know what being 'human' is? As already indicated in this essay, there have been shifts in our understanding of this.

### A Right not to Be Born?

What of the couple who discover that the foetus being carried is so damaged that the child who will be born will have a life of no quality at all? Of course, it is difficult to judge quality. A child who knows no difference may tolerate more than we might objectively suppose. The substituted judgement test, sometimes employed,[36] is not helpful. But let us say that the child's life, to quote an early English case, is going to be 'demonstrably so awful'.[37] The law permits the pregnancy to be terminated (Abortion Act 1967, s. 1(1)(d)). Should we also say that there is a responsibility to do so? Abortion is a rights issue: does it also translate into a matter of responsibility?[38]

Feinberg (1984) argues that biological parents 'do not harm' a child even if the child comes into existence in a state that makes 'life worth living' impossible. But it is still possible, he argues, to talk of a right not to be born. He refers to the 'plausible moral requirement' that

> no child be brought into the world unless certain very minimal conditions of well-being are assured, and certain basic "future interests" are protected in advance, at least in the sense that the possibility of his fulfilling those interests is kept open. When a child is brought into existence even though these requirements have not been observed, he has been wronged thereby. (Feinberg 1984, 101)

Feinberg concedes that not all interests should qualify for prenatal legal protection, but only the very basic ones whose satisfaction is indispensable. But he lists a large number of these including blindness, deafness and even 'economic deprivation so far below a reasonable minimum as to be inescapably degrading and sordid' (ibid., 99). Harris, rightly, finds the list 'astonishing' (Harris 1992, 91).

Are there people who would have been 'better off unborn'? And does this mean that there is a responsibility to abort them? It may be best to start by asking whether it can be better to be 'better off dead'. For Steinbock this phrase suggests that 'life is so terrible that it is no longer a benefit or a good to the one who lives'

---

36  *Re J (A Minor) (Wardship: Medical Treatment)* [1991] 1 FLR 366, 383-384 per Taylor LJ.

37  *Re B (A Minor) (Wardship: Medical Treatment)* [1981] 1 WLR 1421, 1424 per Templeman LJ.

38  See Hursthouse 1991.

(Steinbock 1992, 120). Feinberg offers a thought experiment in which we are given the opportunity after death to be reincarnated 'but only as a Tay-Sachs baby with a painful life expectancy of four years to be followed by permanent extinction or [we] can opt for permanent extinction to begin immediately' (Feinberg 1986, 164). He is of the opinion that we would have to be 'crazy' to select the first option, and that if required to make the choice for a loved one we would also opt for immediate non-existence. However, non-existence is rationally preferable only if all interests, present and future, are 'doomed to defeat'. Such a test works optimally where there is chronic pain combined with such severe mental retardation that the child will not be able to develop any compensating interests.

There are actually two different questions. One asks whether we might be acting wrongly to bring children into existence because of what is wrong with those children; the other whether it is wrong to bring children into the world when we cannot adequately parent them. Mill, writing in 1859, (1972, 239) saw this latter question long before anyone was considering either of the two questions – the former for obvious reasons. For Mill, to bring a child into the world 'without a fair prospect of being able, not only to provide food for its body, but instruction and training for its mind, [was] a moral crime', one against the child and society. It is politically incorrect to ponder the implications of Mill's concern today. It takes us back to the question, considered earlier in this essay, of the licensing of parenthood.

I will concentrate here on the first question. The complexity of this is well brought out by comparing two examples given by Derek Parfit. He invites us to consider the dilemmas faced by two women.

> The first is one month pregnant and is told by her doctor that, unless she takes a simple treatment, the child she is carrying will develop a certain handicap ... Life with this handicap would probably be worth living, but less so than normal life. It could obviously be wrong for the mother not to take the treatment, for this will handicap her child. (Parfit 1976, 76)

One can pause and ask: what if the 'treatment' alters the genetic composition of the child, changing its identity into that of a different person? This has teased philosophers (Agar 1995; DeGrazia 2005; Holtug 1993; Persson 1995; Zohar 1991) but need not detain us. Has a healthy B lost anything of value in being an unhealthy A? Parfit's second woman

> is about to stop taking contraceptive pills so that she can have another child. She is told that she has a temporary condition such that any child she conceives now will have the same handicap, but that if she waits three months she will then conceive a normal child. (Parfit 1976, 76)

In Parfit's view it would be as wrong for the second woman not to take her doctor's advice as for the first woman.

The first case is relatively uncontentious, but the second is far from straightforward, as Parfit himself acknowledges. In his *Reasons and Persons* (Parfit 1984, 358-359) he uses the example of the 14-year-old girl who wants a child. He notes we might say to her: 'You should think not only of yourself, but also of your child. It will be worse for him if you have him now'. But, of course, it will not be 'worse for him', for clearly if she has a child later it will not be the same child. Similarly, if the woman takes the advice she deprives a potential person, albeit one with a handicap, of the chance of having a life. It is his/her only chance: he/she may be glad to have the opportunity. Locke (1987), using a similar example to Parfit's second case, invokes what he calls the 'Possible Persons Principle' – 'in judging the rightness or wrongness of an action or decision we need to take account not merely of those who actually do, or will, exist, but also of those who would have existed if there had been a different action or decision'. However, acceptance of this principle would have enormous repercussions, not least for abortion. If, therefore, the second case can be explained by a more limited (or at any rate different) principle, it would be better to invoke this.

In seeking this, it is well to remember Richard Brandt's observation that 'no person is frustrated or made unhappy or miserable by not coming to exist' (Brandt 1974). Appealing to the concept of deprivation may assist us to understand the differences between being born with a handicap and not being conceived. Steinbock (1992, 74) puts it thus: 'the point of morality is to make people…happy, not to make more happy people'. We may thus be able to conclude that the woman in Parfit's second example also does the right thing if she postpones conception and avoids having a handicapped child. But suppose the second woman is told that any child she bears, now or in the future, will be handicapped, should she avoid conception? Unlike the woman in the second case, she will be depriving herself of the interest in being a mother (though the value of this interest may be diminished in those circumstances), but again it cannot be said that she is depriving anyone else of life.

But if failing to have a child is not wrong, having a child may, in certain circumstances, be wrong. Indeed, the belief that a child may be wronged by being brought into existence in certain circumstances has given rise to so-called 'wrongful life' actions.

The first case is *Zepeda v Zepeda*.[39] The injury claimed here, by a healthy child, was having been born illegitimately. The case was brought in 1963, when considerably greater stigma attached to illegitimacy (in Illinois, where the case was brought, as well as in the United Kingdom). Recovery was denied by courts which, unsurprisingly, feared the floodgates would open if it were permitted. The American courts have since distinguished between being born under adverse conditions and being born with a severe handicap or fatal disease. A clear statement of this distinction can be found in Justice Jefferson's judgment in *Curlender v Bio-Science Laboratories*,[40] a case where a child was born suffering from Tay-Sachs disease:

> A cause of action based upon impairment of status – illegitimacy contrasted with legitimacy – should not be recognizable at law because a necessary element for the establishment of any cause of action in tort is missing, *injury* and damages consequential to that injury. A child born with severe impairment, however, presents an entirely different situation because the necessary element of *injury* is present.

---

39   190 N.E. 2d 849 (1963). See also *Williams v State of New York* 223 N.E. 2d 343 (1966).
40   106 (al. App (3d) 811, 165 Cal Repts. 477 (1980)).

But what constitutes an injury? Is it an 'injury' to be born a girl? Does the answer to this depend on culture and community? Is it an injury to be born gay rather than heterosexual? Or to be born with criminal propensities?[41]

The courts have not been very receptive to wrongful life claims, though they have succeeded in a number of American states.[42] The English courts have rejected the concept. In *McKay v Essex Area Health Authority*,[43] the Court of Appeal expressed the view that 'the difference between existence and non-existence was incapable of measurement by a court'.[44] Ackner LJ said that he could not accept that 'the common law duty of care to a person can involve, without specific legislation to achieve this end, the legal obligation to that person, whether or not *in utero*, to terminate his existence.'[45] Such a proposition, he thought, ran wholly contrary to the concept of the sanctity of human life.

It is not surprising that courts should have had problems with the concept of wrongful life. Their concern are concrete and do not involve 'meditation on the mysteries of life' (as one court put it).[46] But we can delve into more abstract questions. It may be that if one can sustain a reasoned argument for a moral right not to be born that this will provide the foundation for a legal action in tort. My concern, though, is with moral entitlement, and the moral duties of potential parents.

Since we now regard parental responsibility as integral to an understanding of parent/child relations, what are the implications of this before the child is born? Does it cast any light on the constraints, if any, on having children? The law draws the line between parental autonomy and parental responsibility at 'significant harm'. It is at this level that intervention is pitched. Does this offer clues as to what may be expected of those endowed with parental responsibility?

Parental responsibility is a normative standard by which to judge the decisions and actions of parents or of those who wish to become parents. What it will look like will depend upon how it is justified. John Eekelaar, writing of parents' moral obligation to care for their children, has demonstrated that contractarian theories, motivated at least in part by self-interest, cannot really account for the obligation to care (Eekelaar 1991b). He found the true basis for these moral obligations in Finnis's

---

41 This was highlighted in the *Mobley* case in Georgia, USA in 1995.

42 California: see above, n. 40; New Jersey: *Berman v Allen* 404 A 2d 8; Washington: *Harbeson v Parke-Davis Inc.* 656 P 2d 483 (1983).

43 [1982] 2 All ER 771.

44 Ibid., 790.

45 Ibid., 787. 'Wrongful life' has also been rejected in Canada: *Cherry v Borsman* (1992), 94 DLR (4th) 487 and South Africa: *Friedman v Glickson* 1996 (1) SA 1134. Israel has allowed it: *Zeitsov v Katz* (1986), 40(2) P.D. 85, and so has France: *X v Mutuelle d'Assurance du Corps Sanitaire Francais et al.* (2000), JCP 2293 (the *Perruche* case). This case encountered criticism in France from the medical profession, as well as the anti-abortion lobby and disabled support groups, and the government was forced into initiating emergency legislation. The Dutch courts have also now recognised the wrongful life action in the *Molenaar* case (see *X v Y*, Court of Appeal in The Hague 26 March 2003, discussed by Nys and Date 2004, and since upheld by the Supreme Court). The literature on wrongful life is vast: although quite old. I would single out Morreim (1988) as offering particularly interesting insights.

46 In *Curlender v Bio-Science Laboratories*, above, n. 40.

theory of human flourishing (see Finnis 1980, 80-99). Finnis sees the procreation and education of children as 'an indistinguishable cluster of moral responsibilities' (ibid., 83). Eekelaar's arguments have equal force in our context.

To exercise parental responsibility is to put the interests and welfare of children (or future children) above one's own needs, desires or well-being. There may be disputes as to what is in a child's best interests, but there is an irreducible minimum content to a child's well-being, and this must be satisfied by anyone carrying out the role of, or purporting to become, a parent.

This means that the very young should not become parents. Whether it also means that older people should also consider not having children is debatable. The debate has focused on the post-menopausal woman, but applies equally to older men. With more time on their hands, more experience and perhaps more money such people may be excellent parents. Our intuition (or is it our prejudice?) sets its face against them, but the arguments against fertility treatment for post-menopausal women do not stand up to critical examination (Cutas 2007; Fisher and Sommerville 1998). Are couples in their sixties who have children acting irresponsibly? If they can more than meet their child's needs for the 'basic goods' of human flourishing, and if their parenting reaches or excels minimum standards ('the significant harm' test), why should we place obstacles in their way?

## Conclusion

To view the problem through the lens of parental responsibility is to focus on the decision-making process. It is to recognise the commitment involved in bringing a child into the world. It is to acknowledge that having children is an exercise of commitment to love, nurture and care. It is to accept that parents should want the best for their children. To exercise parental responsibility – I use the concept normatively, not descriptively – is to plan parenthood sensibly, and with empathy for the needs and future of the child. It is thus not an exercise of parental responsibility to bring a child into the world whose life will be demonstrably awful. Nor is it an exercise of parental responsibility to bring a child into the world when that child will be cruelly deprived of all, or most, of the basic goods of human flourishing.

I have in the past been critical of those (Onora O'Neill is a good example) who have argued that adults' duties are more important than children's rights (Freeman 1992). O'Neill (1988) believes that taking rights as fundamental in ethical deliberation about children has neither theoretical nor political advantages. In emphasising responsible parenthood, in focusing on obligations, on agents rather than recipients, I do not resile from a commitment to the importance of taking children's rights seriously. Rather I begin to formulate a right overlooked by legislation, international[47] and national – the right to have responsible parents. Once a child is born, responsibility is more recognisable. This chapter has focused on decisions pre-birth. An article in preparation, for publication elsewhere, will examine the right to responsible parents

---

47  It is not in the United Nations Convention on the Rights of the Child of 1989.

The Right to Responsible Parents                               35

as it is tested in important day-to-day decisions on such matters as education, medical treatment, punishment and religious upbringing.

## References

Agar, N. (1995), 'Designing Babies: Morally Permissible Ways to Modify the Human Genome', *Bioethics* 9:1.

Annas, G., Andrews, L. and Isasi, R.M. (2002), 'Protecting the Endangered Human: Toward an International Treaty Prohibiting Cloning and Inheritable Alterations', *American Journal of Law and Medicine* 28:151.

Baker, H. (2004), 'MMR: Medicine, Mothers and Rights', *Cambridge Law Journal* 49.

Benhabib, S. (1992), *Situating the Self* (Cambridge: Polity Press).

Blustein, J. (1982), *Parents and Children* (New York: Oxford University Press).

Bostrom, N. (2005), 'In Defence of Posthuman Dignity', *Bioethics* 19:32.

Brandt, R. (1974), 'The Morality of Abortion' in Perkins, R. (ed.), *Abortion: Pro and Con* (Cambridge, MA.: Schenkman).

Bridgeman, J. (2007), *Parental Responsibility, Young Children and Healthcare Law* (Cambridge: Cambridge University Press).

Brock, D. (1996), 'Funding New Reproductive Technologies' in Cohen, C.B. (ed.), *New Ways of Making Babies: The Case of Egg Donation* (Bloomington: Indiana University Press).

Brock, Sir L. (chair) (1934), *Report of the Departmental Committee on Sterilization* (London: HMSO).

Chadwick, R.F. (1987), *Ethics, Reproduction and Genetic Control* (London: Croom Helm).

Covell, K. and Howe, R.B. (1998), 'A Policy of Parent Licensing' in Institute for Research on Public Policy, *Policy Options* (London: Institute for Research on Public Policy).

Cutas, D. (2007), 'Postmenopausal Motherhood: Immoral, Illegal? A Case Study', *Bioethics* 21:458.

Daniel, J. (1978), 'Child Abuse Screening: Implications of the Limited Predictive Power of Abuse Discriminants from a Controlled Family Study of Pediatric Social Illness', *Child Abuse and Neglect* 2:247.

DeGrazia, D. (2005), *Human Identity and Bioethics* (New York: Cambridge University Press).

Eekelaar, J. (1991a), 'Parental Responsibility: State of Nature or Nature of the State?', *Journal of Social Welfare and Family Law* 13:37.

Eekelaar, J. (1991b), 'Are Parents Morally Obliged to Care for their Children?', *Oxford Journal of Legal Studies* 11:340.

Eekelaar, J. (2000), 'Uncovering Social Obligations: Family Law and the Responsible Citizen' in Maclean, M. (ed.), *Making Law for Families* (Oxford: Hart).

Eekelaar, J. (2001a), 'Family Law: The Communication Message', *Oxford Journal of Legal Studies* 21:181.

Eekelaar, J. (2001b), 'Parental Responsibility – A New Legal Status: Social Parenthood', *Law Quarterly Review* 117:233.

Eisenberg, H.B. (1994), 'A "Modest" Proposal: State Licensing of Parents', *Connecticut Law Review* 26:1415.

Feinberg, J. (1984), *Harm to Others* (New York: Oxford University Press).

Feinberg, J. (1986), 'Wrongful Life and the Counterfactual Element in Harming', *Social Philosophy and Policy* 4:145.

Finnis, J. (1980), *Natural Law and Natural Rights* (Oxford: Clarendon Press).

Fisher, F. and Sommerville, A. (1998), 'To Everything There is a Season? Are There Medical Grounds for Refusing Fertility Treatment to Older Women?' in Harris, J. and Holm, S. (eds), *The Future of Human Reproduction* (Oxford: Oxford University Press).

Floyd, S.L. and Pomerantz, D. (1981), 'Is There a Natural Right to Have Children?' in Arthur, J. (ed.), *Morality and Moral Controversies* (Englewood Cliffs, NJ: Prentice Hall).

Fox, M. and Thomson, M. (2005), 'Short-Changed? The Law and Ethics of Male Circumcision', *International Journal of Children's Rights* 13:161.

Frank, R. (1990), 'Family Law and the Federal Republic of Germany', *International Journal of Law, Policy and the Family* 4:214.

Franklin, S. and Roberts, C. (2006), *Born and Made – An Ethnography of Preimplantation Genetic Diagnosis* (Princeton, NJ.: Princeton University Press).

Freeman, M. (1979), *Violence in the Home: A Socio-Legal Study* (Aldershot: Saxon House).

Freeman, M. (1988), 'Sterilising the Mentally Handicapped' in Freeman, M. (ed.), *Medicine, Ethics and Law* (London: Stevens).

Freeman, M. (1989), 'Is Surrogacy Exploitative?' in McLean, S., *Legal Issues in Human Reproduction* (Aldershot: Gower), Ch. 7.

Freeman, M. (1992), 'Taking Children's Rights More Seriously' in Alston, P., Parker, S. and Seymour, J. (eds), *Children, Rights and the Law* (Oxford: Clarendon Press), 52-71.

Freeman, M. (1997), 'Do Children Have the Right Not to Be Born' in Freeman, M., *The Moral Status of Children* (The Hague: Martinus Nijhoff), Ch. 9.

Freeman, M. (2006), 'Saviour Siblings' in McLean, S. (ed.), *First Do No Harm* (Aldershot: Ashgate).

Freeman, M. (2007), 'Why It Remains Important to Take Children's Rights Seriously', *International Journal of Children's Rights* 15:5.

Freeman, M. and Abou-Doudé, P. (2007), *Journal of Medical Ethics*.

Frisch, L.E. (1981), 'On Licentious Licensing: A Reply to Hugh LaFollette', *Philosophy and Public Affairs* 11:173.

Fukujama, F. (2002), *Our Posthuman Future* (New York: Farrar, Straus and Giroux).

Gil, D. (1978), 'Societal Violence and Violence in Families' in Eekelaar, J. and Katz, S. (eds), *Family Violence* (Toronto: Butterworths), Ch. 1.

Gillies, V. (2005), 'Meeting Parents' Needs? Discourses of "Support" and "Inclusion" in Family Policy', *Critical Social Policy* 25:70.

Gilligan, C. (1982), *In a Different Voice: Psychological Theory and Women's Development* (Cambridge, MA: Harvard University Press).

Gray, J. (2007), *Black Mass: Apocalyptic Religion and the Death of Utopia* (London: Allen Lane).

Harris, J. (1992), *Wonderwoman and Superman* (Oxford: Oxford University Press).

Hart, H.L.A. (1958), 'Positivism and the Separation of Law and Morals', *Harvard Law Review* 71:593.

Hart, H.L.A. (1968), *Punishment and Responsibility* (Oxford: Clarendon Press).

Hartman, R.G. (2005), 'Face Value: Challenges of Transplant Technology', *American Journal of Law and Medicine* 31:7.

Häyry, M. (2004), 'There is a Difference between Selecting a Deaf Embryo and Deafening a Hearing Child', *Journal of Medical Ethics* 30:510.

Holm, S. (1998), 'Ethical Issues in Pre-implantation Diagnosis' in Harris, J. and Holm, S. (eds), *The Future of Human Reproduction* (Oxford: Oxford University Press), Ch. 10.

Holtug, N. (1993), 'Human Gene Therapy: Down the Slippery Slope?', *Bioethics* 7:402.

House of Commons Science and Technology Committee (2005), *Human Reproductive Technologies and the Law* (5th Report), HC 7-1 (London: TSO).

House of Commons Select Committee on Violence in the Family (1977), *Violence in the Family. Volume 1: Report* (First report from the Select Committee on Violence in the Family), HC 329 (London: HMSO).

Human Genetics Commission (2006), *Making Babies: Reproductive Decisions and Genetic Technologies* (London: Human Genetics Commission).

Hursthouse, R. (1991), 'Virtue Theory and Abortion', *Philosophy and Public Affairs* 20:223.

Huxtable, R. (2004), 'Re C (A Child) Immunisation: Parental Rights', *Journal of Social Welfare and Family Law* 26:69.

Jackson, E. (2002), 'Conception and the Irrelevance of The Welfare Principle', *Modern Law Review* 65:176.

Joint Committee on the Human Tissue and Embryos Draft Bill (2007), *Human Tissue and Embryos (Draft) Bill Volume I: Report* (London: The Stationery Office).

*Justice* (1975), *Parental Rights and Duties and Custody Suits* (London: Stevens).

Kevles, D. (1985), *In the Name of Eugenics: Genetics and the Uses of Human Heredity* (Cambridge, MA: Harvard University Press).

Kitcher, P. (1996), *The Lives to Come* (New York: Simon and Schuster).

Knowles, L. and Kaebnick, G.E. (2007), *Reprogenetics: Law, Policy and Ethical Issues* (Baltimore: Johns Hopkins University Press).

Kurzweil, R. (2005), *The Singularity Is Near: When Humans Transcend Biology* (New York: Viking).

LaFollette, H. (1980), 'Licensing Parents', *Philosophy and Public Affairs* 9:182.

Light, R. (1973), 'Abused and Neglected Children in America: A Study of Alternative Policies', *Harvard Educational Review* 43: 455.

Locke, D. (1987), 'The Parfit Population Problem', *Philosophy* 62:131.

Lyon, C.M. (2000), 'The Definition of, and Legal and Management Responses to, the Problem of Child Abuse in England and Wales' in Freeman, M. (ed.), *Overcoming Child Abuse: A Window on a World Problem* (Aldershot: Ashgate), Ch. 6.

Mangel, C.P. (1988), 'Licensing Parents: How Feasible?', *Family Law Quarterly* 22: 17.

Mason, M.A. (1994), *From Father's Property to Children's Rights* (New York: Columbia University Press).

McGee, G. (2000), *The Perfect Baby* (Lanham: Rowman and Littlefield).

McLean, S. (2006), *Modern Dilemmas – Choosing Children* (Edinburgh: Capercaillie Books).

Mill, J.S. (1972), *On Liberty* (Warnock, M. (ed.)) (London: Fontana).

Morreim, E.H. (1988), 'The Concept of Harm Reconceived: A New Look at Wrongful Life', *Law amd Philosophy* 7:3.

Morris, A. and Saintier, S. (2003), 'To Be or Not to Be: Is That the Question? Wrongful Life and Misconceptions', *Medical Law Review* 11:167.

Nys, H.F.L. and Date J.C.J (2004), 'A Wrongful Existence in the Netherlands', *Journal of Medical Ethics* 30:393.

O'Neill, O. (1988), 'Children's Rights and Children's Lives', *Ethics* 98:445.

Parfit, D. (1976), 'Rights, Interests and Possible People' in Gorovitz, S. (ed.), *Moral Problems in Medicine* (Englewood Cliffs, NJ: Prentice Hall).

Parfit, D. (1984), *Reasons and Persons* (Oxford: Oxford University Press).

Persson, I. (1995), 'Genetic Therapy, Identity and Person-regarding Reasons', *Bioethics* 9:16.

Purdy, L. (1996), *Reproducing Persons: Issues in Feminist Bioethics* (Ithaca, NY: Cornell University Press).

Radin, M. (1987), 'Market-inalienability', *Harvard Law Review* 100:1849.

Reece, H. (2003), *Divorcing Responsibly* (Oxford: Hart).

Reece, H. (2006), 'From Parental Responsibility to Parenting Responsibly' in Freeman, M. (ed.), *Law and Sociology* (Oxford: Oxford University Press), 459.

Robertson, J. (1983), 'Procreative Liberty and the Control of Conception, Pregnancy and Childbirth', *Virginia Law Review* 69:405.

Robertson, J. (1994), *Children of Choice: Freedom and the New Reproductive Technologies* (Princeton, NJ: Princeton University Press).

Savulescu, J. (2001), 'Procreative Beneficence: Why We Should Select the Best Children', *Bioethics* 15:413.

Schneider, C., Hoffmeister, M. and Helfer, R. (1972), 'The Predictive Questionnaire: A Preliminary Report' in Kempe, C.H. and Helfer, R. (eds), *Helping the Battered Child and his Family* (Philadelphia: Lippincott).

Select Committee (1977).

Siegel-Itzkovich, J. (2005), 'Israel Allows Sex Selection of Embryos for Non-Medical Reasons', *British Medical Journal* 330:1228.

Smart, C. and Neale, B. (1999), *Family Fragments?* (Cambridge: Policy Press).

Steinbock, B. (1992), *Life Before Birth* (New York: Oxford University Press).

Stock, G. (2002), *Redesigning Humans: Our Inevitable Genetic Future* (Boston: Houghton, Mifflin).

Stock, G. and Campbell, J. (2000), *Engineering the Human Germline* (New York: Oxford University Press).

Swindell, J.S. (2007), 'Facial Allograft Transplantation: Personal Identity and Subjectivity', *Journal of Medical Ethics* 33:449.

Trombley, S. (1988), *The Right to Reproduce* (London: Weidenfeld and Nicolson).

Tronto, J. (1993), *Moral Boundaries: The Political Argument for an Ethic of Care* (New York: Routledge).

Uniacke, S. (1987), 'In Vitro Fertilization and the Right to Reproduce', *Bioethics* 1:241.

Viens, A.M. (2004), 'Value Judgment, Harm and Religious Liberty', *Journal of Medical Ethics* 30:241.

Westman, J.C. (1994), *Licensing Parents: Can We Prevent Child Abuse and Neglect?* (Cambridge, MA: Perseus Books).

Wilson, J. (2007), 'Transhumanism and Moral Equality', *Bioethics* 21:419.

Zohar, N.J. (1991), 'Prospects for "Genetic Therapy" – Can a Person Benefit from Being Altered?', *Bioethics* 5:275.

# [11]
# Does Surrogacy Have a Future After Brazier?

## I. INTRODUCTION

Women have always carried babies for other women, or (perhaps more commonly) for men who are not their husbands or partners.[1] Examples (of sorts)[2] can be traced to the book of *Genesis*.[3] The first modern cases to attract public attention were *A* v. *C*[4] in 1978 (though this was not properly reported until the "Baby Cotton" case[5] in 1985 sensitised us to the problem), *Noyes* v. *Turane*[6] in 1981 and *Stiver* v. *Malahoff*[7] in 1983. All three cases had a sensationalist dimension and attracted media attention: in the first, the surrogate was a prostitute who was approached leaving the magistrates' court; in the second, the commissioning mother was a male-to-female transsexual; in the third case the child was rejected by the commissioning parents (he had microcephaly) but was revealed in a television show[8] to be the child of the surrogate's husband.

The cases coincide with early news (Louise Brown, the first IVF baby was born in 1978) and early concerns about the reproduction revolution. And, it was this, rather than surrogacy itself, which motivated

---

[1] On male domination of reproduction see R. Rowland, *Living Laboratories* (Lime Tree 1992) at 6–14. See also C. Pateman, *The Sexual Contract* (Polity Press, 1988). For Debra Satz "markets in women's reproductive labor are especially troubling because they reinforce gender hierarchies in a way that other accepted labor markets do not" (see "Markets in Women's Reproductive Labor" (1992) 21 *Philosophy and Public Affairs* 107–31 at 110).

[2] The oft-cited Biblical examples are not true surrogacies: the surrogates were slaves (or perhaps concubines: see Genesis XXV, 6).

[3] See chapter XVI, 1–5 (Abram and Hagar) for the best known example.

[4] (1978) 8 Fam. Law 170 and fully in [1985] F.L.R. 445.

[5] [1985] F.L.R. 846. Kim Cotton's story is told in K Cotton and D Winn, *Baby Cotton For Love and Money* (Dorling Kindersley 1985).

[6] No. CF7614 (L.A. Cty. Super Ct. 1981) and see M.A. Field, *Surrogate Motherhood* (Harvard University Press 1988), 1.

[7] See G. Corea, *The Mother Machine* (Harper and Row 1985) at 219–20, 230 and P. Singer and D. Wells, *The Reproduction Revolution* (Oxford University Press 1984) at 118–19.

[8] The "Phil Donahue Show".

2                    MEDICAL LAW REVIEW                [1999]

the government in 1982 into setting up the Warnock inquiry.[9] But it
was moral panic[10] over the "Baby Cotton" affair in January 1985
which led to legislation (the Surrogacy Arrangements Act 1985)[11] and
this, as amplified in 1990,[12] remains the framework of surrogacy law
today.

In 1997 a committee chaired by Margaret Brazier (hereafter
"Brazier")[13] was established to review this law and current practice "to
ensure that the law continued to meet public concerns". The review was
prompted by examples of surrogacy reported in the press in 1996 and
1997.[14] In 1996 also the BMA declared surrogacy to be an "acceptable
option of last resort", whilst stressing that "the interests of the potential
child must be paramount and the risks to the surrogate mother must be
kept to a minimum".[15] This was a long way from its position at the time
of Warnock.

The time was ripe for a review. Surrogacy had divided the Warnock
committee, the majority of which came down in favour of a conclusion
ethically at odds with the pro-autonomy stand in the rest of the
report.[16] And the subject continues to divide: Van Dyck is able to detect
no fewer than seven different feminist positions on surrogacy.[17]

---

[9] Mary Warnock, *A Question of Life* (Blackwell 1985), previously published as *Report of the Committee of Inquiry into Human Fertilisation and Embryology* (Cmnd. 9314) (London: HMSO, 1984).

[10] See M.D.A. Freeman, "After Warnock—Whither The Law?" (1986) 39 *Current Legal Problems* 33–5. The Government insisted that "it was not as a result of the Baby Cotton case that this Bill came forward" *per* the Earl of Caithness, *Hansard*, H.L. vol. 465, col. 925. See also C. Dyer, "Baby Cotton and the Birth of a Moral Panic", *The Guardian*, 15 January 1985 and A. Hutchinson and D. Morgan, "A Bill Born From Panic", *The Guardian*, 12 July 1985.

[11] See M.D.A. Freeman, "The Surrogacy Arrangements Act 1985" in *Current Law Statutes Annotated* (Sweet and Maxwell 1986).

[12] By the Human Fertilisation and Embryology Act 1990, on which see D. Morgan and R.G. Lee, *Blackstone's Guide To The Human Fertilisation and Embryology Act 1990* (Blackstone Press 1991).

[13] The review team was Margaret Brazier, Professor of Law, University of Manchester; Alistair Campbell, Professor of Ethics in Medicine, University of Bristol and Susan Golombok, Professor of Psychology, City University, London.

[14] In particular the Karen Roche case (see *The Independent*, 20 January 1997); also the arrival of the American, Bill Handel, who "advertised" his presence in the United Kingdom (without advertising in breach of the 1985 Act) and let it be known that payments of between £30,000 and £45,000 were available for willing surrogates.

[15] *The Changing Conceptions of Motherhood—The Practice of Surrogacy in Britain* (BMA 1996) at 59.

[16] See Freeman, *op. cit.*, note 10.

[17] J. Van Dyck, *Manufacturing Babies and Public Consent* (Macmillan 1995) at 172–3. See also Joan Mahoney, "An Essay On Surrogacy and Feminist Thought" in (ed.) Larry Gostin, *Surrogate Motherhood* (Indiana University Press 1990) at 183–97.

Med.L.Rev.    *Does Surrogacy Have a Future After Brazier?*    3

There is, the Brazier Report acknowledges, "a policy vacuum",[18] an absence of a "coherent policy".[19] The 1985 legislation had not implemented the Warnock Report in full: had it done so, organisations like COTS and the Surrogacy Parenting Centre could not have operated, and full surrogacy would have been impossible.[20] Surprisingly, neither the Warnock Report nor the 1985 Act addressed the question of payment to surrogate mothers: both the committee and the legislature may have assumed that adoption law would act as a sufficient deterrent to money changing hands.[21] It did not do so: indeed, liberal construction by the courts facilitated the making of adoption orders where surrogates had been paid for their services.[22]

The Brazier Report, looking back to 1985, believes it was thought that surrogacy would "largely disappear",[23] that it would "wither on the vine".[24] Clearly, this has not happened, and, although accurate statistics are difficult to calculate, it has to be assumed that the number of surrogacy arrangements and births is on the increase.[25] And, contrary to early fears, it is only in a handful of cases (the Brazier Report estimates 4–5 per cent)[26] that the nightmare scenario occurs and a surrogate refuses to hand over the child.

## II. BRAZIER'S PHILOSOPHY

The Brazier Report, in the words of the minister who set up the committee, looks to "provide a sensible and sensitive way forward within a framework that inspires public confidence".[27] It believes—and rightly so—that concerns have changed since the days of Warnock. Surrogacy for convenience, roundly condemned by Warnock as "totally ethically unacceptable",[28] is no longer thought to constitute a threat. Today rather, as the report sees it, it is the point at which surrogacy becomes an "acceptable alternative"[29] to other fertility treatment that is the

---

[18] *Surrogacy: Review for Health Ministers of Current Arrangements For Payments and Regulation* (Cm. 4068) (Department of Health, 1998) at i (para 3).
[19] *Ibid.*
[20] *Ibid.*, para. 2.8.
[21] This is the view of the Brazier report: see *ibid.*, para. 3.2.
[22] See *Re An Adoption Application (Payment For Adoption)* [1987] Fam. 81 and *Re M.W. (Adoption: Surrogacy)* [1995] 2 F.L.R. 759.
[23] *Op. cit.*, note 18, para. 3.5.
[24] *Ibid.*, para. 3.44.
[25] Statistics on the number of applications for parental orders are in a table on p. 6 of the *Report* (para. 1.27).
[26] *Op. cit.*, note 18, para. 3.38.
[27] *Ibid.*, para. 1.49, quoting Tessa Jowell M.P.
[28] *Op. cit.*, note 9, para. 8.17.
[29] *Op. cit.*, note 18, para. 4.7.

matter in contention. But, again, we simply do not know the incidence of resort to surrogacy after failed IVF cycles. Nor today, though such concerns were voiced to the Brazier committee,[30] is opposition to surrogacy often couched in terms of the intrusion of a third party into the marriage relationship. It is perhaps surprising that this concern should have eased so much given the constant peddling of "back to basics" and the emphasis on "family values".[31]

The concerns today, as Brazier saw them,[32] are whether the law and practice adequately safeguard the welfare of the child; whether it protects the interests of the surrogate, her family and the commissioning · couple—the report takes it as unproblematic that surrogacy is a service for couples—and whether it should do so; and whether payment of the surrogate is acceptable.

Although contemporary concerns differ from those current in Warnock's day, the ethical issues remain broadly the same. Warnock was concerned with the danger of exploitation: "that people should treat others as a means to their own ends, however desirable the consequences, must always be liable to moral objection. Such treatment of one person by another becomes positively exploitative when financial interests are involved".[33] Brazier acknowledges that it is not payment that makes people into a mere means, that, "on the contrary lack of payment (as in slavery or breadline wages) may be much more exploitative".[34] Despite this, the report advocates allowing surrogacy to continue—regulated, as we shall see—but strongly objects to surrogates being recompensed for their services.

But is it right to indict a service (or an occupation) because of its motivation? A fertility specialist who increases the happiness of many infertile couples may do so for personal aggrandisation or for wealth, but we focus on his/her results, not his/her motives for going into the occupation (or business). The objection may be to earning money by using your body, but no-one has suggested that fashion models, for example, should go financially unrewarded. Brazier's answer to this focuses on the supposed inability of surrogates to foresee the risks entailed. "Payment increases the risk of exploitation if it constitutes an

---

[30] *Ibid.*, para. 4.5.
[31] See Michael Freeman, "Family Values and Family Justice" (1997) 50 *Current Legal Problems* 315–59.
[32] *Op. cit.*, note 18, para. 4.6.
[33] *Op. cit.*, note 9, para. 8.17. On exploitation, see Michael Freeman, "Is Surrogacy Exploitative?" in (ed.) Sheila A.M. McLean, *Legal Issues In Human Reproduction* (Gower 1989) at 164–84. See also Alan Wertheimer, *Exploitation* (Princeton University Press 1996), ch. 4.
[34] *Op. cit.*, note 18, para. 4.23. And see Field, *op. cit.*, note 6 at 26 ("The most oppressive result of all is to allow surrogacy but prohibit the payment of any fee").

Med.L.Rev.    *Does Surrogacy Have a Future After Brazier?*    5

inducement to participate in an activity whose degree of risk the surrogate cannot, in the nature of things, fully understand or predict".[35] The prospective surrogate's autonomy[36] must, it seems, be protected by a healthy injection of paternalism.[37] We do not purport to protect others who are economically vulnerable from entering into dangerous occupations and it is not a satisfactory answer to say that "people choosing to undertake such jobs do so with full knowledge and understanding of such risks"[38] because this is patently not so (since the examples of soldiers is given by Brazier, think of the Gulf War and its aftermath). Poor women have long worked in environmentally dangerous workplaces and where they have been excluded, for example from mines, it is not at all clear that this was to protect them.[39] More obviously, women have always taken risks with pregnancy, and much greater ones than they do now, and have done so for others (men or society at large) but, it seems, risk is only raised as a problem now that there is for the first time the prospect of financial remuneration. It is clear that Brazier would like surrogacy to come to an end. Even if its terms of reference had allowed it to consider the question, it would not have recommended the "full commercialisation of surrogacy".[40] In its view it is not an acceptable occupation: commercialisation would imply a "normalisation of ... a difficult personal choice, with an unknown degree of psychological risk".[41] This may well be true—as yet we do not know—but it overlooks the fact that a surrogate's difficulties should be less than those of a mother relinquishing a child for adoption. On exploitation, Brazier concludes, that "there is not strong enough evidence to warrant attempts to ban surrogacy because of its effect on surrogate mothers", but "there is sufficient cause for concern to make regulation essential".[42] Whether regulation can overcome these perceived problems and risks is itself debatable: much will depend on how this is organised. Brazier's blueprint for this is discussed later in this paper.

Warnock was also concerned with the effect of a surrogacy arrangement on a child. It was "degrading to the child ... since, for

---

[35] *Op. cit.*, note 18, para. 4.25.
[36] On autonomy see S. Dodds and K. Jones "Surrogacy and Autonomy" (1989) 3 *Bioethics* 1–17, distinguishing occurrent and dispositional autonomy.
[37] For agreement see ·L. Purdy, *Reproducing Persons* (Cornell University Press 1996), ch. 11.
[38] *Op. cit.*, note 18, para. 4.24.
[39] And see J. Humphries, "Protective Legislation, the Capitalist State and Working Class Men: The Case of the 1842 Mines Regulation Act" (1981) 7 *Feminist Review* 1–33.
[40] *Op. cit.*, note 18, para. 4.25.
[41] *Idem.*
[42] *Ibid.*, para. 4.26.

practical purposes, the child will have been bought for money".[43] In the Brazier Report this argument translates as "commodification".[44] The Brazier Report does not use the concept of "commodification" in the usually accepted way. In Radin's seminal article it is the effects that surrogacy might have on children generally that is captured by the metaphor of commodification. She writes,

> If a capitalist baby industry were to come into being, with all of its accompanying paraphernalia, how could any of us, even those who did not produce infants for sale, avoid subconsciously measuring the dollar value of our children? How could our children avoid being preoccupied with measuring their own dollar value? This makes our discourse about ourselves (when we are children) and about our children (when we are parents) like our discourse about cars. In the worst case, market rhetoric could create a commodified self-conception in everyone, as the result of commodifying every attribute that differentiates us and that other people value in us, and could destroy personhood as we know it.[45]

This is an argument, though it has rather too much of the "slippery slope"[46] about it, which cannot be ignored. And the effect of surrogacy on the institution of childhood must be of concern. We have fought long enough for children to be recognised as persons (rather than perceived as property), and for their rights to be taken seriously not to compromise this success now.[47] For Brazier it is "legal considerations" (terms of a contract requiring the child to be handed over, in particular) that lead to the conclusion that "any financial arrangement that involves remuneration rather than simply expenses has to be regarded as a form of child purchase".[48] The core value, as Brazier sees it is, what Titmuss called,[49] "the gift relationship".[50] So "bearing a child for others should be seen within the context of a fully informed and free act of giving, and ... neither the child nor the surrogate should be regarded as the subjects of a commercial transaction".[51] There is the assumption

---

[43] *Op. cit.*, note 9, para. 8.11.

[44] *Op. cit.*, note 18, para. 4.34.

[45] M. Radin, "Market-Inalienability", (1987) 100 *Harvard Law Review* 1849-937, at 1926.

[46] On which see F. Schauer, "Slippery Slopes" (1985) 99 *Harvard Law Review* 361-83; W. Van Der Burg, "The Slippery Slope Argument", (1991) 102 *Ethics* 42–65 and D. Walton, *Slippery Slope Arguments* (Oxford University Press 1992).

[47] And see Michael Freeman, *The Moral Status of Children* (Martinus Nijhoff 1997).

[48] *Op. cit.*, note 18, para. 4.35.

[49] R. Titmuss, *The Gift Relationship: From Human Blood To Social Policy* (Allen and Unwin 1970).

[50] *Op. cit.*, note 18, para. 4.36.

[51] *Ibid.*, para. 4.39.

that gifts are unproblematic. Brazier—and the Report is not alone in this—has a model of the altruistic surrogacy with the surrogate as "virtue ethics"[52] personified. She has freely entered into the arrangement and there are no constraints. Nor will there be any problems. But how accurate a picture is this? Pressures and problems will exist, even if they are different ones.[53] Further, what has been overlooked is that the surrogate who has been paid may feel a greater obligation to hand over the child than one who has not. It could well be that in the surrogacy of the future as Brazier envisages it, there will be more "failures" than the 4–5 per cent, which is the current estimate.

Like Warnock, Brazier rejects any suggestion that surrogacy should be prohibited by the criminal law. Warnock was anxious to avoid children being born to surrogates "subject to the taint of criminality".[54] Brazier agrees and adds two other objections: it would constitute an unjustifiable violation of (an assumed but not proved) procreative liberty[55] (this could be justified if there were significant evidence that "any"[56] form of surrogacy resulted in significant harm); and a criminal prohibition could not be effectively policed. As far as this second consideration is concerned two points may be made. First, criminal legislation has functions other than criminal prosecution: in particular it sets moral standards.[57] It is no answer to the criminalisation of marital rape[58] that this would require the state to "police the bedrooms of the nation"[59] (the argument Brazier uses against criminalising surrogacy). The proposition—with which I agree—that surrogacy should not be criminalised is thus not supported by the argument presented. Secondly, what Brazier does not say is that by driving surrogacy "underground"[60] (the undoubted effect of a criminal prohibition), a crime tariff[61] would be created and the price of surrogacy would go up, in all probability as the quality of the service went down. The law would "protect" the market of the criminal entrepreneur. What Brazier does not appreciate

[52] See, for example, P. Foot, *Virtues and Vices* (University of California Press 1978); R. Hursthouse, *Beginning Lives* (Blackwell 1987); M. Slote, *From Morality To Virtue* (Oxford University Press 1992).
[53] See J. Oakley, "Altruistic Surrogacy and Informed Consent", (1992) 6 *Bioethics* 269–87.
[54] *Op. cit.*, note 9, para. 8.19.
[55] On which see J.A. Robertson, *Children of Choice* (Princeton University Press 1994).
[56] *Op. cit.*, note 18, para. 4.38.
[57] See the arguments of Karl Olivecrona in the first edition of *Law As Fact* (Einar Munksgaard 1939), at 150–61.
[58] See *R v. R* [1992] 1 A.C. 599 and *Criminal Justice and Public Order Act 1994*, s.142.
[59] *Op. cit.*, note 18, para. 4.38.
[60] *Idem.*
[61] See H. Parker, *The Limits of the Criminal Sanction* (Stanford University Press 1969), at 277–82.

is that under the scheme it designs this could anyway happen, as the supply of legitimate surrogates, starved of remuneration, dries up, and commissioning parents turn to shady agencies on the margins of the underworld who, for sums far in excess of those quoted in the Brazier report, will arrange surrogacies. Many of these surrogates will be drug addicts and doubtless some will be HIV-infected. We may live to rue the consequences of removing remuneration from surrogates.

## III. BRAZIER'S RECOMMENDATIONS

Brazier recommendations relate to three matters: *payments to surrogates*; the *regulation of surrogacy*; and, *new legislation* to replace the 1985 Act and s.30 of the 1990 Act, tightening up the provisions of these Acts and providing for a new Code of Practice.

### A. *Payments to Surrogates*

It was concern about the "level"[62] of payments being made to surrogate mothers that was a major factor in the initiation of the review. Of course, information was (and is) sketchy but accounts from COTS and elsewhere suggest payments of "£15,000 or more"[63] are being made by commissioning couples to surrogates. Payments reported to Guardians Ad Litem "ranged from nothing to £12,000, averaging £3,800 where payments were made"[64] (and, therefore, though the report does not say so, less than this). In fact in cases known to Guardians Ad Litem (GALs)—those where applications for parental orders were made—in only 3 per cent of cases was payment more than £10,000.[65] The cynic might comment that if there was concern about the "level" of payments it ought to have been because the remuneration appears to be so low! That those who are not applying for parental orders are the "big spenders", as the report suggests,[66] can only be speculation. It is equally possible that they are ignorant of the law—a possibility which the report countenances in another context.[67] The review found a majority of respondents (56%) were against payments.[68] This excluded COTS members who generally favoured payments. A large majority (83 per cent) believed surrogates should not be "out of pocket as a result of their pregnancy".[69] There was less consensus in relation to loss of earn-

---

[62] *Op. cit.*, note 18, para. 3.1.
[63] *Ibid.*, para. 3.4.
[64] *Ibid.*, para. 1.31.
[65] *Ibid.*, para. 5.6 and Annex C.
[66] *Ibid.*, para. 5.7.
[67] *Ibid.*, para. 6.33.
[68] *Ibid.*, para. 5.8
[69] *Idem.*

ings: 75 per cent thought payments should reimburse loss of actual earnings,[70] but only 31 per cent that potential earnings should be compensated.[71] In fact, over one in six respondents wanted to prohibit payments of any kind.[72]

Brazier recommends that payments to surrogate mothers should cover only genuine expenses associated with the pregnancy[73]—a list of permissible expenses is provided[74]—and actual loss of earnings (the difference between the surrogate mother's usual earnings and state benefits).[75] A number of reasons are given to support this conclusion. First, children are not commodities to be bought and sold.[76] Of course, this is right, but Brazier is too readily dismissive of the distinction between payment for the purchase of a child and payment for a potentially risky, time-consuming and uncomfortable service. The Report also overlooks the point made by Laura Purdy[77] that paying a woman to bear a child forces us to recognise the process as socially useful and children as socially valuable creatures whose upbringing and welfare are critically important. Secondly, it is in line with emerging policy in relation to egg and sperm donors, as well as with the law on blood and live organ donation.[78] This inevitably treats the law and policy in these areas as unproblematic, which they clearly are not.[79] But it was outside the remit of the review to question beyond surrogacy, and it is equally outside the scope of this paper to do so.[80] Thirdly, women should not be influenced to become surrogate mothers by the lure of financial benefit. The review found (unsurprisingly) that many surrogates are "primarily motivated by payment".[81] The spectre of surrogacy

---

[70] *Ibid.*, para. 5.9.

[71] *Idem.*

[72] *Idem.*

[73] *Ibid.*, para. 5.24.

[74] *Ibid.*, para. 5.25.

[75] *Ibid.*, para. 5.26.

[76] *Ibid.*, para. 5.11.

[77] *Op. cit.*, note 37, at 47.

[78] *Op. cit.*, note 18, paras. 5.12–5.13. See also Nuffield Council on Bioethics, *Human Tissue: Ethical and Legal Issues* (London 1995) and European Convention for the Protection of Human Rights and Dignity of the Human Being With Regard To The Application of Biology and Medicine (1996), Article 21.

[79] But see L.R. Cohen, "Increasing The Supply of Transplant Organs: The Virtues of a Future Market" (1989) 58 *George Washington Law Review* 1-51; C. Perry, "Human Organs and the Open Market" (1980) 91 *Ethics* 63–71; and G. Crespi, "Overcoming the Legal Obstacles To The Creation of a Futures Market in Bodily Organs", (1994) 55 *Ohio State Law Journal* 1–77.

[80] In relation to organs, I questioned non-marketability in Michael Freeman, "Un Mercato Di Organi Umani?" in (ed) S Fagiuoli, *La Questione Dei Trapianti Tra Etica, Diritto, Economia* (Giuffrè 1997), at 161–203.

[81] *Op. cit*, note 18, para. 5.14.

as a profession is also noted.[82] The fears here may well be exaggerated and regulation could police this. Fourthly, though conceded to be speculative, the report believes it is "not necessarily in children's best interests to learn that their surrogate mother benefitted financially from their birth or from giving them away to the commissioning couple".[83] Clearly, children born of surrogacy arrangements have the right to be told this,[84] but done properly and at the right time, is there any reason to believe that they will be harmed by information that money passed hands? The Report implies that the right time to tell a child of his/her origins is when that child is a teenager.[85] This surely cannot be the right advice and makes one suspicious of the rest of the psychology embedded in the report.

The Report fails to appreciate that withdrawing remuneration from surrogates will only drive potential surrogates away from regulated surrogacy into an invisible and socially uncontrolled world where the regulators will be more like pimps than adoption agencies. There is every reason to control surrogacy and to guard against perceived problems, but most women will expect to be rewarded. Brazier agrees and believes that surrogacy will rarely be undertaken by strangers once its recommendations are implemented. This prognosis is misplaced: surrogacy will continue; it will probably grow as infertility increases; it will go underground and the fees will become larger. We cannot stop women exercising their autonomy, nor can we persuade them that being paid aggravates their exploitation, when common sense tells them the reverse.

## B. Regulation

Brazier proposes that surrogacy should be regulated. This was also the view of the minority in the Warnock Report[86] and it is supported by Singer and Wells[87] and others.[88] Brazier rests its case for regulation on protection.[89] Regulation, it says, "might reduce the more obvious hazards to the child and the others involved (including any children of

---

[82] *Ibid.*, para. 5.17.

[83] *Ibid.*, para. 5.19.

[84] And see Michael Freeman, "The New Birth Right? Identity and the Child of The Reproduction Revolution", (1996) 4 *International Journal of Children's Rights* 273–97.

[85] *Op. cit.*, note 18, para. 5.21.

[86] Wendy Greengross and David Davies (see Expression of Dissent A). See also, D. Davies, "Hire-a-Womb, with Safeguards", *The Times*, 19 July 1984.

[87] *Op. cit.*, note 7, at 126–8.

[88] For example, the Ontario Law Reform Commission, *Human Artificial Reproduction and Related Matters* (1985) and Kim Cotton, *op. cit.*, note 5, at 69 and 186–7.

[89] *Op. cit.*, note 18, paras. 6.5 and 6.6.

the surrogate mother)".[90] The view that regulation is undesirable because its effect would be to aggravate the current situation—in effect the view of Warnock[91]—is dismissed: "the risks of not having a regulatory framework are greater than any entailed by introducing one".[92] Like the minority in Warnock, Brazier would not outlaw surrogacy arrangements made outside the regulated service. Those not using this might find it more difficult to secure a parental order under the new section 30 of the Human Fertilisation and Embryology Act 1990, but that, it is envisaged, would be the only sanction.[93] It is my view that if surrogacy is to be regulated, as I agree it should, then all surrogacy arrangements should be thus controlled. The institution of adoption is a ready-made model: private placements, save within the context of the family, are banned and no adoption order can be made without first being vetted.[94]

Brazier investigates three options for regulatory bodies. It rejects conferring regulatory powers on infertility clinics or the Human Fertilisation and Embryology Authority: it is not right to perceive surrogacy arrangements as "merely another treatment for infertile people".[95] Brazier is right to reject this option. Clinics and the HFEA have medical and scientific expertise and this is rarely required in the context of surrogacy. Other skills are, and these are more likely to be found in adoption-like agencies. It also rejected a new licensing authority on the ground that a "complex and expensive regulatory arrangement"[96] would be "an excessive reaction to current concerns about the practice of surrogacy".[97] It favours instead a "much simpler option":[98] "all agencies involved in surrogacy arrangements would be required to be registered by the UK Health Departments and to operate in accordance with a statutory Code of Practice".[99]

This modest proposal would not require the establishment of any new Authority. Brazier does not make out a strong case for this method of regulation. Given how few surrogacy arrangements and surrogacy births there are, the logic of decentralisation is weak. Even within the control of a Code of Practice, there are bound to be differences of interpretation and whether surrogacy is approved may depend on

[90] *Ibid.*, para. 6.3.
[91] *Ibid.*, para. 6.5.
[92] *Ibid.*, para. 6.6.
[93] Other sanctions are rejected: see para. 7.13.
[94] See Adoption Act 1976, s.11(1), (3) and *Gatehouse* v. *Robinson* [1986] 1 W.L.R. 18.
[95] *Op. cit.*, note 18, para. 6.13. See also para. 7.9.
[96] *Ibid.*, para. 6.22.
[97] *Idem.*
[98] *Idem.*
[99] *Ibid.*, para. 6.23.

geography. On a subject of such concern, should not authority speak with one voice? The case for a single licensing authority (Singer and Wells called it a "State Surrogacy Board")[100] is a strong one.

## C. *Reforming the Law*

Brazier recommends a new Surrogacy Act. This would address in one statute "the main legal principles" governing surrogacy arrangements and offer a surrogacy "code".[101] Rational, as opposed to panicked, legislation is to be welcomed. There are few better modern examples of morally panicked legislation than the 1985 Act (one MP said it "rightly outlaw[ed] the hell and wickedness that exists in America—where women are exploited and handled in an undignified manner for gain"),[102] and the parental order concept, introduced by the 1990 Act, was hastily conceived to respond to a problem of a constituent of its sponsor.[103]

The new Surrogacy Act would both consolidate and reform the law. Thus, Brazier recommends that surrogacy contracts should continue to be unenforceable.[104] The further question as to whether such contracts are valid or void or voidable is not addressed, but such an analytical investigation was outside the remit of the inquiry. The Report envisages the continuation of provisions in the 1985 Act prohibiting commercial agencies from assisting in the creation of surrogacy arrangements, and related provisions prohibiting advertisements.[105] Few will contest this, and Brazier desists from debating the issue. If surrogacy is to be totally regulated, this conclusion must be right. But if surrogacy is to be allowed to continue outside the framework of regulation, the proposal has less to commend it. Fertility clinics are allowed to profit from treating infertile couples. In my view the answer is clear: surrogacy should be totally regulated and the current bans on commercial activity continued.

The new Surrogacy Act would define and limit lawful payments to surrogate mothers allowing, as we have seen, only prescribed expenses and actual loss of earnings.[106] It would also provide for the promulgation of a Code of Practice as a "model of good practice".[107] Although the details of this are to be left for the Department of Health to settle

---

[100] *Op. cit.*, note 7, at 126–8.

[101] *Op. cit.*, note 18, para. 7.2.

[102] Harry Greenaway M.P., *Hansard*,. H.C. vol. 77, col. 45.

[103] Michael Jopling M.P. responding to *Re W. (Minors) (Surrogacy)* [1991] 1 F.L.R. 385.

[104] *Op. cit.*, note 18, para. 7.3.

[105] *Idem*

[106] *Ibid.*, paras. 5.24–5.26.

[107] *Ibid.*, para. 8.1.

Med.L.Rev.  *Does Surrogacy Have a Future After Brazier?*  13

after a consultation process, the Report offers a detailed blueprint in chapter 8. This addresses a number of matters.

Commendably, the first concern is the welfare of the child.[108] The Report does not adopt a consistent line on this. In the discussion of the Code of Practice, as in the Executive Summary, the welfare of the child must be "the paramount concern of all parties to the arrangement, the courts and all other agencies involved".[109] Elsewhere in the Report, we are told that the welfare of the child "must be accorded the highest priority".[110] These are different standards. The paramountcy principle allows no space for other considerations. The child's welfare is more than just the "top item": it "rules upon or determines the course to be followed".[111] But according a child's welfare—in effect, of course, a child yet to be born—the highest priority, it becomes the "first consideration" but not the only one. It is weighted, though by how much is an unanswerable question.[112] A reading of the Report as a whole suggests that it must intend to accord the child's welfare only the "highest priority" (to use language found in other statutes[113] "the first consideration") because the interests of other parties, in particular the vulnerability of the surrogate, are constantly stressed.

The Report also gives its approval to section 13(5) of the Human Fertilisation and Embryology Act 1990[114] which, to say the least, is interesting since few others do.[115] This is the provision which, in relation to fertility services, stipulates that "A woman shall not be provided with treatment services unless account has been taken of the welfare of any child who may be born as a result of the treatment (including the need of that child for a father), and of any other child who may be affected by the birth". It is clear that surrogacy which uses fertility clinic facilities is already subject to the imperative of this subsection.[116] And it is difficult to see how it can bite on those "non-tech" surrogacies which, for obvious reasons, do not. But, though the Report desists from discussing eligibility for surrogacy in these terms, its uncritical approval of section 13(5) must be seen as an endorsement not

[108] Not all will agree: see, for example, Purdy's concern that recourse to a child's welfare is a "trump card" against a woman's autonomy. (see *op. cit.*, note 37, at 193).
[109] *Op. cit.*, note 18, para. 8.3 (see also at ii).
[110] *Ibid.*, paras. 4.46 and 4.50.
[111] *Per* Lord MacDermott in *J* v. *C* [1970] A.C. 668, 710.
[112] On which see Lord Simon of Glaisdale, *Hansard*, H.L. vol. 359; col. 544.
[113] For example, the Adoption Act 1976, s.6.
[114] *Op. cit.*, note 18, para. 4.33.
[115] For criticisms see G. Douglas, "Assisted Reproduction and the Welfare of the Child" (1993) 46 *Current Legal Problems* 53.
[116] See *Principles of Medical Law* (eds.) I. Kennedy and A. Grubb (Oxford University Press 1998), at para. 10.61.

just of its content but also of its ideology. Section 13(5) was introduced and passed expressly to prevent the creation of one-parent families through assisted reproduction, and, implicitly, to prevent lesbian women from receiving treatment services. As Morgan and Lee commented: the provision "has all the hallmarks of a profamilist ideology. Assisted conception is to be, for the most part, for the married, mortgaged middle-classes".[117] Presumably, Brazier intends to rule out surrogacy for homosexuals—and this may well be right—but it ought to say so and to argue the case instead of covertly slipping in such a ban beneath the cloak of a contentious provision. Will a new section 13(5) include also the need of a child for a mother?

The Report does address eligibility, albeit briefly, and not in these terms. It argues that there should be a minimum and a maximum age for commissioning parents. It does not address criteria: the thorny question of surrogacy for post-menopausal women is thus not addressed. If the ethical arguments for not permitting post-menopausal women to receive egg donations are weak, and recent essays suggest they are,[118] *a fortiori* the case for limiting surrogacy to younger couples is unconvincing.[119] It is not clear what the Report has in mind. In 1994 the High Court upheld the decision of a Health Authority not to provide publicly-funded fertility treatment for a woman aged 37 on the grounds only of her age.[120] Is surrogacy to be similarly limited and, if so, on what grounds (the rationing of a scarce resource, surrogates?). Is it envisaged that the maximum age will apply to both men and women? Older women have a better claim to consider parenthood since in the natural order of things they will live longer than their male counterparts. On minimum age, the Report says little but implies that the age at which one can apply for a parental order, currently 18, should be raised.[121] It is anyway lower than the minimum age at which an adoption order can be applied for.[122] But whether the age specified is 18 or 21 (and it surely would be wrong to stipulate a higher age, say 25 or 30) is of no consequence: it is inconceivable that people not at least in

---

[117] *Op. cit.*, note 12, at 146.

[118] See F. Fisher and A. Sommerville, "To Everything There is a Season?"; G. de Wert, "The Post-Menopause: Playground for Reproductive Technology? Some Ethical Reflections"; and I. de Beaufort, "Letter from a Post-menopausal Mother" in (eds.) J. Harris and S. Holm, *The Future of Human Reproduction* (Oxford University Press 1998) at 202–20, 221–37, 238–47.

[119] Where there are no health problems.

[120] *R v. Sheffield Health Authority, ex parte Seale* (1995) 25 B.M.L.R. 1 (the upper age limit set by the health authority for such procedures was 35).

[121] *Op. cit.*, note 18, para. 8.4.

[122] Applicants for an adoption order must be at least 21 years of age though a parent adopting his or her own child need only be 18 (Adoption Act 1976 ss.14 (1A)(1B), 15(1), as amended by the Children Act 1989, Sched. 10, para. 4).

Med.L.Rev.    *Does Surrogacy Have a Future After Brazier?*    15

their twenties would contemplate surrogacy. I have my doubts as to the necessity to specify an age at all.

On surrogates, the Report also indicates criteria: a minimum age (21);[123] a maximum age (no age is mentioned); having had a child and having one still living with her; a minimum period of two years between any pregnancies; a maximum number of surrogate births (one, "save where a commissioning couple seek a sibling for a previous child where the surrogate was the genetic mother").[124] The surrogate is to be provided with comprehensive information about the risks of surrogacy, and to have access to independent counselling and legal advice. The Report also recommends "a period of reflection between any initial approach to act as a surrogate and any attempt to establish a pregnancy".[125] The importance of "free, informed consent" in altruistic arrangements is also stressed.[126] The Report says nothing about the marital status of the surrogate but accordingly overlooks questions which relate to her husband's status, where she is married.

The Report sees the relationship between the surrogate and the commissioning parents as being based on a "memorandum of understanding"[127] (which, though non-contractual, would define and clarify the expectations of the parties).[128] This should record arrangements to secure the future welfare of the child, include agreements about contact between the surrogate and the child[129] (I note not between the child and the surrogate)[130] and/or what the child is to be told about his or her origins. Of course, this suggests that the Report sees contact and identity questions as matters for negotiation between the commissioning parents and the surrogate, rather than as matters of public policy upon which the state has the right to dictate a clear line. On the conduct of pregnancy (matters such smoking and ante-natal care), the Report is ambivalent.[131] Are these matters of negotiation too? The Report says that they are matters to be addressed, but by whom, the regulatory body or the parties to a particular surrogacy arrangement? If regulation is to fulfil its role, then the screening out of unsuitable surrogates, which clearly includes smokers,[132] must be part of its remit.

---

[123] *Op. cit.*, note 18, para. 8.8.
[124] *Idem.*
[125] *Ibid.*, para. 8.6.
[126] *Idem.*
[127] *Ibid.*, para. 8.12.
[128] *Ibid.*, para. 8.14
[129] *Ibid.*, para. 8.13.
[130] *Cf.*, the Children Act 1989, s.8.
[131] *Op. cit.*, note 18, para. 8.13.
[132] On parental smoking as child abuse, see D. Ezra, "Sticks and Stones Can Break My Bones but Tobacco Smoke Can Kill Me: Can We Protect Children From Parents That Smoke?" (1993) 13 *St Louis University Public Law Review* 547–90.

### D. *The Revised Parental Order*

The Report makes a number of recommendations to reform the parental order scheme, currently in section 30 of the Human Fertilisation and Embryology Act 1990. First, it recommends that commissioning parents should only be eligible to apply for an order if they can establish that they have complied with the statutory limitations on payments:[133] otherwise impermissive payments should not be amenable to retrospective judicial authorisation, as is the case at present.[134] However, commissioning parents in breach would remain eligible to adopt the child. The adoption judge would thus retain the power, as now, to give retrospective authorisation to payments.[135] Adoption as a fall back position is far from satisfactory, but with Brazier I have to agree that some solution must be found so that children are not left in an unsatisfactory limbo position. The concept of a residence order only partially assists: the commissioning parents could acquire parental responsibility in this way but would share it with the surrogate[136] (and her husband if the child is produced by means of assisted procreation with his consent).[137] Since this is hardly satisfactory—it is potentially productive of disputes—adoption, however undesirable, would seem the only solution.

Brazier formulates one curious exception to the rule that surrogacy is to go through a registered agency if a parental order is to be sought and made. Where neither the couple nor the surrogate were aware of the requirement that agencies be registered, "their lack of knowledge would not preclude the grant of a parental order"[138] where all other conditions were met. What looks like misplaced indulgence (why should ignorance of the law excuse in this context?) is compounded when, in the next sentence, it is suggested that a judge "might well be disinclined to exercise his or her discretion to grant a parental order" if it were established that the commissioning couple knew their surrogate "was only 16" and no attempt had been made to provide her with advice or counselling.[139] Those using unregistered agencies should therefore be careful to ensure 16-year-old surrogates are counselled or they use 17 or 18-year-olds or, perhaps, there is some other lesson that I have not grasped! To push the realm of fantasy further, what of a *Gillick-*

---

[133] *Op. cit.*, note 18, paras. 7.13.
[134] See s.30(7).
[135] *Op. cit.*, note 18, para. 7.13.
[136] See Children Act 1989 s.12.
[137] See Human Fertilisation and Embryology Act 1990 s.28(2).
[138] *Op. cit.*, note 18, para. 7.23.
[139] *Idem.*

Med.L.Rev.    *Does Surrogacy Have a Future After Brazier?*    17

competent 15-year-old surrogate?[140] If she is artificially inseminated, it is difficult to see what offence is committed.[141] If she receives counselling (after falsely representing her age), would Brazier countenance a parental order?

Secondly, Brazier recommends that parental orders should be obtained only in the High Court to ensure "the effective 'approval' of a surrogacy arrangement is given by judges of the highest experience".[142] I doubt whether this is really necessary or that, should surrogacy continue legitimately, this view will prevail in ten years time.

Thirdly, it is recommended that judges should be empowered to require DNA tests to establish the genetic relationship of the child to at least one of the commissioning couple.[143] As Brazier says, where this is not so, the parties have entered into a pre-natal adoption agreement and the general laws relating to adoption should apply.

Fourthly, Brazier recommends that guardians ad litem should have power to check criminal records to ascertain whether the commissioning couple has any criminal convictions likely to endanger the welfare of the child.[144]

Fifthly, it is recommended that the requirement in the present section 30 that at least one of the applicants be domiciled in a part of the United Kingdom (or in the Channel Islands or the Isle of Man) be replaced by a provision that both should be habitually resident for a period of 12 months immediately preceding the application. As Brazier notes, domicile is a concept of "tortuous complexity" and "habitual residence", though far from simple, is more straightforward.[145]

The proposals for DNA tests (where necessary and it will only happen in the exceptional case), for criminal checks (presumably to establish whether either of the couple is a 'Schedule 1 offender') and for a change in personal connecting factor (though it will affect English domiciliaries who live abroad) should cause no problems.

However, if section 30 is to be revitalised (and it was, after all, a late and rushed amendment in 1990), other changes should be considered. First, if parental responsibility is to be extended to a wider category of unmarried fathers,[146] is it necessary (or desirable) to confine applications for a parental order to couples who are husbands and wives? The government proposals on parental responsibility were made late in

---

[140] See *Gillick* v. *West Norfolk and Wisbech A.H.A.* [1986] A.C. 112.

[141] Sexual intercourse with a girl under 16 is unlawful, but not the artificial insemination of such a girl.

[142] See *op. cit.*, note 18, para. 7.24.

[143] *Idem.*

[144] *Idem.*

[145] *Idem.*

[146] As the Government announced in 1998.

Brazier's deliberations.[147] The Report is aware of the problems exten-
sions may cause but throughout assumes that surrogacy arrangements
are made with commissioning couples and, although it does not specifically say so, implies that they are persons who are married to each
other. Would it be a step too far at this stage to allow those living
together as husband and wife to apply for a parental order? If this
continues not to be allowed, the unmarried couple is forced into the
artificial position of one adopting and the other (or both) seeking a
residence order.[148]

Secondly, the provision in s.30(2) which limits applications to the
period of six months from the birth of the child seems unduly restrictive
and could be relaxed or the limitation period dispensed with totally.

Thirdly, the provision in s.30(4) that at the time of the making of the
order (note not the birth of the child) the husband and wife must have
attained the age of 18 seems, as indicated above, unnecessary. But, if an
age is to be specified, then, in accordance with Brazier's proposals, it
will presumably need to be raised, though, it will be remembered, the
Report does not indicate to what.

Fourthly, the court must be satisfied that the surrogate and the legal
father of the child "have freely, and with full understanding of what is
involved, agreed unconditionally to the making of the order".[149] Where
the surrogate is married, the legal father will usually be the husband
(unless he can prove that he did not consent to the procedure).[150] But if
he did, why should his agreement to a parental order be required?
Where the surrogate is unmarried, the commissioning man will be the
legal father if his sperm was used for donor insemination or in vitro
fertilisation.[151] If there is medical intervention, whether he is the legal
father will hinge on whether the surrogate and commissioning man are
being treated "together".[152] If they are not being treated "together",
and this must be the better view, neither he nor any other man is the
child's legal father.[153] It may be too much to expect from surrogacy
reform that Parliament will look again at these legal parentage rules,
but they are complex, confusing and ill-understood.

Fifthly, agreement cannot be dispensed with, though it is not required
where the person concerned cannot be found or is incapable of giving

---

[147] They are briefly discussed at paras. 7.14 and 7.15. Too much depends on the details of
the new law for its implications to be considered here. I agree with Brazier they are
profound and may necessitate a rethink of the paternity provisions in the 1990 Act.
[148] See *Re A.B. (Adoption: Joint Residence)* [1996] 1 F.L.R. 27.
[149] See s.30(5).
[150] Section 28(2).
[151] This is the common law position and it is not affected by the 1990 Act.
[152] See section 4(1)(b).
[153] And see *Re Q (Parental Order)* [1996] 1 F.L.R. 369.

agreement.[154] This "ground" is modelled on adoption law, but adoption law makes provision for dispensing with agreement if it is unreasonably withheld, and on a number of other grounds.[155] Consideration should be given to extending the model of adoption law to embrace these other grounds. If a surrogate freely hands over a child and subsequently refuses to agree to the making of a parental order, the opportunity to test her change of heart through the unreasonableness provision should be open. Why should she be treated any differently from any other mother who hands over her child and then changes her mind?

Sixthly, the statutory provision is currently filled out by the Parental Orders (Human Fertilisation and Embryology) Regulations 1994, which applies many of the provisions of the Adoption Act 1976 to section 30 applications and orders.[156] Thus, for example, applications are heard in private, a guardian *ad litem* is appointed for the child, and the court has a duty to safeguard and promote the welfare of the child. The child's welfare is the first consideration (as in adoption). However, the welfare checklist in section 1(3) of the Children Act, which explains the paramountcy test, is, we are advised, to be considered.[157] These are matters which ought to be in primary legislation rather than in regulations or guidance, and, if there is to be a new Surrogacy Act, there is the opportunity for a rethink and a reformulation.

Seventhly, Brazier investigates the GAL's role only in relation to criminal searches. The Report overlooks the fact that children cannot be parties to section 30 proceedings. One result of this is that in this "extraordinarily complicated and sensitive area",[158] guardians are not able to instruct solicitors for the children whose interests they represent. The guardian is thus acting without the benefit of legal advice for the child. Section 30 was designed to satisfy the needs of adults, and here it clearly shows. As Cretney and Masson observe: "Despite the appointment of a guardian *ad litem* it appears that there is an expectation that all applicants who meet the basic qualifications for a parental order will obtain one".[159] Not surprisingly the Department of Health guidance envisages that it will be exceptional for a guardian to recommend that an order should not be made,[160] a view which was confirmed by evidence given to the Brazier inquiry by guardians.[161]

[154] See section 30(6).
[155] See Adoption Act 1976 s.16(2).
[156] S.I. 1994/2767.
[157] See para. 3.18.
[158] See J.E. Timms, *Children's Representation: A Practitioner's Guide* (Sweet and Maxwell 1995), at 305.
[159] *Principles of Family Law* (6th edn.) (Sweet and Maxwell 1997), at 947.
[160] L.A.C. (94) 25.
[161] *Op. cit.*, note 18, para. 3.19.

## IV. CONCLUSION

We need to make up our minds about surrogacy. Hitherto, policies pursued have been ambivalent: the 1985 Act sent a strong message of disapproval without attempting to outlaw the practice; the 1990 Act offered new resources to those who commissioned surrogates to bear children for them. The 1985 Act criminalised but did not do so totally, purporting to make a sharp separation between the public commercial world and the private world of the family. The 1990 Act offered new private family law remedies (the parental order), but in so far as other private yet commercial remedies remained (and the sting had already been removed by the judiciary)[162] these were withdrawn (so contracts were declared unenforceable).[163] Neither pieces of legislation was rationally constructed or properly thought through: the first was a response to a moral panic with the surrogate the classic "folk devil";[164] the second was a hasty response to a constituent's problem.

The time is opportune for a new Surrogacy Act. Of the possible approaches to adopt, criminalisation will not work and contract has been rejected. Regulation is clearly the right answer: this was the view of the minority in Warnock and is now the way ahead as seen by Brazier. Regulation is not, however, an easy answer and regulated surrogacy will continue to throw up problems. Decentralised regulation, as favoured by Brazier, is likely to create more and greater problems. One of these will be the thorny question of recompense. If Parliament agrees with Brazier and denies women the opportunity to be financially rewarded for surrogacy services, an unregulated surrogacy with all the evils attendant upon such underground activities will emerge. Brazier would prefer surrogacy to have no future. But the Report points to a future in which it may thrive to the detriment of women, of children and of society.

---

[162] See *Re P. (Minors)(Wardship: Surrogacy)* [1987] 2 F.L.R. 421.
[163] Human Fertilisation and Embryology Act 1990 s.36.
[164] See S. Cohen, *Folk Devils and Moral Panics* (McGibbon and Kee 1972).

# [12]
# Not Such A Queer Idea: Is There a Case for Same Sex Marriages?

ABSTRACT   *Gay marriages (as such) are not as yet allowed anywhere but the demand for them is increasing. Most countries take a liberal attitude towards marriage: few obstacles are put in its way. But objections to gay marriages continue to be raised. These objections are refuted and the case for gay marriage is assessed through the prism of various forms of liberalism. The normative argument for allowing gay marriage is shown to be both strong and consistent with many of the values upheld by the opponents of such unions.*

In Britain, as in other Western democracies, it is very easy to get married — many think too easy. Certainly, it is easier to acquire a licence to marry than one to drive a car. And a higher percentage of marriages crash than do cars. Perhaps, if we required prospective brides and grooms to pass written and practical tests first, marriage would be a more successful institution. Only those good enough at social and sexual intercourse would then be granted the right to marry. Not only is it easy to marry (and more difficult to divorce — in England it will soon become even more difficult to divorce [1]) but we are not over-fussy about whom we allow to marry. So long as they are sixteen, not already married and not wishing to marry a close blood relative or affine, we put few obstacles in their way (we expect 16 and 17-year-olds to have parental permission but, if they marry without, they are still married [2]). Accordingly, we allow murderers and rapists (even those who have murdered or raped previous spouses) to marry; we allow paedophiles and child molesters to marry. We do not stop child abusers or, what Americans call, 'dead beat dads' [3] (those who have reneged on support or other obligations to children) from marrying. Sadists, masochists and fetishists may marry and are not obliged to choose partners with similar inclinations. People who are HIV-infected or suffer from AIDs are allowed to marry [4]. There is special legislation to facilitate death-bed marriages [5]. Transvestites may marry (that the groom is wearing a bridal dress is no impediment to marriage). And transsexuals may marry so long as they marry someone of the other gender from that which they themselves were born in: two 'women' may thus marry if one of them was born a man [6]. Indeed, two transsexuals may marry, provided one was born a boy, the other a girl (English law only requires parties to a marriage to be 'respectively male and female' [7]: it does not insist that sex and gender coincide). There are furthermore no laws requiring persons wishing to marry to prove that they are heterosexual: homosexual men may marry women and lesbian women may marry men (and, indeed, do). And, of course, homosexual men may marry lesbian women. This is right. Marriage is a basic element of social life, and as few obstacles as possible should be placed in its path. It is a central institution through which we express our aspirations

2

about intimate behaviour. Should we then deny marriage to those who wish to enter into unions with a member of their own sex?

## Marriage Defined

One hundred and thirty years ago, in *Hyde v Hyde*, Lord Penzance defined marriage, as understood in 'Christendom' and therefore in Victorian England, as the 'voluntary union for life of one man and one woman to the exclusion of all others' [8]. There has been a lot of social change since 1866 (when judicial divorce was only eight years old): legal responses to polygamy (the marriage in issue in *Hyde*) have become so relaxed that the institution is now recognised for almost all purposes [9]; social and legal attitudes to divorce have changed (adultery will cease to be a legal concept in the near future [10]); since the 1970s the courts and legislature have become much more prepared to accept cohabitation outside marriage as a legal institution [11]. Thus, in 1975, a woman who lived with a man for over twenty years was held to be a member of his family for the purpose of succeeding to a Rent Act-protected tenancy [12]. But the courts have now held twice that the same protection cannot extend to the same sex partner of a deceased tenant [13]. One element of *Hyde v Hyde* thus remains firmly in place: marriage must be between persons of different sexes. We do not allow same-sex marriages. This was affirmed as recently as November 1996 when Ward L.J. said that although some elements of Lord Penzance's classic definition 'may have been eroded, bigamy and single-sex unions remain proscribed as fundamentally abhorrent to this notion of marriage'. Ward L.J. approved a dictum of Sir William Scott, 'a master of ecclesiastical law', from 1795 [14] to the effect that marriage is 'a contract according to the law of nature, antecedent to civil institutions, and which may take place to all intents and purposes, wherever two persons of different sexes engage, by mutual contracts, to live together'. In the 1996 case (*J v S-T (formerly J) (Transsexual Ancillary Relief)* [15] a female to male transsexual had 'married' a wealthy, nineteen-year-old, sexually inexperienced and unhappy theology student and attempted to live a married life with her for seventeen years with the aid of a concealed plaster of paris penis, and donor insemination which enabled them to have two children. The wife throughout had assumed her husband was a man though it appears she realised he had a vagina and, it would seem, menstruated. The respondent's deception went, so Ward L.J. said, 'to the fundamental essence of marriage'. It touched a 'vital corner-stone of marriage implicit in the union of one man and one woman'. It undermined the 'institution' and 'the sanctity and status of marriage' which was, he said 'hallowed' [16]. This is impassioned language, illiberal and moralistic and, it has to be said, out of character with other of his pronouncements, notably his dissent in the more recent case of *Fitzpatrick v Sterling Housing Association* [17]. Noting that 'one cannot engage in a restless search for the views of the common man as if it is to be thought that he only travels on the Clapham omnibus and reads the *Sun* newspaper — or is it the *Daily Mail?* — [18], he held (in a powerful and impressive dissenting judgment) that the homosexual partner of a deceased tenant, if not living together as husband and wife, and this was his preferred view, at least were living as members of a family. This takes English law further than before — even accepting it is a dissenting judgment — but it remains far short of recognising gay unions or advancing the cause of gay marriage. We do not sanction gay marriages.

**The Foreign Dimension**

Nor does anywhere else. Hawaii was thought likely to, though this is now less likely [19], and Denmark, Sweden, Norway, Greenland, Iceland, Hungary and the Netherlands allow gay couples to register partnerships, though the effects of these fall short of the consequences of marriage [20]. It will not be long before an English court is confronted with a same-sex marriage, if not from Hawaii then from somewhere else, or Danish or other registered partnership. We could reject them on grounds of public policy [21] but principle dictates that we should not do so. We've recognised under-age marriages [22] and marriages between uncles and nieces [23] where these marriages were valid by the personal laws of the parties. We've recognised polygamous marriages entered into by English domiciliaries, in one case where the intended matrimonial home was Egypt [24], in another where the husband could not take any additional wives (because of his domicile) [25], and the effect of this latter decision has now been confirmed by legislation and extended to women domiciled in this country whose husbands would be capable of marrying further wives [26]. It may be that initially we will recognise the consequences of such unions only for some purposes, for example succession [27], but not immigration [28] (or in the case of marriages, divorce [29]). There will clearly be characterisation problems (is a registered partnership marriage or contract?) [30]. There are also problems about foreign discriminatory legislation (we would presumably have refused to uphold a miscegenation statute [31] or caste law [32] or law prohibiting monks or nuns from marrying [33] — would we take the same attitude to laws banning gay marriages or uphold them because we uphold the same policy?).

**Gay Opposition**

Although it is likely that courts will first encounter gay marriages (or partnerships) in a conflict of laws context, and although there is not much demand (at present) for homosexual marriages to be legalised in this country — a leading gay bookshop in London told me that books on the subject did not sell [34] — the case for same-sex marriages ought to be addressed. Given the list with which this paper began, it is clear that homosexual men and lesbian women are discriminated against. It may be said that there are more serious and more pressing discriminations [35]. It may also be said that the gay do not want to buy into an institution that they believe is discredited. For lesbians in particular marriage may resonate with symbols of oppression and inequality [36]. But these associations are more likely due to attitudes towards women than to the institution of marriage itself. And this might change — with the whole institution of marriage — if marriage were permitted between persons where no gender stratifications could be imputed. It may be that few would avail themselves of the opportunity to marry were it presented to them. But if we believe that marriage is a social good, and certainly we confer benefits on those who marry, should we deny access because few want it? In the United States parallels are often drawn with the miscegenation statutes which the Supreme Court struck down in 1967 [37]. Relatively few people marry those from other races than themselves, but no-one takes seriously the demands of a bigoted minority who would uphold such bans even today. I respect the views of those from within the gay community who reject marriage as an institution and thus reject it for homosexuals and lesbians [38].

4

I sense a fear that if marriage were allowed the gay would be expected to marry — it is said, ironically, to join mainstream society, though this is drifting away from marriage — so that gays who didn't marry might be further stigmatised. Whether these objections have force will be the subject of continuing debate within the gay community. But whichever view prevails there, it will still have to contend with mainstream objections. It is to these, therefore, that I now turn.


**The Objections**

The first objection is definitional. As Eskridge puts it: 'Marriage is necessarily different-sex, and same-sex marriage is therefore oxymoronic, a contradiction in terms' [39]. Put tersely, can marriage be simply redefined in the law? This was the challenge faced, but not grappled with, in U.S. courts when they were first confronted with 'gay marriages'. Thus, in *Baker v Nelson* the Minnesota Supreme Court interpreted the relevant Minnesota statute governing marriage as one which employed 'that term as one of common usage, meaning the state of union between persons of the opposite sex'. And it sought support in the Old Testament: 'The institution of marriage as a union of man and woman, uniquely involving the procreation and rearing of children within a family, is as old as the book of Genesis' [40]. Two years later the Court of Appeals of Kentucky reached not for the Bible but the dictionary — *Webster* defined marriage as 'the institution whereby men and women are joined in a special kind of social and legal dependence, for the purpose of founding and maintaining a family' [41] and that was that: *cadit quaestio*. The U.S. Supreme Court has not yet had to address gay marriages — though its ruling on sodomy statutes can give little confidence [42] — but in 1987, in upholding the right of prisoners to marry, it said (through Justice O'Connor) that 'inmate marriages, like others, are expressions of emotional support and public commitment. These elements are an important and significant aspect of the marital relationship' [43]. It is significant that the courts here address meaning and content rather than a dictionary definition which encodes historical understanding. But would Justice O'Connor see the applicability of her reasoning to gays?

The definitional argument relies on tradition, on history and on religious sources. It is largely a descriptive claim and, as such, it is not difficult to refute. History is replete with examples of same-sex marriages and unions [44]. Montaigne's *Travel Journal* describes same-sex marriage in Rome conducted at San Giovanni Porta Latina [45]. He adds that the participants were burned, so the practice was not approved. But there is evidence of approval at earlier periods of history. Roman Catholic and Greek Orthodox Churches performed same-sex enfraternisation rituals, glorified the same-sex intimacy of Serge and Bacchus (they were Roman soldiers persecuted for their Christian faith) and developed same-sex union liturgies, which were later published in official church collections [46]. But, even if those who argued against gay marriages on grounds of its novel challenge were not wrong on their facts, they would be presenting an argument that resisted all change. Slavery existed for a long time [47], but longevity by itself is not a decisive argument.

The definitional claim also has a normative dimension. This links marriage to the procreation of children and so rules out same-sex marriage because same-sex couples cannot conceive children. Of course, if there were a necessary link between marriage and procreation, the state could (and to be consistent should) outlaw marriages where one or more partners is sterile or impotent [48]. Post-menopausal women would obviously have to be denied the right to marry [49]. There are, of course, far more sterile heterosexual unions than homosexual ones. It is not always easy to see what opponents are getting at. Hadley Arkes makes the case that 'The traditional understanding of marriage is grounded on the "natural teleology of the body" — in the inescapable fact that only a man and a woman, and only two people, not three, can generate a child. Once marriage is detached from that natural teleology of the body, what ground of principle would therefore confine marriage to two people rather than some larger grouping? That is, on what ground of principle would the law reject the claim of a gay couple that their love is not confined to a coupling of two, but that they are woven into a larger ensemble with yet another person or two?' [50] The idea that once marriage becomes detached from procreation 'anything goes' (marriage to pets is thrown up as one possibility! [51]) is utterly fanciful. Does anyone object to the elderly widow's marriage by suggesting that if we allow it, we might as well allow her polyandry? [52]

John Finnis has joined this debate but what he says hardly advances the cause of those who would rule out same-sex marriage. 'Whatever the generous hopes and dreams and thoughts' of 'same-sex partners' their sexual acts 'cannot express or do more than is expressed or done if two strangers engage in such activity to give each other pleasure, or a prostitute pleasures a client to give him pleasure in return for money, or (say) a man masturbates to give himself pleasure and a fantasy of more human relationships after a gruelling day on the assembly line' [53]. The only sexual activity which is valuable is that which is open to procreation and is within a permanent heterosexual marriage. Homosexual acts as also contraceptive heterosexual acts and all sex outside marriage 'can do no more than provide each partner with an individual gratification' [54]. It is, to say the least, implausible, if not simplistic to see every form of non-procreative sexuality as no better than its least valuable example. As far as marriage is concerned, 'parenthood and children and family are the intrinsic fulfilment of a communion which . . . can exist and fulfil the spouses even if procreation happens to be impossible for them' [55]. This is Finnis's answer to the conundrum of the sterile couple but, of course, it is no answer. Parenthood and children cannot fulfil a couple's inter-personal communion if procreation remains impossible for them.

Finnis maintains that sexual acts between persons of the same sex violate a basic human good, though it is not clear what this basic good is. In an early article [56] he wrote that

> what, in the last analysis, makes sense of the conditions of the marital enterprise, its stability and exclusiveness, is not the worthy and delightful sentiments of love and affection which invite one to marry , but the desire for and demands of a *procreative* community, a family.

By 1996 he was writing of the common good of marriage as itself a basic good [57]. And George and Bradley, addressing the same practice, came to much the same conclusion: marriage is 'an intrinsic (or . . . "basic") human good; as surely marriage performs a noninstrumental reason for spouses . . . to perform [sexual] acts [of the reproductive type]' [58]. They also, in an argument reminiscent of Kant [59] introduce yet another basic good (integrity), leading to the assertion that homosexual acts are wrong because they ignore this good. (In 'nonmarital orgasmic acts . . . persons necessarily treat their

6

bodies and those of their sexual partners (if any) as *means* or *instruments* in ways that
damage their personal (and interpersonal) integrity' [60]).

The second objection to same-sex marriages is that such marriages are bad,
'shameful' [61], a 'mocking burlesque of marriage' [62]. Thus, to Harry Jaffa
'homosexuals even more than Communists are enemies of every good thing we
associate with the Declaration of Independence'. And, 'if sodomy is not unnatural,
nothing is unnatural. And if nothing is unnatural, then nothing — including slavery
and genocide — is unjust' [63]. And Harvey Mansfield contends that homosexuality
is an 'open challenge to society's sense of shame . . . for if the practices of
homosexuals are not shameful, what is?' [64]. Rather more temperately, and
eschewing this natural law position, Richard Posner has argued that 'permitting
homosexual marriage would be widely interpreted as placing a stamp of approval on
homosexuality . . . To permit persons of the same sex to marry is to declare, or more
precisely to be understood by many people to be declaring, that a homosexual
marriage is a desirable, even a noble condition in which to live' [65]. It is Posner's
view that permitting homosexual marriage would 'place government in the dishonest
position of propagating a false picture of the reality of homosexuals' lives' [66]. It is
not clear whether Posner includes lesbians within this or the circumstances in which
he considers marriage 'noble'. At least Posner does not equate nobility and fertility,
though it may be speculated that he would not regard the marriage of an elderly
couple as noble. But what does he think of those who marry (and divorce) often?
Would he describe the marriages of Elizabeth Taylor as 'noble'? Or that of Bill
Clinton and Hillary Rodham? Is nobility what you associate with the marriage of
Charles and Diana? Is 'noble' a word to use about abusive and violent marriages? And
does licensing a marriage give it the stamp of approval? Recall that transvestites,
transsexuals, bisexuals and other non-conventional persons can marry without any
official scrutiny but also surely without the state 'approving' (whatever that might
mean) these statuses. Implicit in Posner's reasoning is that homosexuals should
overlook their sexual orientation and join in the noble institution of heterosexual
marriage. This would be bad not only for them but also for their spouses and for the
institution of marriage.

The third objection that conservatives raise to same-sex marriage is pragmatic. The
argument is forcefully put by Posner. He writes: 'Authorizing homosexual marriage
would have many collateral effects, simply because marriage is a status rich in
entitlements. It would have effects on inheritance, social security, income tax, welfare
payments, adoption, the division of property on termination of the relationship, medical
benefits, life insurance, immigration, and even testimonial privilege . . . These incidents
of marriage were designed with heterosexual marriage in mind, more specifically
heterosexual marriages resulting in children. They may or may not fit the case of
homosexual marriage; they are unlikely to fit it perfectly. Do we want homosexual couples
to have the same rights of adoption and custody as heterosexual couples? Should we
worry that a homosexual might marry a succession of dying AIDS patients in order to
entitle them to spouse's medical benefits?' [67] Posner concedes that neither this
argument nor his other two (one has been discussed, the other relating to 'information
cost' seems too trivial to be worth repeating) is decisive against permitting homosexual
marriage. But since public hostility to homosexuals is too widespread to make
homosexual marriage a feasible proposal even if it is on balance cost-justified, maybe

the focus should be shifted to an 'intermediate solution'. He sees this in the registered partnership model of Denmark and Sweden's homosexual cohabitation law, and prefers the latter which did not then go as far [68].

Posner is right that the consequences attached to marriage which he lists were designed with heterosexual marriages in mind. Of course, they were: such marriages were the only ones allowed. But that is surely not the question. As Eskridge points out, when the state of Virginia was challenged by Loving [69], it could have argued that the incidents of marriage were designed with same-race marriage in mind [70]. The question is not one of consequences, but of what is right. If discrimination is wrong in principle, then appeals to past practice and concerns about speculative dangers cannot make it right.

If the arguments against the recognition of homosexual marriages are so weak — and I have refrained from commenting upon even weaker ones — then why has the cause made so little progress? It could be in part because, as I have indicated, gays themselves have been equivocal about buying in to a 'rotten institution' and fear the effects that recognition of same-sex marriages would have upon gays who opted out. It could also be that the arguments presented in favour have, at least until recently, not been as convincingly argued as perhaps they can be.

## Sullivan's Liberalism

It is to liberalism that conventionally one has turned to entrench the rights of the individual to be different. John Stuart Mill is the classic source:

> If he displeases us, we may express our distaste, and we may stand aloof from a person as well as from a thing that displeases us; but we shall not therefore feel called upon to make his life uncomfortable. We shall reflect that he already bears, and or will bear, the whole penalty of his error . . . He may be to us an object of pity, perhaps of dislike, but not of anger or resentment; we shall not treat him like an enemy of society: the worst we shall think ourselves justified in doing is leaving him to himself, if we do not interfere benevolently by showing interest or concern for him [71].

And it is to liberalism that Andrew Sullivan, one of the most articulate advocates of homosexual rights, turns [72]. His is a call for a return to a classical liberalism that 'wishes to ensure the neutrality of the state' and 'refuses to see the state as a way to inculcate virtue or promote one way of living over another' [73]. He believes that true liberals should only concern themselves with public discrimination and should leave private biases and private discrimination to the conscience of the individual. Liberalism, he argues, has

> most to lose when it abandons the high ground of liberal neutrality. Perhaps especially in areas where passion and emotion are so deep, such as homosexuality, the liberal should be wary of identifying his or her tradition with a particular way of life, or a particular cause . . . Liberalism works — and is the most resilient modern politics — precisely because it is the only politics that seeks to avoid these irresolvable and contentious conflicts [74].

8

Sullivan's goal is limited:

> that all *public* (as opposed to private) discrimination against homosexuals be ended and that every right and responsibility that heterosexuals enjoy as public citizens be extended to those who grow up and find themselves emotionally different [75].

This means an end to sodomy laws, an equal legal age of consent, inclusion of the facts about homosexuality in the curriculum of every government-funded school [76], equal opportunity and inclusion in the military [77] and legal homosexual marriage and divorce [78]. But the converse of public equality is private freedom and Sullivan defends this too, so that discrimination in private employment and housing would not be proscribed. This is not the place to question the public-private dualism which Sullivan treats quite unproblematically (Jane Schacter has done this in an excellent review of Sullivan's book [79]) but it is worth observing that marriage constitutes a test-bed for examining the construction, looking as it does both inwards and outwards.

On same-sex unions, Sullivan is unequivocal. 'Marriage is not simply a private contract; it is a social and public recognition of a private commitment. As such, it is the highest public recognition of personal integrity. Denying it to homosexuals is the most public affront possible to their public equality'[80]. And he adds, 'For liberals, the case for homosexual marriage is overwhelming. As a classic public institution, it should be available to any two citizens' [81]. (In passing it may be noted that this liberalism does not extend to polygamy!). This is the classical liberal position: it endorses toleration, the right to be left alone. But recognition of gay unions requires more than tolerance: it asks also for acceptance. Gays and lesbians are now asking that society recognise their relationships. They seek normative acceptance of their relationships. Thus, as Paula Ettelbrick put it in a recent article

> Lesbian and gay couples want to get married for two primary reasons: (1) for the social acceptance and acknowledgement of their humanity that would be accorded their relationships through marriage, and (2) to receive the same benefits exclusively bestowed upon married couples [82].

The classical political liberalism articulated by Sullivan stops short of endorsement: it cannot endorse a particular conception of the good. Legal recognition of homosexual relationships entails not just toleration of such relationships, but would constitute a recognition that they are as normatively valuable. It is, I would argue, important to establish this if same-sex marriages are ever to be legalised.

Sullivan accepts this for he addresses a number of such normative arguments, though it is not clear whether he appreciates that he has gone beyond the political liberalism of *On Liberty*, with which he began. Thus

> Marriage provides an anchor . . . in the maelstrom of sex and relationships to which we are all prone [83].

Further, it

> provides a mechanism for emotional stability and economic security . . . Not to promote marriage would be to ask too much of human virtue [84].

Recognition of homosexual marriages

> would also be an unqualified social good for homosexuals. It provides role models for young gay people [85].

Further, he argues

> Legal gay marriage could also help bridge the gulf often found between homosexuals and their parents . . . It could do more to heal the gay-straight rift than any amount of gay rights legislation [86].

It would also benefit gay children:

> For them, at last, there would be some kind of future . . . They would be able to feel . . . their emotional orientation was not merely about pleasure, or sin, or shame, or otherness . . . but about the ability to love and be loved as complete, imperfect human beings [87].

He concludes: 'Until gay marriage is legalised, this fundamental element of personal dignity will be denied a whole segment of humanity. No other change can achieve it [88].

Oddly, Sullivan associates these arguments with 'conservatives' [89]. This politics, he says, 'marries the clarity of liberalism with the intuition of conservatism'[90]. They are not arguments based on the liberal goal of achieving 'political equality'. Rather they are arguments that homosexual relationships are good and valuable forms of human association.

### Rawls

But the 'intuition of conservatism' does not point in this way at all. And liberalism does. But it is not the classical liberalism of Mill. Nor that of John Rawls. The current definition of marriage can only break out of its existing straightjacket through a normative debate about the morality and value of homosexual relationships. Yet, these are exactly the arguments excluded by Rawls from public reasoning because they violate the primacy of the right over the good, and contaminate political discourse with non-political values [91]. If homosexuality is immoral, as many believe, then it is not clear why society should condone it by recognising gay marriages even if there is an overlapping political consensus [92] that toleration and equality should be encouraged and promoted. For, while a society may for constitutional or prudential reasons have to tolerate conduct considered by many to be immoral (especially when it takes place in private), it does not follow that it has an obligation to accept or endorse that conduct, for example by making available an institutional resource such as marriage.

### Dworkin

Dworkin's liberalism is more appealing [93]. He emphasises equality and he is critical of the use of majoritarian morality as a justifying rationale for the enforcement of the criminal law. He is critical of the incorporation of majoritarian morality into the formulation of public policy because such an incorporation inevitably entails the unequal

10

treatment of those who deviate from the views of the majority. He was thus famously critical of the Devlin thesis that society had the right to use the criminal law to enforce conventional morality [94]. More recently in his *Tanner* lectures Dworkin has explicitly linked his foundational principle of equality to his critique of consensus-defined state intrusions on private lives.

> Invasions of liberty — criminal laws prohibiting activities or ways of life some people might wish to take up . . . are invasions of equality . . . unless they can be justified as necessary to protect an egalitarian distribution of resources and opportunities by providing security of person and property or in some other way. No laws prohibiting activities on grounds of personal morality could pass the test . . . [95]

Dworkin has addressed the question of homosexuality specifically. Arguing that individuals cannot even if in the majority 'forbid anyone to lead the life he wants, or punish him for so doing, just on the ground that they think his ethical convictions are wrong' [96], he has attacked U.S. anti-sodomy statutes. But whether his reasoning would also embrace the rather different issue of recognising gay unions may be doubted. There is a difference between punishing an activity (of which Dworkin does not approve) and withholding state legitimacy from an institution in which that activity is practised. It is unlikely that a legislature could be persuaded to recognise same-sex marriages without expecting it to bring to bear its own conception of the value of those marriages. Neutrality on normative values will frustrate, if not disable, constructive debate. The liberal concept of equality is not a free-standing principle. If it is to engineer change it must be linked to normative arguments to show that the unequal group deserves equal treatment.

### Raz's Perfectionist Liberalism

More promising yet is the perfectionist liberalism of Raz [97]. Liberal perfectionists hold that 'wise and morally upright governments will choose a conception which understands individual autonomy and (hence) liberty as essential aspects of the human good' [98]. For Raz the value of liberty is intrinsic: it has value in and of itself. 'The main purpose of government . . . is to assist people . . . to lead successful and fulfilling lives . . . to protect and promote the well-being of people' [99]. As I have noted, liberals tend to reject the notion that governments should concern themselves with promoting particular conceptions of the good. Raz refuses to be limited in this way. First, because

> Any judgment that an activity, way of life . . . is either good or bad, . . . is a partial description of a conception of the good [100].

And, secondly, because traditional liberal views of governmental restraint fail to account for the connection between individual goals and societal conditions.

> The goodness of one's life may be enhanced by the fact that one lives in a society of a certain kind.. So conceptions of the good encompass both private ideals . . . and societal conditions which contribute to them . . . [101]

For Raz, rights not only protect against state-initiated coercion, but provide individuals with a range of acceptable options that are necessary to achieve individual autonomy. So, there should be no governmental coercion which interferes with the attainment of autonomy, and the individual must be provided with a 'sufficient range of significant options . . . at different stages of his life' [102]. These cannot be guaranteed by the limited traditional liberal view of negative freedoms (which guarantee only non-coercion on the part of the state). This principle of autonomy imposes obligations on the state (and also on individuals) that exceed this: it requires the state (as also individuals) to promote conditions of autonomy for other individuals through the creation of an adequate range of options. Raz states:

> Fear of uniformity and the denial of individual autonomy has led many liberal writers to insist that the state should have nothing to do with the promotion of the ideals of the good life. This in turn has led to the impoverishment of their understanding of human flourishing and of the relations between individual well-being and a common culture. Instead, one should denounce the rejection of autonomy and the embracing of uniformity as misguided conceptions of individual well-being. Only through a conception of well-being based on autonomy and value pluralism can we restore the true perspective of the role of morality in politics [103].

So, he explains

> A moral theory which values autonomy highly can justify restricting the autonomy of one person for the sake of the greater autonomy of others or even of that person himself in the future. That is why it can justify coercion to prevent harm, for harm interferes with autonomy. But it will not tolerate coercion for other reasons. The availability of repugnant options, and even their free pursuit by individuals, does not detract from their autonomy [104].

Raz addresses homosexual marriages directly. He expresses the view that

> The existence of a society . . . with recognized homosexual marriages is a collective good . . . In a society where such opportunities exist and make it possible for individuals to have an autonomous life, their existence is intrinsically valuable [105].

Raz also uses the harm principle, extended to embrace positive as well as negative freedoms, to buttress his argument. Pertinently he comments: 'It is a mistake to think that the harm principle recognises only the duty of governments to prevent loss of autonomy. Sometimes failing to improve the situation of another is harming him' [106].

One can harm another by denying him what is due to him [107].

Individuals can be harmed if there is an insufficient range of choices that make attainment of an autonomous life possible. For Raz the harm principle is one about 'the proper way to enforce morality' [108]. It is

> derivable from a morality which regards personal autonomy as an essential ingredient of the good life, and regards the principle of autonomy . . . as one of the most important moral principles [109].

12

### Normative Argument

The case for legalising homosexual marriages requires, it has been shown, normative argument. Of course, it is a negative normative assessment (however inadequate, as we have seen) which has stood in the way of such unions being accepted. Those who favour allowing gays and lesbians to regulate their relationships must counter these normative arguments with their own. This requires a normative vision of what functions are important to marriage as an institution. One attempt to construct such a normative argument is made by William Eskridge.

For Eskridge, same-sex marriage would be a normatively valuable institution because it would have a 'civilizing' [110] effect both on gays and lesbians and the rest of society. It would entail a 'greater degree of domestication' [111]. It would offer a 'commitment device' [112] which in turn would reduce promiscuity and reduce risk of exposure to HIV-infection. The commitment device is valuable also because it would reward those who stayed together and discourage drift and dissolution of relationships.

> From a pro commitment point of view, state-approved marriage is good for all couples because it creates additional advantages for the relationship and a big barrier to breakups [113].

The prohibition of same-sex marriage is also anti-procreation.

> By denying same-sex couples the right to marry in the name of procreation and childrearing, the state makes it a little bit harder for gay people to form lasting unions. This, in turn, makes it harder for gay people to raise children and probably discourages some gay people from having children [114].

He argues also that the refusal to recognise same-sex marriages is anti-children. He cites studies to the effect that

> . . . children raised in gay and (especially) lesbian households are as well socialised, as psychologically adjusted, and as capable of forming healthy peer relationships as children raised in different-sex or single-parent households [115].

What they certainly show is that two parents, even of the same sex, are better for children than one [116], and this is now all-too-commonly the case.

The final argument that Eskridge uses is that same-sex marriage would be civilising for society, because it would reduce prejudice and increase 'acceptance and co-operation' [117]. Clearly, that would be a long-term goal.

What this ignores, and what liberalism of all forms glosses over, is that marriage is also about responsibility. The case for allowing gay couples to marry cannot rest on the value of autonomy or on the unjustifiability of discrimination alone. If heterosexual marriage embodies moral aspirations these must go beyond the desire for privacy or intimacy. Marriage is about both privacy and intimacy but it is also about commitment, attachment and caring. Eskridge suggests that marriage offers a commitment device, but he fails to spell out what commitment involves. There is no reason to believe that the values and experiences of domestic life are any different for homosexual couples. And, if their relationships are more fragile than their heterosexual counterparts, is it not possible that the opportunity to go through a commitment ceremony would act as a buttress? The institution of marriage offers structural and cultural support to heterosexual partners: the denial of marriage to gay couples deprives them of this support.

## Conclusion

Overcoming prejudice — which remains at the root of most opposition — will be difficult. For those prepared to engage in a rational debate, the normative arguments are now clear. Of course, there will be fears and concerns, particularly over the effects that same-sex marriage may have on children. But banning the institution is unlikely to assist children, who, whether we legalise gay marriages or not, will continue to be reared by gay parents. Discrimination against the gay adds further to the stigmatisation which such children encounter [118].

If we believe in autonomy, and if we believe that the institution of marriage is a valuable one, one which upholds our highest ideals, it is difficult to justify depriving homosexuals and lesbians of this treasured form of human association.

*M. D. A. Freeman, Law Faculty, University College London, Bentham House, Endsleigh Gardens, London WC1H 0EG, UK.*

## Acknowledgements

This paper began life as a Public Lecture at University College London. I am grateful to those who have commented upon it, particularly Stephen Clark, Nicola Lacey, Andrew Le Sueur, Helen Reece and an anonymous reviewer.

## NOTES

[1] When the Family Law Act 1996 comes into operation. This change deviates from the trend elsewhere in Western democracies.
[2] For the details of this see STEPHEN CRETNEY and JUDITH MASSON (1997) *Principles of Family Law* (London, Sweet & Maxwell).
[3] And see PAULA A. MONOPOLI (1994) 'Deadbeat Dads': should support and inheritance be linked? *University of Miami Law Review*, 49, 257–298.
[4] *Cf* the law of Missouri as described in MICHAEL CLOSEN, ROBERT GAMRATH and DEM HOPKINS (1994) Mandatory premarital HIV testing: political exploitation of the Aids epidemic, *Tulane Law Review* 69, 71–115.
[5] In England the Marriage Act 1983 (but insufficiently so: see CRETNEY and MASSON, *op cit*, note 2, p. 19).
[6] In England transsexuals may not marry in their new gender: see *Corbett v. Corbett (orse Ashley)* [1971] P. 83. Similar prohibitions apply elsewhere.
[7] Matrimonial Causes Act 1973 s.11(c).
[8] (1866) L R 1 P&D 130.
[9] See P. M. NORTH and J. J. FAWCETT (1992) *Cheshire and North's Private International Law* (London, Butterworths), 621–626.
[10] When the Family Law Act 1996 comes into operation. On adultery see RICHARD WASSERSTROM 'Is adultery immoral?' in R. BAKER and F. ELLISTON (1984) *Philosophy and Sex* (Buffalo, NY, Prometheus Books), 207–221.
[11] See MICHAEL D. A. FREEMAN and CHRISTINA M. LYON (1983), *Cohabitation Without Marriage* (Aldershot, Gower).
[12] *Dyson Holdings v. Fox* [1976] 1 Q.B. 503.

14

[13]  *Harrogate B.C.* v. *Simpson* (1984) 17 HLR 205; *Fitzpatrick v. Sterling Housing Association* [1998] 1 FLR 6. The New York Court of Appeals decision *Braschi* v. *Stahl Associates* 543 N.E.22.49 (1989) is in striking contrast. See also *Egan v. Canada* [1995] 2 SCR 513.

[14]  *Lindo* v. *Belisario* (1795) 1 Hag Con 216, 161 ER 531.

[15]  [1997] 1 FLR 402.

[16]  Ibid, p. 439.

[17]  [1998] 1 FLR 6.

[18]  Ibid, p. 27.

[19]  The post-*Baehr* experiences are discussed in THOMAS F. COLEMAN (1995) The Hawaii Legislative has compelling reasons to adopt a comprehensive Domestic Partnership Act, *Law and Sexuality* 5, 541.

[20]  See LINDA NIELSEN (1990) Family rights and the 'Registered Partnership' in DENMARK, *International Journal of Law and the Family*, 4, p. 297. Also valuable is MARTIN D. DUPUIS (1995) The impact of culture, society and history on the legal process: an analysis of the legal status of same-sex relationships in the United States and Denmark, *International Journal of Law and the Family*, 9, 86–1218.

[21]  See C. K. ALLEN (1930) Status and capacity, *Law Quarterly Review* 46, 277–310.

[22]  *Mohamed* v. *Knott* [1969] 1 Q.B.1 (wife 13 or less; parties domiciled in Nigeria).

[23]  *Cheni* v. *Cheni* [1965] P.85 (parties Jews domiciled at the time of the ceremony in Egypt; both Jewish and Egyptian law permits such marriages).

[24]  *Radwan* v. *Radwan* [1973] Fam 35 (the wife had an English domicile and the husband an Egyptian one).

[25]  *Hussain* v. *Hussain* [1983] Fam. 26.

[26]  Private International Law (Miscellaneous Provisions) Act 1995 s.5(1).

[27]  As in the case of polygamy: see *Coleman* v. *Shang* [1961] AC 481; *Re Sehota* [1978] 1 WLR 1506.

[28]  Immigration Act 1988 s2(2) (polygamous marriages are largely denied recognition for immigration purposes). They are, however, recognised for the purposes of deportation! (Immigration Act 1971 s5(4), as amended).

[29]  It took until 1972 before English law allowed matrimonial relief to anyone married polygamously (which included those who had been through a polygamous ceremony of marriage and were thus potentially polygamously married).

[30]  On which see C. M. V. CLARKSON and JONATHAN HILL (1997) *Jaffey on the Conflict of Laws* (London, Butterworths).

[31]  *Sottomayer* v. *De Barros (no.2)* (1879) 5 P D 94, 104. But compare *Conlon* v. *Mohamed* [1989] ILRM 523.

[32]  *Chetti* v. *Chetti* [1909] P. 67.

[33]  *Sottomayer* v. *De Barros (no.2)* (1879) 5 P D 94, 104 (*obiter*).

[34]  Gay's The Word in Bloomsbury.

[35]  As to which see NICHOLAS BAMFORTH (1997) *Sexuality, Morals and Justice* (London, Cassell). See also DIDI HERMAN (1997) *The Anti-Gay Agenda* (Chicago, University of Chicago Press).

[36]  NANCY D. POLIKOFF (1993) We will get what we ask for: why legalizing gay and lesbian marriage will not 'dismantle the legal structure of gender in every marriage' *Virginia Law Review*, 79, 1535.

[37]  *Loving* v. *Virginia* 388 U.S.1 (1967).

[38]  For example, PAULA L. ETTELBRICK (1989) Since when is marriage a path to liberation, *Out/Look*, 2, 9 and NITYA DUCLOS (1991) Some complicating thoughts on same-sex marriage, *Law and Sexuality*, 1, 31.

[39]  WILLIAM N. ESKRIDGE (1996) *The Case For Same-Sex Marriage* (New York, Free Press), p. 8. See also MARK STRASSER (1997) *Legally Wed: Same Sex Marriage and the Constitution* (Ithaca, Cornell University Press), ch. 1.

[40]  191 N.W. 2d 185 (1971): appeal dismissed by U.S. Supreme Court, 409 U.S. 810 (1972). One problem with invoking religion is that of interpreting texts (the standard prohibition in Leviticus has been variously interpreted): another is that it is by no means the case there is a consensus within the corpus of world religions on same-sex marriages (Quakers, Unitarians and some Buddhists apparently find no theological objection).

[41]  *Jones* v. *Hallahan* 501 S.W.2d. 588 (1973).

[42]  *Bowersr* v. *Hardwick* 478 U.S. 186 (1986) (Georgia's sodomy law did not violate the right to privacy, at least with respect to 'homosexual sodomy'. But it has since ruled unconstitutional on equal amendment grounds a Colorado constitutional amendment that precluded 'all legislative, executive or judicial action at any level of state or local government designed to protect the status of persons based on their "homosexual, lesbian, or bisexual orientation, conduct, practices or relationship"' (see *Romer* v. *Evans* 116 S. Ct 1620

(1996) and ANN ESTIN (1997) Gay Rights And The Courts: The Amendment 2 Controversy, *University of Colorado Law Review*, 68, 349–371).

[43] *Turner v. Safley* 482 U.S. 78 (1987).

[44] Eskridge, op. cit., note 39, ch. 2 offers a snapshot of this.

[45] See JOHN BOSWELL (1994), *The Marriage of Likeness* (New York, Villard Books), pp. 264–265.

[46] Boswell, op. cit., note 45, reprints examples of those in ibid, pp. 289–344. But there is no evidence that these were sexual unions.

[47] And see O. W. HOLMES (1897) The path of the law, *Harvard Law Review*, 10, 457, 459 ('It is revolting to have no better reason for a rule of law than that it was laid down in the time of Henry IV').

[48] See ORMROD J. in *Corbett v. Corbett (orse Ashley)*, op. cit., note 6, p. 106.

[49] There have been a number of well-publicised cases in the 1990s of post-menopausal women — even women in their sixties — having children using the new reproductive technologies. In relation to Italy see PAULA GATTORINI (1994) Assisted reproduction in Italy, *Hastings Center Report*, 24(6), pp. 3–4; on France see PAUL WEBSTER (1994) France plans ban on 'aged' mothers, *The Guardian* 4 January, p. 1.

[50] HADLEY ARKES (1993) The closet straight, *National Review* (July 5). 43, 45. See also HADLEY ARKES (1995) Questions of principle, not predictions: a reply to Macedo, *Georgetown Law Journal*, 84, 321–327.

[51] ARKES (1993), op. cit., comes close to making this point. The 'argument' suffers from the standard objections to the slippery slope argument. For conservatives prepared to tolerate homosexuality (e.g. those opposed to sodomy statutes) it may even be self-defeating: there would be a case for rooting out the practice before there were demands to legitimise it by allowing an institution like same-sex marriage.

[52] See CHARLES KRAUTHAMMER (1996) When John and Jim say 'I do': if gay marriages are O.K., then what about polygamy? or incest? *Time*, July 22, 120. See also J. SCALIA's dissent in *Romer v. Evans* 116 S.Cf. 1620, 1635–1636. The benefits and harms of polygamy and same-sex marriage (and monogamy) are highlighted by MAURA L. STASSBERG (1997) Distinction of form or substance: monogamy, polygamy and same-sex marriage, *North Carolina Law Review*, 75, 1501.

[53] J. M. FINNIS (1994), Law, morality and 'sexual orientation', *Notre Dame Law Review*, 69, 1049, 1067.

[54] FINNIS, op. cit., p. 1066.

[55] FINNIS, op. cit., p. 1065.

[56] J. M. FINNIS (1970), Natural law and unnatural acts, *The Heythrop Journal*, 11, 365, 383.

[57] J. M. FINNIS (1996), Is natural law theory compatible with limited government? in Robert George (ed) *Natural Law, Liberalism and Morality* (Oxford, Clarendon Press), 4, 13–14.

[58] ROBERT P. GEORGE and GERALD V. BRADLEY (1995) Marriage and the liberal imagination, *Georgetown Law Journal*, 84, 301, 301–302.

[59] I. KANT (1963) *Lectures on Ethics* (translated L. Infield) (New York, Harper and Row), discussed by MICHAEL FREEMAN (1997) Taking the body seriously? in KRISTINA STERN and PAT WALSH *Property Rights In The Human Body* (London, Centre of Medical Law and Ethics), 13.

[60] George and Bradley op. cit., note 58, 302.

[61] HARVEY C. MANSFIELD (1993) Saving liberalism from liberals, *Harvard Crimson* (November 8), 2. Finnis, op. cit., believes that Socrates, Plato and Aristotle also regarded homosexual *conduct* as 'intrinsically shameful' (p. 1055). This has been challenged by MARTHA NUSSBAUM (1994) Platonic love and Colorado law: the relevance of ancient Greek norms to modern sexual controversies, *Virginia Law Review*, 80, 1515.

[62] Arkes, op. cit., p. 43.

[63] HARRY V. JAFFA (1994) Our ancient faith: a reply to Professor Anastaplo in *Original Intent and the Framers of the Constitution* (Washington, D.C., Regnery), 369 and 383.

[64] Mansfield, op. cit., p. 3.

[65] RICHARD A. POSNER (1992) *Sex and Reason* (Cambridge, Mass, Harvard University Press), p. 311.

[66] Posner, op. cit., p. 312.

[67] Posner, op. cit., p. 313.

[68] The Swedish approach then regarded homosexual union as like heterosexual cohabitation, but a change has since taken place and the Swedish approach is now similar to the Danish.

[69] See *Loving v. Virginia*, op. cit., note 37.

[70] op. cit., note 39, pp. 159–162. See also Strasser, op. cit., note 39, pp. 66–67. An interesting, if unconvincing, contrast is LYNN D. WARDLE (1996) A critical analysis of constitutional claims for same-sex marriage, *Brigham Young University Law Review*, 1, 75–82.

[71] JOHN STUART MILL (1859) *On Liberty* (London, Fontana Press, 1962), p. 210.

16

[72] ANDREW SULLIVAN (1995) *Virtually Normal* (New York, Alfred A. Knopf). See also his reader (1997) *Same-Sex Marriage: Pro and Con* (New York, Vintage Books).

[73] Sullivan (1995), op. cit., note 72, p. 139.

[74] Sullivan (1995), op. cit., note 72, p. 162–163.

[75] Sullivan (1995), op. cit., note 72, p. 171.

[76] Contrast the Local Government Act 1988, s.28 and its reference to 'pretended families'. See also Education Act 1996 requiring sex education be taught within the context of 'moral considerations and the value of family life' (s.403(1)).

[77] See LISA DUGGAN (1994) Queering the State, *Social Text*, 39, 1–14.

[78] Sullivan, op. cit.. note 72, p. 150.

[79] JANE S. SCHACHTER (1997) Skepticism, culture and the gay civil rights debate in a post-civil-rights era, *Harvard Law Review* 110, 684, pp. 692–693.

[80] Sullivan, op. cit., note 72, p. 179.

[81] Ibid.

[82] PAULA ETTELBRICK (1996) Wedlock alert: a comment on lesbian and gay family recognition, *Journal of Law and Policy* 5, 107, 115.

[83] Sullivan, op. cit., note 72, p. 182.

[84] Ibid.

[85] Sullivan, op. cit., note 72, p. 183.

[86] Sullivan, op. cit., note 72, pp. 183–184.

[87] Sullivan, op. cit., note 72, p. 84.

[88] Ibid.

[89] Sullivan, op. cit., note 72, p. 181.

[90] Ibid, p. 186.

[91] See, in particular, JOHN RAWLS (1993) *Political Liberalism* (New York, Columbia University Press). A political conception of justice as fairness is only interested in adopting the basic structure of society so 'that intractable conflicts are unlikely to arise . . . A political conception is at best a guiding framework of deliberation and reflection which helps us reach political agreement on at least the constitutional essentials and basic questions of justice' (ibid), p. 156). On Rawls see SAMUEL SCHEFFLER (1994) The Appeal of Political Liberalism, *Ethics*, 105, 4–22 and LEIF WENAR (1995) *Political Liberalism*: an internal critique, *Ethics*, 106, 32–62.

[92] There is overlapping consensus on the appropriate political responses to debates about 'basic religions and political liberties' and such 'basic rights of citizens in civil society' as 'freedom of movement and fair equality of opportunity, the right of personal property, and the protections of the rule of law', the 'classical problems' Rawls lists (op. cit., note 91, p. XXVII). There is a historical liberal tradition to guide on these questions but this does not exist as regards the recognition of same-sex marriage. Why it does not is itself an interesting question but is outside the scope of this investigation.

[93] RONALD DWORKIN (1978) Liberalism in Stuart Hampshire (ed.) *Public and Private Morality* (Cambridge, Cambridge University Press).

[94] RONALD DWORKIN (1966) Lord Devlin and the enforcement of morals, *Yale Law Journal* 75, 986 (also in RONALD DWORKIN (1977) *Taking Rights Seriously* (London, Duckworth), p. 254).

[95] RONALD DWORKIN (1995) Foundations of liberal equality in Stephen Darwall (ed) *Equal Freedom: Selected Tanner Lectures on Human Values* (Salt Lake City, University of Utah Press) 190, 225.

[96] RONALD DWORKIN op. cit., note 89, p. 302.

[97] JOSEPH RAZ (1986) *The Morality of Freedom* (Oxford, Clarendon Press); JOSEPH RAZ (1994) *Ethics In the Public Domain* (Oxford, Clarendon Press). See also WILLIAM GALSTON (1991) *Liberal Purposes* (Cambridge, Cambridge University Press).

[98] Per RICHARD GEORGE (1993) *Making Men Moral* (Oxford, Clarendon Press), p. 162.

[99] See JOSEPH RAZ (1996) Liberty and trust in Richard George (ed.) *Natural Law, Liberalism and Morality* (Oxford, Clarendon Press), p. 113.

[100] See JOSEPH RAZ (1986) op.cit., note 97, p. 135.

[101] ibid.

[102] See JOSEPH RAZ (1986) op.cit., note 97, p. 20.4.

[103] See JOSEPH RAZ (1994) op.cit., note 97, p. 118.

[104] See JOSEPH RAZ (1986) op.cit., note 97, p. 419. It has been argued (DONALD H. REGAN (1989) Authority

and value: reflection on Raz's *Morality of Freedom, Southern California Law Review* 62, 995 at 1084) that Raz's account of autonomy is internally inconsistent but there is no inherent inconsistency.

[105] See JOSEPH RAZ (1986) op.cit., note 97, p. 206.
[106] See JOSEPH RAZ (1986) op.cit., note 97, pp. 415–416.
[107] See JOSEPH RAZ (1986) op. cit., note 97, p. 416.
[108] See JOSEPH RAZ (1986) op. cit., note 97, p. 415.
[109] Ibid.
[110] WILLIAM ESKRIDGE (1996), op. cit., note 39, p. 8.
[111] WILLIAM ESKRIDGE (1996), op. cit., note 39, p. 9.
[112] Ibid.
[113] WILLIAM ESKRIDGE (1996), op. cit., note 39, p. 112.
[114] Ibid.
[115] WILLIAM ESKRIDGE (1996), op. cit., note 39, p. 112.
[116] For example, DAVID K. FLAKS *et al* (1995) Lesbians choosing motherhood: a comparative study of lesbian and heterosexual parents and their children, *Developmental Psychology* 31, 115; CHARLOTTE J. PATTERSON (1992) Children of lesbian and gay parents, *Child Development* 63, 1025. A good case study is PETER N. SWISHER and NANCY D. COOK (1996) Bottoms v Bottoms: In whose best interest? analysis of a lesbian mother child custody dispute, *University of Louisville Journal of Family Law,* 34, 843–895. More sceptical is PHILIP A. BELCASTRO *et al* (1993) A review of data based studies addressing the effects of homosexual parenting on children's sexual and social functioning, *Journal of Divorce and Remarriage,* 20, 38.
[117] WILLIAM ESKRIDGE (1996) op. cit., note 39, p. 10.
[118] See HELEN REECE (1996) Subverting the stigmatisation argument, *Journal of Law and Society* 23, 484–505 for support.

# [13]
# Questioning The Delegalization Movement in Family Law: Do We Really Want a Family Court?

Open almost any family law treatise, any report on an issue of family policy, and you will find that it contains at some point a plan for the family court ideal. I too have frequently stressed the need for the establishment of a family court. Indeed, I was a member of the Justice Committee on Parental Rights and Duties and Custody Suits[1] which recommended that a family court be set up in England. As to the structure of the court we were content to adopt the Finer Report's recommendations[2] as our own. That report had noted that submissions to it in favour of the family court ideal offered "more by way of enthusiasm than elucidation,"[3] but that is hardly surprising.

Critics of the existing system seem to agree on what is wrong. Inglis put it well when he said in a public lecture, which was subsequently published,

> Matrimonial litigation is simply one phase in a relationship which must continue in a variety of aspects once the litigation is over. Few matrimonial disputes ever completely end the parties' relationship. It is simply redefined for the future.[4]

We are all, I think, agreed that the adversary system has very severe limitations in the area of family law. Manchester will have spoken for many when he wrote,

> Yet surely we are now agreed upon the basic premise of the family court system ... a "caring court" with social and welfare services integrated within it as part of a total team operation.[5]

8 *The Settlement of Disputes*

Words constantly repeated are "civilized" and "humane." Very few have cautioned against the family court. The English law lord and former chairman of the English Law Commission, Lord Scarman,[6] is one to have done so. Rereading his address to the Institute of Judicial Administration in Birmingham, nine years after it was given I am struck by the complacency of its tone and the thinness of its argument. I would not expect Lord Scarman to agree with the thesis that I am about to present. We are, however, agreed that the family court concept contains its own dangers. It is easy to be swept along on a tide of euphoria. It is rather more difficult to stand back and take a cool look at what has happened to the family in the twentieth century and to place moves towards the family court ideal within these welfare-oriented policies. This is what, in part, I attempt to do.

I am not concerned with describing in detail or analysing any particular family court or any posited ideal. Proposals are legion and there are in existence in different parts of the world a number of family courts. In my own country, the United Kingdom, proposals for a family court (but not the same one) have come from Royal Commissions,[7] from the Law Society,[8] from the Justices' Clerks' Society[9] and from the Conservative Party.[10] One of the fullest discussions of the concept emanates from Judge Jean Graham Hall.[11] One of the most articulate and sensitive, from Mervyn Murch,[12] a social administration lecturer. But it is accepted in England that we will not get a family court in the foreseeable future. As much divides current proposals and models as unites them. What does, however, unite all critics of the existing system is a desire to render the legal order more "efficient" and more responsive to the perceived needs of the family. These critics, though ideologically poles apart, share with radical critics of the legal order generally a concern over the impersonality, insensitivity and remoteness of law, not to say its excessive rigidity and formality.

This brings me to the second of my themes. Debates about the appropriateness of adversary justice, about the value of integrating adjudicative and welfare roles in the family court, are discourses about the form of law. These are debates with a long heritage and distinguished pedigree: the classical source is, of course, the sociology of Max Weber.[13] There are pervasive delegalization trends in contemporary advanced capitalist societies.[14] It was Weber who first noted that movements towards greater informalism contained the seeds of their own self-contradiction and were ultimately doomed. If this is right, what effect will the move to the family court have? The annals of legal history are strewn with examples of institutions and practices which have had unintended consequences.[15] Programmes which seem to weaken hierarchies of power may actually establish new channels through which they can be expressed or even strengthened. These new programmes may be rendered necessary by, or be more responsive to, technological or economic change. They may be by-products of new patterns of social administration. Observe the way the decline in the criminal sanction[16] has been matched by the growth of the regulatory sanction[17] spawned by the "new property"[18] state; note the way that the therapeutic state has medicalized deviance.[19] The effect is, what Cohen has called, a "dispersal of social control."[20] State involvement may be less, but intervention is more pervasive. We may be moving away from the era of total institutions only to find ourselves enmeshed in total societies.

This is, I think, a likely scenario for the family court. Few of the family court advocates see it this way and many would not find the consequences I describe distasteful. To some, what I am saying will appear far-fetched. But this is where part one of my thesis reemerges. The twentieth century has witnesses, what Philip Rieff has called, the "triumph of the therapeutic."[21] The emphasis on the family has resulted in its greater surveillance and more intensive supervision. The rhetoric is about family autonomy;[22] the reality is of a more pervasive control than existed one hundred years ago. The two parts of my thesis thus converge.

## THE FAMILY AND THE STATE

The family has not always been as it is now.[23] The current ideal, which attained its fullest flowering in late Victorian times and now seems to be slowly decaying, rests on the companionate marriage, in which the union is one of two individuals rather than two lineages; on the child-centred household; on the quasi emancipation of women; and on the structural isolation of the nuclear family from the kinship system and the community.

In precapitalist societies and in the early stages of capitalism, work and family life overlapped. The household was the basic unit of production: the home was a place of work. There was no clear distinction between the role of worker and of family member. With industrialization and capitalist production the nature of work and family life changed radically. Productive work now took place in the factory. It became increasingly routinized. The factory system at first used women and children but increasing industrialization brought unemployment and women were driven into dependence upon men. Work done in the home was increasingly restricted to looking after husband-workers and producing children. Eli Zaretsky[24] has described how at the same time the family became idealized, as did the familial role of women. The home became a refuge from the demands of capitalist society. In Lasch's graphic phrase the family became a "haven in a heartless world."

> The family found ideological support and justification in the conception of domestic life as an emotional refuge in a cold and competitive society.[25]

The family became a private place to which people, but especially men, could withdraw.

The family was thus exalted. A "cult of domesticity"[26] was engendered, according to Carl N. Degler,[27] by women themselves. It confined women to the home but at the same time it made them the moral arbiters of the family and of whatever else touched its interests. He argues[28] that demands for the recognition of married women's property rights, for divorce laws favourable to women, for sexual self-control on the part of men, for acknowledgment of women's greater stake in regulating pregnancy, as well as for reforms in the larger social sphere, particularly in relation to "social purity" all arose out of the logic of domesticity itself.

The connection between the "cult of domesticity" and the emancipation of women has also been observed by Jacques Donzelot in his *La Police des Familles.* He sees that:

> Birth control and the "liberation" of women rested on women's old social vocation, and on their function as ambassadresses of culture.[29]

Donzelot also sees what Degler does not, *viz.*: that women's roles as cultural missionaries was to some extent the deliberate creation of doctors seeking to make wives and mothers agents of medical influence. Ideas were spread by "promotional goading and attendant blaming of families who, through their resistance, were ruining the members' chances."[30]

The emotional intensification of family life had, as one of its inevitable consequences, conflict. This, the nascent psychological sciences sought to explain and, of course, to prevent and solve. But, as Lasch has argued:

> To enlightened members of the professional classes — and this includes most feminists — knowledge of this kind, promised a preventive science of sexual and social control, which could be used among other things to civilise the poor, to subject them to new controls sincerely disguised as benevolence, and thus to integrate them more fully into the emerging industrial order.[31]

Women saw the advantage of professional intervention in family life. It undercut patriarchal authority. However, it also eroded the traditional prerogatives of women. Thus, as Ehrenreich and English[32] have also demonstrated, women welcomed the substitution of doctors for midwives in childbirth. The overall result was that professionals continually expanded their jurisdiction over family life. Patriarchal authority may have suffered but so did the authority formerly exercised by women themselves. Lasch makes the point that

> in allying themselves with the helping professions, women improved their position in the family only to fall into a new kind of dependence, the dependence of the

consumer on the market and on the providers of expert services, not only for the satisfaction of her needs but for the very definition of her needs.[33]

It is easy to see how society came to be governed by doctors, social workers, psychiatrists, juvenile court judges, criminologists, etc., in short, by the modern apparatus of resocialization. The "helping professions" during the first third of this century came to see themselves as doctors to a sick society. This is graphically portrayed in fictional form in D.M. Thomas's *The White Hotel*.[34] Many have written of the growth of the "therapeutic state."[35] Its influence, its impact on the family has been profound. What the cathedral was to medieval times and the legislative chamber was to the nineteenth century, the hospital, the clinic is to our day.[36]

It is all too common to read of the family losing its functions,[37] as if these had formerly been unproblematic and static. In reality what these commentators have observed is the takeover of society playing the nurturing mother of certain roles played by the family, nuclear and extended, at earlier times in history. I think Lasch has grasped this better than anybody. To socialization of production, he believes, we should add "socialisation of reproduction."[38] This, he claims, "proletarianised parent-hood, by making people unable to provide for their own needs without the supervision of trained experts." Early proponents of children's rights typify this approach.[39] Contemporary advocates of rights for children, Holt[40] or Farson[41] for example, would not see the child-saving movement as bedfellow to theirs at all. It stressed protecting children while they emphasize the importance of protecting children's rights. The divergence between the two comes out distinctly if we examine the early philosophy in practice.[42] The development of a system of compulsory education fits the turn-of-the-century ethos very well.

If the state is to have good citizens . . . we must begin to teach the children in our schools, and begin at once, that which we see they are no longer learning in the home,

wrote Ellen Richards[43] in 1910 in a book intriguingly entitled *Euthenics: The Science of Controllable Environment.* Children were to achieve independence from parental control but they fell increasingly, instead, under the control of the state. In Donzelot's words, "family patriarchalism was destroyed at the cost of a patriarchy of the state."[44]

A second example, which is particularly well-documented, though not beyond controversy, is the development of a system of juvenile justice. The juvenile court substituted prevention for punishment, and close surveillance for judgment. It treated the child's or adolescent's crimes as symptoms of an unhealthy, unhygienic home environment, thus justifying enquiries into the morality of his family and his removal from home if this was deemed necessary. Donzelot describes how parents who called in the

police or social workers in the hope that outside intervention would
strengthen their authority over a wayward child found instead that their
authority was tranferred to an outside professional authority.

> Instead of the desired admonition, however, the juvenile judge, after reviewing the
> results of the social inquiry, decides in favour of an educative assistance that has
> another purpose altogether, since it brings the adolescent into the sphere of the
> tutelary complex, leading to his detachment from family authority and transferral
> to a social authority . . . all in order to prevent him from contaminating his brothers
> and sisters and to enable his parents to devote themselves to the younger children.[45]

Architects of juvenile justice justified their creation on humanitarian
grounds. They may have intended to be humanitarian. They saw
themselves as replacing the undoubted barbarities of the criminal law with
something better. They argued that the juvenile court was to be a friend of
the juvenile offender as well as a confederate of his family. Donzelot
describes this reasoning as "pious representations . . . of reasons that are
much less 'democratic'."[46] Rothman admits that conscience may have
played its part but so, he insists, did "convenience."[47] Donzelot is not the
first to have questioned the motives of the reformers. Platt,[48] Fox,[49]
Ryerson,[50] and Schlossman[51] have all rejected the orthodox interpretation of the development of the juvenile court. Like Platt, Donzelot sees
intervention in the family as a "depoliticising strategy." It was inspired by
a fear of class conflict: it belonged to a general attempt to control the poor.
It was the liberal state's answer to socialist propaganda. It aimed to
convert political debates into administrative procedures. The language
used may have been that of hygiene and health, but political considerations were never far below the surface. The parallels between the rhetoric
about the juvenile court at the turn of the century and the family court in
the last decade are so striking that it is surprising that the implications
for the family court ideal have not been drawn, but I would suggest that
they are there for all to see.

I have given examples from two areas. Others could be cited. I resist
that temptation in order to return to the general issue. Liberals tried to
steer a course between what they saw as the Scylla of conservative
paternalism, which upheld the family as the foundation of the social
order, so that every change was seen as a threat to social integrity, and the
Charybdis of socialism, which wanted to replace parenthood with the
state. But, "in the end," to quote Lasch once again, "they outflanked their
adversaries by creating a therapeutic state which left the family more or
less intact yet subjected to non-stop supervision."[52] The liberal state as a
result has a system of indirect controls which preserves the appearance,
even some of the reality, of private initiative within an overarching
structure of professional supervision. The therapeutic state leaves the
family "'always' 'justified' in theory and always suspect in practice."[53]

## PROFESSIONAL EXPERTISE

The victory of the medical model has meant the elevation of the expert. The effects of this can be seen starkly in the juvenile court. Even where a child has committed a criminal offence, there is reason to believe, and any examination of social enquiry reports reinforces this belief, that in the minds of decision makers the seriousness of his behaviour, what he has *done*, takes a back seat behind an interpretation of what he, and his family, *is*.[54] Individualized justice, the goal of welfare-oriented processes, has been said to result "in a frame of relevance so large, so all inclusive, that any relation between the criteria of judgment and the disposition remains obscure."[55] The social enquiry report is the linchpin of the juvenile court process. Anderson describes it as "the product of an application of social work ideology to the court context."[56] Social enquiry reports are apt to contain value judgments, to make unsubstantiated assertions and often to be based on assumptions which are not supported by the evidence.[57] Writers of the reports, who know no more about the causes of misbehaviour than the rest of us, tend to assemble information which reinforces stereotypes of "causes of trouble" such as broken homes, working mothers, etc., and often to put it into language loosely drawn from psychoanalytic theory.[58] Concepts such as personality disorder, psychopath, impaired bonding, dependency needs are pervasive. The use of theory is random and eclectic.

It is easy to criticize the welfare professionals, social workers, psychologists, child psychiatrists, to attribute this to bad practice. But the problem is deeper than this. As Andrew Sutton has argued, in a recent outstanding article,[59] there has been an unjustified professionalization of issues that are "in fact beyond the present reach of expert under-standing."[60] He is not alone in questioning the expertise used by welfare professionals. It would take me too far away from the subject of this paper to give further details of this. Suffice it to say that Sutton, Morgan[61] and others[62] provide considerable evidence of the inadequacy of the knowledge base upon which assessment and treatment of children, the writing of social enquiry reports and similar tasks proceed. There has been, Sutton concludes, an "unjustified reliance on premature profes-sionalism."[63] In Britain the most detailed investigations into social work practice have followed the deaths (or serious injuries) of children at the hands of parents or other caretakers. A common theme running through all the reports[64] of such enquiries is found in the assertion that the system of child care has failed: there has been a lack or ineffectiveness of communication and liaison between welfare professionals, and between them and the police and medical profession. None of these enquiries appears to have grasped the fundamental nettle, the problematic nature of professional expertise.[65] Such is the power of professional mystique.

14                                    *The Settlement of Disputes*

I have not seen a single proposal for a family court which comes to terms with these issues at all. Take the fullest discussion of the family court in Britain. This is to be found in the Finer report on one-parent families, published in 1974.[66] Though disdainful of American family courts which, it says, are "committed to a social work philosophy which regards family breakdown as a phenomenon to be dealt with primarily by diagnosis and treatment" and which are as much a "therapeutic agency as a judicial institution,"[67] it advocates the use of court social workers. The welfare part of the court would be expected to "demonstrate a commensurate degree of professional integrity and expertise,"[68] commensurate that is with the integrity and formal expertise of the court. But we are talking of different types of expertise: lawyers have formal expertise; social workers aspire to expertise based on empirical knowledge. If Sutton, Morgan and the others are right, the operative words are "aspire to," for it is doubtful whether the knowledge base has as yet been obtained. The Finer report envisages court welfare services providing "assistance for people with marital problems."[69] If by assistance is meant conciliation,[70] so as to civilize the consequences of breakdown, then it is difficult to quarrel with the proposal. The report does not expand on the work tasks it expects welfare services to undertake. It does not, for example, see social workers taking part in the "family court conference," the convening of which it recommends where a maintenance or administrative order has been in operation for two years and the marriage still legally subsists.[71] It does not see social workers as decision makers but rather as handmaidens.[72] They will make social and welfare enquiries and the reports. But the line between informed (or not so informed) opinions and recommendations is a thin one and the experience of juvenile courts, and indeed adult criminal courts which commission reports on defendants, is that they expect, get, and act on recommendations of social workers and probation officers.[73] Indeed, similar evidence is available in the case of courts dealing with family matters where refusals to follow social workers' recommendations are rare and where the courts feel themselves obligated to articulate their reasons for so doing.[74]

## DELEGALIZATION

Moves away from adversary justice and towards a family court are in effect moves towards the delegalization of family dispute settlement. Delegalization can take place on a number of levels and can be motivated or inspired by different goals. The simplification of divorce processes with the introduction in England in 1973[75] of the "special procedure" effected a limited measure of delegalization. It was a response to research which had shown that judicial hearings in divorce were perfunctory.[76] It was motivated also by a desire to rechannel money spent by the state through legal aid subsidizing divorce into other areas of unmet legal need.[77] Much discussion of delegalization[78] is in the context of wresting law away from remote authorities and allowing the masses to participate in the processes of justice. Obviously, movements towards deformalization (as indeed towards formalization) take on different meanings depending on cultural, political and historical contexts. Contemporary moves away from formality in the West may well reflect, in part, the decline in the märket system and the growth of monopoly capitalism. A consequence of the decline of the market has been the rise of state redistribution as a dominant mechanism for allocation (including the growth of the so-called "new property").[79] The rise of monopoly capitalism has meant that the law does not have to be used to promote the ideal of a self-regulating market.

The temptation to approach formalism and informalism as if the effects of each were opposite to the other must be resisted. Weber saw this. He wrote:

> The position of all "democratic" currents, in the sense of currents that would minimize "authority", is necessarily ambiguous. "Equality before the law" and the demand for legal guarantees against arbitrariness demand a formal and rational "objectivity" of administration, as opposed to the personally free discretion flowing from the "grace" of the old patrimonial domination. If, however, an "ethos" — not to speak of instincts — takes hold of the masses on some individual question, it postulates *substantive* justice oriented toward some concrete instance and person; and such an "ethos" will unavoidably collide with the formalism and the rule-bound and cool "matter-of-factness" of bureaucratic administration. For this reason, the ethos must emotionally reject what reason demands. The propertyless masses especially are not served by a "formal equality before the law" and a "calculable" adjudication and administration, as demanded by "bourgeois" interests. Naturally in their eyes justice and administration should serve to compensate for their economic and social life-opportunities in the face of the propertied classes. Justice and administration can fulfil this function only if they assume an informal character to a far-reaching extent. It must be informal because it is substantively "ethical" ("Kadi-justice"). Every sort of "popular justice" — which usually does not ask for reasons and norms — as well as every sort of intensive influence on the administration of so-called public opinion, crosses the rational course of justice and administration just as strongly, and under certain conditions far more so, as the "star chamber" proceedings of an "absolute" ruler has been able to do.[80]

What Weber is saying is important. To the extent that law is set up to protect the weak, it must be formalistic and impersonal and confined by rules. Yet when it is invoked especially to achieve social justice, to protect the weak against the powerful, it is typically an expression of informal "substantive justice."[81] But this can be very easily subverted by the powerful to their advantage. Both law as form and law as substance may be equated with social justice but neither is able to deliver what it promises.[82]

This should alert us to the danger of falling into the trap of thinking that having created a particular structure, it will operate as we expect it to do. Both movements toward formalism and informalism contain within themselves the capacity to turn into something very different from what they appear. Weber depicted the rise of Western capitalism as a movement towards the dominance of formal rationality over substantive rationality.[83] This destroys popular justice. Instead we get bureaucratic centralization and protest against rational legal authority is seen as "irrational." This is why Weber can conclude that any trend toward greater informalism is doomed. "It is by no means certain," he wrote, "that those classes which are negatively privileged today, especially the working class, may safely expect from an informal administration of justice those results which are claimed for it by the ideology of the jurists."[84]

Further insight into what Duncan Kennedy has called[85] a "regime of rules" may be sought in the contemporary Marxist historian, E.P. Thompson. He is writing of eighteenth century England but some of the comments in his coda are of general application.

> . . . People are not as stupid as some structuralist philosophers suppose them to be. They will not be mystified by the first man who puts on a wig. It is inherent in the especial character of law, as a body of rules and procedures, that it shall apply logical criteria with reference to standards of universality and equity. It is true that certain categories of person may be excluded from this logic . . . and that the poor may often be excluded, through penury, from the law's costly procedures. . . . But if too much of this is true, then the consequences are plainly counterproductive. Most men have a strong sense of justice, at least with regard to their own interests. . . . The essential precondition for the effectiveness of law, in its function as ideology is that it shall display an independence from gross manipulation and shall seem to be just. It cannot seem to be so without upholding its own logic and criteria of equity; indeed, on occasion by actually *being* just . . .[86]

This is an important qualification to what Weber argued and it comes from an unexpected source. By stressing the equivocal character of formal law, Thompson is able to argue for the preservation of the "forms and rhetoric of law . . . which may, on occasion, inhibit power and afford some protection to the powerless."[87] His is a plea not to throw out the "baby" with the "bathwater" and it is one we should heed. We must not let our concern about the rigidity, remoteness, insensitivity of traditional legal mechanisms turn us away from the unqualified good in the rule of law. We may find adversary processes inappropriate, even dehumanizing or alienating. Yet the formalism and rule of law which accompanies them provide a measure of protection to the powerless. In our context they are not, as in Thompson's or Weber's arguments, the working classes, but rather women, and especially, children. The rule of law also inhibits power, not least of welfare professionals. Our experience with the juvenile court provides abundant evidence of what is lost when informal procedures and treatment institutions replace traditional court structures and processes.[88] In the United States, realization of this led to the reintroduction of certain rights for juveniles,[89] in effect a partial relegalization of the juvenile court. But at about the same time in Britain, the decriminalization of "children in trouble" was reaching its high-water mark with the *Social Work (Scotland) Act* of 1968[90] and the English *Children and Young Persons Act* of 1969.[91] The British legislature, it seems, had not noticed *Re Gault*.[92] Are those who hanker for a family court similarly blinkered? The hyperbolical language which greets the family court ideal today is so very reminiscent of descriptions of the juvenile court half a century ago.[93]

Too much must not be read into this analogy with moves to the juvenile court earlier this century. To do so would be to divorce the movements from their historical contexts. The juvenile court emerged during the heyday of classical capitalism. The relationship between capitalism and formalism has been so thoroughly analysed[94] that it need not be elaborated upon further here. Capitalism needed certainty, calculability, stability, and formalism promoted this. In this sense the juvenile court was something of an anomaly, perhaps explained by excepting policies concerned with wayward youth from state initiatives generally.[95] But the economic organization of society has changed in the course of the twentieth century. A postindustrial society, a "third wave"[96] has different needs and expectations. To what extent these have been shaped by legal institutions and ideas and themselves influence legal developments are questions which have exercised the minds of a number of contemporary thinkers.[97] Classical capitalism stressed the division between public and private law and, though many jurists resisted the dualism,[98] the pervasive influence, some would say mystification, of the distinction remains deeply embedded in much liberal legal thinking even today. The separation is not easy to defend today and it is in fact widely under attack.[99] Once again legal rights of the individual are becoming dependent on status.[100] There are any number of manifestations of this trend: the rise in administrative law,[101] "the death of contract"[102] and the "therapeutic state"[103] are some of them. The historical setting for the family court is thus one in which status and hence particularistic relationships have reemerged. It is also one in which the patterns of decision making have shifted. Where once they were determined by reciprocal obligations or the wisdom of the market,[104] now they are centralized. There has been a shift, as Kamenka and Tay put it,[105] from *Gesellschaft* law[106] to bureaucratic administrative regulation. They see

the contemporary crisis of law and legal ideology...[as] a crisis of *Gesellschaft* law, a crisis in its capacity to deal with what are seen as the urgent problems of our time and, consequently in its claim to legitimacy.[107]

Whatever the reason and however one characterizes it, there has been an injection of substantive rationality into the formalized law of advanced capitalist societies. The attenuation of the market has necessitated reliance on other extraeconomic mechanisms to extract and redistribute surplus value. It has led to the rise of state redistribution. The "law" thus plays an affirmative role. Under classical capitalist conditions the law played almost a negative part. It promoted the ideal of a self-regulating market and it afforded a measure of protection to the weaker party. The rule of law has often been said to be a precondition of capitalist competition. With the growth of monopoly capitalism the protection offered by the law becomes a barrier in the way of the expansion of economic power. As capitalism becomes less of a market system the structure and content of law, its institutions and practices, undergo a profound change. For example, general rules give way to vague standards.[108] If we examine what is going on in advanced capitalist societies we can understand why formalism has declined. But this does not mean that we can hope to realize the goals (justice, equality, autonomy or whatever) in whose name formalism was attacked. Formalism has declined but not because of intellectual onslaughts upon it. Can delegalization succeed?

There are many delegalization projects of which those concerned with family dispute settlement make up only a small number. There are initiatives to involve the community in policing[109] and to introduce or strengthen the role of lay personnel in the administration of the lower, usually criminal, courts.[110] All these movements share in common a desire to promote the autonomy and self-sufficiency of local social units, whether these be communities, neighbourhoods[111] or, in our case, families, at the expense of the impersonal, bureaucraticized professional power centres. But the dispersal of control into local and traditional structures is perfectly consistent with the support, indeed the expansion of forms of social control which emanate from these power centres. Prison reform is an apt illustration of the process. The increased involvement of medicine and psychiatry in prisons has meant that

> No longer must such institutions be justified purely in terms of vengeance and punishment but as agencies of positive change the prison becomes a "correctional" institution . . . The scientists and the technicians are beginning to win out, not because of some inherent superiority in their paradigm of crime, but by showing that they have the power to be more effective custodians.[112]

The days of prisons as "human warehouses"[113] may be numbered, for,

> In the very near future, a computer technology will make possible alternatives to imprisonment. The development of systems for telemetering information from censors implanted in or on the body will soon make possible the observation and control of human behaviour without actual physical contact. Through such telemetric devices it will be possible to maintain 24-hour-a-day surveillance over the

subject and to intervene electronically or physically to influence and control selected behaviour. It will thus be possible to exercise control over human behaviour and from a distance without physical contact.[114]

Looked at superficially such changes (it is better not to call them "reforms") might appear to weaken hierarchies of power. In reality what they do is to make control more intrusive, more pervasive and more effective. The river may have burst its banks and the water may now flow in new channels. The water now comes at us from a number of directions and its total force may well be stronger than was the original river. The accepted view has been that control, certainly control within capitalism, required formality and impersonality, bureaucraticization and centralism. But today's advanced capitalism is compatible with decentralized social control. Penal developments draw attention to this in striking fashion but what they tell us can be generalized.

Even where the impetus for reform comes from below, from grass-roots sentiment, as to a large extent it does with moves to delegalize family dispute settlement, there is considerable likelihood that developments will be co-opted by the powerful, so that "bad" form takes over "good" substance. Adorno's remarks seem most pertinent.

> Whatever raises from within itself a claim to being autonomous, critical and antithetical — while at the same time never being able to assert this claim with total legitimacy — must necessarily come to naught; this is particularly true when its impulses are integrated into something heteronomous to them, which has been worked out previously from above — that is to say, when it is granted a space in which to draw breath immediately by that power against which it rebels.[115]

Is the result, as Cohen suggests, a "dispersal of social control"? Is the effect, as he argues it is,

> to increase rather than decrease the *amount* of intervention . . . and, probably, to increase rather than decrease the total *number* who get into the system in the first place[?][116]

He is writing of the criminal justice system but the parallels are too close to ignore. We can appreciate the proximity of the two when we return to and examine twentieth century policies towards the family.

We find rampant interventionism, a system of indirect controls and pervasive reliance on professional expertise. We find, in other words, policies which the family court legitimates. I believe, and I think my belief is shared, that the family has suffered from these policies. I believe that the family, particularly its weaker members, will suffer further from delegalization. And yet, if my thesis is correct, the move to a deformalized dispute settlement system in family matters has an air almost of inevitability about it. My article is written in the hope of opening our eyes

20                              *The Settlement of Disputes*

to what we have been doing to the family and what the thrust of contemporary developments will do to the family in the future. Too much has been taken for granted that should be openly debated. Too much that is problematic has been glossed over. I hope my article raises the questions, even if it does not provide the answers.


## NOTES

1. London: Justice, 1975, paras. 85 *et seq.*

2. Report of Committee on *One-Parent Families,* Cmnd. 5,629, 1974, London: H.M.S.O., part 4, sections 13 and 14.

3. *Idem,* para. 4.280.

4. "The Family, the Law and the Courts," 47 *Australian Law Journal* 647, 652 (1973).

5. "Reform and The Family Court," 125 *New Law Journal* 984 (1975).

6. In *The Domestic and Matrimonial Jurisdiction of Magistrates' Courts and County Courts,* Institute of Judicial Administration, University of Birmingham, 1973, 56–64, reported in *The Times,* 16 April 1973. See also Sir Leslie Scarman, *Family Law and Family Reform,* University of Bristol, 1966.

7. Finer, *op. cit.,* note 2, and Houghton, Report of Departmental Committee on the *Adoption of Children,* Cmnd. 5,107, 1972, London: H.M.S.O., paras. 276–279.

8. *A Better Way Out,* London: Law Society, 1979, parts III and VIII.

9. *The Case for a Local Family Court — Reform of the Family Jurisdiction of Magistrates,* 1978.

10. *The Case for Family Courts,* London: Conservative Political Centre, 1978.

11. *Proposal for a Family Court,* London: National Council for the Unmarried Mother and Her Child, 1973.

12. *Justice and Welfare in Divorce,* London: Sweet and Maxwell, 1980. I discuss this in "Towards a More Humane System of Divorce," 145 *Justice of the Peace* 1973 (1981).

13. See *Economy and Society* (eds. Guenther Roth and Claus Wittich) Berkeley: University of California Press, 1968, vol. II, pp. 641–900.

14. As to some of these are Richard L. Abel, *The Politics of Informal Justice,* 2 vols., New York: Academic Press, 1982. These volumes were not available in Britain when I wrote this article. Having now seen them, I realize how much my article would have profited from a study of them.

15. *Cf.* R. Merton (ed.), *Unanticipated Consequences of Social Action: Variations on a Sociological Theme,* New York: Academic Press, 1981.

16. See M. Spector, "Beyond Crime: Seven Methods to Control Troublesome Rascals" in (ed.) H. Laurence Ross, *Law and Deviance,* Beverly Hills: Sage, 1981, 127.

17. See Robert Kagan, *Regulatory Justice,* New York: Russell Sage Foundation, 1978.

18. See C. Reich, "The New Property," 73 *Yale L.J.* 733 (1964); M.A. Glendon, *The New Family and the New Property,* Toronto: Butterworths, 1981.

19. See N. Kittrie, *The Right to be Different: Deviance and Enforced Therapy,* Baltimore: Johns Hopkins U.P., 1971; P. Conrad and J. Schneider, *Deviance and Medicalization: From Badness to Sickness,* St. Louis: Mosby, 1980.

**20.** "The Punitive City: Notes on the Dispersal of Social Control," *Contemporary Crises* vol. 3, 339 (1979).

**21.** *The Triumph of The Therapeutic: Uses of Faith After Freud*, Harmondsworth: Penguin, 1966.

**22.** As in J. Goldstein et al., *Beyond The Best Interests of The Child*, New York: Free Press, 1973.

**23.** See L. Stone, *The Family, Sex and Marriage in England 1500-1800*, London: Weidenfeld and Nicolson, 1977 and E. Shorter, *The Making of the Modern Family*, London: Collins, 1976. ·

**24.** *Capitalism, the Family and Personal Life*, London: Pluto Press, 1976. See also A. Foreman, *Femininity As Alienation*, London: Pluto Press, 1977.

**25.** *Haven in a Heartless World*, New York: Basic Books, 1977, 6.

**26.** The term is Aileen S. Kraditor's. See *Up from the Pedestal: Selected Writings in the History of American Feminism*, Chicago: Quadrangle Books, 1968.

**27.** *At Odds: Women and the Family in America from the Revolution to the Present*, New York: Oxford U.P., 1980.

**28.** Following Nancy Cott, *The Bonds of Womanhood*, New Haven, Yale U.P., 1977 and Aileen Kraditor, *The Ideas of the Women's Suffrage Movement, 1890-1920*, New York: Columbia University Press, 1965.

**29.** Translated as *The Policing of Families*, New York: Pantheon Books, 1979, 221.

**30.** *Idem.* See the interesting critique by M. Barrett and M. McIntosh *The Antisocial Family*, London: Verso, 1982, 95 *et seq.*

**31.** "Life in the Therapeutic State," *The New York Review of Books*, vol. XXVII, no. 16 (12 June 1980) 24 and 27.

**32.** *For Her Own Good: 150 Years of the Experts' Advice to Women*, Garden City, New York: Anchor Press Doubleday, 1978.

**33.** *Op. cit.*, note 31, 27.

**34.** London: Gollancz, 1981.

**35.** See particularly N. Kittrie, *The Right To Be Different: Deviance and Enforced Therapy*, Baltimore: Johns Hopkins U.P., 1971.

**36.** *Cf.* P. Rieff, *Freud: The Mind of a Moralist*, London: Gollancz, 1960, 390.

**37.** See R. Fletcher, *The Family and Marriage in Britain*, Harmondsworth: Penguin, 1973 ch. 5. See also M. Nissel, "The Family and the Welfare State," *New Society*, vol. 53, no. 925 (7 August 1980), 259.

**38.** *Op. cit.*, note 25, 19.

**39.** See, e.g., Charlotte Perkins Gilman, *The Home: Its Work and Influence*, New York: McClure, Phillips, 1903, and Jenkin Lloyd Jones, quoted by Christopher Lasch in *Haven in a Heartless World*, *op. cit.*, note 25, p. 16.

**40.** *Escape From Childhood*, Harmondsworth: Penguin, 1975.

**41.** *Birthrights*, New York: Macmillan, 1974.

**42.** For the distinction, see C. Rogers and L. Wrightsman, "Attitudes toward Children's Rights: Nurturance or Self-Determination," *Journal of Social Issues*, vol. 34(2), 1978, 59. See also M. Wald, "Children's Rights: A Framework For Analysis," *University of California Davis L.R.*, vol. 12, 255, (1979) and M.D.A. Freeman, "The Rights of Children in the International Year of the Child," *Current Legal Problems*, vol. 33, 1980, 1; and *The Rights and Wrongs of Children*, London: Frances Pinter, 1983, ch. 2

**43.** Boston: Whitcomb and Barrows, 1910, 74.

**44.** *Op. cit.*, note 29, 219.

**45.** *Idem*, 158.

**46.** *Idem,* 100.

**47.** *Conscience and Convenience,* Boston: Little, Brown and Company, 1980.

**48.** *The Child Savers,* Chicago: University of Chicago Press, 1969 (a second edition was published in 1977).

**49.** "Philosophy and the Principle of Punishment in the Juvenile Court," 8 *Family Law Quarterly* 373 (1974).

**50.** *The Best-Laid Plans: America's Juvenile Court Experiment,* New York: Hill and Wang, 1978.

**51.** *Love and the American Delinquent: Theory and Practice of "Progressive" Juvenile Justice 1825-1920,* Chicago: University of Chicago Press, 1977.

**52.** *Op. cit.,* note 31, 30.

**53.** *Idem.*

**54.** See J. Lofland, *Deviance and Identity,* Englewood Cliffs: Prentice Hall, 1969, 150. See also E. Schur, *Labeling Deviant Behaviour,* New York: Harper and Row, 1971.

**55.** *Per* D. Matza, *Delinquency and Drift,* New York: Wiley, 1964, 115.

**56.** R. Anderson, *Representation in the Juvenile Courts,* London: Routledge and Kegan Paul, 1978, 25.

**57.** See L. Taylor et al., *In Whose Best Interests?* London: Cobden Trust/Mind, 1980; A. Morris et al., *Justice For Children,* London: Macmillan, 1980.

**58.** It is significant that little serious or sustained attention has been given by professionals to J. Goldstein et al.'s *Beyond the Best Interests of the Child,* revised edition, New York: Free Press, 1980 (first published in 1973), particularly to its idea of the "least detrimental alternative," despite the fact that the book is explicitly psychoanalytical in orientation.

**59.** "Science in Court" in (ed.) M. King, *Childhood, Welfare and Justice,* London: Batsford, 1981, 45-104.

**60.** *Idem,* 48.

**61.** Patricia Morgan, *Child Care: Sense and Fable,* London: Temple Smith, 1975 and *Delinquent Fantasies,* London: Temple Smith, 1978.

**62.** For example, G. Pearson, *The Deviant Imagination,* London: Macmillan, 1975.

**63.** *Op. cit.,* note 59, 95.

**64.** The most famous is the Department of Health and Social Security report into the Maria Colwell case (the Field-Fisher report) published by H.M.S.O., London, 1974. There have been some twenty other reports of enquiries. Eighteen reports are looked at in a new DHSS document, *Child Abuse — A Study of Inquiry Reports 1973-1981,* London: H.M.S.O., 1982. There is a fuller list in D.A. Jones, *Understanding Child Abuse,* Sevenoaks: Hodder and Stoughton, 1982, 290-92.

**65.** A rather similar point is made by J. Howells, *Remember Maria,* London: Butterworths, 1974.

**66.** *Op. cit.,* note 2.

**67.** *Idem,* para. 4.281.

**68.** *Idem,* para. 4.325.

**69.** *Idem,* para. 4.328.

**70.** There is a good description of the Bristol service, the most fully developed in England, in Lisa Parkinson, "Bristol Courts Family Conciliation Service," 12 *Family Law* 13-16 (1982).

**71.** See, *op. cit.,* note 2, para. 4.390.

**72.** I use this sexist expression deliberately since I believe it is within the spirit of the report. Also, I am not aware of a neutral term.

73. See J. Thorpe, *Social Enquiry Reports,* London: H.M.S.O., 1979.

74. See generally 9 *Family Law* 50 (1979), particularly the case of *Re C* (1973) discussed therein. See also *R v. R* (1978) 8 *Family Law* 169 and *J v. J* (1979) 9 *Family Law* 91.

75. Extended to all undefended cases in 1977. See Matrimonial Causes Rules, r. 33(3), 48. See S.M. Cretney, *Principles of Family Law,* London: Sweet and Maxwell, 1979, 159-63.

76. E. Elston et al., "Judicial Hearings of Undefended Divorce Petitions," 38 *M.L.R.* 609 (1975).

77. See M.D.A. Freeman, "Divorce Without Legal Aid," 6 *Family Law* 255 (1976).

78. For example, R.L. Abel, "Delegalization: A Critical Review of Its Ideology, Manifestations and Social Consequences," in E. Blankenburg et al. (eds.), *Alternative Rechtsformen und Alternativen Rechtssoziologie und Rechtstheorie,* Opladen: Westdeutscher Verlag, 27-47 (Jahrbuch fur Rechtssoziologie and Rechtstheorie Band 6). See also now, *op. cit.,* note 14, particularly vol. 1, chs. 7 and 10.

79. *Op. cit.,* note 18.

80. *From Max Weber: Essays in Sociology,* edited and translated by H. H. Gerth and C. Wright Mills. Copyright 1946 by Oxford University Press, Inc., renewed 1973 by Hans H. Gerth. Reprinted by permission of the publisher.

81. *Cf.* M. Horkheimer, *Eclipse of Reason,* New York: Seabury, 1974, 6.

82. See M. Galanter, "Legality and Its Discontents" in (ed.) E. Blankenburg et al., *op. cit.,* note 78, 11, and R. Abel, "Conservative, Conflict and Informal Justice," *Int. J. of Sociology of Law,* vol. 9, 245 (1981).

83. That is why "England" was such a problem for him. See A. Hunt, *The Sociological Movement In Law,* London: Macmillan, 1978, 122-28 for a discussion of this.

84. *Economy and Society,* (eds.) Guenther Roth and Claus Wittich, Berkeley: University of California Press, 1968, vol. II, 893.

85. "Form and Substance In Private Law," [1976] 89 *Harvard Law Review,* 1,685-1,778.

86. *Whigs and Hunters,* London: Allen Lane, 1975, 262-63.

87. *Idem,* 266.

88. See M.D.A. Freeman, "The Rights of Children Who Do 'Wrong'," (1981) 21 *British Journal of Criminology,* 210-29; A. Morris et al., *Justice for Children,* London: Macmillan, 1980.

89. See generally W. Vaughan Stapleton and Lee H. Teitelbaum, *In Defense of Youth,* New York: Russell Sage Foundation, 1972.

90. See P. Brown and T. Bloomfield (eds.), *Legality and Community,* Aberdeen: Aberdeen People's Press, 1979 and A. Morris and M. McIsaac, *Juvenile Justice,* London: Heinemann, 1978.

91. Never fully implemented. The current trend is increasingly punitive though a veneer of welfarism remains. The *Criminal Justice Act 1982* reverses some of the trends embodied in the 1969 legislation.

92. 387 U.S.I. (1967). See also *Breed v. Jones* 421 U.S. 519 (1975) and *cf. McKeiver v. Pennsylvania* 403 U.S. 538 (1971).

93. Juvenile courts were once hailed as the best plan "for the conservation of human life and happiness ever conceived by civilised man" *per* C.W. Hoffman, "Organisation of Family Courts, with Special References to the Juvenile Courts," in J. Addams (ed.), *The Child, the Clinic and the Court,* New York: New Republic, 1927.

94. Notably by M.J. Horwitz, *The Transformation of American Law 1780-1860,*

24          *The Settlement of Disputes*

Cambridge: Harvard U.P., 1977. See also D. Kennedy, "Legal Formality," 2 *Journal of Legal Studies* 351-98 (1973) and R.M. Unger, *Law in Modern Society,* New York: Free Press, 1976, 203 *et seq.*

95. Those who propagated the juvenile court may have been moved by other considerations. See Anthony Platt's analysis in *op. cit.,* note 48.

96. Alvin Toffler's phrase (see *The Third Wave,* London: Collins, 1980). In using his expression, I am falling in with his description of a trend, not adopting his agenda, about which I make no comment.

97. See D. Sugarman, "Theory and Practice in Law and History" in (ed.) B. Fryer et al., *Law, State and Society,* London: Croom Helm, 1981, 70.

98. For example, Hans Kelsen, Léon Duguit and Yevgeny Pashukanis.

99. See R.M. Unger, *Law in Modern Society,* New York: Free Press, 1976; Karl Klare, "Law-Making as Praxis," 40 *Telos* 123-35 (1979).

100. Thus reversing the trend from status to contract depicted by Sir Henry Maine in *Ancient Law.* It hardly needs emphasizing that today's "status" is very different from the feudalistic motion in Maine's historical analysis. See, further, A. Fraser, "The Legal Theory We Need Now," *Socialist Review,* no. 40-41, 147-87 (1978).

101. See the two very different treatments of P. Nonet, *Administrative Justice: Advocacy and Change in a Government Agency,* New York: Russell Sage Foundation, 1969 and L. Scarman, *English Law — The New Dimension,* London: Stevens, 1974.

102. See G. Gilmore, *The Death of Contract,* Columbus: Ohio State University Press, 1974.

103. See N. Kittrie, *op. cit.,* note 19.

104. *Cf.* K. Polanyi, *The Great Transformation,* Boston: Beacon Press, 1944, ch. 4.

105. "Beyond the French Revolution: Communist Socialism and the Rule of Law" 21 *University of Toronto L.J.* 109-40 (1971).

106. There had previously been a move from *Gemeinschaft* law. The terms, of course, derive from Ferdinand Tönnies (see translation as *Community and Association*): similar ideas are found in the writing of Karl Renner.

107. "Beyond Bourgeois Individualism: the Contemporary Crisis in Law and Legal Ideology" in (eds.) E. Kamenka and R.S. Neale, *Feudalism, Capitalism and Beyond,* London: Edward Arnold, 1975, 140. *Cf.* D. Neiken, "Is there a Crisis in Law and Legal Ideology?" 9 *J. Law and Soc.* 177 (1982).

108. See R.M. Unger, *op. cit.,* note 94, 216 and F. Neumann, *The Democratic and Authoritarian State,* New York: Macmillan, 1957. Unger refers also to German writing by Friedrich Dessauer, Justus Hedemann and Rudolf Echterholter (see 292-93).

109. See, for example, J. Alderson, *Policing Freedom,* London: Macdonald and Evans, 1979 or "The Case For Community Policing" in (eds.) D. Cowell, T. Jones and J. Young, *Policing the Riots,* London: Junction Books, 1982, ch. 8, *cf.* C. Moore and J. Brown, *Community Versus Crime,* London: Bedford Square Press, 1981.

110. See Z. Bankowski and G. Mungham, "Laypeople and Lawpeople and the Administration of the Lower Courts," *Int. J. of Sociology of Law,* vol. 9, 85-100 (1981).

111. See, for example, D. McGillis and J. Mullen, *Neighbourhood Justice Centers: An Analysis of Potential Models:* Washington D.C.: Govt. Printing Office, 1977; Frank Sander, *Report on the National Conference on Minor Dispute Resolution,* Chicago: American Bar Association, 1977 (also his "Varieties of Dispute Processing," 70 F.R.D. 79 (1976)); L. Nader, *No Access to Law: Alternatives to the American Judicial System,* New York: Academic Press, 1980. See also Benson Royal Commission on Legal Services, London: H.M.S.O. 1979, Cmnd. 7,648, ch. 43. On the concept of "neighbourhood" see

R. Danzig, "Toward the Creation of a Complementary Decentralised System of Justice," 26 *Stanford L.R.* 1 (1973).

**112.** *Per* Stanley Cohen, "Human Warehouses: The Future of Our Prisons?", *New Society*, vol. 30, no. 632 (14 November 1974), 407 at 410.

**113.** Stanley Cohen's expression. See "Human Warehouses: The Future of Our Prisons?", *New Society*, vol. 30, no. 632 (14 November 1974), 407.

**114.** *Per* Barton L. Ingraham and Gerald W. Smith, "The Use of Electronics in the Observation and Control of Human Behaviour, and Its Possible Use in Rehabitation and Parole," *Issues in Criminology* 35–53 (Fall Issue, 1972).

**115.** "Culture and Administration," 37 *Telos* 93, 101–102 (1978).

**116.** *Op. cit.,* note 20, at 347. See also Stanley Cohen, "Prisons and the Future of Control Systems: From Concentration to Dispersal," in (eds.) M. Fitzgerald, P. Halmos, J. Muncie and D. Zeldin, *Welfare in Action,* London: R.K.P., 1977, 217–28.

# [14]
# Is The Jewish *Get* Any Business of The State?

## Introduction

Whether the Jewish *get*[1] is any business of the state is a subspecies of a much more fundamental question: is religion any business of the state? And, if it is, over what aspects of religion should the state have jurisdiction: faith? doctrine? practice? These are questions deeply rooted in history, in the Reformation and its aftermath, in the Enlightenment and its nineteenth-century legacies, Catholic emancipation, Jewish participation in Parliament, civil marriages, the opening up of university education to non-Anglicans. They are also questions which prick the conscience of the present, when issues like royal marriages (that the law here is incompatible with the Human Rights Act 1998[2] seems to have disturbed no one) or whether religious leaders should continue to occupy seats in the House of Lords[3] (would anyone defend a similar privilege for (say) university vice-chancellors or company chairmen or the chief conductors of the major orchestras?) are debated. The disestablishment question, even in today's largely secular society, is rarely raised: can, we might ask, if we wished to be both mischievous and Kelsenian, the *Grundnorm* change?[4]

These are big issues and they are (unfortunately) beyond the immediate remit of this paper. But the big questions cannot be altogether sidelined. For, if the *get*, a Jewish religious practice, is to be 'the business of the state', what other Jewish religious practices should come within the state's province? Only those which impact on status, thus justifying a control over Jewish marriages?[5] (But how far should this go? Arguably, the ban on *agunot* marrying, upheld by Jewish ecclesiastical authorities, is a breach of the Human Rights Act 1998.[6]) Those which relate to the

---

[1] See Glossary at the end of this chapter.

[2] Bans on marrying a divorcee and marrying a Catholic clearly are incompatible with Articles 8 and 12.

[3] *A House for the Future*, Cm. 4534 (London, 2000). This proposes a reduction (from twenty-six to sixteen) in representation by bishops but would increase religious representation to thirty-one.

[4] Can a just state express neutrality among pluralist conceptions of the good while favouring a particular conception? On the question, see Bruce Ackerman, *Reconstructing American Law* (Cambridge, Mass., 1984), 359.

[5] As in the Marriage Act 1949. This in fact grants Jews privileges and these could, and perhaps should, be removed if the rabbinical authorities refuse to reinterpret Jewish divorce law so as to eradicate its injustices.

[6] This hinges upon whether the rabbinical authorities are 'public authorities' under

366

'public' realm[7] (conceding that the private–public dichotomy is both illusory and state-constructed)?[8] This would make *brit milah*, a quintessentially private act, none of the state's business and that cannot be right (any practice which could harm must be of concern to the state, though this would have no difficulty in endorsing the practice once it situated it within cultural norms and a broad-based interpretation of what constitutes harm[9]).

## Approaches to the *Get*

English law could take a number of different approaches towards the *get*:

- it could recognize it as having the full consequences of a divorce;[10]
- it could refuse to recognize it at all;[11]
- it could recognize it for some purposes but not others;[12]
- it could adopt a laissez-faire policy towards it;[13]
- it could adopt obstructive policies towards it;[14]
- it could seek to assist the process whereby a *get* is given and received;[15]
- it could refuse to assist the *get* process.[16]

section 6(3)(b). The Lord Chancellor (*Hansard*, HL, vol. 583, col. 800) indicated that churches were when they were performing functions 'of a public nature'. This goes beyond *R. v. Chief Rabbi, ex parte Wachmann* [1992] 1 WLR 1036 (the case concerned a declaration by the chief rabbi that a rabbi was morally and religiously unfit to hold rabbinical office). It was held that this was non-justiciable because 'the court is hardly in a position to regulate what is essentially a religious function' and that it should 'be wary of entering so self-evidently sensitive an area . . . [as] adjudicating upon matters intimate to a religious community'. While section 13 (on which, see P. Cumper, 'The Protection of Religious Rights under Section 13 of the Human Rights Act 1998' (2000) *PL* 254) might well confirm the *Wachmann* ruling, an argument could certainly be mounted that in banning *agunot* from remarrying a function of a public nature is being carried out and that this is not one protected by section 13. On human rights issues more generally, see E. Tager, 'The Chained Wife' (1999) 17 *Netherlands Q. of Human Rights* 425.

[7] On public and private, see M. Freeman, 'Towards a Critical Theory of Family Law' (1985) 38 *CLP* 153.

[8] Well illustrated in Susan B. Boyd, *Challenging the Public/Private Divide* (Toronto, 1997).

[9] I have argued this: see M. Freeman, 'A Child's Right to Circumcision', *British Journal of Urology International*, 83 (1999), suppl. 1, 74.

[10] It does this where a *get* can be regarded as effective to dissolve a marriage (as in Israel, provided jurisdictional criteria are satisfied).

[11] But only on public policy grounds.

[12] See *Preger v. Preger* (1926) 42 TLR 281; *Leeser v. Leeser, The Times*, 5 Feb. 1955; and *Joseph v. Joseph* [1953] 2 All ER 710.

[13] But this would ignore the interests of the vulnerable and expose them to unfair bargaining and even blackmail.

[14] This has never been the policy. But if it should be shown that the *get* process is incompatible with the Human Rights Act 1998, it might be argued that this was now the agenda.

[15] The Family Law Act 1996, section 9(3) was so designed, as is legislation in New York, Canada, and South Africa.

[16] This was the policy in England before 1996. An attempt to insert a '*get* clause' into the Matrimonial Causes Act 1973 in 1984 thus failed.

## The Jewish Get *and the State*                      367

My own views on the approach that English law should adopt have changed over the years. Back in the mid-1980s I spearheaded a committee under the aegis of the chief rabbi and wrote a report which examined various models.[17] This recommended that legislation should be passed to facilitate the *get* process where one spouse, usually but not invariably the husband,[18] was recalcitrant. More than ten years later there was legislation passed with this objective in view. It was part of the Family Law Act 1996.[19] The implementation of the relevant part of this Act has been held up for reasons quite unconnected with the *get* provision. As a result, in 2000 there was a private member's bill introduced in the House of Lords (the initiative of Lord Lester of Herne Hill) which seeks to sever the provision in the 1996 Act and pass it as a separate measure.[20] This passed in the House of Lords but failed to make progress in the House of Commons.[21] The provision in the 1996 Act (and the 2000 Bill) is defective in a number of ways. It is accordingly of limited value and may end up as no more than an exercise in symbolic politics. I have expounded on these problems elsewhere[22] and will desist from saying more in this paper than is strictly necessary to my thesis.

My views have changed. The *get* is a deeply flawed institution; it discriminates against women; it has become a vehicle for blackmail and other despicable practices (which the *dayanim* connive at, perhaps even encourage); and the solutions lie within a dynamic interpretation of Jewish law were the halakhic authorities prepared to seek them out. It is sad to reflect upon the dilemma of a religious minority which, having forgotten its liberal heritage, calls upon the dominant culture to bale it out.[23] The world Jewish community, it is clear to me, should not be going cap in hand to the legislatures of the world, but rather rediscovering its own sources, and interpreting these in a principled but creative way to tackle the problem which its halakhic authorities—and not the civil states of the world—have created.[24] The response, so often heard, that these religious authorities can do nothing about the problem, that they are shackled (I

---

[17] 'Divorce and Religious Barriers to Marriage', ms, 1985.

[18] Some wives are known to refuse to accept *gittim*. See Helen Jacobus, 'When a Woman Refuses', *Jewish Chronicle*, 27 Aug. 1999, 22.

[19] Family Law Act 1996, section 9(3): I fully annotated this in M. Freeman, *The Family Law Act 1996* (London, 1996).

[20] Divorce (Religious Marriages) Bill 2000.

[21] See *Hansard*, HL, vol. 614, cols. 1241–63; vol. 615, cols. 505–9; the Bill was talked out by Eric Forth MP when it reached the Commons. The Bill was discussed briefly by David Pannick, 'How to Make a Jewish Divorce a Civil Divorce', *The Times* (Law suppl.), 1 Aug. 2000, 15. On the failure in the House of Commons, see Helen Jacobus, 'Recriminations Follow Failure of Agunot Bill', *Jewish Chronicle*, 28 July 2000, 60.

[22] See Michael Freeman, 'The Jewish Law of Divorce' (2000) *IFL* 58, 59–60.

[23] This statement, first written by me in 1996, was quoted with approval by Wall J in *N v. N (Jurisdiction: Pre-Nuptial Agreement)* [1999] 2 FLR 745.

[24] And see Eliezer Berkovits, *Jewish Women in Time and Torah* (Hoboken, NJ, 1990).

368

avoid, for obvious reasons, saying 'chained') to laws they cannot change, is simply not true. The laws[25] of the *get* have changed and they can change again. Indeed, I would go further: if the *get* cannot be reinterpreted to create a system where men and women are treated equally, where the opportunities for blackmail are eliminated, where barriers to remarriage are removed, the *get* must, like polygamy a thousand years ago,[26] be abolished. It has no more place in a humane religion than do animal sacrifices (which will, of course, never be restored[27]).

But it may be thought I am getting ahead of myself and should offer an explanation of the *get* itself.

## The *Get*

According to Jewish law a marriage cannot be dissolved unless a husband gives his wife and she receives, a bill of divorcement (a *get*). The document is today given under the surveillance of a rabbinical court (a Beth Din), but it is not strictly a religious act, although it takes place in a religious context. The concept was developed by Jews when they ruled themselves. For much of its history the practice of the *get* put Jews ahead of the peoples around them who did not have divorce at all (the small Jewish community in this country did not, with the rest of the population, have to use legislative divorce until 1858 and it would seem their *gittim* were recognized as divorces).[28]

The *get* has always caused problems. These have been exacerbated today with the decline of the tight control of the Jewish *kehilah*, with secularism, and also the decline of marriage. The problem has also come into sharper focus with Jewish acculturation to the norms around them, so that divorce among Jews is much more common than it was only a generation ago.

The problems are mainly caused when a husband refuses to give his wife a *get*. A woman who has been civilly divorced is still regarded, in the eyes of Jewish law, as married. She cannot remarry and if she does so (in a

[25] In this I include both the written law (in the Torah) and the oral law (expounded in the Talmud).

[26] Ze'ev Falk, *Jewish Matrimonial Law in the Middle Ages* (Oxford, 1966) considers this the most important reform ever in Jewish family law. In his view it was influenced by Christianity, which was (rightly) critical of polygyny within Judaism.

[27] There are, however, incredibly *yeshivot* (religious colleges) in Israel 'reclaiming this heritage' in time for the restoration of the Temple.

[28] See M. D. A. Freeman, 'Jews and the Law of Divorce in England' (1981) 4 *Jewish Law Annual* 276, and *Moss* v. *Smith* (1840) 1 Man and G 228. It was only in 1866 that the registrar-general decided that he could not recognize a Jewish divorce as valid. Even so, until 1973 Jews domiciled elsewhere than in the United Kingdom could dissolve their marriage by a *get* (see *Har-Shefi* v. *Har-Shefi* [1953 P 161]). This privilege ended with the Domicile and Matrimonial Proceedings Act 1973, section 16(1); and see now the Family Law Act 1986, section 44(1).

The Jewish Get *and the State*                      369

civil ceremony) any children of the new union are *mamzerim* (which translates roughly as bastards, though the legal discrimination against them
exceeds common law penalties). She is literally chained to her (ex-)husband
(she is an *agunah*). She is a hostage to a dead marriage, and, unfortunately,
like other hostages she can be held to ransom. As I have indicated, it is not
uncommon for women to secure their release by paying large sums of
money extorted from them by acts that amount to blackmail. In one case
reported in June 2000 a *dayan* negotiated a *get* in return for the husband
receiving £30,000:[29] in another widely reported case last year Dayan
Berkovits negotiated a charitable donation in return for a *get*[30] (the document was reproduced in the *Jewish Chronicle* and Berkovits defended his
actions in a subsequent issue[31]). The spectre of *dayanim* participating in
these negotiations is unseemly at best. At worst, it corrupts the whole
process. And, if they only but knew, it alienates. Why should a couple
about to marry agree to a prenuptial agreement, referring any disputes to a
Beth Din, when they become aware of the ways this operates?

The source of the *get* is in the book of Deuteronomy.[32] This takes the
institution of the *get* for granted: it had clearly grown up as a practice.[33]
Deuteronomy codified this custom and introduced a new norm: a man
who had given his wife a *get* was not to be allowed to remarry her upon
the death of her second husband or after that husband, too, had divorced
her. Thus, there is no biblical injunction mandating the giving or receiving
of a *get*.[34] Deuteronomy gives the husband complete discretion. He could
divorce his wife at will, without her consent, and without more than a
semblance of justification. The Talmud subsequently imposed some restrictions upon him. He could not divorce her if she were of unsound mind,
and all husbands who wished to divorce wives had to show fault, although
the minimal nature of this is illustrated by the example given by the school
of Hillel—the burning of his food being apparently sufficient.[35] Concern at

---

[29] *Jewish Chronicle*, 2 June 2000, 1 and 64.        [30] Ibid., 9 July 1999, 27.

[31] Ibid., 16 July 1999.

[32] Deut. 24; 1–4. And therefore post-Mosaic.

[33] It is probable that the concept of the *get* was not known in Israelite society much before
the late days of the Kingdom of Judah. See Yair Zakovitch, 'The Woman's Rights in the
Biblical Law of Divorce' (1981) 4 *Jewish Law Annual* 28, 43.

[34] But there is evidence that a wife could divorce her husband when her basic needs were
not supplied or she was deserted by him. Exodus 21: 7–11 gives Hebrew maidservants this
right, and there is no reason to suppose a free woman's rights would be inferior. See G. R.
Driver and J. C. Miles, *The Babylonian Laws* (Oxford, 1952), i. 292–3, and J. H. Otwell,
*And Sarah Laughed* (Philadelphia, 1977), 121. This seems to have been totally forgotten by
today's halakhic authorities for within it may lie part of the solution to the problem of the
*agunah*. Documents from the Cairo Geniza (10th and 11th cents.) indicate that women there
too initiated divorce suits: see M. A. Friedman, 'Divorce upon the Wife's Demand as
Reflected in the Manuscripts from the Cairo Geniza' (1981) 4 *Jewish Law Annual* 103.

[35] There is a difference here between the school of Hillel, which says just this ('even if she
spoiled a dish for him'), and that of Shammai, where the need for the husband to find
'unchastity' in his wife is emphasized (this is consistent with Deuteronomy, where 'some

370

the unequal distribution of power eventually led rabbinical scholars to take action to mitigate the hardship of wives. In the eleventh century Rabbenu Gershom (c.960–1028) enacted a decree that prohibited a husband from divorcing his wife against her will, subject to specific exceptions. These were wider than what we would understand as the traditional offences.[36] An accompanying decree banned polygamy: this was significant because before this a man could remarry without divorcing his first wife, though if he did not give her a *get* she could not remarry.[37]

The Babylonian Talmud had also given women the power to demand a divorce from their husbands under certain circumstances.[38] These included the possession of certain physical defects, such as a loathsome disease or revolting disfigurement, the husband's involvement in a malodorous occupation, impotence or sterility, refusal to support, habitual unfaithfulness, and apostasy.[39] Further interpretation today would surely extend this list by analogy: one commentator suggested to domestic violence[40] and, if so, then also to sexual abuse of children. But are these interpretations used, since many husbands would surely come within the list? The fiction was also adopted that, although the husband must grant the *get* of his own free will, the Beth Din might apply coercion to him where the wife was entitled, under the interpretation of Jewish law, to a divorce. This was explained by one of the greatest of rabbinical authorities, Moses Maimonides (1135–1204), thus: the recalcitrant husband really desires to comply with Jewish law, but is prevented from so doing by his evil disposition. Maimonides also saw the need to facilitate a divorce for a wife who found her husband repulsive. He wrote: 'they force him to divorce her immediately because she is not like a captive woman who must have sexual relations with one whom she hates'.[41] It is a sad reflection of our times that Jewish law was interpreted more liberally in the twelfth century

---

uncleanness' is stipulated in 24: 1). See, further, I. Haut, *Divorce in Jewish Law and Life* (Hoboken, NJ, 1983), 19. See also James L. Kugel, *The Bible as it Was* (Cambridge, Mass., 1997), 513–18.

[36] The exceptions were (1) physical defects that preclude cohabitation; (2) no children after ten years and he has no other children (this is at issue in the case of *Cheni* v. *Cheni* [1965] P. 85 and is misunderstood in the film *Kadosh* (2000), (3) she causes him to violate a religious precept; (4) she acts immodestly; (5) she dishonours him; (6) adultery.

[37] As to which, see I. Breitowitz, 'The Plight of the *Agunah*: A Study in Halakha, Contract and the First Amendment' (1992) 51 *Maryland Law Review* 312, 323. See also I. Breitowitz, *Between Civil and Religious Law: The Plight of the Agunah in American Society* (Westport, Conn., 1993).

[38] See Haut, *Divorce in Jewish Law*, 25. See also E. S. Nadel, 'New York's Get Laws: A Constitutional Analysis', (1993) 27 *Columbia J. of Law and Soc. Problems* 55, 59.

[39] *Mishnah Ketubot 70a.*

[40] M. Frishtik, 'Physical and Sexual Violence by Husbands as a Reason for Imposing Divorce in Jewish Law' (1991) 9 *Jewish Law Annual* 145 argues for this.

[41] Quoted in Berkovits, *Jewish Women.*

than it is today.[42] Can this be said of any other legal system? It was because of the opinions of Rabbenu Tam, a contemporary of Maimonides, that this liberal interpretation was lost and subsequently forgotten.[43] And the primary objective of Rabbenu Tam was apparently to preserve the institution of marriage and minimize the number of divorces in the intellectual and religious climate of twelfth-century France.

But, these reforms notwithstanding, the position of Jewish women remains inferior to that of men for two important reasons. Firstly, under certain conditions a husband can invoke a procedure known as *heter me'ah rabbanim* (the permission of 100 rabbis), enabling him to circumvent Gershom's decree, which bans polygamy and requires the wife's consent to a divorce. No such procedure is available to the wife, who can never remarry according to Halakha without a *get*.[44] There are modern, if infrequent, examples of the *heter*.[45] Secondly, the consequences of violating Jewish law and remarrying without first complying with the *get* requirement are much more severe for the wife than the husband. A 'wife' without a *get* is still 'married' to her husband—despite a civil decree of divorce. This means that, according to Jewish law, she cannot remarry. If she remarries civilly (or in a synagogue which has relaxed the *get* rules) or if she cohabits, she and her partner are guilty of adultery. She forfeits (in Jewish law only, of course) her alimony rights and, even if her 'husband' subsequently delivers to her a *get*, she is barred from marrying her partner. But the husband, who is separated from his wife without granting her a *get*, is not similarly stigmatized. So, if he remarries in a civil ceremony (or a non-Orthodox synagogue) or cohabits, he does not commit adultery. He is technically 'guilty' of polygamy. And if he has children by his new partner, they are not regarded as *mamzerim* (as hers inevitably would be). Furthermore, if he subsequently delivers a *get* to his wife, he can marry the woman whom he has civilly married or with whom he has been cohabiting. Thus, the consequences of failing to obtain a *get* can be disastrous for a religious Jewish woman: the consequences for a man in similar circumstances are relatively minor in comparison.

Jewish law can be reformed by creative and dynamic interpretation. Further rights could be given to women. Again I have argued this elsewhere, as have others, and these arguments, which are internal to the

[42] My view to this effect was cited by Lord Lester of Herne Hill: see *Hansard*, HL, vol. 614, col. 1244.
[43] According to Berkovits, *Jewish Women*. S. Riskin, *Women and Jewish Divorce: The Rebellious Wife, the Agunah and the Right of Women to Initiate Divorce in Jewish Law: A Halakhic Solution* (Hoboken, NJ, 1989), p. xi, argues that Rabbenu Tam's approach was always a minority position.
[44] And see Breitowitz, 'The Plight of the *Agunah*', 325.
[45] An example formed the basis of *Singer v. Union of Orthodox Rabbis of the United States and Canada* (New York Supreme Court; see www.jlaw.com/Recent/singer/html). The husband paid a $50,000 bribe to the UOR to obtain a *heter*.

372

halakhic system, are outside the scope of this paper.[46] It has to be said, though, that the rabbinical authorities—a self-perpetuating male elite over whom the Jewish community has no control—are resistant to reform. Indeed, insistent that reform is impossible. They refuse to resort to fictions, though Maimonides had no difficulty in doing so, and they themselves have no difficulty when the problem is one they wish to solve. If they have found ways round carrying on the sabbath (the *eruv*) and retaining their whisky over Passover (the sale of *chametz*)—and for both fictions are employed—they could find solutions to the plight of the *agunah* as well (even if again fictions have to be used). Instead, they resort to expedients like the prenuptial agreement. Some have approved 'naming and shaming procedures'. Meanwhile, the chief rabbi claims the problem is exaggerated (there are, he says, only fifteen *agunot* in the country[47]) and prefers to tackle the problem case by case rather than by getting to its causes. The individualistic approach would be hopeless if there were only fifteen cases: no one knows how many there are, and many never surface, but estimates put the figure at least ten times this suggested number.

## Using the Ordinary Law of the Land

So, how is the state to respond? What are the arguments for invoking state assistance to alleviate the problem? The courts first tried to assist in 1969. In *Brett* v. *Brett*[48] a wealthy husband had made it clear to his wife, who was divorcing him not long after their marriage, that he would not give her a *get*. Phillimore LJ made the point that the husband's refusal was motivated by his desire to use it as a bargaining counter against the wife's maintenance demands. Mrs Brett was lucky to find a bench of English judges: the *dayanim*, as we have seen, might have reacted differently. The Court used its power to award financial provision to coerce the husband into granting a *get*. What they did was to increase the sum payable in the event that the husband did not grant his wife a *get* within a stipulated period. They offered no clear justification for this: the reason was just 'obvious'—justice demanded that he not be allowed to treat his wife in this

[46] M. Freeman, 'The Dayanim Must Act', *Jewish Chronicle*, 17 Dec. 1999, 27. For other solutions, see J. David Bleich, 'Modern-Day Agunot: A Proposed Remedy' (1981) 4 *Jewish Law Annual* 167. 'Modern' debates can be traced back to I. Epstein, 'The Problem of the Agunah: An Attempted Solution', *Jewish Chronicle*, 31 Jan. 1936, which provoked a leading article headed 'A Public Scandal' on 7 Feb. 1936.

[47] *London Jewish News* (28 Apr. 2000). Jack Nusan Porter, *Women in Chains* (Northvale, NJ, 1995), believes about 5% of all Orthodox marriages in the United States 'end in the *agunah* stage' (p. xiii).

[48] [1969] 1 All ER 1007. Roman courts in Roman Judaea were involved in compelling Jews to carry out decisions of Jewish courts. See Aharon Oppenheimer, 'Jewish Penal Authority in Roman Judaea' in Martin Goodman (ed.), *Jews in the Graeco-Roman World* (Oxford, 1998), 181, 186–7.

way. It was as if the courts saw the *get* as part of a holistic process of divorce. Questions of jurisdiction and the scope of the Court's powers were not debated. The ruling was acceptable to the British rabbinical authorities in 1969, but they no longer accept it. Although a Beth Din may apply coercion where a *get* is required by Jewish law, they do not accept that a secular court may force a husband to give his wife a *get*. If they do so, the *get* which results is *me'useh* (given under duress and accordingly void). The rabbinical authorities now say that a *get* granted in similar circumstances to those in *Brett* would be *me'useh*. Indeed, they have been saying this since the mid-1980s (when I first became involved with the chief rabbi's committee) and probably for some time before. Whether the change of attitude is retrospective has not been vouchsafed. If retrospective, it is also not clear to when. But, even if the *Brett* solution were acceptable to today's interpretation of Jewish law in England—and note how swiftly changes can come—it would only be of limited value. Not all recalcitrant husbands are wealthy, and some might pay the additional sum seeing it as a burden like tax and their wives would be no better off.

Since *Brett* v. *Brett* the courts have involved themselves on a couple of other occasions. Thus, it has been made clear that if a husband wants a divorce based on two years' separation, the wife can make her consent conditional on the granting of a *get*.[49] And, further, in *N* v. *N*[50] Wall J expressed the view that courts have the power to refuse to permit a decree nisi of divorce to be made absolute on the application of a spouse who is refusing to cooperate in the grant and receipt of a *get*. This *per curiam* remark became the basis for a well-publicized refusal by Judge Viljoen, sitting in the Watford County Court in December 1999, to make a decree absolute where the husband was refusing to give his wife a *get*.[51] These judges are to be applauded, but their humanity and inventiveness reckons without the dogmatism and conservatism of those who interpret Jewish law in England today. I understand that the husband in the Watford case has now given his wife a *get*, but I wonder what the *dayanim* will make of it. Could not the husband say that he only gave his wife the *get* because of duress applied to him by a County Court judge? Is not the *get* therefore *me'useh*?

The courts have been unwilling to refuse divorces on the ground that dissolution of the marriage will cause the respondent grave hardship and that in all the circumstances it would be wrong to dissolve the marriage.[52] This defence only applies to one type of divorce (that based on the fact of five years' separation[53]) and, so far as is known, has never been raised by a

---

[49] *Beales* v. *Beales* [1972] Fam. 210.    [50] At 757.

[51] *O* v. *O* (*Jurisdiction: Jewish Divorce*) [2000] 2 FLR 147.

[52] *Rukat* v. *Rukat* [1975] Fam. 63; *Banik* v. *Banik* [1973] 1 WLR 860. Cf *N* v. *N*, 757 (Wall J envisages 'circumstances' in which refusal to initiate the *get* procedure could amount to hardship).

[53] The Matrimonial Causes Act 1973, section 5, only applies to section 1(2)(e) divorces.

374

potential *agunah*. But it is doubtful if it would bite anyway, since the grave hardship is not caused by the civil divorce but by a refusal to give a religious divorce.[54] When the divorce provisions of the Family Law Act 1996 come into operation (if they ever do), the gravity standard will be lowered: it will only be necessary to show 'substantial' hardship and it will apply to all divorces.[55] *Agunot* will clearly suffer 'substantial' hardships, but again this will not be attributable to the civil divorce order, and therefore it may be doubted whether a court would be right to refuse a divorce to a recalcitrant husband.

These examples of judicial (or potential judicial) intervention all use the ordinary law of the land. They extend no special privileges to the Jewish population.

In the United States—which has, of course, a much larger Jewish population—other judicial strategies have been employed. That these have been successful despite claims that they infringe the First Amendment[56] suggests a fortiori that they should succeed in England. Although I do not think they will, I will briefly discuss them.

First, attempts have been made specifically to enforce civil agreements to cooperate in religious divorce proceedings. These failed initially (usually on the grounds that the contract was too vague[57]), but by 1977 the courts were granting specific performance,[58] even in one case where the husband was prepared to give a *get*, albeit not one from the religious authorities of the wife's allegiance.[59]

A second strategy has been to seek to enforce the *ketubah*. This sets out the obligations that a Jewish husband undertakes with respect to his wife, and is presented by the groom to the bride during the marriage ceremony. One of his promises (the *ketubah* is standardized, and he has no choice) is to pay his wife a certain sum of money upon divorce. The courts have

---

[54] I owe this point to Rhona Schuz, 'Divorce and Ethnic Minorities', in M. Freeman (ed.), *Divorce: Where Next?* (Aldershot, 1996), 131, 135.

[55] Family Law Act 1996 s. 10. It is looking increasingly likely that this Act will never be implemented. It was announced by the lord chancellor in Jan. 2001 that the divorce provisions of the Act will not be implemented, and will be repealed. Ironically, had it been implemented, the English law of divorce would have looked more like the Jewish! (See M. Freeman, 'Divorce Gospel Style', (1997) 27 *Family Law* 413.)

[56] See J. H. Choper, 'The Religion Clauses of the First Amendment: Reconciling the Conflict', (1980) 41 *Univ. of Pittsburgh LR* 673; M. J. Perry, *Love and Power: The Role of Religion and Morality in American Politics* (New York, 1991).

[57] For failures, see *Koeppel v. Koeppel* 138 N.Y.S. 2d 366 (Sup. Ct. 1954); *Margulies v. Margulies* 344 N.Y.S. 2d 482 (App. Div. 1973) (in this case the husband was nevertheless fined for contempt of court in refusing to carry out his promise); *Rubin v. Rubin* 348 N.Y.S. 2d 61 (Fam. Ct. 1973) (where the 'clean hands' doctrine was used).

[58] *Waxstein v. Waxstein* 394 N.Y.S. 2d 253 (App. Div. 1977).

[59] *Scholl v. Scholl* 621 A. 2d 808 (1992) (Delaware Family Court). The husband was prepared to give his wife a Conservative *get*, but she wanted an Orthodox one. The marriage had been celebrated in an Orthodox synagogue and he said he wanted her to suffer 'since she had made him suffer' (p. 813).

regularly enforced the contract. Husbands have raised First Amendment arguments, but these have been dismissed, the courts accepting expert testimony that the delivery of a *get* is not a religious act, merely the severance of a contractual relationship.[60] In the leading case of *Avitzur v. Avitzur*[61] the highest court in New York enforced the *ketubah* in a 4–3 decision, and ordered the husband to appear before a Beth Din. It saw the *ketubah* as analogous to an arbitration agreement, the enforceability of which could be decided on the application of 'neutral principles of contract law, without reference to any religious principle'.[62] It saw the relief sought as 'simply to compel the defendant to perform a secular obligation to which he has contractually bound himself'.[63]

Thirdly, some courts in the United States have construed a husband's refusal to give his wife a *get* as tortious. The claim is that failure to deliver a *get* prevents the wife from remarrying and constitutes as a result an intentional infliction of emotional distress. Courts were initially unwilling to agree to this, but a court in New York in 1990 held that the wife's claim stated a valid cause of action.[64]

Australian courts have employed yet another strategy, that of the injunction. Australia's Family Law Act 1975 gives the courts the power to grant an injunction where it is just or convenient to do so, and to do this unconditionally or upon terms and conditions considered appropriate.[65] As in the United States, in Australia Church and State are constitutionally separated,[66] but this has not prevented Australian courts from granting mandatory injunctions ordering recalcitrant spouses to appear before a Beth Din. In *In the Marriage of Shulsinger*[67] it was said to be 'contrary to all notions of justice' to allow the husband to seek and obtain a civil divorce while refusing to relieve his wife from their Jewish marriage and 'to say that a court can do nothing'.[68] In *In the Marriage of Gwiazda* all

---

[60] *Minkin v. Minkin* 434 A. 2d 665 (N.J. Super. Ct. Ch. Div. 1981). Adultery was alleged by the husband in this case which, said the court, required him to deliver a *get*. In *Burns v. Burns* 538 A. 2d 438 (N. J. Super. Ct. Ch. Div. 1987) this was extended to a case where adultery was not alleged. (Courts in other US jurisdictions have followed this, though not the Court of Appeals in Arizona (*Victor v. Victor* 866 P. 2d 899 (1993) ).

[61] 446 N.E. 2d 136.　　　　　　　　　　　　　　　　　　[62] Ibid. 138.

[63] Ibid. The *ketubah* in this case was a Conservative one, which contains an additional clause in which the parties agree to recognize the authority of the Beth Din of the Rabbinical Assembly. A New Jersey court more recently followed the minority opinion on *Avitzur*: *Aflalo v. Aflalo* 295 N.J. Super. 527 (1996).

[64] *Weiss v. Goldfelder* N.Y.L.J. Oct. 26 1990, 21. Courts were initially unwilling to agree to this tortious claim: see *Perl v. Perl* 512 N.Y.S. 2d 372 (App. Div. 1987). S. D. Gluck, 'The Agunah in the American Legal System: Problems and Solutions', (1993) 31 *J. Fam. L.* 885, 906–13 discusses this.

[65] Family Law Act 1975, s. 114(3).

[66] Commonwealth Constitution, s. 116. A wide-ranging new article is Kent Greenawalt, 'Religious Law and Civil Law: Using Secular Law to Assure Observance of Practices with Religious Significance', (1998) 71 *S. California LR* 781.

[67] (1977) 2 Fam. L. R. 11, 611.　　　　　　　　　　　　[68] Ibid. 617.

376

the court was asked to do, said the judge, was to ensure a party (in this case a recalcitrant wife) submitted to the jurisdiction of a tribunal 'set up well beyond time immemorial ... by the religion of which that party is a professed adherent'.[69]

So far as is known none of these strategies has been employed in this country. Would any of them succeed? Should they do so? There can be no objection to invoking a tort remedy. The contractual remedies may cause greater problems. Although the American courts have overcome the difficulties, English courts might find contractual obligations of the *ketubah* couched in vague language, for example requiring a husband to act 'in accordance with the manner of Jewish men' too uncertain to merit enforcement. English courts might also have problems in upholding prenuptial agreements to appear before a Beth Din. On this, hitherto, there is only a first instance ruling. Wall J in *N* v. *N*, held that 'an agreement made prior to marriage which contemplates the steps the parties will take in the event of divorce or separation is ... contrary to public policy because it undermines the concept of marriage as a life-long union'.[70] I find this persuasive, though it uses a concept of marriage (a lifelong union) which is embedded within Christianity rather than Judaism. And Wall J did concede that agreements had 'evidential weight when the terms of the agreement are relevant to an issue before the court in subsequent proceedings to the divorce'.[71] It was argued that clauses in the agreement could be severed, in particular that the husband's agreement to attend a Beth Din and comply with their instructions was specifically enforceable against the husband as a matter of contract. But the judge held that 'Even if one divides up the prenuptial agreement in this case, and looks at the individual clauses separately, one cannot avoid the fundamental proposition that each is part of an agreement entered into before marriage to regulate the parties' affairs in the event of divorce. The public policy argument, therefore, continues to apply.'[72] The mandatory injunction runs up against the objection that the spouse to whom it is directed is being required to meet religious obligations. It is the clearest example of the state imposing religion on an individual. But Australia, as we have seen, has had no problem with it. And it has to be said that those who refuse to cooperate with the *get* requirement of Jewish law are rarely motivated by religious beliefs (in which I include anti-religious sentiments). As Breitowitz is surely right to notice:

---

[69] Unreported. No. M10631 of 1982 (23 Feb. 1983). My source for this is an unpublished paper by A. Strum, 'Jewish Divorce: What can the Civil Courts Do?' His article 'Jewish Divorce in Australian Family Law: The Enforceability of Jewish Nuptial and Prenuptial Contracts', (1991) 17 *Monash Univ. LR* 182 is most helpful on Australian sources and practice.

[70] At 752.　　　　　　　　[71] Ibid.　　　　　　　　[72] Ibid. 754.

## The Jewish Get *and the State* 377

The unwilling spouse's claim that the *get* law violates his free exercise rights [a reference in the US First Amendment] is further refuted in the vast majority of cases, where his refusal to give a *get* is not motivated by religious beliefs, but out of spite, or as a means of obtaining valuable concessions. Indeed, it is precisely because the husband knows that a *get* is needed that he is able to use it as a bargaining chip.[73]

Perhaps then only the tort strategy would succeed, and success here would depend on surmounting a number of barriers. As indicated already, there can be no objection to an action in tort: the *agunah* is as entitled to protection from intentionally inflicted injury as anyone else. The other remedies, however, raise, as legislative intervention does, the whole question of propriety. The American and Australian courts were not particularly troubled by this; at least the American courts were not once they had convinced themselves that entanglement in religious matters was not in violation of the First Amendment. In the leading case of *Avitzur* v. *Avitzur* the *ketubah* was seen as analogous to an arbitration agreement, the enforceability of which could be decided on the application of 'neutral principles of contract law, without reference to any religious principle'.[74] I doubt whether the analogies are all that close. Most *ketubot* (though not I think the one in *Avitzur*[75]) are in Aramaic, which virtually no spouses will understand. The terms are standard, vague, and archaic. And, most significantly, it is a strange contract where, as here, only one party is a party to it. The Australian court does at least adduce a reason to justify intervention: the denial of a *get* was, said the Court in *Shulsinger*, 'contrary to all notions of justice';[76] the injunction, said the Court in *Gwiazda*, would ensure that 'the court's dissolution of the marriage would be fully effective, not only in theory but in fact'.[77]

So we can return to the question already posed. Is the plight of the *agunah* any business of the state? Is it within the state's remit at all. What arguments are there to justify state entanglement in what appears to be a parochial issue?

### The State's Business?

There are a number of arguments.

First, it is indisputable that we are a multicultural society, a people of different religions and none. There is an established religion, but ironically fewer of its supposed adherents worship in its churches than is the case with several of the minority religions (including Judaism and Islam). Within a pluralistic society mutual toleration and acknowledgement of

[73] Breitowitz, 'The Plight of the *Agunah*', 395.
[75] It was a Conservative one.
[77] n. 69 above.
[74] At 138.
[76] At 617.

378

difference is preferable to the enforcement of a single standard of morality in those areas of life which do not harm others.[78] Those who posit this standard of liberalism envisage the 'others' to be outside the community of the practice in question. But here the flourishing of the lives of members of the community itself, in particular women, are frustrated by rules they have not made and cannot influence. The argument, as developed, says that Parliament and the courts should support the religious institutions of minorities. But there are distinctions to be drawn between non-interference and active support, and also between toleration and endorsement.[79] The case for tolerating the *get* process is strong, though arguments can be adduced against it. It is more difficult to justify upholding what many believe to be a tottering and discredited institution by using state machinery to support it. It is even more difficult to make out a case for endorsement, since that would amount to according legitimacy to the institution and practice of the *get*.

Secondly, it may be argued that the law allows Jews to marry according to their own marriage customs and practices. If, the argument goes, the state assists in the creation of marriages according to Jewish usages, then it should also offer assistance to those engaged in dissolving a Jewish marriage.

A further stage in this argument is that, since Jewish marriages are recognized, so should their divorce rules. This would enable those who marry 'according to the law of Moses and Israel'[80] to divorce according to the law of Deuteronomy (as interpreted or misinterpreted). As in Israel, a *get* would dissolve a marriage:[81] a civil decree of divorce would be otiose. It would follow (and this is not a slippery slope argument) that, since we allow Muslims to marry according to the tenets of their faith, we would also have to recognize the *talaq*.[82] If Jews were to be exempted from the civil laws of divorce, so would Muslims and any other groups with special provision for marriage (Quakers could create their own divorce machinery[83]). There is commendable logic to this argument and Rhona

---

[78] See Bhikhu Parekh, *Rethinking Multiculturalism* (Basingstoke, 2000). A good introduction to the debate is Susan Moller Okin, *Is Multiculturalism Bad for Women?* (Princeton, 1999).

[79] See Joseph Raz, *The Morality of Freedom* (Oxford, 1986); *Ethics in the Public Domain* (Oxford, 1994).

[80] The words of the *ketubah*.

[81] As in *Berkovits* v. *Grinberg (A-G Intervening)* [1995] Fam. 142: we did not recognize it since the proceedings had started in England. That a *get* in England does not dissolve a marriage was confirmed in *Maples (formerly Melamud)* v. *Maples* [1988] Fam. 14.

[82] Even the bare *talaq*, at least where the parties were domiciled in a country where this was sufficient.

[83] They are lumped together with Jews in the Marriage Act 1949, and accordingly section 9(3) of the Family Law Act 1996 applies also to them. Of course, this is merely a quirk of legislative drafting.

Schuz supports it.[84] Does this mean that the *get* would really become no business of the state? Is this laissez-faire solution one that can sensibly be contemplated? I think not. True, it would solve the *agunah* problem at a stroke and all uncertainties about status would go. But the *get* process can only be initiated by the husband. The legitimization of such a discriminatory practice would be unacceptable even if it were lawful. Nor can a particular group in the population be denied access to the courts of the land. With the implementation of the Human Rights Act 1998 the laissez-faire model is ruled out completely.[85] It would have been completely unacceptable anyway to all but a small section of the Jewish population: most of the rest would have no confidence in the Batei Din.

This still leaves the argument that the state allows Jews to marry according to its rules, in its ceremonies, and in accordance with its practices. If it does this, should it not also assist the full dissolution of such marriages? The argument is superficially attractive but it ignores (1) the distinction between creating a facility and assisting an additional remedy; and (2) the real difference between marriage and divorce, the former of which is to be encouraged, the latter discouraged. English law, in common with other systems, has always taken a more liberal attitude to marriage than to divorce: there is no rule of private international law more firmly established than that a marriage will be recognized if it complies with local form[86] (provided the parties have capacity by their personal law[87]). A tighter rein is kept on dissolution of status. There is a pronounced reluctance to refuse to recognize marriages, but public policy[88] (and other grounds[89]) can be invoked to refuse recognition to foreign divorces, separations, and annulments.

A third argument is that where there is a civil divorce but no *get*, a 'limping' marriage is created. The undesirability of this is not contested. It is, of course, a fundamental principle of private international law that a status conferred by a party's personal law should be universally recognized.[90] So, as Schuz puts it, 'the civil law, by its willingness to dissolve marriages which were contracted under Jewish religious law, other than in accordance with that law, exacerbates the problem inherent in the consensual nature of

---

[84] See Schuz, 'Divorce and Ethnic Minorities', 144. Less 'radical' is B. Berkovits, 'Jewish Divorce', (1989) 19 *Family Law* 115 and '*Get* and *Talaq* in English Law: Reflections on Law and Policy', in C. Mallat and J. Connors (eds.), *Islamic Family Law* (London, 1993).

[85] Both because it would discriminate (see Art. 14) and because it would deny access to the courts (see Art. 13).

[86] *Berthiaume* v. *Dastous* [1930] AC 79. The rule can be traced back to *Scrimshire* v. *Scrimshire* (1752) 2 Hag. Con. 395.

[87] The law of the antenuptial domicile of each party.

[88] See Family Law Act 1986, s. 51(3), as interpreted in *Kendall* v. *Kendall* [1977] Fam. 208. Of especial interest is *Chaudhary* v. *Chaudhary* [1985] Fam. 19, 45.

[89] See Family Law Act 1986, s. 51.

[90] See the famous dissent of Scott LJ in *Re Luck's Settlement* [1940] Ch. 864.

380

Jewish divorce'.[91] In effect, the civil courts, when they dissolve a marriage celebrated according to Jewish rites, grant an incomplete divorce. This was why Emery J in the Australian case of *Gwiazda*[92] issued a mandatory injunction to the wife to appear before the relevant Beth Din. The blame can hardly be attributed to the civil courts: the problem is not one of their creation. The solution favoured by some (including myself in the mid-1980s) which has now found its way into legislation (as yet unimplemented) and was embodied in the failed 2000 Bill is to deny a dissolution where it will be incomplete. That this is incompatible with the Human Rights Act 1998 seems to have been noticed by no one, not even initially by the proposer of the 2000 Bill, who is the country's leading human rights lawyer.[93]

A fourth argument for intervention is that the law relating to the *get* offers a potentiality for blackmail by the unscrupulous. A husband can use the threat to withhold a *get* as a bargaining inducement to get an agreement relating to the children[94] or to financial or property arrangements.[95] He can also make the granting of a *get* dependent on the payment to him of a large sum of money. There has been a tendency in the past to hush up these transactions. Women in particular have kept quiet for fear that they will lose their *get* and join the ranks of *agunot*. A B'nai Brith report in Canada in 1987 documented 311 cases where the *get* had been used as a bargaining tool to obtain financial and custodial gains.[96] Evidence has emerged in this country several times recently and the practice is known to be prevalent. Worse still it is connived at, even assisted, by *dayanim*. The argument that the state should intervene to protect the victims of these extortionate practices is compelling, though it is both sad and salutary to report that, if the Family Law Act 1996 is implemented, the scope for such

---

[91] Schuz, 'Divorce and Ethnic Minorities', 144.

[92] n. 69, above.

[93] Possible incompatibility with Article 14 was referred to in the Second Reading debate in the House of Lords (by Lord Lester of Herne Hill, *Hansard*, HL, vol. 614, cols. 1245–8 and by Lord McIntosh of Haringey at col. 1261). As a result, at the Third Reading amendments were passed which purport to rule out such incompatibility: see *Hansard*, H.L. vol. 615, cols. 505–6. I do not believe they achieve this objective. Nor am I convinced that incompatibility with Article 14 is the only problem: it is distinctly possible that the Bill was incompatible with Articles 6, 9, and 12 as well. If the 1996 Act is ever implemented, section 9(3) will be similarly open to challenge.

[94] In *O* v. *O* and in *N* v. *N* the husband's refusal was linked to a contact issue. In *N* v. *N* Wall J did hold that there was a residual discretion not to entertain an application for contact by a husband who was refusing his wife a *get* (see 758–9). But this is only tenable where the refusal was so affecting the child that contact would not be in the child's best interests until the issue was resolved: the child's welfare is the paramount (that is the only) consideration.

[95] But such an agreement would be overturned by a court, were this duress or undue influence to come to its attention. Unfortunately, a woman desperate for a *get* is not likely to disclose this.

[96] B'nai Brith, *The Use of Get as a Bargaining Tool in Jewish Divorce Proceedings* (Toronto, 1987).

practices within English jurisdiction will increase.[97] But does the state need to become involved in the *get* process as such to protect vulnerable women? There are Augean stables in urgent need of cleansing, and if the Jewish community cannot do this, perhaps the state should. I should be surprised if the criminal offence of blackmail has not been committed in at least one of the cases in which a woman has paid out a large sum to receive her *get*. Let the husband be prosecuted. And if it can be shown that the participation of the *dayan* concerned was other than benign, prosecute him too as an accessory.

Finally, there is another possible argument for state intervention, particularly if this takes the form of legislation. A law is an unequivocal declaration of public policy: the symbolic importance of law cannot be underestimated. The educative effect of law, its social engineering potential, is part of the modern experience of law reform.[98] Critics will say this optimism rests upon a 'hollow hope',[99] and the reasons for optimism may not be as great as perhaps they were when law stood in the vanguard of the battle to create equal opportunities. Using law as an instrument of social change tends to work best where there is a readily identifiable victim—there could not be a better example than the *agunah*.[100] Against this it may be said that the authority of a state legislature may not have the impact upon the men involved in these situations that the 'rival' authority of a Beth Din has (Massell's work on Bolshevik legislation and its impact upon the lives of the people of Soviet Central Asia is instructive[101]).

## Conclusion

There is a sixth argument. I excluded it deliberately because it is both weak and insulting. But it is one often heard. The state, it is said, must do something to solve the problem of the *agunah* because the rabbinical authorities either cannot or, worse, will not do anything. Whether it is impotence (as they perceive it), complacency, or lethargy (or a combination), almost no progress is being made. An early initiative of Jonathan Sacks's chief rabbinate was a women's committee.[102] It achieved very little. He has now established a task force and given the job, apparently, to

[97] See M. Freeman, 'Family Values and Family Justice', (1997) 50 *CLP* 315, 348–54.
[98] See Harry V. Ball and Lawrence M. Friedman, 'The Use of Criminal Sanctions in the Enforcement of Economic Legislation', (1965) 17 *Stanford LR* 197. The classic juristic source is Karl Olivecrona, *Law as Fact* (Copenhagen, 1939).
[99] Gerald N. Rosenberg's thesis in *The Hollow Hope* (Chicago, 1991).
[100] See Troy Duster, *The Legislation of Morality* (New York, 1970), 26–7.
[101] Gregory Massell, 'Law as an Instrument of Revolutionary Change in a Traditional Milieu: The Case of Soviet Central Asia', (1968) 2 *Law and Society Review* 179.
[102] This was reported in June 1994 (see *The Times*, 1 July 1994). Frustration at the lack of progress since is reflected in Helen Jacobus, 'For the Sake of our Community', *Jewish Chronicle*, 12 Nov. 1999, 35.

382

a woman who knows little about the subject.[103] The current approach is individualistic, the solving of problem cases as they arise. This does nothing to get to the root of the problem. Prenuptial agreements may[104] coax the potentially recalcitrant spouse into the jurisdiction of the Beth Din. But the Beth Din itself loses more of its claim to legitimacy every time a negative story about its activities or those of one of its *dayanim* is published, and this is worrying often. It is predicted that the number of couples agreeing to a prenuptial agreement will decline.[105] That the rabbinical authorities cannot or will not reform the *get* law is no argument for state intervention.

But does the *get* serve any useful purpose at all today? I doubt it. In cases (fortunately the majority) where it is willingly given and received it adds another layer of bureaucracy to the divorce process. It is neither very expensive nor very time-consuming, though it is a drain on both time and money. The actual ceremony itself borders on the comic, but entertainment value is not proffered as a justification! In cases where one of the spouses obstructs the process, it causes distress. It discriminates against women. It gives a spiteful spouse an additional and unnecessary divorce weapon. It exposes the vulnerable to unseemly negotiation, even to blackmail. Some (men in particular) claim it is a way of evening up a divorce process which they believe at civil level is weighted against them. Even were this true, it would not exonerate or excuse callous behaviour.

The time has come to admit that the days of the *get* are over. They were days when the Jewish *kehilah* was self-governing and when Jews, liberally, recognized divorce, and those around them did not. The *get* could be reformed, but the preferable solution would be an acknowledgement that a divorce granted by the secular authorities of a legal system having jurisdiction of the parties is all that is necessary to dissolve a marriage.[106] Provision could be made to this effect in the *ketubah*. Attempts by the state to get involved will no more solve the problem than sticking plaster will solve cancer. And the *get* is a real cancer in the body of the Jewish world.

---

[103] Mrs Judy Nagler (the appointment is announced in *Jewish Chronicle*, 9 June 2000, 64).
[104] There is a full (if partial) discussion of this by Kenneth Auman and Basil Herring, *The Prenuptial Agreement: Halakhic and Pastoral Considerations* (Northvale, NJ, 1996).
[105] We are told that 70% of couples about to marry agree to a prenuptial agreement.
[106] Rabbi Michael Weil of Paris suggested this as long ago as 1884. See Moshe Meiselman, 'Jewish Woman in Jewish Law: Solutions to Problems of Agunah', in Porter, *Women in Chains*, 61.

The Jewish Get *and the State* 383

## GLOSSARY

| | |
|---|---|
| *agunah* (pl. *agunot*) | chained woman |
| Beth Din (pl. Batei Din) | rabbinical court |
| *brit milah* | circumcision |
| *chametz* | leavened (expanded and interpeted to mean not usable during Passover) |
| *dayan* (pl. *dayanim*) | judge |
| *eruv* | fictional creation of walled city |
| *get* (pl. *gittim*) | bill of divorcement |
| Halakha (adj. halakhic) | Jewish law |
| *heter me'ah rabbanim* | permission of 100 rabbis |
| *kehilah* | community |
| *ketubah* (pl. *ketubot*) | marriage contract |
| *mamzer* (pl. *mamzerim*) | bastard (but not exactly translatable) |
| *me'useh* | void for duress |
| *talaq* | Muslim divorce |

# [15]
# Towards A Critical Theory of Family Law

Inaugurals are strange occasions. Their purpose is, to say the least, equivocal. Tradition has it that a newly appointed professor should present an inaugural lecture. Fortunately, he or she is not expected to present himself of herself in the way in which proponents of new laws in Ancient Greece were. There is no noose round my neck (other than the one which the Government has placed round our collective necks). If you do not like this lecture, you will still have me. This is not a suggestion that inaugurals should precede appointments, but it is an indication of the essentially ceremonious nature of the Inaugural Lecture. After all, such are the pressures on university teachers today, I have given about 100 lectures since I took up my professorial appointment last October. All in all, I have given some 2,000 lectures since I was appointed to a lectureship in 1969 and this is my tenth public lecture in this College. Those who have heard me lecture will be able to calculate that, with roughly a mile and a half covered at each, I could now be in sight of the Statue of Liberty—whether waving or drowning[1] I shall leave you to judge!

But inaugurals are more than ceremonials. They are an occasion when a new professor is supposed to justify his appointment by setting out the ways in which he or she intends to advance learning and disseminate knowledge. Thus interpreted, my lecture today may be seen either as a threat (like President Reagan's "You ain't Seen Nothing Yet"![2]) or a promise, remembering that, like "piecrust," promises are made to be broken.[3] They are also occasions for remembering predecessors and assessing their contribution. Indeed, one of the more attractive of the lecture theatres in college has emblazoned over the board the exhortation "Remember the Days of Old and Consider the Years of Each Generation."[4] As the holder of a personal chair, this is not a duty I have to discharge. I would nevertheless like to pay tribute to all those who have built up the Law School at University College London into what is one of the finest in the country.[5] I hope in some small way I can, through my research, writing and teaching, add to its reputation.

My own interests are in a number of areas: jurisprudence and legal theory (the subject which I was appointed to teach in 1969), the sociology of law (the first compulsory course of which I taught in 1972), the English legal system, private international law, race, nationality and immigration. But I am best known for my contributions to the development of family law, its theories and relationship to social policy and it is therefore appropriate that I should concentrate my efforts today on exploring this subject.

I have called my lecture "Towards A Critical Theory of Family Law." Those familiar with family law will be aware of a paucity of theoretical writing on the subject, at least by those who work from within the discipline of law. The growth (or rebirth) of feminism, a children's rights movement, greater interest in dispute processes and resolution, more attention being given to the relation between state and society inevitably mean that theoretical questions about law and the family cannot long remain unexplored by jurists. Lawyers who remain technicians cannot contribute to the important debates currently raging about the family.

I believe that questions must be raised about the current relationship between state and family, about how, for example, the state mediates gender and generation relations through law. In saying that family law has suffered from an absence of theory, I am both overplaying and underplaying my point. Existing law does, of course, embody some theory and existing legal literature has too often been prepared to take it at face value. The social function of much of that theory, whether implicit or articulated, has been the defence of the status quo and thus of the interests of those who are dominant within society. Look, for example, at the reasoning of Lord Denning M.R. in *Wachtel* v. *Wachtel* in 1973, justifying the resurrection of the "one-third" rule on the grounds that on divorce the ex-husband would have greater expenditure than his former wife. He would "have to go out to work all day and must get some woman to look after the house." The ex-wife, on the other hand, "will not ... have so much expense .... She will do most of the housework herself."[6] Or compare his reasoning in *Button* v. *Button*[7] with that in *Cooke* v. *Head*,[8] or *Eves* v. *Eves*.[9] In *Button* he argued that "a wife does not get a share in the house simply because she cleans the walls or works in the garden or helps her husband with the painting or decorating.[10] But in *Cooke* v. *Head*, where the female cohabitant did "quite an unusual amount of work for a woman,"[11] using a sledgehammer to demolish old buildings, working a cement mixer and doing other "male" activities, demonstrating that she was a crafts*man*, her work was richly rewarded. The message is clear: what women normally do, or are expected to do, has no economic value. But "real" work must be compensated.

By calling for a critical theory of family law, I am asserting that law needs to be socially located and that family law cannot be understood if it is assumed to operate neutrally, ahistorically or cocooned from indices of power. Just as existing theory is designed to shore up the status quo, so critical theory has, I believe, a particular goal as well. Critical family law is an integral part of a struggle to create a more socially just society.[12]

## The Character of Modern English Family Law

Let me first look at the character of modern English family law and, in doing so, briefly at theories which attempt to explain it. In looking for the characteristics of a subject, a number of approaches can be adopted: what it does or is supposed to do (its function); how it does it (its form and content); and what it represents (its ideology). These three approaches are by no means exclusive of one another. In looking at existing theory I shall say something about function; when I venture into critical theory in the second half of this lecture, I shall talk about form and ideology.

To ask questions about the functions of family law is to uncover a hornet's nest. It is a controversial question as to whether it has a function at all and, if so, what that function is. If it has, or is alleged to have, a particular function or functions, a key question is "who says that this is so?". Laws are not bloodless entities: they are not some "brooding omnipresence in the sky."[13] They are made by people, political actors, who have their own interests to protect. These lawmakers have been and remain almost exclusively male, middle-aged to elderly, and in the higher socio-economic classes. Many of those who would ascribe "functions" to family law would attribute these functions to family law in all societies and trans-historically as if function could be isolated from culture, history, structure or power. We must thus treat with caution any attempt to analyse the functions of family law.

This said, one of the clearest expositions of the "functions" of family law in "modern states" is found in John Eekelaar's impressive monograph, ·Family Law and Social Policy.[14] But his analysis falls short of overcoming the problems to which I have just referred. He sees the role of the law ("state intervention") as threefold. The first is to provide mechanisms and rules for adjusting relationships between family members when family units break down. The second is to provide protection for individuals from possible harms suffered within the family. The third is to support the maintenance of family relationships. As he claims, the first two of these functions are relatively uncontroversial. It is "empirically true"[15] that the major thrust of much modern family law purports to be directed at adjustment and protection. But "relatively" uncontroversial is the operative expression. I will say a little about the first two of these "functions" to illustrate some of the problems which a critical theorist of family law inevitably confronts.

Let me look briefly at the protective function of family law. It must not be taken for granted that the law does actually protect weaker members of the family from harm. This may be the official version of various institutions and practices but, as is often the case, the reality may be rather more problematic. Thus, for example, many of the management techniques, such as registers and case conferences, developed to tackle child abuse are thought to be insurance policies to protect the integrity and salve the conscience of adult society, in particular the interests of social workers with the responsibility of protecting children thought to be at risk.[16] If we look at the historical origin of childcare services there is no doubt that a "rhetoric of National Efficiency" played a major part in producing the climate for the introduction of those services. It was not to protect children that these services were developed, but Empire. "The child of today [1916] ... will be the citizen of the coming years and must take up and bear the duties of statesmanship, defence from foes, the conduct and all other necessities for the perpetuation of an imperial race.[17] Countless more similarly telling quotations could be produced to make much the same point.

The problematic nature of protection can also be illustrated by looking at laws which purport to protect women. I will illustrate this by an historical example and a contemporary case, both drawn from labour law. I deliberately go beyond the conventional boundaries of family law (they are themselves problematic and value-laden—there is nothing "natural" about them) because it is clear that state policies towards the family cannot be confined within conceptual fields. Factories legislation which restricted women's industrial work in the nineteenth century, the legacies of which are still with us, was seen at the time as serving the interests of working-class women by protecting them against long hours of work and harsh conditions, freeing them to give their time to homemaking and childbearing, as well as enabling their menfolk to claim a "family wage" to support them and their children.

But was it as simple as this? Protective legislation was not introduced in all areas of work. Was it, therefore, introduced, as has been argued, in areas where women competed with male workers?[18] Or was the legislation really to protect the interests of employers, or at least the most advanced employers, who needed workers in a better physical condition and who were aware that if women were worked too hard they would be unable to produce the next generation of workers?[19] If such legislation was in the interests of

## Towards a Critical Theory of Family Law 157

male workers, which of their interests was it protecting? Did they really want less money brought home? Or was it that working men were afraid that women, being cheaper and more pliable, would infiltrate industry, take their jobs and lower rates of pay for all? Not only would this be a disaster in terms of men's position within commodity production, but it would also liberate women from dependence on men and obliterate gender labour divisions in the home. Heidi Hartmann argues that women (and children) in the labour force "undermined authority relations." She argues that men "reserved union protection for men and argued for protective labour laws for women and children."[20] The problem of cheap competition could have been solved by the unionisation of women and youths but the problem of disrupted family life could not be so solved. Men did not want women to "serve two masters."[21]

This interpretation has been challenged by Jane Humphries.[22] In the case of male colliers, she found evidence to suggest that they wanted state intervention to regulate female and child labour and the "patriarchy first" approach, emphasising patriarchal privileges in having wives at home, was inconsistent with the realities of collier life. She rejects the Marxist-functionalist approach which sees the family from the point of view of capital. The family form, she argues, cannot be explained by showing how functional it is to the capitalist system. "Alternative private or state childrearing agencies, benefitting from economies of scale, could be envisaged which would meet capital's needs for a passive labour force," she rightly observes.[23] Instead she emphasises the strength of working class families enabling them to resist total subordination to capital, a view which is strikingly similar (at least in form) to that of Ferdinand Mount in his *The Subversive Family*, and he was an adviser of Margaret Thatcher![24] The interests served by protective legislation looked at historically may not be the same interests that have supported its retention since. What they were and are now remains debatable.

The debate can, however, be continued by looking at a contemporary case, *Page* v. *Freight Hire Ltd.* in 1981.[25] The case was brought by a female lorry driver against her employers for discrimination under the Sex Discrimination Act of 1975. Her employers would not let her carry a particular load consisting of chemicals. The chemical concerned involved potential risks to those working with it. Both men and women were at risk but women were subject to the additional hazard of sterility and there was also a danger to any child that a woman might be carrying. Ms. Page was 23 and divorced and was prepared to accept the risks and indemnify her employers against them, but was prohibited from doing so. The

Employment Appeal Tribunal held that there was a statutory duty on the employers to ensure the health, safety and welfare of their employees and, therefore, there was no discrimination. What concerned the Tribunal was the danger to any potential foetus. It said: "We accept that the individual's wishes may be a factor to be looked at, although, in our judgment, where the risk is to the woman, of sterility, or to the foetus, whether actually in existence or likely to come into existence in the future, these wishes cannot be a conclusive factor.[26] Protection here meant protection of her (and any potential foetus) and not protection of her rights. If we accept the moral precept of treating persons as equals, a moral principle which equal opportunities legislation purports to embody, we must also respect their capacity to take risks and make mistakes. The *Page* case demonstrates the essential conflict between protection and rights. Nor does it draw the logical conclusion for, as Katherine O'Donovan has pertinently observed, "if all women are to be subjected to control for the sake of future generations, then surely this should give rise to compensation and not to disability."[27]

Much more could be said of the problematic nature of protection. But another of the categories, adjustment, must also be looked at. That family law rules and institutions provide mechanisms for adjusting relationships between family members when family units break down is contentious in that it commits the sin of omission. It implies wrongly that adjustment takes place only where the relationship is diseased or disjointed in some way. It adopts a pathological view of the law. This view is common. The distinguished comparative lawyer, Otto Kahn-Freund, wrote some 14 years ago of how "the normal behaviour of husband and wife or parents and children towards each other is beyond the law—as long as the family is healthy. The law comes in when things go wrong."[28] John Eekelaar echoes this sentiment. "English practice," he wrote, "has been to refrain from formulating general principles as to how families should be managed."[29] As will be seen when I examine the ideology of family law, this view is a distortion of reality. There is clear evidence that not only does the law[30] serve to reproduce social order, but it actually in part constitutes and defines that order.[31] Family law (and not only family law, for labour law, tax law, social welfare law, immigration law and other laws and regulations are similarly creative of such an ideology) produces and reproduces patriarchal relations. The legal form is one of the main modalities of social practice through which actual relationships embodying gender stratification have been expressed.[32] And not just gender stratification, but stratification based on age as well.

## Towards a Critical Theory of Family Law     159

Children appear in the law as legal objects[33] rather than as legal subjects.[34] They are property, rather than persons, a problem population[35] that needs to be controlled. The *Gillick* case[36] is a recent, and apt, illustration of this. The case was seen as requiring a demarcation line to be drawn between the rights of parents and doctors. The case was not seen in terms of an adolescent's rights to birth control. It could have been. The statutory provision which allows a minor to consent to medical treatment at 16[37] does not affect the validity of any other consent,[38] so that a younger child capable of understanding what is involved may also give effective consent. If I am right, the Court of Appeal's decision is *per incuriam* and can be safely ignored by doctors who secure the consent of under-age girls. The *Gillick* ruling is in stiking contrast to the United States Supreme Court decision in *Carey* v. *Population Services International*.[39] The court held unconstitutional New York's legislation which prohibited the sale of contraceptives to minors under 16. The prohibition was struck down because there was no evidence that it rationally furthered the goals of discouraging teenage sexual activity or safeguarding their physical health. Defenders of the *Gillick* decision may resort to paternalistic arguments to support it but these are weak since, given the experimental and extra-marital nature of the sexual activities of adolescents, it must be in their interests, not contrary to them, to use contraceptives.[40]

The *Gillick* case is only one illustration of the way in which the adult-child relationship is constructed by the law. The *Colwell* scandal[41] of the early 1970s makes much the same point. Maria's mother wanted her back from her aunt and uncle with whom she had been fostered for six years. There was never very much doubt in the minds of the social workers involved that ultimately this was the best solution, and the mother's application for the care order to be discharged was unopposed by the local authority.[42] It should have been obvious that this was not what the child herself wanted, but, under the law as it then stood, it was impossible for her views to influence decision-making.[43] In a minority opinion attached to the DHSS inquiry report into the case, a leading social work academic, Olive Stevenson, blamed "the legal and social framework within which the social workers had to operate, in which it was assumed that a parent had a right to reclaim a child if . . . she could prove [herself] to be [a] 'fit person'."[44] That is right but, in an attempt to extricate social workers from blame, Stevenson glosses over the part which they played in creating that framework.[45] Child abuse is a complex issue to which there are no easy solutions. I have written about it widely[46] and have given a public lecture in this college on

160              *Current Legal Problems 1985*

the subject.[47] I shall not, therefore, pursue it any further save to link it to a Bill currently before Parliament which endorses it.

The Education (Corporal Punishment) Bill[48] allows parents of children in maintained schools[49] to opt their children out of corporal punishment.[50] The Government's hand has been forced by the European Court of Human Rights' decision in *Campbell and Cosans*.[51] A Government committed to the "short, sharp shock"[52] (if not yet in the form W. S. Gilbert had in mind in the *The Mikado*,)[53] could not have been expected to go any further, at least until forced to do so.[54] It is not the failure to see a relationship between child abuse and corporal punishment to which I wish to draw attention.[55] It is the way that children are once more seen as legal objects rather than legal subjects. Just as disputes between parents and doctors on contraception are to be decided in favour of parents, so disputes between parents and teachers on corporal punishment are also to be decided in favour of parents. The object (I would like to call her or him a person but this is hardly permissible) is curiously dehumanised to the point of becoming like a piece of land over which there is a boundary dispute.

Let me retrace my steps. I have been talking of the ways in which the legal system actually defines relationships, thus entering the scene at an earlier stage than the resolution of conflict. This is not, of course, to deny that part of the role of family law is adjustment. Once this was limited to sorting out the mess after divorce. Today the typology of problems which is embraced by adjustment is much wider: the problems of cohabitation[56] (the first modern case is as recent as 1972); the problems spawned by the reconstituted family (access, step-parent adoptions, change of name); the problems produced by domestic violence. The responses of the law and legal institutions to these problems, and in particular to cohabitation and domestic violence, are far from satisfactory. I return to domestic violence later when I construct a critical theory of family law.

### Towards Critical Theory

Critical theory about law is usually associated today with a movement in the United States known as Critical Legal Studies.[57] In using the expression "critical theory" I do not intend to adopt entirely the tenets of that movement, in so far as they can be identified, though the basic theorising I use is certainly compatible with some of the thinking associated with the movement.

Just as the principal advance of Dworkin's jurisprudence was to integrate legal theory within political and moral theory,[58] so that of critical legal studies is to demonstrate the need to integrate legal theory within social theory. The exponents of critical legal studies have attempted to introduce into discourse about law the insights and modes of analysis of social theory, in particular the relativity of truth to any given social or historical group.[59] On this view reality is not a product of nature, but is socially constructed. Social arrangements are not unproblematic, inexorable givens. What we see as the social order is thus nothing more than where the struggle between individuals was brought to a stop and truce lines were drawn up. Where I believe critical legal thinking shows an advance is in its attempts, fruitful in many areas, to identify the role played by law and legal reasoning in the processes through which a particular social order comes to be seen as legitimate and inevitable.[60] By identifying and overturning existing forms of legal consciousness, critical legal theorists seek to emancipate the individual.

## A Critical Theory of Family Law

There are a number of reasons why we should want to construct a critical theory of family law.[61] I shall give four. There is, most obviously, the reason that holds for all critical theory: theory is a pre-condition of practical critique. Without theory there can be no coherent explanation. Empiricist studies of family law have flourished in the last decade.[62] We now have greater insight into the "facts," into "living law."[63] But what one finds is determined by the categories one uses. By taking these uncritically from the existing law at best all that these studies have demonstrated is the existence of a gap between what it is assumed the law says should happen and real practice. Sometimes this had led to reform: the introduction of "Special Procedure" in divorce is one egregious example.[64] At other times the reform thrust has been resisted: the evidence produced by the Finer report[65] has not yet led to the establishment of a Family Court.

I am not here concerned with the success or otherwise of reform initiatives. Of course, anyone who hopes to develop critical theory starts with a suspicion that things are wrong and wants reform.[66] The critical theorist cannot ignore the gap between paper rights and real rights. In criticising the biases of the law he or she is bound to be told of progresses towards greater equality, of greater rights for married women,[67] of rights for cohabitants, of equal opportunities legislation.

A true critical response will examine the motive of the reformers (co-optation, for example),[68] the reality of the reform (despite the Equal Pay Act, women now earn a lower percentage of average

*Michael Freeman*

*Current Legal Problems 1985*

male earnings than when the Act was implemented),[69] the effects of reforms (by providing avenues of redress, criticism of inequalities is channelled in law-defined ways and in terms of the law's limited categories and its modes of discourse), its desirability (should cohabitation be treated like marriage?).[70]

But critical theory must go beyond this. Pragmatists have treated the law and the legal system as discrete entities, as natural and unproblematic, and as occupying a central hegemonic position. They have made little attempt to relate the legal system to the wider social order or the State.[71] But family law is principally about the relation of state and society.[72] Much current debate is about state interference into the family, whether it is concerned with marriage, divorce, cohabitation, domestic violence, support, childrearing practices,[73] education, the care of the elderly or the mentally ill,[74] or methods of resolving family disputes.[75] But how can we analyse the legitimation forms offered by the state, how can we advocate limits on state power without a theory of what state action is actually legitimate? Theory is thus a necessary pre-condition of any constructive thought about the subject, or meaningful practice in it.[76]

A second reason why a critical theory of family law is important is to expose policies and concepts, long taken for granted as inexorable givens, for what they are. Concepts like welfare[77] (often a child's welfare is the "first and paramount" consideration[78]; at other times it is the "first consideration"[79]), protection (we are often told that the law of marriage should be extended to quasi-marital relationships to "protect" female cohabitants[80]), rights (parental rights,[81] children's rights[82]) need to be re-examined. What, anyway, is meant by the "best interests of the child"? If, as is likely, it is an unattainable ideal,[83] why are we so mesmerised by it? If we really believe in it, why do we leave decision-making to a group of elderly males with no training or expertise in child psychology? It is obvious that ultimately there is an irreducible element of values in the process. Occasionally, as in *Painter* v. *Bannister*,[84] this is quite explicit. Is our imagery about best interests merely a way of cloaking the fact that judicial fiat is little more than hunch and value-preference? Nor does the evidence suggest that other profes-sionals could do any better.[85]

Underlying the concepts and the changes within them are different forms constituting social relationships. The changes represent different ways of viewing relationships. But what do these different representations signify? Can different legal responses to cohabitation (from akin to prostitution to quasi-marriage) be explained in terms of a perceived increase in the number of those living together in stable unions outside marriage, in terms of greater toleration of pluralistic morality (and, if so, what explains this) or in terms of changes in economic structure?[86] The extent to which changes in economic structure affect the form of law has been too little explored in the context of law and the family. How is it, to take a second example, that the *O'Neill* case in 1946[87] should have led to policies linking a child's welfare to his natural home, while the *Colwell* case in 1973[88] should have been thought to demonstrate the risky nature of natural family life and thus have led to policies linking the child's welfare to substitute care? Both cases were scandals, both led to inquiries and legislation. The differences in the form of legislation cannot be explained by the fact that Denis O'Neill died whilst in the care of the local authority and Maria Colwell died at the hands of her step-father while under local authority supervision.[89]

A third reason why a critical theory of family law is important is that without one it is too difficult to assess the value of new or proposed techniques, practices, or institutions. It is important to question current sacred cows and to relate them to the terms of social life. Conciliation (or at least "in-court conciliation") is currently all the rage.[90] Who could possibly be opposed to a dispute process which takes the acrimony out of conflict? The very mention of the word seems to have an almost mystical effect, ratther like the phrase "clean break."[91] But, whilst upholding the ideal,[92] I would suggest that conciliation is much less structured and much more complex, much less impartial and much more irrational than the received model would suggest. The Finer report (perhaps unwittingly the *fons et origo* of conciliation in this county) posited the legal system as one which "treats people . . . in the last resort as the subject of rights, not as . . . patients for whom the legal process is just another kind of treatment."[93] But is this how practitioners of conciliation see their role? Are the parties litigants or patients?[94] Nor should it be assumed that welfare officers or social workers involved are purveyors of a neutral corpus of knowledge. They have their "images of man"[95] (in most cases rooted in determinism); their beliefs in how the family should function ("a particular familial ideology in which roles are cast and those who do not fit are deemed not to be fit,"[96] Anne Bottomley has rightly observed). Conciliation is part of a shift in the direction of informalism or de-legalisation.[97] The Family Court, most people's goal,[98] is another. But we should not merely accept the inevitability (and desirability) of such moves but closely examine what they signify.

It was Weber[99] who first noted that movements towards greater informalism contained the seeds of their own self-contradiction and were ultimately doomed. Programmes which seem to weaken hierarchies of power may actually establish new channels through which they can be expressed or even strengthened. Observe the way the decline in the criminal sanction[1] has been matched by the growth of the regulatory sanction[2] spawned by the "new property"[3] state: note the way the "therapeutic state"[4] has medicalised deviance. The effect is what Stan Cohen has called, a "dispersal of social control."[5] Informal justice, Foucault has argued, increases state power.[6] "Informal institutions allow state control to escape the walls of those highly visible centers of coercion" (such as courts) and "permeate society," writes Abel in the introduction to an important collection on the politics of informal justice. But it is possible, he argues, "to penetrate the comforting facade of informalism and begin to reveal its political meaning."[7] We must not let our concern about the rigidity, remoteness or insensitivity of traditional legal mechanisms turn us away from the unqualified good in the rule of law.[8] We may find adversary processes inappropriate, even dehumanising or alienating. Yet the formalism and the rule of law which accompany them can provide a measure of protection to the weak. In the context of family dispute processes this means women and children. The rule of law also inhibits power, not least of welfare professionals. It is in part recognition of this that led to a partial re-legalisation of the juvenile court in the United States in the late 1960s.[9] Yet the paeans which proclaim the family court ideal today are so very reminiscent of the fulsome praise heaped on the juvenile court half a century ago.[10]

To read too much into the analogy would be to divorce the two movements from their historical contexts. The juvenile court emerged in the heyday of classical capitalism. Since capitalism needs certainty, stability, calculability, predictability, abstraction, and formalism promotes this,[11] the emergence of the juvenile court is something of an anomaly, perhaps explained by excepting policies concerned with wayward youth from general state initiatives.[12] Today's post-industrial society has different needs and expectations. Capitalism has become less of a market system and more reliant on central control.[13] The drift from status to contract[14] has been reversed and status has become increasingly important in defining the legal rights of the individual. The historical setting for the family court is thus one in which status, and hence particularistic relationships, have re-emerged.[15] It is also one in which general rules have given way to vague standards.[16] It is clear why formalism has declined, but this does not mean that we can hope to realise the goals in whose name formalism was attacked. The dispersal of control can increase, rather than decrease, the amount of interven-

## Towards a Critical Theory of Family Law 165

tion.[17] If we look at the way the family has been colonised by welfare professionals[18] in the twentieth century, we can see the family court as the ultimate legitimation of such policies. Most of those policies were not critically examined and only recently has their impact and its backlash been assesseed: now is the time to pause before further major steps are taken.

A fourth reason for believing in the importance of developing a critical family jurisprudence is to lay bare the myths which surround the development of family law and policy. It is important not only to demonstrate the existence of myths but also, and more significantly, to examine the role of, and motives for, such mystification. It is not new for debates about the family to be governed by myth. The Beveridge report,[19] the foundation of our social security system, ignored the evidence and concentrated instead on what he thought the family *ought* to be doing. Or, to take a second pervasive example, consider the extent to which family policy (the existence of which is questionable but which I assume for present purposes exists) has been predicated on the basis of a husband wage-earner, a wife homemaker and a little over two dependent children in each household unit. Perhaps 10 per cent. of families conform to this model. One of the effects of looking at the household as a unit has been to assume that the "family wage"[20] (a concept in part the product of this myth) is shared and accordingly to provide few remedies for dependents who do not receive their share of the household income. The myth here provides a justification for not intervening in the family—to do so would be to undermine unit-y, though, of course, relief would only be sought when the family harmony was disrupted.[21]

A third example of the use of mythology in family legislation is the folk devil prayed in aid to secure the passage of the 1984 Matrimonial and Family Proceedings Act. I refer, of course, to that mythical beast, Aylesbury's "Loch Ness Monster", "the alimony drone."[22] The evidence shows that it is ex-wives, and the children who usually remain with their mothers, who suffer the greater economic hardships on divorce, and not ex-husbands and their second wives or cohabitants.[23] The Act fails to get to grips with the real issues. It reduces an ex-wife's access to income in the private sphere but fails to recognise that it is precisely in that sphere that she is constituted as a dependent. It conceptualises divorce and its consequences as a private matter while ignoring that access to resources (for example, rights to occupational pensions) are prescribed by state policies.[24] It seeks to cloak women's dependence in rhetoric about child welfare, thus making women emphasise their motherhood to seek support.[25] The Act fails totally to come to grips with the meaning and implications of the unequal economic partnership that marriage constitutes and divorce perpetuates.[26] The inequalities are seen as natural to civil society and not the responsibility of the state. And, to deal briefly with a fourth myth, when women are forced to fall back on social security provision they will find that recent changes in welfare state legislation which purport to be, and seem, favourable to women, in practice achieve less than most think they do. Thus, administrative rules have been changed and affect women far more than men.[27] For example, to claim unemployment benefit parents of small children may be required to produce evidence that adequate child care arrangements can be made should a job be found. A second example is the exclusion of some 40 per cent. of part-time workers, the vast majority of whom are women, from the national insurance scheme altogether because they are defined as "non-employed," that is earning less than a quarter of male average wages.[28] In any case, even those part-time workers who have paid contributions may find they are deemed ineligible for benefit because they are not available for full-time work. In all the discussion about equalisation of benefits, points like these were conveniently swept under the carpet.

## Public and Private—The Critical Divide

In the last part of this lecture, I wish critically to examine the public/private dichotomy[29] which is at the root of so much of the current debate about state and family. Much of the debate focusses on the limits of state intervention into the family. To what extent is domestic violence or cohabitation a private matter? How much autonomy in childrearing practices should parents be accorded? Is the relationship of a divorcing couple and their children any business of the state? What support duties should the state impose on ex-spouses? Is the welfare state replacing the family,[30] or now perhaps should the family replace the welfare state?[31] These questions are constantly being posed.

The debate is often conceptualised in terms of a public/private paradigm.[32] The broad distinction between things which pertain to the state (the affairs of "public life") and things that do not ("private" relations) has a long heritage. It can be traced to Aristotle.[33] Men by nature were intended to live in a *polis*, in which the highest good could be attained. Women, slaves and children did not and could not participate in the full unfolding of goodness and reason which was the "common heritage of co-equal participants in the perfect association."[34] They were confined to the *oikos*, the household, a non-public sphere. The good at which the household aimed was a lesser good. Women accordingly achieved only the limited goodness of the "naturally ruled,"[35] a goodness that was, of course, different in kind from that of the naturally ruling. In the Greek sense of the word, they were *idiots*, persons who either could not or did not participate in the *polis*, the "good" of public life. There is not time or space to trace through Machiavelli[36] to the suffragists (some of whom thought that once "private had become public, politics in the traditional sense would come to an end,)"[37] or to contemporary writers like Hannah Arendt[38] or Karol Wojtyla (now Pope John Paul II).[39] It is important, though, to stress that Aristotle did draw normative conclusions from his analysis, including the justification of dominance of women by men. Why is it, we may speculate, that another of his normative conclusions, the justification of slavery, has received so much more critical attention?

Historically, the Industrial Revolution was a watershed. I say "Industrial Revolution" rather than capitalism because to argue that capitalism requires the separation of home and workplace, with women relegated to the home and excluded from wage labour, is a simplistic interpretation of the historical facts.[40] The tendency towards separation of home and workplace has proved oppressive to women but, as Michèle Barrett points out, "this is because the problem so starkly posed—who was to be primarily responsible for childcare?—was resolved, according to an ideology of gender that pre-dated capitalism, in the interests of men."[41] With women confined to the home,[42] and defined in terms of their responsibilities in the household,[43] the family and the familial role of women became idealised, the home became a refuge from the demands of the economy, a "shelter for moral and spiritual values,"[44] a private place to which people, but especially men, could withdraw. In Christopher Lasch's graphic phrase, "a haven in a heartless world,"[45] a "utopian retreat from the city."[46] The dichotomy between home and the workaday world was almost like that separating heaven from earth.[47] But the home became not only a "walled garden" but a "stifling menagerie."[48] Man was now the breadwinner: his wife the dependent homemaker.

Women are expected to be dependent on men: their role is geared to the household (homemaking, child care, the care of the elderly and handicapped). Their domestic labour is seen as non-productive, not real work.[49] And "sex role is sex rank,"[50] for "as long as woman's place is defined as separate, a male-dominated society will define her place as inferior."[51] The true meaning of "separate but equal" is well understood from the context of race. That most women are now engaged in remunerative employment (albeit over-represented in work which resembles domestic work in the home)[52] is often conveniently ignored. But in the labour market women are a secondary labour force.[53] The construction of a family form in which the male head of household is supposedly responsible for the economic support of his dependent wife and children has militated against demands for equal pay. The "right" of married women to take jobs at the expense of male workers has frequently been explicitly challenged, not least recently with Government allegations that married women at work are a cause of unemployment. You may think that the true cause is just one married woman! The weak position of women on the labour market has the effect of reinforcing their subordination in the home. The notion of the "family wage" has as its concomitant female dependence.

It may be from liberal economic thought that we get the distinction between the economic world of the market (the public) and the non-economic sphere of the home (the private "haven"). But it is in liberal political thought that we find the normative conclusions which have had such enormous implications for the regulation of the family. The history of liberal political thought is one of gradual retreat from a laisser-faire position. It may be interpreted as a search to find a justification for the gradual enlargement of the public realm.[54] The "night watchman" theory of the state is held by some liberals, like Robert Nozick,[55] but they are more aptly characterised as conservatives. Liberals question the legitimate extent of governmental authority: the public sphere, they believe, is properly subject to governmental regulation but not so the private. The state should refrain from intervention in the "private" lives of individuals.[56]

Like it or not, this has been an influential ideology. What, then, are its implications for our subject? Most obviously, by drawing the public/private distinction in this way, liberal theorists deny protection to women and children, and for that matter the elderly, the mentally ill, the handicapped and all others cared for in the "community" (a euphemism for "by women in the home").[57] Within the family, privatisation has meant delegalisation. I have stressed earlier in this lecture that protection is a problematic notion. What I indicated was that the rhetoric of protection should not be mistaken for the real thing and that even the best-laid plans could sometimes backfire. But if women and children are dependents, all that non-intervention achieves is protection of the dominance of men against women, adults against children. When Goldstein, Freud and Solnit tell us that a policy of minimum coercive intervention by the state accords with their "firm belief as citizens in individual freedom and human dignity"[58] we have to ask "whose freedom?" and "what dignity?" In a world of basic structural inequalities of which the family is a microcosm, individual freedom can be so exercised as to undermine not only the liberty of others but also their human dignity. Bill Jordan put the point well when he wrote that "the case against intervention in family life often rests on the freedom of more powerful members (usually husbands in relation to wives and parents in relation to children) to exercise their power without restriction."[59]

The main contacts of women with men and parents with children are in the home. If this becomes a legal Alsatia into which the Queen's writ does not run[60] we risk leaving weaker members of the family to their fate. The idealised notions we long cherished of the family made it difficult for us to believe that the family was a site of violence or abuse. Well-known child abuse cases such as that of Maria Colwell have enabled us to overcome our instinctive reluctance to think ill of the family, at least in cases of non-accidental injury to children. Whether the moral panic instigated by the *Colwell* case, with a vast increase in coercive measures and safety-first policies, can be justified is another matter, but not one I will explore here.[61] Nevertheless, our consciousness of sexual abuse[62] remains muted and our attitudes to violence against women have shifted very little.

Why is violence against women in the home perceived to be a different problem (and different in the sense of being less important) from other violence?[63] We even refer to it differently. We talk of "battered wives' or "battered women" (an acknowledgment of the fact that absence of a wedding ring is no protection). But how many other crimes are characterised in terms of their victims? It is as if we are blaming the victims.[64] We have even set up refuges to which the victims and their children can flee.[65] In what other crimes is the perpetrator left in peace and his victim removed to a place of safety? Some 10 years ago I advocated the establishment of "refuges" for battering men. It still strikes me as preferable to the present absurd solution.

There is some explanation of the ideology which distinguishes private "disturbances" from public violence in the evidence given by the police and Home Office to the House of Commons Select Committee on Violence In Marriage. The Association of Chief Police Officers thought it was important to place domestic violence in its "correct" perspective. "We are," they said, "dealing with persons 'bound in marriage,' and it is important for a host of reasons [none of which they gave] to maintain the unity of the spouses." They go on to express their approval of the provision of refuges for battered wives, but add "every effort should be made to re-unite the family."⁶⁶ The Home Office, discussing the Criminal Injuries Compensation Scheme, which at that time excluded intra-family injuries, argued that "the point at which the State should intervene in family violence should be higher that that which is expected in the case of violence between strangers." It also argued that the State has "no particular responsibility for compensating those who suffer violence in circumstances which are largely . . . under their own control."⁶⁷ The threshold for State compensation is still higher than for other violence.⁶⁸ Marital rape is still not a crime, though defences of the immunity from prosecution are totally discredited.⁶⁹ The commonest, and most entrenched, emanates from Sir Matthew Hale, misogynist and witch-burner extraordinaire.⁷⁰ He emphasised contract, that most private of institutions. "The husband cannot be guilty of rape committed by himself upon his lawful wife, for by their mutual matrimonial consent and contract, the wife hath given up herself in this kind unto her husband which she cannot retract."⁷¹ The paradox of a contract which cannot be retracted brings out the essentially problematic nature of the so-called "private" sphere.

But then the boundaries between state and society, between public and private, are not fixed by nature. They are socially and historically constructed.⁷² Polarising reifies the abstractions. It is the state which decides where the boundaries should be and it constantly redraws these. The private sphere is constituted and reconstituted by the public. The private does not exist outside the state. Each contains the other at the level of social practices and power strategies. To say that a domain is private is not to argue that it is thereby free. The current controversies about the respective realms of public and private, and about the limits of state intervention into the family thus distort and perpetuate a mystifying discourse which sees "the family" as separate from, and in opposition to, the state.

I am thus forced to pose a number of questions. Since the state defines what the private sphere is at any time, since it could just as easily define the same space as public, thus making intervention easier, why does it define a particular area as private? Indeed, why does it define any area as private? Let me take some examples.

The state defines and supports private obligations to maintain. In that sense the private obligation to maintain is not a private matter at all. But then having done this it stops short: the law refuses to interfere in an ongoing family relationship.⁷³ The state does not question how much support a man gives his wife or children, nor does it allow them to enforce the obligation. He sets the standard of living and, to take an extreme example, if he lives in luxury and they in penury, so long as he maintains them, they have no redress.⁷⁴

Conditions of domestic production remain outside the purview of
the law. What does this mean? Most obviously, it suggests a
discrediting of housework. By refusing to support a man's obligation to maintain his wife, it implies that she makes no contribution
worthy of support. This contains an important ideological message
about a wife's subordinate status.[75]

A second example relates to the question of parental autonomy
regarding childrearing practices. The private space is one which has
constantly been narrowed. There have been considerable inroads in
the last 10 years.[76] But why does the state define parental authority
as private? Define it as Plato did[77] or as it is constructed in the
Communist bloc, where parental authority is only a reflection of
social authority,[78] and supervision (intervention would be the wrong
word) becomes natural. The adoption of such an approach would
see the child as public property. By contrast the approach in this
country sees the child as the private property of his parents. The
very concept of parental rights,[79] most obviously the right to
physical possession,[80] expresses this relationship. The fact that
parental rights cannot be adequately enumerated only adds to the
pervasive force of those rights.[81] Parental rights give parents
considerable powers including, in the case of defective newborns,
that of life and death,[82] as well as the power to deprive a child of a
fundamental human right.[83] This is graphically portrayed in the
well-known "Sotos Syndrome" case, and would have been even
more striking had it not been for chance intervention by an
educational psychologist.[84] The *Gillick* case and the Corporal
Punishment Bill, referred to earlier, are further demonstration of
parental power embodied in the law.

What do these two examples (the obligation to maintain and the
doctrine of parental rights) have in common? I would suggest that
the common feature is that by seeing a part for the whole, the
different interests of different members of the family are glossed
over, ignored, obscured. By defining the space as private, the state
mystifies.

Why then is it so important for the state to believe in the unity of
the family? I do not think there is a clear answer to this. It might be
that the power structures embodied in the family are functionally
useful to the state. For example, in the family the child learns what
is expected of him (conformity, obedience) and this helps to mould
submissive citizens.[85] It could also be that belief in the unity of the
family fosters some kind of belief in unity between families, thus
enabling us to pass over class differences.[86] Certainly, despite the
large differences between family living in different classes and
different ethnic groups, we are encouraged to think of *the* family.

172                     *Current Legal Problems 1985*

This is important if state policies are to focus on "the family."[87]

Mention of different interests in the family brings me to my second question. If talk of the "private" is illusory, why do we continue to use such discourse? Whose privacy is it? How is it defined? Who uses it? An English*man*'s home[88] is said to be his castle (in parenthesis, it should not be forgotten that many castles had torture chambers) but responses of different officials (the Supplementary Benefits Commission, the Inland Revenue, the police) do suggest that not all castles are equally impenetrable. The privacy of a woman alleged to be cohabiting will be invaded much more easily that that of a company director suspected of tax fraud.[89] Even within the same organisation, the police, there is evidence to suggest a differential attitude to the necessity to secure a search warrant, depending in part on the socio-economic status of the person whose property is to be searched.[90] Privacy[91] is not, therefore, an absolute: the privacy of some is more inviolate than others.

The definition of "private" can tell us a lot about power relations in a society at a particular time. Writing of the period in the nineteenth century during which the notion of the home as haven emerged, Davidoff and her colleagues make the point cogently. "The home," they write, "represented an extreme of the privacy in which individualism could flourish." But they continue: "If we look more closely . . . we will see that the individualism refers only to the orientation of the master/husband, the privacy was used by him when he cared to invoke it."[92] The right to domestic privacy is more easily invoked by some, for example husbands, than others, for example male cohabitants. The police[93] thus seem more willing to intervene in violence outside the marriage relationship than in violence against a wife. The right to domestic privacy is also less easily invoked outside the setting of the matrimonial home: so the police are more willing to protect women in refuges than those still at home.[94] There are numerous other variables but these are not directly relevant and will not be pursued here.

Does discourse about privacy therefore serve any ideological purpose? I certainly believe it does. Another who clearly does is Joan Kelly.[95] She eloquently and persuasively writes of the problem and its implications:

> "The conception of two social spheres existing side by side simply masked this more complex social reality. It did not describe the society in which it arose so much as reflect it ideologically. Wittingly or unwittingly, it served to legitimate certain of the bourgeois patriarchal practices of that society. At worst, by separating women out of production and making

them 'the Sex', it drew a veil of Motherhood over the forms of women's oppression that bourgeois society intensified: the economic super-exploitation of working women; gross abuse of the sexual advantage this gave middle-class men; subordination of bourgeois women to the property and personal interests of men of their class; and the subjection of women to the demand for ever-increasing population to meet the needs of war and production."

This is offered as historical explanation. It remains, however, essentially accurate. It omits the impact on children, who were similarly oppressed, but she would not, I think, fail to acknowledge this, even if in all the rhetoric about women they are all too often eclipsed. Are there lessons in this for us in 1985? I think there are.

As far as women are concerned we are witnessing an attempt by the "new Right" to re-assert with full vigour the separate sphere of the home. The valorisation of the family, the glorification of motherhood are seen as partial answers to the current crisis. The family is the first line of defence and within it the mother is absolutely crucial. As Carol Smart characterised it in *The Ties That Bind*: "She can prevent delinquency by staying at home to look after the children, she can reduce unemployment by staying at home and freeing jobs for men, she can recreate a stable family unit by becoming totally economically dependent on her husband so that she cannot leave him. *She* is the answer."[96] It is hardly an exaggeration to classify these policies as a "coercion of privacy."[97] And, like Hale's unretractable contract, this suggestive phrase brings out the mythical nature of the separate private sphere.

Why do we, therefore, pretend that women's private space is privileged? It is, I would suggest, to hide the central role that the state, through family law, welfare policies, fiscal regulation, the criminal law, plays in monitoring and controlling sexual ideology and its relation to the family. We are able to overlook this intervention because liberal ideology allocates these matters to the private sphere.

In looking at intervention and the interests this serves it is worth comparing two examples from the mid-1970s. Legislation to provide women a modicum of protection against violent husbands and cohabitants was passed.[98] But injunctions and personal protection orders are no more an answer to domestic violence than a sticking plaster is to a broken leg or "Band-Aid" to Ethiopia. Violent men were conveniently characterised as sick,[99] out of the norm, so that the interests of a male-dominated society were not touched by the legislation. The legislation did not and could not confront the real issues.[1] It necessarily left untouched the real causes of male violence. These are rooted in the subordinate position women occupy within society, in, among other things, economic dependency.[2] That is why it is worth comparing this "successful" legislation with the Finer proposals to introduce a "guaranteed maintenance allowance."[3] That proposal had many defects, not least that it proposed a means-tested benefit. But that is not why it did not get off the drawing board. It failed to capture the imagination of the legislators, partly because of the cost involved but more particularly because it shifted the responsibility of dependence from husbands and fathers on to the state. It threatened, in other words, women's dependency on men and through this the assumed stability of the family unit.

*Conclusion*

At the root of a critical theory of family law is the public/private dichotomy. I have concentrated on it because I believe it overarches. I believe also that many of the reform strategies in the recent past which are conceived within this particular world-view are "cabined, cribbed and confined"[4] by it and that their effectiveness is accordingly limited. Real reform can only come if the dichotomy is transcended.

I have called this lecture "*Towards* a Critical Theory of Family Law." It is not intended to contain either a full-blown theory or a blueprint for action, though I believe there are hints of both. It is offered more tentatively, almost as notes. But it does, I hope, offer insights into some of the directions that critical thinking about law and the family needs to take. I am fortunate to have reached professorial status in the middle of my academic career. I have not attempted, therefore, a summation of my work. what I have tried to do is pinpoint where my thinking is at and the direction in which it might go. A critical theory of family law cannot be encompassed in one lecture. Whether you interpret this as threat or promise, it means that the ideas presented today will, I hope, eventually be developed into a book.

In mythical Slaka—but how mythical?—they have, we are told, a saying: "A good friend is someone who visits you when you are in prison. But a *really* good friend is someone who comes to hear your lectures."[5] I have not been able to test the first part of this saying. So long as the interests of state are identified with the interests of the government of the day,[6] I suppose there is always a chance that I might. Over the years, though, I have had plenty of opportunity to test the second part of the saying. I am flattered by the large

Towards a Critical Theory of Family Law        175

attendance at this lecture. I hope I have given you something on
which to reflect. Thank you for coming and, if you have been doing,
for listening.

## Notes

\* Inaugural Lecture as Professor of English Law, delivered in Chemistry Auditorium
at University College London, February 26, 1985.

[1] See Stevie Smith's poem entitled "Not Waving But Drowning" in her *Collected
Poems* (1975).

[2] A statement uttered regularly during his re-election campaign in 1984 and
affirmed at his inauguration in 1985.

[3] See Jonathan Swift in *Polite Conversation*, Dialogue 1.

[4] The quotation from Deuteronomy XXXII, 7 is found in the Gustave Tuck
Lecture Theatre.

[5] Affirmed in *The Times Higher Education Supplement*, February 15, 1985 (after
hiccup on February 8).

[6] [1973] Fam. 72 at p. 94.

[7] [1968] 1 W.L.R. 457.

[8] [1972] 1 W.L.R. 518.

[9] [1975] 1 W.L.R. 1338.

[10] *Supra*, note 7, at p. 462.

[11] *Supra*, note 8, at p. 519.

[12] A similar sentiment is expressed by S. Rose, L. J. Kamin and R. C. Lewontin,
*Not In Our Genes* (1984) in attacking biological determinism.

[13] *Per* Holmes J. in Holmes-Laski: *Letters*, Vol. II, p. 822.

[14] (2nd ed. 1984), pp. 24–26. This is stated more fully in the first edition.

[15] *Ibid.* at p. 25.

[16] See M. D. A Freeman, *The Rights and Wrongs of Children* (1983), pp. 125–134;
H. Geach, "Child Abuse Registers—A Time for Change" in H. Geach and E. Szwed
(eds.), *Providing Civil Justice for Children* (1983) pp. 40–50; and in the U.S.A., A.
Solnit, "Too Much Reporting, Too Little Service" in G. Gerbner (ed), *Child Abuse*
(1980), pp. 135–146.

[17] See the unpublished paper by C. Rowan, "Motherhood and the Early Welfare
State, 1900–1920," Critical Social Policy Conference 1982. *Cf.* G. K. Behlmer, *Child
Abuse and Moral Reform in England 1870–1908* (1982).

[18] By S. Alexander, "Women's Work In Nineteenth Century London: A Study of
the Years 1820–50" in J. Mitchell and A. Oakley (eds.), *The Rights and Wrongs of
Women* (1976) pp. 59–111.

[19] See M. McIntosh, "The State and the Oppression of Women" in A. Kuhn and
A M. Wolfe (eds.), *Feminism and Materialism* (1978) pp. 254–289.

[20] "The Unhappy Marriage of Marxism and Feminism: Towards a More
Progressive Union" (1980) *Capital and Class*, No. 7, pp. 1–33.

[21] *Ibid.* at pp. 15–16.

[22] "Protective Legislation, the Capitalist State and Working Class Men: the Case of
the 1842 Mines Regulation Act," (1981) *Feminist Review*, No. 7, pp. 1–33.

[23] "Class Struggle and the Persistence of the Working-Class Family," (1977)
*Cambridge Journal of Economics*, Vol. 1, pp. 241–258, at p. 256.

[24] Mount argues in *The Subversive Family* (1982) that "the working class is the true
defender of liberty and *privacy*, because it has no ulterior motive. The material
triumph of the masses—the access they have finally gained to a decent standard of
living—is not to be used for making society more public and collective. On the
contrary, it is to be used for dispersing the delights of privacy to all" (p. 175). There

176            *Current Legal Problems 1985*

are deceptively similar sentiments in M. Barrett and M. McIntosh, *The Anti-Social Family* (1982). See the excellent review article by W. T. Murphy in (1983) 46 M.L.R. 363–379 making the differences clear.

²⁵ [1981] 1 All E.R. 394. An interesting American decision is *Dothard* v. *Rawlinson* 433 U.S. 321 (1977), discussed by C. A. MacKinnon, *Sexual Harassment of Working Women* (1979) pp. 184–186. The Supreme Court upheld a bar on the employment of women as guards in maximum security prisons but would not have allowed the restriction solely as a paternalistic protection for women employees. It concluded that the prison had a discipline interest in excluding guards who could be raped by the male inmates and that only women could be raped (pp. 335–336). The problem in *Page* has also arisen in the U.S.A. It is discussed by Andrade (1981) 4 Harv. Women's L.J. 71, and by Williams (1981) 69 Geo. L. Rev. 641.

²⁶ [1981] 1 All E.R. 394 at p. 398. See, as a further illustration of much the same reasoning, *Turley* v. *Allders Stores Ltd.* (1980) 1 C.R. 66.

²⁷ "Protection and Paternalism" in M. D. A. Freeman (ed.), *State, Law and the Family—Critical Perspectives* (1984) pp. 79–90, at p. 83.

²⁸ In the Preface to J. Eekelaar, *Family Security and Family Breakdown* (1971) p. 7.

²⁹ In *Family Security and Family Breakdown* (1971) p. 76. See also his remark in *Family Law and Social Policy* (1978) p. xxvii, that the law played a "minor role in creating conditions which are hoped to be conducive to the successful creation of families." This sentence does not appear in the second edition (1984).

³⁰ Though, it should be stressed, not the law alone.

³¹ See, further, in a different context Douglas Hay's "Property, Authority and the Criminal Law" in D. Hay *et al.* (eds.), *Albion's Fatal Tree* (1975) pp. 17–64.

³² See similar comments in relation to class by E. P. Thompson, *Whigs and Hunters* (1975) p. 262.

³³ See also R. Dingwall *et al.*, "Childhood as a Social Problem: A Survey of the History of Legal Regulation" (1984) 11 J. of Law and Soc. 207–246. See also R. Dingwall *et al.*, *The Protection of Children* (1983).

³⁴ *Cf.* J. Fitz, "The Child As Legal Subject" in R. Dale *et al.* (eds.), *Politics, Patriarchy and Practice* (1981) pp. 285–302 which, despite the title, is, I think, in agreement with my thesis.

³⁵ *Cf.* S. Spitzer, "Toward a Marxian Theory of Deviance" (1975) 22 *Social Problems* 638 at p. 642.

³⁶ [1985] 2 W.L.R. 413. An excellent discussion of which is contained in *Childright*, issue no. 14 (February 1985) pp. 11–18. See also Tobin's "A Study of Teenage Girls Attending A Family Planning Clinic" (1985) Br.J. of Family Planning.

³⁷ Family Law Reform Act 1969, s. 8(1).

³⁸ Family Law Reform Act 1969, s. 8(3).

³⁹ 431 U.S. 678 (1977).

⁴⁰ And see the remarks of Justice Powell in *Belotti* v. *Baird* 443 U.S. 622 (1979) regarding abortion, that "considering her probable education, employment skills, financial resources, and emotional maturity, unwanted motherhood may be exceptionally burdensome for a minor" (at p. 645). See further Freeman, *op. cit. supra*, note 16, at pp. 263–265. See also H. Rodman *et al.*; *The Sexual Rights of Adolescents* (1984).

⁴¹ This is documented in a number of places, notably in the DHSS Report of Committee of Inquiry into Care and Supervision Provided in Relation to Maria Colwell (Field-Fisher report) (1974). See also, more emotively, J. Howells, *Remember Maria* (1974).

⁴² See DHSS report, *supra*, note 41, at para. 42. The social workers "operated within a legal and social system in which when a child was taken (*sic*) into care the expectation was not that she would remain in care . . . but that she would return to her own family when their circumstances had improved" (*ibid.*).

## Towards a Critical Theory of Family Law          177

[43] But see now Children Act 1975, s. 64. The Children Bill 1974, cl. 52, would have gone much further. On the more recent developments see C. M. Lyon, "Safeguarding Children's Interests?" (1985) *Current Legal Problems Issue on Family Law* (forthcoming).

[44] *Op cit. supra*, note 42, para. 314.

[45] See J. Packman, *The Child's Generation* (2nd ed., 1981).

[46] *Violence In The Home: A Socio-Legal Study* (1979); *The Rights and Wrongs of Children* (1983) Chap. 4.

[47] Published as "The Rights of Children in the International Year of the Child" (1980) 33 C.L.P. 1–32.

[48] There is a full discussion of this in *Childright*, issue no. 15 (March 1985), pp. 11–15.

[49] Parents whose children have assisted places at non-maintained schools will also be able to exercise this right.

[50] Incredibly the Bill actually extends the liberty to beat beyond teachers to any "member of the staff" of a school. The school secretary, caretaker, dinner lady, etc., will in future be able to cane pupils whose parents do not opt them out.

[51] [1982] 4 E.H.H.R. 293.

[52] On this see M. D. A. Freeman, "Short, Sharp Shocks—A Comment" (1980) 130 N.L.J. 28.

[53] Which was with "a cheap and chippy chopper on a big black block"!

[54] Which is likely to happen quite soon. There are cases before the European Court of Human Rights and it seems likely that corporal punishment will be held to be "degrading" and thus contrary to the Convention, Art. 3 (judicial birching has already been so held: see *Tyrer* v. *United Kingdom* (1978) 2 E.H.H.R. 1).

[55] I have done this elsewhere: see *op cit., supra*, note 46: *Violence*, pp. 117–120; *Rights*, pp. 111–114.

[56] *Cooke* v. *Head* [1972] 1 W.L.R. 518. *Cf. Diwell* v. *Farnes* [1959] 1 W.L.R. 624, the leading case until *Cooke* v. *Head*, discussed in M. D. A. Freeman (1972) 25 *Current Legal Problems* 84 at pp. 116–117. On cohabitation see M. D. A. Freeman and C. M. Lyon, *Cohabitation Without Marriage: An Essay In Law and Social Policy* (1983).

[57] A useful introduction to which is D. Beyleveld and R. Brownsword (1984) 47 M.L.R. 359 at pp. 354–369. See also R. M. Unger (1982) 96 Harv.L.Rev. 561 at pp. 561–675 and D. Kairys, *The Politics of Law: A Progressive Critique* (1982). There is also a critical discussion in Lord Lloyd and M. D. A. Freeman, *Introduction to Jurisprudence* (5th ed., (forthcoming) 1985), pp. 709–716 .

[58] This was discernible in *Taking Rights Seriously* (1977) but is clearer in his late writings such as his articles "What Is Equality?" in 10 *Philosophy and Public Affairs*, (1981) his attacks on the economic analysis of law and in *A Matter of Principle* (1985). It is also clear in his projected *Law's Empire*, the first three chapters of which I have been privileged to read in manuscript.

[59] An insight made most forcefully in P. Berger and T. Luckmann, *The Social Construction of Reality* (1967).

[60] On which see P. Gabel, "Reification In Legal Reasoning" in S. Spitzer (ed.), *Research In Law and Sociology*, Vol. III (1980) pp. 25–51.

[61] A beginning has been made. There are first a number of existing essays which may be described as critical into family law. They are J. Rifkin, "Toward a Theory of Law and Patriarchy" (1980) Harv. Women's L.J. 83–95 (also in P. Beirne and R. Quinney (eds.), *Marxism and Law* (1982) pp. 295–301); N. Taub and E. M. Schneider "Perspectives on Women's Subordination and the Role of Law" in D. Kairys, *The Politics of Law* (1982) pp. 117–139; D. Polan, "Toward A Theory of Law and Patriarchy" in D. Kairys, *op. cit.*, at pp. 294–303; M. Schultz, "Contractual Ordering of Marriage: A New Model For State Policy" (1982) 70 Calif. L.Rev. 204–334; F. Olsen, "The Family and the Market: A Study of Ideology and Legal Reform" (1983)

178                    *Current Legal Problems 1985*

96 Harv.L.Rev. 1497–1578 (much the best of the existing literature—unfortunately, it only came to my notice after I had delivered my lecture). In addition, of course, there is a growing amount of feminist literature on the family and law; a few examples of this are A. Sachs and J. H. Wilson, *Sexism and the Law* (1978), K. de Crow, *Sexist Justice* (1975), C. A. MacKinnon, *Sexual Harassment of Working Women* (1979), L. Holcombe, *Wives and Property* (1983).

[62] Good examples of valuable research data are J. Eekelaar and E. Clive, *Custody After Divorce* (1977); W. Barrington Baker *et al.*, *The Matrimonial Jurisdiction of Registrars* (1977); S. Maidment, "A Study In Child Custody" (1976) 6 Fam. Law 195–200, 236–241; M. Maclean and J. Eekelaar, *Children and Divorce: Economic Factors* (1983); J. Eekelaar and M. Maclean, "Financial Provision on Divorce: A Reappraisal" in M. D. A. Freeman (ed.), *State, Law and the Family: Critical Perspectives* (1984) pp. 208–226; J. Masson *et al.*, *Mine, Yours or Ours* (1983); C. Gibson, "Maintenance In The Magistrates' Courts in the 1980s" (1982) 12 Fam. Law 138–141; O. McGregor *et al.*, *Separated Spouses* (1970)

[63] The classic distinction between "law in action" and "law in the books" can be traced (in English-speaking literature at least) to Roscoe Pound. See his "Law In Books and Law In Action" (1910) 44 Amer. Law Rev. 12–36. See also K. Llewellyn "Some Realism About Realism" (1931) 44 Harv.L.Rev. 1222 (his fifth point of departure). The alleged "gap" has been questioned among others, by D. McBarnet, *Conviction: Law, the State and the Construction of Justice* (1981) and D. Nelken, "Law In Action or Living Law? Back to the Beginning in the Sociology of Law" (1984) *Legal Studies* 157–174; and see also S. Henry, *Private Justice* (1983). It is not necessary for me to go into this debate here though my sympathies certainly lie with the critics. Also interesting in the light of critical theory are the remarks of D. M. Trubek, "Complexity and Contradiction in the Legal Order" (1977) 11 Law and Soc.R. 527 at p. 545.

[64] Introduced incrementally starting in 1973 and extended by 1977 to all undefended cases, whether or not children were involved. Though the impetus for the reform was to save money (see C. Gibson, "Divorce and The Recourse to Legal Aid" (1980) 43 M.L.R. 609 at p. 620), the research of M. Murch and his Bristol team certainly assisted the process (see E. Elston *et al.*, "Judicial Hearings of Undefended Divorce Petitions" (1975) 38 M.L.R. 609–640.

[65] On *One-Parent Families* (1974), Cmnd. 5629.

[66] *Cf.* Llewellyn's remarks about realists (*loc. cit. supra*, note 63) (the fourth point of departure explaining why the divorce of "Is" and "Ought" is only *temporary*).

[67] The sort of message that oozes out of Lord Denning's recent writings: see particularly The Due Process of Law (1980), Part 6.

[68] Sarah Spencer and I examine this phenomenon in the context of race relations in our "Immigration Control, Black Black Workers and the Economy" (1979) 6 Br.J. of Law and Soc. 53–81.

[69] Can the social conditions that produce structured social inequality be eliminated through law? Evidence from equal opportunities legislation suggests not. In 1975 women's earnings as a percentage of men's was 72.1%. The Sex Discrimination Act and Equal Pay Act came into operation at the end of 1975. In 1976 the percentage was 75.1%. In 1983 it was 74.2% (see New Earnings Survey 1970–1983 Part A, Tables 10 and 11); also in *Equal Opportunities Commission, 8th Annual Report 1983* (1984) p. 89. The percentage varies with occupation: women police officers earn 90.4% of male police officers' earnings: female sales supervisors earn only 63.4% of their male equivalents (Tables 8 and 9). See also the report in the *Financial Times*, March 11, 1985, quoting Low Pay Unit report, *Women and Low Pay*. Interesting insights from the U.S.A. are found in K. Powers, "Sex Segregation and the Ambivalent Directions of Sex Discrimination Law" (1979) Wisconsin L.R. 55–124.

[70] And also because reform has often generated from the perspective of the

## Towards a Critical Theory of Family Law 179

perpetrator of the original (and continuing) injustice and not from that of the victim. See further, in the area of race relations, the excellent article by A. D. Freeman, "Legitimizing Racial Discrimination Through Anti-Discrimination Law: A Critical Review of Supreme Court Doctrine" (1978) 62 Minnesota L.Rev. 1049–1119. See also his "Race and Class: the Dilemma of Liberal Reform" in D. Kairys, *op cit. supra*, note 57, pp. 96–116.

[71] This is reminiscent of the debate about the merits of socio-legal studies and the sociology of law. See C. M. Campbell and P. Wiles (1976) 10 Law and Soc. Rev. 547–578.

[72] The adequacy of these concepts cannot be explored here. They are thoughtfully by B. Frankel, *Beyond The State?—Dominant Theories and Socialist Strategies* (1983).

[73] See M. D. A. Freeman, *The Rights and Wrongs of Children* (1983) Chap. 7; J. Goldstein *et al.*, *Before the Best Interests of the Child* (1980).

[74] Both of which questions should be embraced by those interested in law and the family: neither are. Tina Lyon and I have tried to do a little about this in our *The Law of Residential Homes and Day-Care Establishments* (1984).

[75] See the important new collection edited by J. Eekelaar and S. M. Katz, *The Resolution of Family Conflict: Comparative Legal Perspectives* (1984).

[76] An excellent illustration of this is contained in P. Gabel and P. Harris, "Building Power and Breaking Images: Critical Legal Theory and the Practice of Law" (1982–1983) 11 N.Y. Univ.Rev. of Law and Soc. Change 369–411 (the illustration drawn from the prosecution of the rape victim Inez Garcia repays study).

[77] *Cf.* M. King, *Childhood, Welfare and Justice* (1981); R. Mnookin, "Child-Custody Adjudication: Judicial Functions In The Fact of Indeterminacy" (1975) 39 *Law and Contemporary Problems* 226. See now R. Mnookin, *In the Interest of Children* (1985).

[78] Guardianship of Minors Act 1971, s. 1.

[79] Children Act 1975, s. 3; Child Care Act 1980, s. 18; Matrimonial and Family Proceedings Act 1984, s. 3 (inserting new s. 25(1) in Matrimonial Causes Act 1973).

[80] D. Oliver, "The Mistress in Law" (1978) 31 *Current Legal Problems* 81–107; D. Pearl, "The Legal Implications of a Relationship outside Marriage" (1978) C.L.J. 252–269.

[81] See B. Dickens, "The Modern Function and Limits of Parental Rights" (1981) 97 L.Q.R. 462–485.

[82] The literature on this concept is now voluminous. On the concept itself see M. Wald, "Children's Rights: A Framework for Analysis" (1979) Univ. of California Davis Law Rev. 255; H. Cohen *Equal Rights For Children* (1980); M. D. A. Freeman, *The Rights and Wrongs of Children* (1983) Chap. 2.

[83] As J. Goldstein *et al.* maintain (see *Beyond The Best Interests of the Child* (revised ed., 1979)). They favour instead "the least detrimental alternative."

[84] 140 N.W. 2d 152 (1966).

[85] See A. Sutton, "Science In Court" in M. King, *op cit. supra*, note 77, pp. 45–104; "Social Services, Psychology . . . and Psychologists" in I. McPherson and A. Sutton (eds.), *Reconstructing Psychological Practice* (1981) pp. 81–108; A. Sutton and G. Moss, "Towards A Forensic Child Psychology" in S. Lloyd-Bostock (ed.), *Children and the Law* (1984) pp. 32–69 (*cf.* R. Dingwall, *ibid.* at pp. 70–78); A. Sutton, "Social Enquiry Reports to the Juvenile Courts: A Role for Love In the Rule of Law" in E. Szwed and H. Geach (eds.), *Providing Civil Justice for Children* (1983) pp. 123–164.

[86] Now 12% (17% of women divorced, separated or widowed). Pre-marital cohabitation has also increased. 24% of women marrying for the first time in 1979–82 had lived with their husbands before marriage (65% of those marrying for second or further time): *Social Trends* 15 (1985) Tables 2.10 and 2.11.

[87] On which see the Monckton Report, Cmd. 6636 (1945).

[88] As to which see *op cit. supra*, note 41. A more recent illustration is the case of Jasmine Beckford, *The Times*, March 29, 1985, described in *The Guardian* March 30,

180                    *Current Legal Problems 1985*

1985, as being in the "shadow" of "Maria Colwell." For the panic that a case can
generate see K. Waterhouse in the *Daily Mirror*, April 1, 1985. The *Sun* has even set
up a hot (*sic*) line (April 1, 1985).

[89] The comparison drawn here is also brought out by V. MacLeod, *Whose Child?:
The Family In Child Care Legislation and Social Work Practice* (1982).

[90] See L. Parkinson, "Conciliation: A New Approach To Family Dispute
Resolution" (1983) 13 Br.J. of Soc. Work 19; "Conciliation: Pros and Cons" (1983)
13 Fam. Law 22 and 25; and G. Davis, "Conciliation: a Dilemma for the Divorce
Court Welfare Service" (1982) 29 *Probation Journal* 183–186; G. Davis *et al.*,
"Divorce and the Resolution of Conflict" (1982) 79 Law Soc. Gaz. 40 and 43. A.
Gerard, "Conciliation: Present and Future" in M. D. A. Freeman (ed.), *State, Law
and the Family* (1984) pp. 281–292.

[91] *Minton* v. *Minton* [1979] A.C. 593. See also P. Symes, "Indissolubility and the
Clean Break" (1985) 48 M.L.R. 44–60.

[92] In an ideal society. One is tempted to draw the parallel with Gandhi's remark
about British civilisation that "it would be a good idea."

[93] *Op cit. supra*, note 65, at para. 4. 285.

[94] Snyder, "Crime and Community Mediation—The Boston Experience: A
Preliminary Report on the Dorchester Urban Court Program" (1978) Wisc.L.Rev.
737. He notes that one of the problems in a mediation programme, which was
basically successful, is the general absence of useful standards to control discretion of
mediating officials (pp. 788–789). This is an important point not properly considered
in this country.

[95] See C. Stoll, "Images of Man and Social Control" (1968) 47 *Social Forces* 119.

[96] "Resolving Family Disputes: A Critical View" in M. D. A. Freeman (ed.), *State,
Law and the Family* (1984) p. 297; See also G. Davis, "Mediation In Divorce: A
Theoretical Perspective" (1983) Journal of Social Welfare Law 131–140; S. Roberts,
"Mediation in Family Disputes" (1983) 46 M.L.R. 537–557.

[97] Or "deformalisation." Olsen (*op cit. supra*, note 61) distinguishes delegalisation and
deformalisation (pp. 1541–1542). She says that whilst deformalisation tries to protect
family solidarity without destroying individual rights, delegalisation threatens
individual rights by refusing to enforce them. Deformalisation, she says, avoids the
"anarchy" of delegalisation. But she admits the deformalisation can have "adverse"
effects on women because it fails to provides full protection to individual family
members. The impact of the "two" strategies is thus similar, so much so that I wonder
whether anything is gained by separating them. I accordingly stick to the language I
have previously used (see my essay in J. Eekelaar and S. Katz, *op cit. supra*, note 75).

[98] See Finer report, *op cit. supra*, note 65, at part 4, sections 13 and 14; Justice report
on *Parental Rights and Duties and Custody Suits* (1975) paras. 85 *et seq.*; Houghton
report on *Adoption of Children* (1972) Cmnd. 5107, paras. 276–279; The Law Society,
*A Better Way Out* (1979) Parts III and VIII; Justices' Clerks' Society, *The Case For a
Local Family Court* (1978); Conservative Political Centre, *The Case For Family
Courts* (1978); Jean Graham Hall, *Proposal For a Family Court* (1973); M. Murch,
*Justice and Welfare in Divorce* (1980), for just the more significant proposals and
blueprints. For more critical comments see E. Szwed, "Family Courts—Are They A
Solution?" in H. Geach and E. Szwed (eds.), *op cit. supra*, note 16, pp. 165–192, and
on family court performance (in the U.S.A.) see the valuable article by M. Paulsen
(1966) 54 Calif. L. Rev. 608.

[99] G. Roth and C. Wittich (eds.), *Economy and Society* (1968) Vol. II, p. 893. He
wrote: "It is by no means certain that those classes which are negatively privileged
today, especially the working class, may safely expect from an informal administration of justice those results which are claimed for it by the ideology of the jurists."

[1] See M. Spector, "Beyond Crime: Seven Methods To Control Troublesome
Rascals" in H. L. Ross (ed.), *Law and Deviance* (1981) pp. 127–157.

Towards a Critical Theory of Family Law 181

[2] See R. Kagan, *Regulatory Justice* (1978).

[3] See C. Reich, "The New Property" (1964) 73 Yale L.J. 733; M-A. Glendon, *The New Family and the New Property* (1981).

[4] See N. Kittrie, *The Right To Be Different: Deviance and Enforced Therapy* (1971); P. Conrad and J. Schneider, *Deviance and Medicalization: From Badness To Sickness* (1980).

[5] "The Punitive City: Notes on the Dispersal of Social Control" (1979) 3 *Contemporary Crises* 339. See now his *Visions of Social Control* (1985).

[6] *Discipline and Punish* (1977); *Madness and Civilisation* (1975).

[7] *The Politics of Informal Justice* (1982) Vol 1, p. 6.

[8] As to which see E. P. Thompson, *Whigs and Hunters* (1977) pp. 258–269. But *cf.* S. Redhead in P. Beirne and R. Sharlet (eds.), *Marxism and Law* (1982) pp. 328–342.

[9] *Re Gault* 387 U.S. 1 (1967); *Breed* v. *Jones* 421 U.S. 519 (1975). *Cf. McKiever* v. *Pennsylvania* 403 U.S. 538 (1971). But on the modest impact of the changes ushered in by *Gault* see M. Sosin, "Due Process Mandates and the Juvenile Court" (1978) 1 *Journal of Social Services Research* 321–343.

[10] See E. Ryerson, *The Best-Laid Plans: America's Juvenile Court Experiment* (1978). Juvenile courts were hailed as the best plan "for the conservation of human life and happiness ever conceived by civilised man" by C. W. Hoffman in J. Addams (ed.), *The Child, The Clinic and The Court* (1927) p. 266.

[11] The relationship between capitalism and formalism has been thoroughly analysed notably by M. J. Horwitz, *The Transformation of American Law 1780–1869* (1977); D. Kennedy, "Legal Formality" (1973) 2 *Journal of Legal Studies* 351–398; R. M. Unger, *Law in Modern Society* (1976) pp. 203 *et seq.*

[12] Though those who propagated the juvenile court may have been moved by other considerations. See A. Platt, *The Child Savers* (1977) or S. Schlossman, *Love and the American Delinquent: Theory and Practice of "Progressive' Juvenile Justice 1825–1920* (1977).

[13] *Cf.* K. Polanyi, *The Great Transformation* (1944) Chap. 4.

[14] A shift (as Kamenka and Tay put it) from *Gesellschaft* law to bureaucratic administrative regulation (see "Beyond The French Revolution: Communist Socialism and the Rule of Law" (1971) 21 Univ. of Toronto L.J. 109–140; "Beyond Bourgeois Individualism: the Contemporary Crisis in Law and Legal Ideology" in E. Kamenka and R. S. Neale (eds.), *Feudalism, Capitalism and Beyond* (1975) p. 140).

[15] It hardly needs emphasising that today's "status" is very different from the feudalistic notion in Maine's historical analysis of *Ancient Law*. See further A. Fraser, "The Legal Theory We Need Now" (1978) *Socialist Review*, No. 40–41, pp. 147–187.

[16] See Unger, *op cit. supra*, note 11 (2nd series), p. 216; F. Neumann, *The Democratic and Authoritarian State* (1957).

[17] See Cohen, *loc. cit. supra*, note 5 (2nd series) at p. 347.

[18] On which see J. Donzelot, *The Policing of Families* (1979); P. Meyer, *The Child and The State* (1983). *Cf.* E. Zaretsky, "The Place of the Family In The Origins of the Welfare State" in D. Held *et al.* (eds.), *States and Societies* (1983), pp. 290–305.

[19] *Social Insurance and Allied Services* (1942) Cmd. 6404.

[20] On which see H. Land, "The Family Wage" (1980) 6 *Feminist Review* 55–77; L. Davidoff, "The Separation of Home and Work?" in S. Burman (ed.), *Fit Work For Women* (1979) pp. 64–97, is also useful.

[21] And see, J. Pahl, "The Allocation of Money within The Household" in M. D. A. Freeman (ed.), *State, Law and the Family* (1984) pp. 36–50. See also her earlier articles in (1980) 9 *Journal of Social Policy* 000 at pp. 313–335; (1983) 31 *Sociological Review* 237–262.

[22] Aylesbury houses the so-called "Campaign For Justice In Divorce." Amongst the publications of this are, *All Disquiet on the Divorce Front* (1980) and *The Financial Anatomy of Post Divorce Man* (1980). But see a partial defence of these publications

182    *Current Legal Problems 1985*

and activities in S. Cretney, "Money After Divorce: the Mistakes We Have Made?" in (1985) *Current Legal Problems Family Law Special Issue* (forthcoming).
   [23] See M. Maclean and J. Eekelaar, *Children and Divorce: Economic Factors* (1983); J. Eekelaar and M. Maclean, "Financial Provision on Divorce: A Re-appraisal" in M. D. A. Freeman (ed.), *State, Law and the Family* (1984) pp. 208–226; B. Doig, *The Nature and Scale of Aliment and Financial Provision* (1982); G. Davis *et al.* "Divorce: Who Supports The Family?" (1983) 13 Fam. Law 217–224.
   [24] But see letter by Frank Field MP, *The Guardian*, December 23, 1983 indicating that consideration is being given to change this.
   [25] Children are now the "first consideration" (s. 25(1) of the Matrimonial Causes Act 1973, inserted by s. 3 of the Matrimonial and Family Proceedings Act 1984).
   [26] See C. Delphy, *Close to Home* (1984) Chap. 6.
   [27] See further, H. Land, "Changing Women's Claims To Maintenance" in M. D. A. Freeman (ed.), *State, Law and The Family* (1984) pp. 25–35.
   [28] Department of Employment, *New Earnings Survey 1982* (1983) Introduction.
   [29] On dichotomies, see A. Katz, "Studies In Boundary Theory: Three Essays In Adjudication and Politics" (1979) 28 Buffalo L. Rev. 383–435.
   [30] See M-J. Bane, "Is the Welfare State Replacing the Family?" *The Public Interest*, No. 70, pp. 91–101 (1983).
   [31] With the return to so-called Victorian values. See further, H. Rose and S. Rose, "Moving Right Out of Welfare and the Way Back" (1982) 2 *Critical Social Policy*, No. 1, pp. 7–18.
   [32] The interpretation of this distinction I adopt is described by Carol Gould as "an older distinction" (see "Private Rights and Public Virtues: Woman, the Family and Democracy" in C. C. Gould (ed.), *Beyond Domination: New Perspectives on Women and Philosophy* (1983) p. 7). She distinguishes instead between institutionalised rules and practices (the public domain) and "individual actions and interpersonal relations where these actions or relations are not institutionally prescribed or defined, but are in principle matters of the individual's own free choice." The interpretations are linked: the one I adopt is much the most commonly used and I see no reason to deviate from it.
   [33] *Politics*, Book 1.
   [34] *Per* J. B. Elshtain, *Public Man, Private Woman* (1981), p. 45. See also S. M. Okin, *Women In Western Political Thought* (1980) Chap. 4. According to Aristotle "to be born female is the most common kind of deformity" (quoted by C. Whitbeck, "A Different Reality: Feminist Ontology" in C. C. Gould (ed.), *op cit. supra*, note 32 (2nd series) p. 70).
   [35] *Per* J. B. Elshtain, "Aristotle, the Public-Private Split, and the Case of the Suffragists" in J. B. Elshtain (ed.), *The Family In Political Thought* (1982) p. 52.
   [36] On whom see J. B. Elshtain, *op cit. supra*, note 34 (2nd series), pp. 91–99. For Machiavelli there were different standards of conduct appropriate to the two spheres (see Q. Skinner, *Machiavelli* (1981) Chap. 3).
   [37] *Per* J. B. Elshtain, *op cit. supra*, note 34 (2nd series), p. 63.
   [38] *The Human Condition* (1958) Part II.
   [39] *The Acting Person* (1979).
   [40] *Cf.* E. Zaretsky, *Capitalism, the Family and Personal Life* (1976).
   [41] *Women's Oppression Today* (1980) p. 165.
   [42] There is a good account of this in N. F. Cott, *The Bonds of Womanhood* (1977) Chap. 2. A good description of how the separate spheres for men and women emerged in the middle classes is L. Davidoff and C. Hall, "The Architecture of Public and Private Life: Middle Class Society in a Provincial Town 1780–1850" in A. Sutcliffe (ed.), *The Pursuit of Urban History* (1983) pp. 326–346. On the construction of the "approved ideal" in literature and art see N. Auerbach, *Woman and the Demon: The Life of a Victorian Myth* (1982).

## Towards a Critical Theory of Family Law        183

[43] On the impact of ideologies of domesticity and maternalism see A. Davin, "Imperialism and Motherhood," *History Workshop Journal* No. 5 (1978); C. Dyhouse, *Girls Growing Up in Later Victorian and Edwardian England* (1980); J. Lewis, *The Politics of Motherhood* (1980).

[44] Per W. Houghton, *The Victorian Frame of Mind 1830–1870* (1957) p. 343. On the relationship between the separation and moral discourse and social control see J. Weeks, *Sex, Politics and Society* (1981), partic. Chap. 5.

[45] *Haven In a Heartless World* (1977) p. 6. But *cf.* M. Barrett and M. McIntosh, *The Anti-Social Family* (1982) pp. 110–126.

[46] See K. Jeffrey, "The Family As Utopian Retreat from the City: the Nineteenth Century Contribution" in S. Teselle (ed.), *The Family, Communes and Utopian Societies* (1972).

[47] *Cf.* A. Douglas, *The Feminization of American Culture* (1977), noting that men saw the marketplace as representing "profane" worldly goods (p. 12).

[48] Per L. Davidoff *et al.*, "Landscape With Figures: Home and Community In English Society" in J. Mitchell and A. Oakley (eds.), *The Rights and Wrongs of Women* (1976) p. 163. On some of the earliest challenges (in the U.S.A.) to the two spheres see the fascinating account by R. Rosenberg, *Beyond Separate Spheres* (1982).

[49] A myth effectively demolished by C. Delphy, *op cit. supra*, note 26 (2nd series), Chaps. 4 and 5.

[50] Per K. Millett, *Sexual Politics* (1969) p. 343.

[51] Per B. Brown *et al.*, "The Equal Rights Amendment: A Constitutional Basis for Equal Rights For Women" (1971) 80 Yale L.J. 891 at p. 893.

[52] Women are heavily concentrated in four occupational groups: clerical workers; service, sports or recreational workers (mainly cooks, canteen assistants and office cleaners); professional and technical workers such as teachers and nurses; and shop assistants. For earlier history see A. Clark, *Working Life of Women in the Seventeenth Century* (1919); I. Pinchbeck, *Women Workers and the Industrial Revolution 1750–1850* (1930) (her Whig interpretation is now very dated); J. Lewis, *Women In England 1870–1950* (1984) pp. 145–217.

[53] See R. Barron and G. Norris, "Sexual Divisions and the Dual Labour Market" in D. L. Barker and S. Allen (eds.), *Dependence and Exploitation In Work and Marriage* (1976) pp. 47–69.

[54] See the essays edited by Stuart Hampshire, *Public and Private Morality* (1978); and *cf.* Mill's classic *On Liberty*; see also R. Wasserstrom, "Privacy, Some Arguments and Assumptions" in R. Bronaugh (ed.), *Philosophical Law* (1978).

[55] *Anarchy, State and Utopia* (1975).

[56] See, for example, D. A. J. Richards, *Sex, Drugs, Death and the Law: An Essay on Human Rights and Overcriminalisation* (1982) Chap. 2.

[57] The debate about state and family rarely takes into account the fact that it is in the area of "caring" for elderly, handicapped, etc., that demands are for *more* state intervention than less.

[58] *Before The Best Interests of the Child* (1980) p. 12.

[59] *Freedom and The Welfare State* (1976) p. 60.

[60] *Cf.* L. J. Scrutton in *Czarnikow* v. *Roth Schmidt* [1922] 2 K.B. 479 at p. 488.

[61] But see my *The Rights and Wrongs of Children* (1983) Chap. 4.

[62] But see now the CIBA publication edited by Ruth Porter, *Child Sexual Abuse Within the Family* (1984).

[63] The literature on the subject nevertheless continues to expand. Since this lecture was given two new books have appeared: J. Pahl (ed.), *Private Violence and Public Policy* (1985) and N. Johnson (ed.), *Marital Violence* (1985).

[64] *Cf.* W. Ryan's *Blaming The Victim* (1976).

[65] The number remains totally insufficient. See V. Binney *et al.*, *Leaving Violent*

184               *Current Legal Problems 1985*

*Men* (1981); M. Borkowski *et al.*, *Marital Violence* (1983); J. Pahl, *A Refuge for Battered Women* (1978); J. Clifton, "Refuges and Self-Help" in N. Johnson (ed.), *op cit. supra*, note 63, pp. 40–59.

[66] House of Commons Select Committee Report, *Violence In Marriage*, H.C. 553, Vol. II, p. 366.

[67] *Ibid.* at p. 418.

[68] The take-up rate is low. This is not surprising since prosecution is normally a condition precedent to the claiming of compensation (see M. Wasik, "Criminal Injuries Compensation and Family Violence" (1983) *Journal of Social Welfare Law* 000 at pp. 100–108).

[69] See my "Doing His Best To Sustain The Sanctity of Marriage" in N. Johnson (ed.), *op cit. supra*, note 63, pp. 124–146. Important recent evidence is provided by Ruth Hall in *Ask Any Woman: A London Rape Inquiry* (1985) Chap. 7 (a finding of 1 in 7 women raped by husbands and more than one-third "forced into sex" who considered this was rape).

[70] See G. Geis, "Lord Hale, Witches and Rape" (1978) 5 Br. J. of Law and Soc. 26–44.

[71] *Historia Placitorum Coronae*, p. 636. Hale's philosopher contemporary John Locke argued that "wifely subjection" had "a Foundation in Nature." And see Carole Pateman's critical analysis in "Feminism and Democracy" in G. Duncan (ed.), *Democratic Theory and Practice* (1983) p. 212.

[72] The political nature of the "private" has been too little explored. But see the valuable collection of essays edited by J. Sittanen and M. Stanworth, *Women and The Public Sphere* (1984), particularly Chap. 18. Further, they differ from society to society. The view has, however, been expressed that the dichotomy is universal (see M. Z. Rosaldo, "Women, Culture and Society: A Theoretical Overview" in M. Rosaldo and L. Lamphere (eds.), *Women, Culture and Society* (1974) pp. 17–42. She proposed a direct relationship between the degree of the subordination of women in a given society, and the degree to which the realms of public and domestic were separated. Drawing on the Ilongots (in the Philippines) she pointed out that where men were more closely involved in domestic life, the distance between men and women, and the degree of authority that men exercised over women, appeared to diminish. See also S. Ortner, *ibid.* at pp. 67–87. A useful discussion is H. Eisenstein, *Contemporary Feminist Thought* (1984) Chap. 2.

[73] Even where there is an "agreement" (unless it is a maintenance agreement within s. 34 of the Matrimonial Causes Act 1973). See *Balfour* v. *Balfour* [1919] 2 K.B. 571. Note Atkin L.J.'s remarks: "The parties themselves are advocates, judges, Courts, sheriff's officer and reporter. In respect of these promises each house is a domain into which the King's writ does not seek to run, and to which his officers do not seek to be admitted" (p. 579).

[74] The case usually cited to illustrate this is the American case of *McGuire* v. *McGuire* (1953) 59 N.W. 2d 236.

[75] See further Taub and Schneider, *loc cit. supra*, note 61 (1st series), at pp. 122–123.

[76] But has this process now come to a halt? There are suggestions (the *Gillick* case is the best example) that it may have done. However, a recent example supporting the thesis in the text is the Surrogacy Arrangements Act 1985.

[77] In *The Republic*, Book 4.

[78] *Cf.* U. Bronfenbrenner, *Two Worlds of Childhood: U.S. and U.S.S.R.* (1970), who (at p. 5) quotes a Soviet handbook (by Makarenko) to this effect.

[79] As to which see J.Eekelaar's classic article "What Are Parental Rights?" (1973) 89 L.Q.R. 210.

[80] Though this must be read in the light of the Guardianship of Minors Act 1971, s. 1, and *J.* v. *C.* [1970] A.C. 668.

## Towards a Critical Theory of Family Law        185

[81] Rather as the overall ideological message conveyed about women is greater and more pervasive than any individual doctrine in itself.

[82] *Re B.* [1981] 1 W.L.R. 1421 and see M. D. A. Freeman, *The Rights and Wrongs of Children* (1983) pp. 259–263.

[83] As in *Re D.* [1976] Fam. 185.

[84] *Ibid.* The Official Solicitor may not intervene: a clear message that the parental decision is not really any business of the state.

[85] *Cf.* L. Althusser "Ideology and Ideological State Apparatuses" in *Lenin and Philosophy and Other Essays* (1972).

[86] A message that certainly comes across in the influential Pelican by R. Fletcher, *The Family and Marriage In Britain Today* (1973).

[87] And the family is a microcosm of the "nation" (the *mother*land). The imagery is particularly striking in war (the country's *sons* fight; "kith and kin" join in or, in the case of the Falklands, are fought for).

[88] The emphasis is too obvious to require further comment.

[89] Interesting insights into the power dimensions involved are found in E. Gamarnikow *et al.*, *The Public and the Private* (1983), particularly in J. Finch, "Dividing the Rough and the Respectable: Working-Class Women and Pre-School Playgroups" at pp. 106–117.

[90] See K. Lidstone, "Magistrates, the Police and Search Warrants" (1984) Crim. L.R. 449–558.

[91] On privacy, see the very useful collection edited by F. D. Schoeman, *Philosophical Dimensions of Privacy: An Anthology* (1984).

[92] *Op cit. supra*, note 48 (2nd series), p. 140.

[93] On police and domestic violence see M. D. A. Freeman, *Violence In the Home: A Socio-Legal Study* (1979) pp. 184–191. R. Reiner notes that the police find intervention in domestic disputes frustrating "because of their apparent uselessness or extraneous character from the standpoint of a specific notion of real police work" (*The Blue-Coated Worker* (1978) p. 178). See also J. Hamer and S. Saunders, *Well-Founded Fear* (1984) Chap. 4, and T. Faragher in J. Pahl (ed.), *op cit. supra*, note 63 (2nd series), pp. 110–124.

[94] See J. Pahl, "Police Response to Battered Women" (1982) *Journal of Social Welfare Law* 337–343. The police are not the only agency to privatise domestic violence. On doctors, see E. Stark *et al.*, "Medicine and Patriarchal Violence: The Social Construction of a Private Event" (1979) 9 Int. J. of Health Services 461–493.

[95] "The Doubled Vision of Feminist Theory " (1979) 5 Feminist Studies 216 at p. 223, reprinted in *Women, History and Theory* (1984) 51 at p. 59

[96] (1984) p. 136.

[97] See T. Stang Dahl and A. Snare, "The Coercion of Privacy" in C. & B. Smart, *Women, Sex and Social Control* (1978) pp. 8–26.

[98] Domestic Violence and Matrimonial Proceedings Act 1976 (but see *Richards* v. *Richards* [1984] A.C. 174, which partially undermines it) and Domestic Proceedings and Magistrates' Courts Act 1978, ss. 16–18.

[99] *Cf.* C. McGrath, "The Crisis of Domestic Order" *Socialist Review No. 45*, 11 at p. 17.

[1] I expand on this in my "Legal Ideologies, Patriarchal Precedents and Domestic Violence" in M. D. A. Freeman (ed.), *State, Law and the Family* (1984), pp. 51–78.

[2] The chart in J. Hanmer and S. Saunders, *op cit. supra*, note 93 (2nd series), on p. 66 is useful.

[3] *Op cit. supra*, note 65 (1st series), paras. 5.104–5.249.

[4] *Per* W. Shakespeare, *Macbeth*, Act II, Scene iv, line 24.

[5] *Per* Malcolm Bradbury, *Rates of Exchange* (1983) p. 128.

[6] A reference to McCowan J.'s summing-up in the trial of Clive Ponting (see *The Times*, February 6, 7, 8, 1985).

# Name Index